THE LOST VILLAGE
OF BARBOURSVILLE

To Judi –

Jeanette Rowsey

THE LOST VILLAGE OF BARBOURSVILLE

Unsung and Vanishing History of the "Best Little Village in West Virginia" (1813-2013)

JEANETTE M. ROWSEY

JRC Publishing
Huntington, WV 25705

Printed in the United States of America

ISBN: 978-0-578-12716-3

CONTENTS

ACKNOWLEDGEMENTS

MANY folksy tidbits and several photographs in this book were mined from the collection of educator and historian Fred B. Lambert. This man amassed an amazing quantity of historical treasure in the form of local reminiscences, photographs, genealogy and Cabell County records before his death in 1967. Although his manuscript notes were never published, his descendants donated what are now known as "The Lambert Papers" to Marshall University Libraries Special Collections Department, so all can peruse the randomly organized fruits of his labor.

Frank Ball was another freelance historian whose work appeared in the *Barboursville Bulletin, Cabell Record, Huntington Advertiser* and other area publications for nearly 50 years. My limited knowledge of Village lore prior to the 1980s came largely from my grandmother's clippings of Ball's "Avenue of Antiquity" series. I was delighted to discover that Mr. Ball had donated scrapbooks of clips and photographs to the Barboursville Public Library. I owe a great debt to him, as well as others who blazed Barboursville's historical trail, including Rick Baumgartner, Maurice Beckett, Carrie Eldridge, Joe Geiger, Frances Gunter and George Seldon Wallace.

Thanks to all the faithful keepers of our heritage in libraries and on websites including: the reference staff of the James E. Casto Local History and Genealogy Room; Linda Larue and the Barboursville Library staff; Heritage Quest Online; Dr. Cicero Fain; the staff of Marshall University Morrow Library Special Collections Department; the KYOWVA Genealogical and Historical Society; Barry Huffstutler, webmaster of Cabell County's "Doors to the Past" website; the keepers of the "Cabell County Family Ties" genealogical website; Barbara Miller who shared an impressive collection of Barboursville clips and memorabilia; Marta Ramey of Ironton Ohio's Briggs Library Hamner Room; the Records Room at the Cabell County Courthouse; the West Virginia Archives and History library and website; Jedd Flowers and Cabell County Schools; and the C&O Historical Society.

My deep appreciation goes to the following individuals who were generous with their time, expertise and memories: Dave and Toril Lavender, Lorraine Powell, Janet Altizer, Roger and Bernice Hesson, Holice Gibson, Wilma Smith, Anne Brady Turman, Barbara Miller, Susan and "Fritz" Hubbard, Roy Goines, Gladys Carter, Ted and Maddie Allen, Connie Jeffries, Marvin Johnson, Walter C.

Wade, Donna Brown, Jack Dilley, Karen and Johnny Nance, Nathan Petit; and my Pea Ridge United Methodist Church kinfolk.

I especially want to thank my family, especially my ever-supportive and loving husband Chuck Minsker and my sons Justin and Evan (whose 2009 suggestion that I write this book switched on a light bulb in my brain that never went out). Although they cannot read the printed word, I must credit my home-office companions Domino and Roofio for their patience, undying affection and wet-nosed reminders to get up and play, without which this writer's posterior would have molded to the shape of a desk chair. Finally, my love and appreciation go to my mom Linda Brady, who was a constant source of inspiration and help; my late "Aunt Pat," Patricia Schultz; Robert "Uncle Buzzy" and Luella Rowsey, cousins Jeff Seager and Suzanne Shriver, Uncle Scott Brady and brother-in-law Don Nash for their interest and guidance; my sisters Sherri Nash and Denise Juan who helped in numerous ways, including putting up with their often obsessive and sometimes irritable sibling for three years; and my aunt Marjolee Brady who paved the way both as the family archivist and its rabble-rousing social conscience. I love you all!

INTRODUCTION AND DEDICATION

FIRST, it is time for some family myth busting.

Back in the early 1970s, when my oldest sister Sherri attended Barboursville High School, there was a particular day that BHS students were excused from school while those of us attending Ona Junior High had to haul ourselves onto Kenneth K. Kilgore's school bus as usual. Indignant, middle sister Denise demanded to know why Sherri was allowed to stay home from school when we were not.

Quick and wily as big sisters can be, Sherri improvised. "It's a holiday in Barboursville."

"What holiday?"

"It's the birthday of the man who discovered Barboursville."

The rest of their conversation would have been lost to memory, but for an act of gullibility that elevated it to the level of "stuff you never live down." As Sherri tells it, Denise marched into her classroom that day and announced to Mr. Hogg that people were celebrating "Clyde R. Barboursville's birthday," in honor of "the man who invented Barboursville."

Fact One: It would have been just as easy to believe Sherri's off-the-cuff revisionist history at that time. Anyone in town could tell you who won the 1953 West Virginia high school football championship, but what about the founder of a town that had long ago been overshadowed by neighboring Huntington? It was perhaps known by some musty old townsfolk (and those intrepid nerds who frequented the town's "blue library"), but certainly not by the clueless Rowsey sisters of Indian Meadows.

Since that time, a few slim local histories have been placed on the shelf at Barboursville's public library. More significantly, now that we have Internet, historical truth is almost instantly provable, or disprovable.

Fact Two: According to our friends at Google:

"No results found for 'Clyde R. Barboursville'."

According to other official sources, Cabell County's Barboursville was established by an Act of the Virginia General Assembly on January 14, 1813. The town was named for James Barbour, who was Governor of Virginia from 1812 to 1814.

James Barbour was born June 10, 1775, was deputy sheriff of Orange County, Virginia, served several terms in the Virginia Assembly before being elected to the United States Senate in 1814. In addition, he was President pro tempore of the Senate during the Fifteenth and Sixteenth Congresses, Secretary of War appointed by President John Quincy Adams, United States Minister to England, and Chairman of the Whig Party National Convention in 1839. He died in a different Barboursville, in Orange County, Virginia, in 1842.

The venerable James Barbour in portrait, presiding over the rapt gaze of Ann Reed (middle), Avana Watson (right), and an unidentified perky young woman when the new library building was dedicated
(Courtesy of Barboursville Public Library)

Cabell County's Barboursville was founded when Mr. Barbour was just 37 years old, one year before he was elected to the United States Senate. As an up-and-coming American statesman, the flesh-and-blood James Barbour probably never ventured through the Appalachian wilderness to the western edge of the state.

Ironically, Barbour's other namesake town and place of burial—Barboursville, Virginia—is now called "one of Virginia's most intact cultural landscapes" by Virginia's Department of Historic Resources.

Which brings me back to West Virginia and this book. As Barboursville observes its bicentennial, I think it is time to give our own cultural landscape some respect. In *The Lost Village of Barboursville* my aim is to point out historical gems from sources that already exist, fill in a few gaps and shine a light on some of the less-celebrated periods of Barboursville's 200-year lifespan. I hope my journey through the past will help readers look with fresh eyes at Barboursville, as a place with a history worth preserving.

I dedicate this work to the memory of two men of the village:

John P. Hogg

Roger Hesson

The first was a delightfully offbeat eastern Cabell County educator. The ultimate "anti-Good-Old-Boy," he opened many young eyes to the real-life importance of history. His distinctive hyena-laugh surely echoed through the halls of OJHS at my sister's announcement of "Clyde R. Barboursville's birthday" —**John Paull Hogg (1945-2007).**

The second man I consider my "fifth uncle"—the family friend whose personality was more indelibly imprinted upon my childhood than are some folks' "real" uncles. He was my Dad's partner-in-shenanigans from junior high on, my first great boss when I worked a student job at Marshall University and most recently— along with his gracious wife "Bernie"—the real spark plug behind this effort. I cannot imagine Barboursville without his sly humor, his generosity, or his beaming smile – **Lion Roger A. Hesson (1937-2011).**

CHAPTER 1

PROLOGUE:
AT 200 YEARS, FINDING
THE SOUL OF THE LOST VILLAGE

I am not a lifelong resident of Barboursville, just one of countless grandkids and great-grandkids who grew up hearing stories around the fireplace.

As a toddler, I moved with my family from Farmdale Road to a big city several states away, "where the jobs are"—a familiar Appalachian tale. Barboursville was where my mom was born and raised, where both my parents went to school and where my maternal grandparents lived most of their lives. Holidays and summers would find us packed into Daddy's company car making the restless slog on old Route 52 from Indiana's flat land to Cabell County, where we divided our time between Long Street and Pea Ridge among folks who cherished their trio of granddaughters.

The hills and trees, coal-strewn railroad tracks, root-buckled sidewalks and old brick buildings of Barboursville seemed far removed from the new housing tracts, parking lots, clipped accents and hurried pace of northeast Indianapolis. Long Street was the place to enjoy my grandmother's buttermilk cornbread and my grandfather's cocoa, toss Christmas paper into the fireplace, catch lightning bugs, roll down the grassy backyard hill, play "drop the clothespin in the milk bottle," make homemade soap bubbles, and giggle endlessly with cousins and family friends.

The old cemetery several blocks away, with its iron plot fences and worn headstones, was eerily fascinating, not just because we had ancestors buried there, but because of the tragic and mysterious neighbors up the hill at the State Hospital (or as we indecorously called it, "the crazy house"). We heard stories of quaint folks living along Water Street and Depot Street, mentions of long-gone Morris Harvey College, Civil War cannonballs—even tales of Jesse James stashing his loot in a cave past the high school.

Perhaps being uprooted from West Virginia at an early age gave me a different appreciation for Barboursville's historic nature, but even as a youngster, I could sense that Barboursville was a place with *character*.

When my family moved back to Cabell County in 1971, nothing much had changed in the village. As I settled into gawky adolescence at Barboursville High School, it was my own perspective that shifted. A sense of malaise seemed to have settled over the town like dreaded dust on my grandmother's fireplace mantle. The prevailing opinion seemed to be that "B'ville" was just your average boring town— our own Hooterville, so-to-speak, complete with water tower. We might have felt superior to Hamlin, Milton and Guyandotte, but compared to nearby Huntington the town was no big deal—our victorious school football and basketball teams notwithstanding.

When I reached age 16 in 1976—the year before Alex Haley's *Roots* became a cultural phenomenon—it seemed family trees and genealogical research were idle pastimes for big shots. Barboursville families like my grandparents might not have been yokels, but they weren't high-society types either, so I really did not know the depth of my Barboursville roots. (Later I found there may have been a few skeletons in the Brady-McComas closet, or at least incidents that folks of that era simply did not talk about.) Moreover, almost nobody, not even the towns-people who had ardently organized events around the United States Bicentennial, seemed to be thinking about the town's own origins or founding families, much less historic preservation. It apparently was not necessary in a place that hadn't seen change for decades.

As I entered my senior year at BHS, local history never crossed my mind. My thoughts were already centered on getting into college and taking my leave. I could not wait to get Principal Childers, his faculty cronies and the whole of Barboursville past the rear view of my very own first car (which, incidentally, was to be a $500 aquamarine Ford Maverick with a black hardtop and AM/FM converter, purchased from an old man on Cyrus Creek).

Then came the 1980s and The Mall happened. Before anybody knew it, this was followed by Cabell County's version of late twentieth century, willy-nilly, All-American Sprawl complete with condominiums, up-market housing devel-opments, mini-storage units, shopping plazas and chain restaurants. Suddenly, Barboursville had a new lease on life and an abundant source of revenue as a regional consumer destination. I was thrilled to settle down in eastern Cabell County in 1987, knowing my husband and I could raise our babies with so many conveniences within a few minutes' drive. Life definitely has its pluses when you're five minutes either way from Penn Station or Pier One. However, at some point, Barboursville started taking the shape of the rest of "Generica" where it keeps getting harder to tell one interstate exit from another.

Jump to 2009: After digging out an 18-year-old copy of Robert Hall's *Walking*

Tour of Barboursville, supplemented with clips from Aunt Margie's family archive, I volunteered to guide our church youth group around the town, as I used to do with my sons' Cub Scouts in the 1990s. By the end of our walking tour, I found myself silently fuming about the obsolete nature of the 1991 tour book. Several historic properties on the tour had already been destroyed—literally replaced by parking lots—and others had been sorely neglected.

Beyond that, there was something else gnawing. There were gaping holes in recorded Barboursville history. The more I researched ready sources on the internet, bookstores, libraries and family albums, the more I was left with the burning questions of an amateur history detective. One family photograph cast a particular spell as a missing link to a forgotten past, this one of my mom posing with her neighbor Keller Washington at her grandfather's home in the early 1940s.

Linda Brady with Keller Washington on
Depot Street in the early 1940s
(Brady Family Archives)

Part of me wanted to jump into the picture and lead the little Bradys, the family member who took the picture, and the dandy-looking African-American gentleman down the porch steps onto Depot Street. Something in me wanted to walk around the town and see it through their eyes. (Would they have dared?)

There were questions I wanted to ask:

- What was Keller's story, and who were the other African American families who lived in Barboursville? Were they connected to former slaves of the area? What happened to the Washingtons and other families who went to the old "colored church" next door to Mom's childhood home on Depot Street? What would it have been like living in Barboursville in those segregated years?
- Why is there what looks like a guard tower in the Community Park? What happened on that property in the years before the park was developed?
- And what about that old State Hospital that operated here after Morris Harvey College and before the West Virginia State Veterans' Home? What was its place in West Virginia's institutions for its most unfortunate people? Who were the residents, where did they come from and what happened to them?

In Barboursville's newfound glory as "the Best Little Village in the State," it is in danger of having its past slip away. Through the decades, in times of both hardship and prosperity, Barboursville simply moved onward and upward, losing an antebellum house here, a cemetery marker there, and so on. Were the answers to my questions already lost to history, save for scattered photographs and artifacts and the memories of a few men and women in their twilight years?

Was this it for Barboursville's history—lost symbols of the past, lost memories, lost opportunities?

Urged on by my journalist son, I decided to fight cultural oblivion the best way I know how, as a researcher and writer. I dedicated my spare time to combing through archives, newspapers, photographs and personal stories far and wide. It has been a fascinating journey—and a lengthy one, spanning more than three years.

I believe the story of Barboursville, West Virginia is worth seeking out and sharing. I hope the reader finds this a well-sourced and well-told Bicentennial history. Following in the footsteps of Fred Lambert, Frank Ball and the other keepers of Barboursville's stories, I know I can only scratch the surface on some subjects. Surely there will be other folks who can fill in the additional details.

Ultimately, it is my wish that our remaining "cultural landscape" will be cared for and preserved.

Travel guide writer Arthur Frommer once put forward his belief that "people simply don't go to a city that has lost its soul. What people want is the sense of being Someplace, not just Anyplace. They aren't interested in communities that have transformed themselves into a sad hodgepodge of cookie-cutter housing tracts and cluttered commercial strips…but they flock to places that have preserved their historic character. . . and saved their soul."

With the village having quietly observed its 200th birthday on January 14, 2013, what better time could there be to unveil some of the memories and mysteries lying within its borders? With this narrative, I offer a glimpse of our local history, both within the context of the towns and cities around it and within the larger American story, that it might capture a sense of Barboursville's distinct sense of place — its "soul," if you will.

CHAPTER 2

OUR SPECIAL CORRESPONDENT FURNISHES AN INTERESTING LETTER (1898-1901)

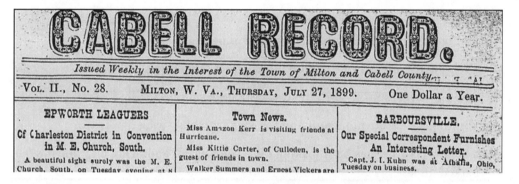

(Courtesy of Cabell County Public Library)

BEFORE traveling all the way to Barboursville's origins, let us ease halfway back in time to the period from 1898 to 1901.

The turn of the twentieth century was a pivotal time. Although the courthouse had already been relocated to Huntington, the village was bustling with the construction of a new rail line. Morris Harvey College was ten years old and thriving. The children and grandchildren of Barboursville's founding families were living well in the nascent industrial age, but still enveloped within a larger farming community.

The *Cabell Record* weekly newspaper launched in Milton in January 1898. The paper featured a weekly gossip column from Barboursville entitled "Our Special Correspondent Furnishes an Interesting Letter." A reporter's name appeared in some of the early issues, "Nellie M.," and for a short period around 1899, the column contained the byline "Jimmy George," then just "George." Eventually it became an anonymously-authored column.

"Our Special Correspondent" mostly detailed the comings and goings of Barboursville society, but a week-by-week reading yields enlightening details of

> CABELL RECORD.
> Issued Weekly in the Interest of the Town of Milton and Cabell County.
> VOL. II., No. 28.   MILTON, W. VA., THURSDAY, JULY 27, 1899.   One Dollar a Year.

village life in the quaint language of the day. Throughout the book, I open each chapter with selected entries from the column as fits the theme at hand.

In the meantime, let us begin our jump into the Fourth Dimension and start our tour of the Lost Village through some sparkling reportage from turn-of-the-century Barboursville and eastern Cabell County— the "Tweets" of their time. They are especially fun to read aloud:

Hoboing has fallen off ninety per cent, since this cold snap set in.

Several young men talk of leaving for the Klondike soon.

Judge Samuels, one of the leading citizens here, is very sick with a nervous affection.

Misses Valet Brady and Maggie Taylor are said to be champions at playing croquet.

Barboursville has the best bucket brigade in the state.

Dick Thornburg is the champion bicycle rider of the town.

The pawpaw crop is as scarce here as Bob Shipe's mutton.

Hunting parties are numerous and are bagging rabbits galore.

The dog poisoner has been making his rounds again, and many a canine has barked his last.

Current Humor: "Why is it that women live longer than men?" "Men break down their constitutions trying to manage women."

The town lock-up hasn't had but one occupant in a year. Doesn't that speak well for our town?

The American Telephone and Telegraph company will put an instrument in at one of the stores here. We can soon talk to Cincinnati, Louisville and Charleston for the money.

Yuley Murphy, the young man who attempted suicide by shooting himself, near Barboursville recently, was in Milton last Thursday exhibiting the pistol ball that was taken from his left lung.

William Simms is in the Philippine Islands, and writes that he is anxious to capture Aguinaldo.

Barboursville has more pretty girls to the square inch than any town in the Western Hemisphere.

Some of the "birds" that captured prizes at the recent big "cocking main" held in Detroit, Michigan were reared in this vicinity and made their owners considerable money…this locality has a great reputation for raising pugilistic roosters.

Barboursville ought to have a brass band.

The temperance element here is said to be organized to prevent the establishment of a saloon. They will take the matter before the county court if council grants the privilege.

Blue Sulphur Springs will be in charge of people this season who will run the hotel in grand style.

A bridge is badly needed to span the Guyan river at this point… (there has been a) petition to the county court for ten years asking for it. It would accommodate the farmers of Pea Ridge, all heavy tax-payers, but make it possible to drive to Huntington without endangering life and property by one's stock frightening at the railroad cars.

From Cox Landing: If you want to learn something about horses, just stop A.T. Clark for a few minutes talk, and he will tell you plenty.

From Martha: the young ladies of this section had a gay 'possum hunt one evening late last week…the young ladies enjoyed themselves hugely and dug hard for possession of the "coon."

A party digging post holes on Davis Creek yesterday found a deck of cards with the Jack of Spades turned up, four feet under ground.

The ghost at the Davis Creek shanty of William and Claude Dillon continues to knock nightly and the boys who occupy the house do not mind it any more. A great many folks visit the shanty and spend the night there. It will knock upon request, and in this way replies to questions. Mr. Henry Stowasser and ex-Mayor Ayers, of Barboursville, spent a night at the shanty during the week and heard the knocking.

The ghost on Davis Creek, which attracted so much notice by its "knocks" was knocked out by the cold weather. A couple of young lads on that creek inaugurated the fraud to gull the people, and they succeeded for a time at least in having good sport over the affair.

A couple of young ladies of Fudge creek…on their way home from Antioch Church, got badly scared at a baby carriage and became unmanageable.

From Blue Sulphur—Why is it when our country boys start to Barboursville for beef for dinner they have to go to Huntington after it, and don't get back until time for supper? What is the matter, Barboursville?

James Causley, an adventurous trapper, moved from the Lord only knows where to the mouth of Heath creek a short time since. His specialty was the trapping of pole-cats, and he had a preparation that attracted these varmints to his place in large numbers, but failed to neutralize their perfume. He did a lively business in securing pelts of this kind, but the neighborhood was in open rebellion against what they termed a "skunk factory," and last week Causley was induced to move to Wayne County, and there is general rejoicing thereabouts. It is said that the fellow made considerable money with his skunk layout.

A man claiming to be the ugliest mortal in the State, was on Merritts Creek, near here, Tuesday, hunting for a farm. He came from Putnam county and was advised to return there and carry his face along.

Fudge creek people are highly religious…meeting houses along the creek are crowded during services.

Beach fork (sic) young men have been drinking cider and raising Cain.

Pea Ridge farmers are after a gang of chicken thieves that have been operating in their midst.

A dejected looking woman, apparently 30, claiming to be Miss Woodall from near Hurricane, was looking for a hare-lipped man here Monday morning. She said they both came here Sunday, were on their way to be married in Ohio, and after occupying an empty shanty below town Sunday night the fellow abandoned her.

"Resolved. That old bachelors be taxed for the support of old maids," was the subject that brought out a heated debate at the meeting of the Irving and Franklin literary societies last Saturday evening.

A fair crowd left this place this morning for Charleston to see Buffalo Bill and his aggregation.

The right of woman suffrage was the subject taken for debate at last night's meeting of the Guild Club, and elicited good arguments.

A Chinaman named Lum Ling, from Columbus, started to peddle in the mountains of Raleigh and Logan counties last week. He retained his 'cue and peculiar attire, thinking it would be a drawing card. It was for irate husbands whose wives and children he had frightened, and he was chased out of the country, glad to escape with his life.

Municipal election not two months off, yet no one has announced themselves for Mayor. Did you ever?

Our Special Correspondent Furnishes an Interesting Letter:
JUNE 28, 1900—Three sons of Dr. G.W. Adams caught a catfish in a hollow log in Mud River Thursday that weighed fifty pounds.

CHAPTER 3

RIVERS, TRAILS AND FIRST SETTLERS (1700S TO 1810)

Upriver and Up a Tree—The Wards

BARBOURSVILLE'S history starts, naturally, with a zig-zagging stream of water—sometimes it's jade green, sometimes muddy brown—that twenty-first-century locals see each day without noticing.

The Guyandotte River is formed by the junction of two creeks in the Cumberland Mountains of southern Raleigh County, and flows northwest to the Ohio River at Huntington. On its way, the 167-mile stream flows through the rugged mountains of Wyoming, Mingo and Logan counties. As the river passes through Lincoln and Cabell counties and nears the Ohio, the slopes become more moderate and the ridges not as high.

(To me, this is helpful to understand when elders or country folk say things like "we went *up* to Hamlin." It sounds odd, since it is obvious on any map that Hamlin is south of Barboursville, but in early days folks had to paddle or pole their way *up*river to go southeast.)

Five main tributaries feed the Guyandotte River, the largest being the Mud River, which originates in Boone County. It is at this point, the mouth of the Mud—once the hunting ground of native tribes, where the buffalo roamed—that Jeremiah and Thomas Ward are said to have found themselves taking refuge against the threat of Indians, at least a dozen feet above the ground in the hollow of an old sycamore tree.

At some unknown time in the late eighteenth century, Jeremiah Ward and Thomas Ward (who was either Jeremiah's son or nephew, depending upon the source) came from eastern Virginia across the mountains to the Kanawha River, then by small boat or canoe down the Ohio River to the mouth of the Guyandotte. The Wards may have first lived in a cave to avoid Indians in the area. One descendent said Jeremiah may have killed the county's last buffalo.

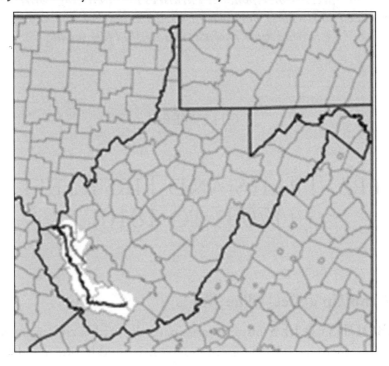

Map showing Guyandotte River and its largest tributary, the Mud River
(Courtesy of West Virginia Humanities Council)

Land Grants and Treacherous Years

To understand what motivated the Wards to settle this particular piece of wilderness in such a treacherous time, the most tangible clue can be found today along U.S. Route 60, about a mile up the Mud River (toward the Mall). On the right-hand side of this busy highway sits an unassuming stone marker that reads:

1772-1929 This stone marks the line where the highway enters THE SAVAGE GRANT—28,627 acres, reaching to the Ohio and Big Sandy Rivers. Granted by King George the Third, of England, in the Year 1772, to John Savage and Other Colonial Soldiers, who served under George Washington, during the Campaign of the Great Meadows, in the Year 1754. Where was shed the first blood of the French and Indian War. This Marker erected by the National Society Colonial Dames of America, of West Virginia.

The Savage Grant highway marker merely hints at more than 50 years of international and domestic intrigue that shaped the region's destiny years before Barboursville became a possibility, much less an American town.

Before 1754, North America east of the Mississippi River was largely claimed by either Great Britain or France. However, portions of territory, including that between the Mississippi and the Appalachian Mountains, were still under the control of native tribes. In an attempt to claim more land and recruit more men for the British Army, Governor Dinwiddie of Virginia proposed that some 200,000 acres of wilderness land be distributed to any soldier who would serve King George's interests. This would benefit the American colonies in several ways, as Eastern land was wearing out, taxes and land prices were high, currency was scarce and immigrants kept arriving.

One of the soldiers who served in what became known as the French and Indian War (under Lieutenant George Washington, no less) was Captain John Savage. At war's end, Governor Dinwiddie offered acreage on behalf of the British crown to Savage and about 60 other soldiers. This transaction has since been referred to as the Savage Land Grant. The boundary of this land was along the Ohio and Big Sandy rivers, including what is now Barboursville.

Though they were rewarded for service in a 1754 battle, many of Savage's brothers in arms chose not to take the land, either selling their claim or passing it along to descendents. You see, before intrepid farmers, trappers and peddlers could make it to the western frontier of the "Ohio Country," they had to survive the mountainous wilds of western Virginia, where remnants of Seneca, Shawnee and Mingo tribesman were still around to be reckoned with.

The 1755 ordeal of Mary Draper Ingles inspired a popular novel that is often assigned to Cabell County high school students. *Follow the River* by James Alexander Thom chronicles Ingles's journey, part of which took place along portions of the Guyandotte River after Shawnee kidnapped her from her central Virginia home. Even after a 1763 peace treaty ended the French and Indian War, years passed before much of the western Virginia land was habitable to white pioneers. And though the Iroquois Confederacy and the Cherokee had signed away all claims to western Virginia land in 1768, there were still brutal clashes across the region for several years. Most notable among these were the 1772 "Bulltown Massacre" by German immigrants in Braxton County, and the 1774 rampage of Mingo chieftain Tah-gah-jute (baptized by the English as "Chief Logan") who took revenge after the savage murder of his relatives by a group of white settlers.

Virginia Governor John Murray, Earl of Dunmore, decided to end the escalating violence with decisive force. He and Virginia land speculator Captain Andrew Lewis amassed 2,500 colonial troops against the natives. Shawnee chieftain Keigh-tugh-qua, known as "Chief Cornstalk," along with approximately 1,200 Shawnee,

Delaware, Mingo, Wyandotte and Cayuga warriors, commenced to attack Lewis's regiment before it could unite with Lord Dunmore's forces. On October 10, 1774, the Indians attacked Lewis's forces at the confluence of the Kanawha and Ohio Rivers in Mason County. Cornstalk's men sustained the majority of casualties. His defeat at the Battle of Point Pleasant signaled the beginning of the end of native presence in the region, although small raiding parties and skirmishes continued through the American Revolution.

Consequently, it was not until decades later that white frontiersmen, including Revolutionary War veterans, began to take advantage of the old British bounty and claim the rich bottomland along the Guyandotte and Mud rivers. After the War of Independence, the new United States Congress borrowed a tactic from old King George, paying Continental Army soldiers in land certificates instead of money for their service. Various states also reserved land to pay their own soldiers. And so, several decades after the Savage Grant was awarded, the western Virginia land grab was finally on.

Which brings us back to Jeremiah and Thomas Ward, who eventually got out of that sycamore tree.

In 1802, Jeremiah purchased land on one side of the Guyandotte, the "Farmdale" side, for a plantation. The Wards apparently had purchased several Savage Grant land tracts, which for them would become a source of wealth and influence. According to Ward family sources, Thomas Ward already owned considerable amounts of land when he and Jeremiah came to the Guyandotte River area. This was most likely a result of service in the Revolutionary War. While here, he bought and sold land in both Cabell and Wayne Counties. At one time, Thomas Ward owned almost all the land from Salt Rock to Martha. Before becoming Cabell County's first sheriff, Thomas made his reputation as the county's oldest maker of salt, which was not only a vital food preservative but also a valuable economic commodity on the American frontier.

What we know about the elder Ward, Jeremiah, is that he evidently yearned for community bonds in the newly tamed land. He and his wife Margaret are listed among the first members of the Mud River Baptist Church, organized in 1807. As one of the first known churches in the county, Mud River Baptist's small congregation was scattered from Branchland in the south, west to the town of Guyandotte, as far north as Greenbottom along the Ohio River, and east to Poplar Fork (currently in Putnam County).

Captain Merritt and his Mill

Meanwhile, across the Guyandotte River from Ward's Farmdale plantation, a retired Revolutionary Captain from Maryland, William Merritt, was hard at work putting in the area's first "public utility." In 1801 Merritt applied to the County

Court of Kanawha—which at that time encompassed most of southwestern Virginia— for an acre of ground on which to build a water grist mill, near a dam he had already built at the mouth of the Mud. According to Cabell historian George Seldon Wallace:

> When the settlers went into a new county it was not unusual for the man of the family to go on ahead and put in a corn crop and then return for his family. After the crop was harvested the problem was to grind the grain… If we should say that the mills were the first public utility in the county… such is the fact. At the time of the organization of this county the Virginia law provided for the condemnation of land for mill sites. And the miller had compensations – he was exempt from military services and until 1819 "the owner or occupier of a water grist mill" was ineligible to serve as a member of a grand jury…In all events the mills and the miller were important in the community. It was a familiar sight…to see a man or boy mounted on a horse, with a sack of grain slung on behind, going to the mill. (Wallace 1935)

Merritt's grist mill was followed in subsequent years by similar mills along Four Pole Creek (by Buffington), Nine Mile Creek (Wintz), Kilgore Creek (Morris) and the Falls of the Mud (Dundas). Highly successful mill operations were built along the Mud at Howell's Mill in 1819 and the Guyandotte River at Martha (operated by Sanders and later Dusenberry) in 1827.

In addition to the land on which his grist mill sat, William Merritt purchased 500 acres across the Guyandotte from Ward's Farmdale land, and the area came to be known by the early settlers as "Merritt's Mill." He became an important man in the community. In April 1809, the first Cabell County Court (forerunner of today's County Commission) met in his home on the bank of the Mud River.

William Merritt and his wife had at least eight children. They and their spouses—with surnames of Turley, Derton, Wentz, Dundas, Rece and Hite— put down roots throughout eastern Cabell County. Another Revolutionary War veteran, Malchor Strupe (1750-1833), apparently joined Merritt in acquiring local bottomland where the Mud and Guyandotte waters mingled. Strupe's son married Merritt's granddaughter.

William Merritt's family lands are still a hub of traffic today, but have undergone a drastic transformation in recent years. In the late 1990s, the state's jail authority contracted archeological investigations of the Merritt family cemetery, because the site for the future Western Regional Jail was the resting place of a number of Merritt's descendants and that of Malchor Strupe.

A photograph of Merritt's mill taken in the late nineteenth century
(Courtesy of Marshall University Libraries Special Collections)

In October 1999, a crew began relocating the Merritt family graves in preparation for the jail's construction. Fifteen buried headstone bases and stone fragments were found, in addition to 25 visible headstones and 13 footstones. Examination of the site uncovered a harsh reality of life in the early 1800s: of the 52 graves identified, nine were those of children, and ten were those of infants. All that remained in the graves were teeth, buttons, pieces of fabric, coffin nails, hinges, handles and bottoms of shoes. (The archeologists at the site also recovered and identified some prehistoric evidence of hearths and fire pits from earlier cultures, but no evidence of houses, supporting the belief that the Barboursville area was no more than a short-term campsite for indigenous populations.) The state ceremoniously relocated the graves of the Merritts and Strupe on another part of the family homestead, replanted trees from the original site and, according to the jail authority, attempted to respect the past and follow best historic practice.

Merritt's investment in the grist mill on the Mud, as well as Ward's primitive salt-making efforts, helped sustain the county's pioneer families and provide them with money, which at that time was "so scarce that hides, furs and salt were about the only mediums of exchange."

Blazing a Trail through a New Nation

It is easy to picture someone like Daniel Boone trudging his way across the river valley in the years after the American Revolution. In fact, Boone himself, *"the rippin'-est, roarin'-est, fightin'-est man the frontier ever knew,"* is said to have walked from westernmost Virginia (by way of Mason County), journeyed east, dusted himself off and met face-to-face in Richmond's halls of government with much fancier men. Boone was one of our area's first representatives in the Virginia General Assembly in 1791, when it was part of Kanawha County:

> George Clendenin, the founder of Charleston, and Daniel Boone, the great Kentucky pioneer and Indian fighter became the first representatives from Kanawha County and incidentally from what later became Cabell County. These men appeared in the Legislative Halls at Richmond, clad in the same garb that they were accustomed to wear at home. The contrast between the western members and the polite aristocracy of the east, was so noticeable that class distinctions became unavoidable. The people of the west were often referred to in later years as "hewers of wood and drawers of water." This only intensified the feeling between the two sections, and helped to form that strong sentiment in the West which later resulted in the new state of West Virginia. (Wallace 1935)

Daniel Boone's legislative stint coincided with the dawn of a new era in land transportation. Hunters, trappers, traders and warriors followed valley trails created by buffalo hooves. Later these same routes were used by teams of surveyors representing the British crown, including a young George Washington. As the frontier moved west and two-way traffic intensified, the trails were widened to accommodate horses, livestock and wagons.

According to regional historian and cartographer Carrie Eldridge, there were just four major trails leading from the eastern seaboard to the mighty Ohio River, all making connection with Virginia's capitol city. After the French and Indian War, one such route slowly stretched its way from Richmond to Lexington, Virginia, through the Blue Ridge Mountains and on to Lewisburg in Greenbrier County.

In 1785, the James River Company incorporated with plans to build both a highway and a canal to connect the Kanawha River with Richmond. (The failed canal way eventually would become the route of the C&O rail line.) The following year the route from Lewisburg to the Kanawha River was cleared and widened. In 1787 the James River and Kanawha Turnpike was authorized. The road was to be six feet wide, with tollgates every four to five miles.

The salt works east of Charleston (said to be West Virginia's first industry) were a strong factor in completing the route between the Kanawha River and present-day Cabell County. Two sources recall that Thomas Ward made small quantities of salt on the river between Salt Rock and Martha, as well as on the Big Sandy, but did not begin to supply the demand of a growing population. Settlers were often compelled to make long journeys to the Kanawha "Salines" in groups of four or five. They carried their provisions with them on horseback, killed game along the route to trade for salt, and returned on pack horses with at most a few bushels of the precious commodity.

The turnpike is believed to have been completed from from present-day Cabell county to eastern Kanawha county as early as 1804, with county roads authorized as early as 1802 by the county courts. The journal of a nineteenth century Barboursville citizen details the "James River and Kanawha" route to the Ohio:

> The "Kanawha Road," which started at James River, a few miles east of White Sulphur Springs, and thence, by way of the Springs, across Green Brier River to Louisburg (sic), and on to Charleston, where it crossed the Kanawha River by means of a ferry, and then came on, by way of St. Albans, Scary and old Hurricane to Barboursville. From here the road crossed the Guyandotte river, below the present bridge and followed the Pea Ridge route to Russell Creek, to the Spring Hill Cemetery on Walnut Hills. It then went by Marshall College and turned to the left and down Fifth Avenue, and followed the Ohio river bottom, to the mouth of the Big Sandy. This old road came through Barboursville on the present site of Main Street, in front of the Court House. (F. B. Lambert Collection n.d.)

According to Lambert, the Kanawha Road stood third in importance of all the roads across the Allegheny mountains: "The great 'National Road' through the northern part of our state, and Ohio, Indiana and Illinois, to the Mississippi river, being the most important of all the routes; The 'Cumberland Gap' route, leading from the Valley of Virginia, through Kentucky was perhaps second in importance; while the Kanawha Route was, unquestionably, third," he wrote.

Influence of Local Settlers

Upon completion of the "Kanawha Road" through the new settlement, the corn that Merritt, Ward and others planted began to supply the area's new settlers with money, as drovers began to drive their hogs from Ohio and Kentucky to eastern markets.

By the time Cabell County was created from the territory south of the Kanawha River in 1809, "scarcely a court convened but one or more roads were ordered surveyed. The people were collected under a superintendent, and assigned a certain road, on or near which they lived, in order to keep it in repair," according to Wallace. These county roads generally traced the routes of major landholders in the area surrounding Merritt's Mill:

McComas. There were the "tall, robust, uncouth and restless" Scotch-Irish McComas brothers of Maryland who came by way of New River to the Guyan Valley in 1779, and their brother Elisha, who settled at Salt Rock. Elisha McComas would later move into south Barboursville, make his mark as a "gentleman justice," a 13-term member of the Virginia General Assembly and a major, colonel and brigadier general of the state's militia. Today the Farmdale Bridge bears his name. As of this writing, two of his descendents hold prominent positions in county and state government, two-term Cabell County sheriff Tom McComas and Randall Reid-Smith, commissioner of the West Virginia Division of Culture and History.

Sanders. There was the wealthy and recently-widowed Martha Green Sanders (referred to by some sources as "Saunders") of Virginia, who began purchasing county land in 1802. Along with her 16-year old son Sampson and the family slaves, she managed several profitable farms along the Mud and Guyandotte Rivers. Thomas Kilgore of Pennsylvania married Martha's only daughter and sold his mother-in-law a huge parcel of prime bottom land along the James River and Kanawha Turnpike roughly ten miles east of Merritt's land. Thomas and Hetty (Sanders) Kilgore settled along the turnpike at a place called Mud Bridge. They raised seven children who married into families with such surnames as Morris, Newman, Simmons and Ball, in what would later become the town of Milton.

Bostick. Manoah Bostick, who would become a major in the War of 1812, was an active land trader who at one time owned some 1,200 acres. After the death of his wife, Bostick would leave the area for Tennessee.

Morris. Edmund Morris was the grandson of London-born William Morris and the son of a Revolutionary War soldier. He came to Mud River and Hurricane Creek and settled in Yatesmont. Edmund's brother was Bishop Thomas Asbury Morris, who became associated with Bethesda Methodist Episcopal Church.

By 1809, the area around Merritt's Mill was still a few years away from town-hood, but was already becoming a center of trade and political activity. The town of Guyandotte, built on a Savage Grant parcel along the mighty Ohio River, would become the county's first town in 1810, and would contend for position as county seat until 1813. From 1809 to May 1810, as the first County Court took place in William Merritt's home, the new county's trustees were Elisha McComas, Monoah Bostick, Edmund Morris, young Sampson Sanders and his brother-in-law Thomas Kilgore.

It is important to keep in mind that the newly created Cabell County was six times as large as it is now, and included all or part of seven current counties—Wayne, Lincoln, Putnam, Mingo, Logan, Boone and Wyoming. The 1810 substitute census for this huge expanse of land lists 487 households, 524 "tithables" (taxable persons including white and free black males 16 years or older, and female heads of households), 122 slaves over the age of 12, and 1,169 horses. It is believed that at least 23 county settlers were Revolutionary War veterans, and there is record of 25 Native Americans living within county borders at that time as well.

As the unofficial town founders, William Merritt and Jeremiah Ward found themselves in a place of great promise, with its gentle terrain, enterprising neighbors and auspicious placement along a national trail and two rivers. Their new settlement, tucked along Virginia's western boundary, was poised to become a thriving American frontier town.

Our Special Correspondent Furnishes an Interesting Letter:
FEBRUARY 27, 1898—Barboursville is noted for the few weddings that occur
in its midst. The youth are said to be hardhearted by Guyandotte young maidens.

CHAPTER 4

A FRONTIER TOWN TAKES SHAPE (1810-1820S)

Consider the word "frontier."

WEBSTER'S dictionary defines frontier as "a region that forms the margin of settled or developed territory," or "the farthermost limits of knowledge or achievement."

As I began writing this chapter, the U.S. Census released its 2010 population estimates. According to *The Herald-Dispatch*, Huntington and Cabell County both lost population between 2000 and 2010, with the City of Huntington losing 4.5 percent of its population since the 2000 count. Cabell County lost out to the eastern panhandle's Berkeley County as the second most populous county in the state (behind Kanawha County). Milton saw a 9.8 percent increase; Hurricane's population jumped 20.3 percent. In the same ten-year span, Barboursville experienced a population bonanza, with a whopping 24.5 percent growth.

"Officials say people are moving to the eastern part of the county because they want newer, larger homes than they can find in Huntington. Others want to escape some of the fees and taxes, that are not imposed in rural areas or in small cities," reported *The Herald-Dispatch*. In light of this explanation, post-millennial Barboursville presents a striking parallel to the early 1800s, when the huddled masses of the eastern seaboard headed west for similar reasons.

Aiding the village's modern expansion has been a 1960s-era running back nicknamed "Termite" Turman, who has presided as Village mayor since 2001. Paul Turman Sr. made the most of Barboursville High School and Marshall College football credentials, as well as family ties in the bridge construction business and halls of state government, to become a championship player in Barboursville's development. And whether clearing the way for 20 acres of apartments, "McMansions" and mini-storage units along Peyton Street, or getting the state to put up half the cost of a $1.6 million "soccer bridge" (his words) off 4-H Camp Road, Turman has been the ultimate frontiersman in his own right. He has redefined and greatly expanded the margins of the Village's developed territory.

Turman has had plenty of help. Barboursville locals today are part of a growing customer base that draws interstate travelers and people from neighboring counties as a powerful consumer magnet. It may be lamentable for lovers of wildlife, the environment and historic preservation, but even those who mourn these natural and cultural losses have taken part in the ongoing march of Barboursville sprawl.

Meat—It's not just what's for dinner

We are all in our way (with apologies to the mayor) fellow "termites," in that we're guided by swarm intelligence to exploit food sources and environments that could not be available to any single being acting alone. Don't believe me? Take one segment of the local economy as a mouth-watering example. Who among us has not joined the weekend swarm to the crowded parking lots of "Red Meat Row?"

Greater Barboursville seems to have achieved critical mass as a twenty-first century "carnivore boom town," with that intoxicating meat-smoke bouquet luring families from their cars, the multitude of customers attracting yet another steakhouse or burger haven, and the general population becoming more protein-infused and cholesterol-laden. Within a single-square-mile swath of real estate at the eastern edge of the village, there are no fewer than a dozen restaurants that specialize in satisfying our taste for beef and pork—whether it is served on a bun, sizzling on a breakfast plate, slathered with barbeque sauce, or cooked in front of us with theatrical Asian flair. Indeed, what is the destructive power of one man with an excavator compared to thousands of men wielding steak knives?

If the reader's taste buds are stimulated by now (*a la* television's drooling Homer Simpson), let your senses reinforce the fact that Barboursville, as an original frontier town, has roots in the animal protein supply chain. The more sinewy citizens of two hundred years ago were not necessarily enjoying the savory harvest, but rather fattening up the product as it went by. In those days, the only way to keep meat fresh was by transporting it live, on the hoof. Most typically, hog-drovers were ushering along great numbers of "America's other white meat" along the turnpike through Barboursville, and corn became an important cash crop. Cornfields lined much of the pike and sales to hog-drovers put cash in family coffers. Before too long, hogs were butchered, processed and packed in Barboursville. Ham and lard were shipped to Pittsburgh and Philadelphia; side and shoulder meat went to Kanawha County to be salt-cured.

Before leaving behind this savory subject and following a more academic path, allow me to conjure up a lively instrumental tune heard on twenty-first century television and radio, almost always accompanied by the languid voice of Matthew McConaughey shilling for the National Cattlemen's Beef Association. From the twentieth-century ballet "Rodeo" by American composer Aaron Copland, the track reintroduces an old fiddle strain called "Bonaparte's Retreat." In addition to fueling one's carnivorous mood and name-checking a European icon, the tune captures the capitalist energy and drive of the times when Barboursville came into its own. Considering that the song was actually played by local musicians of the period, we have a most fitting musical theme to round out our multi-sensory experience. The internet-savvy reader may choose to hop onto YouTube and let any number of old-timey renditions of "Bonaparte's Retreat" provide the soundtrack as we delve into Barboursville's emergence as a center of enterprise in America's "first western frontier."

America's Original "Wild West"

The frontier story has always been about the race to make one's name or fortune while meeting the demand for a new resource — be it juicy steaks, gold, salt, corn, lumber, coal, commercial property or broadband internet reception. Or bear skins.

During the Napoleonic Wars in Europe, several nations' armies demanded the pelts of black bears. The hides were needed to shield fighters from the brutal winters, and to keep the British soldiers in posh tall hats. Therefore, the three-year period from 1805 to 1807 was a busy time to be a trapper in western Virginia. Some 8,000 bear hides were shipped from the Guyandotte watershed up the Ohio River to New York merchants who tapped into those worldwide military markets. This number indicates that the seeds were planted early to incorporate the primitive Guyandotte valley into the world economy with ruthless efficiency. (I mean, think of it—8,000 bear skins, Daniel Boone style, y'all!) Patterns of land acquisition made the region ripe for the picking years before America declared its independence. Economists have mapped how British capitalists resettled the Appalachians in four stages, starting as early as 1763 in the eastern and Ohio River fringes of western Virginia (including the land where Barboursville now sits). The Savage Grant transaction was typical of westward movement into Appalachia through military bounties, grants and sales to individuals.

As part of Southern Appalachia, all of what is now West Virginia was essentially privatized before federal land policy had ever been formulated. After Virginia opened its western lands for sale in 1792, the state sold over two-and-a-half million acres to just 14 speculators. Within less than five years, Virginia flooded northeastern markets with these cheap holdings, throwing our pristine mountain bounty into the hands of a very few individuals.

Therefore, as frontier lands go, the vast Cabell County of 1809 could fairly be included in America's "original wild west," and as such was ever subject to plunder by wealthy outside interests. Private, outside ownership and a succession of extractive industries would have lasting economic, social and environmental impacts on southern West Virginia.

Pathway to the Mississippi

I question whether the hunters, trappers and traders worried about what would happen when their resource of choice was used up. The daring frontiersmen simply moved on to the next big thing. And in 1805, aside from bear skins, the next big thing would have been the seemingly endless land stretching to the Mississippi River after the Louisiana Purchase. This transaction, said to be Thomas Jefferson's greatest achievement in office, effectively doubled the size of the United States as the new century dawned.

Jefferson's Louisiana Purchase involved 14 present-day plains states west of the Mississippi River down to the port city of New Orleans. This acquisition came about through a remarkably fast-and-loose international deal: in 1800, France's ruler Napoleon Bonaparte reacquired Louisiana from Spain in exchange for some territory elsewhere, but found his hands tied in Europe with all the military activity there. He tried to establish a naval base at Santo Domingo in the Caribbean Sea for protection against the British navy, but then a slave insurrection led by the Haitian hero Toussaint L'Ouverture broke out in 1801. Napoleon lost some 70,000 men, Haiti became independent and *(cue music)* Bonaparte retreated, deciding to focus on just conquering Europe. By April 1803, the impulsive emperor made the offer to sell not just the New Orleans area, but the whole of the Louisiana Territory, for $15 million. The Senate quickly ratified the treaty and the House of Representatives appropriated the money. The formal transfer of sovereignty took place in New Orleans on December 20, 1803.

According to historians Findling and Thakeray, the massive land purchase was a hallmark of Thomas Jefferson's presidency (1800-1809), and it ushered in a new century marked by "a blend of high purpose and selfish national interest." Following the Louisiana Purchase, settlement of the West crept along for decades until other treaties, tribal wars and the Gold Rush would eventually open up new frontiers that stretched to the Pacific Ocean.

In the meantime, Barboursville would see its fortunes rise, not only as the connecting point of two thriving Appalachian transportation channels, but also as a way station between eastern powerbrokers and the vast new western frontier.

Life around a Frontier Town

Picture the newly completed James River and Kanawha Turnpike in the years between 1805 and 1830. Along the course that now takes local drivers west from U.S. Route 60 through the length of Main Street and across the river to Farmdale and Pea Ridge, the few residents living along the route could look out their front doors and see more and more of the world pass by. Travelers in wagons, on foot or horseback were at first accompanied by the cacophony and smell of animals on the move.

Drovers of cattle, sheep, hogs or turkeys made their way to eastern markets to feed the taste for meat among America's well-to-do. They started out with their hogs, traveling about six miles per day, and fattening them up en route. Farmers along the road began selling corn to the drovers. William Merritt's son Thomas lived in a house on the east end of the pike (where the Sulzer plant stands in 2013), and his farm supplied feed for hogs and other stock going east. People also continued to bring their corn to Merritt's mill from many miles away. The grinding of the course meal was by turns of the wheel, and in times of low water the turns came slowly. Therefore, the mills were a good place to hear the news and became a great social center.

The surrounding area was fertile farm and timber land. The majority of farmers were from eastern Virginia and Pennsylvania and raised their own flax, hemp and cotton. Sheep, hogs and Shorthorn cattle were raised in (increasingly) great numbers. Farmers tilled their soil in the summer, then logged and sold their timber in the winter, getting from five cents to one dollar per tree.

The few hundred families of the county had to be self-sufficient. The "better class of people," those who lived on the bottoms and plantations around Barboursville, had homes that were built of new logs and floored with lumber cut by whipsaws. According to Lambert's sources, some of the houses outside town limits were of much ruder construction. They were made of round logs, daubed with mud, floored with puncheons and roofed with clapboards weighted down by poles. Windows were few, as glass was taxed, and greased paper was sometimes used to admit light. "The doors were hung on wooden hinges. Light was furnished by candles or pine torches. Every family had its candle molds, and candles were made of tallow, or of tallow and bees wax. The furniture consisted of homemade beds, cupboards, stools, plain tables and split bottom chairs.

Every family had its loom with its small and large wheel, which occupied the women and produced clothing, blankets and such for the family. Cooking was on cranes hung over the fire in Dutch Ovens, or in skillets with lids. Cooking stoves were scarce, even in town, until about the time of the Civil War. Fruits, pumpkins, beans, etc., were strung on strings and dried over the fire."

S 55° E 50 po. 4 feet 6 inches

STREET - 60 feet wide.

| Lot No. 1. | Lot No. 2. | Lot No. 3. | Lot No. 4. | Lot No. 5. | Lot No. 6. | Lot No. 7. |

S 55° E 18 po.

WATER STREET

PUBLIC SQUARE

Jail

COURT HOUSE

N 35° E 18 po.

N 55 W. 18 po.

CENTER STREET

Alley one Pole wide

Lot No. 9. 6 po. by 11

Lot No. 8. 6 po. by 11

Lot No. 10. 6 po. by 12

Lot No. 11. 6 po. by 12

Lot No. 13. 6 po. by 12

Lot No. 12. 6 po. by 12

Alley One Pole Wide

MAIN STREET 60 feet wide

N 35° E - 70 poles, 5 feet, 6 inches.

STREET - 60 feet wide

Lot No. 20. 6 po. by 10

Lot No. 19. 6 po. by 10

Lot No. 18. 6 po. by 10

Lot No. 17. 6 po. by 10

Lot No. 16. 6 po. by 10

Lot No. 15. 6 po. by 10

Lot No. 14. 6 po. by 10

STREET - 60 feet wide

Alley One Pole wide

Lot No. 21. 5 po. by 12

Lot No. 22. 6 po. by 10

Lot No. 23. 5 po. by 12

Lot No. 24. 5 po. by 12

Lot No. 27. 5 po. by 12

Lot No. 26. 5 po. by 12

Lot No. 25. 5 po. by 12

Alley One Pole wide

Lot No. 28. 5 po. by 12

Lot No. 29. 6 po. by 10

Lot No. 30. 5 po. by 12

Lot No. 31. 5 po. by 12

Lot No. 34. 5 po. by 12

Lot No. 33. 5 po. by 12

Lot No. 32. 5 po. by 12

Lot No. 35 - 12 po. by 30 feet

Lot No. 36 6 po. by 30 feet

Lot No. 37 12 po. by 30 feet

Lot No. 38 12 po. by 30 feet

S 35° W. 70 poles 1 foot 6 inches.

N 55° W. 50 poles 4 feet 6 inches.

The surveyor's plan for Barboursville's original streets and alleys is almost unchanged two centuries later.
(Courtesy of Frances Gunter)

"For several years the village expanded slowly. More cabins were added to the infant community as time passed, and every now and then a new harness shop or store would open for business at Barboursville," Lambert noted.

Wresting the County Seat from Guyandotte

In 1809 "Merritt's Mill" got a brief taste of the importance it would assume a few years later. For one year, the County Court carried on its business in the home of William Merritt. In 1810, the county seat was moved to nearby Guyandotte, but remained there only until 1813, when it returned to Barboursville for a long stay. The same year Barboursville was given the status of town by the State of Virginia.

Hard feelings between Barboursville and Guyandotte seep through the fading pages of history, in the form of old political gossip shared by Fred Lambert: "The county formed in 1809, and the public buildings were located at Guyandotte on what is now known as Court Square. However, before the buildings were ready, Thomas Ward – who was the first Sheriff by some kind of chicanery, prevailed upon the Commissioners to hold Court at his house, occupied at the time by William Merritt. This led to an indictment against John Morris for accusing Ward of using improper influence to have the Court held at Ward's house. Thus, the first Court was held at Barboursville," wrote one curmudgeon.

The original county jail structure, in the process of being dismantled during the 1930s.
(Courtesy of Marshall University Libraries Special Collections)

Then there was the matter of the turnpike. "The people of Guyandotte were very much dissatisfied with the route from Barboursville to Big Sandy, claiming that a foreign engineer (Mr. Claudius Crozet, a Frenchman) had tried to kill their town by directing their trade to a point beyond it, making the terminus of the road, as they said, in the woods at the mouth of the Big Sandy." (Guyandotte would correct this "grave mistake" a few decades later, with the completion of an alternate route, the Guyan River Road, which remains one of my favorite "sneaky ways" between Huntington and Barboursville.)

Once Barboursville outplayed Guyandotte for position as county seat, development followed quickly. A plan of the town of Barboursville was laid out for William Merritt by William Buffington, County Surveyor, in 1814. The surveyor's record describes the grid of streets and alleys, which is virtually unchanged to this day: "Lying adjacent to the Public Square, or Court House of the County of Cabell, containing Twenty Acres, exclusive of said Public Square, and laid off into lots, which as number from 1 to 38, with convenient streets 60 feet wide and alleys one pole wide." The plan included the three named streets of Main, Water and Center (now Central Avenue), an unnamed street roughly in the vicinity of Kuhn Street (near the swimming pool and cemetery) and several alleyways. The current public library and the Dollar General Store mark the eastern and southern borders of the 1814 town plan.

Total county expenses for 1814 were only about eight hundred dollars. Each "tithable" paid sixty-eight and three-fourths cents. The first courthouse was built in 1814. The original building had two rooms, one up and one down, and the lower room was whitewashed. It was about 30 to 40 feet square. The courthouse square became a favorite meeting spot to catch up on the news. A jail was added behind the courthouse, constructed of hand-hewn logs and rock.

Stocks and Pillory

"John Coalter was Judge. It is claimed that the people objected to being bothered with fines, judgments, etc., but the Court seemed to think they were necessary and proceeded to administer them," recalled one early resident.

Peter Dirton (sometimes cited as "Derton" or "Dirting") was jailer until his death in 1815. Gunter's book suggests that his son William Dirton married

Elizabeth Merritt, daughter of William Merritt; he later became toll gatherer on the turnpike and built the home on 848 Main Street that stands today. William Miller's written testimony states that the toll keeper's name was John and that the Dirtons were the oldest settlers in the neighborhood, living on the hill near the current Veterans Home.

Wrote G. S. Wallace, "It is interesting to remember that at this time the jail was for the safekeeping of the prisoners and debtors, and that there was a general law which required the justices to mark and lay out the 'bounds and rules' of the county not exceeding ten acres adjoining the jail where every prisoner not committed for treason or felony who gave security to keep the rules had the right to walk for the preservation of his health." This walkabout area for well-behaved prisoners essentially covered the cross streets lined out in Merritt's town plan.

Wallace refers to a court order made on May 2, 1815, appointing commissioners to contract to the lowest bidder construction of the stocks and pillory, to be erected on the public square near the jail. Stocks and pillory (illustrated in this clipart image, together with an official lockmaster, helpless prisoner and ready tomato-thrower) were used for punishment of those who committed minor offenses, and served as a whipping post. It is noted by several sources that these were used in Barboursville for several decades, with the most frequent crime being that of horse stealing.

Records from 1826 showed how punishment was applied for various offenses: "A man named Giles Green, convicted for petty larceny, was sentenced to jail for three months, safely kept on a low and coarse diet, and taken by the sheriff to the public whipping post on the fourth Mondays in April and June at 2 p.m., to be given "fifteen lashes on his bare back on each day well laid on." Another man named John Rickman was convicted of the same crime but given only ten lashes on a certain day each month for three months. Another man stole some flour and meal, and was sentenced to have "ten stripes on his bare back" notwithstanding the fact that the stolen property was returned."

Other recorded offenses were "selling spirituous liquors without license, assault and battery, profane swearing, unlawful gaming, neglect of duty as a ferry keeper, neglect of duty as an overseer of the road, and cashing a hundred dollar counterfeit note. David Witcher Jr., was charged with having willfully and maliciously shot Stephen, a Negro man slave, the property of said David Witcher. . . For this offense he was acquitted."

From its infancy as a town, Barboursville was home to a few freed slaves. "A free man of color," Cuffey Caldwell, owned several lots of town real estate from 1815-1829, some of it deeded by the town's Trustees. Deed records suggest an association between Caldwell and the Merritt or Dundas families. As early as 1815 Jeremiah

Ward (who along with Thomas Ward owned 16 slaves) freed a 60-year-old female, Pegalis Margaret, gave her $30 a year for support and provided for her in his will.

With Barboursville now the seat of legal power, so came the lawyers. The first included Henry Fisher, George Summers, Benjamin Smith, Gideon Camden, David McComas and J. H. Brown. Soon would follow the "ordinaries," taverns and other merchants looking to fill the needs of residents, travelers and those doing business with the Court.

"The Sons of 1791"

Four very young and ambitious men converged upon Barboursville around the year 1813, and all of them would have a major and lasting impact on Cabell County. These men were John Samuels, Solomon Thornburg, Frederick Beuhring and John Laidley. Ironically, all of them came into this world in the year 1791, and Barboursville was chartered around the time of their 21st birthdays. *(At this discovery, the author's inner-Doris Kearns Goodwin got weak in the knees.)*

Though their characters were distinct, their lives would follow a similar trajectory and intersect 25 years later in a consequential way.

Samuels. John Samuels came as a young attorney from the "Valley of Virginia" to Barboursville around 1810. He was eventually elected clerk of both circuit and county, and filled the office for many years. When the General Assembly authorized the town to sell lots in the public square in 1824, Samuels was appointed to oversee the sale as commissioner.

He married Barboursville's Emily Gardner, granddaughter of a French Marquis *(more about her family in Chapter 5)*, and had four sons and a daughter. The couple deeded a Water Street lot in 1835 for construction of the Methodist Episcopal Church. Their oldest son, Henry Jefferson Samuels, was the first Cabell County judge. Their only daughter's name was America, born when Samuels was 50; she grew up to marry the Rev. A. J. McMillion.

The Samuelses were a strong military family: John served in the War of 1812; Joe Samuels, his son, fought in the Mexican War; Alexander Samuels was First Lieutenant in Jenkins's Company in the Civil War, later becoming Adjutant General on General John S. Williams's staff in the Confederate Army. Lafayette "Lafe" Samuels, another son, was a Captain in the Confederate Army, dying at home directly after the war was over. Judge H. J. Samuels was Adjutant General of the State of West Virginia.

John Samuels - Moses Thornburg House, Main Street
(Courtesy of Marshall University Libraries Special Collections)

F.G.L. Beuhring
(Courtesy of Marshall University Libraries Special Collections)

Beuhring. Frederick George Lewis Beuhring was a worldly young man. He came to America from Bremen Germany in 1805 as a 14-year-old, fought to defend Baltimore in the War of 1812 and later joined the import firm of Koeing and Company, the biggest wholesale and importing house in the city of Baltimore. This business took him to the West Indies, Yucatan, and many states of the Union.

Frederick married the boss's niece, Francis Eleanor Dannenberg, and they had four children.

A court order of 1817 shows that Frederick Beuhring lived in Barboursville by that time. Before leaving the village in 1836, he had served two terms as Sheriff. He or his son later established the Beuhring Hotel in Barboursville. Beuhring eventually purchased what became known as the Maple Grove Plantation, located between 7th and 11th streets along the Ohio River, currently the area of Harris Riverfront Park and downtown Huntington. At the time of his death, June 27, 1859, he was a member-elect of the General Assembly of Virginia.

Beuhring's obituary in the *Kanawha Valley Star* offered a detailed tribute to his character:

> "(He was) an adversary, open, frank and fearless. He had a strong innate disgust for everything like duplicity and bad faith. Himself decided and unequivocal, he was always to be found on one side or the other of every question that claimed his attention. Nor was any one, acquainted with him, long in doubt as to the side he espoused. As a master, he was kind and indulgent in the extreme—and as a neighbor had but few equals. To a genuine hospitality he added the most polished manners and rarely failed to make one feel perfectly welcome and entirely at ease. On the subject of religion he very rarely conversed, though he always held to the Lutheran Church. Having no congregation of his own creed near, he always attended and took part in the religious worship in the neighborhood, by whatever denomination conducted; and was one of the most liberal contributors to the support of the gospel as preached by them all."

Thornburg. Solomon Thornburg was born in Sheperdstown, Berkeley County. He arrived from the Shenandoah Valley between 1811 and 1813, and started out in Barboursville as a blacksmith. By 1827, he had attained the title of Commissioner when he, along with John Samuels, John Harmon and William Buffington, ordered that the county be laid off into magisterial districts (which today remain largely unchanged since that time). He was elected to the offices of Virginia assembly, county court and magistrate and, in 1842, county sheriff.

Solomon married Mary M. Staley in 1812, and they had three sons, two daughters and at least 40 grandchildren. Their son James L. Thornburg was educated in county schools and Marshall, lived on the farm with his father, clerked in the William C. Miller store, taught school for a few years, settled below Huntington, and was a surveyor by profession. Another son, Thomas T. Thornburg, operated a store on the corner of Main and Central, and was the county's first Superintendent of Schools.

Two homes of Thornburg family members are shown on the far left
and right-hand sides of this 1920s-era photograph of Water Street.
(Courtesy of Marshall University Libraries Special Collections)

Solomon's great-grandson, Howard B., and *his* son Claud H. Thornburg,
continued the family tradition of educational stewardship, presiding over the
Cabell County Board of Education into the twentieth century. Claud H. also
developed West Virginia's first large housing subdivision, Guyan Estates, on family
farmland near Davis Creek in the 1960s. The Thornburg family burial ground, set
aside along the river in that very subdivision, is a well-kept testament to Solomon's
descendents (as well as a veritable gallery of American tombstone history).

Laidley. The fourth young man, John Laidley, came to town between 1809
and 1810. John was the son of Thomas Laidley, a Scottish man who settled in
Philadelphia in 1774 and took part in the Revolution on the side of the colonists.
After the war, the father settled on the Monongahela River at Morgantown and was
a delegate to the Virginia Convention of 1779.

According to historian Virgil Lewis, Laidley received his early education at
Morgantown. "When but a boy, he learned to set type in the office of an early newspaper of that town. Later he went to Parkersburg where he read law in the office of
his brother, James G. Laidley. Having been admitted to the bar he located for the
practice of his profession at Barboursville, in the then-new county of Cabell." He
served in the army at Norfolk, Virginia, in the year 1814, after which, he returned
to Barboursville, and soon became "a great" Prosecuting Attorney for the county.

John Laidley – *(Courtesy of Marshall University
Libraries Special Collections Department)*

In 1816, he wedded Mary Scales Hite, and had 14 children, five girls and nine boys. Like Samuels, Laidley made a home on Main Street in Barboursville and was elected Commonwealth attorney for Cabell County, a position he held until at least 1852. His children included attorney John Laidley Jr., who would figure into the city of Huntington's creation, and prominent Charleston attorney, legislator and publisher, William Sydney Laidley.

In 1829, Laidley moved his large family to a riverside farm one mile below the town of Guyandotte at the current location of 26th Street, where he engaged in agricultural pursuits and practiced law. Here he resided until his death in 1863.

Around the time of his move from Barboursville to the Guyandotte area, John Laidley represented Cabell County at the 1829-30 Virginia Constitutional Convention, as one of 96 delegates. The imposing delegation included two former presidents, James Madison and James Monroe, and United States Chief Justice John Marshall. The 75-year-old Marshall made an impression that Laidley would not forget.

In 1838, Laidley, Beuhring and other new residents along the Ohio River decided that a subscription school in the county should be known as Marshall Academy, in memory of John Marshall, Chief Justice of the United States. To do this required the passage of an Act by the Virginia General Assembly, so the matter was placed in the hands of Solomon Thornburg, then the representative of Cabell County in the lower House of that body. On his motion made January 4, 1838, it was "Resolved, that the committee of Schools and Colleges be instructed to enquire into the expediency of incorporating the Marshall Academy in the county of Cabell."

The Bill to incorporate Marshall Academy passed the House March 24, 1838, and was passed by the Senate six days thereafter. The first section read, "Be it enacted by the general assembly, that Benjamin Brown, Frederick G. L. Beuhring, James Gallaher, John Laidley, William Buffington, John Samuels, Richard Brown, Benjamin H. Smith, and George W. Summers, be, and they are hereby constituted a body politic and corporate, by the name and style of the trustees of Marshall academy."

Laidley would serve for many years as Marshall's President, and Beuhring as Secretary, seeing the institution rise to College status and raising educational standards for the county as a whole.

In 1856, the Kanawha Valley Star published a lengthy editorial praising the school. An excerpt:

"Turning aside from the din of politics, we take occasion to call the attention of those interested in the work of education, to the excellent institution known as Marshall Academy. It has now been in operation for little more than a dozen years; but in that short period, very many of its students have become prominent and leading men in the learned professions of law, medicine and divinity; and many of them have arisen to high official stations, civil and military, not only in Virginia, but also in other States of the Union. Indeed, it is doubtful whether there is now an institution in the State, that in so short a time, has sent forth so large a portion of leading men. So much for the past of its short history. Its future is still more promising. During the last session, there were nearly a hundred students in attendance…The trustees, Messrs. John Laidley, Frederick G. L. Beuhring, P. C. Buffington, Dr. G. C. Ricketts, and others, are gentlemen whose names give character and currency to whatever they may be connected with." (V. A. Lewis, A History of Marshall Academy, Marshall College and Marshall College State Normal School 1912)

Before Beuhring, Laidley, Samuels and Thornburg left their legacy to the Sons of Marshall, these "sons of 1791"— two attorneys and two businessmen — served their country and helped build a new county seat. During its formative decades, Barboursville was their home.

Were they good friends? Competitors? Fellow worshippers? Smoking buddies? We know little about what antics or conversations transpired between them as young bucks on muddy Main Street. One thing is certain: their achievements indicate that they began their adult lives in Barboursville as smart, vital young men. Together, their legacies fit historian Charles Sellers's characterization of American men of the Jacksonian age, who were "anxious to exercise with wartime vigor the peacetime power of an activist capitalist state."

Our Special Correspondent Furnishes an Interesting Letter:
JULY 7, 1898—George Thornburg and three others passed through Milton in a
surrey on their way to Webster Springs, Nicholas County, for a month's outing.

CHAPTER 5

AMERICAN PARADE ALONG MAIN STREET (1820S TO 1840S)

Completion of the Pike

MAIN Street eventually got less muddy. Most turnpikes were surveyed and improved in the 1820s, and the James River and Kanawha Turnpike was completed between the towns of Guyandotte and Charleston by 1829.

A county map was surveyed and drawn under the direction of John Wood in 1822 before any bridges were built. It indicates three early ferry locations. The first was in the vicinity of "Merrett's Mill" *(sic)* at the confluence of the Mud and Guyandotte rivers. The second ferry on the map is called "Mcginnis Ferry," *(sic)* and appears to cross the Guyandotte River roughly between Aracoma Drive in Pea Ridge and the railroad underpass dog-leg on the Old Guyan River Road. A third ferry appears to the east, across the Mud near Linville Drive, a few hundred feet shy of the present sites of the Lady Godiva strip club and Fellowship Baptist Church *(or as some holdovers from the 1970s refer to it, the Hullabaloo Church, a detail to be explained in Chapter 16).*

The Guyandotte River Company built the first bridge across the Mud River just west of Merritt's Mill, but sold their interest to the James River company a year or two later. That entity rebuilt a more substantial covered wooden bridge in the same location. The state and county set the tolls on the turnpike, with each vehicle, person and animal charged prescribed fees at toll locations set every four miles (those going to a mill or living near a toll booth were exempt). In 1837, a half acre of land just south of the Mud-Guyandotte confluence was deeded by William Merritt's daughter, Elizabeth Merritt Dirton, for erection of the Barboursville

Toll House. Her husband William Dirton became the first toll keeper. (In 1951, the house was moved to its current location on Main Street by Tanyard Branch, to be used as a museum and meeting place by the Daughters of the American Revolution.)

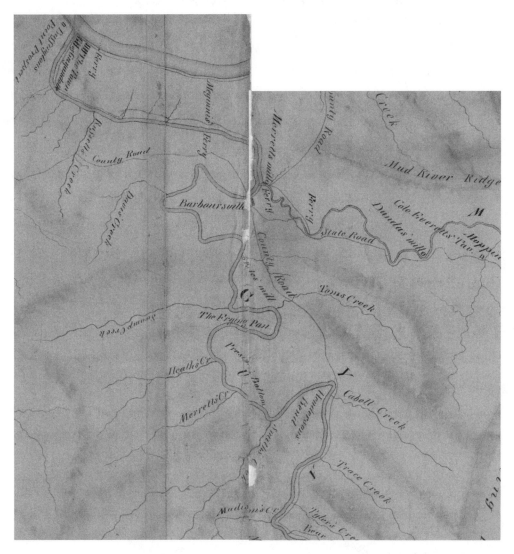

Two panels of 1822 Cabell County Surveyors Map, aligned to show
Barboursville and surrounding districts.
(The Library of Virginia Digital Collection)

Meet the Travelers

Traffic along the pike, also called "The Kanawha Road," was seasonal and spasmodic, especially before 1830. Then the increase in travel became "immense." The

Kanawha Banner, in an editorial dated December 9, 1831, estimated that 2,500 travelers were passing over the road annually.

Fred B. Lambert—who collected and preserved the memories of Barboursville old-timers with the eccentric zeal of a lepidopterist—assembled vivid imagery of the travelers moving east and west on the James River and Kanawha Turnpike during the town's original Golden Age. As the century progressed through the 1840s, road improvements and ever-increasing westward expansion delivered a diverse back-and-forth parade of American characters:

The Dusty Drovers. In the fall of the year, when grain and feed could be cheaply obtained, thousands of hogs could pass along, destined for the eastern quarter of the state. In 1826 alone, some 60,000 head of hogs were driven eastward over the James River and Kanawha Turnpike. The droves sometimes monopolized the road for days, even into December.

The life of the drover was by no means easy. After driving stock sometimes as far east as Richmond or beyond, he often walked back. Drovers received less than a dollar a day for their services, and were compelled to make a certain number of miles per day in order to receive full wages.

Growing corn became a business with many farmers along the route, who were known to ride several miles west to meet the drovers and make a bargain for their crops. The demand for corn tended to impoverish the soil to such an extent that it was literally worn out. This may have been the case in Pea Ridge, reputed to have been so named because the soil was "so poor that it would not sprout black eyed peas."

The Rowdy Militiamen. Three times a year, all roads to Barboursville would fill up with hundreds of county men. Under the Militia Act of 1792, the annual muster day in May served to enroll militia members until after the Civil War. Petit musters were held the second Saturday of April and October. Originally designated as the 120th Regiment of Militia of Cabell County (with a minimum 300 men), the county's regiment would later become part of a brigade with other counties. The County Court nominated officers, with the county subdivided into company districts. Within their representative districts, officers were required to enroll every able-bodied white male citizen between 18 and 45 years of age (with certain exceptions).

In June 1812, the recommendations from Cabell County's court and magistrates were: William Spurlock as Ensign under Captain Daniel France; William McComas under Capt. Noah Scales; Stephen Wilson under Capt. William Buffington; Jesse Toney under Capt. Peter Dingess; and Thomas Morris under Capt. Cadwallader Chapman. By 1846, there were at least six companies in Cabell County, with two battalions and regimental staff. The officers included some familiar county surnames: McGinnis, Shelton, McKendree, Samuels, Maupin,

McCullough, Roffe, Buffington, Wood, Thornburg, Wilson, Brown, Johnson, Hannon, Thompson and Childers.

The militia act provided for fines to be imposed by "courts of enquiry" for various violations. William Miller recalled that a fine of 75 cents was imposed for not attending musters, and that one man was fined five dollars for "not falling into line when required."

Muster day served as a significant nineteenth century social event in early America, at least for men. Since militia commanders often attempted to win their men's cooperation by providing them with alcohol, muster day frequently degenerated into an annual drunken spree. Cabell County's musters "were the time and place when the young cocks demonstrated their fistic abilities," according to G. S. Wallace. Robert Dillon recalled that they had whiskey, fights, foot races, horse races and horse trading at the Courthouse, where men came "for 20 miles and more."

Between the musters and matters of the Court, imagine the whiff of rank testosterone that brought its occasional frenzy to Main Street. Avert your eyes, ladies: "The juries did not like to fine for 'A and B' (assault and battery), and many verdicts were for one cent. Fights were rather popular, and the neighborhood 'bully' was looked upon as a kind of hero. They sometimes chewed off fingers or an ear. Gouging was sometimes practiced. It consisted of skillful application of a long thumbnail, especially grown for the purpose. With a little practice it was easy to remove an eye, or wound the cheek. One of these encounters is said to have taken place on the streets here but it did not result in serious injury."

The Bathing Aristocrats. Happily for those of a more delicate constitution, road improvements of the 1830s ushered in "a wonderful change in the manners and customs of the people. Many more or less aristocratic families moved from Virginia into the Kanawha Valley, and gradually extended to the Kentucky line. Much travel both from the east and the west was attracted to this region, on account of the magnificent mountain scenery, and the fact that road passed through the most celebrated mineral springs of the South," wrote Lambert.

As early as the late 1700s the Virginians had come to the mountain springs, "with their Colonial spleens out of whack and their early-Republic joints creaking," according to Perceval Reniers, author of *The Springs of Virginia: Life, Love and Death at the Waters 1775-1900*. Later, other tourists followed from the east, west and south. Wealthy Southerners, especially those living in a princely fashion due to the wildly surging export value of cotton, would visit as many resorts in a season as time and money would allow. The region of the Virginia Springs contained a collection of "fountains strongly impregnated with minerals, heat, fashion and fame—the Warm, the Hot, the White Sulphur, the Sweet, the Salt Sulphur and the Red Sulphur." The springs were situated along a circuitous route more than a hundred miles east of Barboursville on the turnpike.

By the 1850s, even Cabell County had gotten into the market with its own celebrated Blue Sulphur spring on the Mud River, and there existed another sulphur spring on the Guyandotte, about 18 miles southwest of Barboursville. Those without the means to visit the fashionable springs to the east could enjoy the regional springs, "both of which have… been much resorted to on account of the efficacy of their waters," according to the *Virginia Directory and Business Register* of 1852.

In 1835, one bale of fine Louisiana grade cotton (about 475 pounds worth) would buy the daughter of a successful planter the trip and a fortnight at the premiere Virginia Springs. As described by Reniers, the fashionable pilgrimage would involve ten days cabin passage on the Mississippi River, from Natchez up to Louisville, Kentucky; transfer to another steamer that carried her first to Cincinnati, then on to Guyandotte, Virginia, where our young Southern lady would take the stagecoach. "Landed at Guyandotte, she will pay $11 to the stage contractor for the journey to the White Sulphur, which is east and a little south from Guyandotte one hundred and seventy miles."

Many of the wealthier people (who brought along their Negro coaches, nurses and other servants) had their own private conveyances across the James and Kanawha River Turnpike, "and disdained to ride with the common herd," Lambert added.

The Speedy Stagecoaches. For those tourists and travelers of the middle classes, stagecoach life was plenty tolerable, even enjoyable. In good weather, the stages made from 75 to 80 miles a day, mostly in the daytime. By 1829, the stages were running three times a week. In 1831, two men named Porter and Belden had control of the stage line along the whole route from the Ohio River to Richmond, and as travel increased they put on an extra line of stages. Their company also built and owned the steamer "Guyandotte," which made twice-a-week trips to Cincinnati.

Stage fare from Guyandotte to Charleston was four dollars, with each passenger allowed 20 pounds of baggage. Coaches were fitted with lamps suspended on the sides, enabling them to drive at night. The horses, obtained from the famous Blue Grass region of Kentucky or the Valley of Virginia, were outfitted with fine harnesses with brass ornamentation. Regular relays, or stage stands, were kept along the road, where horses were changed for a fresh team to haul the stage to the next stand. (Mr. Hanley kept a stage stand and hotel in a two-story frame house just above Blue Sulphur Springs near Ona.) The drivers went at a rapid rate and only stopped when hailed by a prospective passenger. A tin horn announced the time for beginning a trip, or the approach to a station.

By 1840, it is said that four to five stage coaches ran each day, each way. Each coach had three seats to carry nine passengers, sometimes with extra passengers riding on top and in front, as well as extras and mail.

Stage travel was not without its headaches. Despite the skill required of a stage driver, sometimes accidents occurred due to a slip in the road or the carelessness (or drunkenness) of the driver. Moreover, the tolls collected for upkeep of the turnpike, intended to be proportionate to the damage done to the road, presented their own kind of hardship. For a time, not only the drivers, but individual passengers were each required to pay a toll at Dirton's tollhouse (then located on the south side of the Mud River), and at each four-mile interval along the route. In 1832, a gentleman traveling over the road stated that the passengers were astonished at this fact and at first refused to pay. Finally, they "yielded to the strong arm of the law, consoling themselves by chanting the Negro melody 'Ole Virginny Never Tire.'"

1837 Toll House

The Famous Politicians. In its heyday, the James River and Kanawha carried eminent statesmen including Henry Clay, Henry Banks, James Madison and Andrew Jackson, who passed through while campaigning for President in 1828. These luminaries traveled to and from White Sulphur Springs, or on to Washington, D.C.

Henry Clay was a nineteenth-century American planter, statesman and orator who served as Kentucky Senator, Speaker of the U.S. House of Representatives and Secretary of State. Clay was said to have been a great favorite along the pike. A Mrs. Ellen Woods wrote of an encounter in Teays Valley: "I have often heard my mother relate that a stranger drove up one evening in a private conveyance driven by a negro servant. He asked for lodging, and as my grandfather never turned anyone away, he was at once invited in. For some reason, Mr. Clay did not introduce himself. Next morning he thanked my grandfather quite warmly, but as the folks had been well entertained by his conversation, he was told that they could not have treated him better if he had been Henry Clay, whereupon he made himself known, to the delight of all."

The Desperate Farmers. Those who were too poor to pay stage fare either walked, rode horseback, or made their way however they could. By the late 1830s, "Immigration to the west increased to such an extent to become a serious matter to the welfare of the "Mother State." An 1835 letter posted by a literary man of Virginia illuminated this trend:

> In enjoying the pleasures and advantages of safe transportation along the great State Road, which traverses this section, there is a spectacle often presented, which awakens a melancholy train of inflections. I allude to the number of emigrants, who allured by the hope, sometimes deceptive, of improving their condition, are bending their toilsome march to the far West. Imagination becomes busy in conjuring up the broken ties of early association, of kindred and country, and we read, in the sorrowful visages of some of these wretched fugitives, tales of mental and bodily suffering, which no language could express. It is true that some of these numberless caravans present the exterior of comfort, and even happiness, but for the most part, it is evidently the last struggle of despairing poverty, to escape from the hardships of its lot. (F. B. Lambert Collection n.d.)

The author of 1839's *The White Sulphur Springs Papers* offered a particular vignette:

> The road passing by the White Sulphur is the great route to the west, by Guyandotte, and for many weeks hundreds of wagons and other conveyances have been going by, filled with emigrants in search of new homes. There is much character to be met with among them occasionally, and it affords the writer much pleasure and interest at times, to hear their original remarks as to the country where they were going, and what they intended to when they got there. I came upon a party one day, who had been bivouacking (*camping without tent or shelter*) on the way; it turned out to be a whole neighborhood, from one of the eastern counties in Virginia on their way to Illinois. They had with them all their farming utensils and furniture, spinning wheels, churns and the like. The boys, a number of them who were large enough, were supplied with guns and walked after the wagons, and furnished the game. The old patriarch of the family, with whom I conversed, said it went very hard

with him to leave old Virginny, but the lands, they had just quitted, were quite worn out, and would not produce sufficient support for their families, which were large. They had collected several hundred dollars among them and were going to buy and cultivate new lands in Illinois. The old man was quite pleased and surprised when I mentioned that the emperor of China ploughed a furrow once a year, from respect to the farmers and agriculture, and calling the attention of one of the boys near him, he said, "Do you hear that, sir, that the king of China was a farmer? And if you keep straight, you may be President of the United States yet." (F. B. Lambert Collection n.d.)

The Wagon Masters. If the stagecoaches preceded the passenger bus, then the predecessors of today's 18-wheelers had to have been the "Old Virginia Conestogas." Fleets of covered wagons hauled "great loads of merchandise going East with the products of the West," and vice-versa. Every wagon was drawn by not less than four horses, and often six were employed, the horses being arranged two abreast. There was hardly any limit to the capacity of the wagon-body and the loading was regulated by the strength of the horses and the conditions of the roads. A train of these wagons creeping along a public road, the white canvas covers conspicuous at a distance, was always an interesting spectacle, wrote Lambert.

A few drivers he remembered by name.

The Hite brothers—Bob, Dick and Bill—were wagoners, and a jollier crowd was said to be hard to find. They always carried their fiddles, and the nights were made merry by the wagoners engaging in 'bull dances' (so called because no women were present). They carried their own cooking utensils and slept around the fires or in their wagons. In the daytime or at night they could be heard for miles, singing Negro melodies, of which they seemed to possess a full repertoire, and of which they never tired. They brought their provisions and feed of the farmers or taverns along the route, cooked their own meals, and drank their own whiskey. They were a rough set of fellows, always ready for a fight or a frolic. The life was a hard one, which only men of the most powerful physique could stand. In addition, the life of the wagoner was not without its temptations, as well as its hardships. The undue use of liquor often caused trouble. Dr. Speece was accustomed to say that some men, who were staid church members at home, left their religion on the Blue Ridge when they went east with their products.

These old Prairie Schooners, as they were sometimes called, often came from as far distant as North Carolina, bringing whiskey and chestnuts, and returning with bacon fattened on the mast, or nuts of various kinds, in which this region abounded. As many as thirty of these wagons have been seen wending their way above Charleston to the East with their heavy loads of salt and other goods, while those coming West were loaded with fruit, plug tobacco, and general merchandise. (F. B. Lambert Collection n.d.)

The Slave-Drivers. The Wagoner's "merchandise" sometimes included enslaved humans in bondage. Included in the immigration from eastern Virginia to the West, great droves of African slaves were moved to Missouri. One early resident recounted to Lambert, "I have seen as many as eight or ten wagons in a group, owned by the same man, and accompanied by as many as 100 slaves on the way to Missouri, to take the boat at Guyandotte."

An "Ordinary" Town

From its earliest days, travel through the center of town made it necessary for Barboursville to have "houses of entertainment," generally called "ordinaries."

The law was rather strict as to who should be granted license for such an establishment. "He must be a man of good character, not addicted to drunkenness or gaming." The Court was to consider "the convenience of the place proposed, the character of the petitioner, for good order, sobriety and honesty, and his ability to provide and keep good and sufficient houses, lodging and entertainment for travelers." The following is a copy of one of the records granting a license to Thomas Morris in 1813:

> On the motion of Thomas Morris, ordinary license is granted him, to keep an ordinary in the town of Barboursville, at the house now occupied by Ben Maxey, who thereupon with Cadwallader Chapman, his security, came into court and gave bond as the law directs. (F. B. Lambert Collection n.d.)

The license fee was usually about 18 dollars per year. The County Court had the legal right to fix all ordinary rates: "Lodging 12 ½ cents; Oats and corn 12 ½ cents per gallon; Horse standing in hay all night 12 ½ cents; Cordial, Cherry Bounce and Gin 18 ¾ cents per half pint (same rate added later for Whiskey and Peach Brandy)."

> The early landlords differed from those in a later day, in that they were not tavern keepers by profession. They were hunters, farmers and ferry keepers. Aside from the fact that they kept liquor for sale, they made little or no extra preparations for their guests. If one house should be overcrowded, the doors of all others were open. The traveler who chanced to stop at one of the first ordinaries "found little to distinguish it from the average mountain cabin. The food consisted of whatever the season afforded – game, fruit and cornbread, ground at the little water mills, was a meal fit for a king. Family and guest

frequently gathered in the same room, told their hunting and Indian stories, and drank liquor from the same demijohn. (F. B. Lambert Collection n.d.)

After the building of the pike, the inns took on "a more mercenary character. The landlords now gave up their other occupations, and became innkeepers by profession. They sought in every way to please their guests," according to Lambert. His records show that Peter Dirton was granted a license in 1814, and his widow Elizabeth Dirton continued to "keep" at her house in Barboursville for several years. In 1815 licenses were granted in Cabell County to John Everett, Samuel Short, Jeremiah Ward, Thomas Morris, Adam Black, George Chapman, John McConahon, John Morris Jr. and Joseph McGonigle. Ben Maxey, Philip Bumgardner, Elizabeth Dirton, William McComas Jr. and Thomas Morris were all "keeping" in Barboursville. Later, John Shelton was licensed to keep at a brick house rented from Thomas Ward near the river. John Hatfield and William Merritt also kept taverns in Barboursville and sold whiskey and other drinks.

Calling the Tune

As traffic and industry grew, the cacophony of hog droves gave way to the more rhythmic clatter of horses' hooves, and sometimes more melodious sounds. At the musters, musicians served up patriotic tunes with fife, tenor drum and bass drum.

A music-loving gentleman named P.S. "Perl" Drown vividly recalled the sights and sounds on Main Street, at Bob McKendree's Tavern in the 1830s and '40s. As "hayseed visitors" on court day crowded the second story porch, they were regaled by local musicians, including the slave 'Babe' McAllister owned by a farmer McAllister, as well as Anthony Riggs, "Samp" Johnson, George Stephens and Jim Peat. Popular tunes of the day included "Ann Hays," and "Arkansas Traveler." George Stephens played "Bonaparte's Retreat from Moscow," "Bonaparte Crossing the Rhine," and "Cold Frosty Morning." Babe McAllister played "Forked Deer" and "Peach Tree."

Spurning the more classic tunes, "the average native of Cabell County at the period of which I am writing, would be far more entertained listening to George Stephen's 'Possum Creek,' 'Soap Suds Over the Fence' or 'Peach Tree' as he played it by ear," Drown noted.

Another nineteenth-century resident recalled that people of the area would visit neighboring farms to take part in each others' "house raisings," "log rollings," "wool pickings," "flax pullings," "fencings," "clearings," "house warmings," "corn shuckings," and "barn raisings."

Dances were frequent. There were many old time fiddlers who played the old tunes with zeal that will never be surpassed. The Old Virginia Reel was the favorite dance. It was sometimes called "French Four." Jack McComas was a famous fiddler, and when he played the "Lady's Fancy," always created a furor of jollity…He would call for "partners for square dance" or the Virginia Reel and start his orchestral talent on that tune, calling the figures on time, changing the keys of his violin to suit the movements appropriate to the dance. "Natchez Under the Hill" was another favorite tune, better known as "Turkey in the Straw"…Throughout the night, as the youths, maidens and parents—all were young again—were eager and impatient for the next set to form. Liquor was cheap and plentiful. Even the groceries kept it, and some of us would be a bit embarrassed to know how often our grandfathers patronized them for this very commodity. (F. B. Lambert Collection n.d.)

The Refining Influence of a French Noblewoman

Amid this atmosphere of hogs, logs, whiskey and fisticuffs, there entered in the 1820s a Boston shipping magnate and his French wife. Between their wealth, family ties and social principles, this power couple would not only shape Barboursville's destiny, but would also help define its most sacred cultural institutions.

In the years before they arrived in Barboursville to open a stage coach inn on the northeast corner of Main and Center, the lives of Joseph Gardner (b. 1774) and Marie Terese Sophie Clotilde Raison de la Geneste (1786-1854) were "both interesting and romantic," as described in a 1902 historical magazine. This is an understatement. According to Joseph L. Miller:

The Marquis Maison De la Geneste, left France and settled in the Island of St. Domingo. Here he purchased three sugar plantations and several hundred negroes – nine hundred I was told by his great grandson, the late Judge H. J. Samuels, of Cabell County. He had…a daughter named Marie Terese Sophie Clotilde Raison De la Geneste, who at the age of fourteen became the wife of Mr. Gardner, a merchant trader sailing out of Boston. Her father opposed this marriage very much on account of difference in family rank. But Mr. Gardner sold his ships and settled down on the plantation in St. Domingo. In 1796 came the Insurrection of the Slaves. By means of a faithful slave they escaped to a United States vessel and later landed at Philadelphia, with only their clothing, two servants, who chose to come with them and some costly jewels that Madame had concealed from the mob. Here they sold a pair of solitaire diamond earrings for two thousand dollars, with which they decided to go to the French, in Louisiana. They went to Pittsburg by stage coach and there took passage on a flat boat loaded for New Orleans. The water was low in the Ohio and near Greenup, Ky., the boat ran aground. Being tired of the slow journey already Mr. and Mrs. Gardner decided to stop here instead of going on to Louisiana. So they rented the largest house in the village and opened an Inn, which became a famous hostelry in that part of Kentucky in the first half of the nineteenth century. Several pieces of costly jewelry were handed down to their descendents, among them a pair of diamond cuff buttons to Judge Samuels. Later they received a partial indemnity from the French Government. From an old letter written at Paris in 1854 I see that the "fifteenth annuity of the St. Domingo Indemnity due the heirs of the late Mq. Maison Dela Geneste" was due in 1852. (D. J. Miller 1902)

Various accounts differ on details of Marie's life, including the spelling of her many names, whether she was an only child or not, and her birthplace—whether Bordeaux, France or Port Au Prince (the city listed on her death certificate). Moreover, we'll never know exactly where she and Joseph concealed the jewels during their adventurous escape to America.

Nevertheless, had it not been for Toussaint L'Ouverture's Haitian insurrection, low water on the Ohio, and Kentucky's comparative lack of appeal, Barboursville as we know it would not exist today.

Joseph Gardner
(Courtesy of Barboursville Public Library)

What we do know about Joseph (pictured in this elegant and somewhat ghostly portrait) and Marie Terese Gardner is that they were people of means. In addition to their jewels and inheritances, once settled in Barboursville they received periodic annuity payments for the loss of the late Marquis Louis's tropical plantation in Santo Domingo, after Joseph petitioned the French Government for restitution.

We can also assume that the couple was patriotic, particularly so during the years from 1806 to 1811, judging by the given names of their offspring. The Gardner children were Mary Evelyn (born 1800), George (1804) Alexander Hamilton (1806), America (1809), Benjamin Franklin (1811), Eliza (1816), Emily (1817) and Joseph Henry (1820). All but Mary Evelyn, who was born in Santo Domingo, were born in Greenup, Kentucky.

We know that Marie Terese was charitable and cultured, donating some of her French Government annuity for the welfare of the town. The Gardner homestead on Main Street (torn down around 1967 to make space for the new Barboursville Baptist Church parking lot) became a gathering place where "one danced to the tune of a classic waltz instead of a ribald hoedown," wrote Frances Gunter.

On Christmas, 1821, the home of Joseph Gardner was thronged with the "beauty and chivalry" of the new town. Belles rested half-mitted hands on the homespun sleeves of their escorts and maintained wide skirts and leg o' mutton sleeves through the crowded room. Their escorts stepped in the measures clad in gaitered trousers, long coats and perchance a stock collar. (Oberholtzer 1922)

Note the signers of a social invitation from June 1823, discovered by the Apple Grove descendents of a "belle" of the region:

The pleasure of Miss Elizabeth Hereford's company is solicited to a BALL at Mr. Joseph Gardner's in Barboursville on the 4th day of July next. Signed John Laidley, F.G.L. Beuhring, John Samuels, Managers (Oberholtzer 1922)

Eliza Gardner Miller
(Courtesy of Frances Gunter)

The Gardner's Barboursville legacy was passed on in large part through their well-bred daughters. (Their eldest daughter and three of the sons settled in Kentucky, while Alexander Hamilton Gardner set off to become a plantation owner in New Orleans.) The youngest three Gardner girls stayed in Barboursville, caught the attention of prominent squires and married well: America became the bride of Cabell County merchant Absalom Holderby. Emily was wed to "Son of 1791" John Samuels, 26 years her senior, and became mother to the first county judge. However it was dark-haired and winsome Eliza *(pictured here, courtesy of Frances Gunter)* who at age 20 would marry 27-year-old William C. Miller and establish home and family with the man called "the pioneer merchant at Barboursville" and "the leading spirit in his time of public improvements in this place."

A quick introduction to the bridegroom's lineage will suffice for now: William Clendenin Miller was born in Gallipolis, Ohio, raised on a large farm in Mason County, Virginia, and lived in our neighboring county's first large brick residence. He was the grandson of German immigrant and Revolutionary War Veteran Christian Mueller. William's father John Miller, having started his career as a hatter in Gallipolis, became a gentleman farmer who was conversant in French as well as German and English. We encountered Miller's maternal grandfather in the previous chapter—Major William Clendenin served as a private under Lt. Col. Daniel Boone in the 1774 Battle of Point Pleasant and was, along with Boone, our region's first representative to the Virginia Assembly. Granddaddy Clendenin also co-founded the city of Charleston and built Fort Lee. John and Sophia Clendenin Miller moved to Cabell County with their sons including William, and a daughter, Margaret, who married Solomon's son Thomas Thornburg.

Just two years after William's 1836 marriage to Eliza Gardner, he received a share of his father's "lands, negroes and other property." In 1840, he began a 20-year turn as Barboursville's postmaster. Miller was known to read the mail to his less-literate neighbors, sharing news of the day from the *New York Tribune* and the *Richmond Times*.

The Gardner, Samuels and Miller families would all settle at the south side of Main Street. Their homes sat across the street, slightly east and presumably upwind of the village tanning yard where cowhides were processed in mass quantities. The land was also opposite the eventual site of a lumber mill (said to be situated near the current Kuhn Memorial Church site), where 36-foot Guyandotte valley timbers were prepared for shipment to Indiana to be made into steamboat hulls.

Despite their coarse surroundings, Harvard-educated Joseph, Marie Terese, their daughters and their daughters' families maintained a cultivated air, and their influence only grew. Marie Terese Sophie Clotilde Raison de la Geneste Gardner would play perhaps her most enduring role in influencing the religious affairs of this burgeoning young town.

Religious Awakenings

A ledger discovered at the Gardner-Samuels homestead in the twentieth century listed members of a Methodist society that met in 1823 in the home of Marie Gardner. (Other surnames on the ledger included McComas, Samuels and Thornburg.) Exactly how Marie came to be a devout Methodist is not known, but a woman's leadership in forming a local Methodist congregation in the eastern United States would not have been unusual in the early 1800s, a time known as the Second Great Awakening.

Women, despite their lack of political or property rights, helped fuel a sweeping nineteenth century movement of American religious revivalism, organizing in response to missionaries and "circuit riders" of the era. Mrs. Gardner's experience could have found its example in the formation of a Methodist congregation in Charleston 20 years earlier: Mrs. Margaret Williams arrived in Charleston and inquired about a religious community. Finding no Methodist meeting established in the city, she invited Rev. William Steele of the Little Kanawha and Muskingum Circuit. The first meeting of Methodists was held in Mrs. Williams' home on January 1, 1804, the founding date of Charleston's Christ Church United Methodist. That same year, the Western Virginia Conference formed the Guyandotte Circuit, and Steele became the first appointed pastor to the Guyandotte Methodist Church.

The Reverend William Steele got around. It is said that he preached the first Methodist sermon in West Virginia. Born in Pennsylvania in 1780, Steele was charged by Francis Asbury, the founder of American Methodism, to the Baltimore Conference which served western Virginia. In 1803, Steele began exploring the area and preaching under assignment by the Redstone District. By 1823, Steele and his family moved to Mecklenburg County, Virginia, and later to Tennessee, Louisiana and Texas, where he died in 1857. William Steele, along with fellow "circuit riders" Thomas Asbury Morris and Asa Shinn (who succeeded Steele in 1804 on the Guyandotte circuit) visited the wilderness settlements to collect pioneers into societies for the worship of God.

As frontier preachers on horseback, their dedication—and their sheer guts in transcending poverty, rugged terrain, harsh weather, ferocious animals, hostile pioneers and flea-ridden sleeping digs—had its example in their Bishop and standard-bearer, Francis Asbury. Between 1771, when he arrived in America commissioned by John Wesley, and 1816, when he died at age 71, Asbury rode more than 225,000 miles on horseback, preaching and teaching a message of salvation. At least one source cites the prospect that Asbury himself may have journeyed to the mouth of the Guyandotte to plant the seeds of Methodism, and it is not outside the realm of possibility. It's more likely, however, that Asbury's effective territorial structure of bishops, conferences and circuits, combined with the draw of large spirit-filled gatherings called "camp meetings" (such as one that took place in 1813 at the current site of Bethesda United Methodist in Ona) brought converts into local Methodist societies.

It is also possible that Marie Terese Gardner and her literate Barboursville neighbors encountered Asbury through his writing; in 1820, his diary was published in book form to represent his years as "the prophet of the long road." Through whatever means Asbury and his fellow circuit riders used to spread the Wesleyan brand of Gospel hope across the Appalachian frontier, Virginia would have more Methodists than any other state by 1800. Church membership continued to outpace the state's population growth well into mid-century.

Other Christian denominations had their Barboursville followers, such as the Jeremiah Wards who worshiped at Mud River Baptist. Lutheran F. G. L. Beuhring, having no nearby congregation, sought out the gospel "as preached by them all," which might also have been the case for other German immigrants who worked and settled in Barboursville during this period. Alongside Steele and his fellow Methodist circuit riders, Baptist missionaries did their part to save souls and serve communities throughout the Guyandotte and Mud river valleys.

In fact, it can be suggested that Baptist and Methodist leaders led the post-Revolutionary charge across the Commonwealth, in the struggle for legal and practical separation of church and state. Virginia's legislative and judicial bodies took decades to sever all Colonial ties to the Anglican Church and its direct heir, the Episcopal Church. This quest for religious freedom no doubt added to the fervor of the Second Great Awakening, and Virginia became an epicenter of dramatic growth for both Baptist and Methodist congregations in America. According to *West Virginia: A History*, Methodists had 281 and Baptists 115 of the 548 congregations in West Virginia by 1850. The Presbyterians trailed far behind with 61 congregations and the Protestant Episcopal, formerly the Anglican, church had only 22. Older denominations such as the Quakers, Lutherans, German Reformists and "Dunkers" were reduced to small fractions of the state's religious adherents.

Whether a community flocked to the call of a Baptist or Methodist preacher tells us something fundamental about the nature of its people. Both denominations had a strong grassroots base of lay leaders in communities and served as vital points for social gatherings. But unlike Asbury's Methodists with their strong central authority and appointed circuit riders, the Baptists churches carried the concept of religious freedom all the way to the local congregation, which selected its own minister and made its own doctrinal decisions.

Methodism tended to appeal to the "natural aristocracy of the areas into which it advanced," due to its deep Wesleyan roots as a movement within the Church of England, as well as its familiar hymnody. In contrast, rural Baptist clergy tended to reflect the makeup of their own congregations. For example, Mud River Baptist's founder John Lee was "very illiterate" at the time he began preaching, "but by persevering industry he not only learned to read but became well acquainted with the scriptures." Much further upriver, Wyoming County residents in 1814 scorned a young Methodist circuit rider as 'proud, ambitious, and too aspiring" because of his fancy dress and presentation.

Although the Mud River Baptist Church attracted worshippers far and wide, and eventually nurtured the growth of many other area congregations, it would not be until after the Civil War that Baptists would regularly assemble in Barboursville. In the meantime, Marie Gardner's seemingly informal role as hostess of the local Methodist society laid the foundation for Barboursville to emerge as a decidedly Methodist town.

In 1824, a small chapel was built and used for worship by the Methodists, on the present location of the Barboursville Cemetery. In 1835, John and Emily Samuels deeded a tract of land to the Methodist church on what is now Water Street. Trustees of the Methodist Episcopal Church (as it was known at the time) were Pat Talbert, John Hite, Charles Rolfe, James Rutherford, William McComas, James Kyle, Luther Ritchie and James Pinnell. The second wood frame church was noted for its two entrances: one for the women and one for the men. "Christians" were invited to sit in the front pews while the "sinners" were to sit in the back.

Through the largesse of Gardner, McGinnis and other prominent families, the Barboursville Methodist Episcopal Church continued to prosper as a "fellowship of kindred minds"—at least until the 1850s, when discordant strains reverberated through the nation over the issue of slavery, and the congregation found yet a third way to dissect itself in the little chapel.

Barboursville on the Map

Over the decades, Barboursville served as county seat for a land mass that would become progressively smaller, as western Virginia's political boundaries were divided and subdivided. Between 1824 and 1867 Cabell County slowly evolved from its original "giant wrist and hand giving the thumbs-up" shape to today's more diminutive outline resembling a sturdy human molar.

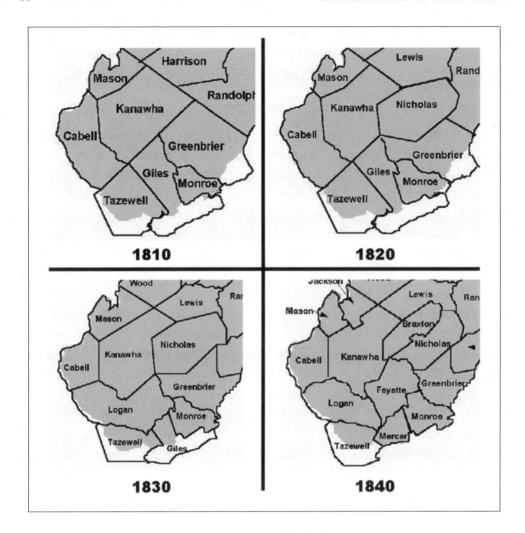

County Maps 1810-1840

The succession of maps illustrate the early splitting and shape-shifting of counties from 1810 to 1840, before Wayne (1842), parts of Boone (1847) Putnam (1848-50) and Lincoln (1867) were taken from Cabell land.

The formation of Logan County in 1824 (with additional land parceled in 1830) divided the Guyandotte Valley watershed roughly in half. By my observation, this feat of political cell division would distinguish the remaining downriver Cabell region as the comparatively tame, temperate and tolerant sister county.

An article by Margaret Thompson, published in the *Herald Advertiser*, offered a succinct contrast between two types of Appalachian settlers, "mountaineers" and "river people." At the risk of over-simplifying, I believe her words capture the enduring cultural divide between settlers in the newly separated Logan and Cabell counties of the 1830s. She wrote:

The mountains kept the Appalachian man isolated for generations from other types of people. There were few roads and what roads existed were narrow, steep and dangerous…He was more than satisfied with his primitive mountain life and protected his freedom and his family fiercely…Due to his cynical background, he had little religious faith in the early years which caused him to blindly accept his fate with a feeling of hopelessness….Later, however, missionaries spread through the mountains until the section became deeply rooted in fundamental religious belief.

The river people in those days were much less isolated than the mountaineers and, accordingly, were more "well-fixed." Unlike the mountaineer…the river settler felt a need for establishing in this new country a social state. He was at heart a materialist and opportunist seeking a good and abundant life in his settlement. He was in part an idealist, trying to establish a social, cultural and religious life along with his home. Self-sufficient like the mountaineer, he developed a more active social life and, being situated on the river, indulged in commerce. River communities usually boasted a tavern, church, school and county court. The river people were influenced by spiritual and intellectual mores with which they came in contact. (Thompson 1971)

By the 1840s, our river town was maturing. In 1838, the stocks and whipping post at the jail were in disrepair and an appropriation was made to have them fixed. The wood frame courthouse was also showing its age. In the 1835 *Gazetteer of Virginia and District of Columbia,* Barboursville was described as containing, "besides the usual county buildings, twenty-five dwelling houses, three mercantile stores, one common school, one extensive manufacturing flour mill, one tan yard, one hatter, two blacksmiths, one tailor and various other mechanics. Population one hundred fifty persons, of whom two are attorneys and one a regular physician."

By the late 1840s, although Barboursville's center of political gravity had shifted with the county's boundaries, the town emerged as a manufacturing and commercial center. Folks from "far up in the valley" still arrived by boat to trade their products from Logan County as well as from Cabell's "Guyan Valley" section (present-day Lincoln County). The flow of traffic east and west along the turnpike through Main Street continued to bring diverse new arrivals. And court dealings still attracted those on both sides of the law from neighboring Guyandotte and around the county. From every direction, more and more folks decided the place was to their liking, and settled in.

As Barboursville prepared to meet the mid-century, four years would bring the village within sight of a new age of promise and splendor.

Our Special Correspondent Furnishes an Interesting Letter:
Two Logan men on a Guyandotte merchantman fell out near here Monday,
and one smashed the other badly, claiming that he had been so ungentlemanly
as to wipe his feet in the assaulting party's mustache. (1898)

CHAPTER 6

FOUR GOLDEN YEARS (1849-1852)

A Sleepy Stream Gets a Closer Look

BY the 1840s, the timber trade was picking up along the Guyandotte River. As more and more families settled the region, some of the oldest and most varied forestland in the world— "great stands of oak, poplar, walnut and hickory," some more than five feet in diameter— were being cleared to plant fields of grain and vegetables, and to build homes and farm buildings. Instead of disposing of the mighty trunks in huge bonfires, as in early days, enterprising pioneers learned that they could sell them to lumber mills to be sawed into boards for factories, furniture and ship hulls.

Men in the Guyandotte uplands worked after harvest into the winter months, cutting down trees, trimming off branches, peeling bark from the trunks and sawing them into long cuts. The river was the only way to move the logs to market, and so grew a profitable seasonable enterprise for the most daring of souls. Men of great strength and skill would lash together dozens of logs into giant rafts, and when the water was right would take a swift ride downstream. After their river ride, the men would either walk the long way home, or try to find transport back on a push boat.

This practice was celebrated by a man who had been a one-time friend of Edgar Allen Poe (before the two had a falling out and became famous literary feudists). Nineteenth-century poet Thomas Dunn English wrote "Rafting on the Guyandotte," after either venturing a trip himself while in Logan County, or just listening closely to tales of local rafters. Published in the popular *Appleton's Journal* in 1872, the poem featured many lusty couplets; here are just a few:

Who at danger never laughed, Let him ride upon a raft. Down Guyan,
when from the drains, Pours the flood of many rains…

Swirling, whirling, hard to steer, Manned by those who have no fear…

If the pins from hickory riven, Were not stout and firmly driven,
Were the cross-ties weak and limber, Woe befall your raft of timber!

Now they turn with shake and quiver, In a short bend of the river.
Ah! They strike. No! Missed it barely; They have won their safety fairly…

Where's the fiddle? Boys, be gay! Eighty miles in half a day! Never a pin
nor cross-tie started, Never a saw-log from us parted…

If among your friends there be, One who something rare would see,
To the loggers' campground send him, To a ride like this commend him…

Making him a happier man, Who has coursed the fierce Guyan,
When the June-rain freshet swells it, And to yellow rage impels it.

RAFTING ON THE GUYANDOTTE.

Rafting on the Guyandotte Illustration in Appleton's Journal.

By 1850, the number of logs carried annually to market on the Guyandotte
and Big Sandy rivers quadrupled in number and increased considerably in price,

according to William Ely, author of *The Big Sandy Valley.* For the most part, the Guyandotte remained a relatively pristine and sleepy stream through a great forest. The river valley, as described by a daughter of Barboursville, was dotted by bottom-land farms and "little log cabins in the hollows, with their wood piles in front, their wash kettles to the rear, their ox carts and omnipresent 'houn' dawgs' trailing in the woodlands close by"…"the sleepy old Dobbins, with mud-bespattered saddle-bags swung over their fat sides, on which the preacher, the teacher, yes and the old country doctor, rode to their appointments."

In 1848, a man named Joseph H. Gill took a ride of his own. On behalf of the Board of Public Works of Virginia, Gill surveyed the Guyandotte from its mouth to Gilbert Creek, 22 miles beyond Logan. He reported on the great wealth of timber and coal he saw along the river, and recommended that the state build a 'slackwater' navigation system from the Ohio River to Logan to clear the river for development of these resources.

A World in Flux

This prospect of developing the Guyandotte for industrial use was certainly not lost on William Clendenin Miller in 1849. As one of the county's most successful men, he was well connected. Serving as Barboursville's postmaster would have kept Miller wholly aware of the events of the day. The world and the nation were going through dramatic shifts, and people were on the move.

Imagine Miller selecting among the news to share with his neighbors as the papers arrived on the mail stage:

With the failure of Ireland's potato crop in the mid-1840s, a tidal wave of hundreds of thousands of poor immigrants was continuing to arrive on America's shores. Political affairs in Europe were still shaking out after an 1848 spread of revolution (not so different from 2011's Middle-Eastern uprisings). The yearning for better living conditions and an end to traditional authority was punctuated by violent upheavals in France, Germany, Italy, Austria and dozens of other countries. All the turmoil in Europe coincided with the abdication of France's last king, the publication of *The Communist Manifesto* in Germany and even more emigrations to the United States.

Back in the United States, James K. Polk (the first President to have his photo-graph taken) decided not to seek re-election in 1848, having met several ambitious goals in a single term. Polk's political career was capped by bringing the two-year Mexican-American War to a conclusion, with Mexico ceding what is now California, Nevada, Utah, and parts of Wyoming, Colorado, Arizona and New Mexico to the United States.

The Whig Party's Zachary Taylor had just defeated Virginia's choice, Democrat Lewis Cass, and was assuming the presidency just as Congress was deeply embroiled in sectional conflicts over slavery. Nobody would predict that President Taylor would make his biggest headlines 16 months later by dying of a sudden illness.

With development of the steam locomotive engine and the telegraph, the Baltimore and Ohio line already stretched from Washington, D.C. to Cumberland, Maryland, and the company was well on its way to connecting railroad lines from the eastern seaboard to the Ohio River. The 1848 discovery of gold in California sent over 200,000 speculators over land and sea to the nation's new westernmost state. Amidst all these geographic and political happenings, the fact that the nation's first women's rights convention had just taken place in New York State may have escaped popular notice.

William Clendenin Miller was certainly conscious of the changes taking place in the world outside Barboursville, Virginia at the dawn of 1849. All evidence shows him to be a visionary and active force in the 36-year-old town.

The Guyandotte Navigation Company

In 1849, after Mr. Gill's river survey, the state of Virginia incorporated the Guyandotte Navigation Company. Along with William Clendenin Miller, others involved in the new company included J. W. Hite, P. S. Smith, H. H. Miller, N. S. Adams, A. M. Whitney, J. Emmons, John G. Miller, Irvin Lusher, J. L. Keller, Sampson Sanders, Solomon Thornburg, John Samuels and Robert McKendree.

From 1831, steamboat service had been extended from Cincinnati to the mouth of the Big Sandy and the Guyandotte rivers. After the 1848 survey revealed the richness of coal and timber resources, Miller's new company was able to attract capital from outside investors. The company planned to construct six lock and dam systems to allow for steamboat navigation, with an eye toward both freight and passenger runs, and to provide turbine power for state-of-the-art mills.

By 1851, the company had quickly completed Dam 1 at Everett's Creek (site of the "Nickel Plant" at Altizer), Dam 2 at the mouth of the Mud (Barboursville), Dam 3 at Smith Creek in Salt Rock and Dam 4 at the "Falls of Guyan" past West Hamlin.

According to a 1933 interview with W. C. Miller's son, J. William Miller, the company obtained the stone for some of the locks from a quarry on the ridge now occupied by the State Veteran's Home. Discovering that there was a small cave near the quarry in which the skeleton of an Indian was found, Miller's son "carried some of the bones home, but was persuaded by an old slave that he would be 'hanted' (sic) and buried them carefully in the back yard."

Orders for a New Courthouse

A few months after the Guyandotte Navigation Company was formed, William

Clendenin Miller, Enoch Underwood, Edmund Rece and Daniel Love were designated as Commissioners by the Court to plan and establish probable costs for construction of a new courthouse and jail, since the original buildings were falling into disrepair. (During this time, Frederick George Louis Beuhring was the Sheriff, and John Samuels the Clerk for Cabell County.)

According to George S. Wallace, William Clendenin Miller personally oversaw the projects to completion: "An order made August 25, 1852 designated Sydney Bowen, William Clendenin Miller and John L. Keller to make a contract and to supervise the building of the new courthouse at a cost not exceeding $4,050. The court directed a jail to be built of white oak logs, not less than 12" thick with a vacancy of 10" wide to be filled with rocks. W. C. Miller and Albert Moore submitted a proposition, which was accepted, to construct a new jail for $3,475." Shortly after the completion of the courthouse, Miller was directed by the court to buy a lightning rod, chairs and carpet, just as the finishing touches of glass windows, blinds and new straw under the carpet were added.

According to J. William Miller, the grounds of the pretty new brick courthouse would host an annual fair, "in which was displayed fruits, vegetables, wines, canned goods, needlework, etc. The livestock was shown on the streets or on lots. About 1852, sorghum molasses was displayed at one of the fairs. It had been made in iron kettles and was thin and dark, but it was quite a curiosity at that time."

A Splendid Home for a Growing Family

An intimate glimpse into Miller's business dealings and family life can still be found in the Miller family letters, which have been preserved and remain with Marshall University's historical collections. By 1852—in the midst of his various infrastructure projects, thriving mercantile business and postal duties—43-year-old William Clendenin and Eliza Gardner Miller had their hands full seeing to the upbringing and education of six young children: 14-year-old Eugenia, 13-year-old Charles, 7-year-old George Franklin ("Frank"), 6-year-old John William ("Will"), 4-year old Joseph Samuels ("Joe") and a new baby boy, Hamilton Gardner, who was called "Hammy." (Later, a second daughter, Florence Gardner Miller, would be born there.)

During these years the eldest, Eugenia, was away at the Greenupsburg Female Seminary, in what is now Greenup, Kentucky. Eugenia received frequent letters from her family. The Millers' high-minded aspirations for their young adolescent daughter shine through in excerpts of correspondence of 1849-1852:

November 18, 1849, Eliza to Eugenia: "Father is getting materials for the courthouse. . . Improvements are still going on in town. The sidewalks are a great addition...I would advise to pursue those studies which your teachers think will be of most importance as they should be the best judges, but amid all your pursuits let the scriptures of divine truth have your first and best attention…I am kept very busy and need your assistance very much yet I will feel perfectly reconciled to your absence if it will only prove to your advantage."

December 29, 1849, William C. to Eugenia: "Mr. and Mrs. Edward Vertegun have a school of twenty-eight or thirty scholars and are getting along well."

September 15, 1851, Eliza to Eugenia on the subject of her school's curriculum: "Astronomy is most exalting and interesting…Do you need tucking combs and some mitts to wear in school?

September 15, 1851, William C. to Eugenia: "I enclose you some Post Office stamps each of which pays the postage of a letter to any part of the United States…When you write and want to pay the postage, wet the stamp and stick it to the letter as you see this one is done."

October 20, 1851, Eliza to Eugenia: "Your pa expected to see you. He went to Guyandotte to see the condition of the river, but finding the water was falling he fortunately concluded not to start, as it is impossible to get anything freighted…Your uncle and aunt are still with us and will remain until the river rises…Try not to think too much of home, you know that it would be a great misfortune to grow up in ignorance. We would greatly prefer that you were nearer to home had you the same advantages. Your pa is very kind and withholds from you nothing that is in his power to promote your interest…try to be reconciled and render yourself as agreeable as possible."

October 26, 1851, Eliza to Eugenia: "The courthouse is a pretty building…We can do nothing to the house this fall for there is no probability of getting lime while the river is so low. . . "

January 4, 1852, Eliza to Eugenia: "Mend your clothes. If you can no longer wear them, send them home; maybe I can make some use of them. I will not deny anything for your comfort or gentility. I have finished this dress with the exception of stitching on the waist the binding around the neck whalebone…the assortment of goods is poor. It is finer and newer than your muslin delaine…If you want a dark calico you may buy it and make it."

February 16, 1852, Eliza to Eugenia: "The Elder preached with zeal. Mary Thornburg joined the church."

March 9, 1852, younger brother Charles to Eugenia: "Ma has not had much time to attend to me. I study some at home. Frank and I have had quite a lonesome time during the winter. The weather has been so severe we have been compelled to stay in the house much of the time…We try to help ma. Ma thinks we take good care of Hammy. He is beginning to talk and crawl. Joe is much pleased with his doll and says sister must write to him again." (Matthews 1949-50)

As construction progressed on the new courthouse on the town square, another brick structure was taking shape through W. C. Miller's efforts. With six children (and one more to come a few years later), it was high time for a new home.

W. C. Miller House
(Courtesy of Barboursville Public Library)

There are reports that Miller began construction of his new house in 1836, but I extracted a piece of information that places its completion date well after that time. A Fred Lambert source indicates that Miller had acquired John Laidley's Barboursville residence after Laidley relocated to the Ohio River. Laidley's may have been the house where most of William and Eliza Miller's babies were born. Miller's middle child "Will," later known by 1930s villagers as "Uncle Billy" Miller, confirmed to reporter Maurice Beckett that his 1845 birthplace was "a large log house not fifty yards from where he now lives."

The stately brick Miller Home completed in 1852, and a singular Barboursville home it was. "This example of Federal style, fashionable in most of the United States until 1830, is a late, simpler version," according to a Cabell County architectural guidebook.

The home at 1112 Main Street remains the oldest standing brick structure in Barboursville. The house stayed in family hands well into the twentieth century. In the sunset of his 91 years, "Uncle Billy" Miller occupied the family homestead as an old widowed gentleman—writing poetry, watching the generations of robins who nested in the yard, and recalling Barboursville's history. The home's character (if not every original element) has been preserved by its most recent entrepreneurial owners. (As of 2013, the building is open to the public as a quite elegant salon and spa, with an artistic rear courtyard and many of the original artifacts and fixtures prominently displayed.)

Both the courthouse lawn and the Miller's front porch would serve as vantage points to dramatic events that would unfold in subsequent years. Today, the red brick house built for William and Eliza's growing brood of inquisitive nineteenth century offspring stands as a monument to his ambitious vision and enduring legacy.

Exodus on the River

At the grassy banks of the Guyandotte River—about halfway between the eventual locations of Guyandotte Navigation Company's Dams 2 and 3—there are no monuments, no statues, no markers of any kind, to commemorate the thing that happened there in 1849. In fact, as a twenty-first century traveler crosses the concrete bridge to Martha Elementary School and Elmwood Baptist Church, there are no remnants of a once-thriving nineteenth century farming and milling community.

The sleepy green river, however, holds a story submerged in its past that, by antebellum Virginia standards, is nothing short of monumental.

Sampson Sanders was one of the richest men in the county. Back in 1813 at Barboursville's founding, he was one of its five trustees as a young man of 27. He was the second child and only son of an aggressive traveling land speculator and slave trader who died when Sanders was 16. Sampson first assisted his mother, then managed his own highly successful farm and mill operation three miles upriver from Barboursville. (The community was later named for his niece Martha Kilgore Morris.)

Sampson grew up among a family of 21 slaves inherited from his father, that grew to 51 adults and children by 1849. This placed Sampson Sanders among the South's top three percent of slaveholders.

At this point in time, several prominent Barboursville families owned one or two slaves each, including the Samuels, Merritt, William C. Miller and Elisha McComas households. The Thornburgs – Solomon, John and Thomas — owned about a half-dozen slaves between them. Other documented slave holders in the vicinity included Sanders's superintendent Martin Moore who lived a couple miles south on the "Frying Pan" farm; the Wilson, Shelton and McGinnis families just west of Barboursville; Buffington of Guyandotte; the Yates and Burdette families of Ona; the Kilgore and Morris families of the Mud Bridge (Milton) area; and Hanley (sometimes spelled Handley) in northern Cabell County. Leading Cabell County, with a peak number of 53 slaves enumerated in the 1820 Census, was the William Jenkins plantation at Greenbottom on the Ohio River.

The full story of Sampson Sanders's relationship to his slaves is detailed in the 1999 book, *Cabell County's Empire for Freedom: The Manumission of Sampson Sanders' Slaves* by Carrie Eldridge, whose scholarly effort unearthed a long-forgotten piece of county history. Eldridge indicates that life for both the black and white Sanders families would have been similar to anyone else's on the frontier: land had to be cleared, houses and barns built, crops planted. "Existing records show the slaves took pride in producing the best crops and livestock in the area. To be a member of the Sanders family was an important position in the county," she wrote.

According to Eldridge's extensive research, Sanders never hired a slave overseer, and he taught several of his slaves to help conduct his business, which involved being able to read, write, "cipher," and even deal with local merchants. As the nineteenth century marched on, this routine would have sharply delineated Cabell County from Richmond, Virginia; by 1832, the state had made it a crime to teach a slave to read.

Sanders had married at age 35, but grew older without any direct descendents, apparently having lost his wife and at least one child to disease. When he put together his last will and testament just a few months before his death at age 63, Sampson Sanders made a decision about his "slave family" that, given Virginia's prevailing attitudes and tricky justice system, was particularly remarkable.

He freed them, all of them.

Not only did he grant his black "family members" freedom from all involuntary servitude—a practice known as manumission—but in his will Sanders provided them with materials from his estate, $15,000 in cash—the equivalent of nearly half a million dollars in 2010—plus horses, cattle, even hives of bees, and three white lawyers to protect them as they made their way to a free state. To ensure that his wishes were understood and carried out, Sanders drew up his will in the presence of several high-profile friends. He appointed "my friends John Samuels, John Laidley, George Gallaher and Cornwellsy Simmons executors of this my last will and testament."

To understand the magnitude of this act, consider the math: In 1850, Virginia recorded 472,528 slaves, of which the Census reveals just 218 were manumitted.

And so it was, just upriver from Barboursville, where the journey began for nearly one-fourth of the totality of slaves freed in 1849 Virginia. The odyssey began with a flotilla of homemade rafts put into the shallow Guyandotte. The group zigged and zagged its way around Barboursville, past the mouth of the Mud and toward the mighty Ohio River. After three days floating downriver, the legally-free Sanders clan, along with their white escorts, their supplies and livestock, came to the wondrous city of Cincinnati. From there, they made the rest of their long journey in a single day, on a fast and thunderous form of transportation they had never before seen or heard—the railroad steam engine.

Cincinnati today is home to the National Underground Railroad Freedom Center, a twenty-first-century riverfront museum that helps make real America's history of slavery, the Underground Railroad and the struggles to secure the freedom of enslaved people everywhere. Visiting the center provides a powerful testament to what happens when dedicated people came together to uncover a lost history and make it authentic and touchable. Nonetheless, I must report that during a 2010 morning exploration of the Center, among the many interpretive exhibits, artifacts and films about freedom's heroes, the term "manumission" was nowhere to be found, it was so rare on a large scale.

According to Huntington native and history scholar Dr. Cicero Fain, "though there were instances of the manumission of slaves, rarely were more than one or two slaves freed at the same time. And, not infrequently, those freed were older slaves. For those fortunate to acquire their freedom, the state of Virginia beginning in 1806 required them to leave the state within 12 months or face re-enslavement."

The Sanders family eventually settled in Cass County, Michigan; just one of their relatives stayed in Cabell County. In 1985, descendent Maurice W. Sanders of Detroit, Michigan, published the story of the freed Sanders slaves and their genea-logical trail as it picked up in the Calvin and Porter townships in Michigan, where they maintained a presence for many years. Excerpts were submitted to the *200th Birthday of Cabell County* published by the KYOWVA Genealogical and Historical Society.

By the time of the 1850 United States Census slave schedules of Cabell County, fewer than 40 slaves remained in eight Barboursville-area households. The largest slaveholding families in the county that year were in Mud Bridge and Greenbottom: Sanders's in-laws the Kilgores owned 24, the Morris family had 18, and the Jenkins plantation held 15 African Americans as property.

Consider the fact that county authorities like John Laidley and John Samuels (himself the owner of two female slaves) honored their dead friend by assuring the success of a well-planned, benevolent exodus of nearly half the county's slave popu-lation. Like Sampson Sanders, were they also freedom's unsung heroes?

Nobody knows how many of our Barboursville ancestors witnessed the extraordinary event, much less how folks on the shore may have reacted to the site of the recently-freed Sanders families floating gingerly atop their handmade log rafts with all their livestock and belongings. As the African American Sanders family—including married couples Solomon and Phyllis, Daniel and Dorcas, Luke and Jane, Moses and Caroline; about 30 children and babies; other single adults; and 87-year-old grandparents Zebedee and Ada—headed to an unknown new home on free soil, they passed around Barboursville for the last time on a cool, clear October afternoon in 1849.

Portrait of a Virginia River Town at Mid-Century

Some years after the Sanders manumission, following the damming of the Guyandotte River and completion of the new brick courthouse, about a hundred of the town's most photogenic residents gathered for a group picture along Main Street.

Nineteenth Century People at Courthouse
(Undated Photo from George S. Wallace)

By 1852, the town was coming into its own, with its new sidewalks and a few prominent brick structures, including the jail (shown behind the courthouse), the Miller home to the east, and the McComas estate about a mile southwest of the public square. Most of the town still consisted of wood frame structures and log homes, including two of the oldest dwellings, the Dirton home up the hill behind the courthouse and the Tom Merritt farmhouse at the eastern edge of Main Street past Miller's.

Turning right from the courthouse, someone taking the short walk west toward Water Street would pass Wilson Moore's store and a few other taverns and establishments on the left, before coming to one of the town's three hotels, the McKendree, on the present site of the First United Methodist church. Irvin Lusher also kept a corner store on Main and Water. Continuing up Water Street, folks would have found homes and establishments on both sides, for this was years before the riverbank slipped away. A public well near the river, the Harrison blacksmith shop, gunsmith Thomas Kyle, John Mills's cooperage and an "Old German's" furniture factory lined Water Street, as well as at least one Thornburg home and the Methodist church "at the bend in the road."

Someone turning left, walking from the courthouse on Main Street would have immediately passed the Miller and Henderson store, later the Miller and Holderby store, a place where venison hams and deerskins from Logan were prepared for shipment to Philadelphia. Crossing Center Street, one would come to the second hotel, originally the site of the Gardner's stagecoach inn, then the Merritt, and later the Holderby Hotel. Just past the south corner of Main and Center was the Beuhring Hotel. (Both hotels are visible in an 1861 Civil War drawing of the 34th Regiment of the Ohio Infantry marching east on Main Street.)

A horse-drawn carriage clopping downhill on Main Street would pass several German residences, including the Krause home, and the German labor force at the Baker and Westhoff tan yard at the creek running south. Valentine Leist (1832-1916) came from Baden, Germany in 1853 and operated a tannery in Barboursville for 60 years. He started out on the north end of Center Street, and eventually purchased the Main Street property on the creek from Baker and Westhoff. One of his sons told Frank Ball that the tannery eventually had 82 vats, each capable of processing 31 cowhides at once, a smelly multi-week process.

The butcher Mr. Freitel had a slaughterhouse behind his shop on the north side of Main between Stowasser and Park Avenues. Along the north side of Main Street were the dwellings of John Merritt, the Dirtons, Abner Wingo, Epps Johnson and the Englishman Octavius Church (1812-1901). Church was the son of a London lawyer who was associated with the British East India Company. After his father's death, Octavius traveled alone to New York as a young lawyer, but settled in western Virginia and purchased hundreds of acres of Cabell County land. According to family sources, he married Captain William Merritt's granddaughter Margaret Ann, and the couple had eight children.

Across from Stowasser Avenue on the south side of Main was a hat factory managed by a Mr. Ritchie. Beyond the hat factory on the south side of Main were a few well-appointed estates, including the Samuels, Gardner and Miller homes.

In 1852, according to *Elliott and Nye's Virginia Directory and Business Register*, the county's two principal towns of Barboursville and Guyandotte both contained about 350 inhabitants each. Barboursville had two town physicians, Doctors

Maupin and McCorkle; Guyandotte had three, and Green Bottom and Mud Bridge had one doctor each.

The economic outlook as described by Elliott and Nye was bright for the county: "The lands are productive of wheat, corn and grass. The surface of the country is hilly but favorable for pasturage. The Ohio River affords facilities of transportation the whole extent of this county, and the Guyandotte, which is now under improvement with locks and dams, will accommodate the interior through which it passes. A graded turnpike passes from Charleston to Guyandotte. Bituminous and cannel coal abound in this county; there is also great quantities of iron ore, with gypsum, salt and lead."

Like the townspeople posing proudly in their Sunday best in front of their fine brick courthouse, Barboursville at 1852 was beginning to resemble a new enlightened America. For more and more village families, the hardscrabble days of working the land had been replaced by opportunity, mobility and an ever-increasing flow of visitors, customers, innovators and investors. Now, with the taming of the Guyandotte and the wealth of natural resources lying upriver, Barboursville's educated and industrious class, men like William Clendenin Miller, may have reasonably believed that the future was indeed golden.

CHAPTER 7

LIFE ON THE CIVIL WAR FAULT LINE (1853-1861)

UNTIL 1861, as citizens of Virginia, our ancestors were subject to the laws of the largest slave-holding state in the nation. State representatives assembled 350 miles away in Richmond, which would become the Capitol of the Confederacy. Yet Barboursville was just ten miles from the "free state" of Ohio. Despite its growing commerce and modern aspirations, Barboursville would soon find itself sitting precariously on the ideological fault line between North and South, abolitionists and slave owners, Union and Confederate sentiments.

Folks in Cabell County might have found themselves challenged to prove their loyalty to Richmond and the Old Dominion, but at the same time most residents remained "out of sight and out of mind" when it came to enforcing Virginia's laws and customs.

I wisely defer to Civil War historians regarding the details of military conflicts across Cabell County. For those seeking inventories of battles, leaders, enlistments, casualties and prisoners, I refer you to Joe Geiger's *Civil War in Cabell County, West Virginia 1861-1865*. For an even deeper dig, an extensive collection of documents can be found at Marshall University through the Rosanna A. Blake Library of Confederate History, curated by Jack Dickinson. The work of these individuals, Civil War reenactors and other experts provide an amazing amount of details as to *what* happened.

The alternative question is *how* exactly did the village end up as a Civil War battleground—or as my lovably irreverent father might have said, "how the *hell* did this happen?" In this chapter, I'll lay out the spiraling convolution of local, state and national events that forced the village into mayhem.

Moral Tensions over the South's "Peculiar Institution"

In the early 1850's, Barboursville was still the home of a single "church house," the Methodist church at the Water Street bend. In all likelihood, it was in that long-gone frame chapel that the debate over slavery slowly began to pull the town's families apart.

The seeds for dissension took root in the 1820s, when two social morality movements—temperance and abolitionism—crossed paths with American congregations.

In 1826, the Virginia Society for the Promotion of Temperance was formed to oppose the use of liquor. Pastors across Virginia initially flocked to the temperance movement. While I have seen no documentary evidence showing involvement of Barboursville church members in this public crusade—this was an "Ordinary" town, after all—public drunkenness would later become a cause of concern to at least two local residents: in the December 1854 issue of *The Guyandotte Herald,* Mrs. Evan Blume and Mrs. Aaron McKendree advertised a temperance tavern in Barboursville, "free from a set of drunken loafers who always lay around a whiskey tavern."

The second morality issue to test nineteenth century congregations was abolition of slavery. Both the temperance and abolition movements challenged clergymen on how the Bible should be applied to society, especially without a specific command in Scripture. Just like abstinence Christians, abolitionists argued that slavery was contrary to the spirit, if not the letter, of the Bible. The fact that many Virginians supported slavery while opposing liquor made the issue all the more vexing. One Baptist editor observed in 1840 that the church could not adopt a temperance oath as a test of membership because antislavery folk used such tests in their churches. This may explain why general interest in the temperance movement peaked; by the early 1840s, the Virginia Society for the Promotion of Temperance was virtually defunct.

The issue of slavery had caused simmering tensions between Northern and Southern churches since the early 1830s, but a meeting of the American Baptist Antislavery Convention in New York accelerated the dispute in 1840. After the Northern Baptist press challenged the qualifications of two slaveholding mission- aries in Texas, some Georgia churches began to chart a separate course for Southern Baptists. Antislavery Methodists began the exodus from the Methodist Episcopal Church in the early 1840s, the crisis coming to a head over the nomination of a slaveholder as bishop. Virginia Methodist leaders played a key role in a deci- sive and divisive General Conference of 1844, when an influential professor and defender of Christian slavery declared Southern Methodism's independence from its Northern connections.

These schisms left Southern Baptists and Methodists free to fashion regional denominations to their own tastes. Examples of how a church in the 1850s would choose its own path dealing with the moral issues of alcohol and slavery can be found in the recorded history of area congregations. In 1853, the Mud River Baptist Church passed a resolution "that the making and selling of ardent spirits for a beverage was morally wrong, but it was permitted for medicine." Two miles due south of Barboursville, Bloomingdale Salem Baptist Church Minute passed its own judgements:

Saturday before second Sabbath in November, 1855: Business included several brethren expressing sorry for use of ardent spirits. All were excused.

February/March 1856: considered cases of blacks Charlotte and Isaac (husband and wife) seeking letters of dismissal for trying to abscond from their master. More charges of drinking were forgiven.

April 1856: Isaac excluded from the church body. (Bloomingdale Salem Baptist Church Minutes 1855-2005 2005)

So where did Barboursville's Methodists stand on the South's "peculiar institution," as slavery was euphemistically termed, in the mid-nineteenth century? The record shows slavery was considered a natural occurrence among the gentlemen farmers of the area, including most of the town's leaders. Consequently, it is not so shocking that the little frame church on Water Street would come to identify itself as the Methodist Episcopal Church, *South.*

It does not appear that the Barboursville congregants immediately felt the impact of the 1844 split in the General Conference. The Northern Methodists of Virginia had created the "Western Virginia Conference" in 1848 in order to strengthen their position in the state, followed by similar organizing two years later by the Southern Methodists. Still, according to historian Henry T. Shanks, "like political discussions, churches were calm in the early fifties."

Spirit of Concession and Compromise

Virginia of the mid-nineteenth century was marked by political disputes on two fronts. The issue of slave ownership cut across the rapidly growing United States, dividing states and territories into Northern and Southern factions. Simultaneously, in the Commonwealth there was growing dissension between the long-settled eastern lands and the "Trans Allegheny" counties to their west.

In Richmond, concerns about equal representation of western Virginia's growing white population resulted in demands for a change to the state's constitution.

Longtime friction between Virginia's eastern and western sections was exacerbated by the fact that easterners were over-represented in the General Assembly, as revealed by the 1840 Census. After nine years of pressure from Lewisburg and Clarksburg, Virginia's eastern opposition finally yielded to the call for a constitutional convention. The result, ratified in October 1851, was known as Virginia's Reform Constitution. It made significant concessions to the west, giving the Trans-Allegheny counties 83 of 152 seats in the House of Delegates. The new constitution also abolished property qualifications as a requirement for voting, meaning that every white male resident who was 21 or older could vote.

For a time, the 1851 Constitution "made satisfying progress toward addressing long-standing sectional differences within the Commonwealth of Virginia."

Meanwhile in Washington, according to Paul Johnson, "the Senate was crowded and enthralled" by the debate over slavery, so much so that the "gigantic brass spittoons attached to every member's desk…had never been in such continuous use." This was an era of high debate in Congress, marked by rhetorical flourishes and history-making oratory, and the "Great Triumvirate" (also known as the Immortal Trio) of colleagues John C. Calhoun, Daniel Webster and Kentucky's turnpike-traveling Henry Clay were "uttering their swansongs." Vice-president Millard Fillmore had assumed the presidency upon the sudden demise of Zachary Taylor in 1850 (who evidently gorged himself during July 4th ceremonies, with fatal gastrointestinal results). Fillmore was ready for compromise over the thorny issues of slavery and potential secession by the South. By September, Fillmore signed five separate Bills of the "Compromise of 1850" into law, turning down the political heat between Northern and Southern factions.

In the Compromise of 1850, the North gained California as a new free state, thereby securing an anti-slavery majority in both Houses of Congress. The major concession to the South was the "Fugitive Slave Law," which declared that all runaway slaves be brought back to their masters. (Abolitionists nicknamed it the "Bloodhound Law," for the dogs that were used to track down escaped slaves.) Though the bills were fraught with details that would eventually re-ignite sectional differences, Henry Clay's Great Triumvirate achieved their final legacy with Fillmore's support.

For a time, people on both sides relaxed, as "the horrific shadow of civil war suddenly disappeared, and they could get on with other things."

Local Preoccupations

From 1853 to 1857, Barboursville's citizens had plenty of other things to get on with. First, the community was certainly grieving, and possibly panicked, by a wave of illness that killed at least 75 infants and children in Cabell County in a single year. Clerks of each County Court began recording deaths in 1853, and

West Virginia Vital Research Records show that on May 5, 1853 "Farmer's child" Hamilton Miller, son of Eliza and William C. Miller, died at 1 year, 10 months. Though little Hammy's cause of death is not decipherable on the preserved document, a number of recorded deaths in the county cited Scarlet Fever as the cause. Other Barboursville lives cut short included: Hammy's 4-year-old cousin William Chapman Miller who died about a week earlier, 7-year-old Martha Elizabeth Hatfield and one-and-a-half-year-old Solomon Jackson Cook. Oscar and Augusta Mather of Barboursville lost two daughters that autumn, 4-year-old Louise Amanda and an unnamed 3-month-old infant.

Church activities were numerous, and the town was a county gathering place for annual fairs on the courthouse lawn. Fourth of July celebrations featured barbequed meat prepared by "expert negro cooks," according to Lambert's sources. The town's lone Masonic Lodge was established in 1853. Solomon's son Thomas Thornburg was "the first man ever initiated, raised, and passed" by No. 13, Ancient Free and Accepted Masons. He would remain secretary of the Lodge for 46 consecutive years.

Work also continued on the Guyandotte River locks and dams. Unfortunately, it had been discovered that the dam at the present-day Martha community could not back water to Salt Rock, nor would the Salt Rock dam back water to the Falls of Guyan. Further, it turned out that the ambitious men of the Guyandotte Navigation Company had rushed into construction without getting clear titles to much of the land needed to build the dams. Several floods destroyed much of the work that had been completed, and the company went bankrupt. A new entity, the Guyandotte Land Company, took up the effort, reconstructed the original dams and completed several others down into Logan County, allowing for small steamboats to traverse the river beginning in 1855.

Soon a man known as Captain Price from Guyandotte began running the steamboat "Major Adrian" to bring out barges loaded with coal; this boat later sank at Heath's Creek. By 1855, the "R.H. Lindsay" began to run on a fixed schedule, conveying both passengers and freight. Old residents of Barboursville recall how these boats made stops there, "when the obliging clerks and Negro porters appeared at the landing to assist the ladies on and off."

Barboursville's local industries flourished, according to Lambert: "There were hatters, tanners, chair-makers, tailors, wagonsmiths and gunsmiths. People came here to trade and dispose of their products from Logan, Lincoln and Wayne counties and from far up in the valley," he wrote. Among the thriving merchants in town was a second industrious family of Millers, unrelated to William Clendenin Miller and his siblings.

John, Christopher and George Frederick Miller were born in the tumultuous little German kingdom of Württemberg in the early nineteenth century. The

"Württemberg Millers" emigrated with their parents to America in 1820, on a ship from Antwerp to New Orleans. They arrived by flatboat at the mouth of the Guyandotte (sources differ on whether their father died en route), and went overland to Logan, but later returned to Barboursville. The elder sons and daughters married Cabell County spouses with the surnames Blake, Bussey, Chapman and Keller. Youngest son George Frederick Miller, who was only two when he came to America, grew up to learn the tanner trade, became a butcher and then a merchant in Barboursville. He married Mary M. Shelton. Like their neighbors, the third-generation American "Clendenin Millers," the first-generation "Württemberg Millers" would also have a great impact on town and county development.

Both families were active merchant traders in Barboursville. In 1854, the two-story Miller Thornburg store was completed on the southwest corner of Main and Center. Built of locally made brick, it stands today, although it has lost the original "stagecoach stand," a recess built into the building where passengers and luggage could be protected from the weather as they unloaded. Just across Main Street (in the general area of the village gazebo) was the store owned by John G. Miller and the Holderbys. Both local businesses established long lines of credit with buyers up north, and extended the same liberal terms to regional farmers. An old Miller and Holderby invoice for $23,000 hints at the scale of this practice:

> Merchants bought goods on a year's time, and sold them to nearly all the farmers on the same terms. They often took notes at the end of the fifth year, in case the farmer was unable to pay; and sometimes continued the same for two or three years, after which they took mortgages. They bought homemade linsey and flax, and tow lines made in 50-yard lengths by the county women, before modern machinery revolutionized the old customs. Wheat was a staple article, as were feathers, rags, ginseng and dried fruits. At times hundreds of bushels of dried peaches were sold here and shipped to the Philadelphia market. Strained honey came in barrels from up the Guyandotte River and is said to have been fine. Bees wax was also sold in large quantities. (F. B. Lambert Collection n.d.)

The promise of a railroad link may have enticed some of the town's business leaders, as had the completion of the turnpike through town a few decades earlier. In 1853, the State of Virginia authorized the Covington and Ohio Railroad to build a line along the intended canal way that originated at Covington, Virginia, passed through the New River Gorge and continued to the Ohio River. Over the next several years, the company contracted work by pick, shovel and mule on numerous tunnels through the Alleghenies. Roadbed work was completed as far as Charleston before the C&O got bogged down in political battles. It seems the citizens of northwestern Virginia, who were already benefitting from the privately-funded

Baltimore and Ohio Railroad, refused to be taxed for an enterprise that would not benefit them directly. Because of an alliance between these and other interests, the General Assembly of 1855-56 refused to aid the Covington and Ohio Railroad, so progress was delayed. Andrew Johnson's Vice-President, John Cabell Breckinridge, would come through later in the decade to speak at the court house in favor of the railroad, but faced opposition.

For the time being, commerce and life in the village throughout the 1850s remained centered on the rivers and the turnpike. Untouched by steel rails and cross ties, the farmland inside and outside of town limits was bucolic. Conveniences such as cooking stoves were still scarce, and Cabell County boys helped their families by gathering wood, building fires, hunting and going to the mill. Robert Dillon described the "Life of a Boy" in this local vignette:

> He went barefooted until Christmas, and one pair of shoes did him. Stone bruises. I have left Sanders mill at midnight, forded the river, and followed a path up Paul Davis Point down by the 'shoot' and on to Four Pole at the mouth of Grape Vine. The owls were a terror. (F. B. Lambert Collection n.d.)

Rising Passions and Deepening Divides

The pastoral tranquility of the early 1850s would not last. The nation's spirit of compromise began to crumble during the presidency of Franklin Pierce, as the insecurities of slaveholders and indignation of abolitionists grew and penetrated into the most neutral locales.

By 1855, hundreds of thousands of copies of *Uncle Tom's Cabin; or, Life Among the Lowly*, by Harriet Beecher Stowe had been sold in the three years since its first printing. Second only to the Bible in nineteenth century book sales, *Uncle Tom's Cabin* featured stories of long-suffering Christian slaves and evil slave-owners, and was credited with helping to fuel the abolitionist cause, laying the groundwork for Civil War.

In the U.S. Congress, the Kansas–Nebraska Act of 1854 gave settlers in those territories the freedom to decide whether to allow slavery. Opponents denounced the law as a concession to the South. They formed the new Republican Party with the aim of stopping the expansion of slavery. The party would soon emerge as the dominant political force throughout the North, and introduce the country to Abraham Lincoln. The new law also made Kansas the epicenter of a crusade on both sides, as "slavers" and "anti-slavers" set up colonies within and outside its borders. Between 1854 and 1856, events in Kansas turned ever more extreme. Pro-slavery Missourians allegedly crossed the border and swamped the elections; this was followed by a thwarted constitutional convention by abolitionists and neutral settlers; followed by the shipment of rifles to anti-slavers by Northern clergymen (including the brother of Harriet Beecher Stowe); followed by a pro-slavery mob attack on a free-soil town in which the governor's house was burned and newspaper presses tossed in the river.

The lawlessness in Kansas so provoked Massachusetts Senator Charles Sumner that he took the floor and heaped verbal abuse on South Carolina Senator A.P. Butler, in a provocative anti-slavery diatribe that took up two whole days on the Senate floor. Butler's nephew, Congressman Preston Brooks, became so incensed by the insults that he approached Sumner at his Senate desk two days after the speech and beat him with his cane so severely that Sumner was "ill at home" for two years. In May 1856, five men in a pro-slavery settlement were slaughtered by a fanatical party led by John Brown, once described as "a man impressed with the idea that God has raised him up on purpose to break the jaws of the wicked." By the end of 1856, the territory became known as "Bleeding Kansas" after 200 people had been murdered.

Just as newly-elected Democrat James Buchanan was settling in at the White House, the U.S. Supreme Court sided forcefully with slave owners in the March 1857 *Dred Scott* Decision. This case was named for a Virginia-born slave who had moved with his master from a free state to a slave territory in the 1840s, and sued for his freedom in the Missouri courts, arguing that his years on free soil made him free. Though Mr. Scott won his case, the verdict was reversed in the state supreme court. After Scott appealed to the U.S. Supreme Court, Chief Justice Roger Taney ruled that as a Negro, he was not a citizen and therefore could not sue in a federal court. The Court's decision also maintained that depriving slave-owners of their property was unconstitutional. With the Supreme Court deciding that Congress had no power to prohibit slavery in the federal territories, the emerging Republican Party was dealt a severe blow, and loyalties on both sides hardened.

The suspicions of slaveholders grew following the Kansas crusades. Some fugitive slaves were publishing their stories and others (most notably Harriet Tubman) helped other enslaved African Americans find their way to freedom via the Underground Railroad. In 1849, a group of freed slaves from Campbell County, Virginia settled in Burlington, Ohio just 16 miles from Barboursville. Cabell County's few dozen remaining slaves were aware of the Burlington settlement, the freed Sanders family, and the work of other abolitionists. The desire to attempt freedom apparently became hard to resist.

Though some county slave-owners had long allowed some of their slaves to borrow the master's buggy and travel by themselves, an event in October 1855 is recounted by Carrie Eldridge, in which "all Roffe's n—s with a good many others started for the Ohio River with the intention of running off," apparently aiming for Burlington. The plan failed to come together, when some slaves discovered Barboursville business man and slave owner Wilson Moore watching them, so "they all concluded to return home." Several county slaves were sold afterwards. Moore was elected county sheriff in 1857.

Ceredo and Guyandotte

As county seat, Barboursville found itself in a rather hapless position as the boiling cauldron of sectional conflict churned ever closer, embodied in the persons of Congressmen Eli Thayer and Albert Gallatin Jenkins. The two incendiary public figures would be instrumental in fanning the flames of conflict, and setting up this location as a proverbial pushpin on a general's war map.

Eli Thayer was a Congressman from Massachusetts who believed that abolitionists like him could help bring about the end of slavery by building a new kind of economic system in the southern states. (Thayer was also connected with the "Kansas Crusade.") Testing his philosophy that steam power could replace slave power, he founded a community on the Wayne County flatlands near the confluence of the Ohio and Big Sandy rivers and named it Ceredo after "Ceres," the Greek goddess of grain. By 1857, the city was fully established with a newspaper and several industries. Proslavery newspapers protested Thayer's Virginia "invasion."

Albert Gallatin Jenkins was born the youngest child of William Jenkins on the family's Ohio River plantation in northern Cabell County. A student at the Virginia Military Institute in Lexington, Jenkins graduated from Harvard Law School in 1850, and began practicing law in Cabell County. A wealthy slave owner and outspoken defender of states' rights, Jenkins was a delegate to the 1856 Democratic national convention in Cincinnati and was elected the district's Congressional representative from 1857 to 1861.

Civil War in Cabell County, West Virginia 1861-1865, by Joe Geiger Jr., details a fateful meeting at the Guyandotte town hall on in July 1857, when Eli Thayer tried to drum up support for his colony. He stressed that Ceredo was intended to be lawful "and that his goal was simply to make a profit" and develop the county's resources. Thayer was successful that day, inasmuch as the local citizens passed resolutions of welcome and encouragement to the Ceredo emigrants. This action elicited praise in abolitionist newspapers as far away as New York and St. Louis.

Virginia's *Richmond Examiner* responded by labeling the citizens of Cabell and Wayne as "bubble-blowers," "Yankee speculators" and "anti-Virginians," suggesting the Commonwealth should withhold all railroad appropriations to this area of the state.

Thirty-six days after Thayer's visit, Congressman Jenkins was asked to address the citizens at the Guyandotte Town Hall. He denounced the colony of Ceredo as an "abolition scheme," and inspired a committee consisting of himself, Owen Moore, Dr. G.D. Ricketts and L. Sedinger to draft resolutions. These resolutions, which passed unanimously, promised "decisive and positive correction of the evil" of Thayer and his ilk, pledged devotion to the Old Dominion and its "time-honored institutions," and asserted that the other counties of Western Virginia "hold no less orthodox sentiments than those contained in the foregoing resolutions."

In fact, "Guyandotte was the only real spot in Cabell County which expressed consistent and solid Confederate support," wrote Matt Prochnow. Cabell County remained deeply divided over the issue of slavery, and tensions continued to increase.

Marshall Turns to the Southern Methodists

On Oct. 26, 1857, Eugenia Miller, now 20 and still away at school—she cited later in life that she attended Vanderbilt—received another letter from her mother Eliza Gardner Miller: "Your dahlias have been prostrated by frost. The last that bloomed was a beautifully variegated purple and white."

By this time, the Millers had buried their sixth child, little "Hammy," and Eliza had given birth to their youngest child, and Eugenia's only sister, Florence Gardner Miller. Their third child "Frank" at age 14 was serving as a page for Congressman Albert Gallatin Jenkins in the United States Senate. Their father William C. Miller, a friend to Congressman Jenkins, was still involved in a number of ventures around the county, including footing the bill for carpentry services at the struggling Marshall Academy.

In 1858, Marshall was in dire financial shape. For its first decade or so, the Academy had received a few hundred dollars each year from the state Literary Fund, channeled through the county's School Commissioners. The trustees (represented by president John Laidley and secretary F.G.L. Beuhring well into the 1850s) were required to report annually to the state fund. According to Virginia state documents, the mission of the Marshall trustees was to keep up "a good school preparatory to entering college and... preparing young men for teachers in the common schools in the county." Relying only on modest student tuitions and whatever unappropriated surplus funding was available through the Literary Fund, these "noble men," John Laidley and the trustees, were so devoted to their work, "that when there was a shortage in the receipts from other sources, they made at the deficiency from their own private funds. When they had provided globes, maps, and philosophical apparatus, they proposed to arrange for the instruction of indigent children."

By 1846, the trustees had become resigned to a pattern of woefully inadequate state investment. "The board of trustees continue to bear testimony, from their own observation, that the present manner of employing the moneys arising from the Literary Fund is unfortunate, and inadequate to the wants of the people, and radically wrong," John Laidley wrote.

After the split between the Methodist church's Northern and Southern factions, financial rescue seemed to be on the horizon for Marshall Academy, with the Southern Methodists taking on the cause. The fledgling M.E. Church South Conference took actions between 1850 and 1855 to make the institution a college, raise funds for building improvements, and assume control of the school. And so in 1857, Marshall Academy, which for 20 years had existed as a chartered institution under the corporate laws of Virginia, passed under the control and management of the Western Virginia Conference of the Methodist Episcopal Church, South.

The Marshall College Joint Stock Company was organized, consisting of 30 Methodist ministers and laymen across the South, each taking one share of fifty dollars each for a sum of $1,500 to support the new Conference Methodist School. This is not to say that Marshall College was slated to become a theological school: a letter from the college's field agent Rev. Richard A. Claughton of Hawks Nest contained the clarification that "we do not expect to teach them Methodism, but Science, and the fear of God. We have no theological department, nor do we desire it."

In 1858, Marshall hired 23-year-old Benjamin H. Thackston to be Principal of the College with the title of President, and Professor of Ancient Languages. He succeeded Academy principal William Boyers, who by that time was owed hundreds of dollars by the trustees and had moved on to teach in Putnam County. Thackston left Prince Edward County, traveled by boat to Guyandotte and walked the remaining distance to the school.

Thackston wrote, "Coming from Eastern Virginia where liberality is a principle of existence, and where education is widely disseminated and commensurately appreciated, I confess to a degree of surprise that this institution has not, before this late day, been permanently established. The facts that it is eligibly situated and stands without a rival in this trans-Allegheny Region of Virginia are a sufficient guarantee that it would be eminently successful. That a College is needed here cannot by doubted."

Even so, the new college's debts hung on, despite numerous entreaties from 1857 through 1859 to Southern Methodist preachers and members of the Marshall College Joint Stock Company to pay on their commitments. Five years in, only five or six of the 30 Southern brethren had paid their share of money. Calls for support of Marshall College were published in the *Southern Methodist Itinerant*, intended to appeal to its readers' assorted sympathies:

January 1858: This is a Methodist College—a Southern institution—dependent, to a very great extent, upon the active co-operation of our Conference. It is situated …immediately below Guyandotte and just above Ceredo. The last named place is a newly located town — located for the avowed purpose of colonizing from the New England States, and filling up that beautiful part of our State with a class of men who are prejudiced against our State Institutions;

hence, it is of greater importance, that our Southern College, in that community, be at once placed on high and safe ground, and that the active energies
of its friends be concentrated in giving it an abiding character and a good
reputation.

February 1859 (in a letter from new trustee president Samuel Kelly): In the wander-
ings of our pilgrimage, we have passed over and seen much of Western Virginia
—its rich virgin soil, and inexhaustible mines of wealth. We have listened to
the sweet music of its murmuring brooks, and the swelling anthems of its
beautiful rivers — the vastness of its soul-cheering beauties and awe-inspiring
grandeurs have deeply impressed themselves upon our mind, and enriched the
treasures of our understanding. It is a great Country — extending from the
Blue Ridge to the Ohio — the beauty and glory of the Old Dominion — the
Switzerland of America — it ought to be the Geneva of Protestant learning. .
. But we want from two thousand five hundred to three thousand dollars to
complete the building and pay a debt already contracted... Come brethren,
preach about it, talk about it, pray about it, and work for it until the work is
done, until Marshall College shall stand forth an honor to our country, and
take rank among the best institutions of our State. Then shall our hearts leap
for joy, when we shall see the noble youths of our country going forth from
our halls of learning adorned with the riches and graces of classic love.

March 1859 (in a letter from Benjamin Thackston): We must remember that it
is this youth that are shortly to assume the reins of government — that they
must soon take their places as conscripts in the great army of humanity, and
that upon them must soon devolve the onerous responsibilities of American
citizens. . . . How necessary therefore that we prepare them, as well we may,
for a position so pregnant with importance to us, and vital alike to them and
to posterity. (V. A. Lewis, A History of Marshall Academy, Marshall College
and Marshall College State Normal School 1912)

The entreaties were to no avail, and Thackston's predecessor William R. Boyer
eventually sued for several years of back pay plus interest. The sale of the College
property was granted. John Laidley, who had founded the Marshall school and
overseen it since the 1830s, would be assigned the sadly ironic task of selling the
Marshall property at auction in the summer of 1864. Mrs. Salina C. Mason was
the highest bidder at $1,500; her family acquired the title to the property, and the
College closed its doors.

Professor Thackston, who had taught at Marshall from 1858 until early 1860,
came to Barboursville to tutor the younger sons of William C. Miller, as well as the
Thornburg boys and a few others who had previously studied at Marshall Academy.

The 1860 Census shows Thackston residing at the Miller residence, where at some point he met our pen pal Eugenia Miller, she of the tucking combs, Post Office stamps and prostrated dahlias. They would fall in love, marry in July of 1861, move to Richmond where Benjamin served as a Confederate in the Auditor's office of the Treasury Department during the Civil War, and later write affectionate wartime letters to each other.

After the war, Professor Benjamin H. Thackston (1835-1918) would return to Cabell County to continue his teaching career in town, and later back at Marshall College after it re-opened as a West Virginia State Normal School, serving as its president from 1881 to 1884. He and Eugenia Miller Thackston (1837-1924) built a home on her father's property at 1124 Main Street in 1869. (The lot now holds a newer brick house, guarded by two cement lions.)

The Noose Tightens

America's Northern Methodists began using Sunday school literature and conference tracts to spread anti-slavery views. Virginia's Southern Methodists found themselves painted into a most "anti-Wesleyan" theological corner of defending slavery. Both conferences attempted to push their boundaries into the other's territory. One Virginia church drew up a resolution to the effect that the "Discipline and Literature of the Methodist Episcopal Church, North, on the exciting subject of slavery, are at war with the best interests of the people of Virginia."

Barboursville's Methodists ultimately got caught up in the struggle. At some point at the Barboursville Methodist Episcopal Church at the Water Street bend, the town's Northern and Southern factions began holding separate Sunday Schools in the same building, with "South" meeting on Sunday mornings, and "North" using the building in the afternoon. Even then, the young people of the two churches still attended both services together, this "mingling of attitudes" provoking the consternation of the elders.

In 1858, Cabell County officials began cracking down on any potential threat of slave escape or rebellion. The county court for the first time constituted patrols under the statute to visit all "negro quarters and other places suspected of having therein unlawful assemblies or such slaves as may stroll from one plantation to another without permission." Guyandotte established a four-man patrol that included W. C. Miller's brother, H.H. Miller.

If preceding events had served to turn up sectional heat, all hell broke loose across Virginia after October 16, 1859, the day John Brown and his followers seized the federal arsenal at Harpers Ferry. Brown's goal was to ignite a slave rebellion and establish a colony for runaway slaves in Maryland. The raid was a disaster for Brown, who became trapped with his men in a small engine house. The local slaves did not revolt as expected, and the first casualty of the raid was ironically a free black baggage handler, shot when he confronted the raiders. Brown was hanged six weeks later for treason in Charles Town, after declaring slavery would not be abolished without great bloodshed.

As the news spread, Virginians began to think seriously of their peril. The Richmond *Enquirer* pointed the finger at "the Northern fanatics…determined to wage with *men and money* the 'irrepressible conflict' to its bitter end." As Brown's body was carried through the free states on its way to Boston, church bells tolled, prayers were offered, and public meetings were held condemning Virginia's execution of the man. Such notable northerners as Ralph Waldo Emerson commemorated Brown, a fact that was inexcusable to most Virginians, who saw the man as "a murderer of the most cruel type and an archenemy of their social system."

The Northern response to Brown's raid had the effect of uniting Virginians. The Commonwealth, wrote Henry T. Shanks, "was in great excitement for the remainder of the year—an excitement which was not created by politicians, for the response of the people was too spontaneous. In the western counties, debates and even fistfights broke out in the schools. An entire edition of the *Richmond Whig* was devoted to the reports of military maneuvers in the different counties; and its editorials commended the warlike attitude."

In several counties, "vigilance committees" were appointed to watch for abolitionists and suspicious characters. Kanawha, Putnam and Cabell counties did not go so far as to appoint such committees, but in December 1859 Guyandotte citizens met to discuss the John Brown raid and passed a resolution essentially stating that any outside interference with slavery would not be tolerated.

By the election year of 1860, Cabell County citizens illustrated their divided sympathies by splitting the vote among three Presidential candidates, each of whom represented a different faction of the Democratic Party after it blew apart in sectional fury at its nominating convention in South Carolina. That summer, the remaining Northern delegates nominated Illinois's Stephen Douglas on a moderate platform that matched his well-earned reputation as an "all things to all men" compromiser. The Southerners nominated Kentucky's John Breckinridge on a slavery platform, and the old Whigs reorganized as the Union Party and nominated Tennessee's John Bell as the de facto candidate for the border states. The new Republican Party chose Abraham Lincoln, Douglas's 1858 Senate seat challenger. In a series of debates with Douglas, Lincoln had established himself as the principled national leader of the anti-slavery, anti-secessionist movement. Once they nominated Lincoln, the Republicans essentially ran a campaign in which the candidate worked behind the scenes—he made no speeches—and left it to the divided Democrats "to commit political suicide."

When the 888 votes of Cabell County's white male citizens were disclosed, Douglas—an 1850 protégé and legislative associate of the popular Henry Clay— had received 46 percent of the county's vote; the new Union Party's Bell received 36 percent; and slavery proponent Breckenridge received 18 percent. Lincoln received *four votes*—less than half of one percent.

After Lincoln was elected, on a minority vote of 39.9 percent, a divided nation sat for months in a leadership vacuum. The outgoing President, Democrat James Buchanan, sat "lazy, frightened, confused and pusillanimous" (in the words of Paul Johnson), and blamed Republicans for the crisis. Almost immediately, the southern states, beginning with South Carolina on November 10, 1860, started taking steps toward seceding from the Union.

A militia group called the Border Rangers formed in Guyandotte on December 10, 1860, most likely in reaction to the election of Abraham Lincoln. The Rangers' stated mission was to protect a Virginia state flag raised on the bank of the Ohio River.

By January 1861, Senators from seven southern states met in Washington and began making plans to form a separate government, followed by a series of emotional farewell speeches on the floor of Congress. With the legislative branch in disarray and the Union already disintegrating, Lincoln was unable to assume office until March 1861.

As Abraham Lincoln grew his iconic beard and waited to enter the White House, he was determined to preserve the Union without appeasing the secessionists. With the South's volatile cotton market, lack of interstate trade and inadequate infrastructure—including a rail system designed solely to get cotton to sea for export—the new President considered the prospect of war to be "so obviously against the rational interests of the South" that is was unlikely, much less inevitable. Yet by the close of 1860, South Carolina had called for the surrender of all federal property within its borders, and President Buchanan had failed to evacuate the 1st United States Artillery from coastal fortifications in Charleston Harbor. South Carolina state troops seized the U.S. Arsenal in Charleston and threatened the federal forces holed up at Fort Sumter.

For its part, the Commonwealth of Virginia, top among the original colonies and provider of most of the great early presidents, at year's end had not joined South Carolina, Georgia, Mississippi, Florida, Alabama, Arkansas, Texas and Louisiana in moving toward secession—yet.

Barboursville in the 1860 Census

A demographic snapshot of antebellum Barboursville—poised blithely at the threshold of bellum—comes to us courtesy of one C.H. Miller, Assistant Marshall, Post Office Cabell Court House, in nine neatly-handwritten U.S. Census schedule pages from June 1860. Enumerator Miller was almost certainly the oldest son of William Clendenin Miller, 21-year-old Charles, who listed his own occupation as

"Clerk," and resided with all his siblings, his parents and Professor Thackston in the W. C. Miller home on Main Street.

Every decennial Census is a product of its time, a gift to posterity that cannot be unwrapped for 72 years. (Tip: If you possess a public library card in Cabell County, you can access many of its genealogical riches free of charge from your personal internet device.) A review of Barboursville and surrounding communities reveals a lot about our Lost Village at that precarious moment.

As Cabell's Census enumerator, C.H. Miller personally recorded data from households in the towns of Barboursville and Guyandotte, as well as the rural post office districts of "Cabell Court House P O" (lands surrounding Barboursville), "Guyandotte P O (area around Guyandotte, including present-day Huntington), Falls Mills, Green Bottom, Griffithsville, Hamlin, Mud Bridge, Paw Paw Bottom, Ten Mile and Thorndyke. His jurisdiction comprised present-day Lincoln County, which was part of Cabell until 1867. For this young man's diligence, attention to detail and penmanship, C.H. Miller should earn the perpetual praise of genealogy buffs and history geeks.

A comparison with nearby communities shows that Barboursville was the most "international" locale in the county, with 16 percent of its heads of household listing a foreign birthplace. (The town of Guyandotte was next with 11 percent, followed by 8 percent of "Cabell Court House," and 5 percent each in Ceredo and "Guyandotte P O." Green Bottom, Hamlin and Mud Bridge housed two percent or fewer foreign-born householders.)

The predominant lands of origin of the Barboursville and "Cabell Courthouse" immigrants were Bohemia (the Stowassers), England (Gill and Vertigans), France (Baum and LeSage), Germany (Henry and Smith), Ireland (Cain and Hessian), Prussia (Westhoff, Long and Diehl), Saxony, Switzerland and Württemberg (Miller). Regarding those of African descent, Barboursville and Guyandotte housed nearly all the county's 11 free black and "Mulatto" (mixed-race) inhabitants. Ceredo in Wayne County, ironically, listed no free citizens of color.

Non-native Virginians made up about ten percent of Barboursville and surrounding households. They included residents born in Kentucky (Algeo, Griffith and Sammons), North Carolina (Blume and Perry), Ohio (Webb, Berry, Justice, Devore, Ross, Scarberry, Webb and Wilson), Pennsylvania (Ferguson and Wintz), Tennessee (Herald, Morrison and Underwood), and the occasional northeasterner such as Connecticut's Lattin, New York's Dusenberry, and Vermont's Thurston. The Ohio River landings of Green Bottom and Guyandotte P O had a greater mix of Kentucky and Ohio-born folks, and Ceredo was about one-third New England transplants. However, compared to the further-inland towns of Hamlin and Mud Bridge (both populated by 96 percent native-born Virginians), Barboursville was considerably less insular, with about a fourth of town residents born outside the Old Dominion.

The relative diversity in the village would suggest that a "live and let live" quality was part of Barboursville's collective DNA from an early period. This may also have made the events to come all the more shocking.

Economically, Barboursville was a mixed bag as well. In addition to its "common" laborers, farmhands, clerks and the like, Barboursville counted 22 heads of household whose net worth exceeded $3,000. Fourteen were in what I term the "comfortable class," with a combination of real estate and personal property up to $10,000, which would be worth an estimated quarter-million dollars in 2010 money. They were: English-born "gentleman" Octavius Church, age 48; Prussian-born tanner Arnold Westhoff, 41; German tanner Albert Becker, 48; physician H. B. Maupin, 43; 74-year-old widow Elizabeth Merritt Dirton; 67-year-old widow Mary Brown Moore; 38-year-old tailor O. W. Mather; Scottish tailor George Proctor, 40; Connecticut-born surveyor Charles Lattin, 51; Scottish timber man R. B. Allen, 36; 34-year-old lawyer H. J. Samuels; 28-year-old hotel proprietor J. T. Hatfield; 30-year-old merchant Joel K. Salmon from New York; and 42-year-old merchant George Frederick Miller of Württemberg. (Those not designated otherwise listed their birthplace as Virginia).

In the upper echelons of net worth, with assets up to $20,000 in 1860 dollars—the equivalent of half a million dollars in the twenty-first century—were 44-year-old merchant (and son of Solomon) Thomas Thornburg; 32-year old farmer (and grandson of Captain William) John Merritt; 35-year-old lawyer (and son of John) Albert Laidley; 69-year-old lawyer (and Son of 1791) John Samuels; and 40-year-old former innkeeper (and son of Martin) Sheriff Wilson B. Moore. The two wealthiest households , whose assets likely would have made them millionaires today, belonged to William Clendenin Miller, 57; and the "Württemberg Miller" household consisting of brothers John G. Miller, 51, and Christopher Sigismund *(sic)* Miller, 54. Just outside town limits lived some of the wealthy descendants of General Elisha McComas. There were much richer men in the county, like the Jenkins brothers and Peter Cline Buffington, but the various Barboursville McComases and Millers were doing just fine.

The 94 Barboursville households enumerated on June 1, 1860—as well as several hundred families living in the surrounding communities—would soon see their marketplace, county seat, transportation center and social gathering place change forever, as Civil War guns and cannons converged on Barboursville.

Remember the *Fannie McBurnie:* Chronology to Chaos

What follows here is a six-month sequence of events that led up to one of the earliest Civil War actions on West Virginia soil:

February 1861. Barboursville's Rev. William McComas becomes Cabell County's delegate to the Richmond Convention, to consider an ordinance of secession.

March 1861. On March 4th, Abraham Lincoln is finally inaugurated. In South Carolina, Brig. Gen. Beauregard, of the newly formed Confederate States of America, begins strengthening artillery batteries aimed at Fort Sumter. Conditions in the federal fort grow dire as food and supplies dwindle.

April 1861. On the 12th, after President Lincoln decides to send a ship to Charleston Harbor with food and supplies—but no arms or ammunition—South Carolina's secessionist forces bombard Fort Sumter. On the 15th, Lincoln asks for 75,000 volunteers to defend the "star-spangled banner" and is answered within days by 92,000 men. On the 17th, an Ordinance of Secession is adopted by the Richmond Convention, "the vote standing 88 yeas to 55 nays." United States Congressman Albert Gallatin Jenkins resigns his seat to become a delegate to the Provisional Confederate Congress. On the 18th, Confederate forces destroy the Federal Armory at Harper's Ferry.

On April 20, Ira J. McGinnis's Border Rangers meet with other militia companies and county citizens in front of the Planter's Hotel in Guyandotte, where they get word of the passage of the Secession Ordinance. The "secession ladies of Guyandotte" have already made a special flag that is raised on the riverbank, and several speakers, including Barboursville's Professor Benjamin H. Thackston, address the cheering crowd. Now-Confederate Congressman A.G. Jenkins rides in to address the militia groups, and the Border Rangers accompany him back to Greenbottom to set up camp and amass weapons and recruits. By the end of the month, a secession flag has been raised at Wayne, and Union supporters in Ceredo form a military force to defend the town.

May 1861. On the 13th, western county representatives hold the first Wheeling Convention and declare the Ordinance of Secession "unconstitutional, null and void." Cabell County does not send delegates, but is represented by the delegates from Harrison County who act under the authority of a convention said to have been held at Barboursville. The secession ordinance is submitted to the vote of the people on the 23rd and is adopted by a majority vote—this after Virginia's Governor has already put the state under Confederate command. In western Virginia, Cabell, Kanawha, Logan, Mason, Putnam and Wayne counties vote against secession, with Cabell giving a majority vote of 650 against it. Still, *The Wheeling Intelligencer* reports that "Guyandotte is a hotbed of secession and the southern folks do about as they please."

On May 29, Cabell County's first Confederate enlistees join McGinnis's Border Rangers at Greenbottom. Numbering about 50, the outfit includes Barboursville volunteers Lieutenant Alexander H. Samuels, 25-year-old farmer Isaac Blake and

17-year-old Private George F. "Frank" Miller, as well as two thirteen-year-old boys from prominent Guyandotte families.

June 1861. Reports in southeast Ohio's *Ironton Register* tell of alarming developments in Cabell County. These include an attack on Proctorville citizens by Guyandotte secessionists, a company of Virginia "State troops" marching through Barboursville toward Guyandotte, and the reading of an act at the Courthouse in Barboursville "by which it (was) made treason to speak in favor of the Union." At least one Union man, a Dr. Litch, is reportedly driven from his Barboursville home. The second Wheeling Convention assembles on the 11th to provide for "The Restored Government of Virginia." Barboursville's Albert Laidley, Cabell's elected representative to the original Virginia Assembly, appears at Wheeling but does not take a seat at the convention.

Note that there are now two state government bodies representing Cabell County, one in Richmond under the Confederacy, and the new "Restored" body in Wheeling.

In late June, Captain Jenkins and his mounted Confederates raid Point Pleasant, capture Union sympathizers and head back to their Kanawha Valley camp at "Coalsmouth" near present-day St. Albans. They are pursued by a hundred Union men from a Gallipolis encampment. The Union force then raids Jenkins's Greenbottom farm, and later arrests about 30 Mason County secessionists, sending them to a prison camp in Columbus.

July 1861. The *Cincinnati Gazette* publishes this special dispatch, picked up by the *New York Times*:

> POMEROY, Wednesday, July 10. The steamer *Fannie McBurnie* was hailed this morning as she came up at Greenbottom, by the notorious A.G. JENKINS. As she neared the shore at a given signal, thirty of his band sprang from ambush near at hand, and ordered her to cast anchor, which she was forced to do, after which they boarded her, and upon search found one box of pistols and a few stores, which they carried off, together with goods taken from passengers. They then told the officer, that as they were particular friends and acquaintances, they would not burn the boat. The above is reliable. (An Ex Congressman Turned Highwayman 1861)

The *Wheeling Daily Intelligencer* writes about the incident in its July 13 edition and includes information about Jenkins's prosperous, easily-accessible farm.

On Thursday, July 11—in response to newspaper reports on the *Fannie McBurnie* incident—four infantry regiments, a troop of cavalry, and a battery of artillery advance into Western Virginia under orders from Major General George B. McClellan of the Union Army, who sends them to "beat up Barboursville, Guyandotte, etc., so that the entire course of the Ohio may be secured to us." On the same morning, the Union's 2nd Kentucky lands below Guyandotte, marches in and takes control of that town, and sets up camp in a wheat field along the Guyandotte River named "Camp Crittendon" (the present Special Metals site in Altizer). Most secessionists leave Guyandotte as Federal pickets occupy all approaches to the town.

As word reaches Barboursville that Union troops have invaded the county, a number of men, including former members of the old county militia, gather in the village to prepare to defend their homes and families, some equipped with only rudimentary weapons such as squirrel rifles and double-barreled pistols. After a Guyandotte rider hastily recruits men from Wayne County, their militia members assemble the morning of July 12 and begin the march to Barboursville. The Union regiment at Camp Crittendon becomes uneasy about the growing militia camp outside of Barboursville. Fearing attack, Colonel Woodruff makes an urgent request for another regiment, and sends forth Federal soldiers to scout the area along the Guyandotte River, confiscate horses from secessionist farms and solicit goods and information from Union supporters in the area.

By Friday afternoon, the Wayne militia has arrived in Barboursville. A Federal scout rides toward town, sent to investigate the Barboursville camp, and narrowly escapes after being fired upon by rebel pickets, losing his horse in the scramble to safe ground. By Friday night, county secessionists and militia members fashion their sleeping quarters on the floor of the Courthouse, as townspeople make their own preparations to defend themselves against the Union invasion.

Meanwhile at Camp Crittendon, Colonel Woodruff has no idea how many Confederate defenders are assembled in Barboursville, and so decides to take immediate action. After midnight, Woodruff offers a few stirring words and sends 316 Federal troops (many of them from Ohio) marching quietly over the six-mile Guyan River Road to the Mud-Guyandotte confluence. The Union forces halt several times as scouting parties go forth. During the night, frightened pickets in Barboursville report that the Union forces are entering the village, someone's gun accidentally goes off and panic spreads, sending some local farmers escaping into the night, before order is restored.

July 13, 1861

As the sun came up in Barboursville on a foggy Saturday morning, the atmosphere must have been charged with suspense. Decades of North-South tension had accelerated into a swirl of political anarchy, rumor-mongering and mob spirit. In just a few months, the town's most genteel citizens had been compelled to defy the United States flag and Constitution. Days earlier, the Union rally and Rebel yell had been heard in two other western Virginia counties, where battles took place in Philippi and Hoke's Run. Now—thanks to the spit-in-your-eye display of a homemade flag on Guyandotte's shore, weeks of aggression by a few dozen Border Rangers and the incendiary comments of newspaper editors on both sides of the fight—the Federal Army now saw Cabell County as a Confederate stronghold threatening traffic on the Mighty Ohio.

Up to that point Barboursville citizens, according to Wallace, still "cherished the illusion that the Federal Government would not resort to war and if there were a war it would be short lived." However, the previous 24 hours had introduced Civil War reality to Barboursville in the form of frightful hearsay, heightened adrenaline and the gathering of every available firearm and hickory club in a two-county area.

Thrust into the role of the town's defenders, a mix of Border Rangers, former militiamen and county residents woke and began seeking out breakfast when they got word that the Kentucky regiment was nearing the Mud River bridge. For safety, the town's women and children sought refuge uphill from east Main Street, at the farm of 59-year-old widow Sarah "Grandma" Blake (the present site of Orchard Hills golf course). A 58-year-old farmer and former militiaman named James Reynolds arrived from several miles up the Mud River, along with his sons Jeremiah, age 19, and Joseph, age 17; they showed up at the William C. Miller home for breakfast, on their way to help the secessionists. Miller unsuccessfully tried to talk the older man out of joining his sons up on the ridge.

At the north corner of Main and Center (as George Thornburg told it years later), Albert Gallatin Jenkins was talking to another officer about meeting the enemy outside of town, to protect "our friends" in Barboursville. Wayne County's "Sandy Rangers," sporting bright red flannels and caps, had also arrived on the scene and joined the others in the morning fog on the hill, the current site of the State Veteran's Home.

The hill offered the rebels a well-protected vantage point, with a two-mile view overlooking the Mud and Guyandotte rivers. The C&O had recently cut the beginnings of a right-of-way into the ridge, creating 45-foot-bluffs on either side. Just a few yards from the river junction was one of Cabell County's two covered bridges; it crossed the Mud just west of the current railroad trestle. Anticipating the arrival of the Kentucky Regiment, the rebels had removed the floorboards from the wooden span, leaving only the "bare stringers and rafters." Colonel Milton Ferguson of Wayne County rode up and commanded the secessionists to reposition themselves behind the hill in a secure but ready formation. On the hill they had dug protective trenches. (Years later, the old Confederate trenches were to be seen plainly until the early twentieth century when Morris Harvey College's McDonald Hall was erected.)

The well-trained and equipped Union soldiers waited until a couple hours after sunrise before making their advance, and then approached the Mud River bridge where they were met with a "tremendous volley from the local militia" that killed one Union soldier and wounded several others. As they scrambled for cover inside and under the bridge and behind abandoned brick kilns nearby, a mule fell through a newly-created gap in the floorboards and its rider clung to the remaining timbers. As bullets continued to storm, the rebels on the hill broke into cheers. The Union companies began a single-file dash across the remaining supports of the bridge, rallied at the road encircling the base of the hill. At the command of Lieutenant Colonel George Neff, the Yankee soldiers began a charge up the side of the hill with their bayonets, "literally dragging themselves up by bushes and jutting turf."

To the local militiamen, bayonets were something new and different. When the Yankees "began to load with butcher knives," they assumed the knives would be propelled at them. One Cabell County fellow named Lucky Savage decided it was time to stop shooting and start running, before turning and finding himself suddenly alone. The Confederates fell into retreat, heading into the hills south of town.

The blue-uniformed Union troops rallied at the place which would become known as "Fortification Hill," and planted the stars and stripes at the summit. Colonel Neff's men proceeded to take the Courthouse as their headquarters and temporary hospital. In the official report the following week, Major George McClellan wrote: "One of Cox's regiments, 2nd Kentucky, defeated and drove 600 of (Governor) Wise's men out of Barboursville, Cabell County, on the 16th."

Descriptions of the retreat vary. On the Confederate side, a Border Ranger provided this account in his diary: "The militia, after delivering one fire, broke and left the field. The Company marched off the hill in order, without firing a gun and marched back to Coalsmouth without the loss of a man or horse. We took the fire of the regiment but no one was hurt of the company." The *Kanawha Valley Star*, on the other hand, described that the militia on the hill "swayed for a moment, a leap was made from their flank and rear, and then the whole body scattered like sparks from a pinwheel."

Over at the W. C. Miller house, 16-year-old John W. Miller, just a year younger than brother Frank of the Border Rangers, decided to arm himself with his old double-barrel pistol and head up Main Street, determined to "go out and put an end to the war." His six-year-old sister Florence cringed against a wall as John took his pitiful gun and set out for the ridge. As he met the militia members in full retreat on Main Street, John quickly returned home. Later Miller would write, "I thought our militia was well trained but lost confidence in them when I watched them in action during this fight."

A Six-Pounder Cannon

Various recollections describe a town in pandemonium that Saturday morning. Over the southern hills, a militia captain's daughter, 13-year-old Mary Lunsford of Tom's Creek, recalled hearing the guns in town while she built a fire in the stove at daylight. By the time breakfast was ready, frightened militiamen were coming back from the fight, too scared to come inside the house. They ate on the run, having shed their guns while fleeing. Early the next morning, about 180 more Union men from Ohio arrived at "Fortification Hill" to assist, and saw blood stains on the bridge and ground, the dead and wounded laid out at the hospital, and "many buildings in town vacant and open, occupants having fled." Rumors flew around the county. A man from Wayne was reporting, falsely, that the Yankees "were killing men, women and children."

There were casualties on both sides; again, reports differ. The Border Ranger diarist wrote that "Mr. Reynolds was killed by the fire and three others slightly wounded of the Militia. The loss to the 2nd Kentucky was four killed and twenty wounded." Gunter's account puts Union losses at five men killed and 18 wounded, and Geiger names three of the Union dead and six of the wounded. The single life lost on the Rebel side was the same James Reynolds of Dry Creek who had break-fasted at W. C. Miller's with his sons. Badly wounded, he was treated by Federal troops at the Courthouse, but died within a day.

Absalom Balangee (or Ballinger) fell over the 45-foot railroad cut during the attack and broke his leg. Using his muzzle-loading shotgun as a crutch, Balangee made his way down Main Street and was then helped up the hill to Grandma Blake's by John W. Miller. That night, after tending to the militiaman's wounds, Sarah Blake put Balangee on a horse and took him to cross the Guyandotte River three miles upriver at Dusenberry's (the old Sanders Mill at Martha). Mrs. Blake's home would later become known as "a way station for travelers, soldiers and wayfaring men during the hectic '60s."

By day's end, the Border Rangers waved their secession flag from a hilltop a mile away before they retreated, vowing retaliation. In the village below and throughout the county, the shock of the morning was replaced with fear of what was to come. A brass six-pounder Union cannon guarded the entrance to the camp at Fortification Hill. *The Wheeling Register* reported that the victors marched through Barboursville "with the banners flying and bands playing airs which the inhabitants never hoped to hear again," as the regiment's flag streamed "from a spire in one of the hot-beds of secession."

Our Special Correspondent Furnishes an Interesting Letter:
MAY 8, 1898—Quite a number of old Union veterans from this section
attended the encampment at Huntington last week.

CHAPTER 8

BARBOURSVILLE'S "CHILDREN OF THE STORM" (1861-1869)

LET us now explore how various townspeople responded during America's long-brewing but alarmingly-sudden Civil War, and what kind of town remained in its wake.

Raids, Ravages, Retaliation—and Four Yankee Teens

Geiger describes the summer and fall of 1861 as a time of unchecked civil chaos in places like Barboursville, especially after the Union men of the 2nd Kentucky left town and moved into Kanawha County. The focus of military action quickly shifted to the east, as troops engaged in Putnam, Tucker, Nicholas, Randolph and Pocahontas counties.

Just a week after the attack on Barboursville, the First Battle of Bull Run in Manassas dispelled any national expectation that the war would come to an early end, as tens of thousands of men faced off in the largest and bloodiest battle in American history to that point. There the Union sustained the loss of 3,000 troops, including 460 dead. The Confederates won the day with fewer losses (387 killed), and a clear route that left Washington, D.C. vulnerable. Both sides woke up to the realization that this war would be longer and more brutal than anyone imagined. On July 22, nine days after the skirmish at Barboursville, President Lincoln signed a bill to enlist half a million men for three years of service.

Military enlistments racked up on both sides during the subsequent months and years. In September a rural Barboursville man, 41-year-old Prussian farmer Anthony Stowasser, enlisted in the Union's 5th Virginia Infantry at Ceredo. Other Union volunteers from the Barboursville area would include mostly farmers and day laborers, including: 16-year-old Frank Adams who also enlisted at Ceredo; French immigrant Joseph Baum; 35-year-old Berry Bias; 30-year-old James A. Bias; three Childers men—Bud, George and William; three Clark men—David, Harvey and William; Nathan (Nathanial) and William Collins; Willis Cornwell; William Cyrus; Samuel Dean; 22-year-old Joseph Eggers; George Fullweiler; John and Peter Harshbarger; 22-year-old blacksmith David Lattin; 25-year-old Charles Shipe; 24-year-old John Webb; 21-year-old Lewis Wintz; and Abram Woodward.

Identified Confederate volunteers from the Barboursville area outnumbered identified Union recruits more than two to one (although it should be noted that each list of veterans was provided by a different man to the *Herald-Advertiser* many decades later, and few of the listed Confederates appear in the 1860 Cabell County Census). In any case, the Rebels were identified as: Fred and John Baumgardner; Harvey Blackwood; Isaac Blake; Lindey Carter; Gabe Crook; George Crump; three Davis men—Joe, John and William; Jesse Dodson; James Dundas; Peter Everett; George Heath; L. Hendricks; 21-year-old day laborer Bird Hensley, William Hensley; 23-year-old laborer Charles Hodge; George and Robert Holderby; Charles Kelley; Charles Lattin; Three men named Love—John, John II and Lon; B.J. McComas; Blackburn McCoy; George McKendree; Thomas Merritt; William Messinger; the aforementioned Frank Miller, 17; Jack Moore; Wilson Moore; John Morris; John Morrow; Physicians Charles and V.R. Moss; John Payne; George and William Rodgers; Thomas and William Roffe (Rolfe); Alexander and Lafayette Samuels; Four Seamonds men—Charles, Jack, Pete and Sampson; Four Sheltons—George, James, John and Monroe; Charles and William Shoemaker; Mark Smith; William Sweetland; John Tassen; Pat and Thad Thompson; 22-year-old Barboursville schoolteacher Edward Vertigans (Vertegaus) and George Vertigans; John Williams; and three Wilsons—Charles, Harvey and Lemuel. Frank Ball wrote of another Confederate enlistee, John Everett, who was killed at age 34 in Bristol, Tennessee.

Not everyone stuck around. According to the obituary of Octavius Church, the English gentleman who married into the Merritt family, when the war broke out, "he being a staunch Union man, emigrated to Minnesota in order to prevent his two sons, then of age, from being forced into the rebel ranks."

In October, the 34th Ohio Voluntary Infantry Regiment came to set up their winter camp in Barboursville. Known as "Piatt's Zouaves" for their rather flashy light-blue, Zouave-style uniforms, this light infantry regiment served as a rear guard to the Union Army and combed the local countryside for Confederates. In addition to the courthouse and jail, the Methodist Church on Water Street was taken over by the Union, used for barracks. There were several engagements around the county between the 34th Reg. O.V.I. and bands of Confederate "bushwackers," including a shooting at Beech Fork and a skirmish on "Poore's Hill" overlooking the current site of Cabell Midland High School. Another Union regiment, the 5th Virginia Infantry, was organized in Ceredo that summer consisting of soldiers from Virginia, Ohio and Kentucky, and part of this regiment was also stationed at Barboursville in late fall.

Drawing of the 34th Ohio Volunteer Infantry Regiment
marching down Main Street in 1861
(Courtesy of Barboursville Public Library)

A rather remarkable drawing exists of the 34th Reg. O.V.I. marching down Main Street in November 1861. Multiple prints have been made of the drawing, including one that currently hangs on a rear wall of the public library. Though the artist's rendering presents the "Zoaves" and other humans as a bit out of proportion, the buildings that line the streets of the village were presented with detailed accuracy, and identified a century later by Frank Ball. The building with a chimney on the left was owned by a German named Kraus, and remained as part of the George Miller house where the public library now stands. The big frame, double-porched building in the left of the picture was the Beuhring Hotel. Both the Miller-Thornburg Store and the Courthouse can be seen in the background.

(Perhaps the most extraordinary thing about the sketch is that it found its way back to Barboursville at all, after being in the possession of the anonymous artist for decades. Eventually, in the late 1800s, a very influential son of (who else) William Clendenin Miller had a chance meeting with the man while dining at a cafeteria in Pittsburgh. The stranger learned in their passing conversation that Joseph Miller was from Barboursville; he had been just 13 years old when the sketch was made. Shortly after the Pittsburgh conversation, a delighted Miller received the sketch by postal carrier.)

A person in Cabell County did not have to be a militiaman or a recruit to become swept up in the increasingly violent conflict. Area residents might become part of the Union or Confederate cause as informants, prisoners, or dispensers of vigilante justice. William Clendenin Miller himself was held prisoner by the Union for a time at Guyandotte, according to a 1933 interview with his son. During this time, 16-year-old "Will" had packed and prepared to enlist, but when his father returned from POW status, he refused permission for his third son to do so, sending him off to Kentucky instead. William C. Miller was able to protect his family and prepare for the worst; during the war, a pot containing gold and silver pieces was kept hidden beneath a large flagstone at the front door of the Miller home (another account describes the hidden riches as silver tableware).

Less fortunate was wealthy secessionist Henry Shelton, who owned a plantation home on the current Ridgelawn Cemetery property at West Pea Ridge. Members of the Union-leaning Achilles Fuller family—after hearing rumors that Shelton had taken one of their sons to turn over to the Confederates—paid a September visit to the house of the 43-year-old father of seven and shot him dead. The Fuller boy later showed up unharmed. No official action was taken to arrest the killers, but Shelton's sons would dispense their own justice a few months later.

As if civil turmoil, vigilantism and occupying forces weren't bad enough, Barboursville's transportation routes suffered irreversible devastation. On September 29, waters crested on the Guyandotte and a major flood forever destroyed the slack-water navigation system of wooden locks and dams that had been championed and built by Barboursville's business visionaries. What remained of Dam 1, at the Roby Branch of the Guyandotte, was irreparably breeched by Union soldiers. Roadway traffic fared no better. According to Evan Wiley Blume, Barboursville's Mud River Bridge washed out, was rebuilt and later burned up during the war: "Jim Sedinger set it afire to keep the Yankees from crossing in."

Such was life in Barboursville in the second half of 1861, and it was not a time for the faint of heart. My mother and aunt relayed a bit of hazy Civil War lore passed down to them in their childhood—that their great-grandmother's hair turned snow white after gunshots thundered outside the house where she was hiding. Being something of a delicate flower myself, I find such a reaction quite understandable given the circumstances; but as I discovered, not every Barboursville woman withered amid the danger.

Emmy Cox at the beginning of the Civil War
(Herald-Advertiser clip courtesy of Barboursville Public Library)

On Sunday, November 10, 1861, 17-year-old Margaret Emily "Emmy" Cox, the adventurous stepdaughter of a Barboursville horse-trader, spurred her horse to a gallop into the dark. A "natural born Yankee" and skillful rider, Cox knew of a column of Confederate troops that had entered the county, and took it upon herself to warn selected neighbors, lest they be taken prisoner by Jenkins's Cavalry unit. In true Paul Revere fashion, Emmy cried out to the startled bearded faces peering out their windows along Little Seven Mile, "The rebels are coming!" In this way she raced on to the next farm, and the next, riding six miles that night from Barboursville to Cox's Landing on the Ohio River.

It is possible that Emmy simply happened upon the Cavalry that day, or she may have witnessed neighbors being captured by the Confederates, who charged into Barboursville at full speed before continuing across the Mud River and into Guyandotte. She was acquainted with men involved on both sides of the conflict, and was brazen about thwarting the Rebels even if she knew them personally, according to a 1978 resurrection of the account by Rick Baumgartner in *The Herald-Advertiser*. To the chagrin of her sister Sarah, who "thought I ought to leave the war business to the men," Emmy didn't like to work in the house when there was "so much excitement outside," as she put it.

Emmy Cox may have known about the Union recruit camp, "Camp Paxton," that had been recently established in Guyandotte. It is highly probable that she knew the three Barboursville boys training there, Frank Adams and the Felix brothers, two Swiss immigrants who resided at the time with their parents near the intersection of Main and Water Street. Seventeen-year-old Arnold and 16-year-old Werner were the only offspring living with surveyor James Felix and his wife Julia during the 1860 Census count. The brothers were encamped at Guyandotte, having just signed up with the brand new 9th Virginia (Union) Infantry.

The 9th Virginia Infantry was formed by New York-born Congressman Kellian Whaley, a lumberman living in Wayne County who filled the seat vacated by Albert Jenkins. On October 22, the recruit camp was moved from Ceredo to Guyandotte, and 130 or so untrained men descended upon the town. By November, their numbers had been depleted somewhat by a furlough and an outbreak of measles, and they were poorly supplied and without uniforms, but their presence had no doubt alarmed Guyandotte's secessionist citizens.

While Emmy Cox made her ride to Cox's Landing, the force of about 700 horsemen led by Colonel John Clarkson, (including Company E consisting of Albert G. Jenkins's Border Rangers) approached Guyandotte for what was termed a "morale boosting mission." Jenkins's men and boys had not been home since spring, and the fact that a Union regiment was forming there must have been infuriating. That same day a side group, consisting of Private George Shelton and a few of his friends, split off at Barboursville and made a detour to the Russell Creek home of Achilles Fuller, who had killed Henry Shelton a few months earlier. Fuller was summarily executed in his doorway, whereby the Confederates "gave a rebel yell" and rode back up the turnpike past the Shelton home.

That evening the Cavalry encircled the "deceptively peaceful" town of Guyandotte, where some of the callow Union recruits were returning from worship services. Others were relaxing and eating dinner in the homes of welcoming residents (who may have signaled the Union troops' locations to the Confederates). The Border Rangers with the help of local volunteers seized the suspension bridge and secured escape routes along the riverbank. Major Whaley's recruits, most of them boys from Lawrence County, attempted to resist, then escape, but were quickly overcome by the Rebels. When it was over, ten were killed, at least ten wounded and dozens captured. Confederate losses were limited to three killed and five wounded.

The Union regiment's physician, Dr. Jonathan Morris, also captured, tended to the wounded prisoners. Among them were Barboursville's teenaged Felix brothers, one shot in the face, where the ball "entered near the mouth and lodged just under the skin in his neck." A few minutes later his brother was brought in having been shot through both arms, with a fractured left ulna.

The next morning, the Confederates tied all the prisoners together in a closely-connected two-by-two formation except for the wounded men, who were mounted on horses. Then they herded the Union prisoners out of town and up Guyan River Road. The civilians were forced to march at the head of the line behind Major Whaley, and the march began at a full run through the muddy center of the road. Secessionist women wearing locally-designed Confederate aprons heckled the prisoners as they passed.

Civil War re-enactors join the forced march of Union prisoners from Guyandotte during the sesquicentennial observance of Guyandotte Civil War Days, November 6, 2011
(Photo taken by author)

The men heard cannon fire echoing from Guyandotte as they approached Barboursville. The bound prisoners were untied and mounted on the horses along with Cavalry riders to enter the village. The Confederates stopped to gather up their captives of the previous day. Among the civilians taken prisoner were Barboursville residents Constable John W. Alford, 61-year-old farmer William Hinchman, 61-year-old gunsmith Thomas Kyle, 41-year-old storekeeper Matthew Thompson, 45-year-old courier Frank Morey and someone identified by *The Ironton Register* only as "Mr. Fraddle" (a surname that sounds suspiciously like that of town butcher Julius Freutel).

The grueling march continued, with the Barboursville civilians now added to the roped assemblage of "Damned Yankees" (soldiers) and "Tories" (civilians), moving south to Chapmanville (where Major Whaley made his escape) and then on to Newbern, Virginia, where the remaining prisoners were ordered into cattle cars and transported to southern prisons. Newbern is nearly 200 miles from Barboursville; three prisoners died during the march. The civilian prisoners were released and allowed to go home about a month later, on December 14. The soldiers would be held longer. Sixteen-year old Private James Franklin Adams, from just outside of Barboursville, was taken to a prison in Salisbury, North Carolina, where he would remain for more than 15 months, before being paroled in a prisoner exchange and rejoining the war effort.

On the morning of November 11, just after Clarkson's Confederates withdrew from Guyandotte with their prisoners, a steamer on the Ohio River carrying about 200 Union soldiers of Ceredo's 5th Virginia Infantry stopped at Proctorville to pick up members of the Lawrence County Home Guard. Acting in response to reports about the sneak attack on the 9th Virginia, the boatload of men disembarked and entered Guyandotte, then began targeting the homes and businesses of known Confederates and those suspected of collusion in the previous night's attack. A combination of Union and/or Home Guard members began torching the places, destroying many buildings in and around the town center in the name of "military necessity," or vengeance, or both.

Frank Adams, Emmy Cox, Arnold and Werner Felix—all younger than 18—were compelled to channel their passions for the Union cause when most of their peers were secessionists—making them teenage rebels against the rebellion.

What became of Barboursville's Yankee adolescents?

Werner Felix was fatally wounded in another battle in 1864. Older brother Arnold Felix married Venilah Burns of Lincoln county and the couple raised at least 12 children in the town of Thorndyke in Union Township. Later Census records list Arnold Felix's occupation as "painter." Descendent June Ashworth revealed in KYOWVA Genealogical Society's Cabell County Bicentennial book that Arnold lived until 1902 and that he and his wife had 67 grandchildren.

Private Frank Adams would go on to fight heroically in at least two major Civil War battles, ultimately earning a Congressional Medal of Honor, before marrying Emily Elizabeth Merritt and raising six children. In the 1990s, a bronze marker was placed on Adams's grave in East Pea Ridge's Oaklawn Cemetery by the Medal of Honor Society.

For the first two years of the Civil War, the feisty Emmy Cox continued in her self-appointed rounds as "Cabell County's Paul Revere," and moved to Guyandotte to help her mother run a hotel. There, the young woman who once swore to her Confederate-leaning girlfriends, "I wouldn't have a rebel for a beau if I never got married," met First Lieutenant William Hill Newcomb, a Union commander who had participated in the Second Battle of Bull Run. They married in 1866 and built a home at 206 Buffington Street in Guyandotte. There she raised four sons (including the co-founder of Huntington's Anderson-Newcomb department store), and lived on to tell her tales of Civil War adventure. Margaret Emily Cox Newcomb died at the age of 87 in 1930.

The Divergent Loyalties of the McComas Clan

An enduring slogan of Civil war lore is "brother against brother, father against son." Across the embattled states there were millions of divided families. In Barboursville this was the case among several, including the Baumgardner, Lattin and Samuels men.

According to his obituary, Barboursville's Henry Jefferson Baumgardner "was attending Lebanon University when the Civil War broke out and he enlisted in the Union army. He was the only one of 21 close relatives to cast his lot with the North, all of his brothers and other close relatives enlisting in the Confederate army. First promoted to corporal, he was afterwards elevated to the post of a brevet lieutenant on the field of action. He was wounded at Fredericksburg, Md., a month before the battle of Gettysburg, losing the use of one arm."

Lafayette and Alex H. Samuels, two of the sons of John and Emily Gardner Samuels, served the Confederates, with Alex elected second lieutenant of the original Border Rangers. Alex Samuels was captured and confined in various prisons in early 1863, re-enlisted, and was eventually killed in action in 1864. "Lafe" Samuels died at home shortly after the war ended. Their brother Henry Jefferson Samuels, known as H. J., organized the Cabell County Petroleum Company and not only opposed the secession ordinance, but campaigned against it throughout Cabell County. This caused him to be forced out of the county at the beginning of the war. Later he was appointed Adjutant General of Virginia's provisional government, and upon West Virginia's statehood was elected Circuit Court judge.

An impressive home at the southern edge of town, William McComas's "Mulberry Grove," stood for over 150 years on what is now Peyton Street, as a silent testament to family division at the highest levels. Though the McComas men did not literally face off on the same field of battle, one can only speculate as to how their opposing allegiances affected relationships in the family, and vice-versa.

It is not known what McComas man strolled across the lawn in this undated photo from the William Wallace collection. It is irrefutable that each of the sons and grandchildren of Elisha W. McComas walked boldly along his or her own path of conviction, family loyalty be damned.

William McComas Home, "Mulberry Grove"
(Courtesy of Marshall University Libraries Special Collections)

The General. Cabell County trustee, Virginia Assemblyman and Brigadier General Elisha McComas and his wife Annie French were known to have raised five children to adulthood, including sons David, William and James, and daughters Rebecca (m. Keenan) and America (m. McKeand). "General McComas" (as he became known after the War of 1812) deeded the 400 acres in south Barboursville to his eldest son William. The General's military and political standing helped assure that his particular line of southwest-Virginia's Scotch-Irish McComases "lost their rough edges, absorbed formal learning," and became "people of substance and reputation," in the words of family biographers.

The Minister. Gen. Elisha's eldest son William McComas was born in 1793 in Giles County. He attended private schools, and Emory and Henry College. He subsequently became both a practicing attorney and an ordained Methodist minister. In February 1812, 19-year-old William married 17-year-old Mildred Ward, the daughter of the county's first sheriff, salt-maker Thomas Ward. The McComas-Ward union produced at least six independent-minded offspring over a 21-year span. Those who grew to adulthood at Mulberry Grove included Elisha Wesley, William Wirt, Hamilton Calhoun, Rufus F., Benjamin Jefferson and Irene Octavia. (It is also documented by Cabell County historian George S. Wallace that Rev. McComas fathered an illegitimate son, Evermont Ward, through a liaison with his wife's younger sister. Evermont Ward would emerge later in West Virginia history as a celebrated jurist and land speculator in southwestern West Virginia.)

Rev. William McComas was elected to the Virginia State Senate (1830-1833). He went on to win election under the Whig banner as a representative in Congress from 1833 to 1837. He would return to Richmond as Cabell County's appointed delegate to the 1861 Virginia Secession Convention, where "Virginia had convened her renowned jurists, profoundest thinkers and literary characters, among them being men who had held high positions in the councils of the State and Nation." There, Rev. William McComas would vote on the county's behalf, *against* secession.

The Judge. David McComas was born two years after William. Also schooled as a lawyer, David won fame as a brilliant jurist, was active in the Whig Party and served for five sessions in the Virginia State Senate, beginning in 1830. In the last decade of his life, he presided as a judge of the General Court of the State of Virginia, and served on the Eighteenth Circuit Court in Cabell County. David married Cynthia French, a Captain's daughter. They had no children and do not appear to have lived in Barboursville. Judge McComas was described as "a jolly man, full of wit and humor, but a most negligent man about his dress." An 1831 speech David McComas delivered in the Richmond state house, upholding South Carolina's right to break from the Union—perhaps the first out-and-out secession speech on record—would be published and circulated widely among Confederates just prior to the outbreak of the Civil War.

The Quiet McComas. General McComas's third son, James McComas was a farmer living in Cabell County's "Paw Paw Bottom," near his sisters' families in 1860. The progenitor of at least two twenty-first century Barboursville sons who made their mark in county and state government, the sectional leanings of this son of General Elisha are unknown by this author.

The "Governor." William's oldest son, born about 1822, was named after his grandfather, but was referred to as Elisha Wesley McComas, Wesley, or "E. W.", and after he moved west became known as "Governor McComas." He studied at Ohio University in Athens, Ohio; studied law and was admitted to the bar in 1841. Soon after that, at age 20, he married Ariana P. Holderby of Guyandotte. E. W. was commissioned as Captain in the Eleventh Virginia Infantry, and served in the Mexican-American War, where he was wounded and captured, then discharged in 1848.

Throughout his professional life, this oldest son of the General Elisha's oldest son had a knack for walking away from his past, while simultaneously parlaying his experiences into ever more illustrious positions. Drawn to politics after his Mexican-American war ordeal, E. W. McComas was elected to the Virginia Legislature, served as Senate President for two years, and in 1855 had the distinction of being chosen lieutenant governor of Virginia on the ticket with Governor Henry A. Wise, to serve a four-year term, even sitting for an official portrait that once hung on an official wall in Richmond. In 1857, E. W. McComas suddenly resigned as lieutenant governor halfway through his term. The admitted reason for his resignation was ill health and a desire to seek a new climate, but his intimate friends said that his resignation was largely prompted on account of a difference with Governor Wise about John Brown's activities in Kansas. No formal explanation of his resignation was ever uncovered.

E. W. McComas soon turned up in Illinois, where he spent the run-up to the Civil War establishing a law practice, soon becoming a leader of the Chicago bar. He made his reputation in a notorious murder case, in which newspapers reported on "Governor McComas" being chosen as counsel for a man named Jumpertz, who had been charged with cutting a woman into pieces and packing the remains into a trunk shipped to Chicago. When Jumpertz was pronounced not guilty and allowed to go free, it not only created a sensation in Illinois, but also gave Elisha Wesley McComas a national legal reputation.

He would quickly change careers again: When famous inventor Cyrus H. McCormick bought the *Chicago Times* in 1860, he placed "this brilliant young Virginian" in charge of its editorial management. McComas distinguished the *Times* as a Democratic paper until the war began, when:

> Governor McComas remained a resident of Chicago for several years, throughout the period of the war, and during that time not only continued his newspaper work but also his practice as a lawyer. He was on intimate terms of friendship with Stephen A. Douglas, and his beautiful tribute to that great statesman after his death was widely read and appreciated. Throughout his residence in Chicago Governor McComas was a prominent figure in nearly every public occasion. He had the courtesy of the heart which distinguished the true type of the old Southerner, and as an orator his services were much in demand. It is recalled that on the visit of the Prince of Wales to Chicago Governor McComas was chosen to deliver the address of welcome. (Kansas State Historical Society 1918)

After the war, E. W. McComas returned to Mulberry Grove and lived there until 1868, looking after the affairs of his father until the Rev. William McComas died. In 1868, Governor McComas moved again, settling with his family on a farm near Omaha, Nebraska. In 1870, he went to Fort Scott, Kansas and lived there the rest of his life, winning "a special place of esteem in the hearts of all the local citizens. His great ability and advice were invoked upon every important occasion of public concern." Elisha Wesley McComas also wrote and published several books, entitled respectively: *A Rational View of Jesus and Religion*; *The Divine Problem;* and

A Concept of the Universe. In his later years, when his wife Ariana was an invalid, McComas was said to have shaped his later life out of consideration for her care. Upon her passing, a biographer noted, "her decline had been a protracted one, but her physical sufferings were wonderfully light and her death most painless and peaceful."

The Doctor. The second son of Rev. William, Dr. William Wirt McComas, was born around 1827. He grew up to become a practicing physician in Giles County near Pearisburg in 1860, where he had a wife, Sarah French, and four young children. At the beginning of the Civil War he would command a Confederate artillery company there. At the 1862 Battle of South Mills, in Albemarle County, North Carolina, William Wirt McComas was killed in action at age 35.

The Union Lieutenant. Hamilton C. McComas was born in Parkersburg on November 9, 1831. "H. C." apparently joined Elisha Wesley in the Mexican American War and, like his eldest brother, struck out on his own in the Midwest and achieved national renown. Described as "tall, dignified and professionally successful," H.C. was a lawyer living in Monticello, Illinois in 1860 with his wife and young baby Charles. Though he apparently maintained contact with the family, Hamilton was the only McComas brother to enlist with the Union, as Lieutenant Colonel of the 107 Illinois Infantry.

After the war, he continued his law practice in Illinois, then moved on to Kansas, and later served as a judge in St. Louis, Missouri. At some point he and his family traveled to New Mexico to examine some silver mine investments. In 1883, Judge H. C. McComas and his wife were attacked and killed by Apaches in the desolate New Mexico Territory, and their 6-year-old son Charlie kidnapped, shocking his Cabell County relatives and mystifying the news-reading nation.

The Nebraskan. Less is known about the sectional leanings of William's son Rufus F. McComas, who was born in 1833, squarely between the delivery dates of his older Union and younger Confederate brother. Perhaps choosing to avoid the conflict altogether, Rufus moved to Nebraska and does not appear in the 1860 Cabell County Census. Rufus turns up in the 1880 Census as a "Farmer/ Steamboatman" living with wife Betty Simpson and four children in eastern Nebraska. By 1883, Rufus apparently located in Silver City, New Mexico with brother Hamilton as part-owner of several mines, but chose to avoid the doomed Lordsburg Road excursion of H.C.'s family.

The Confederate Prisoner. William's fifth known son, Benjamin Jefferson McComas, born about 1835, was a member of the Cabell County Bar, and would serve with the Confederate Forces under General Jubal Early. Benjamin Jefferson McComas was captured at Cedar Creek in the Shenandoah Valley campaign, and sat out the rest of the war in a Yankee prison camp. Upon his release, Benjamin returned to his law practice in Cabell County.

The Teacher. William's and Mildred's youngest child and only daughter, Irene Octavia (1843-1913), was a 17-year-old living at Mulberry Grove in 1860. She was a Confederate sympathizer and then an embattled Barboursville school teacher who married General George McKendree after the war.

Attack on the Miller Home

In 2009, the owners of the William Clendenin Miller home made an accidental discovery (as reported in *The Huntington Quarterly*). "A friend of mine grew up in the house next door," said Kriska Adkins, one of Picasso Salon and Day Spa's original owners, "and when we bought this house, he told me it was haunted. He also said that supposedly it was hit by a cannonball during the Civil War. A couple of months into construction, we had to tear out one of the old fireplaces, and when we did, a cannonball rolled out of the chimney." In 2011, the six-pound cannonball sat on a stand at the salon's front desk, where customers and guests could handle the weighty artifact, which harkens back to the second strategic Civil War action in the village.

This second incident took place on September 8, 1862, between some of the 2nd West Virginia Volunteer (Union) Cavalry, commanded by Colonel William H. Powell, and a portion of the 8th Virginia Cavalry, C.S.A., under Albert Gallatin Jenkins. The Union troops, never forgetting the Guyandotte raid, kept Cabell County under close (if not steady) watch, including the county seat of Barboursville. Jenkins had continued to lead raids throughout western Virginia and eastern Ohio, and the various actions and threats of his company against "peaceable citizens," as well as random attacks by Confederate guerilla parties, kept border towns in a state of anxiety throughout the war. Prisoners continued to be taken throughout the county on both sides. The two forces seem to have clashed in town more than once on September 8, according to a Border Ranger account:

> After inquiring from the citizens, we found that all they knew was that they saw an officer and eight or ten men turn the corner and they supposed they were merely the advance of some regiment coming to take possession of the town. We concluded to ride into the town and take a look at them. We rode in as far as Thornburg's store on top of the hill where the officers ordered a charge, having seen a blue coat. We found them at Hatfield's Hotel. About half of them went over the River Bank and the rest ran in all directions, the boys firing at them as they ran. We caught two of them before they could get out of the Hotel. Lieut. Brown, the officer in command of the Yanks, hid in a bake oven in the back yard of Oscar Mather's house. This was the Sabbath Day and Church was going on at the time in Southern Methodist church. Three or four bullets struck the building and the preacher did not have time to dismiss

the congregation. The congregation was found getting toward home as fast as they could possibly go, without waiting for the benediction… (Wallace 1935)

According to an account by J.J. Sutton, a private in the West Virginia Cavalry Volunteers, a late night action at the Miller home may have disrupted significant Confederate plans in the Kanawha valley. Major Powell had learned from two Confederate prisoners on September 7 that Jenkins had over a thousand cavalry camped near Barboursville. He then was informed that Jenkins was using William C. Miller's home as his temporary headquarters. Determined to capture Jenkins, Powell led several companies of the 2nd West Virginia to charge the Miller home on the night of September 8, finding it to be "guarded by at least 50 Confederate soldiers, which fact could not be observed by the extreme darkness of the night." Powell's men drove the Confederates away, and later reported that "Col. Jenkins and his staff escaped by the rear door and through the garden," although Jenkins's actual presence at the house that night was never ascertained.

During the charge, one Union soldier, First Duty Sgt. Braxton P. Reeves of Lawrence County, Ohio, was shot and killed. His body was placed on the porch of the Miller home until after the Confederates left the area and his regiment could retrieve it.

The raid on the Miller house may have been the last deadly military clash in the village, but Barboursville's people would remain vulnerable throughout the war to a series of short-term Union army occupations, as well as periodic attacks by increasingly autonomous and desperate bands of Confederates.

Messy Affairs of County and State

It is uncertain how any county business could have been conducted during this time. According to G. S. Wallace, "Many of the prominent citizens and largest property owners were out and out secessionists. Some of these men left the county and cast their lot with the Confederacy. After the beginning of hostilities, Federal forces occupied Cabell County and continued therein until after the war. The presence of these soldiers and the changes in the government put the Union element in full and complete control of the county government."

All the county officers elected to two-year terms in 1860 were "strong Southern sympathizers," and county records "were silent" until 1862. Court records of 1862 confirm that John Laidley Jr. was elected as prosecuting attorney to fill the vacancy caused by the resignation of Ira J. McGinnis. Barboursville's 23-year-old John Witcher—a former store clerk taken prisoner the day of the Guyandotte raid—was appointed clerk of the court, and Thomas J. Merritt was made deputy clerk. A few months later Witcher would become second lieutenant in the Third Regiment of the West Virginia (Union) Cavalry, at once ensuring both vigorous action against roving Confederates, and a total loss of continuity in the business of the Court.

In the spring of 1863, Union man B.D. McGinnis was named to fill the unexpired term of his secessionist cousin, Border Ranger Ira J. McGinnis. In the absence of the sheriff, J.B. Baumgardner was appointed to the office of collector of county taxes, commissioned a few months later to collect State taxes as well, and given the tax tickets for 1861 and 1862. "Fatty," as Baumgardner was known for his large physique, friendly nature (and obviously thick skin), kept a hotel at Barboursville. His new job tested his reputation: on one occasion, he was fired upon by someone near the Everett place near Ona; another time, a "Rebel" named Spurlock relieved Fatty's deputy of $2,247.23. The Legislature found it necessary to pass three separate acts dealing with Fatty's office.

Around the same time, another Barboursville man, 46-year-old blacksmith Greenville Harrison, was serving as commissioner of revenue. While he was at work in the courthouse, a band of unknown "Rebels" swooped down on him and took away his tax books. The incident brought about the removal of the courthouse to Guyandotte, where enough Federal troops were stationed to provide a modicum of security no longer present in Barboursville. Court records from that time until 1864 were never to be found. On August 9, 1864, Cabell County's board of supervisors pronounced, "the Court House of this county is in the possession of the military authorities and not in a suitable condition to enable the Board to hold their meeting therein. The board ordered that meetings be held at an office of the recorder in Guyandotte until otherwise ordered.

Added to its inability to keep a sheriff or collect revenue, the on-again-off-again presence of Federal troops and Confederate raiding parties, and the insult of moving county business out of its relatively new brick courthouse—Barboursville was experiencing the simultaneous legal thrashings of the American Civil War and West Virginia's statehood movement. Although tensions between eastern and western Virginia had been brewing since the 1790s, the window of opportunity for West Virginia, the "child of the storm," to achieve independent statehood would never have opened without the catalyst of Civil War, argues Joe Geiger.

As the war raged, the Wheeling Conventions set in motion the following events: In October 1861 a vote was held in the counties of western Virginia on a proposal to form a separate state to be called the "State of Kanawha." It passed overwhelmingly, with State records showing a vote in Cabell of 200 for and none against. In January 1862, Ohio County minister and convention delegate Gordon Battelle proposed that the new state constitution provide for the gradual abolition of slavery rather than the immediate abolition, and this became the basis of the Willey Amendment. In July 1862, the West Virginia Statehood bill was passed by the Senate, changing the slavery provision of the West Virginia Constitution to allow for the gradual emancipation of slavery. On January 1, 1863, President Lincoln's Emancipation Proclamation freed all slaves in areas of rebellion, but did not apply to states loyal to the Union, including the future state of West Virginia.

So West Virginia officially entered the Union on June 20, 1863 as a paradox—a Union state that did not abolish slavery for nearly two years after Lincoln emancipated all Southern slaves. This meant that slaves were now officially free in Virginia, but would not be fully emancipated until February 3, 1865 in West Virginia. Not only that, but free African Americans who were not already here as slaves would soon be forbidden to live in West Virginia, due to passage of a December 1863 law forbidding residency of any slave who entered West Virginia after its formation.

For any Cabell Countian who had championed the abolitionist cause, this unintended consequence of the governmental process must have been a real head-scratcher. But by now, the topsy-turvy state of affairs was merely par for the course in a place whose center of political gravity had been pulled in so many directions— from Richmond, Ceredo, Guyandotte, Harper's Ferry and Wheeling, Virginia, as well as the state of Ohio and the District of Columbia.

War Grinds to a Bitter End

The tide was turning against the South. Jefferson Davis had seriously mishandled international diplomacy and internal politics, with severe military consequences. Each of the 15 Confederate states had raised its own forces and decided when and where they were to be deployed. Many of their leaders considered the rights of their state more important than the government of the Confederate States of America. In one instance, Davis's Navy secretary complained that 'our fate is in the hands of such self-sufficient, vain, army idiots.'

Once the North penetrated into southern land, the Confederate capital Richmond gradually became "a snakepit of bitter social and political feuds," as the interests of the states diverged and it was "everyone for himself." As described in Johnson's *A History of the American People*, many of the elites who instigated secession left "Armageddon" long before the war's end. However, someone forgot to tell the ordinary Southerners, who continued to fight the war with extraordinary grit and endurance.

At Antietam, in the bloodiest single-day battle in American history, 23,000 soldiers (out of almost 100,000 engaged) were killed, wounded or missing after 12 hours of savage combat on September 17, 1862. The battle marked a turning point: the failure of the Confederates' first northern invasion gave Lincoln the opportunity to issue the preliminary Emancipation Proclamation. Paradoxically, Cabell County's Confederate recruits increased dramatically on that very day.

If wars are truly lost by one side running out of money, the Confederates were probably doomed from the beginning. They had no indigenous gold or silver supplies and no bullion reserves. Davis's treasury secretary had kept printing paper currency, so much so that by 1864 one gold dollar would buy more than 20 Confederate dollars. By the time Davis appointed a competent replacement, it was too late and the South's finances were beyond repair. People cut themselves off from paper money altogether and began to barter in-kind. The only people with means to move around were those like William C. Miller who had prudently held onto gold and silver.

In a 1927 interview, William C. Miller's son recalled:

> We did not have any high prices during the war until people began to speculate in gold. This started about 1863, when gold went to 263. And in those days goods were bought on long time, from six months to 12 months. Merchants would go to the large cities and lay in large stocks, of sufficient quantity to last a year; and this panic of 1863 occurred in April after the merchants had all "stocked up" with this high price goods and the panic came increasing prices 100 percent. (F. B. Lambert Collection n.d.)

The villagers who were not enlisted as part of the crushing military machinery were at best living a frazzled and threadbare existence.

Benjamin Thackston wrote to his wife Eugenia in August 13, 1863:

> I will get some things from the government in the way of uniforms. I have got two nice red flannel shirts for $4.37 each. You can use the old one for your maid. I am still boarding myself. I have taken Mr. Caldwell of Clarksville who was wounded in the second Battle of Manassas to room with me. He is clerk in the Assistant Quarter Master General's office at a salary of $1,000 a year. He is very poor and I did this as a matter of accommodation to him as his salary is not sufficient to board and clothe him comfortably. We hardly ever have boiled victuals. We live principally on eggs, fried meat, onion, cymlin tomatoes, etc. We only have two meals a day. I am not making enough to keep us comfortable. (Matthews 1949-50)

In a letter from Eugenia to Benjamin on October 20, 1863:

> I had winter socks in readiness long ago. I delayed making your vest for lack of material for the back. Our cloth is now in the loom. I think perhaps you need new drawers…If you want to sell the jeans I can get $10.00 per yard for it. I have not made arrangements for shoes for Eliza (the maid). Your leather is still in the tanyard. (Matthews 1949-50)

Geiger cites at least two more raids on Barboursville in 1862 and 1864, in which Confederate guerillas performed such mischief as stealing or shooting horses, swiping all the leather from the tannery, robbing stores, burning Union stables, kidnapping the sheriff and other public officials, and disrupting the 1864 election. Judge H. J. Samuels observed that horses and vast quantities of valuable contraband goods were finding their way to "Dixie" on steamboats stocked with empty boxes and barrels by Southern sympathizers. Samuels wrote a letter in late 1864 urging the government to help drive out the rebel pests. He had a business motive in expelling the guerillas, so that petroleum and coal could attract "a large migration of capitalists to this region."

Samuels credited one man with leading the effort to clear out the Confederate bushwackers, Barboursville's former court clerk, Major John Witcher, adding simply, "They fear him."

Major Witcher's 65-member cavalry unit was formed in December 1862 and included a large number of Cabell County men. In a region where Federal troops would come in, stay temporarily and then move on, Witcher and his men provided more continuous protection for county citizens who were under threat of being "completely overrun with (Confederate) cut-throats and robbers." More importantly, they knew the lay of the land. One of Witcher's men boasted (bringing to mind actor Tommy Lee Jones in *The Fugitive)* that they knew "every bridle path, rock, house and hollow log in Cabell, Wayne and Logan counties." One pursuit in the dead of winter had Witcher's men riding 40 miles in 12 hours, "without stopping long enough to get anything to eat for either men or horses." Witcher had to return home that time by swimming the Guyandotte River, during which time his horse drowned.

Witcher's men captured a captain, 3 lieutenants, 60 privates, 40 horses and many small arms. One man, Border Ranger Lieut. George Holderby, was captured in Barboursville trying to hide at the home of one of his relatives by imitating pillows—"lying crosswise at the head of a bed."

A few surviving accounts describe the ordeal of transporting Confederate prisoners to the state prison in Wheeling during the spring and summer of 1864. One example comes from the diary of William Dusenberry:

May 30, 1864: Shelton prisoner…takes Mrs. Shelton to Point Pleasant on my way to Wheeling…Shelton had a ball and chain on. Jumped overboard, ball, chain and all. We had the boat stopped but could find nothing of him. He is either at the bottom of the river or had loosened the chain, dropped the ball and then swam to the shore.

May 31, 1864: I found the rivet-head that Shelton had cut off his shackle.

June 1, 1864: Lying at Wheeling. Took prisoners to State's Prison. Auditor refused to pay (fee) for guarding prisoners, just expenses. (Dusenberry n.d.)

An article in the *Wheeling Intelligencer* cited the arrival of about 70 Confederate prisoners from the southern region and described them as "the dirtiest, scraggiest, most cadaverous looking set of vagabonds that we ever saw."

On May 9, 1864, Brigadier General Albert Gallatin Jenkins, colonel of the 8th Virginia Cavalry, was captured near Dublin, Virginia after being shot, a musket ball shattering his left arm. It was Jenkins's second major injury, the first being a head wound sustained at Gettysburg in 1863. In Dublin he was taken to a nearby home that had been established by the Federal troops for wounded officers. On the thirteenth, Jenkins's arm was amputated near the shoulder. At first, Jenkins seemed to improve but then developed pneumonia, and rapidly bled to death at age 41 from secondary hemorrhage. Thus ended the life of the once-celebrated Congressman, who had helped introduce the American Civil War into Cabell County.

By the end of 1864, Generals Grant and Sherman led their troops to demonstrate forcefully that resistance to the Union was futile. The Deep South was demoralized, with large swaths of crops and infrastructure destroyed, people starving and prisoners subjected to the worst atrocities.

By March of 1865, it was reported that Cabell County was mostly quiet, most of the guerillas having been captured or killed. Any remaining trouble was chalked up to deserters from both sides and fellows who were already considered ne'er-do-wells before the war started.

On April 2, 1865, Grant's Army captured Richmond and the state capital was evacuated. A quarter of the city's buildings were destroyed in fires set by retreating Confederate soldiers, with Union soldiers putting out the fires as they entered the city. Benjamin Thackston, according to his obituary "served out the war in the official life of the Confederacy, and was in the last line troops defending Richmond before its fall." His wife Eugenia Miller Thackston was with him and witnessed the burning of Richmond. They returned to Barboursville.

Confederate General Robert E. Lee surrendered his Army of Northern Virginia on April 9, 1865. In an untraditional gesture—done partly in anticipation of peacefully restoring Confederate states to the Union—Lee was permitted to keep his sword and horse. As news of Lee's surrender reached Confederate forces across the South, they surrendered as well. The American Civil War was over, six hundred thousand men having died in the four-year fight.

On April 14, 1865, less than a week after Lee's surrender, President Lincoln was shot by John Wilkes Booth. Lincoln died early the next morning, and Andrew Johnson became president.

A Slow Return to Peacetime

After the war ended, "citizens of the Guyandotte Valley, as well as others in Southern West Virginia, were apparently treated, not as brothers in a victorious cause, but instead as defeated citizens of the Confederate States of America," wrote H. R. Smith. Abraham Lincoln had meant to bring Confederates peaceably back into the fold and reunify the nation, but did not live to serve out his second term. Congressional Republicans decided to inflict punishment on the former Rebels through draconian Reconstruction policies.

Similarly, on the home front there were punitive laws on the books, and scores to settle. The prisoners taken after the Battle of Guyandotte sought remunerative justice:

> In 1864, Julius Freutel, J. B. Alford, Thomas Kyle, C. Dusenberry, and Robert Ross brought separate suits against Thomas J. Jenkins, George W. Holderby, Peter C. Buffington, Robert Holderby, John Chapman, Hurston Spurlock, Milton J. Ferguson, John N. Clarkson, Warren P. Reece, Calwellsey (sic) Simmons, Joseph W. Morris, Wilson B. Moore, Henry Buffington, John N. Buffington, Leander Gilkerson, James Ferguson, Burwell Spurlock, Vincent A. Witcher, James R. Morris, John Plymale, Henry Everett, John S. Everett, James Everett, Peter Everett, Henry C. Poteet, V. R. Moss, Charles K. Morris, Charles L. Roffe, Godfrey Sights, William A. Jenkins, and Charles Shelton, and levied attachments on the lands of P. C. Buffington and the Jenkins... The declarations in each case charged that the defendants had conspired together and were making war against the government, and in the first three cases alleged that the plaintiffs had been arrested and taken to Richmond, Virginia, and in the last two cases the declaration alleged that the defendants had destroyed their property and had taken in the Ross case his hogs, sheep, cattle and bacon. In the Dusenberry case the jury returned a verdict in his favor for $10,000 and in each of the other cases the jury returned a verdict in favor of the plaintiff for $30,000. (Wallace 1935)

In addition, former Confederates were further disenfranchised through the "Test Oath," a state act requiring all public officers to swear "that I had never voluntarily borne arms against the United States; that I had voluntarily given no aid or comfort to persons engaged in armed hostilities thereto...that I have not sought, accepted or attempted to exercise the function of any office whatever, under any authority in any way hostile to the United States." Later this act was extended, and teachers, physicians, and all persons whose business was done under a license from the state were required to take such an oath. Needless to say, state, county and town governments were run by Union men for several years.

Irene McComas
(Herald-Advertiser clip courtesy of Barboursville Public Library)

During the war, school and church had ceased in large measure to function in Barboursville, according to Helen Hanna. The village soon formed a common council under mayor John B. "Fatty" Baumgardner, and a public school system was put into operation. William McComas's daughter, Southern sympathizer Irene Octavia, had been teaching for several years, but on May 27, 1867 she was ordered to "desist from teaching" after refusing to take the Test Oath.

The only churches left standing in the county after the war were the Mud River Baptist and the Barboursville Methodist Church, South. The federal government had taken over the Barboursville church for barracks and hospital use, and later allotted an indemnity of $1,800 for damages during the war. The Northern Methodists in Barboursville finally made a physical break from their former brethren and erected a building on Main Street for the Steele Memorial Methodist church. The Steele, Dirton and Sidebottom families were members of this new church. Not long after, Baptist and Episcopal congregations began using space in the courthouse for religious services.

John Witcher's service to the Union in Cabell County and elsewhere brought promotions in rank. He was even said to have accompanied General Grant around the time of Lee's surrender. After the war, he was elected as Cabell County's state delegate in 1865, to secretary of state in 1866 and Third District representative to the U.S. Congress in 1868. After failing to be re-elected in 1870, Witcher moved west.

By 1867, the West Virginia Legislature was on a path to progress. It ratified the Fourteenth Amendment to the United States Constitution, granting full citizenship to African Americans. The state assumed control of Marshall College and reopened the former academy as a "state normal school" dedicated to the training of teachers. That same year, Cabell County assumed its current compact shape when Lincoln County was formed from the county's southeastern acreage.

At the close of the decade, sectional divisions had eased, somewhat. After the House of Delegates voted 22 to 19 in favor of Fifteenth Amendment to the U.S. Constitution, the State Senate ratified the amendment by a vote of ten to six (with six either absent or abstaining), and African Americans gained the right to vote. Consequently, many conservative Republicans joined with Democrats to re-enfranchise the former Confederates through the Flick Amendment.

By 1869, Barboursville's courthouse square was once again the social center of town, and the village's brass band began practicing there. By year's end, the United States celebrated the completion of the Transcontinental Railroad, and a man named Collis P. Huntington was named president of the Chesapeake and Ohio Railroad Company.

In the larger scope of the Civil War, Barboursville's troubles were small potatoes compared to the massive, gory bloodbaths of Antietam, Fredericksburg and Gettysburg. Compared to Guyandotte, much of which lay in ashes, the village escaped major physical damage outside of manly wear and tear on some of its buildings. The incidents at Barboursville and Guyandotte don't even make the cut among 59 "major events" included by state historic preservation officers in West Virginia's *Sesquicentennial Civil War Calendar*.

Nevertheless, Barboursville was among the first Virginia towns to feel the seismic effects of Civil War, as it was caught in the middle of a boiling cauldron of abolitionism, secessionism, and the curious urge of men to address problems through violence. Although the fighting in Cabell County may not be considered "historic" on a national scale, the effects on Barboursville were deep, personal and lasting.

Our Special Correspondent Furnishes an Interesting Letter:
John B. Baumgardner, "Fatty," and who is it that does not know him
in this end of the state, has been ailing ...but can yet appreciate a good
joke and has a number of new ones on hand to tell his guests, that
are always treated nice at his hotel.

CHAPTER 9

VILLAGE BOOMS AND BUSTS (1870-1897)

Dawn of a New Age

THE pictured segment from a southern United States map, prepared in 1861 for *Harpers Weekly*, shows Barboursville's relative prominence among ante-bellum towns of the region. For at least a few years after the map was published, the village remained the central place for rural families within riding (or floating) distance to trade goods, socialize, conduct county business and perhaps seek out the services of a doctor, druggist or lawyer.

By 1867, the year Barboursville was officially incorporated by the state Legislature, Lincoln County was formed, shrinking Cabell to its final size of 282 square miles of land. Less than a decade later, the population within Cabell's boundaries suddenly soared. Two new municipalities sprang up and flourished—one a former stagecoach stand on the Mud River, and the other a stretch of Ohio River flatland just west of Guyandotte. Smack in the middle between Milton and Huntington sat our small village, which would begin to look more and more like a relic from the eras of Jefferson and Jackson.

The Civil War decade not only represented a time of great social reckoning, it marked the historical divide between early America and modern America. In the years after President Lincoln's death, the military cadence of "When Johnny Comes Marching Home" eventually gave way to Gilbert and Sullivan's frolicking tune, "Hail, Hail, the Gang's All Here."

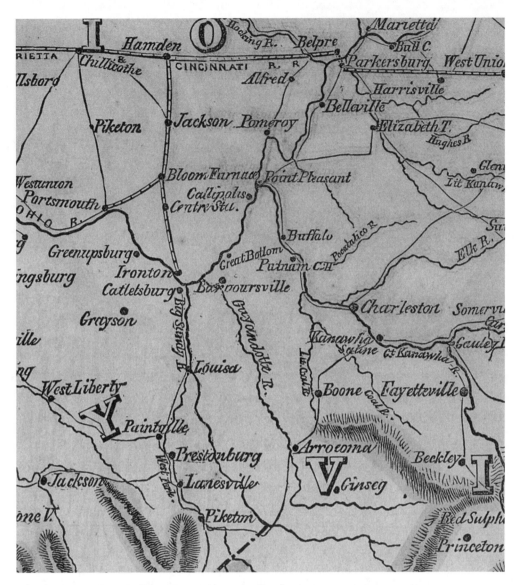

A segment of a Harpers Weekly Map of the Southern States,
showing Barboursville's relative prominence in 1861
(*Library of Virginia Digital Collections*)

It is helpful to comprehend the sheer scope of change in the late nineteenth century, when America rose from the ruins of war and the consequences of Southern "reconstruction," to become the world's industrial leader. From the 1870s through the 1890s, the relationship between the nation's political and industrial leaders was transformed, eventually remolding the economy and the landscape itself into the America we largely recognize today. Against this backdrop, the little village of Barboursville rolled through the ups and downs of three dizzying decades.

America's population grew from less than 40 million at the end of the Civil War decade to over 75 million at century's end. This natural increase (through baby-making) was compounded by lower infant mortality, longer life expectancy and continuing waves of mass immigration—first from northern and western Europe, and later from southern and eastern Europe. The nation began taking on the characteristics which continue to define American today, described by historian Paul Johnson as "huge and teeming, endlessly varied, multicolored and multiracial, immensely materialistic and overwhelmingly idealistic, ceaselessly innovative...all the great strengths and weaknesses of the mature republic."

Politics of the era featured high voter turnout among eligible men, and close contests between Republicans, Democrats and occasional third parties. Republicans dominated most presidential races. Beginning with the 1869-1877 administration of Ulysses S. Grant—who showed greater genius as a military general than as chief executive over a scandal-ridden government—a cloud of corruption and ineptitude in Washington, D.C. hung on for decades, arguably undermining the moral authority and power of the presidency itself. Historians refer to this era as The Gilded Age, after a satirical 1873 Mark Twain novel that makes fun of the greed and corruption of the upper classes.

Cabinet members, state legislatures and Congressmen were prone to increased influence (and sometimes outright bribery) by the business sector, giving rise to powerful and wealthy interests. These were led by steel magnate Andrew Carnegie, oil baron John D. Rockefeller, the Big Four of the railroads and other still-famous names like the Astors, the Vanderbilts and J. P. Morgan. These were men who wielded political muscle with impunity. As super-rich tycoons, they spawned competitively-opulent lifestyles, the invention of labor-saving devices, manipulation of the markets and abuses of the workforce (and in reaction, new labor and political movements). The late nineteenth century captains of industry are credited by historians with having a much greater impact on the American public than almost all the presidents of that era.

During these three decades, the United States economy grew at its fastest rate in history. The iron ore fields of the northern states and the coal deposits of the Alleghenies were joined together in production of steel rails at Chicago and other northern cities, resulting in a thick coast-to-coast network of transportation and communication lines. The output of wheat, corn and other commodities increased exponentially. Crops and man-made products began to reach once-remote segments of the population in unheard of abundance, enabling even Americans of humble roots to participate in the world's first consumer society. Comforts denied to most of humanity throughout history—food, housing, warmth, refrigeration, light and power—were made available to the masses in less than a single lifetime.

Barboursville's Shifting Labor Patterns

Whereas in 1860 an ambitious young American would have set his sights on a large and successful farm, by 1900 he was much more likely to seek a job. This gradual change was mirrored in Barboursville, West Virginia. The United States was taking in about 15 million new acres of farmland each year, and the center of gravity of rural labor was steadily moving westward—from western Virginia in the 1840s to Indiana by 1900.

The transformation can be observed locally by looking at the occupations held in the Barboursville magisterial district, first in 1870's Census schedules, then in 1900. Farming as an occupation went from almost half of area households in 1870 to less than a third in 1900. At the same time, differences between the village and its surrounding communities grew more distinct: within town limits fewer men— less than ten percent—were identified as farmers by the turn of the century. Work as "farm laborer" doubled in the outlying district by 1900, comprising about one fourth of occupations in rural areas surrounding the village, while at the same time shrinking to just seven percent in Barboursville town limits.

Simultaneously, education took on a more prominent role in the village. In 1870, fewer than two percent of Barboursville workers listed their occupation as "school teacher." In 1900, teachers (of both white and "Negro" races) made up four percent of the district's rural workers, and nine percent of village workers. Overall, career choices opened up for Barboursville's young men, and even a few women were earning wages. The need remained for a few blacksmiths, carpenters, hotel and boarding house keepers, doctors, lawyers, ministers, tanners and domestic servants. Sawmill work in the village seems to have gone by the wayside, while mechanization and other modern conveniences turned a few enterprising Barboursville folk into dressmakers, salesmen and deliverymen. Pioneers in the district's "modern" workforce circa 1900 included German-born stenographer Robert Floding, 24-year-old dry goods saleslady Elba Chapman, Mrs. George B. Miller who ran an ice cream parlor, and following in her father's footsteps, 18-year-old railroad telegrapher Mabel Townsend.

With the completion of the Chesapeake and Ohio Railroad, those working in railroad occupations rose from about three dozen in 1870 to nearly a hundred at the turn of the century. Several Barboursville men, both established citizens and new arrivals, latched onto opportunity as C&O surveyors, civil engineers and land agents, and established themselves as the town's new "upper crust." As the bridges were built and the tracks laid down, labor was at first predominated by Irish immigrants (including my great-great grandfather), to be followed by African-American laborers and Italian American stone masons who built later sections. In addition, there were night watchmen, engineers, firemen and brakemen who kept the trains running in and out of the Barboursville depot. Some of these men would settle in and plant their families as permanent town residents and future leaders.

Indeed, it was the railroad more than anything else that both "boomed" and "busted" the village of Barboursville.

Roots of A Striving New Generation

Just as the close of the Civil War ushered in a new industrial age, it also marked the disappearance of Barboursville's first influential generations. All four "Sons of 1791" were now gone: Solomon Thornburg had died in 1854. F.G.L. Beuhring passed away in 1859 at his residence on the Ohio River. John Laidley practiced law until his death in 1863. The last one to go was John Samuels. In December of 1869, his Main Street farmland—over 160 acres—was parceled off to several heirs, including his son, Judge Henry J. Samuels.

Samuels's brother-in-law and neighbor, William Clendenin Miller, still dwelled in the area, but eventually had experienced enough of town living. His aristo-cratic in-laws, Joseph and Marie Gardner, had both passed away in the 1850s. His greatest construction projects —the Guyandotte lock-and-dam system and the Cabell County Court House—had been either degraded or destroyed during the war. And he had paid the price for being friends with Congressman Jenkins, being held as a Union prisoner, having his house hit by cannonballs and his porch used to park a soldier's corpse, not to mention the emotional toll the war had taken on his wife Eliza, eldest daughter Eugenia Thackston and his other children. In August 1870, Miller sold his Main Street lot to Albert Laidley—the son of the man he may have purchased it from in the first place—and relocated to a farm on the outskirts of the village.

As the local stage was being reset for the new era, there were still a number of affluent men from established county families living in the district—including farmers John Thornburg, Patrick Morrison, David Harshbarger (later to be identi-fied with the new town of Milton), Jefferson McComas, Charles K. Morris and Charles Roffe, as well as the two unrelated Millers now in their sixties—the afore-mentioned W. C. Miller and Würtemburg's John G. Miller—living in and around the village. John Merritt now headed the family's prosperous milling operation on the Mud River. Thomas Thornburg was the richest retail merchant in town; Joel Salmon and H. Poteet were also running successful stores.

Other families had seen their fortunes fall after the Civil War, including the Moores, Sheltons and others who were defendants in Cabell County's anti-Confed-erate lawsuits of 1864.

Throughout the rancorous and litigious years of post-war restitution, it was (as usual) a good time to be a lawyer. Barboursville's richest attorneys included retired Circuit Court judge H. J. Samuels and Judge James Ferguson. Also occupying the Court House on Main Street for most of the decade were Clerk Joseph S. Miller

(William's son), and Circuit Judge Evermont Ward (the alleged offspring of Rev. William McComas and his sister-in-law "Risky" Ward).

Both James Ferguson and Evermont Ward were colorful characters who had practiced law since 1840. James H. Ferguson started out as an apprentice or "bound boy" to the wealthy Germans John and "Sig" Miller. He launched his first career as partner in a Barboursville shoemaker's shop. He practiced law in Logan, then practiced in Barboursville for several stretches, relocated to Charleston later in life, and had a number of years when his whereabouts remained a mystery. Ferguson took a succession of wives—first Elizabeth Derton, then Elizabeth Ong, and finally Elizabeth Creel—and fathered a number of children. According to a Lambert transcript, "Judge Samuels stated that he met a women claiming to be the mother of J. H. Ferguson. He gave her ten dollars to keep her from seeing Ferguson because she seemed to be of low birth. This occurred in Logan. He seems to be an illegitimate child…Judge Ferguson's wife taught him to read and write."

Despite Ferguson's sketchy personal biography, G. S. Wallace maintained that the staunch Union man—who was attorney for the plaintiffs against Buffington, Jenkins, Moore, Shelton and the other Confederates—"was easily the most commanding figure in the county at this time and continued a successful practitioner until he was a very old man." As a state legislator in January 1865, ardent Unionist and universal suffrage advocate James H. Ferguson of Cabell County presented a joint resolution in the House, creating a joint committee of eight "to inquire into the expediency and constitutionality of providing the immediate abolishment of slavery in West Virginia." The resolution was tabled.

After a proposal to call a West Virginia Constitutional Convention was carried, an election was held in October 1871 to select delegates. James H. Ferguson was defeated by Evermont Ward who, along with Thomas Thornburg, helped frame the Constitution of 1872, the present Constitution of this state. Ward would preside over a notorious Barboursville murder case four years later, and would dabble in the curative arts, becoming "famous as the inventor and owner of a proprietary medicine known as "Ward's Magic Relief."

The passing of Barboursville's Revolutionary War veterans, their sons, and attorneys like Laidley and Samuels who shaped the county in its early years, signified the phasing out of men who "operated within the framework of the English common law." Many of these old values remained with the well-rooted Merritts, Thornburgs and other "early Barboursville" progeny. Yet a new generation of capitalists, aligned with the new competitive era, acquired land in and around the village as the promise of the railroad finally became a local reality.

Railroad Starts and Stops

The colossal new continental railroad system loomed large in the American conversation. It was, as a matter of fact, the driving force behind the nation's new coal-steel complex and sophisticated financial markets in major cities like Chicago and New York.

Anticipating completion of the railway, the old James River and Kanawha Turnpike Company had asked Cabell County to accept responsibility for the section of the pike within its borders, and abandoned maintenance of the national road just after the Civil War. From 1865 on, the county struggled to maintain its roads while it waited for rail transportation to arrive, a wait that would last eight inconvenient years.

Before the war, the federal government had helped subsidize the Illinois Central, and by 1870 the government provided more than 100 million acres of land as a direct subsidy for railroad construction. States also gave acreage and money, bringing the total of direct government aid to railroads to over $350 million in the years from 1861 to 1890. As a result of the power of a handful of wealthy capitalists—with former peddler Collis Potter Huntington wielding perhaps more political influence than even Carnegie or Rockefeller—railroad companies became legally privileged in a number of ways. Government gifts to the railroad included charters from state legislatures, special banking privileges, right of eminent domain to legally force land sales, tax exemptions and protection against competition, not to mention the federal lands given on a prodigious scale.

This is not to say there was an overall plan for an efficient national transport system; railroads tended to be designed and built to profit the men who ran them. But Americans gloried in their new railroad network and all the new possibilities that came with it. George Pullman, who founded the Pullman Palace Car Company, introduced his sleeping cars widely by the 1870s, built an entire town south of Chicago to house his workforce and introduced automatic couplers and air brakes. New refrigerator cars made growers in California competitive with Eastern farmers, and made possible a meat-packing industry whereby livestock was transported to Chicago or other central points for processing, and the products distributed throughout the nation. As other new advances were introduced (such as barbed-wire fencing and the harvesting combine, both of which had a gigantic impact on ranching and farming), the country began to build, and think, on a much grander scale.

Back at home, there were stumbling blocks to that great day of connection with modern times. In addition to Appalachian terrain that made the work of track-laying different from the western plains (where rails and cross-ties could be slapped down along huge swaths of flat land with relative ease), there was the political complication of West Virginia's recent statehood. The railroad was now the property of two states, so the legislatures of Virginia and West Virginia had to cooperate to pass two identical acts consolidating the Virginia Central, the Covington and

Ohio, and other small railroads, into the Chesapeake and Ohio Railroad. Progress on connecting the east coast of Virginia with the Ohio River was further delayed when financing the C&O through stock sales turned out to be impossible. Gen. Williams Carter Wickham was made president of the C&O in the hope he could interest outside capitol. Wickham turned to the notorious railroad builders known as the "Big Four" (Leland Stanford, Mark Hopkins, Charles Crocker and Collis P. Huntington), who were hurrying to connect the tracks of the Central Pacific and Union Pacific to create a transcontinental railroad. Collis P. Huntington, who had a knack for dealing with Congress and New York financiers on behalf of the railroads, was recruited by Wickham, and went with him to survey the Virginia-West Virginia route in 1869. Soon after, Huntington himself became president of the C&O.

Between 1869 and 1871, Collis P. Huntington employed Albert Laidley as a land agent for the C&O in Cabell County. Laidley—who during that period bought from W. C. Miller what may have been the Barboursville romping ground of his early childhood—purchased 17 farms along the Ohio from the mouth of the Guyandotte River west, and conveyed the land to Mr. Huntington. Reserving enough land for C&O use, Collis P. deeded the remainder of acreage to an entity called the Central Land Company. Through his agents, Huntington began plotting out a grid of streets and avenues for the new city named after him.

Meanwhile, completing the C&O through West Virginia's terrain was turning out to be a slow and tortuous task. Work on the required fills, cuts and tunnels was still performed by men using picks and shovels. Many of the laborers were newly freed black slaves from Virginia. Construction of the mile-and-a-half Big Bend Tunnel in Summers County ended up taking three years and a thousand men contracted by the C&O, hundreds of whom lost their lives laboring in dangerous and foul underground conditions. According to Cicero Fain, countless numbers of anonymous men were killed by silicosis, falling rock and nitroglycerin explosions, and were unceremoniously covered, along with the dead mules, in landfills at either end of the mountain.

A remote roadside statue in Talcott, West Virginia above the tunnel's entrance commemorates former slave John Henry, a real man whose fabled race against a steam drill during the C&O's Big Bend project made him the subject of a famous American folk ballad. *(It's about a 300-mile round trip drive from Barboursville; in case you ever decide to go on an afterschool pilgrimage with your kids, be sure to pack dinner.)*

During this period, from 1870 to 1872, grading and masonry work that started before the war in Cabell County was nearing completion. Barboursville is documented as housing fewer than ten railroad workers in 1870, mostly Irish and Swedish immigrants, about half of them skilled stone masons. (About 30 ex-slaves enumerated in the Census district were not engaged in railroad work, but employed for the most part as live-in servants or farm hands at the homes of affluent, by-now-familiar, families.)

In addition to Albert Laidley, several distinguished Barboursville gentlemen, including former Civil War officers from both sides, found common cause and lucrative careers with the C&O railroad's completion. Former tanner George Frederick Miller was working in 1870 as a railroad contractor, as was a new village arrival named Robert Bibb. Other Barboursville men whose fortunes rose with the C&O included three prominent village names: Kuhn, McKendree and King.

In 1872, Capt. James I. Kuhn came to Barboursville as the agent for an eastern syndicate, to arrange and settle the title of 200,000 acres of "valuable real estate and coal lands" on the Guyandotte and Twelve Pole Rivers. A Republican, former sheriff of Brooke County (in West Virginia's northern panhandle), and Captain in the First Virginia Union Regiment, Capt. Kuhn would settle on the north side of Main Street with his sisters, and would take a wife but remain childless.

Major George W. McKendree was a civil engineer who surveyed the C&O Line and
purchased land on the current site of the Barboursville Community Park.
(Herald-Advertiser clip courtesy of Barboursville Public Library)

A couple of years later, former Confederate Major George W. McKendree surveyed and developed the Huntington and Big Sandy Railroad from Huntington to Catlettsburg; he would later survey the Guyan Valley railroad. The son of Barboursville hotel keeper Robert McKendree, George came of age at the corner of Main and Water Streets, and was privately educated. He embarked upon his profession as civil engineer at the tender age of 17. As early as 1860, he was surveying the new C&O line at Covington Virginia, and after the war became division engineer of the Richmond and Allegheny branch. In 1874, Major McKendree married Miss Irene McComas, former beleaguered schoolteacher and granddaughter of county pillars Elisha McComas and Thomas Ward. George McKendree purchased General John Witcher's "Clover Valley" farm, and built a family home for Irene and their young children on the southern edge of the village, the current site of the Barbourville Community Park.

Thomas W. King, a plantation owner's son and Confederate Army veteran from Fluvanna County, Va., would arrive in the late 1880s as a foreman, and later a bridge carpenter, for the C&O. He followed the rails over the mountains and bought some Main Street property from the Samuels family. There, he and his wife Sarah raised three sons who would also grow up to have "responsible railroad jobs."

On January 29, 1873, after four years of ponderous work, West Virginia's C&O crews working eastward met with their counterparts who had been building westward. The task of completing the rail line from the Atlantic to the Ohio was achieved at last. Later that day, a special train loaded with distinguished guests and officials of the C&O arrived at the Hawk's Nest railroad bridge from Richmond, and a ceremonial driving of the last spike officially dedicated the completion of the rail line. The train continued on after the ceremony, reaching the new city named for Collis P. Huntington, where a gala celebration was planned. The *Huntington Herald Dispatch* reported that a telegraph failure prevented the announcement from reaching the city of Huntington in time, so that when the train of dignitaries arrived at the Huntington Station, only a small number of people were on hand to greet them.

However, a transcript of the *Argus* newspaper of February 1, 1873, indicates that Barboursville was ready and waiting for the railroad V.I.P.'s. Decades of turnpike-honed hospitality had taught the villagers what it takes to welcome weary travelers on a cold January night:

Our people were much excited on Wednesday last (Jan. 24) by a telegram to the effect that the long heralded train with the happy excursionists would pass through Barboursville en route from Richmond to Huntington during the evening of that day. In a few hours afterwards the station was crowded outside and inside, with eager and curious persons to see the sight and enjoy the fun. In the meantime some gentleman prepared a nice basket of egg nog and whisky toddy to which a basket of large and finely flavored apples and a box of fine cigars were added.

In a telegram containing the above facts, together with an invitation to stop was sent the party on the approaching train. The invitation was accepted. As the train stopped a hearty cheer from all present arose on the midnight air in favor of those who had, under the most trying difficulties, laid the last rail of a great road, which connects the Atlantic Seaboard with the prairies of the west. Everything passed off pleasantly, the excursionists seem to feel perfectly content. They said that it was the first treat that had been offered them on the road.

The city of Huntington soon saw an influx of emigrants from New York and New England, but the town was hit hard during the Panic of 1873, and for nearly six months workers on the C&O were paid in railroad scrip in lieu of money. Despite a cost of nearly $24 million, an enormous amount of money for that time, C&O trains would not run regularly for about six months following the opening of the line. Completion had been rushed, with makeshift construction in several places along the route, so several sections of track had to be re-laid and permanent fills and retaining walls constructed, after the opening of the line. During its first years of operation, the C&O experienced constant problems, such as a huge rock slide in 1875 that blocked all rail traffic for three weeks. In March of 1888, the east span of the railroad bridge into Guyandotte was knocked loose by a train; later that same year the west span went down, killing the engineer. For many years, the line was not very profitable.

Still, by February of 1875 the Chesapeake and Ohio Railway was running several regular routes through Cabell County, as advertised in the *Huntington Advertiser*. An express train that connected with the steamers *Bostona* and *Fleetwood* left Huntington daily at 9:50 a.m., included an overnight stay in White Sulphur Springs, and arrived by dinnertime the next evening in Richmond. An "accommodation train" between Huntington and Kanawha Falls ran four hour trips in each direction three days a week, stopping on signal at Guyandotte, Barboursville, Milton, Hurricane, Scott, Scary and other "intermediate stations" to the east. In addition, a mixed freight and passenger train from Huntington to Kanawha Falls ran three days a week, leaving Barboursville eastbound at 3:35 p.m. and westbound at 7:18 a.m.

After years of waiting and the difficulties—not to mention the future consequences—of completing the C&O, Barboursville was once again a link on America's most important transportation network.

A Man with a Printing Press

In the new expanding America, with fewer inhibitions on enterprise than ever before, abuses of financial power became commonplace. During this period of ruthless competition, American businessmen adopted British scientist Charles Darwin's phrase "survival of the fittest," to justify their push for laissez-faire government policies. Overproduction of goods and raw materials, overcapitaliza-tion of railroads and feverish speculation in securities would bring about a great depression known as the "Panic of 1873."

Newspapers and magazines grew to report on these abuses. Between 1850 and 1880, the number of daily newspapers grew from 260 to almost a thousand nation-wide. In the Gilded Age, the press became more successful in uncovering the worst abuses of capitalism than either of the political parties or any governmental bodies.

Barboursville became home to its own political mouthpiece, in the form of a weekly paper. A single issue of a publication named the *Cabell County Press* can be found on microfilm in the state archives in Charleston. Dated June 10, 1873 from Barboursville, West Virginia, the paper was "published every Tuesday by the Cabell County Press Printing Co. at $2.00 a year—in advance." The slogan just under the publication title reads "INDEPENDENT IN ALL THINGS, NEUTRAL IN NOTHING."

Though an editor or publisher's name does not appear on the preserved micro-film, the 1870 Barboursville Census lists a young man of some means named Harvey M. Scott, age 26, living on Main Street in between the George F. Miller and Albert Laidley residences. Scott's occupation was listed as editor, and he lived with wife Delphine and 10-month-old son Harvey. On the same property lived 18-year-old printer Harvey Bailey, which suggests a combined dwelling and printing press operation. Harvey Scott no longer lived in Cabell County by 1880, but he is as likely as anyone to have been the editor of the *Cabell County Press.*

The unnamed writer pulled no punches in regard to a Republican State Convention in Columbus, Ohio, and its failure to "censure Gen. Grant for signing the salary grab bill, without whose signature it could not have become a law," continuing:

> It was the most disgraceful piece of bargain and corruption ever known in the history of American politics. Think of it, citizens of the Republic, and rise up in your might at the proper time, and by your votes forever consign to oblivion the men you have lifted to places of trust, and who betrayed you by perpetrating this gigantic robbery upon the public Treasury. The Congress of the United States increase their pay five thousand dollars, but fearing the President would veto the bill they increase his pay one hundred thousand dollars and thus secure his approval of the bill. Some members, actuated by principle and fearing their constituents, have refused to receive the increase. General Grant, however, takes it as freely as he takes his drinks, and as he has taken everything else ever offered to him." (Cabell County Press 1873)

The local write-ups also provided a snapshot of town life in the new railroad era. Among the village news of the day:

ABOUT OUR CITY LEVY—The amount of tax levied last year for the use of the corporation of Barboursville was something over $1,000...This might be modified this year from the fact that the levy last year, besides covering all the expenses for schools, was made to cover the indebtedness of the corporation for purchase of lot and building schoolhouse, amounting to nearly $600, and other indebtedness to individuals, of probably $250. One source of revenue, however, is cut off from the present council. They derive nothing from license to sell liquor, while the amount realized by the old council was something over $250.

BARBOURSVILLE ITEMS: We were pleased to meet our old friend Dr. V.R. Moss on our streets again. The Doctor and his lady have been absent for several weeks in Teay's Valley, and the latter, who has quite a severe attack of pneumonia, is rapidly improving.

We have a new Mayor. The old one having resigned. J.B. Baumgardner, Esq., was appointed by the Council to fill the vacancy.

At the last meeting of the Council it was ordered that advertisement proposals for making a sidewalk from Main street out to the depot, be published...

It was also decided to give notice to applicants for teachers for the public school here, requiring applications to be filed with the Recorder...

The streets are in first-rate condition, and the town is now in a very fair financial condition....

C.E. Myers has opened a first-class saloon next door above the post office. Charley is a very popular caterer, and will do a prosperous business.

Mrs. Newberger has left us, having disposed of her property here (house and lot) to Mr. Wm. Derton. She left in high dudgeon last Tuesday, and it is said that one of our very popular landlords grieves over her departure. His grief, we understand, measured by dollars and cents, amounts to about thirty dollars. He is willing to be comforted.

POLITICS: "Candidates plenty, cash scarce." (Cabell County Press 1873)

Also in the June 1873 issue, J. H. Harshbarger, L. J. Hoback and D. I. Smith published notices announcing candidacy for "Sheriffality of Cabell County." A large advertisement by Thomas Thornburg, Barboursville Market, listed prices for items from food staples to live chickens to cotton yarn. Public notices of

"Commissioners Sale" of estates alluded to debts that might have been connected to the old anti-Confederate suits against Moore, Roffe and other estates. Smaller advertisements, called "Professional Cards" touted the services of several men:

> W. R. Alexander, Physician and Surgeon. Would respectfully offer his professional services to the citizens of Barboursville and surrounding country. He hopes his past experience in the large hospitals of New York city, consulting the most approved methods of treating diseases, together with his steady habits and proper professional attention to those who may favor him with their confidence will entitle him to a fair share of public patronage. Special attention given to diseases of women.

> W. R. Julian, Resident Dentist, Barboursville, West Va., Office at Dr. Alexander's Drug Store. Work from the country solicited, and calls promptly attended to.

> Joseph S. Miller, Lawyer, Cabell Court House, West Virginia

> C. W. Smith and T. B. Kline, Attorneys at Law, Cabell C. H., W.Va. – Will practice in the counties of Cabell, Lincoln, Wayne, Boone, Logan, Putnam, Mason and adjoining counties, and also is the Court of Appeals and the United States District Court at Charleston. Prompt attention given to the collection of claims. (Cabell County Press 1873)

Amid the politics, gossip and advertisements, a letter by John Thornburg, secretary of the Methodist Episcopal Church South, reflects the earnest style he was known for:

> In view of the probability of the transfer of Rev. Wm. Gaines Miller from this to some other field of labor, we cherish with grateful remembrance his deep piety, his untiring efforts as a minister and pastor, and his uncompromising devotion to the best interest of the Church, and that wherever he may be sent, we will follow him with our prayers and kindest regards, and not withstanding many embarrassments here thrown in his way on some portion of his work, we cheerfully and cordially endorse his course as a minister and a gentleman. (Cabell County Press 1873)

The New City of Huntington

From the time Huntington was incorporated in February 1871, Barboursville would evermore be contrasted with its municipal neighbor. By the end of the year, people were flocking to the new city and homes and businesses seemed to appear overnight. It was noted several years later by a Virginia newspaper that, "When C. P. Huntington started the town of Huntington, W.Va…it attracted a great deal of attention. It was the first town to spring up and assume city shape and style within a few years."

When the C&O made its western connection, Huntington already had a population ten times that of Barboursville. Unbeknownst to anyone at the time, people and capital would continue to pour into Collis P. Huntington's "jewel city" for more than 80 years.

Created by one of the nation's most powerful men (with the assistance of Barboursville's Albert Laidley), the city was in many ways an archetype for the conspicuous consumption, explosive growth and sheer "bigness" of the Gilded Age. The railway owners were kings of the new economy, more influential in their way than even Carnegie or Rockefeller. According to historian Samuel Morison, rail tycoons "had the point of view of a feudal chieftain. Members of state legislatures were their vassals, to be coerced or bribed into voting 'right' if persuasion would not serve...Collis P. Huntington, Leland Stanford, and their associates...wielded a power over public opinion comparable to that of slave-owners over the old South."

Along with the C&O, a powerful and sustaining force for Huntington's early commerce came from the White Collar Line of steamboats. When the first passenger train reached Huntington from Richmond on Jan. 29, 1873, these "sidewheelers" were already in service, with schedules from Cincinnati to Pomeroy, Ohio. The railroad connection brought a heavy flow of passengers, freight and mail. To handle it the White Collar Line had a good-sized steamboat leaving Cincinnati "upbound" every weekday. By 1880, the *Bostona* and the *Fleetwood* were known as fast boats with highly-capable captains, stewards and "first-class cuisines." Leaving Cincinnati at 4 p.m., and relying on their distinctive steam whistle tones to communicate with passing boats in the dark of night, the steamers were expected to be at Huntington the following morning before the departure of the eastbound C&O train, and they usually were.

The city of Huntington was certainly a source of pride for Collis P., but it was never his home, just one more trophy in his coast-to-coast empire. From its wide streets that copied the new western standard (and seemed to anticipate the invention of the automobile), to the well-designed city grid that provided a ready palette for architectural achievement, the Ohio River terminus had all the makings of a future industrial metropolis.

Barboursville's homes of even its most well-to-do families—the William C. Miller home, the George Frederick Miller residence built in 1865, and the Derton Home built in 1870—were based on styles of an earlier era and stopped short of any architectural flourishes. Huntington would show no such restraint. As early as 1874, men such as William "Coin" Harvey (whose striking Italianate home yet stands on Third Avenue, albeit in sad condition) and St. Cloud's Henry Chester Parsons (whose gingerbread Victorian remains a west Huntington showplace) were setting the tone in Cabell County for gorgeous construction befitting a capitalist aristocracy.

For most of the 1870s, however, the growing young city of Huntington would more closely resemble a wild west town, with dirt streets, frame buildings and its own "great bank robbery," complete with a Barboursville connection.

What About Jesse James?

"There's a cave over that hill where Jesse James stashed his loot after he robbed the Huntington bank."

My cousins the Seager boys and later my buddy Jill—village dwellers in the 1960s and '70s—told about this place of mystery located on the other side of the mountain from old Barboursville High School. When and how the local school-kid story originated, I do not know. My oldest cousin Jeff tried to make a solo trek there in his youth, but could not locate the cave. Jill was more successful in finding the clandestine hangout, along with some high school friends (who may or may not have been cutting class on a school day). She's the one who took me there, once our children were big enough to hike from the amphitheatre in the new Community Park, where the "Jesse James Cave" is nowadays quite accessible to the clued-in and well-shod.

I don't know that the rock formation could be classified as a cave, *per sé*. There are definite "cavelets" where a small animal or a brave/foolish person's arm or leg could gain entry. And evidence suggests it's still a popular "secret hangout," judging by the occasional piece of litter awaiting pick-up by an ambitious Wolf Cub Scout with his trash bag and trusty barbeque tongs (*"Mrs. Rowsey, was this Jesse James's beer can?"*) Alas, the connection between this Barboursville "cave" and the James gang is a fiction, albeit a harmless one with the added power of inspiring a Digital Age youngster to go outside and walk someplace.

A book entitled *Missouri Caves in History and Legend* offers a viable explanation for the proliferation of "Jesse James hideout" stories across nineteenth century America. As outlaw gangs pulled robberies during this cutthroat era, sightings of the notorious Missouri criminal Jesse James multiplied (not unlike late-twentieth-century "Elvis sightings"). When "show caves" in mountainous states began to compete for tourists around the turn of the century, even a made-up James Gang saga could serve as a lucrative draw. Apparently, tons of places have Jesse James cave legends.

So no, Jesse James almost certainly did not rob the Huntington bank in 1875, much less stash his loot behind Barboursville. But this does not negate the historical link between the village, the "Great Huntington Bank Robbery," and the James Gang.

At least one credible historian suggests that Jesse's brother Frank James and gang member Cole Younger (both former Confederate bushwhackers from Missouri) were involved in the heist. Ted Yeatman's extensively-researched book *Frank and Jesse*

James: The Story Behind the Legend contains over 500 pages of documentary evidence and biographical details about the gang, including several pages on the West Virginia incident.

Yeatman describes a 26-year-old drifter named Thomas J. Webb who met Thomas Coleman "Cole" Younger in Ohio. The two were joined by Tom McDaniel "and probably by Frank James" before taking a train to West Virginia to scout possible robbery sites. After ruling out the B&O and C&O trains as well as banks in Wheeling, Grafton, Parkersburg and Charleston as unsuitable targets, the men came to the town of Huntington, which was scheduled to receive an Adams Express package at its bank containing one hundred thousand dollars (as they learned from sniffing around these parts beforehand). The fact that the city was named for "robber baron" Collis Potter Huntington didn't hurt, as it offered the opportunity for the publicity-savvy James brothers to polish their reputation as self-styled Midwestern "Robin Hoods."

According to Yeatman, the gang arrived in Huntington a few days before making their move and were greeted by Father Quirk of Saint Joseph's Catholic Church; he thought they were in town for a Methodist conference. They stayed in Guyandotte homes over the weekend, where they were reportedly observed reading the Bible and presumed by observers to be pious men.

A 1971 article about the robbery in the *Huntington Herald Advertiser* offers little knowledge of the gang members' identities, but rounds out the story with local recollections. To summarize both sources: two men entered the Huntington Bank with revolvers in hand. Cashier Robert Oney was held up and forced to open a safe. After a short standoff, he relented and handed over the safe's contents. When the robbers learned from Oney that the Adams Express delivery was already in Cincinnati, they forced the young man to show them the express receipt to prove it. During the heist, a black bank messenger named Jim returned from the post office and was also taken prisoner. Oney and Jim were tied up and frog-marched across the street. A neighboring storekeeper who had seen the bandits enter the bank was about to go for help when two other men rode up in front of his store, bought a cigar from the man and warned him not to say anything about what was happening at the bank.

When bank president John H. Russell returned, Oney yelled and the robbers jumped on their horses and rode hastily from the scene. Sheriff D.I. Smith was alerted. Along with the bank president and another man, the Sheriff chased the robbers on horseback. The three came so close to catching the robbers that at one point the bandits dropped a sack of nickels to speed their escape. Telegrams were sent to Catlettsburg and all points between there and Louisa, and to Charleston, Barboursville and other locations. Soon, a posse of at least a dozen men took off in pursuit.

At this point, an unambiguous Barboursville link appears in both historical accounts:

> George F. Miller of Main Street, Barboursville, executive vice president of the bank, organized a posse of about 15 men from the village and followed the bandits far into Kentucky. Most of the men from Huntington returned the following night, but Miller continued his search. Four days following the robbery, Miller was still in pursuit of the gang. He sent this telegram to John Russell: "We are at West Liberty. Have 15 fresh men and horses after the parties. Think they will overhaul them. They have gone toward the Cumberland Gap..."

Once back in Huntington, the bank president found less than $20,000 was missing. About a month after the robbery, authorities in Tennessee brought a man into custody carrying about $4,500 in cash, some of it bloodstained. Thomas Webb was identified as the robber, brought to Cabell County, tried and convicted of the crime. Webb was sent to the state penitentiary where he died without ever identifying his accomplices.

Though there were no casualties during the Huntington Bank robbery, the city was nevertheless thrown into an immediate uproar, according to the *Advertiser*. "Even today, there are those who like to believe that Jesse James himself performed the daring daylight robbery," reported the newspaper a century later.

Perhaps a more worthy historical quest would be to lay speculation aside, get our heads out of the cave, and identify the Barboursville posse members who answered the telegraphed call and joined George F. Miller in his relentless 80-mile pursuit of the James-Younger gang members.

The George F. Miller Confusion

Moving beyond the Jesse James cave legend to documented history, we find ourselves at what Frank Ball called a "sturdy old edifice" on the north side of Main Street at Stowasser Avenue, the home of Huntington Bank vice-president George Frederick Miller Sr.

I find it more than slightly ironic that the two longest-standing homes in Barboursville were originally occupied by George F. Miller—and not the same George F. Miller, mind you, but two unrelated and equally notable men. This has apparently been a source of confusion to at least three people with greater historical credentials than yours truly. It only became more mind-boggling as I uncovered more Census data, genealogies and other documents. I lost weeks of writing time as I tumbled into a genealogical rabbit hole of quadruple-helix Miller namesakes.

Submitted for the potential sanity of future Miller researchers, this is my best effort to set the record straight and disentangle the "G. F. M.'s."

Main Street home built by George Frederick Miller Sr.,
as it appeared before a 1969 restoration

Main Street home built by George Frederick Miller Sr., after restoration
(both photos courtesy of Lorraine Powell)

George Frederick Miller Sr. (1817-1892) As recorded in the *Barboursville Bulletin* by Frank Ball, the home at the corner of Main and Stowasser was built about 1865 by Würtemburg's George Frederick Miller. (This home was purchased by the Stowasser family after Miller's death. Now the home of Mrs. Lorraine Powell, the Miller-Stowasser home underwent historic renovation in the late 1960s and early 1970s. The new owners not only restored the original woodwork and fireplaces, but furnished the home with local antiques, including items from the former Price Hotel on Central Avenue.)

George F. Miller Sr. married Mary Shelton in 1843 and had five children, four of whom lived into adulthood. One son was a Barboursville merchant named—confusingly—William Clendenin Miller, who was born 12 years after his neighbor William Clendenin Miller and Eliza Gardner had a son named George F. Miller.

Census data pegs George Frederick Miller Sr., as the man most certain to have been the posse leader who tracked the Huntington Bank robbers. A couple years after his James Gang manhunt, the former tanner and merchant became Cabell County's sheriff, immediately following the term of D.I. Smith, who was his son-in-law.

George Franklin Miller
(Courtesy of Frances Gunter)

George Franklin Miller (1844-1922). The 1870 census establishes that this son of William Clendenin and Eliza Gardner Miller had already moved to Indiana (where he married a wealthy young lady named Catherine and worked as a book-keeper) by the time of the James Gang incident. His 1922 obituary is perhaps the most reliable account of his life and legacy. George Franklin Miller was known as Frank Miller to his friends, was born in Barboursville, August 24, 1844. As a boy he served as page to Congressman Jenkins. While only 16, "Frank" Miller enlisted with the Confederate army and had an enviable war record. At the close of the war, "Mr. Miller moved to Cincinnati and there engaged in business. After a few years, he moved to Indianapolis and took up a very active political and social life. He was elected to the city treasurer's office and filled the position admirably for a great number of years," before passing away in his late seventies.

Given the name similarity and the passage of a hundred years, it is little wonder that the two men seemed to have accidentally become one in the historical record: The section on "Centennial Homes" in Gunter's Barboursville history features the same youthful portrait of George F. Miller under the Miller-Stowasser Home description as appears in Joe Geiger's biography of Confederate Captain George F. Miller. (I'm betting with Geiger that the portrait is young Frank as a Confederate Cavalryman.) But then Geiger refers to his Confederate soldier as "George Frederick Miller." To make matters even more befuddling, Yeatsman's James Gang history describes posse leader George F. Miller, as "executive vice president of the bank and a former confederate cavalryman." Despite these conflicting accounts, Census records prove that they were two entirely separate men.

George Frederick Miller Jr. (1848-1910) With these identity issues settled, it's time to add a third Main Street George F. Miller to the illustrious mix: Sheriff's son G. F. Miller Jr. received an early education at Marshall Academy, was taught by professor B.H. Thackston, and entered business at an early age. In later years county historian George S. Wallace would describe him as "the most outstanding businessman this county ever had."

George Frederick Miller Jr.
(George S. Wallace)

Sometime before 1880, George F. Miller Jr. was hired by his father as deputy
sheriff. He married Lucy B. McConnell of Catlettsburg, Kentucky, and the
couple had four children, eventually relocating to Huntington. According to Don
McMillian, Miller became vice president of the First National Bank and held valuable real estate in the new city. A mansion was built for Miller in 1885 on the
northwest corner of 6th Avenue and 11th Street; according to McMillian, the
carriage house remains today at 523 11th Street (currently home to the Prudential
Bunch Reality offices) across from the Trinity Episcopal Church. His first wife died
in 1889, and he remarried soon after. In 1906, he was a partner to Charles Lloyd
Ritter in the creation of the Frederick Hotel in Huntington, which was named
after him. As Gilded Age Cabell County biographies go, not too shabby for a small
town boy.

But wait—there's another genealogical twist.

No sooner had I successfully unraveled the three George F. Millers (and gotten
past the two cross-named William Clendenin Millers), when I was confounded
by this: In 1890, George Frederick Miller Jr.—now a 42-year-old Huntington
widower with three sons, including one George Donald Miller—married Captain
George Franklin Miller's baby sister, 35-year-old Florence Gardner Miller. They
wed in the Methodist Chapel on the north side of Main Street next to the courthouse. It is not known if the groom's son George D. Miller, or father-of-the-groom
George F. Miller Sr., or brother-of-the-bride Captain George F. Miller witnessed
the ceremony. Perhaps in attendance was the groom's 39 year-old first cousin
George R. Miller, also of Main Street.

There was an additional discovery in the 1870 village census of yet another
one. An Irish-born laborer with $40 in personal assets was living near the Hatfield
Hotel on Center Street with his wife. Blame the hours of genealogical double-takes
and re-checks, but I found myself chuckling at the notion of this unassuming
immigrant walking into any village establishment and introducing himself as
George Miller.

Barboursville Babylon—The Meehling Affair

Be advised—this next historic episode contains graphic and disturbing imagery.

Barboursville in 1876 was shaken by a crime that was grizzly, scandalous, and
unprecedented in county history—made all the more shocking by the convulsive
Saturday night reaction of citizens on the public square.

Minutes of the Bloomingdale Baptist Church hint at what transpired between
Württemberg-born farmer Charles Meehling, his wife Matilda and a hired laborer
named Ed Williams:

February 19, 1876: Sister Matilda Meehling excluded from the church, as she was instrumental in the death of her husband. (Bloomingdale Salem Baptist Church Minutes 1855-2005 2005)

Judge Evermont Ward's sentencing statement to Matilda Meehling at the Cabell County Courthouse is so detailed and emotionally wrenching in its nineteenth century operatic eloquence, that little else needs to be added. Here it is in its entirety, as reproduced in G. S. Wallace's *Cabell County Annals and Families:*

Matilda Meehling, you have been indicted, tried by a jury of your country and convicted of murder in the first degree. Murder with malice aforethought; of willful, deliberate, premeditated murder. Of the correctness of this verdict there is not only no reasonable doubt, but not even the shadow of a doubt.

The atrocity of your crime is almost without a parallel. The deed of which you have been convicted is one of the foulest that blackens the annals of time. You were a poor girl, in the humblest walks of life. An honest, industrious young man, with no fortune but his own strong right arm and manly resolves, led you to the altar. You there gave him your hand, and, he supposed, your heart. He vowed to love protect and cherish you and forsaking all others cleave alone unto you, and he paid this vow to the Most High. He made you the partner of his bosom and the mother of his children, and provided you with reasonable comforts. He purchased a handsome little farm, on time, payable in numerous small installments, improved it; stocked it and had paid all but a small pittance of the purchase money. He doubtless looked forward with bright expectancy to an early period in the future when he could have a comfortable little home for his loved ones and owe no man anything. But alas for human expectations, he employed Williams as a laborer, not dreaming that he was taking an adder into his bosom—a serpent into his Eden, to mark his happiness and destroy his life—but it was so.

Williams dishonored his house, defiled his bed, and with his bloody-minded and adulterous wife, conspired his death. After the intimacy between yourself and Williams commenced the presence of your lawful husband could no longer be brooked. He became a "Mordicai the Jew at the Kings gate." You could not consent to have your pleasures broken or circumscribed.

Twice you attempted to poison him, and twice you failed, by administering overdoses, and although you witnessed the terrible suffering he had to undergo on account of your cruel and inhuman act, your iron heart never felt the soft touches of pity. You saw his hands withering, his limbs paralyzing and his frame wasting from the effects of the poison. Grim Death was slowly and certainly doing his work, but too tardily for your inpatient spirit. You could not leave to time his taking off, but you urged your associate to speedy work—the deed must be done this night—this very night. You could not let the hallowed Sabbath pass. He follows your evil counsels and in a few hours afterwards, the dreadful deed was done. A deed which time cannot erase or the ocean's waters wash out. A deed as deep, as foul, as black as any recorded on history's page. Whilst your poor husband is sitting by the fire, all unconscious of impending evil, he sees the uplifted axe, and has but time to say "Oh! Don't kill me"" and blow after blow falls on his head, mashing it as if it were to a jelly. Next the head is almost severed from the body with a butcher's knife.

The evidence does not show how he obtained this knife, but your little boy of too tender years to be sworn, whilst sitting on my knee told me that you gave him the knife. He is now taken by the head and heels and buried in the dung and filth of the stable and animals are turned in to trample upon his already mangled remains. You return, wash up the blood and you and your associate inaugurate a new administration; take the superintendence of affairs and all goes merrily, although within sixty or seventy yards of this horrid spectacle. In a few days your husband is missing—an alarm is felt by the neighbors, but none by yourself and Williams. Suspicions, however are aroused and fall in the right direction. Williams and yourself are arrested and committed to jail. All turn out to make search, and in the stable, buried in the dung, trodden over by the horses, there is found the mangled remains of a man who had lived amongst them, and commanded their respect and esteem, exhibiting a spectacle the very thought of which is sickening to the human heart. They were justly indignant, but let feeling carry them too far, they did not wait for the sentence of the law but took judgment into their own hands. This was wrong. The law should have been permitted to take its course, for while it reveals its terrors to the guilty offender, it is, at the same time, the staff of honesty and the shield of innocence.

They came in mass to the jail, took Williams and hung him. You were then brought and the vote taken in your case, and at first there was no dissenting voice. But after a moment's pause, some noble and manly-spirited fellow said "No Gentlemen, no —she is a woman; for the honor of her sex spare her, forbear and let the law take its course." Every soul yielded silent acquiescence, the crowd dispersed and you were returned to your cell and now the law has taken its course; its sentence is written and it becomes my painful duty to pronounce it upon you.

And now, twice your life has been saved solely on account of your sex. You are a women, and a woman is Heaven's best, divinest gift to man. She is his acknowledged superior in all of the excellencies and refinements of life. She is pure. She is tender. She is kind. She is affectionate and loving, and man masculine, not only loves, but adores her, and the more so, as she is part and parcel of his own being; taken from his side to be his own equal—under his arm to receive his protection—from near his heart to be loved. He regards her as a being dwelling in an atmosphere pure and serene, and made a little lower than the angels. But like the angels who kept not their first estate, she sometimes becomes fallen, and when she falls great is the fall. When she once turns fiend, she becomes a fiend incarnate.

Twice, I repeat, your life has been spared because you are a woman; once by the mob and once by the jury. I do not condemn but appreciate this feeling. Mercy is the darling attribute of the Ever Living and Just. But this mercy was not shown on account of your supplications for it—not in answer to your imploring cry of "That mercy I to others show, that mercy show to me?" but simply on account of your sex. It may be mercy to you to have your days prolonged as it gives greater opportunities for a preparation to meet the Judge of all earth; but still your fate is hard, very hard indeed. You are to be excluded from society and housed with its outcasts, without regard to race, color or previous condition, and doomed to hard labor and course diet all the days of your life.

It is no small matter to give up our worldly enjoyments, but with you they are pretty much at an end. Your neighborly visits. Your social meetings and your church goings are now a thing of the past. When you leave this place, you will have gazed perhaps for the last time upon the features of your aged father, and your little children, whom you leave in the world without a mother's oversight, and with no father, save the Father in Heaven, who (thanks to his holy name) will ever be a Father to the fatherless. When you leave us, you leave us no more to return amongst us. Your counsel, in his eloquent appeals for mercy in your behalf begged that you might be permitted to return, even though it be when your locks were whitened by time and your frame bent with age and infirmity. This cannot be; but were it possible, there would then be nothing to interest you. All things would be strange—passingly strange. The farms and road would be changed, the little saplings would be trees, the old people gone and the young people old. They could afford you no pleasure; but if they could, that pleasure is forfeited. Your body must remain in the damp cells of the penitentiary until it is consigned to the colder chamber of the grave. And Matilda, when your earthly imprisonment ends, you will still have another trial to undergo before the Great Judge, the righteous and unerring Judge, whose eye extends over all the transactions of the children of men, and "without whose knowledge not a sparrow falleth to the ground." He will judge without jury or witnesses and from his sentence there is no appeal. Oh, Matilda! Prepare to meet thy God. Give up all hope or expectations of wordly pleasure. Such hopes will prove delusive and false, and the veriest of vanities. Send your petition to the Throne of the Heavenly Grace. Rely not on your own merits, for we are all without merit; but plead the Merits of One whose atoning virtues are sufficient to blot out the sins of the whole world. The sentence of the Law is, that you be taken to jail, and the sheriff of this county convey you from thence to the public jail and Penitentiary House of the State and that you be therein confined during your natural life. And may you there learn to unlearn what you have learned amiss. (Wallace 1935)

The 1976 history compiled by Barboursville's General Federated Women's Club states that Matilda was saved from execution when Dr. Randolph Moss reported that she was pregnant, adding "time proved that Dr. Moss was wrong in this."

As a woman, Mrs. Meehling would have been among a small minority housed in the Gothic stone fortress of tiered cages known as the West Virginia State Penitentiary, which opened in 1867 with 840 barred five-by-seven-foot cells for men and just 32 for women. (The penitentiary operated continuously for 129 years.) The GFWC history reports that Matilda died seven years after being confined in the Moundsville penitentiary; if this is true she would have been about 35-years-old. One source describes the typical prisoner diet during that period as "dry, undercooked beans, potatoes and water." Internet stories abound of cruel punishments (as early as the 1880s), suicides and undocumented inmate deaths at Moundsville. Today the abandoned penitentiary—the place where the earthly vessel known as Matilda Meehling ceased to contain her tortured soul—has become a favorite destination for thrill-seeking tourists and students of the para-normal, as one of America's "most haunted" sites.

And what of Ed Williams, and those who took the law into their own hands before he had a chance at trial?

A 1909 *Huntington Herald-Dispatch* story, entitled "Cabell County's Greatest Tragedy and First Execution," covered the incident that Judge Ward's otherwise-elaborate speech gave merely a sentence—"They came in mass to the jail, took Williams and hung him." It seems that once the "Actors in the Drama" were mostly gone 33 years later, the *H-D* editors saw fit to reproduce the full story on Page 1, with apologies for its sensational elements, "that there may be drawn a lesson from it which might, in the end, tend to avert many of the crimes which are committed."

Anyway, according to the newspaper, here is how the lynching went down—hold on to your hat:

Old County seat the Scene of Violence. At that time Barboursville being the county seat, and a rival numerically with Huntington, was noted for the quietude which usually prevailed within its antiquated precincts. Most of the members of the Cabell county bar resided there and with the usual number of other professional gentlemen, a high order of intelligence prevailed. Everything was plodding along after the ordinary undisturbed routine when an excited messenger appeared on the streets bearing the message that the body of Charles B. Mehling *(sic)*...had been discovered in a terribly mutilated condition...This was on Saturday evening, about the time that the week's work had been completed and the men of the community had settled down in their quiet home for rest, and the industrious housewives were making the usual preparations for the approaching Sabbath.

The news which the messenger brought spread like a prairie fire and in almost as little time as a dozen of these lines could be written excitement had mounted to the highest pitch, the streets being crowded with the aroused inhabitants of the little town. Everybody knew Charley Mehling...While this excitement was apparently at its height, there entered the town Sheriff D.I. Smith, accompanied by some of his deputies, having in charge a man and a woman, whom they proceeded to lock up in the old county jail. Many recognized the prisoners as they were passed along the streets as Matilda Mehling, the wife of Charles Mehling, and a worthless fellow, said to be a mulatto, by the name of Ed. Williams, who had been held under surveillance for a day or two, as suspects of having criminal knowledge...

A Mob Begins to Collect. It was near night fall when these prisoners were locked up in the jail, and though the hour for the closing meal of the day had arrived, all thought of such refreshment had been passed, so great was the sensational developments of the hour, and from every direction excited men, and even women and children were seen entering the town, until finally there was collected the largest crowd that was ever gathered there, all claiming to get a look at the incarnate friends who seemed so unnatural as to have participated in such a brutal murder as that with which they were now charged, at the same time cries could be heard from every quarter, "Hang the demons," "Burn them at the stake," etc.

The Mob Does Its Work. In the meantime, older and conservative heads were occasionally found in the crowds, and they seeing that mob violence was destined to prevail, proceeded to plead for order, and allow the law to prevail. Among these were Rev. George W. Young, the pastor of the M.E. Church, South, Capt. J.I. Kuhn, prosecuting attorney L.C. ("Kooney") Ricketts...and a few others. Rev. Young and Capt. Kuhn, seeing that a lynching was imminent, sought entrance to the jail and told the prisoners that they would better confess their crime, which Williams proceeded to do, relating the most horrifying facts relative to the tragedy. By this time the mob had crowded about the court house and jail and then cries for vengeance upon the prisoners seemed universal. The populace had gone wild, every semblance of reason or judgment had disappeared until many joined in the tumult with that lack of reason as though they had escaped from a lunatic asylum. Ropes had already been provided, and as Capt. Kuhn and Rev. Young emerged from the jail they were faced by the infuriated mob. For a moment the jail was locked and resistance met the mob, but it was only a moment, when at the demand of the leaders of the mob, jailer Jim Shelton opened the door and the maniacal crowd rushed in and seized the male prisoner who was upon his knees praying for mercy from the mob and his Maker.

Williams was dragged from the jail and to the front yard of the court house where a rope had been tied to a projecting branch of a shade tree and an oil barrel placed under to serve as a scaffold. The man was hurriedly placed on the head of the barrel and the noose adjusted around his neck, when a moment of suspense followed. Prosecuting Attorney Ricketts was pleading at the top of his voice to spare the man's life, Rev. Young was also pleading for order to prevail, while Captain Kuhn, then a young, stout man, was exerting himself to prevent the improvised scaffold from being knocked from under the victim. Finally a man inserted a huge hickory cane in the bung hole of the barrel and forced it from under the man and he fell and dangled in space for a few moments when he was strangled to death.

Cry for the Woman's Life. "Bring out the woman," was the cry following, but in the meantime she had succeeded in convincing the physicians that she should not be hanged—could not be executed without placing the blood of murder upon the hands of the mob, and she was spared.
The mob lingered about the scene until shortly before midnight when it dispersed, but not without first having declared vengeance upon any one who might attempt to remove the body of Williams.

A Ghostly Scene on Sabbath. Sunday was approaching when the children of the town would have to pass by on their way to Sunday school and would witness the ghastly scene of the suspended body, with all of its distorted features. Capt. Kuhn procured some muslin and groping his way to the scene, climbed upon a box which he carried with him and in the pitchy darkness drew the muslin over the body so that on Sunday morning it was seen swinging back and forth under the force of the wind, completely enshrouded in white, but later in the day it was removed and hauled out of town on a wagon, meeting on the main street a hearse containing the body of his victim… (Cabell County's Greatest Tragedy and First Execution 1909)

The Meehling murder stands out as a horrific crime—it was also revealed that Williams and Mrs. Meehling considered killing Melinda's four-year-old son who was awakened by the killing. They decided that a mere threat would scare him into silence, which it did until the boy was assured at the trial that neither his mom nor her "fiendish paramour" would no longer be able to harm him.

Curiously, the Ed Williams hanging was said to have been one of *two* vigilante actions to occur on the Courthouse lawn in Barboursville. Was there actually a second hanging from the mulberry tree on the village square? I have found no solid documentary evidence of a second incident, although several local histories contain a vague and undocumented reference to a Negro man being hanged at the square. The possibility cannot be ruled out that this account of a second lynching could have been created from, or confused with, the mob justice against Ed Williams, the man "said to have negro blood in his veins." So questions linger, both about a second lynching incident in Barboursville, as well as what role that race might have played in the release of prisoner Williams and the frenzied rage of the crowd that night.

In any case, while it was not the only domestic evil to take place in the village— a Fred Lambert source, Perlina McComas, divulged that a man in town "went crazy and murdered his wife with an ax"— the Charles Meehling murder certainly stands (and may it ever) as the most notorious and macabre in Barboursville history.

As such, here is an appropriately eerie postscript, courtesy of the GFWC village history: "It has been reported that the particular branch of the mulberry tree that held the hanging rope for Ed Williams died before the rest of the tree."

The Charmed Childhood of the McKendree Twins

As we emerge from the slime of wickedness and vigilantism, what better time for a revitalizing tonic of joy and innocence from the Lost Village? On balance, late nineteenth-century Barboursville should not seem like a screening of *The Postman Always Rings Twice* or the mob scene from *Frankenstein* any more so than an episode of *Little House on the Prairie*. Happily, such a cheerful child's-eye-view of village life was also captured for posterity.

In 1876, a few months after Matilda Meehling was sent up the river to Moundsville, 32-year-old Irene Octavia McComas McKendree found herself "with child" for the first time. In November of that year, she and George McKendree became parents of twin girls, Mary and Mildred.

McKendree twins 1890s
(Herald-Advertiser clip courtesy of Barboursville Public Library)

Mary McKendree Johnson (pictured on the left) grew up to be a Congressman's wife in Parkersburg. She wrote a book in the 1920s, *Representative Men and Women of Cabell County*. Twin sister Mildred McKendree Henderson began writing her Cabell County memories into notebooks in the mid-1940s. After her death, Henderson's daughter collected her mother's notes and in1974 had them typed into a manuscript. Huntington's *Herald-Advertiser* reproduced excerpts of Mildred's childhood remembrances of her early days at "Clover Valley" (on the current Barboursville Community Park acreage), and her move to Main Street as a wide-eyed six-year-old.

"Father bought the Clover Valley farm from General John Witcher in 1877. It was part of the old Lewis Rolf (*Roffe*) farm before the Civil War. This piece and the Charley Moore place and land up to Dusenberry Dam section was all (Roffe) land and joined the William McComas home farm near Barboursville.

"On the (*Roffe*) farm was the "Grove" which was a famous place for gatherings, day picnics and basket meetings. Here the county families came and spent the day. Large swings would be put up and sometimes platform dances would be held, with local fiddlers furnishing the music.

"There was an old storehouse still standing there in the 1880s and dances were held in this building also. The dances in that day were mostly square dances, and any kind of floor would do to "cut loose on." I can hear Charley Dodds tuning his fiddle still. Many religious meetings were held at the Grove where long benches would be placed and a "preaching stand" made. People came from miles around with their baskets of food.

"Our home had large wooden hooks on the walls, high enough to be out of reach of children. These were for guns to rest on and the guns were always loaded.

"As a child I was very muscular—had a grip like an eagle's claw, Papa used to say. My ambition was to be a circus lady, ride bareback and walk the tight rope, balance myself on the wire and fly through the air. Papa taught us many tricks. We had a trapeze on the limb of one of the big cottonwoods and a wire stretched between the flowering cherry and a cedar.

"In 1882 we lived in the village of Barboursville, a few miles from Clover Valley. Mary and I were six years old when we left Clover Valley for town living... Houses were strung along each side of the road which was Main Street. Stone stiles and hitching posts were in front of the homes and narrow flat stones made sidewalks. We lived in a large white house with French windows opening out on broad porches and surrounded with several acres of grounds. A long walkway through a grape arbor led to the well. This was near the street and anyone passing by could open the gate and get a cool drink of water.

"Sometimes the hogs, taking advantage of the ditch in front of the house, made themselves a wallow and during hot days would lie almost covered in mud and grunt in contentment. Strange as it would seem now, we thought nothing of it. It made no difference if the cows grazed in the streets, horses stood hitched to the posts of the fences and the hogs wallowed. We could just walk around them.

"Our neighbors had children our age, so Mary and I had playmates nearby. The tintype photographer came to town and spent several weeks if business was good. He would put up a tent in some vacant lot. The townspeople and country people came for the pictures, bringing along the whole family.

"One of our greatest days was when the tightrope walker came to town. He usually came in on a morning train, and the children would follow him around in great anticipation of the event to take place in the afternoon. Several hours were spent stretching the rope across the street from Mr. "Fatty" Bum's hotel (John R. Baumgardner, Barboursville hotel and saloon keeper who weighed 375 pounds) across to the brick house on the corner. All eyes were glued to the roof where the rope walker appeared in tights and velvet trunks and spangles and began his perilous feat. Sometimes one came to town who could afford to have a band play while he was performing. Money was collected before the show started.

"The town was justly proud of (its own band) the Barboursville cornet band, led by Albert Poteet. They made a fine appearance in their green uniforms with scarlet satin lining, and were most accommodating—playing on public occasions and serenading newlyweds and important visitors.

"Every so often the Italian with a performing bear or a grind organ and monkey came along. We called them all Italians, and indeed for years, I thought that was what Italians were—men with bears and organs and monkeys. I didn't know there were any other Italians.

"Dentists went from town to town, usually in a covered wagon, and the visits were made known in advance so people could come from hills and hollows. Most emergency tooth pulling was done at home by a member of the family or by the village blacksmith. We had patent medicines such as Lightening Relief, Hot Drops and all kinds of tonics and blood purifiers in addition to garden and wood herbs. Mutton tallow and camphor were rubbed on the chest for colds. Poultices were tied on the wrists. Favorite remedies were hot whiskey toddies, hot tansy tea, onion juice syrup and a quid of tobacco tied on for bee stings.

"There was a large sawmill just below town and hauling huge logs to the mill gave work to many townspeople. The mud, at times, was terrible and most of the hauling was done with oxen, sometimes using a dozen yoke. Drivers had long "blacksnake" whips on hickory sticks with crackers on the ends of the whips. When the mud was unusually deep the drivers walked on the side-walks directing the oxen by "Gee and Haw" and cracking the whip over them so loudly it sounded like a gun shot.

"Heavy shoes for common use were made by the town cobbler, and we wore boots with brass caps. Hooped skirts stood out so far that a young man would have to stoop over to shake hands with a girl wearing one. To get near enough to kiss was out of the question. The girls would dance around and their grapevine hoops hit the gentlemen's limbs; they would rebound in the opposite direction to such an extent that anyone with whom they came in contact was in danger of being knocked down. It was quite an art to sit down in a hoop skirt without the hoops flying up over the wearer's head.

"In the summer, everyone went to the depot to see the trains pull in. The rail-road was an interesting part of our life—the only part that went out into the big world and daily came back to us. As the engine stood in the station, puffing and gasping, we had a feeling of admiration for the power of this great thing.

"In our little town we knew all of the trains by name and not by number. I remember the "Bob-tail," the Fast Flying Virginian," "The Vestibule," the fast freight and the slow freight, the fast train and the slow train. We knew the whistles and their meanings—the whistles for the cut or the crossing at Wilson's Mill and for the bridge below town. We knew how much time we had to get to the depot to get the newspapers from the news butchers. There were quick shrill blasts that meant something was on the tracks, usually a cow, sometimes a child. We knew the engineers, firemen and brakemen by name. Some of the engineers had a special way of whistling. Some played tunes, or what was taken to be tunes and word got around that J.B., running No. 6 would play a certain tune, and we would stop our play to listen for the tune when J.B.'s train went through...

"Hand brakes were used in that day and brakemen ran along on top of the cars, jumping from one to another and braking each car for the stop. At a certain distance before the entrance to a tunnel or low bridge were warning signals to the brakemen. These were tall frames with a bar over the track from which a row of cords hung down, low enough to strike the brakemen on the head, warning him of danger, and he would "duck." This way they were warned at night." (Baumgartner, Mosaics from Barboursville's Past n. d.)

Here are items from *The Huntington Advertiser*, some followed by comments of Mildred McKendree Henderson:

Nov. 7, 1885—the street lamp posts have arrived and they are daisies.

Nov. 17, 1885, Barboursville—A game of baseball was played last Saturday between the "Red Caps" and a picked nine, both of this place, resulting in a score of seven to six, in favor of the Red Caps. Barboursville has good baseball material.

"The ball players on the Red Cap team were George McDermitt, Ralph, Henry, Jack and Lake Blume; Wilton and Clifford Pinnel, Ed Hovey, Tom Holroid, Garland and Tom Merritt, and Walter and Phil Leist. George Alexander was catcher on account of his enormous hands. He caught without gloves. The uniforms were homemade of red and white calico, with full trousers gathered at the knees. The waists had collars trimmed in white stripes. Some of the boys played barefooted."

Dec. 5, 1885—the contract for lighting the street lamps has been awarded by council to H. J. Lusher at $8.50 a month.

Feb. 20, 1886—The mayor has offered a reward of $5.00 for the apprehension of the miscreant who broke the globe and stole the oil can out of a street lamp.

Nov. 7, 1886—the telephone lines between Huntington and Barboursville give perfect satisfaction. The telephone is in Bright's Drug Store.

"The only drugstore in town was Bright's. My memories of this store are limited to TULU chewing gum and pretty bottles. The gum came in little sticks. We were not allowed to chew gum, and I had a hiding place under the top of the gate post where I put my gum before going into the house."

Jan. 29, 1887—The public pump at the corner of Main and Water streets is a perfect nuisance and should be cut down and thrown over the bank.

"This was a large pump with a square wooden platform around it, and it had a long trough for watering horses. There were many teams in town, especially on court days. At this time horses would be hitched all over town, to fences, tree and hitching posts." (Baumgartner, Mosaics from Barboursville's Past n.d.)

The Rough and Rowdy "Guyan" Boatmen

With steamer traffic steady along the Ohio River, the fickle Guyandotte River once again came to life. A survey of the Guyandotte, approved by Congress, was completed in 1874 by Arthur L. Cox of Barboursville. He learned that about $400,000 worth of farm and forest products floated out the river annually. In addition, 300 tons of merchandise was shipped upriver in push boats. Funds were provided in 1878 to dispatch a small crew to clear a better channel for the push boat traffic. Crews of 12 to 25 men moved up and down the river, removing snags with dynamite and axes, dragging boulders and loose stone from the channel. Congressman John E. Kenna reported that 20 percent of logs floated down the river were lost the year before the channel was cleared. By 1883 not a single log was lost on its way from the head of the watershed to the Ohio. Soon, small steam boats began to travel the Guyandotte again as well.

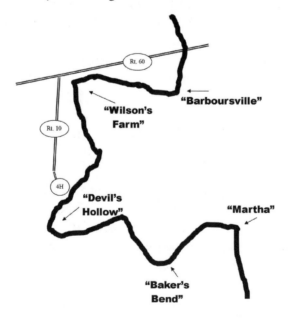

Locals named the bends in the Guyandotte River around Barboursville,
according to Maurice Beckett.
(Illustrated by author)

Raftsmen on a log raft near Altizer, circa 1900
(Courtesy of Marshall University Libraries Special Collections)

The trip around the village of Barboursville must have been particularly challenging. Local writer Maurice Beckett "talked to old people who had seen the steamboats and heard their mournful whistles. All the big bends of the river were named. There was the bend at Martha, then Baker's Bend, Devil's Hollow, Wilson's Farm and Barboursville." Beckett recalled from his swimming days that most of the river was easily wade-able in the summer, but was much deeper in the bends. "At most bends the river had, in its long history, cut into the hills, forming tall cliffs and cluttering the shore with great rounded boulders. Barboursville, however was built on the ancient Ice Age deposits of the Teays Valley and, where other river bends were topped by rock cliffs, those of the village were of clay."

Lambert's collection includes first-hand recollections of a few Guyan boatmen, including the Godby brothers, James and George, of "Chapmansville," *(sic)* Logan County. They owned a few steamboats in the mid-1890s, including the *J. T. Hustler,* and ran six or seven months each year. The Godby brothers also had a line of eight to ten push boats from Guyandotte to Logan, which carried passengers "only when they insisted. It took two days to go to Logan. We sometimes brought wheat to a mill, at Barboursville, for grinding, but were slow in getting it hauled and delivered on time. We often waited an hour or two, so had to quit…. We preferred the upper freight because rates were better. We ran night and day till we reached about six or ten miles, after which we only run in day time, because customers lived out in the hills, at least part of them did, and freight might be stolen."

According to Sam Bias, it took five to six days and about six men to push a large boat to Logan. He described the punishing labor that went into the trip and some of the men who took it on:

> They had to haul boats around the dam, or unload and carry the goods. Skids were put under the boats and all the men helped put it over the dams. At other times they hired oxen, or made a windlass. Raftsmen often brought consider- able quantities of ropes with them. Ropes were often wrapped around trees to check rafts by degrees to land them. One steered the boat, and about four pushed. The men started at upper end of boats and gradually walked back. They generally had pads on their shoulders to keep from hurting their shoul- ders. It took about six days from Guyandotte to Logan.

> A man named Chambers and another man named Conley, Dave Lester of Logan were raftsmen. Mack Johnson had a store on East side below the Falls. Dave stopped and had 3-4 dozen eggs cooked and ate them all. Once a constable, Andy Dick tried to arrest him and others above the Falls 200-300 yards. Dick was shooting at him as he swam. John Justice, Ben Justice, etc., were large men, almost giants. One of them brought down a whole bear, sold it in Guyandotte about 1875. My father served some at his hotel in Guyandotte.

> Cooking was done on (the) bank. They took along skillets, pans, etc. My father and Tuck made shingles on Tom's Creek. Corn bread, bacon, pickeled pork, etc., after the war. Potatoes, no canned goods. Often fished at night and had fish next day. Fried in bacon grease. Fished til midnight, used hook and line. Had a gun. Often killed ducks. I killed a bald eagle just above the Falls. It had been catching Lewis Midkiff's geese. It measured 7 feet on wings. (F. B. Lambert Collection n.d.)

The treacherous bends curving around Barboursville would offer repeated opportunities to see and hear these freight-runners laboriously winding their way up to, or down from, the Guyandotte Valley. Judging by their somewhat roman- ticized writings, it seems that both McKendree twins were fascinated by the late-nineteenth-century behemoths who forged the Guyan. Mary wrote in 1929:

> The most colorful part of the picture in an earlier time was to be found in the river life…And those boatmen! They were a picturesque crew some fifty years ago. Guiding their narrow, awkward, serpentine crafts with creaking rudder and heavy poles, they strained and sweated, sang or swore, as they negotiated the tricky bends in this river of winding curves.

> The boatmen were regular fellows and "took theirs straight." Good old "Red Eye" in the big brown jug was usually important cargo. It was anodyne to banish memory of the hardships, the icy contacts with the water, and the child

of the blasts, which swept from the mountains down the shallow gorge. These boatmen were master hands at swearing, and they were often so boisterous that children playing along the banks ran away in fright as they heard these raftsmen sweeping by, yelling and swearing lustily. Yet, they were only a lot of mountaineers taking their trips as high adventure.

Their singing is a vivid memory with those who have heard it. They sang such rollicking tunes as, "Dance, Boatmen, Dance!" "Big Black Dog on a Sourwood Mountain," "Little Brown Jug," as well as the plaintive old ballads, centuries old, brought over by their ancestors when they crossed the Atlantic.

Sometimes the wind and current overcame these boatmen, and they snubbed their cables around trees on the bank, seeking friendly shelter and food at a farmhouse along the way, to start the following morning, at break of day. When they were at journey's end, and their hard trip behind them, then did they often let their high spirits run riot. These same high spirits have been known to land them occasionally in the caravanserie presided over by a none too genial host, the Cabell County jailer. (M. M. Johnson 1929)

Later, sister Mildred recalled the raftsmen and their equally hard-working and hard-carousing counterparts on the steamboats:

The work also was very heavy on the steamboats that plied the inland waters. The boats stopped at any landing where they were hailed. Farmers sent droves of stock, grain and all sorts of produce by boat. The work of the roustabouts was hard, and it was said the steamboat captains gave them cocaine, as that drug causes great physical strength while it lasts. Then the roustabouts could sleep it off when there was a lull in loading or when there was a long distance between landings.

It was customary for the river men to celebrate after a trip down the river, when they were safe in the valley of the Guyan. Sometimes they spent days or even weeks going home after a hard trip down the Ohio with rafts of logs. We called them "Loganites" or "Logan Knights." (Baumgartner, Mosaics from Barboursville's Past n.d.)

Among The President's Inner Circle

Before William Clendenin and Eliza Gardner Miller passed away (in 1886 and 1888, respectively), they got to see most of their seven children grow up to marry well and launch successful careers (with the exception of youngest son Hamilton who died at ten months, and daughter Florence who became the second Mrs. G. F. Miller Jr. after her parents died). However, it was their fifth child, Joseph Samuels

Miller (1848-1921), a man whose public ascent burnished the Miller family legacy, who may have provided his parents' twilight years with their greatest satisfaction.

Joseph was born the same year as future brother-in-law George F. Miller Jr. Schooled on Main Street by sister Eugenia's beau, Professor Thackston, Joseph attended boarding school at the Beach Grove Academy in Kentucky. (As a 12-year-old likely away at school, Joe might well have been the sole Miller child unscathed by the Civil War hostilities at home.) He studied law and was admitted to the bar but never practiced. While only 21 years of age, Miller was appointed to complete the unexpired term of William Merritt as Clerk of Cabell County Circuit Court; the following year he was elected for a four-year term. Two years later he was elected as Clerk of the County Court on a full Democratic ticket. In 1875, he married Florence Tice of Hagerstown, Maryland. In 1876, Miller was elected as State Auditor and successfully held his office for eight years.

During Miller's tenure as State Auditor, West Virginia's Capitol—which was first located in Wheeling, then moved to Charleston, and then back to Wheeling—moved back again, after a statewide election in 1877 established Charleston as the permanent seat of government. In the meantime, the young auditor was making an impression on New York's Democratic governor Grover Cleveland. At the end of his second term, Miller himself was preparing at age 36 to become a gubernatorial candidate in West Virginia, but the young up-and-comer withdrew around the time Democrats nominated Cleveland as their Presidential candidate.

Grover Cleveland was seen as a self-made man who had distinguished himself for firmness and integrity, and won the general election as the man who would oversee "the reorganization of Federal power of a party virtually excluded from it for nearly a quarter of a century." Cleveland also became the second man elected in a 32-year string of mostly mustachioed United States presidents. Chester Arthur, the man who preceded him in the "presidential soup strainer club," was described by opponents as a disreputable character put on the Republican ticket to appease party bosses. Vice-President Arthur was elevated to the presidency in 1881, four months into the James Garfield administration, after Garfield was shot and killed by a disgruntled office-seeker.

A rather glowing political biography of 1892 describes how Grover Cleveland met the challenges of his first pre-inaugural period:

"To most men, the lack of all experience in public life in a Federal office would have been a serious drawback on the threshold of an Administration which was to bring back to the country the policy of a party long excluded. But it was rather an advantage to Grover Cleveland. He had none of those prejudices, those likes and dislikes, which incessantly surround the men who have had many years experience in the somewhat artificial and insincere life of Washington. He did not know personally any large number of those with whom he was destined to deal. But he had patience, the faculty of investigating everything with care and of deciding it on its merits, and he had an insight into men and their characters which is rare ..." (Hensel 1892)

Grover Cleveland named his cabinet the day after his March 1885 inauguration. In addition to the Attorney General and a handful of Secretaries, "the choice of men to fill those offices popularly recognized as of the second grade" telegraphed Cleveland's reform-minded philosophies. Among these few dozen second-tier directors, President Cleveland "with his characteristic sagacity in the selection of men called a vigorous, clearheaded and able executive officer in the person of Joseph S. Miller" to head the Internal Revenue system. Miller would serve in this position during the first Cleveland administration, which ended in 1888, when Republican Benjamin Harrison of Indiana (America's last bearded president) was elected to a single term, despite losing the popular vote to Cleveland. (Cleveland won back the presidency in 1992.)

Joseph Miller and President Cleveland apparently enjoyed fishing together on the banks of the Potomac River. Miller wrote a humorous poem about a fishing experience with Cleveland that was published in the *Washington Chronicle,* and is reprinted in Gunter's *Barboursville.*

Joseph S. Miller
(Courtesy Frances Gunter)

According to Gunter, Miller convinced Cleveland and some of his friends to invest in coal lands in Wayne County. Upon his return to West Virginia, Miller became one of the men who purchased rights-of-way for the Norfolk and Western Railroad Company, which came through the town of Kenova.

In 1891, Joseph Samuels Miller built a Queen Anne house on Kenova's Beech Street, which paralleled both the railroad line and the Ohio River. In 1904, the home was the site of a gala wedding and reception for his only daughter Lavalette (for whom the Wayne County community of Lavalette is named). At the time of his death in 1922, Miller was President of the National Bank of Kenova. Miller's home, once visited by President Cleveland, is listed on the National Registry of Historic Places. Owned by the current mayor in 2012, it is better known in the twenty-first century as Kenova's Pumpkin House.

Losing the Courthouse

> "An ox cart was slowly clumping its way down the crooked river road that separated Barboursville from Huntington. It did not carry the usual load of tan-bark or newly-hewn railroad ties. On it, and carefully secured were the court records of Cabell county. Huntington was growing and Barboursville had met its first, heartbreaking setback." (M. E. Beckett 1935)

Huntington's exponential growth as the center of population began to spur demand for the courthouse to be relocated and a campaign to move the county seat to Huntington began in the early 1880s. A vote to do so was taken in 1884, but the move was defeated by a narrow margin. Voters narrowly approved the change in the general election of 1886, but the offices were not actually moved until December 26, 1887. Even a lengthy fight in the state Supreme Court failed to halt the inevitable blow. So after nearly 73 years as county seat (with the few brief interruptions cited earlier), all of Cabell County's records, ledgers, papers and books were moved to Huntington.

A young Mr. Salmon walked behind the county clerk's records. Captain Thomas West Peyton III walked behind the wagon conveying the circuit clerk's records from Barboursville. A few years earlier Peyton had been deputy to the last "Clerk of County," Moses Shephard Thornburg (Solomon's nephew), and was elected to circuit clerk in 1884 after the offices of circuit and county clerk were divided.

The official "demotion" of Barboursville meant not only the loss of court business, but the continuing decline of Barboursville as a center of social activity. Three years earlier, the town's original social center, the old Merritt Mill, had ceased all operations after an 1884 flood gutted the building and ruined its sawmill and carding machinery—it would never operate again. With the town's political decline, the hotels would surely lose a steady stream of visitors into the village. In Barboursville's business center, hostelries like the Hatfield, the Charles Ryan, the Blume, the Baumgardner House (presided over by town character and gracious host John B. Baumgardner); and the Price House (*pictured*) would need to find some new customers for their accommodations, and soon.

Members of the Stowasser and Price families pose in front of the
Price Hotel on "Center Street" where the Village Medical clinic now stands
(Photo courtesy of Wilma Smith)

Barboursville Takes on a New Identity

Within weeks of the "heartbreaking setback," plans were made to find a use for the abandoned buildings on the old village square. On May 14, 1888, five Barboursville businessmen formed a corporation for the express purpose of establishing and conducting a Seminary. The Barboursville Seminary, a school which soon became Barboursville College and later, Morris Harvey College, began with five dollars in the treasury.

Barboursville immediately took on the task of forging a new identity. Pastors T. S. Wade and G. M. F. Hampton were elected president and vice president by the school's board of trustees, and were given less than a month to transform the old courthouse and grounds into a college building and campus in time for classes to begin on September 12. The summer of 1888 was a busy time not only for the founders of the seminary but also for the village fathers. Barboursville had to be transformed into an upright "college town," and at the same time students had to be recruited to populate the pending institution.

COLLEGE AT BARBOURSVILLE.

Guyandotte, W. Va., July 21st. 1888.

DEAR BROTHER:

Divine Providence has opened the way for the establishment of a Male and Female College, at Barboursville, W. Va., under the auspices of our Church.

It is proposed to furnish first class Collegiate Culture at the lowest possible expense, and build up a home institution that will command the respect and patronage of the people at large. The first Session will open on the 12th. of Sept. 1888 with a faculty qualified to meet all the demands of the work.

The organizaton of the institution will be completed soon. After an informal consultation of the trustees, we are prepared to announce, that

REV. G. M. F. HAMPTON, A. B.

will CERTAINLY be a member of the faculty.

We urgently request that you bring this matter prominently before your people and do all in your power to secure patronage for the institution. It is important that the enterprise be extensively advertised at the earliest possible moment.

All persons interested in higher education and who are willing to help build up a home institution by their patronage, are cordially invited to correspond with the undersigned, who will cheerfully give desired information.

VERY RESPECTFULLY.

T. S. WADE, Chair'n. Com.

Eight weeks before classes first were held at the seminary, school president T.S. Wade, above, had this broadside posted in nearby Guyandotte.

College of Barboursville Broadside 7-21-1888
(Herald-Advertiser clipping courtesy of Barboursville Library)

As Rev. Wade was beating the bushes for students and patrons (see reproduction of Guyandotte broadside), the village's two remaining saloons, "Uncle Fatty Bum's" and J.C. Snead's, were voted out. The courthouse became the administration building and lecture hall. The bars were removed from the county jail and it became the men's dorm. Property on the ridge behind the courthouse, yet overgrown with brush and "well peppered by Union soldiers' Minnie-balls," held potential for future expansion. Right next door, on the northwest corner of Main and Center, was the Blume hotel, which "could be easily procured, for business was dull." The Blume was purchased to serve as a college boarding house and women's dormitory. The Methodist Episcopal Church South had erected a lovely new brick chapel in 1884 on property deeded by Bailey Thornburg and Nettie Samuels Thornburg, using $1,800 allotted by the federal government for Union Army damages to the Water Street church building during the war. The local congregation would soon make this chapel available for use by the new school.

The former Blume Hotel served as the boarding house and girl's dormitory.
In this photo from the late 1930s the original hotel lettering can still be seen.
(Courtesy of Barboursville Library)

By this time, Barboursville was home to at least three other organized Protestant congregations: the Methodist Episcopal Church – North, which broke from the original congregation, became Steele Memorial Methodist and had a building on Main Street. The Episcopalians had been authorized, as well as the Baptists, to use the courthouse for services since 1869. The Trinity Church and Parish was formed in Barboursville and held services once a month, but eventually began alternating between the village and Huntington—ultimately planting itself permanently as Huntington's Trinity Episcopal Church. Barboursville's Baptists were still without a building, meeting in private homes until 1890, when a children's Sunday School was conducted over Poteet's store on the corner of Main and Center.

A county record of Sept. 1, 1888 documents the sale by the Barboursville Seminary of the "E. W. Blume Hotel, previously John G. Miller Store House, to Thomas Thornburg, George F. Miller, George Blume, George McComas, H. J. Samuels, H.C. Poteet, S.G. Preston, J.H. Jackson, T.S. Wade, trustees," who "shall establish and maintain a college under the patronage, care and supervision of the Methodist Episcopal Church South, in which all white persons of good moral character making application may obtain a classical, or inferior grade of education, without regard to religious profession, social or property qualifications...this cause shall not prevent the trustees from dispensing of this rule in favor of ministers, their families, or other meritorious or charitable cases."

Built in 1884, the chapel of the Methodist Episcopal Church, South,
sat at the west side of the old courthouse and served students of the new college.
(Courtesy of Wilma Smith)

Only 25 students were enrolled by September 12, but by the time the first catalog went to press, the body had grown to 130 students. Seventy percent came from Cabell County, half of these from Barboursville. Nine other West Virginia counties, as well as the states of Kentucky and North Carolina, sent their young ladies and gentlemen to experience "culture at the lowest possible expense." The new faculty set about their purpose, "to throw around the pupils the hallowed influence of Christian religion without trying to bias their minds in favor of any particular denomination."

In 1889, due to lagging finances, the seminary was renamed Barboursville College and passed into the hands of a group of five stockholders, who each invested $200. They were E. W. Blume, Henry Poteet, Henry Stowasser, Charles H. Miller and "Frederick" Miller. A year later the stockholders turned it over to the Western Virginia Conference of the Methodist Episcopal Church, South. Once again (as with the struggling Marshall Academy 40 years earlier), the Methodist Church took the lead in rescuing a local institution of higher learning.

The college catalogues of 1889-95 reflected the prim influence of the faculty and village leaders, who were determined not to lead the village's young charges into temptation:

> "Students must not visit each other in their rooms nor go strolling about town after 7 o'clock (winter).

> "Company must not be entertained except on Friday evening, and then not later than 10 o'clock. This rule forbids young ladies to attend church or sociables, or to walk the streets or to take strolls, or to hang over the fence with young gentlemen.

> "Worthy students may study in their rooms. There shall be no dancing nor attending of dances.
> "Girls and boys must not study together in chapel.

> "No drama shall be presented from the stage of the college." (Mrs. Philip Richmond 1976)

By 1890, Barboursville College not only occupied the courthouse square, but had rapidly transformed the identity of this resilient town. Considering that only about three percent of Americans of the "appropriate age group" went to college, it was a prestigious achievement. The school would later be renamed for a Fayette County benefactor, and would remain an anchor of village life until the mid-1930s.

The Gilded Age Goes Out in a "Panic"

While Barboursville was coming to terms with its new standing as a "dry village," a saloon-free cradle of higher learning, Guyandotte was becoming known as a hub for the regional timber industry. As the 1890s approached in this "fast buck" era, logging became an even bigger industry in the hills and hollows. The Maine-based Little Kanawha Lumber Co., which had a sawmill at Portsmouth, Ohio, had the first large logging operation in Logan County. In 1889, the company started to acquire timbering rights in Logan and Wyoming Counties, West Virginia Huge rafts would be tied near the shore of these towns while the loggers waited for a steamboat to take the logs downstream.

"At Guyandotte when the timbermen anchored their rafts, the good people of the town anchored themselves safely at home," wrote Rodney White. Guyandotte, and Catlettsburg to the west, offered whiskey, crapshooting, women and song to keep the men entertained. But by 1893 the carousing, and much of the Guyan Valley timber industry itself, would come to a halt, at least temporarily.

During Cleveland's second administration, a series of bank failures and industrial collapses ushered in the worst depression the country had seen (or would see again until 1929). Known as the Panic of 1893 or the "Cleveland Panic," the crash was the result of the treasury's gold reserve being depleted by an excess of imports and liquidation of American securities after a panic in London. Prices and wages hit rock bottom and markets dwindled. The Gilded Age gave way to a several years of soup kitchens and ragged armies of the unemployed. The 1894 Pullman Strike near Chicago was a particularly ugly episode marking the harsh division between business and labor, which in turn would help sweep in the Populist and Progressive eras.

Cabell County suffered severely, like the rest of the country. According to Wallace, economic conditions continued to be bad until the end of the century. "Before commercial timbering operations had begun, a lack of cash was a chronic condition. It was only the relative plenty of cash in 1892 and early 1893 that made its scarcity in late 1893 and 1894 seem so critical," wrote Dr. Edwin Cubby of Marshall University.

Fortunately, Barboursville's young college hung on through these lean years, as did the village.

If there was a silver lining to an otherwise miserable decade, it was that the wounds and hatreds of the Civil War were finally put to rest. "Waving the bloody shirt"—the political practice of reviving old sectional grudges for electoral gain—had ceased to be an effective tactic by the 1880s. Common cause, industrial pursuits and time had healed the rancor between former members of Cabell County's Border Rangers and the Union's "Bloody Ninth." During the 1890s, aging veterans of the Civil War and their loved ones began to come together through Confederate and Union organizations to look after destitute comrades and purchase final burial plots for the fallen. (These groups would foreshadow the nation's future veterans' associations and government assistance agencies.) As a final footnote to the war, the remains of Albert Gallatin Jenkins were moved from Greenbottom to a distinguished new Confederate plot in Huntington's Spring Hill Cemetery.

By the mid-1890s, another major chapter in American history ended. A report in the 1890 U.S. Census entitled 'Progress of the Nation,' analyzed the course of American westward expansion and settlement since the first Census in 1790. This report officially concluded that the American frontier—legally defined by Congress as land occupied by more than one but less than six persons per square mile—was no longer worth measuring. Historian Frederick Jackson Turner presented an essay that invoked 'Progress of the Nation' to the 1893 Chicago World's Fair, declaring that the frontier was gone. Thomas Jefferson had predicted after the Lewis and Clark expedition that it would take 100 generations for the frontier to fill up. It had taken only 80 years.

With railroads crisscrossing the United States from coast to coast, Barboursville was just one junction town along more than 160,000 miles of rail line. The young town of Milton outpaced the village in population growth, and both towns were already dwarfed by Huntington. (*See population charts.*) By the late 1890s, Barboursville had, for most intents and purposes, assumed its twentieth century status of bedroom community.

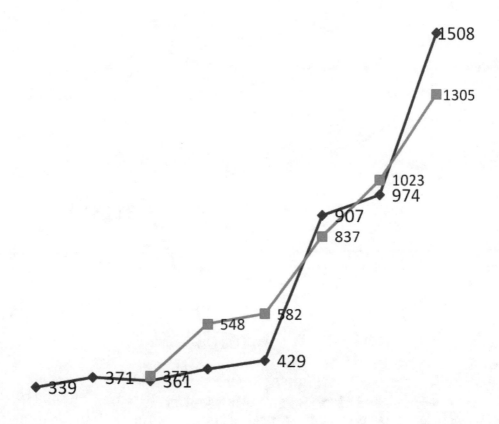

Population 1860-1930

—◆—Barboursville   —■—Milton

Population Line Charts 1860-1930 Barboursville - Milton (Data courtesy of Connecticut State Library online collection of Decennial Population Counts Based on U.S. Census, with Composition and Characteristics of the Population for States, Counties, Cities, Townships and "Minor Civil Divisions" http://www.cslib.org/pathfinders/censusstats.htm#Decade)

Population 1860-1930

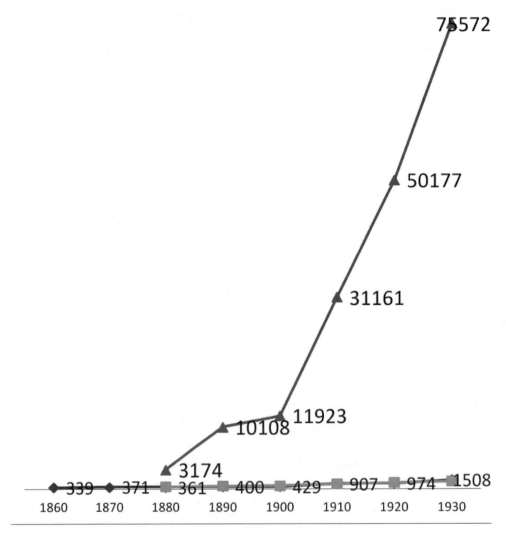

Population Line Charts 1860-1930 Barboursville - Milton - Huntington (Data courtesy of Connecticut State Library online collection of Decennial Population Counts Based on United States Census, with Composition and Characteristics of the Population for States, Counties, Cities, Townships and "Minor Civil Divisions" http://www.cslib.org/pathfinders/censusstats.htm#Decade)

CHAPTER 10

HERE LIES MARY E. BRADY: A FAMILY SAGA

THE waning years of the nineteenth century provide an apt "resting place" in our march through the Barboursville timeline. This chapter and the next will look at the sweep of history through the lives of some less-celebrated village families.

For now, I will (mostly) give the omnipresent Millers, McComases and Thornburgs a rest, as I open the family closet and shine a light on the checkered past of my own Brady-Moore ancestors.

Mary Brady Tombstone *(Photo by the author)*

179

Just a few paces from a chain link fence that separates the Barboursville "baby pool" from the old village cemetery, lie some of the sturdiest old headstones to be found there, in the Brady family plot.

Buried alongside her husband near the family monument, the matriarch of the Barboursville Bradys, Mary Emaline Moore Brady, remains a mystery in many ways. Unlike Eugenia Miller or William Dusenberry, she did not leave behind a collection of letters or a box of diaries, and I am unaware of any preserved family photos.

Nevertheless, Mary provides a great example of just how much family lore can be found by anyone with time and tenacity—not only to tap into the magic of Google, but spin microfilm reels at the public library, peruse the offerings of the KYOWVA genealogical society, power-lift deed books at the courthouse, or spend a nearly-silent Friday afternoon in the Special Collections library at Marshall. For every tombstone inscription or street name, there is a potentially rich biography to be found using mostly-free resources found within Cabell County. Consider this an invitation to take a (nearly-free) vacation into the past and insert your own roots story into the historic mix.

Through discoveries I happened upon in these places, I became intrigued by the life of my great-great grandmother. I can't speculate as to how Mary Moore Brady felt about the fluctuating fortunes of her time, much less what must have been a deep vein of family tragedy. Although she may forever remain a shadowy female presence in an era of men, I have come to regard Mary as the lynchpin in a Barboursville family saga that spans two centuries.

Out of the "Frying Pan"

Local golfers are familiar with a public course opened in 1973, the Esquire Country Club located off Heath Creek Road. Internet reviews of the 18-hole, 72-par course are mixed; my favorite description came from the *Herald-Dispatch*: "Relatively flat, but requires the use of all clubs in your bag." The golf course and the housing development that more recently sprang up around it sit island-like within a deep bend of the Guyandotte River, once known as "The Frying Pan" farm *(as is labeled on the 1822 county map)*.

Around 1813, Martin Moore (1775-1850), his wife Mary Brown Moore (1793-1877) and their oldest children came from Albemarle County, Virginia to the thinly-populated McComas District in Cabell County. As discovered by my aunt, Mary Brown was the daughter and granddaughter of Revolutionary Patriots. It is assumed that she and Martin came to Cabell County with considerable assets. Martin was first employed as superintendent for Sampson Sanders, and bought the Frying Pan farm, where he lived for 38 years.

Like their neighbor Sampson Sanders, my ancestors owned slaves. A Sanders nephew, Sampson Simmons, recalled traveling downriver around the Frying Pan as a young child, and "seeing old Martin Moore's negroes fanning the chaff out of wheat, by four of them taking hold of the corner of a sheet and waving it back and forth in the wind." He told of the slave couple, "Old Uncle Tom and Aunt Dinah, splendid negroes" who raised 20 children for their master. "Uncle Tom was a Baptist preacher of no mean ability, and had the high respect of all the white people in the neighborhood. He would make appointments to preach in different neighborhoods, and the white people would take all their slaves and go to hear him preach," wrote Simmons.

Unlike Sampson Sanders, Moore's loyalty to his slaves went only so far: "Mr. Moore, at one time, had a debt of two thousand dollars on his place and the mortgage was about to be foreclosed, and he sold two of Uncle Tom and Aunt Dinah's boys off for one thousand dollars each, and paid it off," said Mr. Simmons. Still, when Martin passed away in 1850, it was Uncle Tom who officiated at his burial.

Martin and Mary Brown Moore had 11 children and owned 9 slaves in 1830; by 1840 they had seven children living at home and owned 17 slaves. In 1850, when Martin's life ended, it seems at least six of his children had preceded him in death. Martin and Mary's children included Shelton Moore, Willis Moore, Margaret Shelton, Wilson B. Moore, Martin Moore Jr., Louisa "Lou" Moore (who married New Yorker Thorn Dusenberry in 1849 and moved to Louisville), Amacetta (who married John S. Everett and was the mother of two girls) and Frances "Fanny" Moore. Two of Martin's sons (most likely Shelton and Willis) emigrated to the West and were said to have died while serving the Confederate Army. There is speculation that Willis fathered an illegitimate child in the village. Martin Junior married a woman named Sarah and had two children, Samuel and Elizabeth.

Less than a year after the Sanders slaves rafted to freedom, the Moore slaves met a more customary fate: Tom and Dinah's family was split up, most of them sold for inheritance money. Before his death, Martin had already given six of the slaves to his children: a girl, Malinda, went to Amacetta Everett; to Martin Junior went a slave named Henry; a slave who bore the documented name of "Darkey" was given to Margaret Shelton; to Louise Dusenberry went a girl named Martha; the boy John was given to his daughter Frances Moore: and 8-year-old "Priscilla" was given to Wilson. A 1940 piece by Helen Kent references Will Book #2, Records of Cabell County, The Estate of Martin Moore, December 1850, and shows the names of the remaining slave family members, with their price of sale: Tom and Dinah sold for $200, Edmond $700, Isaac $700, Squire $700, Judie $325, Scipio $400, America $275, and Elias who sold for $275.

The year of his father's death, the Census taker found Wilson B. Moore living in Barboursville as a hotel keeper and married to the former Mary Jane McCallister. She was the great-granddaughter of Revolutionary War veteran James McCallister, a son of Ireland. Wilson and Mary Jane had two young sons, John and Charles, two or three lodgers, and the young slave girl assumed to be Priscilla.

In 1851, Wilson's 58-year-old mother, widow Mary Brown Moore, moved from the Frying Pan farm into a log and frame house just north of Main Street, across Center Street from the old county jail. That same year, Wilson and Mary Jane Moore's third child, Mary Emaline, was born.

One of a Million Irish Refugees

Meanwhile, a 15-year-old Irish lad, James Samuel Brady of Philadelphia, was embarking upon a journey that would ultimately bring him to Barboursville. According to a handwritten history furnished by his son:

> James Brady Sr., our grandfather, married Margaret Bryan, in Ireland near Dublin. He died leaving two children, James and John Brady...After the death of his father in Ireland, his aunt brought him over here to visit and he staid (sic) here till he was 17. He then went back over to visit to his mother but didn't like it. His aunt, a Mrs. Ryan, lived in Illinois (and) ran a dairy. We don't know anything about John, our uncle. He staid (sic) in Ireland. (F. B. Lambert Collection n.d.)

If the third-generation family account is correct, James Brady would not have been typical of the 600,000 desperately-poor Irish immigrants who came to America between 1846 and 1851, during the height of the potato famine. Many landed at ports in New York or Philadelphia, and few would have had the luxury of traveling back to their home country for a visit. Considering that passenger manifests listed dozens of similarly-aged Irish immigrants named James Brady, it's virtually impossible to verify my great-grandfather's story or trace my great-great grandfather's origins.

The great wave of Irish refugees took advantage of cheap passage to America, escaping further misery and dreaming of a better life. In fact, the same brand of anti-Irish racism that was used to justify Victorian England's domination over Ireland was seen in America's anti-immigrant "nativist" politics of the mid-nineteenth century. Like African slaves, Irish people were stereotyped, caricatured with ape-like features in early political cartoons, and generally held to be an inferior class of human. They were relegated to the lowest rungs of the employment ladder in jobs considered too dangerous even for black slaves, because the loss of a slave was an out-of-pocket expense for the slave-owner.

Whatever it was that brought him to America, James Brady found himself among a steady pool of Irish laborers ripe for exploitation. Discrimination and low skill levels limited the jobs the Irish immigrants could be hired for. According to the

Historical Society of Pennsylvania, the Irish were generally not directly recruited by railroad companies, but by independent contractors who were responsible for laying certain sections of track. In some cases, employment agents, some of them unscrupulous swindlers, recruited immigrants just as soon as they got off the ships and transported them immediately to work on canals and railroads, laying down tracks and expanding railroad lines across the eastern United States, armed with only picks and shovels.

THE TORCH

INSPIRATION RIDGE

James Brady engineered a C&O railroad cut on the old Fortification Hill, renamed "Inspiration Ridge" by early twentieth century students and romantics. *(1933 BHS Yearbook image courtesy of Barboursville Public Library)*

Like so many others, James ventured into an industry that was in its formative stages. A contract to lay track meant that a gang of railroad laborers worked from sunrise to sunset at a furious pace in harsh conditions, cutting down trees, removing stumps, cutting rock, leveling the ground, blasting tunnels, and building bridges and retaining walls. Accidents and death from exposure or disease were common, as laborers lived in close quarters in makeshift labor camps with inadequate nutrition, minimal supplies and poor medical care. Wages were dependent upon the amount of money the contractor obtained from the railroad company. It was not unusual for profit-driven contractors to hire double the number of hands necessary to complete a job to drive down individual wages and increase the pace of construction. Often treated as expendable, some Irish miners eventually resorted to violent labor riots on the rails, further fueling perceptions of the Irish as a drunken and disorderly group.

What is known for sure about James Samuel Brady is that he not only survived more than a dozen years of hardship and toil on the railroad, but proved worthy of becoming a contractor himself. He became associated with the company Ryan and Austin in the grading of two miles of the C&O railroad at Cotton Hill, Fayette County, before arriving with pick, mule and cart to engineer the final cut through the north end of "Inspiration Ridge" in Barboursville.

This happened in the late 1850s, right around the time that Mary Emaline Moore was living through her own set of harsh circumstances.

A Youth Tossed in Turmoil

Back in Cabell County, Mary's father Wilson Moore was a man on the rise in 1850. The stone wall in front of the courthouse was built under his direction, and he ran a store across Main Street between Center and Water streets. Mary's youngest brother, George Wilson Moore, was born in 1853, the same year their father was made the county's Deputy Sheriff.

Death seemed to hover over the extended Moore family. During the 1850s, Mary E.'s aunts, uncles and cousins succumbed to various fates. Although there are long gaps in Cabell County's death registry, a piece of Moore family information comes through a preserved letter from trusty correspondent Eliza Gardner Miller, written to daughter Eugenia in June 1852: "Fanny Moore died last night of consumption. Her brother Martin's death is expected every day of the same disease, which will be ten children Mrs. Moore has lost."

Judging by a comparison of 1850 and 1860 Census records, it is likely that disease also claimed young Mary's aunts Amacetta Everett and Sarah (Martin Junior's wife) and a young cousin also named Mary. What deadly ailments might have decimated Martin Moore's heirs? Several diseases were frequently cited in early Cabell County death records, particularly "consumption," scarlet fever, diphtheria and cholera. Most are illnesses that could be prevented today, or else quickly treated at the local urgent care center.

"Consumption" is an old term for tuberculosis (TB), which would waste away or "consume" its victims. TB is transmitted through the air by droplets from the throat and lungs of people with active disease. The symptoms include coughing, sometimes with sputum or blood, chest pains, weakness, weight loss, fever and night sweats. Other illnesses that took the lives of nineteenth century villagers have either been eradicated by vaccines, or prevented through what are now basic measures of hygiene. According to the World Health Organization, cholera is an acute bacterial intestinal infection caused by ingestion of contaminated food or water. It has a short incubation period, from less than one day to five days, and causes watery diarrhea and vomiting that can quickly lead to severe dehydration and death if treatment is not promptly given. Scarlet fever was once a very serious childhood disease. This disease is caused by the same bacteria associated with strep throat, and starts much the same way with sore throat and fever, but is distinguished by a "sandpapery" rash on the neck and chest that spreads over the body. Untreated, it can lead to the complication of rheumatic fever that can damage the heart and cause death.

Then there were the awful complications from minor childhood accidents. In 1853, Mary's 6-year-old cousin Samuel Everett Moore (Martin Junior's son) died from inflammation after his ankle was badly bruised from getting caught in the crack of the puncheon floor in one of the county's rustic schoolhouses.

If little Mary and her brothers were becoming aware of life's fragility, they were also getting acquainted with Barboursville farm life. In 1855, Wilson Moore purchased the Thomas Merritt farm at the east end of Main Street, including the weather-boarded log house where Mary would live out most of her days. The Moore acreage ran from the top of the hill at the present-day Orchard Hills golf course to Mud River, and comprised perhaps 200 acres. The sloping land was productive, the old house underwent improvements, and Wilson's mother, Mary Brown "Grandma Moore," moved into her own dwelling on the farm property. In April 1855, Mary's youngest sibling Eliza was born.

A Cabell County, West Virginia death record posted by the Church of Jesus Christ of Latter-day Saints, indicates that "Percilia Moore" died on December 14, 1856 at age 16. This seems to close the chapter on the life of the inherited black slave child "Priscilla," since the age progression jibes with both the last will and testament of Martin Moore and the 1850 Census slave schedule for the Wilson B. Moore household. Curiously, in the death record no race is given for the deceased Percilia, and Wilson B. Moore's name is entered after "Father's Name." There is no burial place, cause of death or mother's name indicated. This piece of evidence does not necessarily establish a biological relationship between Wilson and Percilia. It may suggest that during her short life Percilia was a close and cared-for member of this antebellum Barboursville household. In any case, nobody can know for sure if she and Mary Emaline shared a bond that could be described as "sisterly."

In 1857, as sectional tensions were growing between the town's abolitionists and slave-holders, Wilson B. Moore was promoted to Sheriff of Cabell County. Then in December 1858, when Mary Emaline was just seven years old, her mother died. As with other relatives, the cause of Mary Jane McCallister Moore's death is a mystery; she was just 31 years old. With Percilia gone, Mary Jane's death left Mary's father and elderly grandmother behind to raise five children.

Into the Fire—Savage Times for the Moore Men

In 1860, 41-year-old Cabell County Sheriff Wilson Moore had assets valued at $14,000, his three oldest children (including Mary) were attending school; his two youngest children spent their days at home on the east Main Street farm. According to the U.S. Census slave schedules, Moore owned another slave at that time, a 35-year old male of mixed race. Wilson's mother was 67-years-old, living on the farm and most likely rearing the children. As cited earlier, Wilson was already busy with slave-surveillance around the county, in addition to whatever normal Sheriff duties were still taking place, as Cabell County's social order dissolved into pre-war upheaval.

By the time Mary Emaline was about 11 years old, her father had taken up the Confederate cause, abandoned his role as Sheriff, and joined up as a private in Company E of the 8th Virginia Cavalry Regiment under General Jenkins. He was almost certainly in the defensive position at Fortification Hill when the Union Troops invaded. "Uncle Billy" Miller recalled that the old Moore log house across from the Courthouse as well as the Beuhring Hotel were torn down and "put into the fortifications on the hill." The village's women and children headed uphill from the Moore farm to the Blake place for protection. If young Mary's hair did indeed turn white with fright, as Brady lore puts forth, this would have been the logical time and place.

Wilson Moore gained certain notoriety for his actions during the Battle of Guyandotte in November 1862: After the ambush of the Proctorville boys and other Union recruits at Guyandotte, some who tried to swim across the Guyandotte River were shot at from the riverbank. Later, witnesses described the fate of a Yankee recruit who was attempting to swim across the river when the former sheriff of Cabell County told the youth that he could surrender and avoid being harmed. When the recruit reached shore, according to a witness, Wilson Moore aimed his revolver and discharged its contents into the young man's head, "literally blowing his brains out, mutilating his head in a shocking manner."

Throughout the war, Wilson was said to be involved in other regional skirmishes and was captured with two other Border Rangers, according to two Lambert sources. According to an account given years later by Mary's son Charles, the men were being conveyed up the Ohio to prison at Camp Chase in Wheeling by boat, "when the federal guards on the boat became intoxicated. Under the shades of night Moore and Reece tied a rope to Vaughn, who could not swim, and all jumped over-board. They swam ashore and made their escape." A letter from a Cabell County man named E. Walton to his daughter, dated April 3, 1864, corroborates the incident: "They caught W.B. Moore and Warren Reece and had them on a steamer, taking them to Wheeling. Nine miles below they jumped over-board and swam ashore and made their escape…A soldier was killed by someone near where they was taken and they was suspected for shooting him, and it is supposed that if they had not made their escape they would have been shot at Wheeling."

On April 28, 1864, just weeks after her father's daring river escape, Mary's little sister Eliza died. The cause of the nine-year-old's death is unknown as courthouse records of the time were lost. During the same year, as the Rebel cause was sinking into defeat, Wilson Moore was one of the 31 Confederate defendants sued in Cabell County for acts against the government, kidnapping, theft and destruction of neighbors' property. Mary Moore would have been about 13 when these things happened.

When Wilson Moore's Confederate service ended, he continued courting trouble. A man named P.H. Childers described an incident in December 1868:

(Wilson Moore) was a widower, and had a sweetheart over in Ohio, whom he visited, crossing the river at Dog Ham bar. A boy named West would ferry him over and back. There was a scandalous story got out about Moore and his girl, and Moore claimed that West had started the story. One Sunday he got his nephew, James Shelton, to go with him to the West home to settle the trouble. The boy, Stephen West, was not there at the time, but had gone, with the only gun in the place. Moore gave a beating, even an old woman *(sic)*, then he and Shelton went down on the river, and while they were gone, the boy with the gun came in. He set the gun at the door while he was looking around. Moore and Shelton rode up. Some words were passed. Moore threatened to come in; the boy said if he did he would stay in. Moore jumped from his horse and started to the house. West took up the gun; Moore drew his revolver and told him to "run, or I'll shoot." They were about twenty feet a-part, and both fired about the same time. Moore's shot struck near West in a log of the house. Moore turned back to the fence, and when he came to the fence he fell across it and dropped over the fence dead. West crossed over the river, but came back and surrendered. He was tried in the Circuit Court and was cleared. Moore's body was taken to his home, and an inquest was held, when it was found that six buck shot had pierced his heart. (Childers 2008)

There is a damaged obelisk monument in the Barboursville Cemetery where Wilson Moore was laid to rest. Each of the four sides of the marker is engraved with the name of a different family member, and Wilson's weather-beaten side of the stone faces east. Facing west, in clear lettering, is "Mary Jane, Wife of W.B. Moore." The side facing south reads in part, "Eliza, Dau. Of M.B. and M.J. Moore."

Monument in Barboursville Cemetery memorializes
four members of the Moore family
(Photo by the author)

The name on the fourth, north-facing, side of the obelisk is nearly impossible to make out with the naked eye, due to 14 decades of weather damage, but the date of death is easier to read, and it is a distinctive date—February 29, 1871. (Very weird, because Leap Days don't fall on odd-numbered years—a grieving family's mistake, or a conspiracy for the ages?) As fate would have it, a flip through the pages of a randomly-selected Lambert notebook uncovered another family tragedy.

John Thomas Moore, Mary Emaline's oldest brother, was a young man when he purchased the southeast corner lot at Main and Center from Joseph S. Miller for $200. On this lot was erected a "frame store house." That corner is where events began to unfold on the night of Tuesday, February 28, 1871:

BARBOURSVILLE NEWSPAPER ARTICLE MARCH 6, 1871.

HOMICIDE. KILLING OF JOHN THOMAS MOORE Last Tues. night between the hours of 12 and 1 o'clock, one of the most unprovoked and brutal murders was committed here that we have ever known.

The town was full of raftsmen from up the Guyandotte river and the noise and confusion early indicated that a large number of the party were bent on having a spree. On the same evening a party of negroes had rented the hall in Mr. J. Thomas Moore's new building for the purpose of having a ball. A party of raftsmen endeavored to force the door open and the negroes called on Mr. Moore to protect them. He appeared and told the white men to leave, that it was his property and he would defend it. Seeing his determination to do so they left and went to the Burnett House.

After the ball was over and all supposed the trouble ended, and as Mr. Moore was returning to the hotel where he was boarding, and while passing the sitting room door of the same, a young man by the name of Stratton, who it appears had been engaged in the disturbance up at the hall ran out and after exclaiming, "Here's the (damned) protector of the n—s" he ran up to him and plunged a knife into his right breast. A general melee ensued between some of the friends of Moore who were present, and two men who belonged to the party of timbermen were wounded by pistol balls. There were six or eight shots fired, two of which only, as far as we can learn, taking effect. Moore was carried into the parlor of the hotel where he died in less than five minutes. The wound was probed to the depth of five inches and the medical gentlemen who examined it said that it was made with a sharp pointed dirk-knife.

A coroner's jury was immediately impaneled from the information elicited, young Stratton was arrested and sent to jail, together with a man named Sellers. On the following day an examination was had before Squire Childers and Stratton was sent on for trial to the next term of the Circuit court here in

May and Sellers was released. A motion to give bail was refused and the prisoner was remanded back to jail. We withhold the testimony taken before the examining court as we deem it inexpedient to publish it at this time.

There was considerable excitement after the occurrence all over town and we have heard no one speak of the affair except to brand it as a most outrageous dastardly act. We have attempted in the foregoing to give the details of this melancholy affair in as fair and impartial manner as we are capable of doing. There are a great many rumors in regard to it, but from all we can learn the above statement is about as near correct as we can obtain. (F B. Lambert Collection n.d.)

OBITUARY. John Thomas Moore was the oldest son of W.B. Moore whose tragic death about two years ago will no doubt be remembered by many of our readers. The writer served several years in the Army with him and recalls many instances of disinterested acts of kindness during "the times that tried men's souls." In physique, general appearance and manners the son was the exact prototype of the father. Generous, kindhearted and brave, his untimely demise has cast an untimely gloom over the entire community that time alone can efface. Cut off in the springtime of life, he now sleeps in the cold embrace of death. The charmed circle is broken, another link is taken away and our ears will never more be gladdened by welcome sound of his footsteps. We miss the genial greeting of our friend and can hardly recall the fact that he has passed away.

Mr. Moore was born on the 11th of August 1846 and was consequently 24 years 6 months and 17 days old at the time of his death. He was to have been married the following week to an estimable young lady of this place, whose heart-felt grief over the body touched a sympathetic chord in the hearts of all.

Ere the star of his happiness had reached its zenith, in the full flush of manhood, he was called to another sphere, where no distinction can be known but all must appear on a common level. "Earth to earth, dust to dust" is the fiat of the Great Dispenser of all our destinies; then how very important it is that we should always be ready for that solemn event.

Rev. J. C. Crooks preached the funeral sermon at 1 o'clock last Thursday, and the body was then escorted to the grave by a large concourse of our citizens.

The occasion was one of deep solemnity and the bereaved family have the sympathies of our entire community. (F B. Lambert Collection n.d.)

Years later, a woman of Barboursville who would have been a young teenager in

1871 told Fred Lambert that the killer Stratton was from Logan and that he "went up for life." John Thomas Moore was preparing to marry Lucy Dundas when he was killed, and this witness remarked that Miss Dundas never married.

In the following decades, the lives of Mary's remaining two brothers would be cut short as well. Charles's death record of 1888 indicates murder as the cause of death. George Wilson Moore's date and cause of death remain unknown but turn-of-the-century Brady family history, as told to Fred Lambert, referred to Mary as the only surviving child of Wilson and Mary Jane Moore.

As of 1871, after the loss of her mother, sister, father and oldest brother, one would hope that Mary Emaline's Grandma Moore, well familiar with family loss, would have been a source of comfort to the young woman. (Frying Pan Farm matron Mary Brown Moore outlived all but one of her children and many of her grandchildren.) Of course, we'll never know just how Mary Emaline grieved, or exactly what year James Brady entered her life.

It is documented that the hardworking Irish railroad contractor James Brady had arrived to complete the C&O before the Civil War. A rare and precious nugget of Brady oral history was passed down to my Aunt Margie years ago by her great-aunt Valette Brady, who apparently heard it straight from her mother Mary E. Brady: the C&O line ran through the Moore property on the east end of Barboursville, Mr. Brady apparently took notice of young Miss Moore at some point, and the two began having conversations over the fence.

James S. Brady and Mary E. Moore were wed in October 1871 by the Rev. John C. Crooks, the same man, who preached her brother's John's funeral eight months earlier.

Land Deeds and Diapering Cloth

Even before James and Mary Brady were married, legal proceedings and settlements took place around the estate of her dead father. Complicated litigation and land transfers arising from the anti-Confederate lawsuit against Moore continued to shake out for years. After John was murdered his estate had to be settled as well. The heirs—Charles, Mary and George—inherited these and other family lands, and were named in several court decrees as both "party of the first part" and "party of the second part" as acreage was passed along. Assisted by such agents of the court as Thomas Thornburg, Thomas J. McComas and John B. Laidley, Mary and James became well-versed in the land business.

As the 1870s and 1880s unfolded, Mary gave birth to seven healthy children. During these years, with the same event-marking regularity as a late-twentieth-century family collecting "Precious Moments" figurines, the Bradys accumulated tracts of prime Cabell County land

In 1872, James and Mary's oldest son Charles M. Brady was born. The same year Mary and her brothers acquired the Wilson Moore property across from the courthouse. She then sold her share to brother Charles for $400.

In 1873, James, Mary and her brothers acquired over 300 acres of land on Trace Creek from the McCallister trustees (presumably an inheritance from her maternal grandparents), as well as the deed to their deceased brother John's corner lot on Main and Center.

Second son George Wilson Brady was born in 1874. That same year, James and his brother-in-law Charles purchased 255 acres along the Guyandotte River at Martha for $1,800 when local diarist William Dusenberry and his family went into bankruptcy. (This land included the present day Chaffin Estates.)

Oldest daughter Margaret M. Brady, known as Maggie, was born in June 1875, just weeks after Mary Brady and Charles Moore acquired 262 more acres between Martha and Barboursville on the Guyan River, purchased from John and Flora Witcher for $6,100.

Daughter Valette was born in 1879, and Mary acquired 29 acres on the Mud River from her brother Charles Moore.

The 1880 Census shows 39-year-old farmer James and Mary living on Main Street with four children. At age 7, Charles was attending school. Daughter Lucy was born in Oct 1881.

In 1882, Mary acquired acreage on the Guyan River from C.L. and Mary Roffe. Son James T. Brady was born in March of 1883, and youngest child Walter F. Brady was born in 1885. At some point, the family moved to the farm at Martha, and in 1890 James acquired 400 additional acres from the Roffe estate.

Town and Country Living

Nearly a century after the Brady marriage, *Barboursville Bulletin* correspondent Frank Ball talked about days gone by with their children Valette Brady, Walter Brady and Lucy Brady Conner. They told him about their father James loading the children into a wagon and heading for Barboursville in the 1890s so they could take advantage of better schools. Lucy recalled childhood days on the Martha farm, "of her father sliding sacks of grain and other produce down a chute into a boat anchored in the river, and then shoving off to Guyandotte markets. James Brady drove his livestock into Barboursville's C&O Depot where there was a stock pen, and loaded them into stock cars "for markets over east or downriver to Cincinnati or Louisville." Daughter Lucy also remembered the Logan County raftsmen floating into the Guyandotte raft boom with the spring raises when she was a child.

As the Brady children grew, the family seemed to split its time seasonally between the Main Street home place, the farmlands up at Martha and the "low bottom" fields along the Mud River. The Brady work ethic was in full flower but the children, in keeping with the times, veered away from full-time farming life in adulthood. Instead, the now-Senior James Brady tended the farmland and dabbled in the "business life" embraced by his sons.

Moore-Brady home on north side of east Main Street in the nineteenth century
(Courtesy of Marshall University Libraries Special Collections)

The Brady children tried their hands at different occupations. George W. Brady's career was especially well-documented; he was featured as one of Kanawha County "representative citizens" in a book published in 1911. According to his biography therein, James and Mary's second-oldest son "was reared on his father's farm three miles distant from Barboursville and attended the public schools and later the Morris Harvey College for two years." George was then associated with C. Davis in the meat business at Huntington, then took charge of a restaurant for H.O. Via. After three years as a clerk in a general store, he went back to the home farm for two years to help out. He accepted a clerkship in the McDonald Collier Company store until a mine strike caused the store to close, then served as a company store clerk at Powellton. In 1904, he purchased a business in partnership with F. B. Irwin, and in 1907 purchased Mr. Irwin's interest." Around age 40, George W. Brady Sr., "retired" to the large white frame house that still stands on Depot Street, with his wife the former Reba Sevy and three children. From then on, "Dude," as the sharp dresser was known, would manage the rental houses he owned, consult, and spend the days hobnobbing with other Barboursville gentlemen at the corner store—all the while keeping his career savings buried in jars in the family farmyard.

Valette, as a county schoolteacher, was the first Brady career woman. She would remain a "spinster," or unmarried woman, and lived at the Moore-Brady home place on Main Street until her death in 1972, at age 93. (Shortly thereafter, the husband of one of James and Mary's grandchildren sold the property to Sturm

Machinery—now owned by global firm Sulzer Metco—and heavy industry took the place of one of the village's first homes.)

Son James T. Brady began working in the 1890s for "old man Biederman's" store on the corner of Main and Depot street, as he made his way through Morris Harvey Academy. Shortly after the turn of century, "James Senior" and "James Junior" bought Mr. Biederman out, and the two Bradys continued the store, eventually moving their business to "downtown Barboursville." Over the decades, the younger James Brady would adjust his inventory to provide what villagers most needed, from shoes to dynamite to refrigerators to hardware. He married the daughter of Captain Drury Allen, made a pleasant family home on the second floor of the store building, doted on his children, gave them nicknames, and spent his autumn years in public service, helping oversee village and county affairs.

In the 1900 census, Mary E. Brady was listed as "farmer" and head of household, living with her three grown daughters at the Main Street place, while James S. Brady occupied the Guyandotte River farm in McComas district. On Census Day 1910, 72-year-old James was living on Main Street with Mary and three of the adult children. In addition to his involvement in his son's store, the old man served on the Board of Directors of the First National Bank in Barboursville.

"Hurled Into Eternity"

As Mrs. James Brady, Mary's adult years appear to have been filled with as much satisfaction as her youth was filled with distress. However, one more headline-making stunner was in store, when her Irish railroad-building husband was taken from this world at age 79:

AGED CITIZEN OF BARBOURSVILLE IS KILLED BY TRAIN. James Brady Sr., Hurled Into Eternity When Struck by F.F.V. Flyer. WAS ONE OF PIONEERS OF CABELL COUNTY. Failed to Notice Approach of Train Until Too Late to Save Himself.

James Brady Sr., aged 79, a pioneer citizen of Barboursville, and a man well known throughout the county, was struck by Chesapeake and Ohio F.F.V. train No. 2 at the depot in Barboursville yesterday evening about 5:30 o'clock and was hurled to instant death.

His head was crushed in, causing death and both of his limbs and his back were broken but his body was not mutilated to any extent. He was hurled into the air and his body knocked over one hundred feet, going thirty-feet into the air.

Mr. Brady, who had retired from active life, was going after his cows in a pasture across from the depot in Barboursville. A freight train was passing on the west-bound track and he was standing on the right rail of the east-bound track waiting to get across when the flyer suddenly slipped upon him from around the curve. Persons standing nearby yelled to him but he did not realize his danger until the engine was almost upon him. He could even then have escaped but instead of falling back, he apparently lost his self-control in the face of his impending danger and started to jump across the track and was struck by the engine and hurled to death.

His body was later removed to his home, only a short distance from the Barboursville depot. The funeral arrangements have not yet been announced.

Mr. Brady had been a resident of Barboursville for many years, having come to this county when the Chesapeake and Ohio railroad was built, he being a contractor on the construction of the line.
He was born in Ireland but came to America when a young man and made a success of all his undertakings. He was held in the highest esteem by all those who knew him and was beloved for his many fine and admirable traits of character.

He is survived by his wife and seven children, four sons and three daughters, among them James Brady Jr. well known merchant. One of his daughters, Mrs. Summers of Milton had just arrived at her home yesterday on a visit to her parents and was in a serious condition last night from the shock over the tragic death of her father. (Herald-Dispatch 1912)

In a short note published in the *Herald-Dispatch*, we finally get a hint of Mary's "voice," that of a gracious turn-of-the-century lady:

CARD OF THANKS. Barboursville, W.Va. May 13, 1912. We wish to extend our thanks to the good people, who remembered us in our hour of sorrow, through the death of our husband and father, and who so kindly aided us in various ways with thoughtful deeds and acts of kindness; also for the beautiful flowers that were so thoughtfully sent in. Respectfully, Mrs. J.S. Brady and Children (Herald-Dispatch 1912)

Mary passed away six years later at age 67. A tiny funeral notice in *Herald-Dispatch* mentioned that services would be held at her home, conducted by the Reverends Huddleston and Coffeeman. A few days later, the Barboursville community column in the *Huntington Advertiser* noted that "the funeral of Mrs. James Brady, Sr., was one of the largest ever held at this place."

Our Special Correspondent Furnishes an Interesting Letter:
DECEMBER 8, 1898—Brother W. W. Gardner, the colored minister,
closed his revival at the African Baptist Church last Sunday. He had great success.
Six souls converted, and a large attendance of white people.

CHAPTER 11

BEYOND THE SLAVE KITCHEN: BARBOURSVILLE'S AFRICAN AMERICAN FAMILY HISTORY

IN discovering the lost history of Barboursville, I came face to face with a bleak fact; that is, I am a documented descendant of slave owners, white people who owned black people as property. Countless offspring of Cabell County "men of influence"— Miller, Jenkins, Morris, Moore, Kilgore, Shelton, Wilson and Thornburg—had at least a great-great-great granddaddy who kept slaves.

Recognizing this irreversible shame, I decided the only suitable response was education. By helping to solve some family mysteries, my research might help reconnect somebody to a missing branch on a family tree. (That was my initial thinking, anyway.) At the same time, uncovering the history of local African American families could shine a new light on the "black experience" in Barboursville. Although Barboursville's African American neighbors made up a fairly small fraction of the total population, without them our history, and the village itself, would be something else altogether.

And so my search began. To better understand the role race played in "what made Barboursville Barboursville," I began by plotting the identities of African American individuals across 14 decades of county slave schedules, Census data and court records. Through these snapshots in time I identified more than 300 documented souls who inhabited the village at one time or another. Patterns emerged that replicate our nation's black history on a small scale, from the existence of "free persons of color" and slaves of the antebellum period, to records of black and "mulatto" residents of the late nineteenth century, to stories by and about the "negro" and "colored" residents of the early twentieth century.

What started out as my attempt to find family links between the Barboursville slaves and their post-emancipation counterparts quickly evolved. First of all, I discovered there is no such thing as "the black experience" in Barboursville, but rather a variety of experiences, each built on those who had come before. Not only did my fact-digging mission reveal something of Barboursville's particular nature as a community, it drove home one important fact: black history in Barboursville did not begin and end with slavery—not by a long shot.

Debunking the Slave Kitchen

As irony would have it, it is impossible to cook up this historic dish without leaving a broken eggshell or two.

Through the mist of time, the sole landmark touted as a relic of African American life in Barboursville is the awkwardly-named "Kuhn slave kitchen." This weathered, white-washed building on the Presbyterian church parking lot made its way into the historic walking tour and became one of the places that motivated me to write this book in the first place. There is just one thing – the kitchen has an identity problem.

At the risk of jeopardizing another historic Barboursville structure, one fact must be pointed out: it would have been impossible for the little building to house a slave kitchen serving the Kuhn family. It could have been a slave kitchen serving another family in pre-Civil War years, or could have been used by paid domestic servants after that period. It does sit on land once owned by James Kuhn. However, as observant readers of Chapter 9 may have already deduced, former Union Captain James Kuhn could not have owned slaves in Barboursville for the simple reason that he did not arrive in the village until 1872, several years after West Virginia's slaves were emancipated.

Furthermore, referring to "the Barboursville slaves" as a generic reference to all non-white villagers of the past misrepresents most of the African Americans who inhabited Barboursville during the nineteenth century. Although at least several dozen spent all or part of their lives providing domestic service to white families (either paid or unpaid), the "slave kitchen" does not fully symbolize the various doors of opportunity opened by African Americans in the village, both before and after emancipation.

Fortunately, at least one other Barboursville historic structure exists as a counterpoint to the "servants kitchen," and stands in silent tribute to the upward mobility of post-bellum black families—more on that later.

This recently-placed marker, while well-meaning, doesn't reveal the actual lives
of African Americans buried on current and former cemetery land.
Notice small stones in the background, some with the initial "S" that could
have symbolized "slave," but more likely stood for "Smith."
(Photo by the author)

Barboursville's "Free People of Color"

Going back to Cabell County's early decades, it's impossible to speculate how
living in a western Virginia river town alongside people like Marie Gardner, John
Laidley, William Clendenin Miller, or the German immigrants would shape the
worldview of a nineteenth century boy or girl; certainly they would have left an
impression. Similarly, growing up beside a national thoroughfare like the James
River and Kanawha Turnpike would have opened one's eyes to the great diversity
of American life. It follows, then, that contacts between white and black villagers
would have an indelible impact on members of both races.

Barboursville was certainly not immune to Virginia's prevailing racial attitudes and laws. Unlike eastern Virginia, however, people of the antebellum town were exposed to African Americans living in more varied circumstances: Enchained west-bound slaves forced to sing as they marched along the Midland Trail. The Ward and McComas plantation slaves working the soil near the Farmdale and Peyton roadways. Sampson Sanders's "family members" moving about independently and conducting business with local merchants; fiddler 'Babe' McCallister entertaining in front of McKendree's tavern; county slaves periodically sold off at the courthouse; the old family hand who shared folk wisdom with the young Miller sons. In addition to these examples, there were a few black men and women who were not "owned" by anyone.

Certain African Americans in Barboursville were designated in the Virginia tax rolls as "free persons of color." It turns out that hundreds of free black and multiracial men and women lived in Virginia and other southern states. They recently became the focus of genealogical research by Paul Heinegg and others, and their stories have produced a more complete understanding of the types of connections between free people of color and white citizens in the early 1800s.

Prior to the 1830s, when large plantations locked down most of the south as a "slave society," the legal line between freedom and slavery in Virginia was more permeable. Though most people of color were desperately poor, a few were able to build stable, even comfortable, lives based on connections with influential Caucasians. An African American's legal status and social standing could be determined by such things as an exemplary work record, parental origins (whether through coerced, casual, or long-term and loving interracial relationships), service for the Continental Army, or heroism on the wild frontier. Consequently, individual cases of manumission were commonly accepted in some Virginia communities.

The 1810 Cabell County tax list indicates a free Negro named Daniel Grimby. His whereabouts within the county's large land mass were not identified, and he remains "a mystery man of color." "Pegalis Margaret," the 60-year-old female who was included in the will of Jeremiah Ward, lived out her last years as a free woman with her own Barboursville home.

An early village property owner named Cuff (or Cuffy) Caldwell is particularly intriguing. Though little is known of his personal route to freedom, documents indicate Caldwell may have been freed by the Dundas siblings who came from Alexandria to settle in Barboursville and Blue Sulphur. A free man by the same name appears in Virginia tax lists of Augusta County in 1810, 1813 and 1814. Between the village's founding and 1818, at least four of the 38 lots laid out in the original town plan were deeded to Cuff Caldwell by William Merritt and other village trustees. The choice location of these lots (on the corners of Main and Center and nearby alleys) hint that Caldwell was a tradesman of sorts; Cicero

Fain's research cites that he was a carpenter. Deed records of 1822 show Solomon Thornburg sold half of Lot 16 to this "free man of color." In 1829 Caldwell died, and the same lot was deeded to Eliza Dundas.

Even after Richmond imposed racial constrictions in the 1830s, making it illegal to teach African Americans to read and prohibiting interracial "mixing," other slaves of the Barboursville area found freedom as a result of memorable episodes. Charles Love reported on the auctioning of a slave girl owned by a Colonel Simmons, after a courtship was detected between the young woman, named Eliza, and a white widower previously married into Simmons's family. The widower bought Eliza for $1,800 and then freed her.

There is also the historic puzzle of free couple Stephen and Annie Witcher, whose lives are glimpsed through tidbits of information that span several decades. Presumably the same man shot by his master (who was subsequently acquitted, as referenced in Chapter 4)—Stephen appears in the Appraisement Bill of Estate of Daniel Witcher as one of six slaves sold. The price on "male slave" Stephen was $400, less than the monetary value of younger male slaves, suggesting he was not in prime physical condition by that time, perhaps disabled by his gunshot wound. By the time of the 1860 Census, 60-year-old Stephen Witcher had gained his freedom and was living as a farmer just outside village limits along with 70-year-old "mulatto" Annie Witcher. Though neither could read nor write, Witcher's personal property was valued at $150. Ten years later, the 1870 Census enumerator found farm worker Witcher, 70, and Annie (then listed as age 90) sharing a household in town limits with another African American family, 38-year-old domestic servant Harriet Stewart and her three young children.

A reminiscence by Sampson Simmons, who would have been a young child in 1850, suggests Witcher became a free man well before Civil War times:

> Uncle Steve and Aunt Annie were two freed negroes who lived in Barboursville. He was a very large man, and she a very tiny woman. She baked ginger bread for sale, and also kept cider. We small boys were permitted to go to town on Court days and holidays with a few half dimes in our pockets to spend for ginger bread and cider at Aunt Annie's. (F. B. Lambert Collection n.d.)

The couple apparently lived long enough to become familiar personalities to several generations of white villagers. A Barboursville news item transcribed from the March 11, 1875 *Huntington Advertiser* describes a man who was most likely the 75-year-old Witcher, still alive but struggling with age and infirmity:

> BADLY BURNED—An old and crippled negro of this place, well known as "Old Uncle Stephen" got up at a late hour last night to fix the fire and attend to his invalid wife; and after he fixed the fire to his satisfaction, leaned himself

against the mantel piece to receive the benefit of the fire he had just lighted. The blaze being larger than he had expected caught hold of the tail of his shirt, and he, being old and stiff, could not extinguish it until it had burned the shirt off his back. The burn is very serious, and will be apt to go hard with the old man. He is, at this time, under the treatment of Dr. Beardsley, of this place. (F. B. Lambert Collection n.d.)

Aside from the Witchers, we find record of a free African American woman living in Barboursville in 1860. Twenty-one-year-old laundress Nancy Anderson and a one-year-old son named Edmund lived in town as well—making Barboursville home to at least four of 24 free Cabell Countians of color that year, with most of the others residing in Guyandotte.

"A Society with Slaves" in Virginia's "Slave Society"

Of course, the majority of African American villagers never experienced freedom until at least 1863— 1865 if they were still living in the new state of West Virginia.

Studies by local historians Carrie Eldridge (who researched the Sanders slaves), Karen Nance (the Jenkins slaves) and Cicero Fain (post-bellum Huntington) make the case that mid-nineteenth century Cabell County was clearly a "society with slaves"—being one in which slaves were present, but not central to the overall economy of the region—as opposed to the "slave society" typified by the plantation economies of eastern Virginia and the Deep South. As such, there were a range of management practices among the county's slave-holding families, with the extremes of physical violence and sexual coercion uncovered at the Jenkins plantation on one end, and the extraordinary manumission of the Sanders slaves at the other. As Fain points out, a relatively "loose structure of the institution" in Cabell County between 1840 and the late 1850s provided a number of slaves with the opportunity to socialize, worship and even travel independently.

Still, for some of the region's enslaved people in the 1850s, sanctuary beckoned from nearby Ohio. Free communities in Lawrence County were within a few hours' reach on foot and over water. These included both Burlington and "Quaker Bottom" (as modern-day Proctorville was known) where fugitive slaves were aided along the Underground Railroad. Following John Brown's 1859 raid on Harper's Ferry, slaves from the Cornwellsy Simmons and Charles K. Morris farms south of Barboursville tried to escape several times. Morris was concerned enough about further runaway attempts that he relocated his family and all his slaves to Wytheville, Virginia.

With the onset of the Civil War, Virginia's able-bodied Confederate sympathizers (including slave patrollers like my star-crossed ancestor Wilson Moore)

were called away into the rebel army, providing the more daring slaves with opportunities to flee. During 1861, northern cities such as Louisville, Cincinnati and
Pittsburgh experienced exponential growth in their African American populations.

Back in Barboursville town limits, the situation may have been a bit different. By
1860, William Clendenin Miller, John Samuels, Wilson Moore, John Thornburg
and Thomas Thornburg were the only documented slaveholders in the village, and
each owned no more than two adult workers. Among these five households (all
located on Main or Water streets) lived a total of four African American men ages
26 to 35, three female slaves from 17 to 60 years old, 8-year-old Priscilla/Percilia in
the Moore household, and four infants age three and younger.

At least a few of these individuals may have stayed put in Barboursville until
war's end, if J.W. Miller's account is a valid indication:

> I never witnessed any of the cruelties Harriett Beecher Stowe tells us about
> in Uncle Tom's Cabin. The slaves were respected and honored by all regard-
> less of the station they occupied in life. They received their freedom with full
> honor; they helped to carve this country out of a wilderness and no man can
> say aught against them. I call to mind a Negro man my father raised from a
> small orphan boy. When he received his freedom we were glad to know he was
> ready to take his place in the world. He was an expert cook, his first salary was
> eight dollars a month as steward on a steam boat, his wife was chamber maid
> at a good salary, and when he wrote me, "I have a son named after you and a
> daughter named after your sister," it pleased me to know he remembered old
> home folks. (J. Miller 1925)

A State in Limbo

As the Civil War ended, Cabell County's dwindling slave population was left in
a two-year state of legal limbo—living in a new Union state that was nevertheless
not free. Most of the remaining enslaved men, women and children had already
been separated from their blood relatives; now their masters (whether cruel or
"benevolent") were being sued, taken prisoner, or dying on distant battlefields.
What the African-American "lost villagers" decided to do after 1863, and where
they went, has largely remained a mystery.

We do know that the decade was marked by the wholesale out-migration of
African Americans. The new state was a legal no-man's-land; West Virginia had not
only been uniquely exempted from Lincoln's 1863 Emancipation Proclamation,
but the new legislature then passed a law to forbid the residency of any former slave
who entered the new state. Under the Willey Amendment to the constitution ratified on March 26, 1863, children born to slaves after July 4 of that year would be
free from birth. Any older West Virginia siblings, or slaves 10 and younger, would

have to wait until age 21 to be free. Slaves between 10 and 21 years old would be free when they turned 25, according to the revised West Virginia constitution.

While the Mountain State delayed the promise of emancipation for two years, the South's newly-freed population was already on the move, discovering both the possibilities and the limits of legal freedom. Large numbers of ex-slaves took to the southern roads after the war, looking for lost friends and relatives who had been sold away, and seeking opportunities to provide for themselves and their families. The federal Freedman's Bureau was formed by Congress, working with individuals and churches in both the north and south to teach African Americans how to read and write—a basic right that had been denied to them for decades, and which now gave them the ability to locate loved ones through the newspapers. Jubilation gave way to practicality as former slaves sought paying work, negotiated business contracts and strove for land ownership, "the ultimate key to inclusion in the new America."

The effects of post-Civil War policies and Southern Reconstruction were felt nationally. From the time of Lincoln's death, the nation's leaders had wrestled bitterly with the intermingled consequences of the South's physical destruction and the granting of new rights to former slaves. After passage of the Thirteenth Amendment, President Andrew Johnson (a southern Democrat) pardoned many of those who had been Confederate leaders. Republicans in Congress, many bent on further punishing the demoralized South, were outraged at the pardon and impeached President Johnson; he escaped removal from office by a single vote. Congress subsequently made changes to the Constitution, with the Fourteenth Amendment affirming that citizenship cannot be denied on account of race, and the Fifteenth Amendment granting African Americans the right to vote.

By the late 1860s, African Americans outside of the Mountain State began to enter political life at every level of society, a state of affairs that was simply beyond the comprehension of the old Southern establishment. Defying the new Constitutional guarantees, white southern Democrats responded with over-whelming violence, initially against Republicans of both races, but later focused exclusively on their black neighbors. The Ku Klux Klan emerged throughout the south by 1870.

Within just a few years, the efforts of Southern freedmen to gain a foothold in the post-war society were met with blatant racial hostility and increasingly restric-tive "Black Codes." By the 1870s, West Virginia would offer a somewhat more welcoming alternative to what became the effective re-enslavement of black share-croppers in the Deep South.

By 1867, a new day was dawning in the Mountain State. Black West Virginians younger than 21 years of age were provided with schooling in certain communi-ties (although not yet in Cabell County). Two counties away, a young man began attending a night school for former slaves. Early in life he had moved with his mother and siblings from Franklin County, Virginia. He began working alongside his stepfather in the Kanawha County salt furnaces and mines, his family living in impoverished conditions. He soon found work as a houseboy for a woman who taught him to read and write. After attending school in Malden, he made his way on foot to Virginia's Hampton Institute, graduated at the top of his class, then returned to West Virginia as a teacher. Later, he moved on to establish a school in Tuskegee, Alabama. Through his educational methods, writings, speeches and philanthropy, Booker T. Washington established himself as the most respected African American leader of the early twentieth century.

By 1868, African Americans in West Virginia still could not vote or serve on juries, but they had achieved such basic rights as being able to gather in public, and could leave the State and then return. They also had the same legal right to trial as whites, and could marry. James Johnson, a slave who had escaped his Wytheville owner and made his way to Guyandotte around 1860, wed Mary Wilson on April 4, 1866, in the first black marriage recorded in Cabell County. He later purchased acreage between Altizer and Barboursville on the Guyan River Road and raised a dozen children in "Johnson Hollow."

Post-Bellum: Who Remained?

Tracing the genealogy of African Americans born into slavery is beyond challenging. With the exception of "free persons of color," black men born before 1850 were not enumerated in the federal Census in the same way as white men; instead, they were tallied on personal property assessments in the same manner as livestock. In 1850 and 1860, enslaved African Americans were included in separate "slave schedules" that included approximate age, gender and color, but no names. Therefore, it is impossible to know just how many local slaves remained in Cabell County after they were emancipated.

Fortunately, some records exist that identify specific individuals and families.

The most noteworthy group had belonged to Charles K. Morris and Martha Kilgore Morris, the couple who inherited almost 2,000 acres of Sampson Sanders's homestead in the community that would be named in honor of said Martha (Sanders's niece). After the escape attempts and the specter of emancipation threatened their "property" in 1859, the Morrises had taken the family slaves and other belongings over the Blue Ridge mountains to Wytheville. After the war the Morris family returned to the McComas district of Cabell County, and a contingent of faithful former slaves accompanied them back "home."

For their loyalty and service, the African American Morris men (who, like many freedman, took the last name of their former owners) were provided employment and land, including George Morris whose property was valued at over $1,200, making him easily the wealthiest black man in the county in 1870. Melinda Morris Goode and her husband lived on 30 acres on Holland's Branch until they died and were buried, according to their wishes, alongside their former owners in the Morris family cemetery. Farm workers Samuel and Benjamin Morris headed large households in Barboursville in1870 and 1880, as did a former Kilgore slave who lived with Charles K. Morris for many years. Laborer John W. Kilgore is found in village Census records from 1880 to 1910, along with his wife Ada and several daughters who grew up in Barboursville. This former slave was described by Frank Ball as a noted jokester of the village, known for beginning sentences with "Nation and fire, Ada!"

Another "town character," Harrison Epps, was described as a "towering ex-slave who had to have specially built shoes to encase his huge feet." According to Frank Ball, Epps was "famous…for his laugh, the loudest and longest in Barboursville." In 1870, Harrison and Sophia Epps were farm and domestic servants living with Samuel Dusenberry in McComas district. In 1880, Epps lived with W.T. Thompson in town, and at age 54 was listed in the Census rolls as a servant.

A white neighbor of the Morris family on the Guyandotte River, dentist and diarist William Dusenberry from New York, the man whose family had purchased the mill and dam from the Sanders estate, commented on the 1869 travels of "Black William." In describing this man who traveled back and forth on the Ohio River as far as Cincinnati, Dusenberry often used a common racial epithet. In the same journals, however, Dusenberry mentioned that the former slave had been his overnight guest, bearing produce and gifts from his journeys to treat Dusenberry and other white families of the area. Fain cites the travels of "Black William" as an illustration that some of the county's free adult males had the resources, social contacts and acumen to successfully navigate their way around the region.

For women and children, however, this type of freewheeling exploration would have been much more difficult, if not impossible. It is my conjecture that some of these former village slaves did not leave or sever ties with Barboursville, at least not for several years.

I'll let the reader decide if the record supports my assumption, which is based on what I'll call the principle of "fuzzy post-bellum arithmetic." My amateur reasoning is based on the fact that many ex-slaves could only guess how old they were. Once black and "mulatto" citizens finally appeared by name in the 1870, 1880 and 1900 census schedules (the 1890 federal census records were unfortunately lost in a fire), either the census-takers were being careless, or else those born into slavery—including the scholarly Booker T. Washington—never knew their birthdates.

Taking into account this phenomenon and the fact that census schedules often provided "guesstimates" with respect to the ages of the newly-freed citizens, I think it is reasonable to overlook some age discrepancies across the decades—such as the fact that Barboursville's free woman Annie Witcher was shown to be age 70 in 1860's Census schedule, and 90 years old in 1870. Therefore, I surmise that a few Barboursville slave women or children of 1860 *may* have still lived with their former owners as of 1870. One possible scenario involves a motherless 3-year-old "mulatto" female living in the William C. Miller household in 1860; in 1870, 14-year-old Bettie Adams, also of mixed race, resides with the Millers. It is certainly within the realm of possibility that Virginia-born Bettie Adams remained with William and Eliza after emancipation.

Consider also the case of Patsy Dean. The 33-year-old "Patsey" Dean listed in the 1870 census headed a household in Barboursville's business district with five dollars in personal property and the following children: 2-year-old Annabella Dean, 8-year-old Susan Miller, 7-year-old Henry Wheatfield, 13-year-old Marcellis Miller and 16-year-old Frederick Wheatfield. The children were all identified as "mulatto," and were all born in West Virginia before emancipation. In the 1880 Census, Patsy is found (this time listed as age 40) keeping house in Barboursville. Annabella and the Miller and Wheatfield youngsters are no longer present, but there are three new children in the Dean household, 7-year-old Harvey, 5-year-old Gertrude and 2-year-old Clarence, as well as a boarder, 39-year-old barber Jesse Nelson of Kentucky.

Later newspaper accounts suggest that Patsy stayed in the village after living there as a slave, leading me to wonder if she had gained her freedom and then remained in town so she or the youngsters could be found by other freed kin. During those first free years, could Patsy have taken the "mulatto" Miller and Wheatfield children under her wing, settling in safe and familiar Barboursville until their parents could find them?

The following newspaper clips tell the rest of Patsy's story, revealing the poignant truth of a 60-year family separation:

> Mrs. Patsy Dean is an old colored woman at Barboursville. In 1839 she and her sister, who were both slaves in Virginia, were separated. They endeavored to ascertain each others (*sic*) whereabouts after the war, but were unsuccessful until within the past few weeks, when Mrs. Dean discovered her long lost sister at Middleport, Ohio. She is Mrs. Caroline Reloford, and will visit Mrs. Dean the coming week." (Cabell Record January 5, 1899)

Less than three months after the sisters' expected reunion, came these accounts in *The Cabell Record* and *The Huntington Advertiser*:

> "Patsy" Dean, a venerable colored woman, who was known far and wide, died

at Barboursville yesterday morning. She lived there when slavery was in existence. (Cabell Record March 30, 1899)

AUNT PATSY IS DEAD – AN AGED COLORED WOMAN OF BARBOURSVILLE BREATHES HER LAST YESTERDAY. Mrs. Patsy Dean, an aged colored woman, died at her home in Barboursville yesterday after an illness extending over a period of several weeks. Aunt Patsy, as she was familiarly known, was well liked and it is safe to say that she has nursed fully three-fourths of the white people of the ex county seat when they were children. Aunt Patsy's age was not known definitely, but she has frequently said that she remembered well when Andrew Jackson was first elected President of the United States. Judging from this she must have been at least eighty. Her remains were laid to rest at Barboursville cemetery this afternoon and a large part of the white population of the town turned out in honor of this good old woman. (Aunt Patsy is Dead 1899)

And what of the other women and children who appeared in the Barboursville census of 1870? Almost all of them lived in the homes of white families. There was 15-year-old Sallie Hamlin in the household of Judge Henry Jefferson Samuels; 15-year-old domestic servant "Catherine" (no last name) with the Blake family; 50-year-old Permilla Davis in the William Merritt household; domestic servant Lucinda Maghee living with two young daughters in the household of Irish railroad worker Anthony Buck and family; 15-year-old "Rosie," a domestic servant in the Charles K. Morris home; a 12-year-old boy, Clawence Price, living in the Albert Laidley home; and domestic servant Francis Price of Louisiana living with her 3-year-old son in the home of wealthy matron Ann Wilson.

On the face of it, the 1870 living situations of African Americans in the village seem little different from slavery days. With the possible exception of Clawence Price and Rosie Morris, none of the adults or older youth are shown as being able to read or write. All but Francis Price were born in either Virginia or West Virginia. Nearly all disappeared from public record a decade later. Only Lucinda Maghee (McGee) and her children appeared in the village Census by 1880.

Two particular households, however, seemed to foreshadow the change that was to come. The first inkling that Barboursville would become home to a new class of free African American "outsiders" was the arrival of two entrepreneurial men and their wives. Virginia-born Lewis Marshall, a 26-year-old barber, and Lucy Marshall, 30, of Kentucky shared a house with 39-year-old drayman Anderson Nelson of South Carolina and Jane Nelson of West Virginia. The second example was a "free-standing" household of four, 36-year-old railroad worker James and 23-year-old Matilda Boice, both of North Carolina, along with their daughters, 4-year-old Mary L. Boice, born in North Carolina, and 2-year old Anna, born in

Tennessee. In all three families, the wives were "keeping house" rather than working for other households. At some point, these families also moved on; with the lone exception of Lewis Marshall, none of the six appear in Barboursville census records after 1870.

Outside of the two "independent" black households, African American life in Barboursville of 1870 appears to be practically unchanged from antebellum times—except for the near absence of adult males. A handful of white families either housed live-in servants or otherwise "took in" black women and children. The community was not yet providing formal education for these "colored" youth (at least not as documented in village records). As with the rest of the South, local evidence suggests an unsettled decade for most of the village's freed black residents.

New Citizens Migrate to Cabell County

The post-war arrival of "new" African Americans in some ways paralleled the journeys taken by William Merritt and other early settlers of the Appalachian region: the man of the family would make a solo exploratory trip on foot or horseback, evaluate the suitability of a prospective locale, and then return to retrieve family or friends (sometimes sending for them through a third party instead). Leaving their known communities would likewise expose the freedmen to difficulties and dangers, but instead of the wild animals and hostile native tribes of old, there was now the harsh reality of racism in new environments (even the storied "promised land" of Ohio).

After the passage of the Flick Amendment, removal of the Confederate test oath, and the ratification of Fifteenth Amendment— black males in West Virginia were political enfranchised for the first time ever, just as white male Democrats were regaining their voting rights after several bitter years on the outs. Some Ku Klux Klan activity is known to have taken place around West Virginia (including some parts of Cabell County) from 1867-70, not only to keep blacks from voting but to ensure that ex-Confederates *could* vote. On the whole, political attempts to prevent African Americans from voting in West Virginia were marginal at best.

Fourteen Cabell County men of color (26 percent of the total black voting population), took part in the 1870 state election. Dusenberry's diary noted great excitement among former slaves near Barboursville on that election day. Not everyone shared their enthusiasm. In the area around Ousley's Gap between Barboursville and Salt Rock, the sight of an African American man casting his vote allegedly caused a white Democrat to voice his disgust, saddling that hill along McComas road with a derogatory racial nickname that has hung on among locals for over a century. The name "N— Hill" has hung on, no doubt inspiring a variety of rumors involving the lynching of an unknown black man. The election day origin story, having been described by members of the prominent Swann family and recorded by old faithful Fred Lambert, seems most credible.

Just as freedom's promise was materializing for some of West Virginia's new citizens, out-of-control violence was seriously undermining the rights of African Americans throughout the old Confederacy. Martial law was declared for a time in sections of the Deep South to protect Republicans and freedman from the KKK and Confederate veteran "rifle clubs," who were determined to turn back the clock on Reconstruction. Despite civil rights legislation passed in Congress, black men in the South (who actually comprised voting majorities in five states in 1867) continued to lose access to the polls through extreme intimidation. Many who had been elected by their brethren to state and local offices were expelled or flagrantly murdered. White Republican sympathy for the "plight of the Negro" began to wane by the mid-1870s. When the Freedmen's Savings and Trust Company, chartered by the Federal government to teach former slaves the value of thrift, failed in 1874 Congress did nothing to bail out the stricken depositors.

There was a precise endpoint to Reconstruction; Southern whites referred to it as "the Redemption." After the disputed presidential election of 1876, a political bargain known as the Compromise of 1877 was made between the Republican Party of candidate Rutherford B. Hayes and the Democratic Party (whose nominee was a northerner, Samuel Tilden). In essence, Hayes made a number of concessions to Southern Democrats in exchange for gaining the White House. As part of the deal, Hayes agreed to remove all Federal troops from southern states, essentially abandoning the cause of freed slaves and leaving vengeful white southerners to make and enforce their own rules. From then on, a systematic campaign of intimidation, terror, segregation and fraud—including various state and local statutes known as "Jim Crow" laws—undermined the Constitutional rights granted to ex-slaves after the war. This trend continued well into the twentieth century.

As early civil rights leader W.E.B. Du Bois put it, "The slave went free; stood a brief moment in the sun; then moved back again toward slavery."

In contrast, Cabell County, though not always the sunniest racial environment, was at least shaping up as a place of comparative tranquility for the newcomers. Though the majority of railroad laborers were still white immigrants, ex-slaves were already beginning to abandon the eastern Virginia farms and plantations for the opportunity to earn good wages, and in some cases respect for their skills and hard work, building the C&O railway. Soon, the new city of Huntington would attract men like itinerant preacher Nelson Barnett, who spread the word to his people in Buckingham County that honest work could be found at the western end of the line. As Cabell County (especially Huntington) continued to grow, so did the proportion of African American residents. The county's black population reached 6.5 percent of the general population by 1880, a seven-fold increase over 1870.

In Barboursville's census district, a full 6.1 percent of the enumerated population was African American in June 1880. By my tally, there were exactly 100 black and "mulatto" inhabitants in the district—all the easier for my fellow eggheads to draw a mind's-eye pie chart using the following *italicized* numbers: *Nineteen* men between the ages of 16 and 35 were railroad employees boarding at two different buildings or encampments. *Two* black males were among the seven prisoners housed at the Cabell County jail. In contrast to 1870, just *four* adults (Rose Godby, Hester Robinson, William Gibb and Harrison Epps) were living as servants within white households (the Samuels, Shipe, Thompson and Thornburg families). The remaining *75* African Americans—including *44* children and youth under 18— lived in 14 different single-family dwellings sprinkled throughout the village.

African American heads of household (and their wives) who settled in the district between 1870 and 1880 included: farmer Phillip (and Lucy) Brown of Louisiana; laborer George (and Clara) Grover of Kentucky; hotel cook Taylor (and Mattie) Fliggins of Virginia: farmer David (and Celia) Hamler of West Virginia; laborer John (and Amanda) Kilgore of West Virginia; housekeeper Harriet Norris of Virginia; housekeeper Fannie Payton of West Virginia; "washer woman" Adeline Pullins of Virginia; railroad employee Marshall (and Annie) Scott of Virginia; and farmer Charles (and Fannie) Simmons of West Virginia Four households—those of single housekeepers Patsy Dean and Lucinda McGee, farmer Benjamin (and wife Mahala) Morris, and railroad employee Lewis Marshall—were headed by adults who had also been village residents in 1870. With the loss of the 1890 federal census schedules, it is not known how long most of these families stayed in Barboursville, much less what kind of treatment they encountered while living in the village.

Though most were lost to public record after 1880, some evidently found the village a suitable place to live for several decades. Few, however, had greater longevity in the village than Martha Banks Fliggins.

The Arrival of Mrs. Mattie Fliggins

Once passenger service was introduced on the C&O, the route from Huntington to Clifton Forge began to transform nondescript stations along the way into places of discovery for black migrants hopping off to purchase food and sundries, or to seek out jobs or acquaintances. The more accommodating stops along the rail line became, in the words of historian Cicero Fain called, "hubs on the collective black migrant network."

Newlyweds Taylor and Mattie Fliggins could not have picked a better day to get their first impression of Barboursville. They arrived in the village from Huntington (the place where they met), on the very first passenger train to come through on the new C&O tracks, as Mattie later told William C. Estler. That Sunday morning, the two stepped down from the train just as "a great celebration" was going on in connection with the new railroad service. They decided to take their combined savings and settle in the village, purchasing "a little place facing what is now Main Street" for $500. Mr. Fliggins found a job as a cook with the Blume Hotel.

In a *Herald-Advertiser* article published a few years before her death, "Aunt Mattie" told the story of her life to Mr. Estler. Described as "remarkably well-preserved, devout, soothsayer to the troubled and possessor of much homely wisdom," Mrs. Fliggins demonstrated a detailed memory of her early years.

Born July 24, 1839, Martha Banks was the daughter of Washington and Adeline Banks, and property of plantation owner Clayton Caldwell of Craig County, Virginia. A slave until age 25, Mattie was a young child when her father was sold to what she called a "N— trader who took him away to Alabama." Yet she recalled her owner as "one of the greatest men she has ever known," and described some bright moments in the Caldwell slave cabins, built "town-wise along a 'street' not far from the big house."

High spots in the lives of slaves came during homecomings or at Christmastime. During Christmas week the festivities reached great heights with dancing from late in the evening to early in the morning. As a reward for trustworthiness, fine work and obedience, slaves were all permitted to attend dances during the festive week. Aunt Mattie's uncles, Uncle Dick, Uncle Jerry and Uncle Harry played the violin, harmonica and banjo for dancing. Dancing would last until 4 o'clock in the morning when the exhausted parties would return in the early faint-grey of dawn to their cabins, knowing they would not be required to work hard during Christmas week. The white folks would be present too, adding their shouts at times to the merrymaking.

But amid the fun and gay times, for the disobedient slaves there would be no present from Santa. If the slave had too many marks against him, he was not given a pass to the dance. If he would even try to go to the dance, he would be prey for the patrollers. Aunt Mattie said that patrollers were bands of white men appointed by the state or county government that sent incorrigibles and disobedient ones to the whipping post. Mr. Caldwell never sent a slave of his to the whipping post although several were caught by patrollers according to Aunt Mattie. (Estler 1935)

In her early teens she was chosen as personal servant to Miss Harriet Caldwell, the "young mistress of the house" who was three years younger than Mattie. After the end of the Civil War, of which Mattie said she had only a "vague impression," she continued to serve Miss Caldwell, caring for her dresses and accompanying her on trips, and was a trusted confidant. When Harriet became the bride of "young blue-blood" Andrew Hannah, Mattie accompanied the couple on their wedding trip to Canada, where the former slave saw the greatest body of water she had ever seen and felt the wind from Lake Erie.

After three months in Canada, the Hannahs came through Huntington on their return trip, and were so impressed with the thriving railroad center that they stayed a while. Andrew set up a general store on Third Avenue near Ninth Street, where Mattie helped out until she met a young man her age from Wytheville who worked in the C&O roundhouse. Taylor Fliggins was "of steady nature and thrifty," and he and Martha Banks were married on March 4, 1875 by J. D. McClintock. The Hannahs returned to Virginia and the Fligginses relocated to Barboursville where they began to raise a family.

Her childbearing years must have been a heartrending phase of life for Fliggins. Between Census and vital statistics records, I identified names of children born to Mattie and Taylor Fliggins: Two boys, Meshak (born around 1884) and Richard (born around 1885), appear in the 1900 Census as teenagers. A son Henry was born around 1886 and died before age 5 of whooping cough. A daughter Fannie was born in 1888; she died at 8 months, also of whooping cough. The Estler article says Mattie gave birth to a total of seven children, several lost in childhood due to the fact that they were "jest porely," and one child accidentally killed when a neighbor's child turned a chair over it, crushing its skull.

The Fliggins family moved to Dayton for a short period in the early twentieth century, where they kept a hotel until another family tragedy, this one of an ominous nature, soured their view of that Ohio city. One morning they searched and then found the body of son Emory Mishack (called "Mish") in a canal after he had been carrying a large sum of money. In Mattie's words, "Well, nobody knows just what happened." The only Fliggins child to outlive his mother was Ervin, born before 1890; he lived close to his mother in Barboursville, and died in 1942 of a heart ailment. Whatever happened to her husband Taylor and how long he lived is not known; he last appears as a hotel cook in the 1900 Barboursville census.

Aunt Mattie made up for her losses by raising eight children other than her own. Two months ago she took the ninth, a curly-headed little (boy), fat and healthy. Today he sleeps in a great basket a safe distance from the fire in her hearth, well fed, happy and with plenty of kick in his feet...Aunt Mattie adopted Annabelle McDonald, the most talented of her family, when she was three years old. Annabelle lived with Aunt Mattie until she was 25, is married and now lives in Elkhorn. Julia Harris came from North Carolina to Aunt Mattie when she was four years old and still lives in Barboursville, in her early twenties. One of the adopted children died. Nora Belle Banks, who she raised from the age of two to the age of 16, the time of her death. Mary Davis came to Aunt Mattie at the age of ten; she married and now lives in Ashland. Ollie Banks was the child of a cousin in distress who came to her charge, then came Maggie Walker, Myrtle Ellen and a number of others. The new baby has been named John Wesley… (Estler 1935)

As Mattie grew older, she not only became a surrogate mother to African American orphans, but a trusted matriarch of sorts to Barboursville's upper class. Estler wrote of folk wisdom, mysterious old-time curatives, and huge dinners given for the "white folk of the town," in which "she set a fine board and waited on her friends, piling the table full of the best things imaginable."

The Thornburgs and many other prominent people of the community were present. In her prime she was caterer to all large company dinners on holiday occasions. No wedding could go over properly without her supervision. When a house full of company was expected, Aunt Mattie was called to take over the kitchen and no guest left with appetite unsatisfied.

Mrs. E. E. Spencer, now president of the Barboursville Woman's Club, remembers when Aunt Mattie used to humor her and her sister (they were the Misses Bess and Dolly Miller). Often they left the home of their father, William G. "Uncle Billy" Miller and went to Aunt Mattie's on Saturday nights when the moon was right where she would wash their hair "to make it grow and keep from splitting." Then she would cut out a bit from the nape, whisper a charm, and give them the lock and a magic potion which they would carry to Tanyard branch, a winding creek in the hollow, to put under a secret rock for the voodoos to eat. (Estler 1935)

Census records of 1900, 1910 and 1920 indicate that Mattie took on a succession of jobs in her autumn years—including midwife, wash woman, and as a domestic servant living in the household of Captain Drury Allen. By 1930, Mattie had mostly retired to the home she owned on the alley behind the current Masonic lodge. There she became remembered among townsfolk (a few yet living in 2012) for dispensing stories and old-fashioned remedies from her stoop. According to Estler, the elderly woman kept a cow and "many, many dogs—small and well groomed which she keeps in a little village of kennels behind her house."

This lifelike image of Mattie Fliggins was drawn in 1935 by
Herald-Advertiser staff artist Irvin Dugan.
(Courtesy of Huntington Public Library)

Current nonagenarian Anne Turman, or "Happy Brady" as she's known to relatives, is the daughter of store-owner James T. Brady and granddaughter of both Captain Allen and James S. Brady. She vividly remembers "Aunt Mattie."

"She would take in young girls, black girls that needed help, you know, and helped 'em a whole lot.

"She lived in a little wooden hut along in there. She did our laundry here. Of course, Uncle Edley Allen had the laundry and mom always sent the sheets there," she said in a recent interview. "We had the first washing machine, I think, in Barboursville and it had a ringer on it. And my dad said, 'I don't want to hear of the kids being around that – they'd catch their arms in it.' So my mother never used that washer. She sent the sheets to the laundry and Aunt Mattie carried, in a basket, our clothes down to the alley. She always washed them and brought them back," said Mrs. Turman.

Gladys Carter of Huntington could legitimately call Mrs. Fliggins "Aunt Mattie," as one of her biological great-nieces in Barboursville, and shared vivid memories of the older woman: "From my understanding even back then, she was a very sweet person…and she took in children. I guess you would say they were orphans, because I remember this one was named Julia…seems like to me, Julia had a brother, his name was R.T. And she raised him to a certain age. They left here finally, and I know Julia went to California."

Mrs. Carter shared a specific recollection of sitting with Aunt Mattie before she died. "She had a swing on her porch, and you could look down the alley (to Main Street where Gladys lived). Aunt Mattie was sick, and Martha and I—Martha was probably about 12 and I was about 8— we went down there to check on her, but then it was kind of dark (inside) and Aunt Mattie was sick. She would be in bed and we would go in and check on her, then we would go back out and sit on the porch and swing. If we would see Mom or Dad either one coming, we would scramble to get back in the house. It's funny now, but back then we was kids…kind of I guess (scared) by her being sick and everything—we would go in and sit with her a little while, then we would say 'lets go back out on the porch.'"

Mattie Fliggins died October 16, 1938. Her funeral was at the Methodist Episcopal Church, South, where her body laid in state before burial in the Barboursville cemetery. She left behind son Ervin, a grandchild, her niece Octavia Sorrell, and the Sorrell descendents.

Before her heart finally gave out at age 99, Martha Banks Fliggins offered Estler this explanation for her advanced age: "It takes some folks a heap o' time to get ripe enough to get in God's storehouse."

"Moments in Early Negro Education"

The education of Barboursville's African Americans before 1900 is a subject that offers far more questions than answers. Preserved records of the Barboursville school district are, for all practical purposes, devoid of information about the education of "colored" pupils. Biographical writings and African American histories of the region are barely more helpful, citing only scant mentions of Barboursville. Within this shadowy realm, in the way one person's offhanded comment becomes another's piece of informational treasure, a few references shed some much-needed light.

Huntington's esteemed Carter G. Woodson (founder of Black History Month), and his professional peers worked diligently to assemble a satisfactory history of *Early Negro Education in West Virginia* in 1921, and were themselves frustrated by the fact that "only meager information" could be obtained through state and county records. Relying heavily on personal questionnaires and interviews, Woodson's study provided important facts about the quest for education in cities and towns across West Virginia. The book contains two mentions of Barboursville.

Early Negro Education in West Virginia explains pre-emancipation trends in the schooling of western Virginia slaves, and follows the trail blazed through sections of West Virginia by "benevolent white friends" who worked to teach groups of the newly freed. These friends included Union soldiers, missionary teachers, Freedman's Bureau workers and others. While they may not have all brought with them the highest instructional methods, Woodson gave them credit for providing something even more important: "inspiration which set the whole body of Negroes

BEYOND THE SLAVE KITCHEN: BARBOURSVILLE'S AFRICAN AMERICAN FAMILY HISTORY   217

throughout the State thinking and working to secure for themselves every facility for education vouchsafed to the most favorite element of our population."

Like other less industrialized areas, Cabell County trailed behind Kanawha and other northern counties in founding black schools, which relied quite literally on a critical mass of pupils. By 1867, West Virginia counties such as Cabell were just beginning to organize their white public schools, and compulsory education was still more than 20 years away. Through the urging of the State Superintendent of Public Instruction, a succession of laws were passed to address the schooling of black children. These laws spelled out exactly how many pupils were required in a district to establish and keep a "Negro" school open:

> In 1866…the legislature enacted a law providing for the establishing of public schools for Negroes between the ages of six and twenty-one years. These schools had to maintain an average attendance of sixteen pupils or be closed. As Negro communities were not very large and the number of children were small, many Negro children scattered throughout the State were denied the opportunity to acquire an education. This law, therefore, was amended in 1867 so as to authorize local boards of education to establish a school whenever there were more than fifteen Negro children between the ages of six and twenty-one. The attitude of the State was that of separation of the two races in the schools, but the first two laws bearing on Negro schools did not make this point clear. Upon revising the constitution in 1872, however, it was specifically provided that whites and blacks should not be taught in the same school. Thereafter, however, the whites and blacks sometimes used the same school houses. As the school term consisted of only four months of twenty-two days each, the whites would open school in September and vacate by Christmas, when the Negroes would take charge. No further changes were made in the school law until 1899, when it was further amended to the effect that the trustees in certain districts should establish one or more primary schools for Negroes between the ages of six and twenty-one years and that these officials should establish such Negro schools whenever there were at least ten Negro pupils resident therein, or for a smaller number, if possible. (Woodson 1921)

Against this legal backdrop (and with a nod to Public Broadcasting's Henry Louis Gates Jr.), I offer three fragments of information discovered along the bumpy and foggy road to progress, "Barboursville Moments in Early Negro Education."

Moment #1: Future Speaker Tests Future Preacher. Educational opportunity in West Virginia followed as a result of employment on the Chesapeake and Ohio Railroad, according to Woodson. Sometime after the 1867 formation of a school in Point Pleasant (with funding from the Freedman's Bureau), he added, "Negro schools developed in Cabell County, the first and most important being in Guyandotte and Barboursville. Rev. I. V. Bryant began the first school in

Guyandotte in 1873, after qualifying for the service in an examination conducted at Barboursville by the late Champ Clark, who at that time was President of Marshall College in Huntington."

That single Barboursville citation by Carter G. Woodson provides the first of our three Lost Village moments. The teacher's examination itself was not such a big deal, as there was a great need for adults willing to do the job. Former superintendent Fred Lambert explained how easy it was back then for someone to get a license by taking a nominal examination: "Conducting these examinations the County Superintendent would sometimes meet the applicant on the road, give him a few oral questions, fill out his certificate, collect the fee, and deliver it at once."

In this case, for whatever reason, the superintendent of Barboursville township schools did not interact with the black teaching candidate. The Marshall College president who did administer the test was a young white man, 24-year-old James Beauchamp Clark, whose name means little these days unless you're obsessive enough to Google it. It turns out that soon after the Barboursville examination, "Champ" Clark left Marshall to receive his law degree in Cincinnati, relocated to Missouri, and was elected to Congress. He served as the Democratic Speaker of the U.S. House of Representatives from 1911 to 1919.

The young man taking the examination was Isaac Vinton Bryant of Lawrence County, Ohio, just 17 years old at the time. Four years later, "I. V." Bryant would be licensed to preach, becoming one of Huntington's preeminent black pastors and community leaders, on a par in his day with Reverend Nelson Barnett. The same year he was certified by Champ Clark to become a Cabell County teacher, young I. V. Bryant established a school for black students in a cabin in between the towns of Guyandotte and Huntington. At that time, the black population was small enough that the two towns, still separate municipalities, had to cooperate to meet the numbers required to keep the school open. Not long after, the Huntington city council would approve a new Negro school in a nicer donated building.

I. V. Bryant served as an important aspirational role model for late-nineteenth century black citizens of the county. Throughout his life, I. V. Bryant articulated two urgent needs of black people: "A well-rounded Christian education and the ownership of property. If these things could be achieved, black people could compete with white people in a predominantly white society."

Perhaps not surprisingly, I found neither Bryant nor a "negro school" in Barbourville district records of the time. Nevertheless, it must have operated at some point in the 1870s—who am I to question Carter G. Woodson, a man represented by his own life-size Huntington statue, the Father of Black History Month?

Moment #2: Algeo's Complaint. Whatever "Negro school" may have existed in Barboursville in the early 1870s, keeping it going in the early years must have presented an irksome challenge, as voiced by a local educational reformer in 1875.

William Algeo (pronounced "Al-Joe"), a white man, was an early Cabell County abolitionist, teacher and postmaster, as well as superintendent of schools in Cabell County at that time. In our second "moment in Negro Education," a cryptic statement attributed to Algeo hints at shifty doings by the local establishment.

One of the Lambert notebooks contained the following entry: with two colored schools in 1875 in Guyandotte and Huntington, Mr. Algeo "complains of injustices of law requiring 25 pupils for colored school, when only 10 often compose a white school. Got the negroes to move near Barboursville, and promised them a school, but the law changed, and he was accused of misrepresenting facts."

Year	White Total	"Colored" Total
1867	432	6
1868	415	8
1869	408	11
1871	330	0
1873	387	0
1874	378	0
1875	412	0
1876	433	0
1877	443	6
1878	437	9
1882	370	108

An 1863-1883 *Record Book of Free Schools, Barboursville Township*, donated to Marshall University's Special Collections department, does nothing to clear up the matter. The Record Book does verify that Algeo was the elected superintendent. It also contains "Reports of School Commissioners on Enumeration of Youth" for 11 different years following West Virginia statehood; these records show the number of male, female, white and "colored" youth counted in township sub-districts. (These figures probably did not include tuition-paying village families, who at first shunned the very idea of free schools.) In any case, the figures from Merritt's record book seem to indicate a complete absence of African American youth in the district between the years 1871 and 1876. In the view of a reformer like William Algeo, it is a rather discouraging set of numbers—until the reader skips forward to 1882.

Moment #3: "Leading Colored School in Barboursville." Both the census and school board enumeration reports indicate sudden and explosive growth of the "negro" population in the Barboursville district between 1878 and 1882. During that same period, state law reduced the number of children required for a black school in a community to 15, and the court system helped broaden educational opportunity in areas where local school boards were intransigent. Thus opens the curtain on our third "moment," comes by way of Theodore Wilson, another black educator from across the Ohio River.

Like I. V. Bryant before him, Theodore Wilson represented two significant trends identified by Carter Woodson—African Americans who came to West Virginia from other states to teach, and black preachers who doubled as schoolteachers:

> From Ohio…came as many (West Virginia teachers) as were obtained from both Virginia and Maryland. Although the Negroes were early permitted to attend school in Ohio, race prejudice had not sufficiently diminished to permit them to instruct white persons in white schools. Looking out for a new field, their eyes quickly fell on the waiting harvest across the river in West Virginia. These workers from adjacent States, moreover, served the people not only as teachers but also as ministers of the gospel. They were largely instrumental in establishing practically all the (black) Methodist and Baptist churches in the State, and while they taught school during the week, they inspired and edified their congregation on Sunday. (Woodson 1921)

Theodore Wilson's family biographer wrote that, in 1884, "one of the leading colored schools of Cabell County, West Virginia, at that time was located at Barboursville and (Theodore) Wilson taught there for a while." Again, I found no village or township sources referring to this Mr. Wilson. However, a series of articles in *The Ironton Tribune* in 1938 not only cited the school, but also referred to three prominent men of Barboursville who were associated with Wilson and his family.

Theodore's father was known early in life as "George Beuhring." As an eight-year-old, the man who would take the name George Wilson was sold to Frederick Beuhring, the "Son of 1791," after he purchased the big farm on the Ohio River (now part of downtown Huntington). The biographer wrote:

> Mr. Beuhring must have been a farsighted businessman, and perhaps a more humane one too than the average slaveholder of his day…he permitted Mr. Wilson to have some time to work for himself and even permitted him to receive pay for his labor for others. In this way Mr. Wilson was able to lay aside a little cash for the comfort of his family and in preparation for the day of freedom which he doubtless saw ahead.

> The farsightedness of Mr. Beuhring was further shown by a proposition he made to Mr. Wilson just before the outbreak of the Civil War. That was the chance he gave to the latter to secure his freedom by purchase. In other words,

he offered Mr. Wilson the opportunity to "buy himself"…Mr. Beuhring agreed to manumit, i.e., make out papers of freedom for Mr. Wilson upon the latter's payment of six hundred dollars. Or rather Mr. Wilson was to pay three hundred dollars in cash and the rest when and if he became financially able to do so. (Hall 1938)

After emancipation, the Wilson family crossed the river and settled in Rome, Ohio (despite initial threats by the Ku Klux Klan), and George's children were able to attend "schooling facilities" in the Rome and Union townships. It came to pass that George's son Theodore Wilson was prepared to enter the teaching profession in 1876, at age 19. He secured a school in Huntington, and found support and encouragement in the "progressive attitude taken by leading business and professional men on the question of education."

Moreover, their wisdom was further shown by their sponsorship of schools for the colored citizens such as that to which Mr. Wilson was called…Naturally his success was due in part to the support given him by the leading white citizens of the city, and no one could show greater gratitude for this support than Mr. Wilson himself. Of his own accord he has listed the names of the following gentlemen who he says were his "ardent supporters" during the thirteen years of his work there. (Hall 1938)

Among the 16 supporters named by Theodore Wilson were George F. Miller and B.H. "Trackston." Owing to the absence of such a name in the nineteenth-century U.S. Census, this must have been the reporter's misspelling of "Thackston," the Barboursville school master who headed Marshall College in the early 1880s.

If the staunch Confederate son-in-law of William C. Miller was in fact an influential supporter of "colored education" in the 1880s, it then raises another question: During those obscure years between 1867 and 1884, could it be that Benjamin Thackston offered assistance to the cause of "negro education" in Barboursville, his place of residence? If nothing else, it speaks volumes about the complicated nature of nineteenth century race relations, that former slave-holders were recognized as "ardent supporters" of African American trail-blazers such as Theodore Wilson.

Scattered across two decades, these three "moments in early negro education" reveal precious little. But in the absence of other information, the fact that a few "negro education" pioneers and their white neighbors focused time and effort on the cause during such a tumultuous period is *something*—especially when you consider what was happening in other parts of the nation. If nothing else, these tidbits serve as pinpoints of light on a foundational time for Barboursville's new African American citizens.

The philosophy of racial uplift espoused by I. V. Bryant and other black leaders of the era included the idea of both education and property ownership as keys to liberation. This ideal would indeed come to fruition in Barboursville, from Depot Street to Main Street and beyond. In less than two decades, these ambitions would not only be realized, but surpassed, by two men who measured success by each 10-cent shave and 25-cent haircut.

"A Wheelbarrow Full of Dimes"

"Two black men had the first barber shop in Barboursville on Depot Street" around 1881, according to Harry B. Washington.

Barbers Henry and Jerry (Jeremiah) Hicks have not been previously commemorated in Barboursville's historic publications. All that was written of a two-story house on Main Street was that "negroes lived there." They didn't seem to leave the same impression on white neighbors as the familiarly maternal "Aunt Mattie." Jeremiah Hicks was not referred to by white sources as "Uncle Jerry." However, through a patchwork of public documents, as well as conversations and correspondence with gracious descendents, the legacy of Barboursville's most progressive and enduring African American family can be told.

According to Jerry Hicks's great-grandson, family genealogist Marvin Johnson of New Jersey, it was passed down that "Jerry was a slave who came directly from Africa to the United States…his father was Billy Hicks who was a full blooded African chief." Henry is missing from Jerry Hicks "official" family tree, but the Washington family roots story, together with census and county records, strongly suggest that the two men were brothers. In 1880, Henry (age 32) and Jerry (age 29) were living as neighbors with their wives and children in Roanoke, Virginia. William Hicks, 50, and Winnie, 52, shared a home with Henry and his family. All three men were employed as "laborers." By 1882, the brothers were in Barboursville, West Virginia.

Why did the Hicks brothers decide to set up shop by the little Barboursville depot, at a time when Huntington had a much larger and thriving black community? As someone who moved from a large Midwestern city to Cabell County at an impressionable age, I have long appreciated the opportunity for someone here to become "a bigger fish in a smaller pond." I am guessing that Jerry Hicks would have been able to relate.

Ted Allen, who was born in Barboursville and now lives in the suburbs south of Chicago, Illinois reasoned that his great-grandfather must have found a sense of tolerance in Barboursville, "because he came there in a position to render a service…and they probably didn't have any barber shops in Barboursville then."

Unlike the black manual laborers and domestic servants typical of 1870s Barboursville, the Hicks brothers brought an ability to read and write along with a marketable skill, a thrifty nature and an entrepreneurial spirit that served them well. Upon his death, Jerry A. Hicks would be described as the "colored barber, whose razors scraped the faces of Cabell County officials when the county seat was located in Barboursville." There was another source of income, according to Mr. Allen. Perhaps owing to his father's storied African traditions, Jerry Hicks "had his special talent (for concocting) an array of things for different afflictions. He had herbs and stuff, so he was known for that."

Although I could not pin down Barboursville Census data on older brother Henry Hicks, his great-grandson Harry B. Washington wrote down an oral history of Henry and his wife Mary Elisa. Census data might show a few discrepancies in dates and figures, but Washington's handwritten composition provided some helpful insights into Henry and Mary's Barbourville associations. Mary Elisa, originally from Louisiana, apparently had a cousin in Burlington, Ohio, who helped her find a job in West Virginia.

"She worked for the mayor of Barboursville by the name of Herbert King, and the Vallandinghams who owned the bank. The bank sold Mary Elisa a house across the street from the mayor," Washington wrote.

A Cabell County Deed Book details the sale of a Main Street property across the alley from the stately Miller-Stowasser home on December 25, 1882, by former village druggist (John Samuels's son-in-law) R. D. Bright, to Jerry and Henry Hicks for "$250 cash in hand."

The brothers most likely subdivided the Main Street lot, where Hicks built a two-story home on the eastern side at 901 Main Street, and Henry's family lived at 905 Main Street.

"They said he would collect dimes and put them in a cigar box, and when he got ready to convert them he had a big wheel barrow full of money, Ted Allen said of his great-grandfather Jerry. "He took it down to the bank on Main Street and converted it into cash…and built a house."

"It was a very nice home," said former next-door neighbor and family friend Gladys Carter. "It had an entrance hall that took you upstairs and the other side took you to the living room. Then from the living room you could go into the dining room then you would go down like a step and you were in the kitchen, a very nice place."

Ted Allen was born in his great-grandfather's house and grew up there. "We had a cistern in the back where you could pump water from the back porch, and an ice box. I remember as a kid (before electricity or indoor plumbing), we used to have our Saturday baths in the kitchen in the wash tub. We would have to put wood and coal and stuff in the stoves to cook. And then we went from that to gas. I remember all that, and I remember going to the outhouse and not really wanting to go. It was one of the oldest houses on the block, but for its time it was modern.

My great grandmother did the laundry for the railroad and my great grandfather did the barber shop. So they were quite well off, I guess."

Frank Ball's renowned historical strolls down Main Street, published in *The Barboursville Bulletin* of the 1960s and1970s, failed to turn up much of anything on the Hicks homestead. He did, however, relay an anecdote that hints of an unspoken social segregation between the Hicks family and some of their white neighbors, the kind that breeds false assumptions: "I have been told that when the owners were being assessed for part of the Main Street paving fronting their property, it was suspected that Jerry Hicks would be the 'weak link,'" Ball wrote. "He was a barber with a little shop on Depot Street…and it was thought that he was not too 'well-heeled.' At any rate, the solicitor made his rounds and returned. And, Lo, Jerry Hicks's name led all the rest."

Though most of their descendents are now scattered, the family lines of both men would be woven into the fabric of Barboursville life for more than a hundred years.

Henry and Mary had one daughter, Amanda, and three sons, Luke, Mose and Edward. According to Harry B. Washington's family story, Luke grew up to work at the Old National Bank in Huntington, Mose worked at the Huntington Hospital, and Edward worked at the Horse Racing Track. Amanda married a C&O worker who came to the village, and spent most of her days in Barboursville. There was another daughter, Mary A. Hicks, who died in 1906 at age 17 of "consumption," according to state death records.

Jerry and Hattie Jordan Hicks raised children Arlena, Matthew, Bessie, Allie, Earnestine and Hattie. (A son born in Virginia, John W., does not appear in the Barboursville census records.) Arlena married William W. Scott, and Lillie married Barboursville's George Hamler, both couples raising children in the village. Matthew picked up his father's trade by age 18, working as a Barboursville barber before moving to Chicago and operating a fur company, according to family sources. Matthew married Mattie Jackson and she preceded him in death, leaving no children. Bessie married John L. Brown and settled down in Hackensack, New Jersey. Two years after Bessie moved to New Jersey, sister Hattie was married there to James Roberts, and spent the rest of her life as a resident of Jamaica, Queens, New York. Allie attended West Virginia State College, became Mrs. Chester R. Rudisell and spent most of her years in Logan. Earnestine was a dressmaker living with her parents in 1910; her life is lost to family and public records after that time. Today, Jerry and Hattie's progeny exceeds one hundred, according to family genealogy.

In 1920, after nearly 40 years plying his trade in the village, Jerry Hicks died of heart disease while attending church services just a few doors down from his old barber shop. His widow, Hattie Jordan Hicks, passed away in 1931. Henry Hicks date of death is unknown, but his widow Mary Elisa Hicks, after living for 60 years in Barboursville, died in 1928. All are believed to have been buried in a section of the village cemetery that, according to Allen. no longer exists.

From the 1880s, the Hicks families saw to it that their children received a proper education in the village. As the curtain rose on the 1890s, Henry and Jerry would provide yet another foundational structure to the changing community of Barboursville.

Deeds to "Higher Ground"

In 1888, the county seat moved to Huntington, and village leaders were scrambling to rebrand the old public square as a seat of (white) higher education and moral fiber. Around that same time, West Virginia's African Americans were asserting themselves in the political, education and religious spheres. The period between 1888 and 1891 was a time of great cultural ferment in West Virginia, and Barboursville's families were not to be left out.

African American churches built "from scratch" blossomed within the post-bellum decades, and defined their communities in important ways. From the 1870s, Huntington's Mount Olive Baptist, First Baptist and Ebenezer Methodist Episcopal church sites roughly marked the boundaries of what would become a growing black residential concentration in the city. Black marriage ceremonies, which had only been legally recognized for a few decades, became a significant privilege and precious benefit to church congregants. Church leaders helped maintain social decorum among a rapidly growing migrant population, and found new opportunities for status and stature, some making their voices heard in political arenas.

In Charleston, a group of 49 black delegates from across West Virginia convened in September 1888 to nominate their own election ticket, making the 1888 general election the "first major election in the state in which African Americans became a significant voting force." By 1890, Huntington's black leaders demonstrated interest in local and statewide political affairs, and a few were able to rally enough voter support to acquire some "low-level municipal positions," such as postal carrier and assistant street commissioner.

African Americans in West Virginia made great gains in the field of education. With the growth of population, it had become increasingly evident that the state needed to train more black teachers. In 1881, the legislature contracted with Storer College in the eastern panhandle to prepare young black people to enter the teaching profession, but western counties still relied on teachers from colleges in Ohio or other states. Around 1890, summer schools were operated in Charleston, and some African American educators were able to attend teacher institutes with their white counterparts. A group of black Baptist leaders in the state began advocating for a public college. The state Superintendent and Governor were "in a receptive mood," and found a way to secure funding through a land grant act.

On March 1891, legislation enacted with a helping hand from Cabell County's former Judge James H. Ferguson created the West Virginia Colored Institute in Kanawha County. Later renamed West Virginia State College, the school became one of the leading black public institutions in the nation. A site was originally envisioned in St. Albans, but met with white resistance from that community. Soon after, Governor Fleming and his staff located a "negro colony" along the Kanawha River where residents welcomed the idea. The campus was seated on 80 acres from the estate of former plantation owner Samuel Cabell, who had notoriously produced a family with his former slave Mary Barnes. The children of this interracial union were generously provided for in Mr. Cabell's will, and grew to be an 1870s rarity—educated, professional-class citizens, including doctors and teachers. The former plantation became the town of Institute.

Huntington established its first black high school in 1891. On Thanksgiving Day that same year, members of a "study group" of black men and women came together at a Methodist Church in Charleston to launch the West Virginia State Teachers Association. This organization would span six decades in support of better education for West Virginia's black youth, beginning as a body of clergymen and educators concerned with the "general social uplift" of African Americans in the state.

Barboursville's families no doubt took in all the developments: a progressive black movement was flowering in this corner of West Virginia. With Cabell County's center of social and political attention shifted to Huntington, village leaders had worked hard to redefine Barboursville as a cradle of learning and a newly "dry" town. And the C&O continued transporting new African American workers and their families past the depot, where they caught a glimpse of this tranquil little village. Together, these facts must have spelled opportunity. *Something* inspired the following transaction:

February 6, 1891—William and Mary Derton to Jeremiah Hicks, Henry Hicks, George Hamler, Samuel Goodlow, and David Hamler, trustees of the First Colored Baptist Church in Barboursville. $50.00 cash in hand. At "Station Street" in said Town, 378 feet n. of the intersection of Station and Main. *(Cabell County Court House Deed Book 35)*

I located the deed record while searching the origins of this church. Before I became aware of the Hicks family, I remembered it as the empty "colored church" next door to the house where my mom grew up. I heard about it as the rustic little chapel where 3-year-old Linda Lou Brady was discovered by her parents one Sunday after slipping away from her room, walking the few steps from house door to church door, and situating herself in a pew to surround herself with the spirited prayers and hymns of the congregation.

What I was not expecting in my research was a second black church in Barboursville. In the Cabell County deed index was another group of "colored church" trustees. Just eight days after the Hicks-Hamler-Goodlow purchase, a different group of African American men purchased the current site of the Barboursville Public Library:

> On February 14, 1891—West half of lot 14 in Barboursville. Colored Methodist Episcopal Church of Barboursville (by Trustees) to Robert Davis. Trustees Rev. R. W. Williams, William M. Morgan, William Black, Elijah Tucker, Robert Davis….lot conveyed by H.C. Simms, Executor of last will of John G. Miller for $100 paid. (*Cabell County Court House Deed Book 35½, p. 373*)

The west half of Lot 14 apparently changed hands again within the year, and eventually reverted back to the "Württemberg Miller" offspring. A chapel for a Colored Methodist congregation in Barboursville was not to be, and Davis, Williams, Morgan, Black and Tucker slipped from village history.

The "First Colored Baptist Church," on the other hand, would anchor Barboursville's black families for more than 50 years. Renamed The First Baptist Church of Barboursville, its congregation and the Hicks family would plant more seeds of political and educational empowerment, helping transform the village into a small-town haven for other African American families.

Racial Snippets from *The Cabell Record*

As Fain noted, the establishment of a black church in a community provided legitimacy and the opportunity to help educate whites, as newspapers started to cover weddings, baptisms and other church accomplishments. This was as true in Barboursville as it was in Huntington, and may have been responsible for fairly frequent and respectful coverage of African Americans in the village, at least as compared with reports from surrounding towns. A patchwork of "colored" life and events, as reported by white writers inside and outside of the village, is found in these turn-of-the-century dispatches for *The Cabell Record*:

> JANUARY 27, 1898—Colored children near Barboursville walk seven miles daily to attend school.

> FEBRUARY 10, 1898—An additional batch of colored men arrived last Saturday night to work on the C&O Railway, west of Ona, laying steel rails.

FEBRUARY 24, 1898—The colored school has had a good teacher in Mr. Capehart, of Guyandotte, the past year, and the class in his charge has been a large one and profited much by his instruction.

MAY 19, 1898—The colored troops seem to want to fight nobly.

JULY 10, 1898—The colored Baptists held all day services Sunday, Rev. Stratton of St. Albans officiating.

AUGUST 4, 1898—Our public schools, which will begin about October 1ˢᵗ, will be taught by J.W. Wilson, principal and Misses Belle Bias and Leona Merritt as assistants. The colored teacher has not yet been named.

AUGUST 25, 1898—Mr. Capeheart, a young colored man of Guyandotte, will teach the colored school again this year.

NOVEMBER 17, 1889—The colored Baptists have been holding a revival, which has been in charge of W.W. Gardner, of Pittsburgh.

JANUARY, 5, 1899—Morris Boyer, a colored tramp, had his feet frozen badly last Sunday night, from exposure, near Guyandotte.

JANUARY 26, 1899—The colored people have had a good school here this season, and their children have gone regularly.

FEBRUARY 2, 1899—The colored school closed yesterday.

JULY 20, 1899—Rev. Stratton, of St. Albans, pastor of the colored Baptists here, baptized several converts here in the presence of a large crowd. Many colored folks were present from Huntington.

AUGUST 3, 1899—A force of colored men have been laying steel at the C&O between Barboursville and Guyandotte. Big improvement.

AUGUST 3, 1899—The Board of Education met last Saturday and selected teachers for the public school for the coming term as follows. . . Teacher at colored school, Miss Lena Hicks.

AUGUST 24, 1899—The colored Baptists will paint and otherwise improve their church on Depot street.

MARCH 8, 1900—The colored laborers working on the Guyan Valley Railway suffered severely from the recent cold weather. They are from North and South Carolina, unused to such frigid weather, and came here thinly clad to brave such blizzards. One of them was taken off a mule here frozen badly. He had rode from Laurel Hill, and after he had been thawed out returned to that place again. A number of men have frozen ears and feet.

MARCH 8, 1900—A colored man who had been ill but a short time at the laborers' camp above here, died Monday, and his remains were interred in a near-by cemetery.

JUNE 28, 1900—The colored folks are preparing for an extensive celebration of the Fourth here.

AUGUST 2, 1900—(a) colored man had a gash in (his) neck in fighting with another darkey. Dr. Adams took ten stitches to close the wound.

AUGUST 2, 1900—A colored laborer, employed by Contractor Allen, was drowned in Guyan River, near here, while bathing last Sunday, and his remains were shipped to his home in Virginia for interment.

AUGUST 16, 1900—Miss Hicks appointed to colored school for coming year.

SEPTEMBER 13, 1900—The colored citizens organized a political club Monday evening at their school house.

SEPTEMBER 20, 1900—The Colored Republicans Club elected Jerry Hicks, President; Matthew Hicks, Secretary, and Dave Hamler, Treasurer.

MARCH 14, 1901—A colored fellow who is boarding at Mrs. Mattie Fliggins' broke out with smallpox Sunday evening, and the town authorities at once took precautions to prevent the spread of the pest by quarantining the house (contracted on New River).

APRIL 4, 1901—Colored fellow at the Fliggins house…improving nicely

APRIL 25, 1901—An aged colored man, Ras Carter by name, who was raised by General McComas, who lived here in the early part of the last century, was here from Mason City several days this week. It had been sixty years since he had been in this section, when he was a slave, and Monday he collected fifty cents that a party owed him at that time.

APRIL 25, 1901—The smallpox patient—Tom Taylor, the colored

fellow—was able to leave his bed yesterday, is convalescing. (Town discontinued quarantine.)

Contrast the Barboursville reports with the *Cabell Record's* news items from outside the village, some of which were more bigoted, to say the least:

FROM MILTON—"Uncle Tom's Cabin" play produced in Milton tonight under a mammoth tent with a capacity for seating 2,500.

FROM GUYANDOTTE—Uncle Tom's Cabin troupe, the 187th on the road, gave a fairly good presentation of the well-worn drama at the wharf Monday evening to a fair sized audience, in a well-equipped floating palace (by proprietor Mr. Eisenbarth).

FROM HURRICANE—Barber "Payne" was locked up here Sunday morning on account of a darkey rumpus with Frank Cosby.

FROM LINCOLN COUNTY—The Lincoln county people along Guyan say "all coons look alike to them."

FROM McCOMAS DISTRICT—Inez, the post office near N— Hill, has had quite a colored population. Lately, three to every white inhabitant. The track laying force, mostly colored men of the G.V.R.R., have been stopping there with their cars. They annoy no one and make matters pleasant of an evening with their songs.

Barboursville Families:
Hamler, Hill, Smith, Washington and Whirls

Cabell County's African American community was growing exponentially. Huntington's rise was not just in sheer population numbers, but in its metropolitan mix of industrialization, poverty, educational opportunity, residential concentration, political activism, recreational outlets, criminal activity and church organization. Possibly more accustomed to a rural lifestyle, and probably attracted by the presence of loved ones, a handful of families opted for a slower pace of life in Barboursville.

Five notable households were established in Barboursville by the turn of the century. Members of the Hamler, Hill, Smith, Washington and Whirls families distinguished themselves from other African Americans in the village, particularly the hundreds of temporary laborers who stayed in boarding houses or construction camps during completion of the railroad. In addition to the Hicks households and the various "kinfolk" of Mattie Fliggins, these five families lived in Barboursville through the years most closely associated with the South's "Jim Crow" era. Their children were both "churched" and schooled in the village.

Early railroad workers lay tracks for the Guyan Valley Railroad
on the old McComas Farm near Peyton Street.
(Courtesy of Frances B. Gunter)

Perhaps most significantly, these families achieved the one dream that was a hallmark of black aspiration. In addition to securing what I.V. Bryant called "a well-rounded Christian education," these families owned homes on Barboursville's Main Street, as well as Barbara Street, Huntington Avenue and Depot Street.

Hamler. At least three generations of Hamlers lived in the village. David Hamler seems to have been a Cabell County slave who remained. His marriage to Celia Wilson of Pea Ridge occurred in Cabell County in 1875; both were born in Cabell County and both listed 42 as their ages when married. It appears they had been born into slavery in 1830s Cabell County, established a family shortly after emancipation, and married when the opportunity presented itself. They were living on the outskirts of the village as of the 1880 Census, with 45-year-old "mulatto" David listed as a farmer and 44-year-old "black" wife Celia "keeping house." Their two sons, 15-year-old Edward and 13-year-old George were both working as laborers but had attended school in the previous 12 months and, unlike their parents, could read and write.

In 1886, Celia Wilson Hamler died of unknown causes. David remarried at 49, taking 40-year-old Katherine (Katie) Whirles of Roanoke as his second wife in 1890, with the noteworthy I.V. Bryant officiating. David and son George became fellow trustees of the "First Colored Baptist Church," along with the

Hicks brothers and Samuel Goodlow, when the Depot Street lot was purchased in 1891. By 1900, the couple owned a home in Barboursville town limits, and David Hamler continued work as a laborer at least until age 60. By the time Katie Whirles Hamler died in 1919, David had also passed away.

David and Celia's oldest son Edward married Mattie Payne and raised a family living in the Jefferson District of St. Albans as of 1910. He lost both a 17-year-old son and his wife to tuberculosis. In 1930, Edward was still living in Jefferson. Youngest son George Hamler stayed in Barboursville, and in 1896 married Lillie B. Hicks, the daughter of Jerry and Hattie. George and Lillie had five children, Calvin, Warner (who seems to have died in childhood), Estelle, Matthew and Bessie Lucille. In 1900, the family was living in Bath County, Va., where George was employed as a coachman. The family returned to Barboursville by 1910, where George worked as a yard laborer for the C&O. By 1920, George and his family had relocated to Guyandotte.

Private Calvin Wendell Hamler
(Courtesy of KYOWVA Genealogical and Historical Society)

The Hamlers were one of two Barbourville families of color to demonstrate their patriotism when the "Great War" ignited across Europe. In 1917, Congress passed the Selective Service Act requiring males between the ages of 21 and 31, including African Americans, to register for the draft. Even before the act was passed, many African American males from all over the country joined the war effort.

George's oldest son, Calvin Wendell Hamler, served in the segregated "colored ranks" in World War I. This unfocused image of Private Hamler, with civilian clothes and what appears to be a cigarette dangling from his mouth, was found in the *Honor Roll of Cabell County, West Virginia* (a fragile leather-bound volume housed at the KYOWVA Genealogical and Historical Society).

Private Donald Hill
(Courtesy of KYOWVA Genealogical and Historical Society)

Hill. The WWI *Honor Roll* features a sharper image, this one of Private Donald Hill, the middle child of William Henry ("Scott") and Lucy Ann (Anna or "Annie") Hill of Barboursville. The Hill family spans over 60 years in the village.

"Of all the colored people in Barboursville, there were none better than Scott Hill," wrote Fred Lambert. Lambert and Frank Ball both preserved some of the family history and genealogy of William Henry "Scott" Hill, who was born in Logan County in 1859, in the waning days of slavery. An undated newspaper story was written by Ball, after Mr. Hill had "long since passed his days of usefulness as a workman," tells of Hill's roundabout and complicated journey from slavery to freedom, from childhood to old age, and from the upper Guyan valley to the mouth of the Mud.

"Uncle Scott," as he was familiarly known, was born the property of Lorenza Hill, prominent orchardist and farmer of the Guyandotte valley. Lorenza Hill, owner of several slaves, lived on a large tract of land across the river from the little mining town of Kitchen in Logan county...

Mr. Hill remembers well the excitement created by the Civil War and the frantic movements attendant thereto. His owner was a blender of the best whiskies in the valley and his home was widely visited by soldiers and citizens alike who sipped the choice brandies and exchanged the news of the day.

Hysteria in border states ran high during the war, and it was thought best by some slaveholders to move their slaves farther south for safekeeping. It was rumored that Union soldiers were taking the slaves by force and freeing them. So Lorenza Hill, whom Uncle Scott affectionately remembers as "Ole Boss," started with his slaves on a long journey into Virginia.

Uncle Scott's memory of this trip and stay in Virginia is rather painful. To begin with, it meant the sacrificing of "Old Baldy," a steer of which the slave children were exceedingly fond, to furnish meat for the journey. En route, Uncle Scott's uncle and three of his uncle's children were sold. Tearfully, his mother parted from her brother and her nephews and niece as the trip to Virginia was resumed.

Ole Boss left his remaining slaves with a planter in Tazewell county and returned to Logan. A year in Virginia found Scott's father and mother greatly overworked, and they and their children greatly underfed.

This treatment was in direct contrast to that given them by their owners and the mother had the nerve to "strike." She hired herself to a neighbor slaveholder that her children might be fed. And in the fall of 1864, wartime hysteria had subsided somewhat and Lorenza Hill returned to Virginia for his slaves. They were overjoyed at seeing him. They were sure they would be well fed and treated kindly. In return, they would work hard for Ole Boss.

A year after the trip back from Virginia, the slaves of Lorenza Hill were surprised and not a little dazed when he tried to convey to them the fact that they were free. They didn't want to leave Ole Boss. They had no place to go. So they lived on with him and worked for him as usual. Uncle Scott stayed with his former owner until he was 21. And the slaves who were sold en route to Virginia returned often to visit the Hill farm.

At the age of 21, Scott hill left the valley and went to Springfield, O. there he met and married Annie Morris, who was born the slave property of Charles Morris of Martha, near Barboursville. (F. Ball, Unknown n.d.)

Fred Lambert's manuscript picks up the story from Logan: "Mr. Hill came, on a push boat, from Logan County, in 1889, and rented land of Charles K. Morris, about a half mile, from the railroad station, at Martha." *(Fred Lambert did love his commas.)* "He staid *(sic)* there a year, and then moved to N— Hill, and rented land of Dick Roberts, staid *(sic)* there a year, then moved to an old house, just above Amaziah Ross's, and the bridge, at Martha. He moved to Barboursville, in 1892."

Between 1883 and 1907, William Henry (Scott) and Lucy Ann Morris (Annie)

Hill had 13 children, 12 who lived long enough to be named: Arnold Arthur, Harry Gordon, George Clifton, John Isaac, Mary Jane, Bernie, William Henry, Donald Franklin, Annie Marie, Randolph Virgil, Edna Hortense and Virginia Dare. Henry passed away at age nine; Bernie and Virginia died as infants. In 1901 *The Cabell Record* reported, "Arnold, the oldest son of Scott Hill, a hard working colored man of this place, was drowned in the Ohio River near Guyandotte last Sunday while bathing." He would have been just shy of 18 years.

Annie and Scott Hill posing in front of their home, date unknown.
(Courtesy of Barbara Miller)

Census records show that Scott Hill was employed as a railroad laborer in 1910, then as a farm laborer or gardener. Annie worked as a domestic. According to Ball, "In his younger days, Mr. Hill pushed a cart about town selling fish to the citizens. For many years he was a familiar figure as he wheeled about the village, and his 'feesh, fresh feesh,' became a by-word among the youngsters. In addition he was a great hog raiser, and he made arrangements for swill from many of his neighbors who were glad to accommodate him."

In 1930, 71-year-old Scott and 68-year-old Annie were still living in their house on Barbara Street. By the time of Ball's report some time after that, Scott would sit "patiently by the bedside of his invalid wife daily, musing on the past. Friends have lately installed a radio for the aged couple by which they may hear directly from the outside world." Scott Hill died at age 81, and Annie died one year later. Both were buried in Barboursville.

After the couple's passing, the home on the southwest side of the village was occupied by their son George Clifton Hill, until 1955. A Mrs. Anna Gibbs of Columbus, Ohio (whose name appears as informant on both Lucy Ann's and George's death certificates), was probably daughter Anna Marie. Son Randolph V. Hill appears in Huntington's 1940 city directory, married to a woman named Maggie and working as a porter. No further record was found of WWI-veteran Donald, or of Scott and Annie Hill's other children.

According to Roy Goines, "Mr. George Hill, he lived there and he was by himself, and lived right next to a wooded area behind McClung Street...I was only about six or seven years old at the time. I remember my uncle would take me up there...he had a little coal fireplace where he would keep his house warm in the wintertime. I don't remember that he had any electricity or anything like that." Never married, George Hill worked for the state road, died in 1955 at age 68, and was buried in Barboursville Cemetery near his parents. An etched outline of his hunting dog "Rambler" adorns George C. Hill's flat gravestone.

Smith. Charley Smith was born in 1894, a couple years before Privates Calvin Hamler and Donald Hill. Charley was the middle child of Henry and Lillie Smith, who by 1900 moved their young family from Paw Paw bottom (near Salt Rock) to Barboursville, enabling Charley's older siblings, Ollie, Willie and Mollie, to attend school that year. He and the three younger sisters Grace, Junia and Goldie (born about 1902) would wait until they were about six or seven before joining the seasonal weekday walk across town to the "colored school."

Charley's father Henry Smith can be found in county census records in 1870 and 1880, his youth spent as a servant in the John E. Morrison household in McComas District. Henry and Lillie Smith married in 1888. Henry was a 41-year-old farmer in Barboursville District in 1900, but at some point passed away, leaving Lillie to raise the children alone. When Charley was about five, his 8-year-old sister Mollie died of consumption. Three years later, 14-year-old brother Ollie died of typhoid. By 1910 Charley's mother owned her own home on Depot Street, living with brother Frank Williams and the four remaining children. The family lived in Barboursville until sometime after 1910.

Evidence suggests that education was as important to the Smiths as it was to the Bradys, who also moved their children into eastern Barboursville from the southern farmland. Even though Willie and Charley were working odd jobs in 1910, 15-year-old Charley was a student. His younger sisters Goldie and Junia would go on to compete in the first Douglass High School debate contest in 1917. By 1920, the family's situation had changed. Lillie and her family had moved to Eighth Avenue near Guyandotte, the youngest daughters finishing high school and Willie living with his mom and driving a coal truck for a living. By this time, middle child Charley Smith had also passed away.

Barboursville Cemetery marker of Charley Smith, who died at
age 17 years, 2 months and 9 days (1894-1911)
(Photo by author)

What is unique about Charley Smith, this young African American whose life ended at age 17, cut short by typhoid fever, is his tombstone in the Barboursville cemetery. Like my second-great grandmother Mary E. Brady, Charley Smith had the posthumous fortune of being buried under one of the sturdier, more readable monuments in the local burial ground. Charley's still-upright headstone, complete with its slanted cross and backward-stamped "S," might serve to represent most of the black Barboursville family members whose identities were never carved in stone, as well as those whose names disappeared from the cemetery decades ago. The headstones of his siblings are nearby, in various sad states of brokenness.

Washington. The next family, like the Hamlers, were linked by marriage with the Hicks family. Like the Hills, they were linked to folks in Logan County. And like the Smiths, they lived on Depot Street.

Charles Washington came from Roanoke County, Virginia with a good C&O job, and was described by his grandson as "a tall and very strong man with a very pleasant look." It's not certain when he arrived in Barboursville, but by 1892 he had fallen for Henry and Mary E. Hicks's daughter Amanda. They were married in the village by Rev. C.W. Shearer, exactly 15 months after Amanda's father and uncle purchased the church lot on Depot Street.

The Washingtons had one son, Keller, and four daughters, Claudine, Enola (or "Nola"), Lillian, Essie and Henrietta. The family moved away from Barboursville for some time in the 1890s, and then returned. By 1900, Charles purchased what was probably Henry Hicks's former Main Street home and filled it with children. I have not been able to determine when Henry passed away, only that Henry's widow Mary Elisa, and 76-year-old family patriarch William "Billy" Hicks, were living with Charles and Amanda Washington in 1900.

Between 1920 and 1930, Charles bought a house at 972 Depot Street. He gained further railroad experience as a fireman, brakeman, pump man and station engineer at Barboursville. Amanda, in addition to caring for the family, worked as a "wash woman" in town. Three of the daughters were married in Barboursville, then moved away—Claudine became Mrs. Joseph V. Clark of Fayette County, Lillian became Mrs. Dennie Lawson of Boone County, and Henrietta became Mrs. Thomas Layne of Lawrence County, Ky. Nola married Arthur Whirles in Logan. Essie appeared in the Census at age 11 but must not have reached adulthood, as she was not named in her nephew's family history.

After working 50 years for the Chesapeake and Ohio Railroad, Charles Washington died in 1937, leaving the Depot Street home to Keller and his wife, the former Mary Ferguson of Logan County. They had seven children who split time between Barboursville and the Aracoma coal camps, where Mary continued to work for years as a cook, going down on the train and coming home on the weekends. Left to his own devices, Keller acquired a reputation through the twentieth century as a rascally but well-liked neighbor, with notorious connections and a few secrets (to be unwrapped in Chapter 13, as the Lost Village's second century unfolds).

Whirles. James Edward "Edd" Whirles was the son of David Hamler's second wife Katie Whirles Hamler, making him the step-brother of George Hamler. In 1910, Whirles was a 26-year-old laborer, married with a teenage son, and living with David and Katie Hamler in Barboursville. His wife Viola Castle was born in Ohio, as was their son Arthur. In 1916, 21-year-old Arthur Whirles married Charles and Amanda (Hicks) Washington's daughter "Nola"—they lived in Logan, where Arthur was working as a painter. This marriage produced a daughter, Helen. Edd and Viola eventually purchased a nice home on Barboursville's west side, where they lived for nearly three decades. In 1930, they were both working for a local country club, Edd as "custodian of golf links," and Viola as a housekeeper.

In 1939, Edd was stricken with an unknown malady that caused him to be taken to "Lakin State Hospital for the Colored Insane" in Mason County. He would remain there for three years and seven months before succumbing to heart disease.

As the place where James Edward Whirles spent his final years, it is worth noting that Lakin Hospital was unique among all-black mental health institutions in the United States Opened in 1926 and operated as a segregated institution until 1954, Lakin was known as a place of respect, compassion and "family spirit," populated entirely by African American staff and administrators as well as patients, who helped look after one another, grow food, and maintain the facility. They had access to a variety of personal services on the premises—an island of self-sufficiency within a mostly-white rural county. From its inception, Lakin required that even non-professional staff have at least a high school diploma, a standard that exceeded "white" West Virginia hospitals of the era, according to former staff psychiatrist Mildred Mitchell Bateman. According to a former staff member, "At a time when the vast majority of psychiatric care for black Americans was markedly substandard, Lakin seems to have been a serious attempt to accomplish the 'equal' portion of the 'separate but equal' doctrine."

The fact that an institutional environment such as Lakin's was possible in western West Virginia—and nowhere else east of the Mississippi—is a testament to the educational advocacy and leadership that took root in the 1880s. These efforts culminated in several state-funded institutions essentially being run by and for African Americans, including the West Virginia Colored Orphan's Home in east Huntington.

The culmination of forces that began taking root in southwest West Virginia in the 1880s helped turn a migrant coal digger into Carter Woodson, a destitute child laborer into Booker T. Washington, and a Kanawha River plantation into a nationally-esteemed "Collegiate Institute." By the time of Mr. Whirles's demise, a village that had housed farm hands, washerwomen and fish peddlers now included children who had grown up in this new reality.

The Legacy of Reverend William Washington Scott

The Hamler, Hill, Smith, Washington and Whirles children, many of them sons and daughters of former slaves, were taught in Barboursville by men and women who held higher education as a precious, hard-won privilege. Perhaps the most remarkable was William Washington Scott:

In comparison with some of the other Southern states, Louisiana has sent but few of her sons into the mountains of West Virginia. Mention must be made of at least one earnest worker from the State, however, in the person of Rev.

William Washington Scott, who is a progressive man and has made a place for himself in religious and educational life.

Mr. Scott first saw the light at Bastrop in Morehouse Parish, La., on July 30, 1874. His father, Rev. Edward Scott, who still survives (1922) combined farming and preaching. He was the son of John Scott, who was a Cherokee Indian, and his mother's maiden name was Martha Bates. The mother of our subject before her marriage was Miss Annie Casey, daughter of Washington Casey and Amanda (Scott) Casey. Amanda Scott was of mixed ancestry, so that Rev. Scott represents a trinity of races, Negro, Indian and Caucasian.

Young Scott grew up on a farm and attended the public schools of Bastrop. After leaving public school it was necessary for him to make his own way in school, but he did not permit this to discourage him, as he was spurred on by a great aim, and would not reckon with defeat.
He did high school work at Monroe, Louisiana, and at Greenville, Miss., where he worked before and after school hours to earn his living expenses and tuition.

Reverend William Washington Scott (1875-1938)
(Courtesy of West Virginia State Archives)

After that he pursued short courses in the Moody Institute, Carnegie College, Ohio University, West Virginia Collegiate Institute and Iowa Christian College, Oskaloosa, Iowa. He has the B.D. degree from the theological department of Iskaloosa, where he did his theological work.

He began teaching at an early age in the rural schools of Louisiana and for 25 years has been active in educational work. Prior to leaving he was principal of the public school of his home town on Bastrop one year.

Most of his school work since coming to West Virginia has been in the public schools, though he taught for a while in the West Virginia Seminary and College at Red Star. Among the places he has taught may be mentioned Barboursville, Ethel, Logan, Latrobe and Layland.

Mr. Scott gave his heart to God when he was a mere boy of thirteen and was baptized into the membership of St. John Baptist Church, Bastrop, Louisiana. He immediately felt called to preach the Gospel, but it was some years later, after making preparation, and after coming to West Virginia, that he was licensed to preach in April, 1902, and on December 28 of the same year was ordained to the full work of the ministry at Barboursville.

As pastor he has served several churches. The Barboursville church has availed itself of his services at different times amounting to five years in all. He served as pastor of St. Paul, St. Albans from 1904-8, the Coal Street Baptist Church, Logan 1914-16, the First Baptist Church of Lorado 1916-19. He was also pastor at Yolyn for a while. Mr. Scott has been a builder wherever he has gone, both in his church work and in his school work. At all of the largest places, where he has served as pastor, church houses and parsonages have been erected, and under his preaching and influence many have been led to Christ, saved, and added to the church. Mr. Scott came to West Virginia in 1901. On January 21, 1903, He married Miss Arlena May Hicks, daughter of Jeremiah and Hattie Hicks, of Barboursville. They have four children: Cecil, Freda Louise, Hattie Beatrice and Eula Geraldine Scott.

In politics Mr. Scott is a Republican. His secret order affiliations are with the Masons, Odd Fellows, Pythians and Fisherman. His standing in his denomination may be inferred from the fact that he has served for years as Clerk of the Guyan Valley Baptist Association, President of the Tenth District Sunday School Union, Vice-Moderator of the Mt. Olivet Association and member of the Executive Board of the State Baptist Convention. Mr. Scott has had unusual opportunity to study conditions on different fields and he is of the opinion that the things most beneficial to the race are religion, education, and the ownership of real estate. He now (1922) contemplates taking up evangelistic work. (A. Caldwell 1923)

The above biography appears in an African American "Who's Who" entitled *History of the American Negro, West Virginia Edition, Volume VII*, published in 1923 by A.B. Caldwell of Atlanta. The volume was the last in a seven-year collection featuring "representative men and women of the race." Previous volumes featured first-hand information provided by pastors, lawyers, doctors, business owners and others in Georgia, Virginia, North Carolina, South Carolina and Washington, D.C. Mr. Caldwell intended to build a body of work directed to "those ten million American citizens…whom we know as Negroes," in response to his observation "that, daily and hourly, the press of the country grinds out matter of one kind of another pertaining to the Negro. Much of this is characterized by shallowness and levity, and deals in an exaggerated way with their crimes and foibles; while that which deals with the achievements and accomplishments of the better and more successful element of the race passes almost unrecorded and without notice."

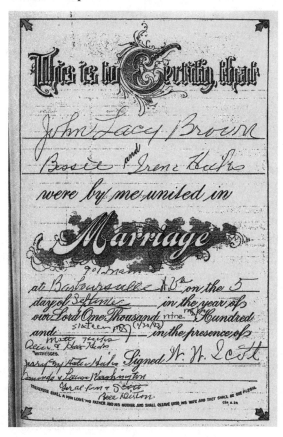

Marriage Record signed by W.W. Scott
(Courtesy of Marvin Johnson)

In *Volume VII*, Caldwell featured 115 men and 3 women from the Mountain State, acknowledging that the book "does not include all the important men and women of the race in the State, but it does include many of the noblest and best." Reverend William W. Scott is one of 11 men and women who lived in Cabell County—all the others were from Huntington, including pastors C.C. Barnett and I.V. Bryant. William Washington Scott was the only Barboursville resident to merit inclusion in the publication. As a Baptist, a Republican and a member of various "secret orders" of the day, he was typical of the great majority of those profiled in West Virginia.

After William W. Scott met and married Jerry and Hattie's daughter, village schoolteacher Arlena Mae Hicks, they had son Cecil (or "Ed" according to the county register of births) in Cabell County, followed by three daughters, all born in St. Albans. They were Frieda Louise, who married Walter Calloway and moved to Chicago; Hattie Beatrice, who married Vivian Lamont Rotan of Fayette County and had ten children; and Eula Geraldine, who married Theodore Roosevelt Allen of Huntington and had three children before Mr. Allen died in a car wreck. Later Eula remarried and relocated to Chicago.

William and Arlena made Barboursville their lifelong home, keeping 901 Main Street in the family well after Jerry Hicks passed away. The Reverend Scott officiated the occasional wedding, including a 1916 ceremony for sister-in-law Bessie Irene and groom John Lacy Brown—their grandson kept the family Bible containing a certificate of marriage signed by the preacher. Rev. Scott's record of ministry with the "First Baptist Church of Barboursville" was lost with other church records.

Vivid memories of the church itself rest with descendents and neighbors who grew up in the plain but tidy little chapel, memories of gaslights, a pot-belly stove, organ music, high-backed pews and fidgety children.

William and Arlena's youngest daughter Eula Geraldine was the organist and pianist. "We didn't have a piano, we had an organ that you would pump with your feet," said her son Ted Allen. He and his friend Roy Goines both remembered "Onward Christian Soldiers" being an old standby. "We sang that one to death" Ted added. As young boys, they took part in another timeless church custom: "Roy and I used to cut up all the time at church. We'd go home and get our little butts kicked. I would be the one that instigated everything and we'd start giggling and the parents would say, 'I can't wait to get you at home.'"

The children and grandchildren grew up to enter business, education, art, journalism and medical professions—the kinds of careers that reflected Reverend and Mrs. Scott's ideals. The couple's commitment to education that began with Lena's turn-of-the-century appointment as the village's "colored school teacher" later manifested itself in physical construction.

In 1909, Reverend Scott purchased about 9,000 square feet of land for $97 cash from P. A. and Susie Harris. A few years later, William. and Arlena deeded the property to village trustee J. T. Thornburg for use as the Barboursville Colored School. One of dozens of one-room schoolhouses in Cabell County, the building and land became the property of the Board of Education, Independent School District of Barboursville, from 1914 to 1953. The General Federation of Women's Clubs history states that by 1922 the school had 25 students and a teacher, Ruth

Martin, who commuted from Huntington. Students completed school work through the eighth grade at the school, and then rode the school bus to Douglass High School.

William Washington Scott, described by neighbors as a "tiny man," walked with his students from Main Street to the remote corner of Maple and Huntington Avenues, into the one-room schoolhouse they called their own. The Sanborn Map Company published fire insurance maps of Barboursville in 1922 and 1934, clearly labeling the "Colored School" as the only building on the west side of Huntington Avenue. In 1944, several years after Rev. Scott's death, the Sanborn Map indicated the structure was vacant. In 1953 the school district sold the property to private owners.

Since then, Scott's former one-room school house has been occupied by a succession of families, surrounded by other dwellings, built onto and encased in vinyl siding, but it still stands, and is still discernible by its shape as the old "Barboursville Colored School." With the loss of the Barbourville's First Baptist Church property, and the recent demolition of Huntington's Colored Orphan's Home, the fact that William and Arlena Scott's investment has been preserved—however accidentally—is cause for commemoration. Any historic tour of the village should be capped off with a respectful drive past this unsung monument to early twentieth century "racial uplift," the legacy of the Hicks and Scott families.

Mixed Origins and Labels of Race

One advantage in studying Barboursville's African American history is that the number of families of color is small enough to wrap one's brain around, but large enough to see patterns across multiple households. One trend worth looking at is the racial origins of families who settled in the village, including William Washington Scott, whose genetic makeup was described in his 1923 biography as "a trinity of races, Negro, Indian and Caucasian."

From 1850 until 1930, Census enumerators were instructed to record the color of free inhabitants as either black, white or "mulatto," a word used to describe "all persons having any perceptible trace of African blood." (The lost 1890 Census required an even more complicated classification of biracial individuals.) By 1930 the instructions changed again, and "a person of mixed White and Negro blood was to be returned as Negro, no matter how small the percentage of Negro blood." It was not until the year 2000 that Americans had the option of indicating two or more races on their Census forms.

According to Barboursville's Census takers, while the transient railroad workers comprised both "black" and "mulatto" inhabitants, most of the first "post-emancipation" settlers were black, including Harrison and Sophia Epps, the Flligginses, Kilgores and McGees. Later waves of African American settlers in the village were more often identified as "mulatto," like the Hamlers, Francis Price, the William Good family of Main and Long Streets, and the Washingtons.

In some cases, the same person's race would be reported as "B" for black one decade and "M" for mulatto the next. In addition to the information gap created by the loss of the 1890 Census schedules, local researchers are thrown for a loop by the fact that 1900 Barboursville Census-taker W.H. Stowasser classified every non-white villager as "B," and ten years later enumerator Ira Hatfield identified every one as "M." Is it any wonder, then, that Americans of mixed European and African ancestry have had to rely so heavily on passed-down oral history to piece together their family trees?

As with William W. Scott's racial "trinity," family lore may highlight the more exotic or adventurous background stories. Harry B. Washington relayed this account of his great-grandmother Mary, who married African-born Henry Hicks:

> On a plantation in the State of Louisiana, a man by the name of Glassco Brigham had children by one of his slaves. One was Mary Elisa Brigham, she was half White and half Black. She was very nice looking and was very smart. At the age of 21 years old she ran away from the plantation. She and several other slaves hitched a horse to a wagon and headed for Galveston, Texas. Halfway there she tied the horse to a tree, gathered their belongings and continued on to Texas. She had saved up money to buy a ticket to West Virginia. She had a cousin living in Burlington, Ohio who was (an) Indian by the name of Henry Todd. He helped Mary Elisa find a job in Barboursville, West Virginia…Henry Todd, who lived in Burlington, Ohio, was a Cherokee Indian, a descendant of Mary Todd Lincoln, Abraham Lincoln the President's wife. (Washington 1996)

Scott Hill was another of the Barboursville residents whose Census classification as "black" or "mulatto" alternated with each decade. His origin story indicates some white ancestry, and is actually a bit perplexing . Fred Lambert's handwritten manuscript, "A Barboursville Colored Man – William Henry ("Scott") Hill" contains proofreader's marks, with the edited result reprinted here as such (additions are underlined and deletions stricken through):

> He was born Feb. 5, 1859, a slave and son of Lorenza Hill, of Big Creek, Logan County, West Virginia, and Mary Hill, daughter of Lorenza Hill, and a slave woman Julia. Scott Hill's parents were Hiram Hunter, later known as Hiram Hill, after his master, Lorenza Hill. He had been a slave of a Mr. Hunter, of Virginia. Hiram and Mary Hill were the parents of sixteen children, three of whom survive. (F. B. Lambert Collection n.d.)

I won't try to unpack Scott Hill's familial origins as told to Fred Lambert, but suffice it to say that Logan County's "Ole Boss" Lorenza somehow figures into the Hill lineage. This would help explain Lorenza's rescue of Scott, his mother and siblings from dire conditions and near-starvation in Virginia.

Given the fact that Census classifications of race (following the dictates of white society) "removed" any white ancestry from those with biracial or multiracial origins, I found it interesting that the descendents themselves viewed things differently. For example, Harry B. Washington wrote, "Amanda (Hicks) met a man who was a Fireman and Brakeman on the old C&O Railroad. She married him, Charles Washington, a white man."

A few decades later in the mid-1920s, another man who fit a similar description would relocate with his wife to Barboursville, at the invitation of Mattie Fliggins.

The Sorrells: Finding Refuge from "Jim Crow"

Roy Goines said of Mattie Fliggins, "She was instrumental in my grandmother and grandfather coming from Virginia to live. She was my grandmother Sorrell's aunt. Grandmother Sorrell was a Banks; her father's sister (Mrs. Fliggins) lived in Barboursville. And my grandfather was white, and being married to my grandmother, who was black, created problems down in Virginia. . . So Aunt Mattie Fliggins living up here said, 'Well, Fred, why don't you and Octavia—why don't you come up here and live in Barboursville? Things aren't quite as prejudiced. . .we don't think you'd have too much of a problem if you were to come up here. So that prompted Grandmother and Grandfather Sorrell to come from Virginia and live in West Virginia."

Roy's boyhood friend Ted Allen concurred: "I think (Fred Sorrell) was Caucasian. He had blue eyes and blonde hair… He would go in the beer joints and no one questioned his race."

The atmosphere in the Commonwealth of Virginia wasn't simply prejudiced; it was legally hostile to couples of mixed race as well as citizens of indeterminate ancestry. As absurd as it sounds today, Virginia's self-described "white supremacist" society upped the ante on existing Jim Crow restrictions. A set of "high-society" white Virginians became preoccupied during the 1920s with what they called "the danger of racial amalgamation." "Anglo-Saxon Clubs" were organized and supported by Virginia newspaper editors as a genteel and respectable alternative to the Ku Klux Klan. Their members were elite white Virginians who were "obsessed with genealogy and pristine bloodlines," according to historian J. Douglas Smith.

The group succeeded in passing the 1924 Racial Integrity Act which required mandatory registration of all Virginians, a year in the penitentiary for willfully lying about one's color, mandatory presentation of racial certification to local registrars before a marriage license could be issued, prohibition against whites marrying anyone save another white—and the definition of a white person as one "who has no trace whatsoever of any blood other than Caucasian."

J Fred Sorrell
(Courtesy of Barbara Miller)

The director of Virginia's Bureau of Vital Statistics, an Anglo-Saxon club member, began to enforce with a vengeance what was called "the most draconian miscegenation law in American history." He also appealed to other states to pass similar legislation, predicting that a concerted national effort "might hold off amalgamation for five hundred years." This same man used government resources to distribute 60,000 copies of a pamphlet entitled *Eugenics in Relation to the New Family and the Law on Racial Integrity* to schools, health workers and ministers across Virginia. In the pamphlet he decreed "Let the young men who read this realize that the future purity of our race is in their keeping, and that the joining of themselves to females of a lower race and fathering children who shall be a curse and a menace to our State and civilization is a crime against society, and against the purity and integrity of their future homes and the happiness of their future loved ones and themselves."

In the face of a backlash, determined to identify even the slightest trace of black ancestry in white Virginians, and convinced of their own superiority, members of the Anglo-Saxon Clubs doubled down; they succeed in passing another law in 1926. Virginia's Public Assemblages Act mandated the separation of the races in all public places. It was just after this time that Fred and Octavia Sorrell are believed to have moved from Albemarle County, Virginia to Barboursville, West Virginia.

Conditions as a whole within West Virginia were markedly better. Though not immune to racial exploitation and violence, West Virginia was ahead of the curve when the state legislature passed the Capehart Anti-Lynching Law in 1921. While Virginia's Bureau of Vital Statistics was pursuing a pseudo-scientific campaign of racial "purification," West Virginia's Negro Bureau of Welfare and Statistics was working to help African Americans purchase farms and make other economic gains. One historian stated that, "In southern West Virginia, blacks came closer to finding economic equality than in any other coalfield, and perhaps anywhere else, in America."

Still, racial segregation in the United States was never seriously challenged during this era, even by staunch advocates of better conditions for African Americans. And despite fewer restrictive laws in West Virginia, social customs and company policies helped the white establishment distance itself from people of color in various Mountain State towns and cities, including Huntington. Cicero Fain described the gradual formation of rigid lines dividing white and black neighborhoods through restrictive real estate covenants, word-of-mouth understandings and occasional acts of retribution against those who would not fall in line.

In Barboursville, Fred and Octavia had an easier time of it. Aunt Mattie's social connections most likely smoothed the way, and the Sorrell family found the village a fine place to live for more than seven decades. By 1930, they had rented the former Henry Hicks home at 905 Main Street with their children Howard, Claudia, Dorothy, Louise and Martha. Fred worked as a farmhand, and Octavia as a cook for a private family. In the years that followed, the Sorrells would accommodate a large household of children and grandchildren. They became fondly-remembered neighbors in the village, working for the Estlers and the Millers. Fred became a deacon in the Colored Baptist Church. Octavia became known for her singing, whether guest-soloing at village churches, or letting her voice ring out in holy praise on the sidewalks of Main Street as she made her way to and from her work for the Estlers and other Barboursville families.

The Old Dominion's loss was Cabell County's gain. Fred and Octavia's Barboursville family line extended to the late twentieth century, when two remarkable family achievements touched Marshall University.

The Sorrell's only son worked for 35 years as a maintenance worker and service engineer at Marshall. Even after his retirement in 1974, he would be called back to consult or help on special projects. Nobody knew the physical workings of the campus like Howard Sorrell. This man never drove a car. He caught the bus from Barboursville to work every day. He personally built an unpretentious one-story residence on the Hicks-Washington-Sorrell lot at 905 Main Street. (The cinder-block structure serves as a child care center in 2013.)

A much larger but equally unpretentious building on the east end of Marshall's campus houses the physical plant, facilities planning and management, and receiving departments. Clearly seen across from Joan C. Edwards Stadium on 20th Street by drivers, students and game-day tailgaters, the maintenance building was named in honor of Howard Kenneth Sorrell after he retired. It became the first building on Marshall University's Campus to be named for a living person.

Octavia Sorrell in her sunset years
(Courtesy of Lorraine Powell)

Howard Sorrell never married, but was a great friend to his neighbors, not to mention a fellow Herd fan, fishing buddy and youth mentor. After retirement, Sorrell took it upon himself to become an unofficial village ambassador to new African American families who moved into Barboursville. He was the last descendent of the late nineteenth-century settlers living in the village when he died in 1996.

Howard Sorrell's nephew and Fred and Octavia's grandson, Roy Goines, also made a name for himself at Marshall. *(His story of athletic and academic achievement on both sides of America's segregation line appears in Chapter 14.)*

Good Neighbors

It certainly should be acknowledged that the African American households in Barboursville remained a small presence in the village—some would say *unthreateningly* small—and that claims of a relatively tolerant community are based on stories and evidence gleaned from those who were content enough to stay, rather than those who quietly "moved on down the line." The fact that black and mixed-race households dwindled after 1920 could be attributed to a variety of reasons, ranging from race-based isolation and incidents of prejudice to more race-neutral factors like the loss of work opportunities or boredom with small-town living.

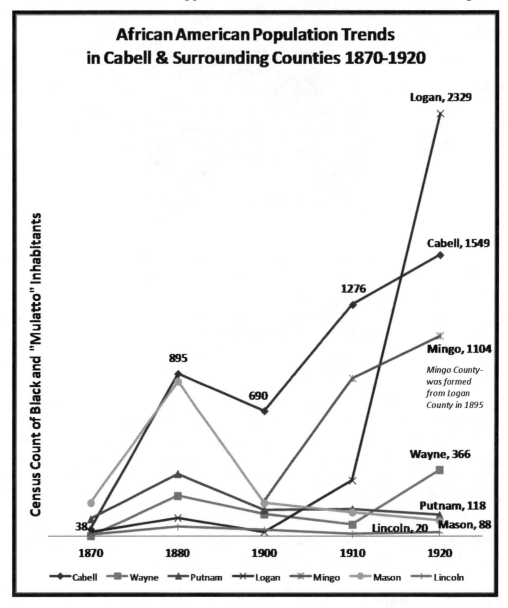

County Population Trends
(U.S Census Data)

Nevertheless, compared to other communities, Barboursville seems to have offered stability during a tumultuous period of black migration. The following chart, showing the population shifts in Cabell and surrounding counties between 1870 and 1920, illustrates the trends among southwestern West Virginia's coalfields, railroad lanes and rural farmlands. In this context, it becomes more clear how groups of African American workers and their families might come and go, or stay away from some places entirely.

Segregation was a way of life for the Fliggins, Hicks, Hamler, Hill, Smith, Washington and Whirles families of Barboursville. There were some doors that would never be open. Beyond the folks who lived next door, employers and other white associates of these families, others may have kept their distance. It is likely that many held on to the attitudes of nineteenth century Southern white culture, as expressed in a boyhood remembrance by Maurice Beckett: "I delivered the newspaper to "Aunt" Mattie (Fliggins) and was always slightly afraid of her, poor lady, for she was very black and very negroid, and my little life had not included other "negroes.""

Yet even in those times, Barboursville had just enough—maybe more than just enough—influential white residents to negate the ugly effects of America's "Jim Crow" social codes. They did this simply by being neighborly: men of the county court patronizing the Depot Street barber shop, Roderick Bright selling a Main Street lot, Belle Dirton standing witness at a family wedding, P.A. Harris conveying the deed for a schoolyard, the "large white attendance" passing through the Depot Street church doors for a Baptist revival.

Within the village, with all its prejudices and false assumptions, a community of African Americans emerged from the shadow of slavery, lived and worked among white neighbors, worshipped freely, banked their earnings, reached for and owned their piece of the American dream. Harry B. Washington was one of the last two "black pioneer" family members to live out their days in the district. In his handwritten family history he echoed the sentiments of others I spoke with, representing four generations in the village:

"I love this little town of Barboursville where Seven Black Families were welcome to live and die in peace."

Our Special Correspondent Furnishes an Interesting Letter:
FEBRUARY 24, 1898—*Young boys at Huntington, Guyandotte, Barboursville,*
Ona and other points hang on moving trains with a recklessness that can have
but one result, and that disastrous.

CHAPTER 12

TURN-OF-THE-CENTURY BUSTLE (1898-1920)

A Diverse Mix in the Village

IN 1880, Huntington had ten times as many people as Barboursville. By 1900, Huntington's population had grown to 30 times that of Barboursville. Over in the "Jewel City," Third to Sixth Avenues sprang up with buildings in Queen Anne, Gothic Revival and Italian Medieval styles, as well as the new Renaissance-inspired county courthouse with its gold-leaf cupola. While Huntington represented the metropolitan ideal, Barboursville was the same old nineteenth century "market town," hemmed in by the Guyan and the Mud. Although it was something more than a whistle-stop along the C&O, the village had become the county's "third-fiddle" municipality, having been outpaced by both Huntington and Milton in population.

If the *Cabell Record* gossip clips featured in Chapter 2 are an indication, villagers were just fine with small town status. Having settled into its role as a college town with Methodist ties, the town played host to debating clubs, monthly "musicales," educational societies, fraternities and sororities. The business leaders formed a Board of Trade, and young men joined the Junior American Mechanics lodge.

Members of the Methodist Episcopal South continued to share their chapel with college students, who were expected to attend services every day. The "colored" Baptist church on Depot Street was a social center for black families, and the white Baptists were raising money to build their own house of worship.

Hotels, dormitories and private boarding homes accommodated college students, laborers and businessmen. In addition, farm folks, villagers, river men, and all classes of workers on the C&O hoofed it up and down Main, Center, Depot and Water Streets. Judging by Barboursville's under-utilized "town lock-up" just behind Center Street, the mix was largely harmonious. There was purportedly a trouble spot down by the river, according to "Our Special Correspondent" who wrote, "A battle with brick took place on the Bowery, a street leading to the ferry, Monday evening, and one man was slightly hurt."

Barboursville's gossip columnist, perhaps giving voice to certain smug inhabitants of a "dry village," also offered this bit of verse about the imbibing classes in other West Virginia towns:

> *Many Parkersburgers quench their thirst with wine,*
> *At Charleston they're stuck on Central City beer.*
> *A Loganite wants whiskey straight,*
> *Because it brings him cheer*
> *Hamlin boys will take theirs half and half,*
> *And say it brings queer dizziness;*
> *Huntington boozers have no choice,*
> *They just take the whole business.*
> *(The Cabell Record 1899)*

A more wholesome spirit was celebrated in turn-of-the-century Barboursville, reflecting pride not only in its college culture, but enthusiasm for the "base ball" team associated with the school. The late-nineteenth century sport had spread through the nation's colleges and local clubs as a serious pastime, and teams formed in Barboursville as early the 1880s. By 1901, a Barboursville team was going up against teams of young men in places like Guyandotte and Milton. In May 1901, *The Cabell Record* reported, "The Barboursville College base ball nine defeated the club connected with Marshall College by a score of 9 to 5."

Whereas young Barboursville men a century earlier had been plotting out streets, shouldering muskets, pushing plows and hauling rocks, the shortened workday brought as many new generations of village men prepping grass fields, leading practice drills, "tossing the old horse hide," and thinking up sports clichés. As villagers settled into the twentieth century, sports and sports fandom became lasting obsessions.

In 1901, the college found itself on solid financial footing for the first time, after a Fayette County coal field developer and his wife responded to Southern Methodist appeals and endowed the Barboursville College with a $10,000 gift. The school was immediately renamed Morris Harvey College after its benefactor. In the decades to follow, the school would be able to expand its academic and athletic facilities.

The steamer *Guyandotte* was making regular trips upriver, and logging operations and push boats continued sending commerce downriver. On the east end of town, an older woman named Hattie Anderson owned about 80 acres up Blake Hollow in the Hash Ridge area. There she kept a boarding house for timber men from Lincoln and Logan counties who would walk up the hollow and stay overnight before their slow slog back up the Guyan.

Birds-eye view of Morris Harvey main campus in 1906.
Notice the cluster of students lounging on the triangle-shaped piece
of ground between the chapel and the administration building.
(Courtesy of Wilma Smith)

Construction was also underway on the Guyan Valley Railroad. Day laborers, many of them black, stayed in lodgings owned by Henry Adams, James Davis and Max Walton. On the opposite side of the creek from Anderson's, Captain Drury Allen purchased about 100 acres of the old Peter Blake farm from Nettie Thornburg in 1900. In addition to his work subcontracting for the railroad, Captain Allen put up an untold number of laborers at construction camps on his property.

"Houses rent well in this town. There is always a demand for them, and never enough to satisfy the seekers. People like this place and our population would be much more than what it is if there were more dwellings," wrote Our Special Correspondent.

A Line to the Coalfields

J.L. Caldwell, who owned mineral rights and timber in the region, was an early promoter of a new rail line to run through Cabell, Lincoln and Logan counties. In July 1899, a survey party for the new Guyan Valley Railroad Company set out with their compasses, transits, levels and calculation tables to decide where to lay the new tracks. Chief Engineers George McKendree and James French surveyed the land from Barboursville to Logan County, along with Doug French, James Blume, Lake Blume, Floyd Alberts, Tom Miller, Stephen Davis, Grant Shipe, Beamer Davis and others. Major McKendree is said to have influenced authorities to abandon the original plan to run the line through Blake Creek in favor of building the rails along the Guyandotte River—which just so happened to cross McKendree's land (current Barboursville Community Park) and the farm of his wife's people, the McComases of Peyton Street.

The children of Barboursville's Thomas King were also immersed in the railroad business. Daughter Ethel married a railroad yard foreman, Mr. Long. Son Wallace King was an attorney who supervised the purchase of timber for bridges and other railroad construction. James King oversaw the maintenance of way department, and Herbert King spent years obtaining rights-of-way for much of the Guyandotte Valley branch. According to Frank Ball, it was on one of these trips that Herbert King met the lady he later married, Lula Spurlock of Midkiff in Lincoln County. "Once as he was crossing the Cabell-Lincoln county line near Salt Rock, his horse reared and he was thrown into the next county, to hear him tell it," reported Ball.

Work on the new line to Logan County began in 1900 under the supervision of William Kelley. Drury Allen subcontracted masonry for chief contractors Carpenter and Wright of Virginia, and built the bridges and overpasses along the line. Allen and his wife, the former Annia Friend, daughter Annie G. and son Edley H. had moved around Virginia and Kentucky before arriving in the Barboursville area, where they settled for life. According to Allen's granddaughter Ann Brady Turman, her mother "Annie G." spent time living with the president of Morris Harvey College at the old Dirton home as a student. Captain Allen eventually tore down the old Blake log house and built a new frame home that preceded today's Orchard Hills clubhouse. Over the years, the Allens raised several adoptive and foster children, and at one time hired Mattie Fliggins as a live-in servant in their busy home.

News snippets in the *Cabell Record* from 1898 to 1901 hint at the impact of railroad construction and the conditions encountered by workers who passed this way:

Some of the contractors on the N— Hill and Salt Rock road are paying their laborers but 80 cents a day, from which they have to board themselves. And the work is the hardest kind, too.

A disastrous freight wreck occurred at this place Friday night...no one was hurt.

A force of colored men have been laying steel at the C&O between Barboursville and Guyandotte. Big improvement.

Freight traffic has been immense on the C&O line of late.

The old Baumgardner hotel has been rented by the railroad contractors, in which to house their employees until substantial shanties can be erected for that purpose.

Hundreds of men, mostly colored, car loads of mules and tools have been arriving here to work on the Guyandotte Valley Railway.

The male members of the Italian colony are hard at work breaking stone on the McKendree hill for the abutments for the first railroad bridge, and they break the English language in an awful style.

Mr. Allen, who is here to put the foundations on the railroad bridge piers has moved his family to the dam.

A yard with several switches will be built at Barboursville, and that place made the headquarters of the Guyandot (sic) Valley Road. (Cabell Record 1898-1901)

The Guyan Valley Railroad merged with the C&O in 1903, allowing completion of the link from Barboursville. The Norfolk and Western had already opened up coal fields through Wayne County to Williamson in the early 1890s.

The addition of a rail line to Logan County was a significant development.

On September 9, 1904, a large crowd in the town of Aracoma welcomed the first train from Barboursville; the town would be renamed Logan in 1907. The arrival of the Guyandotte Valley Railroad boosted Logan County's coal production from 500 tons in 1904 to 272,080 tons in 1905. The Island Creek Coal Company, formed from modest beginnings in Holden, West Virginia, grew to be one of the top five producers in the country and a subsidiary of the mammoth Occidental Petroleum Company.

The Williamson-Logan Field was geographically linked with three other coalfields discovered in West Virginia: the Kanawha and New River Field, the Winding Gulf Field and the Pocahontas Field. By the early 1900s, the southern West Virginia coalfields would employ 100,000 men. Commercial coal mining changed the complexion of southern West Virginia. Between 1890 and 1910, West Virginia was the only southern state to increase in total population. In addition to large numbers of Austrian, Hungarian, Italian, Russian and Turkish immigrants, an influx of African American migrants filled Logan and Mingo counties.

As the new center for the nation's extractive industries, southern West Virginia became a hotbed for headlines. The rapid growth of a migrant labor population fueled interracial tensions, crime, squalid living conditions and communicable disease epidemics. In 1902, a feisty Irish-American dressmaker and schoolteacher, Mary Harris "Mother" Jones, campaigned to unionize 7,000 miners in Kanawha Valley. In 1906, over 600 miners were killed in eight separate mine disasters across the state.

Removed from the turmoil at the northern terminus of the Guyan Valley line, the train station at Barboursville expanded as a hub of passenger travel. In addition to regular traffic on the C&O main line from Huntington to Charleston, large numbers of shoppers and businessmen now made their way from Lincoln, Logan and Boone counties to Huntington and other destinations.

The arrival of the "GV" line changed the nature of local freight handling, as members of the Brady family recalled to Frank Ball:

> Package freight handling was a mammoth job in the "Gay" Nineties. Teamsters didn't take their turn, but answered the call of Station Agent William Townsend, as he yelled to them that their produce had been "unearthed" from among the layers. The "nominee" would then pull his team out of line, load up, Melissa, Pea Ridge, Martha, Inez, Salt Rock, Roach, West Hamlin, or wherever. But the Valley Rails changed all this, leaving packaging freight to local hauling, largely. (Ball, Avenue of Antiquity Series 1973)

In 1910, the Chesapeake and Ohio moved other operations into Barboursville. The company dismantled an old freight house in Kanawha County, rebuilt it at Depot Street and established what would become the C&O Reclamation Plant. The "C&O Shops" provided employment for many years, producing rails, ties, joints and bars to meet the heavy demands of the railroad system. In 1912, the Dirton siblings sold land to the railroad to provide additional right-of-way.

As the C&O was rapidly expanding between 1890 and 1908, scores of standard design train stations were built throughout its network, including a combination passenger-freight station at Barboursville's Depot Street. Few company records were preserved from this era so the actual date of construction is unknown, but judging by the schedules chalked onto the bulletin board in the photograph, the station was built before completion of the Guyan Valley line. Beckett described the Barboursville depot as being about 40 feet wide and a 100 feet long, elevated to the level of the freight car openings with a long adjoining walkway, a passenger waiting room and two ticket windows.

Then there was the building's original color. The caption of a photograph found in the collection of the Chesapeake and Ohio Historical Society—"C&O passenger station at Barboursville, West Virginia, with horse and wagon, circa 1900. Orange with white trim paint"—indicates the Barboursville station was built during what is known as the Chesapeake and Ohio's "Orange Period." Brightly-painted orange passenger cars and train depots were favored by the men who took the company's helm in the 1890s, after Collis P. Huntington lost financial control of the C&O. A visual reference can be found a few hours' drive (or a few seconds' Google-search) away: Alderson, West Virginia has repainted its old depot building the period orange shade, making it one of a few remaining C&O stations to show-case the standard turn-of-the-century color scheme.

Barboursville Depot circa 1900
(Courtesy of the Chesapeake and Ohio Historical Society)

As a young boy, Maurice Beckett of Lee Street would cut through his neighbors' yards on Saturdays to meet his father, a railroad agent working on Depot Street. There, while waiting for the end of Hal Beckett's shift, Maurice took in the sights, sounds and distinctive smells of the depot, and observed the impressive feats of the engineers, telegraphers and caboose men. Years later, an essay by Beckett captured the interplay between passenger and freight traffic on the two lines that defined the rhythm of village life:

(The Guyan Valley passenger train) was a small train with two passenger cars, a postal car, and two express or freight cars…Each day the "GV" passenger train went to Logan and back, whistling at countless road crossings and stopping as often as each 5 miles to load and unload passengers and express items; it also carried mail. There were stops at Barboursville, Martha, Roach, Salt Rock, Branchland, Hart's Creek, and many other hamlets or cross roads…. Railway employees rode the local line free.

From Barboursville one could travel to Huntington or Charleston to board the "Name Trains" for Cincinnati or Chicago, or for Washington and points East. These big, elaborate trains were The Virginian, The Sportsman, and The George Washington. Their beautiful locomotives were the ultimate in steam engine construction with great driving wheels almost as tall as a man, and capable of starting or stopping their 12 or more cars with such ease that a glass of water on the diner's table was not spilled. Their Pullman designed sleepers were comfortable and convenient, the porters were polite…and the food served in their diners, though expensive, was excellent…

Down the GV by day and night came ponderous coal trains to join the main line at Barboursville. Two types of locomotives were used for this haul: the "Mallet" (pronounced "Malee"), and the "Mike," which, I was told, was really a "Mikado." The 4-cylinder Mallet was the strong workhorse and pulled up to 100 loaded hopper cars of coal down the valley easily. Many times, however, these great trains were pulled by a Mike, which had two cylinders. This should not have mattered for it was down grade. The problem lay in entering the main line of the C&O. Due to its heavy traffic there were many times when these coal trains had to stop and wait their turn, for practically nothing stopped the Name Trains on the main line aside from accident or error and these were rare. So, the Mike and its followers would come to a clanking halt short of the main line and watch the signal pole for a "go ahead." All outbound traffic in the village was effectively blocked. (M. Beckett, The Railroad n.d.)

By 1916, railroad travel in American reached its peak; 98 percent of United States passenger travel was by train, and 77 percent of freight was carried by rail. Barboursville may have been just one of hundreds of North American "train towns" but local commerce, like the locomotives, was moving at a fast clip.

"B" Stands For…

Brick-making. George Edgar Thornburg (1846-1927) was one of Barboursville's leading businessmen at the dawn of the twentieth century. He had a hand in several local enterprises, including serving as president of the new Teays Valley and Guyandotte Telephone line. After donating land across the river for construction of the new Pea Ridge Methodist Episcopal Church, South, Thornburg turned his attention to the northeast corner of Main and Center. He and his wife, the former Nancy "Nannie" Wilson, may have just intended to build a respectable home, but in doing so the couple left a fine Barboursville legacy in what is inarguably the village's most ornate building.

The George Thornburg building, constructed in 1900, is seen in this photo from the 1930s.
(Courtesy of Marshall University Libraries Special Collections)

In March 1901, the George Thornburg house was built. If the Miller-Thornburg store and Morris Harvey campus buildings served as calling cards for Barboursville brick, Thornburg's corner home was a celebration of it. It is described in *The Cabell County Architectural Guide* as "an excellent example of the Queen Anne style," boasting a tower with a conical roof, a wraparound porch and an abundance of ornamental detailing.

Small brick-making plants had lined the Guyandotte River for years, even before the Civil War, after two resources were found in abundance here. First, there existed the necessary supplies of natural gas to provide the intense heat needed for firing kilns. Secondly, the trifling Barboursville soil, barely suitable for growing crops, held thick layers of red and reddish-brown clay between the topsoil and the bedrock. This provided the raw material for "a very good grade of red building brick."

In 1904, George Thornburg founded a large modern brick factory on Peyton Street, named either the Guyan Valley Brick Company or the Barboursville Brick Company (sources differ). The plant was capable of producing 75 types and colors of brick and tile. In 1909, after a nationwide financial panic destabilized the company, Thornburg's son-in-law, Mordecai Clarence Johnson, entered into the business, sold stock and re-organized it as the Barboursville Clay Manufacturing Company.

Mordecai Johnson had come from Sissonville, West Virginia to Barboursville in 1896 as a college student, taught school and took classes, and graduated from Morris Harvey after four years to become a pastor for the Methodist Episcopal Church, South. "M.C." married George and Nannie's only child, Minnie, in 1898; this marriage produced two children, Edgar and Thelma. Mordecai and his family spent several years assigned to churches around West Virginia and Kentucky. They returned to Barboursville by 1909 and lived at Main and Center with George, Nannie and a few live-in servants for more than a decade. In 1913, M.C. and Minnie's son and George and Nannie's only grandson, 12-year-old Edgar, died of accidental causes, described in the county death register as "burn by powder."

Hotel Edgar at the south side of Main St. circa 1910
(Courtesy of Barboursville Public Library)

As the nineteenth century wood frame buildings in Barboursville's business district were gradually replaced, fire-resistant, locally-manufactured red brick became the construction standard. A stately two-story brick elementary school was built in 1903. In 1906, D. Blain Shaw built a two-story structure on south Main Street across from the college. The building took up nearly half a block and housed the Edgar Hotel, Earl Spencer's grocery, and later the Brady Hardware store. In 1914, Mordecai Johnson built the three-story brick on Central and Brady that would house a grocery store on the first floor, the telephone office on the second floor—where Belle Dirton served as faithful night operator on the switchboard, and a Miss Ramsey of Merritt Street worked as the "Hello Girl"—and meeting space on the third floor. In the alley behind Johnson's telephone building was the new brick jailhouse and fire station, built around 1915.

During peak production, the Barboursville Clay Manufacturing Company would produce nearly 80,000 bricks a day. A crowning achievement was the 1921 sale of Barboursville brick for a White House remodeling project. In the mid-1920's the company was sold and remained under ownership of the Wiseman family for more than 50 years. A second, lesser-known, brickyard existed for some years on the eastern edge of the village, on old Merritt farm property near the Route 60 underpass. According to John Merritt, it was built about 1917, and Bob Kyle was the first Superintendent. But the company George Thornburg built at Peyton Street operated for 75 years. By the 1970s, it was the only red brick manufacturer in West Virginia.

Bank. In September 1905, The First State Bank opened for business. The board of directors consisted of George Thornburg, president; U. G. Shipe, vice-president; H. S. King, C. R. Morris, B. V. Davis, F. B. Enslow, and a 31-year-old transplant named Phillip Alexander Vallandingham.

According to a profile written by Fred Lambert, P.A. Vallandingham came from a long line of Welsh descendents concentrated in and around the state of Kentucky since the early 1800s. He settled in Barboursville, purchasing the site on north Main Street that once belonged to Octavius Church, and embraced community life. Frank Ball revisited the origins of the bank in 1958, as part of a full-page feature on 50-year Barboursville family businesses in *The Herald-Advertiser*:

The bank was opened for business Saturday, September 2....J.I. Kuhn came in and deposited $15.00 and the First State Bank was in business....(P.A. Vallandingham) was a farmer in Cleveland's day when 5-cent tobacco and 4-cent butter discouraged him and he decided to learn the banking business. He worked for (the bank in Owenton) for a year free, paying his own room and board partly from proceeds of a tobacco crop that he sold for 7½ cents a pound. He then got on the payroll of this and another bank or two for a few years.

W.E. Sullivan, an Owen County business man, became interested in him and came into West Virginia to search for a good location for a bank with a view of setting Mr. Vallandingham up in the banking business. Beginning at Ansted in Fayette County, he worked his way back to Kenova. He decided that Barboursville was the best bet. And the judgment of Mr. Sullivan has proven good. "The people of Barboursville and vicinity were then as now as he described them: substantial, honorable, and trustworthy businessmen and farmers," says Mr. Vallandingham.

Somewhere along the line, Mr. Vallandingham had obtained possession of a horse and buggy. He drove into town from the west, sold his horse and buggy, and went into the banking business with the proceeds. At least that's the way some of the old villagers tell it. Here he met and married a fellow Kentuckian, Miss Willa Bowden, then a teacher in Morris Harvey College.

The First State Bank occupied a small building next to the one it occupied now, for a year. In 1906 a vault was bought to replace the small safe and the building in which the bank is now located was built…the brick came from George Thornburg's brick plant in Barboursville. Mr. Vallandingham was cashier for many years. He became president in 1932. He has stood before one of the windows for 53 years…His son, Granville, has been vice president for the past several year(s) and Mr. Vallandingham's son-in-law R.E. Defibaugh *(married to daughter Betty)*, has been cashier for some years. Both the Vallandinghams have been Barboursville mayors. Phillip Vallandingham, son of Granville, fills in for his grandfather.

Mrs. Granville Vallandingham works in the bank occasionally helping out with the bookkeeping. At first, Mr. Vallandingham was the entire working force. But when the work became too heavy he inquired of the Morris Harvey College president who would be an adept girl to aid with the books. The authorities recommended Miss Willa B. Moore, a local girl. She began in 1907 and is still there. And it is doubtful if any of the Vallandingham family know as much about the books as she does. "She has been a faithful employee," Mr. Vallandingham remarked.

Ball wrote, "the Vallandingham dynasty is set for probably another fifty years," and in this prediction he was correct. In 2012, a fourth generation of Vallandingham men serve as First State Bank executives. From Captain Kuhn's first $15 deposit in 1905, the family business grew to a $288 million, multi-branch, community institution.

It has been pointed out that Mary Willa Bowden was a "Renaissance woman" in her own right before she became Mrs. Vallandingham in 1910. According to grandson Jack Dilley (who provided the photograph), she received her Bachelor of Arts degree from Kentucky State College in 1900, the first class to have female graduates. (That school is now the University of Kentucky.) When she took a position at Morris Harvey in 1901, she specialized in English instruction but was also proficient in Latin, French and German, and a lover of literature.

Mary Willa Bowden Vallandingham
(Courtesy of Jack Dilley)

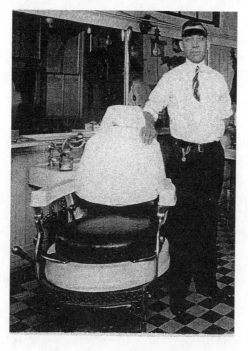

Charles May at his Barber Shop
(Courtesy of Barboursville Public Library)

If one could describe a twentieth century "power couple" to succeed Joseph and Marie Gardner, the Vallandinghams would almost certainly be that pair. Not to be overshadowed by her husband's banking business and public service (he was

Barboursville mayor for two terms and served on the county school board), Mrs. Vallandingham was a charter member of Kuhn Memorial Presbyterian, a charter member of the local Daughters of the American Revolution, a Barboursville PTA president, and organizing president of the Barboursville Women's Club.

Barber. In 1900, a teenager named Charles May got work laying railroad tracks about a mile or two south of Barboursville, and worked with the Guyan Valley crew until they got to Big Creek. According to Frank Ball, "his first barbering attempts were made when he was a laborer on the section force up the Guyandotte when he would throw a burlap sack around his victim's shoulders and clip an overgrown mop of hair. For these he got whatever the trade would bear, which was little. After a few months of this...he moved into town and set up shop."

The Charles May Barber Shop on Central Avenue was opened in 1908 in single-story frame building that had in the previous century housed Justice of the Peace J. Lusher, Moses Thornburg's law office, and Dr. McConkey's medical practice. According to May's son Samuel, Charles *(seen in this undated photo courtesy of the Barboursville Public Library)* was the first barber to use electric clippers, and in 1908 was allowed to use them only between the hours of 6 and 9 p.m.

May was joined by his brother Oscar, and had a three-chair shop for more than five decades. In later years May diversified, adding a beauty shop and dry cleaning operation in the same building, before it was razed in 1958. Charles May and his wife Grace raised at least seven sons and daughters on Central Avenue. In a family reversal of career paths, son Everett May started out following his father in the barbering business, then left the trade for the railroad life, working with the C&O signal department and moving up to become foreman of the reclamation plant's signal shop on Depot street.

Business. In addition to the brick factory, Charles May's barbering business and The First State Bank, at least two other locally-owned businesses spanned more than 50 years.

The oldest was James T. Brady's store, which operated on Depot and Main Streets from 1899 to 1923, before locating in the former Edgar Hotel, with James and Annie (Allen) Brady and their children occupying the second story of the building.

Another business that stayed in the same family for decades was Updyke's dry goods store. In 1907, 40-year-old Fabious I. Updyke brought his wife Rosie, his teenage sons Chauncey and Cecil, and his mercantile experience from the coal town of Keystone in McDowell County. He took over a store building from W.S. Spencer near the corner of Main and Central and went into business with the help of his sons. Upon their father's death in 1931, Chauncey took over the department store, and Cecil ran a shoe store next door. For years, Chauncey Updyke kept the store with few employees, with the exception of Mrs. Ora Stafford, who worked there on and off for over 35 years.

Other village businesses flourished in the early twentieth century. By 1910, the village boasted a few additional general stores, butchers Bob Shipe and J. H. Meador, grocers Evan and Lake Blume and Thomas Merritt, and tobacco merchant J. C. Ellis. Former postmaster and Civil War veteran's son, Wilhelm Heinrich "Henry" Stowasser, opened an art and picture shop in 1908 called the Peerless Art Company with his son Garfield. The art business gradually turned into a variety store.

During the 1890s, George R. Miller (son of Würtemburg's John Miller) and his wife Mollie opened an ice cream parlor on the current library site (the same spot where the "colored Methodist church" almost came to fruition in 1891). A favorite meeting place for Morris Harvey students, "Miller's Famous Ice Cream Parlor" drew fans from Kentucky and Ohio. According to Linwood McCormick, the Millers had ice brought in on the train and stored in an ice house in the back. At some point neighbor Octavia Sorrell was brought into the operation and perfected the preparation of various ice cream flavors in hand-cranked ten gallon ice cream makers, and later taught the craft to her son Howard.

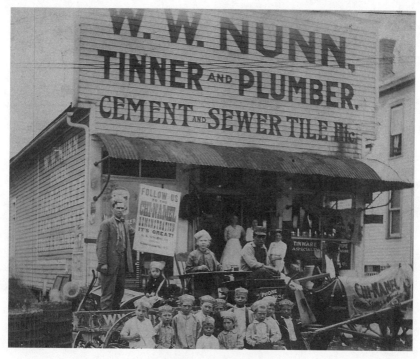

"Chi-Namel" Promotion
(Courtesy Bob Doss)

Finally, there was 38-year-old plumber William W. Nunn of Central Avenue, who took part in early marketing demonstrations sometime around 1910. The Ohio Varnish Company had come out with a new durable paint called "Chi-Namel," which featured tiny brush-wielding Chinamen in its print notices (ads that would surely be deemed racist in today's culture). A letter in the *Hardware Journal of 1910* lauds the company for coming up with the lucrative idea of having personal demonstrations to boost retail sales. Apparently, Barboursville's Mr. Nunn and his employee Cline Doss climbed aboard the Chi-Namel bandwagon—or more literally, embellished a horse-drawn wagon with promotional signage, added some local boys and girls wearing little "Chinaman" caps, and hit the Barboursville streets, P. T. Barnum style, to generate local buzz about the product. By 1920, Nunn had moved on to become a hardware man in Guyandotte.

Baptists (and other church-goers). After decades of meeting in private homes, store buildings and the courthouse, Barboursville's white Baptist congregation was formally organized in 1900 with 19 members. They started a building fund in 1902, which a few years later culminated in the erection of a chapel at 947 Main Street. The church was located next door to the home of P.A. Vallandingham, who became the men's Sunday school teacher. As pictured, the building was originally red brick with a belfry, but was remodeled and enlarged several times before the congregation built its current building across the street in the early 1960s.

Barboursville Baptist Church c. 1905
(Courtesy Barboursville Public Library)

An early Barboursville Baptist pastor was George Walter Huddleston of Fayette County, who served as a Baptist Association preacher and missionary in various locations before taking charge of the Barboursville flock from 1909 to 1913. He then became City Missionary in Huntington, and later served throughout the southern Guyandotte Valley.

In subsequent years at Barboursville Baptist, according to early churchgoer Maurice Beckett, "we were a small church and the poorly paid preachers came and went with assured regularity; many of them young, poorly trained, and indifferently educated." One constant in the church, Beckett wrote in an evocative five-page essay, was the "immense and important outpouring of time, talent and religious feeling that has gone into the hymns of the Christian Church. Prior to World War I most of the small town and rural population...knew and sang far more hymns than any other form of music."

In addition to passing along the old songs of faith—"Onward, Christian Soldiers," "Nearer, My God, to Thee" and the like—Barboursville's churches held revival services at least yearly. By the 1920s:

> The two Methodists and the Baptists Church spaced their (revivals) so the populace had the opportunity to attend one at a time, each congregation faithfully backing the services of the other."

Postcard Image of Steele Memorial Church 1907.
(Courtesy Barboursville Public Library)

Sometimes, depending on the facilities of the minister in charge, they were held in large tents which were capable of holding more than the church. Tents were also cooler in the summer. The pastor of a given church very rarely held its annual revival; the normal procedure was to hire a minister from another area, particularly one who was skilled in this highly emotional field. (M. Beckett, The Barboursville Baptist Church n.d.)

Rev. Samuel Steele of the original (Northern) Methodist faction relocated from Illinois to Barboursville in 1901, where he succeeded preachers of the previous century including Jeremiah Engle, J. C. Sidebottom, "Walking Joe" Bedford, L. D. Bryan, J. B. Shaw, Albert Craig, D. H. Rutter and H. H. Shaw. In 1907, Steele achieved his vision of having a "northern" church built on the south side of the village, where a majority of the old Union families lived and where he believed the church would attract new members. Taking the seats, pulpit and bell from the original "northern" chapel on Main Street, Reverend Steele had it rebuilt (*as pictured*) on McClung Avenue (at the present Church of Christ site). The move caused a further split in the congregation, but the families who remained grew to sustain the village's second Methodist church, and it became today's Steele Memorial United Methodist Church.

Like other towns in states bordering the Mason-Dixon line, Barboursville would ever after remain a village with two Methodist churches. The 60-year-old rift between America's Methodist Episcopal Church" and Methodist Episcopal Church, South would take almost as many years to heal, beginning with the 1905 publication of a joint hymnbook between the two denominations. In 1939, the nation's northern and southern Methodists were reunited, simply renamed the Methodist Church. In 1968, the General Conference brought the Evangelical United Brethren into the big theological tent and renamed it the United Methodist Church.

Still in 1910, Barboursville's southern Methodists were the most culturally influential in the village, with their chapel housed on the Morris Harvey campus, hosting students in mandatory worship, helping to turn young collegiate men into pastors, and receiving the beneficence of prominent village families. Barboursville, West Virginia seemed to be *the* place for a Methodist preacher to raise his family (and get a free college education for his children); the 1910 Census documents at least seven M.E. South clergymen living in town limits: Charles A. Powers of Central Avenue, William M. Hiner (retired) of Water Street, Felix K. Struve of College Avenue, John B. F. Yoak of McClung Avenue, H. H. Pownall of Merritt Street, A. E. O'Dell of Main Street, and Mordecai C. Johnson at the Thornburg home at Main and Center Streets.

There were other Protestant church groups in the village. The 1910 Census schedule lists a Rev. Rush F. Patterson of Cottage Street who headed the Apostolic Holiness church. This is probably the same "Pilgrim Holiness Church" of the 1920s that Beckett referred to, "which held its frequent revivals as it saw fit," and "was attended by those Mennnonite-like people whose women wore extra-long dresses and long sleeves, and many of their husbands wore beards." (Based on an official website source, this church was formed in 1897 by Cincinnati converts from both Methodist and Quaker traditions.) Trinity Episcopal Church may have had Barboursville members hosting occasional services in cooperation with their Huntington counterparts. Finally, there was fledgling interest in a Presbyterian church, initiated in 1914 when 13 local members organized a small congregation.

1909 Bridge Over Guyan River
(Courtesy Barboursville Public Library)

Bridges and Buggies. Traffic in and out of town improved significantly in 1909, when a steel bridge ordered by the county court at last spanned the Guyandotte River from Main Street to Farmdale Road. It was one of three Industrial Age bridges out of the village. The 1883 steel bridge across the Mud had been built by the county to replace the original wooden bridge destroyed during the Civil War. Sometime between 1900 and 1908 the C&O line was relocated and the current overpass at the Main Street-U.S. 60 junction was built at the place where the old turnpike originally entered Barboursville.

The addition of the "Farmdale Bridge" finally did away with the old ferry, which had been located about 200 yards downstream from the corner of Main and Water Streets. Mrs. L.D. Cummings recalled taking walks out to Pea Ridge about a year before the bridge was completed:

The fiord at Barboursville had to be used to cross the Guyandotte River. It was a little below where the old bridge now crossed the river. We waded across, and usually walked to the foot of the hill where Oaklawn Cemetery is now located.

After the bridge was built, a few houses were built in Farmdale and the road was improved out Pea Ridge. Most of the traffic to Guyandotte and Huntington was along the Guyandotte River.

Even though Henry Ford introduced his Model T to America in 1908 and sold over half a million of them in 1916, automobiles were still seen by most Cabell County citizens as "toys for the wealthy." And so the streets of Barboursville would not be paved until 1916.

Ramsey M. Cackley operated a livery stable at Central Avenue, which in the early part of the century was still referred to by some as "Center Street." He kept horses, rented buggies, and was quite adept at transporting his passengers through the unpaved, muddy Barboursville streets. (later he would run a scheduled bus service between Barboursville and Huntington.) Even as "horseless carriages" began to make an appearance in Cabell County, Cackley's horse and buggy proved to be more reliable transport for folks such as newlywed Betty Carper Steele, who married in 1915. Her father-in-law the Rev. Steele had hired a motorized "jitney" to carry the couple off for their honeymoon trip, but the automobile driver had to wait on the opposite side of the Farmdale Bridge for its passengers to cross over in Cackley's buggy.

As the twentieth century reached its teens, even with its muddy and rutted streets, Barboursville had shaped itself, in its mix of churches, rail lines and red brick landmarks, into the village we largely recognize today.

Signs of the Times

By 1912, the nation's government and political parties had also been transformed in short order, and America was at the peak of what became known as The Progressive Age. Theodore Roosevelt assumed the presidency in September 1901 after an anarchist's bullet ended the life of William McKinley early in his second term. From then on, the relationship between government and Big Business began shifting.

The young, vigorous and wildly popular Republican Teddy Roosevelt sought to check the worst abuses by the "malefactors of great wealth" and give a "square deal" to farmers, laborers and common citizens. Roosevelt became known as a "trust-buster" for his aggressive curbs on the power of large corporations. Supporting labor unions in their demands for better wages and shorter hours, the president also enforced an eight-hour day for federal workers. He championed laws and established federal oversight to improve deplorable conditions in meat-packing, food processing and drug manufacturing, and set aside millions of acres of public land in the interest of environmental conservation.

Theodore Roosevelt's administration put America on a stronger international footing to intervene and keep smaller Western Hemisphere countries on their feet, and pushed through construction of the Panama Canal. Perhaps through sheer force of personality, and by joining the interests of urban progressives and rural populists, the Republican Roosevelt took the torch of reform away from liberal Democrats and socialist movements, and easily won another term. At the end of his second elected term in 1908, Roosevelt declined to seek a third term, hand-picked his Secretary of War as his successor on the ticket, and took off on an extended African Safari.

Republican William Howard Taft easily won the 1908 election. At 300 pounds, Ohio's "Big Bill" was history's most rotund American president. From Roosevelt he inherited an up-sized, well-educated and public-spirited civil service sector, and he carried out a number of T. R.'s policies, including 90 anti-trust suits. Politically, however, Taft was the opposite of gregarious "Rough Rider" Teddy. He was said to be less energetic in his pursuits, more inept in dealing with Congress, and he did little to inspire the public imagination. Eventually, some of his foreign policy decisions so angered his predecessor that Roosevelt was persuaded back into the political arena to run against the Republicans in 1912 on a Progressive ticket.

Self-styled "Bull Moose" Roosevelt did not succeed in winning back the presidency, but his third-party run had the long-term effect of squeezing liberal and progressive elements out of the "Grand Old Party" for good. The Democratic Party fielded "a new sort of candidate" in the serene and scholarly Woodrow Wilson, and won the three-way election.

In his charmed first term, Wilson convinced the Democratic Congress to advance many principles similar to Roosevelt's and Taft's, including child labor laws, the Federal Reserve Act, Federal Trade Commission Act and, with ratification of the Sixteenth Amendment in 1913, a national income tax. He eventually became an advocate for a women's right to vote. One area in which the Virginia-born Wilson did not take a forward-thinking stance was on the issue of race: he extended segregation to almost every federal department, and greatly disillusioned the black leaders who had supported his candidacy.

Racial attitudes on the whole took an uglier turn throughout the country in the second decade of the twentieth century. Huge increases in immigration from eastern Europe seem to have fueled a national backlash, as did migration of African Americans into America's large cities.

A heavyweight boxing match took place in Reno, Nevada on July 4, 1910 between white prizefighter James J. Jeffries and black boxer Jack Johnson. The event took on extraordinary national significance. The fight was hailed as "The Fight of the Century" when Jeffries sought to reclaim the championship from Johnson, who had challenged and defeated a white heavyweight champion two years earlier. Farmer Jim Jeffries, coming out of boxing retirement, was dubbed "The Great White Hope," and many whites across the country saw a potential Jeffries win as a demonstration of superiority of their race. Twenty thousand spectators attended the event, and hundreds of reporters covered it. Even the *Herald-Dispatch* got into the act, with an operator receiving Associate Press bulletins at the end of each round, then announcing the results by megaphone from the second story of the Fifth Avenue newspaper building. After the white man Jeffries went down in the 15th round and Johnson was declared the winner, race riots ensued across the country (and at least one Cabell County altercation was reported). Venomous editorials and legal decisions left no doubt about the depth of racial animosity in American society.

The growing scientific field of genetics led some political leaders to embrace the notion of controlled breeding to favor "advanced" races. Even President Roosevelt warned during his presidency that immigrants and minorities were too fertile, and that Anglo-Saxons risked committing "race suicide" by failing to keep up baby-for-baby.

Even though hundreds of thousands of Europeans were entering the United States each year between 1905 and 1914, Barboursville was becoming less diverse racially and ethnically than it had been in antebellum times. In contrast to the waves of eastern Europeans flocking to West Virginia's mining counties, the 1910 and 1920 Census schedules show only a handful of foreign-born heads of household in the village, most of them aging family patriarchs from the western European countries of England, Germany, Italy, Ireland and the like.

A Late Centennial Observance

> Barboursville, formerly seat of Cabell County, spent her one hundredth birthday yesterday in a quiet and sedate manner. No formal recognition of the centennial was held and not many persons were aware that January 14th marked the close of her one hundredth year. (Barboursville 100 Years Old, 1913)

It is understandable that Barboursville was not ready to observe its Centennial. For one thing, the town's birthday fell in the dead of winter. For another, there was a lot of work underway to bring the village up to twentieth century standards and accommodate the influx of new residents. "The contracts have already been placed and there are no vacant houses to be found in the entire town, every one being filled up and all by the men and their families who will make the very important and costly changes there," reported *The Herald Dispatch*.

Paving work was taking place across the bridge on the Pea Ridge side of the James River and Kanawha Turnpike, as Guyan riverbank rock was crushed for the road bed (pictured). The completed road would be paved in brick in 1914.

Paving on Pea Ridge
(Courtesy Bob Doss)

Due to ever-increasing coal shipments, the C&O Railroad invested at least $150,000 to make Barboursville the terminal of its Guyan Valley division in 1913. This involved building a connecting link between the main line and the G.V. line, permitting the eastbound coal trains to pass directly onto the main line without the necessity of going all the way to the Huntington yards.

It was a year of speculation in new ventures. In 1913 there were published reports of renewed effort to revisit a possible oil well around Salt Rock with more modern drilling machinery, after attempts decades earlier found only "a dry hole" there. After an early spring hot spell, "twenty prominent men of the college town" announced plans to put up cash for a "thoroughly modern ice and cold storage plant," and sent 30-year-old miller Earl Spencer on an information-gathering trip.

Chicago-born brothers Albert E. and William F. May had arrived in Barboursville early in the decade, and saw opportunity. They owned an electrical generator that was powered by natural gas and set up on the hill next to the Farmdale bridge. They also owned the first water system. In 1913, water mains were laid and a water supply tank built above the college. This enabled the town to replace the volunteer bucket brigade and fight fires using a hose and drum on a "fire cart" that could be pulled by two men. The May brothers would eventually attract even more business with a new flour mill at the corner of Main and Water Streets.

Another enterprising transplant was David Blaine Shaw of Philippi, son of former Morris Harvey president, state legislator and Southern Methodist David William Shaw. Once the impressive Edgar Hotel was built, the young real estate agent decided to diversify. In 1911, *The Herald Dispatch* reported that Shaw bought *The Cabell Record,* noting that he also was publishing *The Barboursville Budget,* a Democratic paper. "Some of Mr. Shaw's Huntington friends assert, jocularly of course, that he is building up a newspaper trust and that he expects to enter politics, and be able to catch 'em comin' and goin.'"

By March 2013, Barboursville's Board of Trade was headed by D. Blaine Shaw. The board was making plans with Morris Harvey College and the Women's Club for an "auspicious occasion" to celebrate the Centennial on the first week of June. Noting that Barboursville's population had grown from 400 in 1903 to 1,200 in 1913, Shaw "spoke entertainingly of the coming celebration" in an interview with *The Herald-Dispatch.*

Scheduled with Morris Harvey's annual commencement in mind, the event would also mark West Virginia's fiftieth anniversary, the 25th anniversary of the college—"and incidentally, the fact that just twenty-five years ago Barboursville ceased to be the county seat of Cabell county, voluntarily transferring that honor to Huntington because it interfered with the town's educational advancement and she didn't want it anyway," reported *The Herald-Dispatch* with a straight face. According to the article, Shaw promised "a feast of reason, a flow of soul and other things satisfying to both the mental and physical self."

June arrived with an elaborate five-day schedule of Centennial events, highlighted by Morris Harvey class day recitals, baseball and concerts on "Class and Music Day" Monday, the Southern Methodist ministerial institute and literary contests on "Ministers and Literary" Tuesday; Morris Harvey commencement exercises and track and field events on "College Day" Wednesday; and a "sunrise cannonading," band concert, parade and distinguished speakers on "West Virginia Day," as Thursday was themed. The week was topped off by "Barboursville and Cabell County Day" on Friday. This final day featured more cannons, parades, brass bands and speakers, plus a free barbeque and "Kentucky Burgoo" dinner, dynamite exhibitions, trap shooting, a balloon ascension, an "Old Soldiers" campfire, and of course, a grand fireworks display.

According to the report in *The Herald-Dispatch*, registry books showed about six thousand people were in the village during the week, and the event was "a great success from every standpoint." Although Governor Hatfield and U.S. Senator

Chilton were no-shows, other dignitaries and speakers graced the podium at the college campus, and their remarks were captured for posterity.

Barboursville Centennial 1913
(Courtesy Bob Doss)

On the final morning, West Virginia University president Thomas E. Hodges recalled that, as a former president of Marshall College, the first vote he had ever cast in the county was for the removal of the court house from Barboursville to Huntington. After congratulating the town on having traded the county seat for a fine educational institution, Hodges "brought his hearers to a startling realization when he predicted that before the next century had passed by, gas and oil would be only a memory in West Virginia; our great wealth of coal would be gone and unless some plan of re-forestation was brought about that the timber forests would be barren."

> He declared that the real wealth of the people is not those resources but the soil, which is here to stay and upon which the prosperity of the future generations would have to depend. "If properly conserved, the soil will always be good and the prosperity of our descendents will be insured," said Dr. Hodges. (Celebration over and Barboursville feels justly proud 1913)

The other featured speaker was the Honorable George J. McComas. The Huntington attorney, and great-grandson of both Elisa McComas and Thomas

Ward, took his rapt listeners on a journey to the time of their town founders. Like Dr. Hodges, McComas offered his own observations on societal change. I'll leave it to the reader to decide which speaker was most in step with the march of history:

> He took up at length the character and individuality of the early settlers of Barboursville and community and declared that the people of that section today should draw particular inspiration from the splendid accomplishments of the men who have gone before, who, evidenced their valor and heroism by establishing a solid foundation of civilization "along those shores where the wild savage roamed and the wild savage was monarch of all he surveyed."

> "These men believed in God and their strong right arm," said Mr. McComas as he detailed the wonderful achievements of the men of one hundred years ago.

> And in this connection, Mr. McComas impressed the fact that there was nothing in the lives of these early settlers more worthy of serious consideration than the home life which they established in the valley. "The ultimate outcome of any people depends on the virtue and love of home," he said.

> "They lived in the best and sweetest communion with nature that has exalted from that day to this and their characteristics in this regard, were largely responsible for the well-founded civilization they established.

> "They took their places in invention, statesmanship and other marks of civilization but to us they left no greater heritage than the purity of the home."

> Mr. McComas called attention to the different conditions existing today from those of the pioneer days when a father maintained such a close supervision over children and when there was no danger of race suicide.

> "I fear that the father of the present day does not look after his boy as the father of those days did. You can do more for your boy by seeing that his steps are properly guided than you can by devoting your whole attentions to the assembling of a fortune to be left to him that would probably induce him to riotous living and worthlessness."

> He commended to his hearers the home life of the men who laid the foundation of that civilization. "The homes were filled with healthy boys and girls then and there was no danger of race suicide."

> He took a curt fling at the woman's suffrage movement which has attracted many women from the cradle to the legislative lobby, and declared that the

mother of the early days who rocked the cradle and smoked her corn cob pipe did more for the advancement of civilization than the suffragette type of the present day. (Celebration over and Barboursville feels justly proud 1913)

On the final evening, Professor Fred B. Lambert "read a very comprehensive and interesting history of Barboursville and Cabell county. It was a fine paper and it was directed that it be published in the newspapers and put into pamphlet form."

In the last late night hour of Barboursville's Centennial Celebration on Friday, June 6, 1913, "the balloonist made another ascension, putting off the fireworks from the balloon."

Entry into Europe's "Great War"

President Wilson's early successes and legislative triumphs on the domestic front—introducing to America what historian Paul Johnson called "big, benevolent government"—became overshadowed by international conflict, first in Mexico and then in Europe.

Though buried deep in the recesses of national consciousness, tensions existed in those times between the United States and our Western Hemisphere neighbors, both north and south. A diplomatic crisis with Canada, of all places, had been narrowly averted by President Taft in 1910, after a turn-of-the-century treaty dispute over the Alaskan boundary left Canadians bitter and resentful toward the United States Instability and turbulence in several Caribbean and Central American countries led to economic and military interventions by both the Taft and Wilson administrations, with mixed results. During the Mexican Revolution, Wilson sent United States troops to occupy a Mexican port city in 1914, and to defend the border in 1916 after New Mexico was raided by the infamous "Pancho" Villa. (These events somehow escaped my awareness of early-twentieth century events. To my pop culture-infused brain, the only previous references to this period were the 1978 Warren Zevon song "Veracruz" and the 1986 slapstick comedy ¡Three Amigos!)

Barboursville had at least one young man among the one hundred thousand-plus troops carrying Woodrow Wilson's guns. Sergeant Andrew J. Perry of Army, Company F, 51st Infantry, is one local soldier who earned a year's worth of military experience at the Mexican border. The expedition has been referred to as a "dress rehearsal for the Great War," because it provided soldiers with invaluable training. At the same time, it revealed the Army's appalling lack of preparedness.

With the first Mexican occupation in 1914, Wilson signaled a decisive shift away from American isolationism. At the same time, his administration was keeping a cautious and wary eye on developments in Europe. In July, the assassination of Archduke Franz Ferdinand in Sarajevo by a Serbian activist incited

Austria-Hungary into declaring war on Serbia. Disputes, treaties and alliances among the European countries were nothing new, but this time Germany acted with crushing force to back Austria, Russia mobilized on behalf of little Serbia, France allied with Russia, and within months Belgium and Britain were pulled in as well. Having no direct quarrel with Germany, even after that country embarked on an aggressive two-front war against Russia and France, the president initially issued a proclamation of neutrality and urged Americans to remain impartial.

At first, the country balanced the optimistic opinion that Europe's latest troubles would be short-lived, with the divided emotions of United States citizens—sentiments were generally pro-Ally in the East, South and West, and more neutral in the Midwest with its higher concentration of German Americans. By 1915, the war on the western front became a war of positions and trenches, what *The Oxford History of the American People* called "a ghastly, blown-up version of the Union and Confederate lines." The tide of American opinion began to turn when the Germans began to wage war in the air, on the sea, and under the ocean with submarines, or "U-boats." In May, the British passenger liner *Lusitania* was torpedoed, without warning, by a U-boat off the coast of Ireland, killing 1,100 hapless civilians including 128 American men and women. The horror of this event stilled the voices of many American pacifists, but Wilson remained unswayed through the 1916 election.

By 1917, Wilson's neutral stance had been tested by a final futile attempt to mediate in Europe. Following a tight electoral victory, the president toured the country to promote military preparedness as the only way to keep America strong and safely out of the conflict. Congress eventually provided funding to strengthen the armed forces, as massive slaughter continued on the European continent. More than a million French, British, German and Russian lives had already been lost by this time. Diplomatic relations were finally broken between the United States and Germany in February, after that country began unrestricted submarine warfare on American ships sighted in German-declared war zones. The final straw seemed to be the March 1917 British interception of the "Zimmerman Telegram," in which Germany proposed a plot to collude with Mexico and Japan in attacking the United States, and brought to light the nefarious practices of German spies and secret agents within American borders.

On the evening of Monday, April 2, 1917, Morris Harvey's baseball team was feeling the effects of the "hardest practice seen on the local field for several seasons." Barboursville's Red and Black "ball tossers" had been getting into shape for several days, and were sacrificing the upcoming Easter break to compete for the best positions on Coach Beckelheimer's promising squad. A few miles away, the thoughts of Huntington's most stellar businessmen were centered on an upcoming drive to raise a whopping $200,000 for a "Y.M.C.A. plant" in the city. At the same time in

Washington, President Wilson was stepping up to the podium and reviewing with Congress the failure of his efforts to restore peace. The eloquent 28th president declared:

> With a profound sense of the solemn and even tragical character of the step I am taking and of the grave responsibilities which it involves, but in unhesitating obedience to what I deem my constitutional duty, I advise that Congress declare the recent course of the Imperial German government to be, in fact, nothing less than war against the government and people of the United States…

> It is a fearful thing to lead this great peaceful people into war, into the most terrible and disastrous of all wars, civilization itself seeming to be in the balance. But the right is more precious than peace, and we shall fight for the things which we have always carried nearest our hearts…America is privileged to spend her blood and her might for the principles that gave her birth and happiness and the peace which she has treasured. God helping her she can do no other. (Morison 1994)

War was declared on Good Friday, April 6. This was followed a month-and-a-half later by passage of the Selective Service act, which obliged nearly 24 million American men to register for service. Cabell County established three draft boards, appointing three men on each. The territory outside of Guyandotte District was represented by Dr. L. C. Morrison and J. H. Harshbarger of Milton, and Rev. Urban V. W. Darlington, Bishop of the Methodist Episcopal Church, South, who lived in Barboursville. Villager Herbert King served on the County's Legal Advisory Board, which rendered service in connection with the selective service law including administration of questionnaires to all men ages 18 to 45. According to local historian Ernest Midkiff, Cabell County had 4,325 registrants. In May, about 30 county men volunteered to attend officers training at Camp Benjamin Harrison in Indiana. At the first call for troops in September, Cabell was one of three West Virginia counties whose volunteer enlistment in the National Guard exceeded the draft quota. As a consequence, no county men needed to be drafted at the first call.

Of the total 2,887 service men from Cabell County, at least 62 Barboursville enlistees served our country from 1914-1918, according to newspaper accounts and the *Cabell County Honor Roll.* They included: Private Lacy Charles Anderson, Corporal Gilby Maynard Angel, Lieutenant George Raymond Ayers, Private James Bates, Private George Baumgardner, Private James E. Black, Private Eli Bledsoe, Private Clifford Burks, Sergeant William H. Burks, Private James L. Butcher, Seaman Charles Lyal Clay, Sergeant Frank Coman, Corporal Joseph E. Cooper,

Corporal Quan Coyner, Private Charles Henry Davis, Corporal Russell Dirton, Private E. W. Ferguson, Private Omar Ferrell, Private Arnold Ford, Sergeant Jessie Ford, Private Reeve Gibson, Corporal Vivian Gothard, Third Yeoman Earl M. Haddot, Private Calvin Wendell Hamler (colored section), Private Levi A. Hatfield, First Class Seaman John Henzman, Private Donald Hill (colored section), Second Lieutenant Leonard Keyser, Private Alvie Lewis, Private James Lewis, Sergeant Paul E. Love, Private E. B. Mallory, Corporal Eustace C. May, Corporal Harry McCutcheon, Private Harry W. Merritt, Private Charles Joseph Miller, Private John Kenneth Morris, Sergeant Riley Mullins, Sergeant Andrew J. Perry, Private William Poindexter (volunteer, colored section) Corporal Gordon A. Powers, First Sergeant William Otto Reid, Private Clarence Roffe, Private William R. Ruley, Private Arthur Sharp, Private Clair W. Smith, Private Paul E. Smith, Sergeant Zeb V. Stafford, Private Hobart Caylor Stanley, Sergeant-Major Henry M. Stanley, Private Roy Staton, Private Alvis A. Stone, Private Hugh Stover, Private Clarence C. Swann, Midshipman James Robert Tague, First Quartermaster Mitchell A. Tagul, Corporal Forrest Calvin Thacker, Private Harry Franklin Toothman, Sergeant Chauncey Lee Updyke, and Private Walter H. Walker.

Nettie Woodyard of the Army Red Cross Nurse Corps

On the day the United States entered the war, President Wilson appointed a war council to run the American Red Cross. A Huntington Red Cross chapter was organized, from which would grow several dozen auxiliary units throughout the city, and branches at Barboursville and Milton. According to the *Honor Roll*, "the very flower of womanhood and girlhood at Huntington and Cabell County responded to the call." As the war continued, American Red Cross employees and volunteers provided medical and recreational services for the military at home and abroad. About 20,000 Red Cross nurses provided much of the medical care for the American military during World War I.

The kind and slightly care-worn face pictured here is that of 49-year-old Nettie Swann Woodyard, who entered service in 1917 as an Army Red Cross Nurse, the only woman from Barboursville to appear in the *Cabell County Honor Roll* . The "Great War" was the first conflict in which nurses had professional training, and this seventh child of village blacksmith Benjamin Franklin Swann and Rachel Morrison Swann received hers as a 1916 nursing graduate of Huntington General Hospital.

It is not clear what led this middle-aged lady into the Red Cross Nursing Service Corps, but it is plain that Nettie was well-acquainted with human loss. The family history, census and cemetery records that exist sketch faint outlines of her life as a woman who had married William J. Woodyard of Wytheville, Virginia in 1893, and gave birth to a son, Willie Swann Woodyard, nine months later. Her son died at age three, and her husband disappeared from local records before 1900, leaving Nettie both childless and single, either through divorce or widowhood (sources differ). By 1910, she was living with her parents and sister on College Avenue and working as a sales lady dealing in medicines.

Nurse Nettie Swann Woodyard pictured in Cabell County Honor Roll
(Courtesy of KYOWVA Genealogical and Historical Society)

A March 1918 article in the *American Journal of Nursing* lists Nettie Swann Woodyard as a Reserve Nurse for the Army Nurse Corps, assigned to the U.S. Army Base Hospital at Camp Jackson in Columbia, South Carolina. Whether Nettie served overseas in a field hospital or at another base before this assignment, I do not know. Though governed by military discipline, nurses had no official authority. They could not direct orderlies or corpsmen, handle administrative problems or head up wards. The nurse corps could only provide direct care and comfort to wounded and dying young men as they returned to the safety of the mainland.

(Worth mentioning here is an interesting historical side note. It concerns an unintended World War I legacy having to do with an unmentionable product. Women of the world can thank WWI Red Cross nurses with development of—*avert your eyes, gentlemen*—the sanitary napkin, after busy American nurses in European field hospitals found a practical use for a newly-invented cellulose bandaging material. Thus, the Kotex was born and the Kimberly-Clark Company made its fortunes.)

Based on her reported assignment date, Nettie Woodyard would have arrived at Camp Jackson well into America's entanglement in the war, and would have been immediately confronted with cases of shock, hemorrhaging, infected wounds, and inhalation of poisonous mustard gas. The work must have been harrowing. Medical journals cite some of the illnesses the camp's staff attempted to treat that year, including a meningitis epidemic, a measles outbreak, and at least two mysterious cases diagnosed as the deadly Anthrax infection seen among British troops.

Then came a wave of influenza that at its onset resembled nothing worse the common cold. The illness first appeared early in the spring of 1918 in military camps throughout the United States and in pockets across the globe. Few took notice in the midst of the war, but by late spring the epidemic was hitting young men in military camps especially hard. Several hundred soldiers quickly fell ill at Camp Jackson and were admitted to the base hospital. More became infected and the hospital where Nettie was stationed was soon overflowing with men too ill to stand. Stories were told of healthy young Americans of 20 to 40 years old (the most susceptible age) suddenly developing the flu and dying within hours from a "most viscous type of pneumonia." A large section of the South Carolina camp became an extension of the hospital. More than 5,000 persons were treated for influenza and at least 300 died from the disease in Camp Jackson alone.

The Influenza Pandemic of 1918-1919, also known as the "Spanish Flu," has been cited as the most devastating epidemic in recorded world history, killing more people in a single year than in four years of the Black Death Bubonic Plague of the 1300s. Estimates put global mortality from the 1918-19 influenza pandemic at anywhere between 30 and 50 million, more people than were killed in the war. An estimated 675,000 Americans were among the dead. In West Virginia, the flu sickened thousands. Huntington saw as many as 3,000 estimated cases and nearly 200 deaths.

Maurice Beckett, who was five years old in 1918, wrote of his own families and others in Barboursville—including the local grocer—being knocked down, but not wiped out, by a nasty strain of the flu that fall. The disease was suspected to have entered the village through the Depot's crowded waiting room. Beckett's grandfather was reached on the "party line" after the food in the small family icebox ran out, and "Pa" Beckett supplied milk, meat and eggs by horse and buggy from his Fudges Creek farm to the Beckett's Lee Street front porch, until Maurice's parents were back on their feet.

Nurse Woodyard survived the pandemic at Camp Jackson, and returned to West Virginia. According to family historian George Swann, she had a career as a school teacher in addition to her WWI nursing assignment, and lived in Marlinton in Pocahontas County for many years before coming back to live in Barboursville. She spent her twilight years at the Swann family home at the current site of Call's insurance office on Central Avenue, next to the Village of Barboursville Elementary. Nettie Swann Woodyard passed away in 1945 and is buried in Oaklawn Cemetery.

From Tom's Creek to Belleau Wood—
Barboursville's Gold Star Son

Two miles south of the village, McComas Road offers a landscape of rolling hills, green fields, and single-family homes surrounded by plenty of elbow room. It is to the credit of those along the old "Barboursville Turnpike" around the Lower Fork of Tom's Creek—including the Swanns, Hashes, Hinchmans, Sharps, Adamses, Sowardses and Shoemakers—that so much of the old farm acreage is still intact. The smattering of older houses and barns along McComas Road still render a vision of the world Private Roy Staton probably knew for 17 years.

Born on June 6, 1900, the youngest child of Nathan and Elizabeth Staton (or Staten—both spellings appear in official family records) and the grandson of Achilles Cleton Staton, was still "Baby Staton" when the census-taker passed through on June 26. Looking at Roy's photo as a young man, it could be the face of any rural Cabell County boy who ever hunted in the hills, fished the creeks, helped his father mow the bottom land, and dreamed of seeing the world.

Private Roy Staton pictured in Cabell County Honor Roll
(Courtesy of KYOWVA Genealogical and Historical Society)

Based on records in the *Honor Roll of Cabell County*, Private Roy Station was both Barboursville's youngest person to serve in the Great War, and Cabell County's first non-officer to volunteer in the Armed Forces, entering service less than a month after his 17th birthday, on July 1, 1917. This was before the local draft went into effect, and just ten days before General John Pershing, commanding the newly-established American Expeditionary Forces, requested three million men.

Young Roy entered the 16th Infantry Regiment of the 1st Division, Company L. Prior to being committed to battle, the 16th Infantry Regiment of the 1st Division (which would become known as the "Big Red One") began training with the French 47th Division "Blue Devils." In November 1917, the 16th Infantry became the first United States regiment to fight and suffer casualties in the trenches during World War I, when it repelled a German night raid in Bathlemont near the French-German border.

As part of the Allied command, United States forces took on the "Huns" to attack German supply lines and reverse gains by the Central Powers east of Paris. By 1918, the situation in France and Belgium was particularly shaky. Determined to "bleed white" the French troops in a battle of attrition (the war killed or wounded half of all Frenchman between 15 and 30 years old), Germany had advanced and seriously threatened the North Sea ports and Paris.

Battle-tested by the time of his 18th birthday, Private Staton was part of a machine gun detachment contributing to the 85,000 United States forces in the Second Marne offensive in July 1918. In this operation, America joined British and Italian troops assisting the French, as the Germans repeated an earlier push across the Marne River toward Paris. The Allied Supreme Commander authorized an enormous counter-offensive on July 18, launching 24 divisions of the French Army alone, as well as some 350 tanks, to attack the Germans from three different directions. Selected to break the most sensitive part of the German line were the 2nd American, the 1st Moroccan (French) and Roy's division, the 1st American.

It was there that Mrs. Staton's youngest son found himself in an ocean of armed humanity. I calculated that Private Roy Staton was the same age that day as my youngest son nine decades later—snug in East Pea Ridge, bed-headed and flannel PJ'd at Christmas break, slouched on the living room couch planning college visits, with an iPod, a stack of new books, Play Station games and balled-up Hershey Kiss wrappers on the coffee table, and the family dog stretched out on the next cushion. In contrast, how did Roy Staton of McComas Road experience his last 24 hours?

This description by First Lieutenant L. Janda of the 9th Infantry Regiment of the 2nd Division may come close:

Night fell early in the forest and a steady rain set in. The road became muddy and slippery and as we approached the center of the woods congestion became terrific. The French were trying to pull out while the Ninth, and Twenty Third

Regiments, Marines and rolling stock were struggling against fatigue and time, to get into position in time for H hour. The men had settled into a dogged silence, the whole Regiment strung out in a single file, going up the road in the ditch alongside of the road, each man holding on to the belt of the man ahead of him so that contact might not be broken. They were too tired to care much what happened. Collapses were frequent. A man would silently drop and the column would close up again. Brains were stupefied but somehow the bodies kept on going.

Suddenly, at 4:35 to the dot, a livid flame seemed to shoot up out of the entire forest behind us and seemed to hang there as our guns opened up one continuous roar of bombardment that was deafening. Instantly the front came to life. There was a wild clattering of machine guns and lights of various colors flying in all directions. At the same time the Regiment surged forward. I believe that the First Battalion must have been literally pushed over the German first trenches by the sheer weight of men behind it. The din at this time was terrific. Vocal commands and whistle were out of the question--arm signals alone were of any use. (The Great War Society 2000)

In constant attacks over four days and nights against seven separate German divisions, the 1st Division broke through their entrenchments. United Press Staff Correspondent Fred S. Ferguson was with the American forces on the night of July 20. He reported, "Smashing counter-attack after counter-attack, the allies are still sweeping forward, rolling up the German armies between the Aisne and Marne. The important railway from Soissons to Chateau-Theirry is now domi-nated by the French and American artillery, which is dropping shells over it on a wide front. This is a serious blow to the enemy, these railways being the principal means of communication in this region. I passed a full mile of German prisoners, four abreast, marching to the rear under guard of French and American soldiers."

On July 21, the *Huntington Advertiser* carried this 12:05 a.m. dispatch from Paris: "The German retreat across the Marne has been complete, the war office announced this morning. The entire south bank has been cleared of the enemy. Further advances have been made between the Aisne and the Marne. More than 20,000 prisoners have been taken on the whole front, and over 400 guns have been captured."

The counter-offensive in northeastern France roared on for 23 days and nights. Staton's division, the "Big Red One" suffered 7,000 casualties. Sixty percent of its infantry officers were killed or wounded, and in the 16th Infantry nearly all the field officers were casualties. Private Roy Staton was killed in action on July 19, 1918, his remains never identified.

The Second Battle of the Marne developed into a significant Allied victory. After it became clear that the Germans had failed in their offensive, a number of

German commanders, including Crown Prince Wilhelm, believed the war was lost. Casualties were higher among the German forces than the Allies. France suffered 95,000 casualties, Germany 168,000, with Britain incurring 13,000 losses and the United States 12,000.

It was recognized that Allied resistance to the German offensive had been significantly bolstered by the presence of fresh American troops, unbroken by years of war. War correspondent Floyd Gibbons wrote of the American troops, "I never saw men charge to their death with finer spirit."

World War I essentially ended a year later, when the Germans and the Allies signed the Treaty of Versailles on June 28, 1919.

In 1924, the Cabell County War Memorial Association built a "triumphal arch" memorial to county's 91 dead and all who served in the World War, a quarter-scale replica of the one in Paris. A tree was planted along Memorial Boulevard between West 5th and 13th Streets for each soldier who gave his life in the war; many still provide shade along what is now known as the Ritter Park jogging path. Roy Staton's name can be found on a plaque near the base of the Memorial Arch, the closest thing to a West Virginia grave marker for Barboursville's only fallen soldier of World War I.

In 1928, American Gold Star Mothers, Inc., was established by 25 mothers of soldiers killed in "The Great War." The association lobbied for a government-sponsored pilgrimage to Europe for mothers with sons buried overseas, realizing that many could not otherwise afford the trip. In 1929, Congress enacted legislation that authorized pilgrimages to the European cemeteries "by mothers and widows of members of military and naval forces of the United States who died in the service at any time between April 5, 1917 and July 1, 1921. (During the Congressional hearings, the popular view was that the maternal bond surpassed the paternal bond, so no trips were offered to the fathers.) By October 31, 1933, when the project ended, 6,693 women, about a third of those determined to be eligible, had made a two-week pilgrimage to the final resting place of their sons.

Elizabeth Morrison Staten (as the name appears on her 1947 death certificate), might have been eligible to take advantage of a government-paid pilgrimage to northern France by luxury liner with other elderly Gold Star Mothers. However, I do not know whether she or any of the Staton/Staten relatives ever had the chance to go abroad. If so, they might have made their way to Paris and then 50 miles by automobile to Belleau Wood, a 200-acre site permanently maintained by the American Battle Monuments Commission.

Belleau Wood contains vestiges of trenches, shell holes and preserved relics of the First World War and adjoins the Aisne-Marnes American cemetery. Nearly 2,300 American graves in the cemetery include 250 Unknowns. On a hill overlooking the cemetery is an 80-foot-high limestone chapel erected over the original frontline trenches. Once inside the chapel's ornate oak doors, one would pass through a vestibule to an altar of Italian marble surrounded by five arched alcoves. Each alcove contains a stained-glass window and some of the engraved names of Americans missing in action. Among the 1,060 names on the "Tablets of the Missing" is that of Private Roy L. Staton of West Virginia.

In his short life, Private Roy Staton of Tom's Creek did his part to reverse the treacherous tide of the Central Forces. In his heroic death he exemplified the 1st Division's motto, "No mission too difficult, no sacrifice too great—Duty First!"

Our Special Correspondent Furnishes an Interesting Letter:
MAY 17, 1900—A horse that he was shoeing stepped on Tom Anderson's foot last
Friday, mashing the large toe and making a painful injury.

CHAPTER 13

TUCKED AWAY (1920S-1940S)

Motoring into the Modern Age

CONSIDER the changes that took place in America within five years after World War I ended: The eighteenth and nineteenth Amendments to the Constitution were ratified, prohibiting the sale of alcohol under federal law, and granting women the right to vote. Music was first broadcast over radio. In the White House, the "Democratic Era" of 1913 to 1921 came to end when Warren G. Harding was elected. Harding signed the Johnson Act into law, further restricting immigration into the United States.

Huntington was continuing to grow in size and grandeur. The population in 1920 exceeded 50,000 and continued its rise toward a new metropolitan ideal. In addition to the Memorial Arch, magnificent stone churches were taking shape along Fifth Avenue, and mansions in the fashionable Staunton Road, Southside and Southern Hills neighborhoods offered a feast of architectural styles.

Barboursville itself was beginning to "take on a metropolitan appearance," according to reporters. By 1919, water works improvements, new gas lines, street paving, electric street lights, a new city hall and a new high school were either completed or well underway. According to the *Herald-Dispatch*, "All real estate offered in the old town is selling at fancy prices. The lots that are on sale are going fast, and new additions have been opened at the outer limits of the town."

Still, in the early 1920s, the pace of transportation through the village was slow. On Main Street, under the "enormous and spreading sycamore tree" by Tanyard Branch, Bill Herndon still operated a blacksmith shop where he forged shoes and placed them on the hooves of local horses. Townsfolk saw an occasional horse-drawn wagon or, less frequently, a "T-Model Ford" rattling by on Central Avenue.

One member of the town's Board of Trade was particularly influential in modernizing the area. William Nathan Clay, a carpenter and farmer of 150 acres in the Martha community, served as a popular magistrate from 1912 to 1936, and later in life filled other county offices. "Squire Clay," as he was known, also served as a member of the West Virginia House of Delegates in 1917-1918. During his term at the statehouse, the Squire ushered through a bill to authorize a paved road from Barboursville's Main Street to the Lincoln County line at Salt Rock, and this road was built in 1921.

It would take until 1926 for the C&O Railroad, under court order, to pay for and construct an underground passageway—the Central Avenue viaduct—under the Guyan Valley line tracks. Until that time, an eight-foot raised crossing was described by the U.S. district court judge as "a poorly-kept grade crossing...sufficiently high to prevent a view of what was coming on the other side of the street, before starting up the grade to this crossing."

Other members of the town's "wideawake" board of trade, especially W.W. Nunn, D. Blain Shaw and George R. Thornburg, were credited with launching a spirited campaign for the betterment of the town. Other men of note included two former newspaper men, town physician Dr. Thomas Hallanan, real estate agent J. Jerome Haddox, and postmaster J. W. Wilson, "whose home place is now on Pea Ridge, so rapidly growing into a fashionable community."

One singular development sealed the village's fate as a bedroom community. Just as ancient insects became perfectly preserved and fossilized in amber, Barboursville's business and residential district was similarly "frozen in time" by another hardening substance—specifically the ribbon of hot-mix pavement that would become U.S. Route 60. Years before downtown Huntington found itself rather isolated by the Interstate Highway System, our lost villagers learned what it was like to be tucked away. As the century-old James River and Kanawha Turnpike became obsolete, Main Street was carved out of the new traffic flow of U.S. Route 60. America's new high-speed parade motored around rather than through Barboursville, just a few yards beyond the C&O tracks.

The villagers adapted. In 1921, Wiatt Smith reported:

"Barboursville is rapidly taking on a suburban aspect. Many residents of the town come daily to Huntington to work, and, now that the journey can be made readily in half an hour by private automobile or motor bus, Barboursville folks come in to shop and go to the picture show and for many similar purposes. It is interesting to note that it takes ten minutes longer to travel from Main Street, Barboursville, to Ninth Street by automobile, than it takes to travel from Main Street, Guyandotte, to Ninth Street by street car...

this is to further emphasize the likelihood that some day Barboursville may be part and parcel of Huntington." (W. Smith, Barboursville: Some Interesting Historic Facts About Former County Seat 1921)

By 1923, Henry Ford had sold two million Model T automobiles. One Barboursville man was particularly fascinated with these machines. Vernon Sharp, born in 1900 in Branchland, the son of lumberman and mechanic Otto Sharp, grew up in Tom's Creek (like his fallen contemporary Roy Staton). According to Sharp's daughter Patricia, Vernon purchased a used Model T in the early 1920s, disassembled it in his parent's front yard, then replaced all the parts, teaching himself the auto repair trade. In 1924, Vernon married schoolteacher Velva Morrison and bought property on Farmdale Road, where they reared four children and lived for the rest of their lives. The Sharps were active and charitable members of the Church of Jesus Christ of Latter-Day Saints, and were typical members of Barboursville society.

Sharp's Service Garage opened in 1924. It was torn down to make way for the new national road, then rebuilt at the corner of Farmdale Road and U.S. Route 60, where it stood as a local landmark for nearly seven decades. My husband remembers, from his days as a Channel 13 news videographer in the mid-1980s, shooting a story about Vernon Sharp when the elderly gentleman still pumped gas for customers at what was the area's last full-service "filling station." He was duly impressed with Sharp's collection of Studebakers in the old garage, and our young sons enjoyed the quaint "muffler man" sculpture that greeted motorists out front, on the current site of Rite Aid pharmacy.

Fast Times at Farmdale Road

Given 30 years of "dry town" status, the village's comfortable separation from the wickedness of Huntington's "city life," and the collection of retired Methodist ministers residing there, one would expect that Barboursville dodged what Morison called the "wild drinking and loose morals" of America's post-war, pre-Depression years.

Not quite.

Two local voices, folksy Frank Ball and eloquent Maurice Beckett, picked up the torch from Fred Lambert and carried on as community historians for the twentieth century. Thanks to both men, we have two "guy on the street" perspectives of village life in the 1920s. Their unvarnished anecdotes probably reveal more than either the Board of Trade or the pious descendants of Marie Gardner would have divulged about idle time on Barboursville's fringes, from the depot to the river.

Wrote Beckett:

I guess that Barboursville had a bit of everything. We had our own, well-known bootlegger, who saw that those who desired it did not go thirsty. Later there was one quiet citizen on the outskirts who was found to be producing a good grade of spirits in his attic. His wife was a placid and church-going lady whose friends were convinced that she was ignorant of the upper operation. On weekend afternoons a woman and her two teen-age daughters could usually be seen walking the side streets of the village. Frequently they were interviewed by some of the lonely and uninhibited young men who desired company. (M. Beckett, Barboursville History 1996)

Fairground Racetrack at Farmdale
(Courtesy Barboursville Public Library)

Beckett also recalled a nationwide craze that took hold locally, just as the horse was being superseded by the automobile as a means of transportation. Decades before the annual Oktoberfest/ Fall Fest carnival descended on Farmdale Road with its caravans of ride equipment, vendor trailers and transient operators, today's "Sadler Field" featured an earlier playground with its own shady element:

This was the era, too, of the race track and the fairgrounds, which lay in the bend of the Guyan in Farmdale, across the river. It lasted but a few years until the approaching Great Depression doomed it, and the grandstand burned, but it was a lively place for that brief time....As small boys, we used to sit on

Inspiration Ridge and watch the fireworks from the fairgrounds. (M. Beckett, Barboursville History 1996)

Linwood McCormick noted that horses raced daily in the summer, and were shipped from all over the United States, and even Cuba, in special padded boxcars. McCormick was one of the local boys who led horses from Depot Street, down Main Street, and across the bridge to the fairgrounds. Mary and Keller Washington shared how their sons also worked to drive the horses to the track, adding that many times the mud was so deep that both boys and horses would sink to their knees.

Exact dates of the track's existence are hard to pin down, but Frank Ball offered this account:

In 1921 they parlayed it as the Huntington Tri-State Fair Ground with the only mile race track in the state as a sideline. Business and civic leaders in Huntington and Barboursville backed its coming as a great blessing while some were decrying the "menace" farther out the road called the Guyan Country Club. Eventually, the race track became a reality with the "fair ground" as a sort of blind. The racing game brought some of the most degraded people of America among us. I wonder if there was any such individual as an honest one who followed the ponies: owner, rider, bettor or trainer.

But the money flowed freely during the two or three years in the early 1920s that the ponies raced to the yells of the spectators. There were Flibertygibbet, Ouch, Sway, Ting-a-ling, Scalion, Addie Wolf, Black Monkey, Black Hackle, and one-eyed Rustler. Some of them were owned by men with backing; others were shipped COD from racetrack to racetrack and some citizen with a few hundred dollars cash was persuaded to pay the express bill and get the plug off the car. Such a nag was old Jack Hanover, in truth, a steeplechase racer, but owned by a Negro who believed old Jack had what it took to race at the level. Frank Harshbarger paid the unloading bill—$150 I believe. The Negro gave Frank a lien on Jack Hanover and we all went over to the track to see a "local" horse run. He ran like a cow; always behind, and we all lost hope that he would ever win a race. The session ended without a win and the town boys began calling Harshbarger "Jack Canopener."...But after nearly 50 years, Frank hasn't heard the last of Jack Hanover. Men following the racing game through the racing record saw long after where Jack Hanover had finally won a steeplechase race—and it made big news in our hamlet. Jack must have been scared at something.

Seems that the "fair grounds" across the river in Farmdale failed purposely or naturally and the giant wooden grandstand burned one night. The paper the next morning gave details of the fire and said that plans were already drawn and in the hands of stockholders for the erection of a large steel grandstand. Boy, wasn't that quick. Nothing further materialized and the money that once went through the pari-mutuel machines began trickling back to grocery stores and other businesses and kids who had gone hungry began eating higher up on the hog. And it seemed those who profited most by the short life of the mile race track were not able to hold onto it very long. Somehow, it got away from them.

As to the racetrack and fair sidelines, every concession stand operator agreed that fewer people bit at the tricks of their various trades here than anywhere else they had ever worked. They would give that old "come on" spiel for a while; then curse the day they arrived in our locale. I have heard circus men from two-ring shows down to the colored minstrels say the same thing and that the only reason that they stopped in Barboursville was that it was a junction and when they played the "valley" they almost had to stop or lose a day.

P.S. Harshbarger says that they not only nicked him for the express bill but that he had to pay the nag's feed bill while he was here losing races—about $300 total. Wow! (Ball, Ye Olde Racetrack 1970)

Tivoli Theater, 1937
(Courtesy Donna Brown)

In addition to the short-lived racing enterprise, there were other signs afoot that Barboursville was joining America's growing leisure class. The Guyan Golf and Country Club was established alongside Pea Ridge in 1920. And in 1926, two years before Huntington's Keith-Albee Theater opened—a "bizarre, astonishing and exotic piece of architecture" second only in size to New York's Roxy Theater at the time—a Barboursville family brought showbiz on a much smaller scale to Main Street.

Carpenter S.V. Anderson and his oldest sons built a two-story yellow brick building on the north side of Main Street along Tanyard Branch and named it the Tivoli Theatre, after a world-famous musical variety circuit of the era *(pictured here during the flood of 1937)*. Later the building was leased to the ubiquitous Alpine Theatre Circuit, then to Arthur Crissman. He named it the Criss Theatre, the identity it kept until the 1950s, when television most likely rendered obsolete the only movie house in village history.

Just as sporting and shows were achieving more respectability in small town America, national Prohibition was changing the drinking habits of Americans everywhere, with unintended consequences that would result in the amendment's repeal in 1932. This brings us to the "Roaring Twenties" enterprise of bootlegging, and the double life of one of Barboursville's unforgettable characters.

Memories and Mysteries—Keller Washington and His Notorious "In-Law"

Keller Washington

The only son of African-American railroad worker Charles Washington and barber's daughter Amanda Hicks was born in the 1890s. He lived in Barboursville until his life ended in the late 1950s. When Keller Washington was 24, he married 16-year-old Mary Ferguson of Logan County, and they settled into the Barboursville family home to raise three sons and four daughters. Originally an odd-jobs laborer and railroad "section man" with the seventh-grade education typical of most Cabell County men of his generation, Keller was hired by Vernon Sharp and became a mechanic at the Farmdale Road service garage.

If all the villagers who ever encountered the man were to lay their "Keller stories" end to end, the result would not necessarily raise the esteem of Barboursville's African American role models, but it would surely be entertaining. A portrait of a dapper, unconventional and fun-loving man with a hard-working wife emerged out of conversations with several Barboursville friends and neighbors.

As a young lady brought up in Barboursville's "Board of Trade" society, Ann Brady Turman saw the Washingtons from the opposite side of the color line: "Mary was a dear old lady, dear woman, but now that Keller, he was something He worked over at Sharp's garage for years…Mary cooked up at Logan for the coal camps for years, and then she used to cook for my mother some. Yeah, she was such a good person. But Keller—oh honey, he'd just do anything, he didn't care."

My uncle Scott Brady was a young boy on Depot Street in the 1950s. He mainly remembers Keller for his car—a sharp, two-toned green Mercury. He also carries a vivid and comical sidewalk memory of the older man and a white neighbor sitting in chairs side by side, intently staring down at the ground where a red ant was fighting a black ant, the men having placed bets on the outcome.

To the African-American children of the village, Keller was a teller of tall tales. Said Roy Goines, "I remember him so well, going out to visit with him. He'd have that coal going in that fireplace, and we'd sit up and talk. Mrs. Washington, his wife, worked in Logan. She'd come home on the weekends. I always found that to be so odd, but that's the way they lived. He worked over at Sharp's Garage over on Route 60 in Barboursville, worked there for the whole time I knew him…I'd go out and listen to all the lies he could tell!"

Roy's cousin Gladys Carter added, "I remember when we would go out to their house in the summer time and sit there until after it got dark, and he would tell all these things and we would be scared to go home."

Ted Allen remembers the Washington family as unique because of their oldest child. "Harry B. had an interesting background; he ran away from home when he was a kid. He ran away from home and got with the circus and he became a musician and they tell me that they were on a trip somewhere on a train and he fell off the train and knocked out all of his teeth. He continued being a musician and became a dancer. About that time the Second World War started, so he joined the Navy and he got out and became a fireman in Huntington. Before he became a fireman he bought some property somewhere and had a rooming house for veterans."

When he was nearly 80 years old in 1996, Harry B. Washington furnished a handwritten family history to my friend Janet Altizer. He revealed what sounds like an idyllic Barboursville childhood:

> …I think of all the nice boys I played with when I was growing up…There was a racetrack ¾ miles around it, a large corn mill, C&O shops and the Morris Harvey College…I remember the college foot ball team. Bugger Dickerson and I was the Ball Team's mascots…When I was a young boy I traded a camera to Earl Mays for a tenor guitar, he showed me three chords on the guitar, I would play and tap dance on the corner of Main and Center Street. Everyone would stop, flip a coin to me and would enjoy my dancing. (Washington 1996)

In his later years, Keller's son continued to play a number of instruments, and twice a week livened up the dance floors at Yesterday's and DeSoto's. (I suspect I must have twirled past the old gentleman at some point in my waning disco days.)

The details of Harry B.'s lineage and his parents' background might be taken with a proverbial grain of salt, due to his advanced age at the time he wrote them down. All the same, his family history links both Keller and Mary to a notorious figure in West Virginia history. As Harry B. told it, in addition to raising and selling bird dogs to "rich people from Virginia, North and South Carolina and Georgia," Keller "made a living for his family by going to Kentucky for whiskey and he would get on a coal train with the whiskey and take it to the Sheriff Don Chaffin *(sic)* of Logan, WV."

Don Chafin (1887-1954) became such a significant West Virginia figure as the leader of the "defending forces" in the Battle of Blair Mountain—the largest armed United States insurrection since the Civil War —that his Logan home is listed on the National Register of Historic Places. Chafin's legendary iron grip on Logan county politics and law enforcement made him a rich, influential and ruthless man by the time he was 30. (Incidentally, Don Chafin relocated to Huntington in his 40s, bought a ten-story bank building on 9th Street and 5th Avenue, renamed it the Chafin Building, and lived in its penthouse until his death at age 67, having re-invented himself as a regional philanthropist.)

Don's father, Francis Marion or "F. M." Chafin had set the political stage by serving as Logan County sheriff in the 1890s and sending his son to college (including a stint at Marshall), after which 21-year-old Don returned to Logan to run as a Democrat for the county assessor's seat. He won that office in 1908, just as the rise of the "Million Dollar Coal Fields" was ushering in a period of unparalleled growth and change in southern West Virginia. Don Chafin then catapulted himself into a 16-year fiefdom. With financial support from coal company operators, Chafin deployed a large force of deputies to keep labor organizers out of the county. United Mine Workers of America members hated him so much that he was shot and wounded when entering a UMWA headquarters building in 1919. Two years later, in addition to arming public law officers with machine guns to stop the march of organized miners from Marmet to Logan, Chafin arranged for three airplanes to drop homemade bombs on miners during the Battle of Blair Mountain.

As described by author Howard B. Lee, Chafin was "a mountain feudal lord to whom every coal operator in the county paid tribute, and of whom every miner within its borders stood in abject fear."

Chafin was also alleged to be related to Mary Ferguson, who married Keller Washington in Logan in 1917 and spent most of her adult working life as a cook in the Logan coal camps. The public marriage record lists Mary's parents as William Ferguson (born in 1878) and Nellie Lawson of Logan. In his memoire, Harry B. referred to William as "Jube" Ferguson, adding that "Jube Ferguson's father was a white man of Logan County who was the Deputy Sheriff." Now, it would be mathematically impossible for Don Chafin to be Mary Washington's grandfather as Harry B. claimed, but Sheriff F. M. Chafin (born in 1855) could have easily fit the description. If true, this would have made Don Chafin Mary Washington's biological uncle. This possible family link might explain how Keller Washington could have had unfettered access to deliver bootleg Kentucky whiskey to Logan.

There is another obscure but interesting connection between Barboursville and the notorious "Czar of Logan." In 1923, Don Chafin purchased the old Blue Sulphur Hotel that stood on the bank of the Mud River three miles east of the village (across U.S. Route 60 from the Mud River Baptist Church).

Blue Sulphur Springs was an abandoned tourist attraction with an interesting past. From the early days of the James and Kanawha River Turnpike, the 35-acre property had been known as a summer camping resort for "people of a pious nature." On July 4, 1885, George J. Floding had a grand opening for his new three-story hotel there, and a railroad station was nearby to accommodate the guests. At the turn of the century, it appears the old resort very nearly became site of the state's "Colored Orphanage" in 1900. According to the institution's first director, "The growth of the institution made necessary a larger plant. Through the generosity of Mr. G. W. Flooding (sic) and friends of the institution, a beautiful site and building with 36 rooms were secured at Blue Sulphur Springs. Certain antagonisms made another move necessary."

The once-celebrated hotel had been shuttered for about a decade when Don Chafin purchased it. His brother-in-law Walter Green Fraser, a railroad employee living in Barboursville, remodeled and re-opened the hotel for business. After 1923, according to Frank Ball, occasional dinners and dances were well-attended, but business soon declined and the Chafin/Fraser enterprise was abandoned.

With the daily purchase of ice from Huntington, ice water was
considered "a delicacy of the day" at the Blue Sulphur Hotel in 1901.
(Newspaper photo courtesy of Barbara Miller)

Make what you will of this timeline: National Prohibition was enacted in 1920, ushering in the era of the bootlegger, the speakeasy, and Keller Washington's purported job as a whiskey runner for Sheriff Chafin. In 1923, Chafin took some of his coal company wealth and bought Cabell County's old Blue Sulphur Hotel. Dinners and dances took place at the hotel on "special occasions." In late 1924, Chafin was charged and convicted for illegally selling liquor in Logan County, and spent ten months of a two-year sentence in a federal penitentiary. Thereafter, the old Blue Sulphur hotel closed for good.

Whether there is any illicit link between this sequence of events will forever remain a mystery of those hush-hush days under the Eighteenth Amendment to the U.S. Constitution.

Downriver Impact of the Coal Boom

In 1927, 83-year-old William Miller was again living in his childhood home on Main Street. As the youngest son of original village postmaster William C. Miller, "Uncle Billy" had become known as the town's history collector. (His 1925 narrative history of the Barboursville community is still featured on the village's official website in 2012.)

One day in December, Miller received a letter from an unknown "colored man" of Saginaw, Michigan:

Dear Sir:

Do the steamboats still run on the Guyan River and do trains run from Guyandotte to Barboursville? Are there any of the Merrits, Millers or McComases alive?

How many churches are there in Barboursville now? There was only one when I was there but I understand that there are two colored churches now.

Miller speculated that the sender was a former Sanders slave, one of the dozens of "Ethiopian servants" *(the newspaper's euphemism)* who were liberated in 1849 and set out on log rafts to find free land in Michigan.

A postcard circa 1910 shows a Mud River splash dam at Barboursville.
(Courtesy of Wilma Smith)

In his reply, Miller simply wrote, "If you could see some of the trains that come down the Guyan Valley now, you would think the steamboat days on the Guyan are over."

It would have been burdensome for old Mr. Miller to describe all the ways the village had changed. For one thing, Barboursville was now home to six houses of worship, the "colored" school and church, and the new James I. Kuhn Presbyterian

Church (built in 1925 on real estate that Captain Kuhn's widow left to the small congregation upon her death in 1914). The trains never did run from Guyandotte to Barboursville. Instead, they crisscrossed each other a block away from the Miller home, carrying passengers, workers, and tons and tons of southern West Virginia coal.

The river itself might have been unrecognizable to the Michigan letter-writer. In the timbering boom that lasted from the 1880s to the 1920s, the Lower Guyandotte River watershed—740 square miles of land drained by the river between Logan and Huntington —had been almost entirely stripped of its ancient oaks, poplars and other hardwoods. The corporations that financed the felling of the virgin forests had made little effort to replant the trees. Lumber companies that purchased land upriver in the nineteenth century, after the inhabitants refused to give up just the surface rights, had simply re-organized to take full and profitable advantage of the coal seams that lay conveniently beneath the denuded ground.

Season after season, millions of logs had been harvested, pooled behind booms or splash dams along the Mud and Guyan rivers, and then released in a tide to flush their way toward Ohio River sawmills, ramming their way through each bend in the river. Over decades of timbering and with each flash flood, the steep and bald slopes upriver left the river choked with mud like never before in human history, obliterating mussel beds under tons of sediment and killing fish populations.

Water Street in Barboursville, perched precariously on a cliff formed, not of rock, but of Ice Age mud and clay, was particularly prone to erosion under these conditions. Yet even into the 1920s, the Guyandotte River at Barboursville was still considered swimmable by some:

> In the 1920s the Village Fathers decided to erect a public beach along the deep hole of water at the bend. Wooden steps were built down the side of the cliff next to the May's mill. A path led to the sandy beach where in the spring young men set a wooden diving board. For one or two summers the town people who wanted to swim came down the steps, past the great pile of corn cobs behind the mill, swam, then returned to their homes to change their clothing. The lack of a dressing room, plus the habits of some of the scantily clad gamins made them change their minds. Soon Barboursville's "beach" was used only by the boys.

> Up the river at Wilson's Farm, people were sometimes not so lucky. It was a longer and deeper hole than at Barboursville and the waters in their swift created a "dead" pocket where the exhausted swimmer, being over his head, could not fight the current to the safety of the shore…These drownings happened with regularity in the summer. (M. Beckett, The Guyandotte River n.d.)

In the next two decades, as one of several important arteries in the vast
Appalachian network of bituminous coalfields that spread across parts of eight
states, the Guyandotte River would become further degraded by an ecological
"one-two punch" of instant mining towns and coal processing.

The Logan Coal Field consisted of mines along the Guyandotte River and its
tributaries (including Island Creek and Buffalo Creek), from western Wyoming
County to southern Lincoln County. Between the 1880s and 1930s, coal companies built dozens of self-contained towns for their workers, many of them near
the route served by the Guyan Valley rail line. Everything in a coal town was
built and owned by the company: schools, churches, stores, recreational and residential structures. Prior to the Great Depression, 90 percent of southern West
Virginia miners lived in company-owned towns, without benefit of their own civic
institutions. By 1931, the largest group of coal miners in the Logan field were
native born white Americans, followed by African-Americans, Hungarians, Italians
and Poles. The company-supplied housing for mining families ranged from the
well-constructed homes of Holden (called the crown jewel in the Island Creek
Coal Company empire) to tight little rows of shacks in the obscure and segregated
African American or immigrant enclaves. The well-being of company town families would generally rise and fall with the dizzying swings of the industry.

A 1920s photograph of the May brothers' Valley Mills operation
perched audaciously on the river bank at Water Street
(Courtesy of Wilma Smith)

Maurice Beckett described the eventual downstream impact of these developments:

> The years and the river flowed on. All along its valley the towns grew and dumped their raw sewage into the river. Even this it seemed to handle, although fewer people swam in it for that reason. Then came World War II, and instead of shipping lump coal to the Ohio Valley to grind and treat for the high temperature boilers it was ground and washed at the mines. The acid and fine dust from the process ran into the river, killed the fish and turned it black. No one strongly objected for it was war time and the fuel was needed, but the river died. Few fish but mud cats and carp remained. The sand bars turned black with coal dust. (M. Beckett, The Guyandotte River n.d.)

Like Don Chafin's largesse, the river pollution that flowed down from the Logan Coal Field was simply the by-product of an industrial transformation that enriched Cabell County in a number of ways. Inextricably linked by the sullied river and the dusty tracks, Barboursville was only 60 miles from the city of Logan, but the two points along the Guyandotte River valley were worlds away in many respects. Beyond the depot and the newspaper headlines, villagers had little sense of the pitch black of a mine, the conflict between operators and unions, and the Dickensian desperation of "stranded" out-of-work miners and their families.

Economically and socially, Cabell County further separated itself from its coal-extracting neighbors to the south and joined the Midwestern cities and Kanawha Valley as an industrial center. International Nickel, American Car and Foundry, Standard Ultramarine, and Owens-Illinois Glass Company became major employers in the county. As Appalachian coal was carried toward the great steel mills of Pittsburgh and Chicago, the automobile factories in Detroit, and the electrical power plants and factories of the Great Lakes and Ohio River regions, Barboursville got its own small but significant piece of the action. By the late 1920s, Barboursville identified itself not just as a residential haven, railroad hub and college community, but also as a manufacturing town.

One business in particular provided decades of employment stability and helped the village avoid the worst effects of the Great Depression.

The Crash

Those who study the economic freefall of 2008 can find comparisons to the Crash of 1929. After an early-century progressive streak, there were four years of ineptitude and scandals under President Warren G. Harding, followed by Calvin Coolidge whose catchphrase was "the business of America is business." In 1928, millionaire Herbert Hoover carried the Republicans to their third consecutive presidential victory. He privately worried about "the fever of speculation" that accompanied America's post-war prosperity, but took pains to maintain a spirit of optimism, even amid warnings of the financial debacle to come.

Long before there was such a thing as a "subprime-mortgage-backed-derivative," and before the twenty-first-century masters of high finance were inventing high-tech ways to bend the rules, the decade of the 1920s was in essence a time of *no* rules, other than the law of supply and demand. Over-speculation in the stock market had become rampant by the end of the decade. Among the many get-rich-quick schemes were stock pools, in which a group of men would get together and buy a block of shares in a company—any company—and then trade shares back and forth among themselves in order to hike the price and pull in outsiders, before dumping the stock on the market. Unregulated, these types of activities led to quick profits by the winners, sucker bets for the losers, and decimated businesses all around.

Barboursville was not immune from "speculation fever." According to Maurice Beckett:

> In 1926 the nation was caught up in a hot air balloon ride of real estate euphoria. In Florida, underwater lots were sold to northerners who had never seen them. Real estate promoters near the cities opened subdivisions for an expanding population which had not yet begun to expand. One just development east of Huntington became so over-extended that the promoter took his life. Nor was Barboursville exempt, for there are always those who hate to see apparent riches pass them by. In north Barboursville adjoining the railroad and the old cemetery, a subdivision was opened. A lot auction was held in which the big attraction was the promised ascension of a hot air balloon. As I recall, the balloon did not ascend and neither did the subdivision.
>
> Dad, who was already involved in a real estate and insurance business as a sideline to his railroad job, joined a large group of village men trying to subdivide a farm to the east about two miles. It was a dismal year for the Becketts. In 1926, his business life became so entangled that he left his job as a station agent and started a real estate and insurance business in nearby Huntington. All around him businesses were collapsing and in less than two years his collapsed with them. He was able to return to the railroad as a telegrapher. (M. Beckett, 850 Lee Street 1996)

When America's economy collapsed after the stock market crash of October 24, 1929 (a day that became known as "Black Thursday"), the coal industry buckled as well. West Virginia miners—most of whom already knew low pay and poor living conditions in a region which no longer had enough farmland to sustain life—found themselves in the cold grip of poverty years before the rest of the nation. The beleaguered companies began selling off the miners' houses and abandoning the depressed coal town settlements, leaving residents without community services such as education, police and fire protection.

As a world-wide depression deepened, President Hoover exhorted faith in the "trickle-down" system of supporting commerce by feeding in money at the top. He encouraged private charity, but resisted direct government relief to citizens or public works programs. The number of homeless migrant laborers exploded, as men decided to travel for free by freight train and try their luck far from home. By 1932, when Franklin Delano Roosevelt was elected by one of the largest popular margins in history, two million men were roaming the country looking for work or handouts. Based on recollections of my mother and aunt, Barboursville's Depot Street sidewalks and porches received their share of visits from America's legion of hungry, unemployed "hoboes."

The general picture in post-Crash West Virginia was statistically twice as bad as the nation at large. When Federal Relief Administration field representative Howard O. Hunter addressed the West Virginia House of Delegates, he brought to their attention the fact that in 1932 (the depth of the Depression), one of every six persons in the United States was dependent upon public relief agencies. In that same period, one West Virginian out of every three existed on public relief. By the time Mr. Hunter addressed the Legislature, he said there were still nearly half a million West Virginians dependent upon public relief for their food and shelter.

"May I say that this does not take into account other thousands of people who are unemployed, but who through the resources of friends, relatives and their own ingenuity, have managed to stay away from the public relief office," he added.

Mr. Hunter's agency was contending with the fact that West Virginia was one of a handful of states in which there were serious charges of political resistance to, and interference with, federal relief efforts:

> At its best, public relief is still a discouraging and unpleasant matter. It is particularly discouraging when it is done on such inadequate and hand to mouth basis as it has been necessary to do it in West Virginia.

> Some of the stories we have heard and some of the things we have seen in West Virginia about the conditions in some of these relief families would make your hair stand on end. There are true stories of conditions which, if published, would almost amount to a national scandal. Children by the thousands have stayed at home this winter instead of going to school because they have no shoes and clothing. Thousands of children in families in this state never see a bottle of milk. Other thousands of people are living in shelters which are a disgrace to the state. It was impossible to put many thousands of men to work in this state on our civil works program, for instance, until the federal government had made a special grant of money to purchase clothing.

In other words, this is the most real and most critical situation that has ever been faced in this state and it is even more critical to these half a million people who are entirely dependent on public aid for their very living.

Now, who has paid for what has been done for these people? The serious question which I am presenting to you today is the fact that the state of West Virginia, as far as any practical action goes, has ignored this problem. Ninety-six per cent and more of all the money that has been spent for public relief in this state for relief the past year has come from the federal government. The other small amount has been squeezed out here and there from local communities. The state itself has yet to show any evidence of a sense of responsibility for this great problem. (West Virginia Archives and History 2012)

Through the 1930s, against this backdrop of business failures, political squabbles, delayed government action and widespread human misery, one would expect that Barboursville suffered along with the rest. To a certain extent this was the case, but villagers might have appreciated the fact that things could have been so much worse, especially considering the stark reality in the southern "hollers." In Logan and Mingo counties, which had split off from Cabell a century earlier, conditions were described by federal relief workers as worse than the worst urban slums in the United States. Just outside of Williamson, one doctor reported, "children are sleeping on the floor in corners of old shacks, rat-ridden, filthy and open to the four winds of Heaven. They're marked for death here—marked by the hundreds."

Barboursville weathered the 12 years of the Great Depression with a much smaller measure of human tragedy. Nevertheless, two events of the 1930s tested the resiliency and resolve of our Lost Villagers. In 1937, Cabell County residents were among more than 25,000 people in the region affected by record flooding on the Ohio River; 6,000 were left homeless in Huntington alone. In town, the banks overflowed at Tanyard Creek and at the mouth of the Mud and Guyandotte Rivers. On top of a shattered economy, the 1937 flood was just one more indignity, as was the loss of Morris Harvey College in 1935.

Morris Harvey Relocates to Charleston

Forty-seven summers after village leaders rallied and founded a new college in the vacant courthouse, the building and original town square were once again abandoned.

Despite an ambitious building program that brought a modern gymnasium and two imposing dormitories to "Inspiration Ridge" and another large dormitory and athletic field to the south side of town, the board of trustees had voted as early as 1926 to move the college to Charleston as "Kanawha University." The trustees eventually relented to the pleas of villagers. (This appeal, according to Maurice Beckett, was punctuated by a fraternity performance at the annual Zeta Kappa "minstrel," with young men slowly parading framed portraits of the school's dour-looking past presidents across the stage.) Barboursville had been able to plod along for another nine years as a college town.

The Great Depression meant declining enrollment and dried-up endowments. The growth of state-supported Marshall College ten miles away made the advantages of relocation crystal-clear. A prominent group of educational leaders had recommended Charleston as "the most propitious location for a college east of the Mississippi river," and the capitol city had already secured resources and space.

An unpublished essay written by former MHC student Maurice Beckett in 1980 pays tribute to the administrators and teaching staff who dedicated themselves to providing a meaningful education in the increasingly dingy main building, "when it became obvious that its days were limited."

Other than a handful of village residents who were on the faculty, most of the teaching staff lived and ate in the dormitory. They included Mr. and Mrs. Pangle who taught social studies, he a small man with a misshapen arm and she a "wispy, sallow little woman." There was also Dr. Pond who taught math, Dr. Summers who taught history, Professor Stout who taught English, and Dr. R J. Yoak who taught the required Bible class. If any one member of the rapidly-changing faculty held the college together it was, according to Beckett, Ashley C. Blackwell, a pleasant, polite, cultured (and chain-smoking) man who guided the fraternity and taught chemistry "conscientiously and well" for 14 years. Blackwell was vice-president of the institution upon its removal to Charleston.

The last president of Morris Harvey College in Barboursville was Leonard Riggleman, a 1922 graduate who hailed from Randolph County. In 1964, a Morris Harvey Alumni Banquet featured a speech by J. B. F. Yoak Jr. who "roasted" his old classmate with these remarks:

> When C&O Train, No. 13, steamed into Barboursville that evening in September, 1916, it little realized what a personage it had brought to our little city. Neither did those who met the train realize it as they passed him by, un-noticed, as they looked for promising students who might make good members for the Phi Delta or Pieriean Literary Societies.

> Who would have thought that this country boy, dressed in his first store-bought suit—it was purple-striped and he wore yellow shoes— carrying a battered suitcase, which held all his belongings, would in fifteen years be the President of the College? (Yoak 1964)

(Morris Harvey reunion gatherings took place in the village until at least

1979, a time for MHC family members and friends far and near to revisit old memories. In the meantime, the main college building would become the home of Barboursville Junior High. Around 1940, fire claimed the bell tower and gabled roof, and the old courthouse building was remodeled.)

After the college was vacated, 21-year-old Maurice Beckett came up with his own solitary tribute to mark the end of an era:

> It was, as I recall, an evening in June of 1935. That day Morris Harvey College had closed its doors in Barboursville forever, and gone to greater things in Charleston, W.Va. However, when it closed its doors, it did not lock all of them. I had graduated from Marshall College, where I had played my trumpet in the band. I felt that some requiem should be made to Morris Harvey. It was about 10:00 o'clock, and the streets were almost empty. Trumpet in hand I entered the back door of the building, which had housed both courthouse and college for over 80 years. I walked past the empty bursar's office. The dark passageways were tomb-quiet. Up the stairs I climbed, finding my way from habit, my steps sounding out in the darkness. I passed Dr. Yoak's Bible classroom to my right, and Prof. Blackwell's chemistry lab on the left. I suppose Bible classrooms have no odor but all chemistry labs smell of acid. I crept past the dark assembly room: Wade, Marshall, Atcheson, Meek and McClung were surely gone. I climbed the final stairs, past some faintly visible chalk marks which said, "Think," to the auditorium on the 3rd floor. It was probably in this largest of the old courthouse rooms that a few unlucky men had been condemned to death, to hang on the local gibbet. I remembered it for more enjoyable and recent occasions—bats and all. I could still, in my mind's ear, hear Maxie Moore playing the piano. Now I went to the door of the belfry—it was unlocked—and out on the platform facing Main Street. The only person in sight was a state trooper, changing guard. I raised my trumpet and put my Barboursville soul into the bugle call…TAPS. (M. Beckett, Morris Harvey College n.d.)

Barboursville's "Bread Basket"

The loss of the college changed the identity of Barboursville once again. Yet even as Morris Harvey was in its slow decline, an industry on the east side of the village took on growing significance. A familiar corporate presence played a huge role in maintaining the security and stability of area families through the Great Depression.

As the numbers tell, the most important employer in Barboursville remained the Chesapeake and Ohio Railroad. In particular, by the time of Stock Market Crash the company's Barboursville Reclamation Plant was serving a vital system-wide function. Even in the worst of times, keeping hundreds of miles of C&O

tracks maintained through the repair, replacement and recycling of various parts and devices provided good, steady work for men of the area. Through the subsequent decades of railroad consolidation—the "Chessie System" years of the 1970s, and into the mid-1980s under the corporate behemoth known as CSX Transportation—the plant continued to provide jobs for over 100 people who helped keep the tracks in running order.

Straddling the main line on 45 acres of railroad property, the Barboursville "shops" expanded from a simple supply house in 1923. Expansions were made onto the old freight building, and other buildings sprang up to house a machine shop, boiler shop, blacksmith shop, signal shop, car shop, carpenter shop, track reclaiming shop, and rail sawing mill.

The last known view of Main Street from the top of the
former courthouse, taken in the late 1930s
(Courtesy of Barbara Miller)

Based on my own tally of "bread-winning" men and women living in Barboursville town limits, this table of top-ranked village livelihoods in the years 1920, 1930 and 1940 best illustrates the changing nature of the workforce in the "tucked-away" years:

		1920 Town Census	1930 Town Census	1940 Town Census
Number of Adults Listing a Paid Occupation		281	495	443
#1	Ranked Occupation or Employer (% of Barboursville Workers So Employed)	C&O Railroad (24%)	C&O Railroad (32%)	C&O Railroad (28%)
#2	Ranked Occupation or Employer (%)	Brick Plant (11%)	Public Schools (6%)	Public Schools (10%)
#3	Ranked Occupation or Employer (%)	Tie (6% each): • Merchant/ Stores • College	Tie (5% each): • Road Construction • Merchant/ Stores • Farm/Diary	Carpenter/Building Trades (8%)
#4	Ranked Occupation or Employer (%)	Tie (5% each): • Carpenter/ Building Trades • Farm	Tie (4% each): • Carpenter/ Building Trades • College	Tie (7% each): • Government "New Deal" Work Programs • Manufacturing jobs in Huntington factories
#5	Ranked Occupation or Employer (%)	Tie (4% each): • Domestic/ Servant • Public Schools	Tie (3% each): • Brick Plant • Domestic/ Servant • Garage/Auto Mechanic	Tie (6% each): • Brick Plant • Merchant/Stores

The corner of Depot and Main remained a social center as the company provided activities for its workers and their families. The plant supplied paying customers for corner stores and other local businesses. In 1933, Flossie and Charlie Thompson opened a restaurant and grocery on the corner, offering hearty plate lunches for 25 cents each. Across the street was Burgess's East End Grocery, where the neighborhood gentlemen would sit in the back room around a pot-bellied stove, dressed in their suits and starched shirts, solving the problems of the world. Perhaps supplanting the Morris Harvey athletic lineup, the C&O sponsored baseball and basketball teams.

Within the noisy sprawl of the Barboursville "shops," the men were able to sustain family life and sharpen their work skills in an atmosphere of camaraderie and respect. One man in particular seemed to set a congenial tone. Missouri-born William Walter Constance worked his way up from a Midwestern railroad blacksmith to supervisor of the Barboursville plant. Mr. Constance had a personal management principle, according to Frank Ball, "that if you went easy with your men when you had little for them to do they would come through for you when you were in a pinch…I never knew his theory to fail. Once I helped load a car of bolts in 25 minutes that would have taken more than an hour to load ordinarily."

Call it loyalty to their boss, deep appreciation for an honest day's work, or the old Barboursville work ethic—the workers of the Reclamation Plant weathered uncertain days and threats by the line's president to move the shops elsewhere. In February 1936, they responded to a catastrophic plant fire with extraordinary grit:

C&O 1931-1932 BASEBALL TEAM. Front Row (left to right) includes: Stanley Thompson, Irwin Gieske, Tommy Thompson, Harry B. Washington, Julius Vietz, Kelly Wilson, Gail Chapman. Back Row: Charlie Thompson, Carl Hinchman, "Iron-Head" Burgess, Joe Childers, Harold Luster, Tommy Thompson, Ed Smith, H.C. "Twenty" Lantz, Everett May, Walton Grove
(Courtesy of Donna Brown)

The men were sitting cozily by their firesides this bitterly cold night when the town's fire siren out on Inspiration Ridge gave a three-alarm fire signal. Those in town went to their doors to see a great black smoke rising from the plant. The southwest corner of the old building was on fire!

There was a surge of all available employees toward our bread basket. A fire unit from Central City was called as was the Milton Volunteer Fire Department. Our car-and-hose was handy and our town's Dodge truck with two hoses and two chemical tanks was soon on the scene. But all was in vain. A stiff north-easterly wind drove the fire into the unburned sections of the building, dry from years of age, and quenching it was hopeless. Men gave their attention to saving the contents.

Across the switch track from the flaming building stood the office carrying records over the past 13 years. Imagination painted an ugly picture of the results should it burn.

On the switch track, ten feet from either the office building or the burning building stood a boxcar loaded with oil and other flammable materials. And on the main line waiting for an incoming freight, was a booster engine.

By the mere throwing of a switch, the engine could have pulled the explosive car to safety saving the shop office. But it wasn't on the engineer's schedule and he had not orders to move a gasoline laden car in our town. So he sat in his engine cab a mere 50 yards away and watched our frantic appealing efforts. Heat held the firemen at too great a distance for water to reach all the car.

The eaves of the car began smoking. An explosion was imminent. A small blaze appeared. Hubert Adkins, a blacksmith helper, grabbed a fire extinguisher and went into the inferno between the car and the freight building and had a stream of cold water turned on him as he extinguished the blaze. The strong wind eventually carried enough fire toward the building and, fortunately, away from the car, to save an explosion and the office. The real hero of the fire, the blacksmith helper, left the embers an hour or two later with his song unsung and his worthy efforts unnoticed, largely.
This was in depression days. What would it mean? Millions were out of work. This had been our meal ticket through fair days and foul. Now the working site of half our men had gone up in smoke. And "moving" the shop became a certainty now in both the minds of the employees and the populace.

It is amazing what men can do in emergencies. Every nook and corner of every building left standing was utilized. The platform of the old building was saved and work was performed on it in mild weather. The welder went into the planner building. The signal shop moved upstairs over an old storage room. "Rights" were overlooked in operating machinery that would run until the fire-damaged lathes and millers could be renovated. Within three or four weeks, every man was back on duty and we were beginning to build anew from scrap iron. (Ball, C&O Reclamation Plant Fire Recalled 1979)

Walter Constance was Reclamation Plant supervisor from 1923 until his sudden death from a cerebral hemorrhage in 1937, the year after the fire. In 1946, the C&O built a nine-hole golf course with sand greens between the north end of Depot Street and Route 60 for the recreational use of employees, their families and guests. They named it the Constance Memorial Golf Course.

A New Deal Legacy

Fortunately for beleaguered Barboursville, the sounds of hardworking men extended beyond the rail yard and brick plant, thanks to a wave of federal civil works programs.

In his first hundred days in office in 1933, President Franklin Delano Roosevelt had taken bold, aggressive action to help the "forgotten man." The president was aided by First Lady Eleanor Roosevelt, who traveled around the country and reported back on the appalling and heartbreaking conditions she witnessed. FDR was granted broad executive power by Congress, and took to the radio waves to set forth a comprehensive—some would say controversial, a few would even say communistic—scheme of national reform, relief and recovery policies. In his "fire-side chats" to the American people, he referred to this collection of policies as the New Deal.

The President quickly enacted a broad set of emergency measures and policies (including a push for the Constitutional repeal of Prohibition). Several monumental achievements of the FDR administration continue today. The National Labor Relations Act set up a board (NLRB) to enforce provisions such as collective bargaining. The Fair Labor Standards Act of 1938 banned child labor and set a minimum wage. The Social Security Act provided a system of old-age pensions for workers, unemployment insurance, and aid for dependent mothers and children, the blind and physically disabled.

Other New Deal initiatives failed to sustain Congressional support, and have been obscured by the passage of time. Thirty miles northeast of Barboursville, one such example of a Rooseveltian "pet project" sits today along the Kanawha River, near the Toyota Motors Manufacturing facility. The experimental town of Eleanor (named for Mrs. Roosevelt, who visited the settlement several times) is worth checking out—the original town hall contains some photos and memorabilia, and the local Dairy Queen serves up a yummy homemade lunch. Originally named the Putnam County Farm Project, Eleanor was the third "rural-industrial community" to be funded by the Federal Relief Administration. The settlement consisted of modern houses sitting on modest farm plots, each with its own chicken pen, as well as schools, health programs, and homesteader-planned industries. The town provided a brand new start for 150 displaced West Virginia miners and their families who were carefully selected from a thousand applicants. Like the storied Arthurdale, West Virginia, and a few dozen other "resettlement communities" across the country, Eleanor represents one of the New Deal s most "radical" programs, that of relocating destitute Americans into planned collectivist communities.

Many less-dramatic New Deal social welfare policies led to substantial and enduring changes in the way West Virginia dealt with its poor and unemployed, creating a new network for public assistance and a new attitude toward the unfortunate. New Deal programs provided stimulus spending for public health programs, libraries and cultural activities, including publication of the book *West Virginia: A Guide to the Mountain State* in 1941, a statewide Historic Records Survey. and a concert orchestra in Huntington.

Civil works programs—specifically the Work Projects Administration (WPA), the Public Works Administration (PWA), the Civilian Conservation Core (CCC) and National Youth Administration (NYA)—created jobs for untold men, women and teenagers in the Barboursville area. As a matter of fact, the old McKendree Farm just south of town (long before it became the Barboursville Community Park) was put to use as a "pre-CCC" conditioning camp for some of the state's most impoverished and malnourished young men. According to state news clips, this happened at about the same time Morris Harvey College vacated the village:

June 11, 1935: Bruce McCutcheon, 26, resident of the transient bureau, was killed today when he fell from the rear of a truck while on route to a transient camp near Barboursville. He was registered at the bureau as the son of Samuel McCutcheon of Kanawha county. (Associated Press 1935)

August 7, 1935: Four young men, whose ambition it was to enlist in CCC camps of the state, have been "graduated" from the state conditioning camp for young men at Barboursville this week and have been accepted in the forestry service. More are on the road to the required physical condition and more than 100 who had been turned down because of underweight, due mostly to undernourishment, will later be "graduated."

The camp was established by the state department of public welfare for young men who aspired to positions in the CCC camps but were unable to make the grade because of physical deficiencies. There are 50 in the Barboursville camp now and 50 more are to enter training this week.

The men work near the camp at forestry and agriculture, on the state farm that provides produce for the Huntington state hospital and other state institutions. Special attention is paid to diet and exercise. Thorough physical examinations are conducted frequently. Records show that the men gain on an average of 11 pounds in three weeks. They undergo modified Army routine.

The condition of the young men on entering camp is due to lack of normal privileges in their home life, usually because they are members of families that have undergone extreme hardship. All are from the relief rolls.

In the CCC camps they are put to interesting and educative work and upon the expiration of their terms of enlistment are turned out physically fit and ready for positions in everyday life that will take them and their families off relief. (Associated Press 1935)

In 1940 alone, the Barboursville area had at least two people employed by the PWA, six by the NYA, and eleven young men of the area working for the CCC. Nationwide, the Civilian Conservation Corps put 2.5 million unmarried men to work maintaining and restoring forests, beaches and parks. Workers earned just a dollar a day, but received free meals, education classes and job training at CCC camps, including "Camp Cabell" outside of Milton. The largest single CCC effort in West Virginia was the mine-sealing program, in which half of the state's 1,700 abandoned mines were sealed to reduce acid runoff into streams and rivers.

The Civilian Conservation Corps helped lift up my own great-uncle, a young man who at age 10 lost his mother to tuberculosis, saw all his belongings swept away in a Cabell Creek flood and, like many local men of the era, dropped out of high school to help make ends meet. The skills provided through the CCC camp helped Uncle Bill get on at a lumber company in Columbus, Ohio, where he made a successful life with a management job, lovely home and devoted family.

The Work Projects Administration (sometimes called the Works Progress Administration) provided temporary employment for eight million Americans who constructed or repaired schools, hospitals and other projects. Toward the end of the Great Depression, within the 1940 Census schedules for the town of Barboursville and two neighboring districts—taking in the area roughly bordered by Blue Sulphur to the east, Davis Creek to the West, north to Route 7 and south to Doss Hill Road—I identified 110 men and women working for the WPA. This represented seven percent of the workforce within village limits. In the rural sections just outside of Barboursville, where about 30 percent of men were still doing some sort of farm work, and 26 percent commuted to manufacturing jobs at places like the Reclamation Plant, Brick Plant or Nickel Plant, a full nine percent had WPA jobs that year.

The toil and sweat of this temporary workforce resulted in some of the area's most durable architecture. Native stone buildings were erected through the Work Projects Administration, including the 4-H building across the Davis Creek Bridge in 1936, built along with a campground for the youth of the county with help from the Farm Bureau and county teachers. The State Road Commission sponsored the 1940 WPA construction of a storage building near the intersection of U.S. Route 60 and Merritts Creek Road. Both still serve the public. (Other county structures erected by the WPA include a therapeutic center for crippled children at Milton's Morris Memorial Hospital, and Huntington's Ritter Park Rose Garden.)

The departure of Morris Harvey College and Academy, as well as consolidation of the Barboursville village and district school boards, provided the greatest opportunity for WPA labor. On the southern end of town, where the former MHC boys' dormitory, Billingsley Hall, housed the first eight classrooms for "Barboursville Joint High School," the WPA contributed a 12-classroom annex. Then in 1938 and 1939, WPA workers razed Billingsley and built in its place an auditorium, gymnasium, library, home economics room, shop, offices and dressing rooms—the nucleus of what most graduates remember as the "hallowed halls of old BHS."

Cabell County 4-H Building at Davis Creek, built in 1936
(Courtesy of Barboursville Public Library)

It was through the WPA that some otherwise-destitute Cabell County families were able to put food on the table and shoes on their children's feet, while helping to build for the long term. Coincidentally, the work programs and CCC camps also improved the health, self-esteem and discipline of a generation of young men who would soon be called to serve in an unexpected overseas war.

By 1941, when the nation's unemployment rate had fallen to 9.7 percent (from a high of 24.75 percent in 1933), Roosevelt had by most accounts restored the people's faith in their government. During his second term, FDR remarked in a fireside chat how his policies had saved American capitalism by purging its worst abuses and accommodating the greater public interest.

"We in America know that our democratic institutions can be preserved and made to work," he said. "The only sure bulwark of continuing liberty is a government strong enough to protect the interest of the people, and a people strong enough and well enough informed to maintain its sovereign control over its government."

FDR pointed out in the same 1938 radio address that democracy had disappeared in certain European nations during the worldwide economic decline because their governments had said, "We can do nothing for you."

Nation is Pulled into a Second World War

By the end of the 1930s, the country was just digging itself out of the Great Depression. Americans had little interest in conflicts abroad, but inescapable trouble was looming in the Eastern Hemisphere. As early as 1936, political and military leaders in Italy, Spain, Russia, Japan and Germany were simultaneously stirring up old rivalries, deceiving their Western counterparts and riding a tide of economic resentment and nationalist hatred. Within less than a decade, events would reveal a handful of foreign men as some of history's most sadistic villains.

Mussolini, Franco, Stalin and Tojo were bad enough—each peppering the globe, respectively, with fascist dictatorship, military rebellion, political repression and imperialist aggression—but Adolf Hitler combined all their nefarious traits, and worse. A rather unimpressive-looking specimen himself, this German veteran of WWI rose to national power in 1933 and secretly began building the machinery to achieve the vision of a superior and conquering "Master Race."

From 1937 to 1945, fueled largely by the paranoia, racism and insatiable ambition of their "Fuehrer," a resentment-filled German society somehow metastasized into co-conspirators in Hitler's "Third Reich." Once Hitler consolidated German power, he unleashed upon the world a new form of efficient, mechanized and systematic Evil.

In short, World War II was the result of the rise of the Nazi military, Hitler's "annexation" of Austria and Czechoslovakia, and a series of secret pacts with Mussolini, Stalin and the warlords of Japan. Their actions spawned an "Axis" of belligerent countries that forced themselves in one way or another upon a majority of the world's nations. The war officially began in September 1939 when Hitler's army invaded Poland. German forces continued to attack countries on the European continent, and entered a defeated and demoralized Paris in June 1940, where Hitler set up a puppet government over defeated France.

By October 1940, after Nazi air strikes battered the cities of Great Britain in preparation for an invasion there, America's stance of neutrality quickly dissolved. Through the passage of the Lend-Lease Act, President Roosevelt received authority from Congress to sell, transfer, or lease war goods to the government of any country whose defenses were vital to the United States defense. In June 1941, Joseph Stalin became an unexpected Ally after Hitler broke a non-aggression pact and began invading Russia. The popular (and now three-term president) FDR proclaimed that the United States would become the "arsenal of democracy" for the Allied forces, and began strategizing with Britain on how to best defeat Germany.

A feverish United States effort to build a "two-ocean navy" revitalized American industry. The Selective Training and Service Act of 1940 created the country's first peacetime draft and formally established the Selective Service System as an independent Federal agency. Still, as of 1941 American citizens were largely determined to stay out of combat.

While the European battles were raging, tensions were mounting globally. Japan was pushing to expand its totalitarian empire into Indonesia, the Philippines, and other European colonies in the Pacific. President Roosevelt responded by receiving Philippine forces into the United States Army, appointing General Douglas MacArthur to command forces in the Far East, and freezing all Japanese assets in the United States By October of 1941, Japan's war minister Hideki Tojo was elevated to Prime Minister. He presented the United States with a demand to "unfreeze" Japanese assets, cut off aid to China and leave the Philippines alone.

On November 26, with their ultimatum to the United States unanswered, the Japanese secretly sent out six carriers with 423 planes, two battleships, two heavy cruisers and eleven destroyers in the direction of an island launching point a few hundred miles north of Pearl Harbor on the United States territory of Hawaii.

At 7:55 a.m. on December 7, 1941, bombs and aerial torpedoes began raining down on the sleepy United States Naval harbor in Honolulu. By the end of that bloody Sunday, there were 2,403 Americans killed and 1,178 wounded at Pearl Harbor in the surprise attack that cost the Japanese only 29 planes and pilots. On the same day, Japanese bombers struck Manila and Guam.

As the awful details of the disaster poured in, Americans reacted with shock and anger. In the sad way that many of us remember exactly where we were and what we were doing the morning of September 11, 2001, the attack on Pearl Harbor imprinted itself on an entire population.

My mom vividly remembers running home from Cotton and Marie Thompson's house on Depot Street, and calling to her parents to turn on the radio because Pearl Harbor was bombed. Linda Brady was just four years old and had no idea what that meant but knew from the voices on the radio and the faces of her grown-up neighbors, that something really bad had happened. Aunt Margie, then five years old,, describes her recollection of the day: "We had just come home from being in the woods looking for a Christmas tree and I couldn't wait to come home to listen to the Sunday comics read over the radio by the mayor of New York. I had to stop listening to the comics so we could hear about the bombing of Pearl Harbor."

Within one day of the attack, the United States declared war on Japan. This in turn led to a December 11 declaration of war against the United States by Axis partners Germany and Italy. And so America geared up quickly and without fanfare, to engage in what became the deadliest military conflict in history.

During World War II, 15 million Americans served in the armed forces— more than a tenth of the United States population. All men between 18 and 45 were liable to military service, although exacting physical and intellectual fitness standards disqualified some. Ten million men served in the U.S. Army, many of them drafted in as General Issue infantrymen, or "G.I.'s," under the command of the legendary General George Patton. America's forces were rounded out by volunteer recruits: four million in the navy and coast guard, 600,000 in the Marine Corps, and about 275,000 female nurses in the "Waves," "Wacs," "Spars" and "Lady Marines."

Barboursville's young men responded in a big way. The pages of Cabell County's newspapers were dotted with photos of young men (and a few women) in uniform, with announcements of their overseas assignments, marriages, furloughs, awards or casualties. Of Barboursville High School's 1944 graduating class of 92 seniors, 16 boys had stars next to their names indicating they missed commencement exercises because there were "in service." In 1945, another 16 boys out of 85 BHS graduates were away in military service.

Extraordinary Service—the Daniel Family

America's economy was suddenly galvanized, but a sense of national austerity prevailed as gasoline, tires and some food products were rationed for the war effort. George Brady Jr. temporarily moved his young family from Depot Street to a South Charleston apartment so he could be closer to his job in the chemical industry.

The level of volunteer effort put forth by the youth of Barboursville staggers the modern imagination. Members of the BHS Future Farmers of America chapter—those who had not already left school to go to war—intensified their service efforts on the home front. In the 1943-44 school year alone, under the leadership of teacher William Garrison, a group of 43 students grew 62 acres of crops, raised 4,227 head of livestock, and brought in gross income of nearly $24,000 from local food production. This was on top of classes, their usual school club activities and a conservation program that included planting 2,000 trees, tending 48 acres of "cover crops," plus collecting scrap paper, rags, metal and other re-useable waste.

In another wing of BHS, the school's band director, Joe Lusk, led his 46 young musicians in learning the works of Sousa and the like, and performing in a large number of patriotic occasions connected to the war effort, such as bond drives and community war rallies. The band was recognized for distinguished service by the Music War Council of America, and invited to play for wounded veterans at the Ashford General Hospital in White Sulphur Springs.

For sheer motherly sacrifice, I doubt anyone could match Alma Pearl Daniel, a former schoolteacher remembered by her daughter-in-law as being the happiest "when she had eight pairs of muddy shoes on each side of the family's gas heater."

The eight sons of Alma and her husband John Wesley Daniel grew up on a 117-acre farm just south of Martha. In 1937, when "times were tough," 17-year-old

Elmer saw the military as a way of moving on in life. He was the first in the family to enlist in the Navy. His older brother Charles was turned away for being underweight so, according to family members, he "went home and ate a lot of bananas" until he was able to make the cut. Third brother "Georgie" first joined his two older brothers on the USS Blue, but the Navy separated the three after Congress passed the "Sullivan Act." This law prohibited siblings from serving on the same vessel, and was enacted after five American brothers named Sullivan were killed in a 1942 Japanese torpedo attack on their ship.

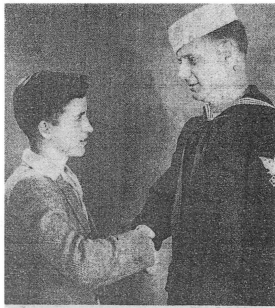

Herman W. Daniel, left above, the seventh son of a Barboursville family to enter the Navy, was greeted yesterday at the Huntington recruiting station by Shore Patrolman W. A. Hicks, right, an old friend, formerly Barboursville chief of police.

Herman Daniel
(Undated Huntington Publishing news clip courtesy of Barbara Miller)

By 1945, seven of the eight Daniel brothers were in service. Charles was a chief torpedo man's mate in the Pacific who narrowly missed the Pearl Harbor bombing while he was on shore leave. Elmer spent eight years on active duty as a damage control chief. Howard "Reece" Daniel was a chief electrician. Virgil was a signalman during the Battle of Normandy. Cecil was a chief gunner's mate. At age 17, Herman became the youngest of the brothers to enlist and served as a data processing specialist. Youngest brother Dorsey was too young to enlist during the war, but collected mementos that his brothers sent home from their worldwide travels.

The modern Guyandotte River bridge at Martha is dedicated to the service of the seven Daniel brothers. In all, John and Alma's sons gave a combined 125 years of military service. Fortunately, all lived through the war to tell their tales of adventure. Before her death in 1977, Alma was given a letter of appreciation by the Secretary of the Navy. There may have been other cases of seven or more siblings serving in a branch of the United States military at once, but this measure of family dedication was certainly rare.

Barboursville's World War II Honor Roll

Barboursville's citizens would later see fit to build a Memorial Wall of Honor with the names of men and women who took their places around the world in defense of the United States and in service to the Allied countries. Such was the patriotism of the time and the town. For several years, the lighted Honor Roll wall graced the Main Street side of the old Miller-Thornburg store, where passersby or those waiting at the bus stop could recognize the hundreds who served. (The Honor Roll was purportedly vandalized in the early 1970s; the sign was later recreated through the efforts of village leaders and several BHS graduates of the 1940s and 1950s, and erected near a footbridge at the old public square.)

WWII Honor Roll on Main Street
(Undated photo courtesy of Barbara Miller)

What follows is an alphabetical listing of who are known to have served in the Second World War from Barboursville, including all the names that appear on the Honor Roll display. *Note: Casualties marked with double asterisks do not appear on the local Honor Roll, but were found in a search of the West Virginia Veterans Memorial Database.*

Billy Adkins, Earl Adkins, James A. Adkins, Moses Adkins, Raymond W. Adkins, Vernon Adkins, W. Paul Adkins, Albert M. Adkins Jr., Everett "Gay" Alberts, Roy C. Alberts, Paul S. Algeo, Betty Jane Allen, Dewey "Dee" Allen, Edward H. Allen, James "Dinky" Allen, E. Earl Altizer, Frank Altizer Jr., James "Jim" Anderson, Joe Lee Anderson, Junior Anderson, Ray O. Anderson, F. "Whistle" Arbaugh, Leo Arbaugh, Clarence "Sleepy" Armstrong, Richard R. Armstrong, Robert J. Armstrong, Paul Ashworth, Dr. Thomas Baer, Peter H. Baer, Phillip A. Baer, James "Jimmy" Bailey, Albert O. Ball, Seth W. Ball, Charles J. Barett, Joseph "Pete" Barett, Lewis H. Barrett, Donald J. Barry, Earl T. Bates, Harry M. Bates, James "Biggy" Bates, John "Johnny" Bates, Noah M. Bates, Edmund Baumgardner, F. Bricky Baumgardner, Gilbert Beach, Raymond Beach, Donald "Bob" Bias, Clarence Black, Clayton "Clate" Black, Walter H. Black, Cledith C. Bledsoe, Elmer Bledsoe, Hedrick Bledsoe, Wyatt F. Bledsoe, Albert Bowen, Clarence Bradberry, Earl J. Bradberry, Herbert S. Bradberry, **Robert C. Bradberry,** Mary Lou Brady, Robert "Bob" Brady, James "Chink" Brady Jr., Roy Brown, Elmer Browning, Troy "Trogan" Browning, John Brumfield, John C. Brumfield, Jonny C. Brumfield, L. Faye Bryan, Jack W. Buchanan, Clyde "Mophead" Burgess, Douglas "Billy" Burgess, Forty "Jay" Burgess, Robert "Mag" Burgess, Earl "Buddy" Burke, Edgar "Pete" Burks, Walter W. Burks, George Burks Jr., **Eustace Butcher Jr.,** J. W. Butcher, William L. Butcher;

Dale H. Camper, A. T. Carpenter, *Denver Carter*, George M. Cartmill, Roy M. Casey, Ernest "Squirley" Cazad, William "Bill" Chambers, Fred Chapman, Eddy Chapman, Harvey "Pete" Chapman, Lawrence Chapman, Paul E. Chapman, Westley M. Chapman, Carl Childers, Harry Clark, Paul Clarke, Algie V. Clay, Lee W. Clay, Robert "Bob" Clay, Donald C. Coffey, Edward G. Coffey, Carrol M. Collins, Donald C. Collins, Herbert Collins, Harold Collins, Oley E. Cooke, Eloise Coyner, R. Dana Coyner, Clarence Crowe, Charley Cumpston, Harold L. Cumpston, Hunter "Peeley" Cyrus, Cecil Daniel, Charles E. Daniel. Elmer W. Daniel, George A. Daniel, Herman Daniel, Howard "Reece" Daniel, Virgil W. Daniel, *U. V. W. Darlington Jr.*, Lee "Junior" Davis, Frank "Ted" Debore, H. Paul DeJarnett, Joe B. Dickenson, S. "Booger" Dickenson, J. D. Dilley, Lyle Dilley, Robert "Bob" Dilley, William M. Dimmer, Clarence "Fat" Drye, Eugene "Gene" Duckworth, Earl F. Duff, Albert F. Eggleston, Kennedy Lee Elder, W. B. Elder, James R. Eldridge, Billy Ellis, Billy E. Ellis, Bruce Ellis, Bruce L. Ellis, William "Bill" Estler, Chester Fannin Jr., William "Bill" Ferguson, James A. Finley, Benjamin Flescher, Haskell "Doug" Ford, James H. Fowble, John Frye, Clayton Fuller;

Delbert L. Gibson, James Gibson, Paul M. Gibson, Clare S. Gothard, Lester K. Gothard, Lyle C. Gothard, Merrel Gothard, W. Sandy Gothard, Thurman Lee Grass, Hunter "Jack" Greene, William F. Greene, Herman Paul Groves, **Billy E. Gwinn,** Calvin W. Hale, W. "Bill Hambleton, Pansy Hamlin, Carl C. Hampton, James A. Harbour, Bert Harris, Jack Harris, D. "Toots" Harshbarger, Louie "Fat" Harshbarger, Merle W. Harshbarger, Roy L. Harshbarger, *Homer Hash*, Bruce B. Hash, Jesse "Tort" Hash, Leonard Hash, Naomi M. Hash, James "Jack" Hatfield, Leon Haynes, Clifford T. Henderson, E. Raymond Henderson, Virgil C. Henderson, Herman

R. Hensley, Richard Herdon, William "Bill" Herdon, Willis H. Hertig, John "Jonny" Hicks, W. "Buddy" Hicks, W. A. "Bill" Hicks, Alford Hinchman, Wetzel "Doc" Hinchman, William "Bill" Hood, Edward W. Horn, **Aubrey F. Hughes,** Bernard R. Hunt, William "Bill" Hunt, Charles M. Hunter, Wallace "Pete" Hurt, William Hutchinson Jr.;

James "Jimmy" James, Homer L. Jefferson, James Jefferson, Wallace Jefferson, Woodrow G. Jefferson, Thomas M. Jeffery, Howard "Whitie" Jobe, Hubert Jobe, John D. Johnson, John E. Jordan, Linord W. Jordan, Goodhue Kail, Joe Kail, John E. Kaiser, Carroll "Pat" Kelly, Merle I. Kelly, Herbert "Booty" King, Wetzel "Slats" King, "Bill" Kingery, Robert Kirk, John H. Kuhn, S. Earsel Kuhn, Vivian L. Kuhn, Frank V. Kyle, Frankie "Mike" Kyle, Jack Kyle, Charles E. Lambert, Homer F. Lambert, George W. Leist, Vernon Lewis, Everett Lipscomb, Glen S. Lipscomb, Sally W. Long, Robert "Bobby" Love, William "Bill" Love, Harold Lusher, Eugene "Pete" Luster;

Richard Mallory, Hysel "Hotfoot" Mallory, Newman "Sim" Mallory, Charles A. Marken, Joseph "Joe" Markum, Marvin W. Markum, Ernest C. Martin, Wilmont Martin, Amos Matthews, Clinton "Bearcat" May, Ray C. May, John B. Mayes Jr., Shelby L. Mays, Walter H. Mays, Charles R. McCallister, Everett McCallister, Fred McCallister, J. Lawrence McCallister, W. Arvil McCallister, Harrold McCarty, Larvil O'Neal McCarty, M. G. McCarty, Dexter McCloud, **Chester B. McCloud**, Kenneth Lee McCloud, Carol McComas, Linwood McCormack, Thomas "Max" McCreary, Charles F. McCue, Freddie McDonie, Robert "Bob" McDonie, Frank McLaughlin, Carroll Merritt, *Harry Midkiff, Donald E. Midkiff, Earl E. Midkiff, Fred Miller, Raymond C. Miller, Wallis W. Miller, Clifford Milton, Ronald Milton, C. Mason Mitchell. James "Jack" Mitchell. Lee Roy Mitchell, Nathan Mitchell, *George Morris, Joe Morrison Jr., John W. Murdock. Phil Murray, Ernest R. Murray, David T. Myles;

Clifton A. Nash, George G. Neal, Jack S. Neal, John S. Neel Jr., *Joe C. Nelson, Glen Nelson, Evan Newman, Hugh Newman, Lantz Newson, Harold Nicholas, **Paul W. Park, Earl C. Parry, Robert "Bob" Patterson, Hobert Patton, Homer Patton, James M. Patton, Clyde F. Paul, Richard Payne, Riley Payton, Chester Penson, Edward P. Perry, Francis A. Perry, Harry E. Perry, James "Ham" Perry, James E. Perry, Ralph L. Perry, Rhodes B. Perry, Russell B. Perry, Ralph "Bill" Petrie, Albert M. Peyton, Alden Peyton, Dr. Robert Peyton, John "Jackie" Peyton, George Pinson, L. Clay Pinson, William Pinson, *Robert T. Plybon, Oakie O. Poling, Homer Porter, Roy Powers, Seward S. Price, Robert Ramsey, Beyson Rawn Jr., Charles Ray, Clinton Ray, Charley Rayburn, Eddie Rayburn, Ezra Rayburn, Harold Rayburn, L. Howard Rayburn, Paul Rayburn, R. Everett Rayburn, James E. Riblett, Walter Riffle, Susie Riley, John Ruley, Francis "Frank" Rupe, J. Bryce Rupe, Finley W. Russell, Clayton Rutherford Jr., John F. Ryan;

Robert K. Safford, Harrold Sallards, William "Bill" Samuel, Earl "Bob" Sang, Glen F. Sargent, William Sargent, Lloyd Scarberry, Harry E. Schrader, Carl N. Shephard, Younger Shephard, Meldal Shephard, Donald E. Shepherd, Raymond Shepherd, Clinton Short, Robert W. Showwalter, Harold Smallridge, Charles A. Smith, Cledith Smith, Dennis Smith, Edward "Ed" Smith, Herbert "Bert" Smith, Paul C. Smith, Robert "Bob" Smith, Robert "Don" Smith, **Rufus Raymond Smith, William "Bill" Smith, Walter F. Smith Jr., George Songer, *Oscar W. Songer, Orville Sowards, James T. Spradling, Gus Stackpole, George Stanley, James Stanley, Edward D. Steele, William "Bill" Steele, Fred E. Steele Jr., John Stevenson, Basil G. Stewart, Edward Stollings, Noble R. Stoud,

Robert S. Stover, Norman A. Strank, Lewis Strathman, Neal Stroud, Stephen "Steve" Sturm, Richard Sullivan, S. S. Summers, Everett Surgeon, Ben Swann, George Swann, Robert L. Swann, Woodrow Swann;

Gene Taylor, Chalmer Templeton, Clyde Tensley, **Edward "Ed" Tinsley**, James "Jimmy" Thacker, Glen "Blackie" Thompson, Paul Thompson, Jack "Tub" Toler, Lewis "Pig" Toler, Lonnie "Pig" Toler, Ralph "Babe" Tooley, Russell L. Tooley, Charley Triplett, W. Jean Turley, Rolland Turman, Samuel "Sam" Turman, W. "Bill" Vandel, Ezra "Ez" Vannatter, Thomas "Tom" Vannatter, Harold V. Vass, Torryson W. Vass, Amerose Vittitoe, Blaine Vittitoe, William H. Waggoner, William "Bill" Wagoner, Ernest E. Wallace, Robert Wallace, W. Junior Wallace, James E. Walls, Kenneth Ward, Melvin Ward, James W. Warden, Joseph "Joe" Warden, Raymond Warden, Russell L. Warden, Walter W. Warden Jr., Harry B. Washington, Norman "Mommy" Watson, Harry J. Watts, Marvin Bennett Watts, Earl L. Weatherholt, Lee Roy Weekly, Bailey W. Wentz, Harvey W. Wentz, Lowen N. Wentz, N. Kendall Wheeler, Jack Whitehall, Harold C. Wilcox, James E. Wilkerson, James R. Wood, Bernard Woodling, Eugene "Doc" Worley, William "Peg" Worley, Fred Wroten, Linford Wroten, *J. Beale Yoak, Dale M. Yoak and J. Doyle Yoak.

Worldwide Struggle Forges the "Greatest Generation"

American forces provided needed fortification to war-ravaged Britain and the other Allies. President Roosevelt and British Prime Minister Winston Churchill proved to be inspiring war leaders with strong strategic commanders, but they and the other Allies fought a grim defensive battle well into 1943. The tide had begun to turn when military forces from Canada, Free French Forces, the United Kingdom and the United States participated in the Invasion of Normandy landings on June 6, 1944. The final year of World War II was marked by what General Dwight D. Eisenhower called "the dirtiest kind of infantry slugging," as a series of battles as costly as any since the Civil War stretched through the cold, wet European winter.

As German resistance finally began to crumble in the spring of 1945, Allied armies penetrated Germany, Austria and Poland where they made the horrific discovery of the concentration camps. Multitudes of Jews, gypsies and other men, women and children had been rounded up since 1937 for torture and extermination by the sadistic enforcers of the Third Reich. By the time they were found at Buchenwald, Auschwitz and other locations of wholesale atrocity, entire communities of families had been systematically murdered, and the remaining survivors were discovered penned up, naked, diseased and starving.

Just as victory appeared certain, America and its Allies suddenly mourned the death of their leader, four-term President Franklin Roosevelt, who died of a cerebral hemorrhage on April 12 while he was drafting a speech. The final words from his writing pen: "Let us move forward with strong and active faith."

Within three weeks of Roosevelt's death, Italian dictator Mussolini was captured and killed by his own countrymen. Two days after, Hitler died a coward's death in a Bunker under Berlin, shooting his mistress and then himself. Victory in Europe was declared on May 7 and May 8, 1945, when the WWII Allies formally accepted the unconditional surrender of the armed forces of Nazi Germany.

Japan surrendered in late summer, after the United States dropped two atomic bombs on the cities of Hiroshima and Nagasaki, killing as many as 140,000 people in Hiroshima and 80,000 in Nagasaki.

A young Barboursville man was able to describe the surrender of Japan from a close vantage point:

Fire Controlman (first class) Raymond Miller, 25, is back home from the Navy after witnessing, at a distance of only a few feet, one of the most significant events in the world's history—the abject surrender of Japan aboard the mighty battleship Missouri in Tokyo Bay Sunday, September 2.

Controlman Miller, a veteran of more than three years of Naval service, stood virtually at General MacArthur's elbow when the articles of surrender were signed. The controlman was a crew member of the Missouri, upon which he served the latter months of the war.

The weather was warm and the sun shone brightly when Japan's emissaries, General Yoshijio Umezu of the Imperial Staff, and Foreign Minister Mamoru Shigemitsu signed away the Nipponese empire, Controlman Miller said.

"The entire ceremony took only about 10 minutes and there wasn't much formality about it," the controlman said. "The Japs were rushed on board and rushed right off. I remember that the Jap soldiers looked shabby and runty in their uniforms. The American and Allied officers towered above them.

"It almost seemed as if the tallest officers in the United Nation's forces had been chosen especially to make the Japs look mean and insignificant...General Wainwright looked thin and worn from his confinement in the Jap prison camps.

"General MacArthur looked brawny and informal. So did Admiral "Bull" Halsey. On the other hand, Admiral Nimitz was neat and dignified. I particularly noticed his grey hair." (Barboursville Tar Watched Japs Give Up In Tokyo Bay 1945)

Over the course of World War II, Barboursville's greatest generation lost at least 17 of its brothers in the line of duty. The following men were either born in

Barboursville, attended Barboursville High School, or lived in the village upon their enlistment:

1942: Staff Sergeant Harry F. Midkiff was killed in action in North Africa and buried in the American Cemetery of North Africa. Twenty-three-year-old Army Private Chester B. McCloud was stationed near Lakeland, Georgia when he was killed in a car accident. Private Paul W. Park of the U.S. Army died in Walter Reed Hospital in Washington, D.C.

1943: Robert C. Bradberry was killed in action at sea while serving as a Coxswain in the Coast Guard. Thirty-five-year-old John Beale Yoak, a seaman with the Merchant Marine, was reported missing at sea on July 18.

1944: Denver M. Carter of Lesage was killed in France at age 22. Aubrey F. Hughes was 27, married to the former Evelyn Steele, and serving in an Army Engineer Battalion, when he was killed in action in St. Raphael, France; this happened while his company was bulldozing a port area for a landing strip and ran over a mine field. Homer Hash, one of six children of John H. and Lena Peyton Hash, was a Second Lieutenant in the Army Air Corps who flew a twin-engine bomber. During a trans-Atlantic flight from Brazil to Europe, Hash's plane crashed upon its high-speed landing in Dakar, West Africa, inflicting fatal injuries; he was 25 years old. Private Edward Lee Tinsley lost his life in battle in Metz, Germany at age 21. Army Sergeant Eustace Butcher Jr. was just 19 years old when he was killed in Germany on Christmas Day.

1945: Twenty-year-old Private Billy E. Gwinn, son of Charles and Hattie Gwinn, was killed in Germany. Oscar William Songer died at sea in the Pacific; his name is inscribed on the Tablets of Missing in Honolulu. Just three weeks before the war ended in Europe, Warrant Officer George E. Morris died at age 23 in a non-battle-related plane crash in Belgium.

Other, undated, casualties of the war included Urban V.W. Darlington, a Private in the U.S. Air Corps, as well as Navy men Robert Theodore Plybon and Rufus Raymond Smith.

All told, it is estimated that as many as 70 million human lives were extinguished in World War II.

America's Big Mid-Century Rebound

The speed of President Harry Truman's political education cannot be overstated. This inconspicuous-looking Midwesterner had been FDR's vice president for just 82 days when he assumed the office of Commander in Chief.

Keeping in mind that President Roosevelt had made little effort to keep Truman "in the loop" regarding domestic, military or diplomatic matters before his sudden demise, consider the fruits of Truman's on-the-job training from April 12, 1945 to September 5, 1945: He managed a European peace treaty with Churchill's British successor. He quickly grasped that Russia's Joseph Stalin was breaking promises he had made to the Allies and aggressively setting up local communist governments wherever his armies penetrated Axis territory—it turned out that "Uncle Joe" was framing out the Iron Curtain and planting seeds of the Cold War before the "hot war" had even ended. In July, Truman oversaw the culmination of four years of research on uranium fission that ushered in "the atomic age" with the first test explosion in New Mexico. Less than a month after the nuclear test, aware that Japan's military leaders were determined to wage a "fight to the finish" strategy with 10,000 suicide planes, Truman ordered the use of America's two A-bombs on Japanese cities.

As soon as war ended, Congressional pressure forced a hasty demobilization of American forces and the Truman administration implemented the 1944 "G.I. Bill of Rights" to aid veterans in securing housing and education. On September 5, President Truman went before Congress and outlined his "Fair Deal," a program of domestic legislation to manage the new peacetime economy.

Truman's first term and 1948 re-election were a testament both to his judgment and America's new position as the world's most powerful nation. Home to just seven percent of the world's population, the United States had 42 percent of post-war global income and half the world's manufacturing capacity. At the end of the 1940s, America had not only found its way out of the Great Depression, but per-capita income in the United States was the highest in the world. Perhaps the most confounding argument against Stalin's Communist Party line was the fact that nothing was succeeding like American Democracy.

As a small town within a peaceful and prosperous nation, Barboursville emerged from the Depression, the loss of its college and a World War with its residents standing tall. Manufacturing was strong in the county. With cars in many driveways, and reliable bus and taxi service at hand, the tucked-away village was a comfortable yet convenient distance from Huntington (whose population peaked at 86,353 in 1950).

Village merchants survived and maintained influence in county affairs. Hardware man James T. Brady presided over the three-man Cabell County Court (forerunner of today's County Commission). Other "downtown Barboursville" businesses in 1947 included the South Side Grocery, Barboursville Appliance, E.A. Mahaffey Construction Company, Perkins Plumbing, Clay's Barber Shop, Kennedy's Ice Cream, Drugs, Fountain and Sundry owned by Ezra J. Ward, The Green Lantern Fountain Service, Barboursville Cab, Updyke's Department Store, Luster and Wagoner's Stop and Shop Market, the Gulf Service Station on the corner of Center and Main, Hash's Beauty Shoppe, the Barboursville Pharmacy, and Jack Burton Plumbing and Light Fixtures.

Central Avenue facing north in the late 1940s
(Courtesy of Barboursville Public Library)

Civic groups in the village, from the Lions to the Masons, Chamber of Commerce, Daughters of the American Revolution, Farm Woman's Club, Woman's Club and Men's Club, were active, strong in membership and poised for a bright future.

In October 1949, the other groups joined the Woman's Club in kicking off a drive for a library building, Members of the library committee included Mrs. Lyal Clay, Mrs. W. H. Brownfield, Mrs. W. H. O'Dell, Mrs. Harold Bowen, Mrs. Harry Hatfield, Mrs. C. N. Fannin, Mrs. W. D. Bourn, Mrs. Archie Foster, Mrs. Roy Browning, and school principals John Fife, O. R. Powers and H. E. Berisford. It took only a year-and-a-half before the goal was reached. The former John G. Miller house at 728 Main Street was acquired for the library. In 1951, the town's books were hauled down the sidewalk by boys from the Junior High School.

Barboursville Woman's Club members have a Tea. From left to right, Mrs. Bowen, Mrs. Sang, Mrs. Clay, Mrs. Browning, Mrs. Patton, Mrs. Bowden, Mrs. Haynes and Mrs. Wallace. *(Courtesy of Barboursville Public Library)*

Village residents took on a second cultural pursuit in the late 1940s, when the Barboursville Chapter of the Daughters of the American Revolution began looking toward preservation of the abandoned 1830s toll house that sat on the bank of the Guyandotte in between the Farmdale and Mud River bridges. Mr. and Mrs. Lacy C. Anderson donated a 64-by-196-foot lot along Tanyard Branch on the north side of Main Street, next door to Anderson's Criss Movie Theater. Fundraising, technical planning and volunteerism were in full thrust as townspeople donated materials, equipment and services to help restore the old building and make it functional as a DAR headquarters, complete with gas, water and electricity.

Barboursville approached the mid-point of the twentieth century with the buildings on William Merritt's original Public Square once again fully occupied. Now, however, the large brick structures were host to completely divergent—and strangely juxtaposed—populations. Over four decades, these establishments would gradually reshape the identity of the village.

The next two chapters will look at Barboursville through the prism of these two institutions. First we'll survey the origins and highlights of the village's proud public schools. Then we'll take a look past the walls of the State Hospital, a mysterious but constant presence in "Institutional Barboursville."

CHAPTER 14

WE'VE GOT SCHOOL SPIRIT

Barboursville's Champion Generation

THROUGHOUT my formative years, there were these names peppered into my mom and dad's occasional conversations about high school: Maddox. Wookey. Curry. Thompson. I somehow felt like I knew them without ever having seen them. Just regular guys, I am sure, but somehow the stuff of town legend, a legend that seemed to grow a little more with every BHS class of 1954 or 1955 reunion.

The Barboursville High School classes of the late 1940s and 1950s enjoyed a multi-season hot streak on the football field. The pinnacle was the 1953 West Virginia Class A Football Championship, when Coach Richard "Dick" Ware led 36 young men to a 27-0 win over Benwood. The following year at the title playoff, a one-point loss to Follansbee broke a string of 28 consecutive wins by the Pirates Varsity.

A year-and-a-half later, the 1955 *Treasure Chest* yearbook was dedicated to the BHS football team:

We have never heard of such a thing being done—but, if there ever was a more deserving or noteworthy group of young men, we salute them too.

Everyone knows the amazing record compiled by the Pirates…This story is not, however, to inform you of that record, but to pay tribute to the coaches and departing senior members. There is not enough space in this book to sing all the praises due these gallant sportsmen. We hope in your later years that you will turn back and read these words and maybe it will bring into your life some pleasant memories of the good ole' days.

BHS 1953 State Football Champs (Top Row left to right) Head Coach Richard Ware,
Rhiney Sang, John Plybon, Nugent Sharp, John McGlone; (Middle Row left to right)
Edward Riffle, Ronald Petrie, Ronald Langham, Dick Spencer; (Bottom Row left to right)
Russell Lane, Jim O'Lynn, Jack Steinbrecher, Lanny Perry.
(From 1953 Treasure Chest Yearbook)

First, let us mention the coaches. We firmly believe that they are, without
doubt, the best to be found. HEAD COACH RICHARD WARE—despite
all the attention heaped on him, this perfectionist has managed to remain
the same modest and likeable person he was when he first set out to travel
the rocky road every coach must travel…Unlike most coaches, Mr. Ware did
not put football above school. How long shall we remember his views on this
subject: "First, you are a gentleman; second, you are a scholar; and third, you
are an athlete." (The Treasure Chest—Barboursville High School Yearbook
1955)

BHS 1953 State Football Champs (Top Row left to right) Paul Adams, Larry Perry, Wayne Chapman, Jerry Jefferson, Don Midkiff; (Middle Row left to right) Paul Hess, George Porter, Jimmy Wood, George Hankins, Bernard Terry; (Bottom Row left to right) Dale Dean, Bob Barrett, Charles Booth, Harry Burgess.
(From 1953 Treasure Chest Yearbook)

BHS 1953 State Football Champs (Top Row left to right) Elwood Adkins, Jim Maddox,
Tom Parker; (Middle Row left to right) Frank Wookey, Gene Vanscoy, Kenney Keller,
Assistant Coach Chasey Wilson; (Bottom Row left to right) Robert Bills, Jim Myers,
Richard Plybon. Ron Tickfer and Assistant Coach Edward Smith were absent when this
team picture was taken.
(From 1953 Treasure Chest Yearbook)

Through a decade of gridiron glory, the entire district got caught up in the
excitement of Barboursville athletics. Football put the village back on the map, as
something greater than the little dot next to West Virginia's largest city.

Years of lovingly-kept alumni scrapbooks and reunion records (several assembled by the gracious Barbara Stephens Miller, Class of '53) tell of much more,

however, than a single-minded focus on tackles and touchdowns. Rather, there is the sense that Barboursville's elementary boys and girls of the 1940s shared a special confidence and camaraderie that carried through their autumn years. The prosperity of post-war America, the village's investment in its young people, and a close-knit group of caring and seasoned educators seem to have nurtured these particular sons and daughters into Barboursville's "champion generation," and perhaps its best ambassadors.

The success of the Barboursville Pirates—both athletically and academically— did not happen overnight, but was built upon decades of effort that surely would have impressed good ole' Coach Ware.

Nineteenth Century Schooling

District Superintendent Fred B. Lambert, 1910
(Courtesy of Barboursville Public Library)

At last, here is the "Lost Village" rock star himself. Ever the historian, Fred B. Lambert cared enough to include information about the early schools in *The First Annual Catalog and Statistical Report of the Barboursville District Public Schools*, where this photo appears. As district school superintendent in 1910, Lambert compiled, wrote and published the book with the help of local advertisers. Five decades later, educators Orville R. Powers, Mr. Griffis and Mrs. Sam McConkey filled in some missing details by interviewing older members of the community and contributing another historic digest of village schools.

Frontier Education in Cabell County. Lambert reached way back before Cabell County was formed, to cite the legal underpinnings of its public education system. The first school law of any kind was the Aldermanic School Law passed by the Virginia General Assembly in 1796, that gave power to a Board of Aldermen to locate and build school houses at the expense of the county. According to Lambert, it is not likely that the law was put in force in Cabell County for several decades, as there existed no authentic record of a common school in the county until 1823.

Before county records existed on "common schools," the very first schools in the area were most likely taught at private expense, possibly in association with a religious congregation. One of West Virginia's earliest Methodist ministers identified William Paine of England as the man who taught the first grammar class in Cabell County sometime around 1811. Lambert speculated it was "not improbable that it was at Barboursville…as this was the only settlement near his home large enough to afford a grammar school," but another source puts Paine's class closer to the vicinity of Howell's Mill.

Lambert wrote of Cabell County's frontier schools:

In those days the schools were held in any old house obtainable, and only at such times as some itinerant teacher would come along. They were generally held in the fall of the year, in order to avoid both summer work and winter weather. The frontier custom was for some of the farmers best qualified to the task to spend a few weeks or months of "the most leisure season of the year" in teaching children of the neighborhood, whose parents might choose to send them at a small expense, say $1.25 a quarter, payable in work or provisions. "In this way some of them succeeded in obtaining such an education as was then thought to be necessary among the common people, for the course was very short and superficial," Lambert said.

Early teachers came from various places, Ohio, Kentucky, Pennsylvania, and some from the Valley of Virginia. Sometimes they were men of considerable culture, but ordinarily they were ignoramuses of the lowest type. Their knowledge consisted of a smattering of arithmetic, the simplest English, and the ability to write a miserable scroll with a good quill pen. Of history and the other branches of an ordinary English education they knew but little. They were as uncultured as they were unlettered. In the very early days they dressed in the usual garb of the border—cow hide shoes, "a full set of gray domestic cotton cloth, with a broad brim drab hat." They generally appeared in the early autumn, going from house to house soliciting signers to their "article." The rate was about a dollar a month with board included.

The typical local school houses were about 14 feet wide by 16 long made of logs. The houses were often used for church purposes, such as old Mt. Zion on Pea Ridge. The roof was of boards weighted down with a pole. Most often the bare ground was the only floor…In the front end hung a door swung on wooden hinges and fastened by a latch. At the other end was the chimney, from five to eight feet in width, made of flat rocks daubed with mud, and finished up with sticks and clay. At one side a log was cut out nearly the full length of the house. A puncheon or plank was set under this in a slanting position on wooden pins driven into holes bored in the log below, or hung against the wall by wooden hinges. This formed the writing desk at which the boys stood and practiced their copies with the goose quill pens and homemade ink..

A boy was typically taught to spell, read and "cipher" to the rule of three. A student privileged to learn grammar and geography was considered quite learned. Girls were usually taught simply to read and spell imperfectly, and rarely could write. (F. B. Lambert 1910) (F. B. Lambert Collection n.d.)

Seven schools were reported to the state in 1824, with just 36 children in Cabell County receiving free tuition to attend them. This only included schools for poor children from the county's large expanse, and for whom the school commissioners paid the tuition from Virginia's Literary Fund. As explained in the 1930-31 Cabell County report to the state, "Commissioners embrace all those children within the meaning of the word 'indigent' that are orphans and without property, as also those children whose parents are known to be poor." In 1827-28 there were 20 schools in the county, to which 25 poor children were sent at the state expense. The next year there were 24 schools and 205 children received free instruction. In 1829-30, 25 children were taught at a total cost of $41.21. And in 1831-32, Cabell County had 35 common schools, 400 poor children, and 276 sent to school for an average of 38 days. As school books were expensive and scarce, Lambert noted, this year-to-year variation continued until the Civil War.

Barboursville's "Common" and Private Schools. A "common school" in Barboursville was said to exist as early as 1832, according to more than one source; there was also a primary school in Guyandotte at the time. My great-grandfather, George Wilson Brady Sr., was aware of the old building; it may have been the original chapel used by the Methodists between 1824 and 1835. Brady helped to move part of the old school/church building across town to use the timber in an existing construction around 1928, and said the old building was made of hand-hewn timbers mortared and joined with wood pegs. The old building stood on the southeast corner of the Barboursville Cemetery near the Brady grave plot, which would put its location at the site of the community swimming pool.

When Marshall Academy was founded, it was not conceivable for most families of the area to send their children. An 1840 report contained the following item: "Board in respectable families near the Academy can be had for $30.00 the scholastic year of ten months." There was, Lambert cryptically noted, "animosity toward the Academy and this did not cease until long after the Civil War, and it seemed that some of the early county superintendents shared this feeling."

In 1850, county superintendent Thomas Thornburg wrote, "there is in the county generally want of good school houses and capable teachers and for these reasons there are some children who fail to get to go to school."

There is evidence of a few early schools on the outskirts of Barboursville. Solomon Thornburg had a private school built on his Davis Creek farm for the education of his children. Lambert cited a school at Pea Ridge as early as 1845, at Old Mt. Zion church opposite the Millard Thornburg property. This was taught by a man named Elijah Simmons, of whom Robert Dillon provided the following detail: "Children say he would throw clubs or sticks at them." Mt. Zion may have been the same building that sat on the Henry Shelton Farm, where Fred Baumgardner and Rufus Hensley first went to school in the late 1850s, taught by "an old English Woman, Mrs. Frances Cook," using the Blue Back Speller and quill pens.

As the village matured, private schools were established separately from the "common schools" by Barboursville's well-to-do families for their own children. David McGinnis was named by several sources as one of the early village teachers around 1840. Others who taught in the mid-nineteenth century were identified as a Mr. Simpson, a Mr. McClelland, Mr. and Mrs. Edward Vertegan, Mr. and Mrs. Joseph Foster, Miss Fannie Chapman, Jared Armstrong, Dr. V.R. Moss and James Thornburg. P.S. Drown recalled being taught in the 1850s by Charley Simpson at the Court House, along with pupils O.S. Mills, George Thornburg, William Miller, William Martin and George Merritt.

During the 1850s, as Marshall Academy was struggling to stay afloat with help from the Southern Methodists, Thomas Thornburg became Cabell's first County Superintendent. Serving as school commissioners with him were John Laidley, Thomas Brannon, John Morris, John Samuels, Henry Barrett and James McComas. In 1854, in an Auditor's Report of the State for the Virginia Literary Fund, Thornburg reported on behalf of the board that the means at their disposal "are inadequate for the education of all the indigent children in this county. The commissioners acknowledge that in many respects they have failed to perform their duty, but promise in future to be more attentive."

The school built by William C. Miller and taught by B.H. Thackston was a small brick building next to Miller's home. Thackston—perhaps the county's most distinguished educator of the era—appears to have dedicated himself to private schooling in whatever space he could arrange:

> I taught in the Masonic Hall about 1860 and 1861 in an office in the yard of
> Dr. Seashole, near Capt. Kuhn's residence, on the Wingo property. Afterwards

I taught in W. C. Miller's yard in an office there. The Miller's Florence, my wife's sister who married George F. Miller, Joseph Rece, son of Milton Rece (for whom the town of Milton was named), Harvey Harshbarger, Bailey Thornburg, Mrs. G.E. Thornburg, George F. Miller and his sister Mrs. Bayless Poague, the Holly Boys, one of whom is Mayor of Charleston. (Marshall) wanted me for Principal; but I declined, as I lived at Barboursville, and thought my family would be a nuisance to the school and vice-versa. (Lambert Interview with B.H. Thackston)

Tom and Frank Peyton who lived east of Barboursville were also said to attend the Miller private school, where tuition was $2.00 per month prior to the Civil War.

B.H. Thackston
(Courtesy of City of Huntington Website)

During the war, the State Fund of Virginia was cut off and "common" schooling seems to have ceased altogether in the village. The only schools taught were subscription schools for those families who could afford private tuition. Marshall Academy had succumbed to its unpaid debt, and a fortunate few like young Joseph S. Miller left the state to attend private boarding schools. However, wartime commitments and sectional divisions meant that most young people did without formal schooling during the years of disarray in the county.

New State, New Educational Foundations. A legislative act in December 1863 provided for free schools in West Virginia, but Cabell County was slow to put them into operation. In Lambert's analysis, local parents had long associated free education with the paltry and underfunded "pauper schools," and objected to having their children enrolled by a commissioner; this prejudice lingered for several years after the war.

Decades earlier, the county supervisors had divided the county into five townships: Barboursville, Guyandotte, Union, Carroll and McComas. The formation of Lincoln County in 1867 absorbed most of Carroll township; the remaining portion in Cabell County became Grant Township. Schools in Barboursville town limits were independent from the outlying township. In 1872, "townships" were renamed "districts," and two others were added over the years. County schools were managed by a three-member board of education in each district. The school term lasted four months in 1863, when William C. Dusenberry was appointed as superintendent.

William Algeo
(Courtesy of Marshall University Libraries Special Collections)

Dusenberry was succeeded in 1865 by Superintendent William Algeo, who had the honor of establishing free schools in the county. A member of the Masonic Lodge at Barboursville, he was described by Lambert as a remarkable man:

> In scholarship he was probably above the average of his day. In disposition he was eccentric. Wherever he went he carried his book usually a Latin grammar of which he was a close student. He lived in a little cottage at N— Hill. Here he produced berries and other small fruits which he marketed in a basket at Barboursville, walking the entire distance reading a book on the way. In his general reading if he came to a word he did not understand he immediately went to a neighbor's house, Mr. Daniel Swann's, to consult a dictionary.

Having obtained the information for which he came he at once departed, speaking to no one.

He was full of energy. Mr. Algeo was present at the first meeting of the school commissioners in Barboursville District, and had to use every effort possible to prevent the levy from being voted down. He visited the schools, encouraged the people and the teachers, and was ever ready to assist in any educational reform. (F. B. Lambert 1910)

By fall of 1865, C.H. Hall of Proctorville was teaching free classes in an upstairs room of the old Merritt Hotel, as part of a patchwork of small classes in the area, including the rural schools at Pea Ridge, Booten's Creek, Cox Landing, Fairview/ Wilson, Wildcat and Watson, and classes in the homes of James McDermot, Mrs. Neuberger, Irene Octavia McComas (until the notorious "test oath" firing), Benjamin Thackston and Helen "Kate" Jewell. It is hard to determine when and where private education gave way to the new free schools, but Algeo is credited with bringing it about one community at a time, as well as encouraging the provision of separate schooling for the "colored" students of the district.

By 1867, state leaders realized the progress of the free schools was hampered by a lack of sufficiently qualified teachers. A Cabell County Delegate, J. H. Ferguson, persuaded the West Virginia legislature to purchase the old Marshall Academy from its private owners and establish it as the state normal school for teacher training. The county supervisors contracted to purchase the property from the Mason family, and county voters approved a levy to meet funding requirements.

The "Alley School." The independent school district of the town of Barboursville was established in February 1867. In June, the common council of the village—consisting of mayor John "Fatty" Baumgardner, recorder C.W. Hall and councilmen Samuels, Salmon, Dick and Merritt—met to put the town's school system into operation. By 1869, Village Lots #32 and #38 were condemned (converted to public use) and Barboursville's first public school building was constructed. William Merritt's town plan of 1814 concurs with the recollections of old-timers in the 1950s history, in that the school was located on today's Musgrave Court across from the current Fire Department. The log house of Jance Lusher, a wagon repair shop and a blacksmith shop stood nearby.

"The alley school," as they later called it, was the village grade school from 1870 to 1903. A two-story wooden structure, it consisted of one room up, one room down and a stairway that went up from the center of the building. The school was furnished with large two-pupil seats, a "recitation bench," a blackboard and a pot belly stove.

Early teachers were George Blume, Joel Donahue, Elmer Swann, Mr. Vertegan, Ike Weed, Leona Merritt-Turley, Maggie McGinnis, a Mr. Melrose, W.H. Parrott,

Mrs. A.D. Hoff, 18-year-old Nettie Swann Woodyard and William Algeo himself. Like generations of American students from the 1830s to the 1920s, Barboursville pupils relied on the series of Illustrated Readers and "Eclectic Spellers" written by William Holmes McGuffey of Ohio.

By 1873, the various village schools were consolidated into one, and the school term lasted a full five months. The concept of free public schooling had evidently gained full acceptance by that time. Barboursville pupils included George, James, Walter, Valette and Charles Brady; the Blume children; Norman Blake; the Thackston boys; John Eggers; Jim Wilson; Etta, Maggie and Amizette Poteet; Tom and Bess Miller; Dolly Spencer; Willa Moore; Ella M. Rexrode; Ethel Bennett; Mamie McKinnon; Georgia Shepherd; and John and Tom Thornburg.

By the time schooling became compulsory in West Virginia in the 1890s, Barboursville families were outgrowing the Alley School. The new Barboursville College housed an academy for primary students, and Miss Etha Nash had a private school, but the need was great. At the turn of the century, the town set its sights on a parcel just across Center Street, and Ira Adkins of the county board of education assisted in the acquisition of a large lot. In the fall of 1903, a beautiful four-room brick building, Barboursville Elementary School, was completed and occupied.

Solomon's Legacy

Few families would influence local school matters over a longer span of time than the "thrifty Thornburgs" of Barboursville and Davis Creek. In addition to his role in the creation of Marshall Academy, "Son of 1791" Solomon Thornburg was largely responsible for the 1827 division of magisterial districts within the county. This dictated the general placement of the county's common school buildings for more than a century.

Marshall University's Special Collections library holds an old ledger book that belonged to Solomon's son, Barboursville merchant (and brother-in-law of William Clendenin Miller) Thomas Thornburg. The book is filled with meticulous pencil entries logging every penny spent by Thornburg on various categories of essentials, gifts and precious few indulgences. As the first school superintendent from 1849-1860, Thomas minded the district's money and served in that capacity cheaper than any of his successors; his salary amounted to only $15 or $20 per year. By 1888, Thomas Thornburg also served as one of the original nine trustees of the Barboursville Seminary (which became Morris Harvey College).

One hundred years after his uncle Thomas became district superintendent, Davis Creek farmer Howard B. Thornburg took up the mantle and served on the Cabell County school board. He would hold this office from 1949 through 1965. Upon his death in January 1966, *The Herald-Advertiser* published an open letter to his widow Ersie Hefner Thornburg from the supervisors of the Guyan Soil

Conservation District, which H.B. helped to organize in 1942. The letter spoke of his "invaluable experience, integrity and faithful service," adding, "We will miss Howard B. Thornburg's guidance for years to come."

H.B and Ersie's son Claud H. Thornburg (Solomon's great-grandson), was elected to his father's vacated school board seat in 1966 and served until 1990. A retired farmer, Claud was developer of Guyan Estates, described in his obituary as "the first large housing subdivision in West Virginia."

For more than three decades in the nineteenth century and four decades in the twentieth century, nearly every decision regarding public education budgets, employee actions, purchases and school construction in Cabell County took place under the diligent watch of a Thornburg man. It is hard to imagine how Cabell County's public schools—not to mention two institutions of higher learning—would have been built and sustained without their stewardship.

Evolution of Village Schools

High School. Seven years after Barboursville High School opened its doors, the 1934 senior class yearbook staff, with a precious absence of irony, wrote of the "Glorious Past of Barboursville High School." That year's annual also introduced the words to Barboursville's instantly-nostalgic football fight song (sung to the rousing "Notre Dame" tune):

> *Come on let's give a cheer for old B.H.S.,*
> *Winning or losing we're at our best.*
> *Take that old ball down the field,*
> *Keep right on fighting, don't ever yield.*
> *Cheer, cheer for old B.H.S.,*
> *Winning or losing we're at our best.*
> *When the game is over we'll shout out the victory.*
> *Rah! Rah!*

Up until the fall of 1925, local high school classes were conducted at Morris Harvey College. In 1924, the boards of the Barboursville magisterial district and the town (Barboursville Independent District) merged for the purpose of establishing a common high school. The residents of the town and surrounding district authorized the board to purchase Billingsley Hall on the south side of town from Morris Harvey, paying for the purchase by direct levies. In 1925, the Board decided to take over one year of the high school work, so the ninth grade pupils were consolidated with the seventh and eighth grades to form the Barboursville Junior High School. At first these students were taught in the graded school (elementary) building with the following faculty: Chester N. Fannin, Principal, Mrs. Edna Ball and Mr. John Fife.

In 1926, the other three grades of high school were taught on Morris Harvey College campus in the old Blume Hotel (known then as the Music Hall), until Billingsley Hall was remodeled for additional classroom space. By 1927, Barboursville High School officially opened its doors at the Main Street location, with six homerooms, six grades and six teachers, including Chester Fannin, who simultaneously served as the school's principal.

In 1929, a cornerstone with the inscription "Barboursville Joint High School" was laid at the northwest corner of the new eight-room building on the south side of town. Athletic director H.C. "Twenty" Lantz—a top West Virginia athlete of the 1920s who got his nickname when he scored 20 points in a Morris Harvey basketball game—coached the Pirate football, basketball and baseball teams. In 1930, a major athletic milestone was recognized when the football team played on the new "King Field," a property given to the school by the Lions Club.

Barboursville Elementary
(photo courtesy of Barbara Miller)

Elementary. In 1932, Barboursville was an independent school district serving only students inside town limits. That year, seventh and eighth graders were moved from the high school and added to the Elementary program, and F. E. Morris, a full-time teacher, became principal of Barboursville Elementary. Without benefit of a secretary or office space, Morris raised the school from second to first class rating.

In 1933, the county unit system came into effect, improvements were made to the library and playground, and students outside of town limits began attending Barboursville. Eight additions and refurbishments to the building took place between 1933 and 1973, including a rebuild in 1942 after a damaging fire forced the school to use other village buildings for several months.

Junior High. In September1936, the Junior High School was established in the lower level buildings of the old college, and the seventh, eighth and ninth grade classes were moved there, 480 students in all. In 1941, wings were added to each end of the building. After a fire gutted the building in 1942, the old bell tower was lost in the refurbishment.

By the 1950s, the school consisted of four additional buildings: the 1884 Methodist Church/Morris Harvey Chapel became the library, which was attached to the main building by a small enclosed walkway. The old Blume Hotel/Music Hall to the east became an annex known as the "B" building. An industrial arts building was located behind the main building. The three-story Morris Harvey athletic facility, built on the Center Street hillside in 1923, held the gym and dressing rooms for the BJHS Pirates.

Scions from the Stock of Morris Harvey

Barboursville's secondary schools were not so much built as they were grafted onto the stock of Morris Harvey College. Successive Barboursville classes were rooted in existing buildings—the college Music Hall, the south side boys' dormitory—until both the High School and Junior High stood independently after the loss of the college and academy in 1935.

The connection between the private Morris Harvey College and Barboursville's public schools went beyond shared real estate. After the college was uprooted and transplanted to West Virginia's capital city, it is significant that a core group of MHC's devout sons and daughters stayed and dedicated themselves to nurturing an educational legacy in the village. It seems somehow fitting that the high school annuals of the 1930s were named *The Torch;* the "Harveyan" flame was carried forth by young men and women who made the leap from MHC graduates to Cabell County educators.

All but one of the Barboursville High School faculty members in the 1931-1932 annual *(pictured)* came from Morris Harvey, with several completing their Masters degrees not at nearby Marshall, but at West Virginia University. As the years rolled on, more and more teaching posts in Barboursville's schools would be filled by Marshall graduates. Yet several Morris Harvey constants (including Fred

B. Lambert) taught multiple generations of Barboursville students. Here are just a few who shared long tenures and influenced countless students:

=THE TORCH=

Faculty

NOVA M. WALKER
   A. B. Marshall College—Home Economics.
      H. C. LANTZ
         B. S. Morris Harvey College—Mathematics and Athletics.
            FAY BRYAN
               Morris Harvey College—Geography and History.
                  C. N. FANNIN, Principal
                     A. B. Morris Harvey College, M. A. University of West Virginia.
                     English.
                        PAULINE E. CATON
                           A. B. Morris Harvey College.
                           Graduate Student of West Virginia University—Mathematics.
ETHA E. NASH
   A. B. Morris Harvey College.
   Graduate Student University of West Virginia—Social Science.
      JOHN T. FIFE
         B. S. Morris Harvey College.
         Graduate Student University of West Virginia—Chemistry.
            NANCY E. BOWDEN
               A. B. Morris Harvey College.
               Graduate Student of the University of Cincinnati—Latin—French.
                  J. DOYLE YOAK
                     A. B. Morris Harvey College.
                     Graduate Student West Virginian University—Social Sciences.
                        BETTY ALLEN VALLENDINGHAM
                           A. B. Morris Harvey College—English.

1932 BHS Faculty
(Courtesy of Barboursville Public Library)

Glennah Powers received her A.B. degree from Morris Harvey, spent 35 years at Barboursville Elementary, and became "dean of Barboursville teachers." Quaintly attired in a prim lace collar, brooch, full-length black skirt and ankle boots, she appeared to be the quintessential Victorian spinster schoolmarm, but also had a playful side. My mother remembers how Miss Powers encouraged her young pupils to master a large vocabulary. Linda Brady also told me of times when principal Orval P. Powers (her nephew) would visit her class and drill the students on various spelling words; he was unaware that Miss Powers was sneakily writing, then erasing, the answers on the chalk board behind him. Upon her retirement, "Miss Glennah Powers" Day was observed in Barboursville, where she was recognized for "her high ideals and inspiration to both her pupils and fellow workers."

Dorothy May Stackpole (1914-1997), great-great granddaughter of Marie Therese and Joseph Gardner, received her Bachelor of Science degree from Morris Harvey and taught for 38 years in the region, ending up at the campus where she started. She taught algebra at Barboursville Junior High and is credited with initiating the school's counseling program.

Alberta Cummings (1896-2003) began her high school and college studies at Morris Harvey before embarking upon a 47-year career as a county teacher. The home economics teacher at Barboursville Junior High, Mrs. Cummings was also a prominent leader in the state and county 4-H organizations—at one time she visited the home of every 4-H member in Cabell County. In the early 1960s, both Stackpole and Cummings were recipients of the Valley Forge Classroom Teachers' Medal for Freedoms, presented to United States teachers "doing exceptional work in teaching responsible citizenship and a better understanding of the American way of life."

Truby V. Hager (1907-1988) may have been the final "Harveyan" to teach at Barboursville. Mrs. Hager was remembered as a wonderful English teacher by both my mom (Class of '54) and her youngest brother (Class of '70). Her likeness last appeared in the faculty section of the *Treasure Chest* yearbook in 1970.

Most notably, principals Chester Fannin and John Fife carried the torch of the old alma mater into "old BHS."

Chester N. Fannin (1901-1968) was born in Fairmont, West Virginia. He came to Barboursville as the prototypical Morris Harvey undergrad, the son of a Methodist minister who grew up living in various communities around Kentucky and West Virginia. Upon receiving his A.B. degree from MHC at age 23, he began teaching at Barboursville elementary, and two years later assumed additional duties as principal at the high school, located in the old Blume Hotel/Music Hall. During this time, Fannin was completing the requirements for a Masters degree in English from WVU, which he received in 1928. The following year, he became the first principal at Barboursville High School and served in that capacity for ten years.

In 1977, BHS chemistry teacher Mary Lee Fleming wrote a tribute to Fannin, drawing on her personal memories as a member of Barboursville's first graduating class of 26 seniors:

Largely through the initiative and effort of Chester N. Fannin, Barboursville High School was established. Just out of college, he had been made principal and eighth grade teacher at Barboursville Elementary School. That was the year I was in the eighth grade and the year I feel I really learned to study under his tutorage. In those days Diploma Tests in every subject were conducted for all eighth grade students in the county at the end of the year. There was intense rivalry between schools for the best scores. Mr. Fannin and the entire class returned to school after supper many evenings that spring to train for spelling matches, arithmetic drills, and the like.

The following year another grade was added and our first junior high began. It was housed with the six lower grades in the same building. Mr. Fannin was still principal and taught English and history for the junior high students. One of his great concerns was that students who lived on the south side of town could only get to school by crossing the railroad tracks, sometimes crawling between the railroad cars when a train was standing. Two school days that year he sat at the crossing on Central Avenue and recorded the number of pedestrians, cars, and other vehicles using the crossing. As a result of his many endeavors in this direction, the underpass was built.

In 1927, two years after the ninth grade was added, a six-year high school opened its doors in the building next to the present junior high, which is now used as the Adult Education Center. There were only six home rooms, one for each grade. Six teachers provided the curriculum for all. Mr. Fannin was our principal, our dean, our disciplinarian, and, most of all, our counselor and friend. I still believe he was the best teacher I ever had! (The Treasure Chest - Barboursville High School 50th Anniversary Yearbook 1977)

In 1939, Fannin went on to serve as an assistant superintendent for Cabell County Schools until he retired from the school system in 1966, then served as assistant professor of education at Marshall until his death at age 67.

John T. Fife (1902-1971) was born in Putnam County and spent much of his childhood in Virginia. Other than that, he had a great deal in common with his Morris Harvey classmate Chester Fannin. They each lived out their lives in Barboursville homes less than three blocks from their alma mater. They each raised two sons. They both were active members of the First United Methodist Church. Like Fannin, Fife graduated from MHC in 1924, taught at the Barboursville schools and Morris Harvey Academy as a young man, and completed his Masters at WVU. In 1937, Fife became acting principal of the three-grade Barboursville High School. From 1939 to 1967, John Fife was the school's principal.

Although there were surely plenty of sophomoric nicknames ascribed to the man, John Hogg (Class of '63) described him as "The Man in the Dark Blue Suit."

Quiet, unassuming by nature, omnipresent… a firm hand, a harsh lecture, an attempted joke…a willingness to listen, a reassuring smile, forceful when necessary, lenient when possible. The foundation of BHS is concrete and steel. But its soul is that of John T. Fife—and for many, his spirit still wanders through his hallways. (The Treasure Chest - Barboursville High School 50th Anniversary Yearbook 1977)

Reporter Dave Peyton referred to his former principal as "Mr. Barboursville High School" in a write-up about a retirement event in Fife's honor. The interview turned to the educator's philosophies about teaching, and about Barboursville's student body:

Above all else, the principal holds to the premise that young people are inherently good and pure and will remain that way if given proper guidance.

Furthermore, Mr. Fife said, he believes students, through knowledge, will inherently come to the belief in the existence of God.

"In the biology classes I used to teach, we would discuss living things, which are composed of matter. This matter is composed of molecules. The molecules are composed of atoms. The atoms are composed of protons, neutrons and electrons. But that was as far as we could go. And all the students came to the conclusion that there was some greater power than man at work in the universe."

He is fond of his students at Barboursville. He says cliques have never been prevalent there and he believes the large number of students spread over a wide area of the county is the most important barrier to the formation of small, select groups in the school.

And Mr. Fife's basic belief in the goodness of students has won him the respect of those thousands who have graduated from the school.

That respect was demonstrated Friday during Class Day activities when Mr. Fife was presented a new, 1967-model automobile as a gift from students, alumni, faculty, members and friends. (Peyton 1967)

Excellence In and Out of the Classroom

Principal Fife, in discussing how much the school system had changed since the early 1930s, told the *Advertiser*, "In those days, there were no buses, no attendance officers and no dropout problems. The only ones who came to school were the ones who wanted to."

When the 1940 U.S. Census schedules were made public in April 2012, I noticed something surprising.

The Census collection in 1940 for the first time included the highest grade completed in school. Compelled to go beyond casual observation, I tallied up and charted the education levels of adult heads-of-household and wives (if married), both in Barboursville town limits and the two surrounding districts. Remarkably, fewer than 20 percent of "providers" in the village had completed high school, and less than 15 percent in the outlying communities had done so. Fifty percent of the village householders, and 70 to 80 percent of those in rural Barboursville district, had an eighth-grade education or less in 1940. Wives were much more likely than their husbands to have completed high school, surely due to the necessity of able-bodied boys to serve in the war or help provide for their families in the early part of the century.

In terms of high school completion, the contrast between pre- and post-war Barboursville was dramatic. As the Depression ended and farm work in the district gave way to good factory wages, the influence of dedicated educators helped grow a tradition of pride and excellence in Barboursville schools. The school community grew to include Martha and Pea Ridge families whose children attended the junior high and high school. The B.H.S. "minstrel shows" and "musicales" of the 1930s reflected the lingering Morris Harvey College influence. As these gave way to high school senior plays, junior high West Virginia Clubs and elementary school May Pole dances of the 1940s, Barboursville embraced the cultural strivings of its children.

Barbara Miller's collection of school memorabilia yielded some delightful photographs of Barboursville's Champion Generation in their tender years. Norman Rockwell himself could not have painted a more reassuringly wholesome vision of mid-century Americana. I am pleased to display my favorites:

Left: Donna Turman, Donald Fannin and Rheta Booth were captured here in perfect, elegant character in a Barboursville Elementary production of "Huckleberry Finn."

Right: Young Max Hatfield as Pinocchio, surrounded by five hooded girls. Okay, there is nothing particularly Rockwellian about this 1940s image. It could just as easily be the picture of a strange Eastern European cult—or the perfect heavy-metal album cover.

In 60-plus years of Barboursville Pirate depictions, these young buccaneers with hoop earrings who graced the B.H.S. auditorium stage (including Lloyd Lewis, Jim Arnold, David Gerlach, Ronnie Beaver, Keith Markin, Bill Curry and one unidentified classmate) were not the most menacing.

One young lady Pirate not only excelled in class and represented the school in the county Spelling Bee, but played a major role in the long-term "branding" of Barboursville. In 1949, Chamber of Commerce president D.B. Nelson awarded a $25 savings bond to 12-year-old Betty McMellon for her winning entry in a Barboursville slogan contest: "The Best Village in the State." A sign with her catch-phrase was affixed to a tiny Chamber of Commerce "headquarters" on the north corner of Main and Center, next to the taxi stand. McMellon's grade school brain-storm evolved into the slogan still in use six decades later, "The Best Little Village in West Virginia."

As the 1950s progressed and ushered in the post-war "Baby Boom" generation, middle America was focused on the educational, moral and physical fitness of its youngsters. As the state's "Best Village," Barboursville was no exception.

In 1950, Barboursville elementary led the county in reading scores. Herbert Nutter served as the Junior High principal; his wife kept a private kindergarten on Park Avenue, walking her children to visit Miss Sue Alexander, read the books and see the new record player at the public library. Junior High teacher Beulah Fisher Toney sponsored one of the state's most successful West Virginia Clubs, inspiring ninth graders to learn about the state's history, culture and geography. Between 1947 and 1963, 65 of Cabell County's 70 "knights and ladies of the Golden Horseshoe" were Mrs. Toney's Barboursville students.

With an emphasis on protecting the delicate moral fiber of these youngsters, the Barboursville branch of the public library joined the Huntington Library in a unique 1954 promotion. The nationwide effort was supported by Women's Clubs, PTAs and clergymen across the United States, with the mission to remove lurid and "obscene" comic books from the hands of children. In a well-publicized campaign to swap ten "bad comics" for one "good book," the local library gave boys and girls their pick of titles such as western stories, *Treasure Island, Heidi* or *The Bobbsey Twins*. The only requirement was that they bring in ten comic books that appeared on the "objectionable" list of the Cincinnati Committee on the Evaluation of Comics. The offending titles included horror and crime comics, *Mad Magazine* and other material believed by social leaders of the day to be a source of moral corruption and a gateway to juvenile delinquency.

That same year, elementary school principal Orval P. Powers helped establish Barboursville Little League baseball and served as the village league's first presi-dent. Pea Ridge residents George Buchanan and Maxine Booth did much of the planning for the league, according to Frank Ball; Holice "Wormy" Gibson has also been recognized for his contributions to the fledgling youth sports league. Two decades before a federal law known as Title IX banned sex discrimination in school academics and athletics, Maxine Booth may have been a catalyst for four girls being able to play in an otherwise all-boys' league. The first girl to play for the

Barboursville Insurance team was Cheryl Hoskins, followed by Wendy Smith, Judy Bailey and Sarah Ferguson, who was the sole female home-run-hitter, according to Ball.

Like the pictures in the widely-used school readers of the day—*Dick and Jane, Tom and Betty*—it appears that Barboursville of the 1940s and early 1950s contained increasingly-suburban boys and girls who were high-spirited but well-behaved, well-groomed and—well, White. In the yearbooks, in the classrooms and on the school grounds, there was no other skin color to be seen. School segregation was the law of the land. After the last school bell rang and the last bus returned to its garage, however, playtime in Barboursville was slightly more color-blind.

Segregated at School Time, Integrated at Play

There were two athletic young villagers who grew up with the "champion generation," but never suited up for the Pirates. This is the boyhood story of Main Street next-door neighbors Teddy Allen and Roy Goines, African American youngsters of Barboursville.

Teddy was the grandson of Rev. William Washington Scott and great-grandson of barber Jerry Hicks. Roy, two years younger than Teddy, was the grandson of the Sorrells and the great-great-nephew of Mattie Fliggins. Like almost all of Barboursville's children, they were brought into this world by either Dr. Bourne or Dr. Curry, and grew up playing with Bill Curry, Dicky Spencer and Jimmy Maddox, as well as the Foster, Sang and Thompson brothers.

"We used to be adventurous all over town as young boys, we were all over the place," Allen recalled. "I learned how to play baseball and football with people that were right there in the village. Johnny Sharp was an Army American back in the '40s. He taught me football and Eddie Rayburn taught me how to box. We used to go down to the—I did anyway—to the (Barboursville Elementary) school house where they had shuffle board in front of the school, and another building behind the school and we could play ping pong. I didn't feel entirely comfortable, (but) when I would go there I would play ping pong."

"One playground was right there adjacent to the school, and another little play spot that we used was right behind the Presbyterian Church on Main Street, close to where Phil Vallandingham lived, a little lot there that we played baseball," added Goines.

"I remember a special relationship with Bill Curry, who is the son of the original Dr. Curry who lived on the street next to the Presbyterian church. Anyway, Bill and I were both athletically motivated. We loved to rough it up. So Mrs. Curry—I remember her being in her kitchen window, and Bill and I were outside with the football and we'd have one-on-one's that went something like this: Bill would be on the goal line and say 'Roy, you can't get across.' And then I'd trade and I would be on the goal line and Bill would say, 'I'm coming.' And we would bang around. And I remember Mrs. Curry saying to me after we were a little bit older, 'I was so scared that you boys were going to hurt one another out there, you were so rough.'"

As boys of the late 1940s, Teddy Allen and Roy Goines took part in the kind of rambling outdoor play with other neighborhood children that seems to have disappeared in the post-Millennial era. According to Goines's cousin Gladys Carter, girls' life in the village was less freewheeling, yet for kids of all races and genders Barboursville had a recreational outlet that was not available in Huntington, the Criss "movie house" on Tanyard Creek.

"I didn't play with any of the kids, but we were allowed to go to the movie and we weren't segregated or anything," Carter told me.

Goines, like my parents and others of the Champion Generation, shared fond memories of the Criss.

"Teddy and I would go there on Saturday nights and watch the movies until they turned it off. Probably no more than about a hundred times. Roy Rogers, Gene Autry, Hopalong Cassidy—oh boy. Eddie Rayburn ran the projector there. That was a meeting point for all the boys. We would go there, and Eddie was instrumental in buying balls and bats. And we'd go to the playground and play, and Eddie was so good with us youngsters as we were growing up there.

"But you couldn't go to the Keith-Albee Theater in Huntington. You couldn't do that. In Barboursville, I could go to the movie house and we weren't told to sit in any particular spot, and everything was normal there, except for the fact that you couldn't go to school.

"With segregation, that relegated me to catching a school bus and going to school from Barboursville, rather than walking to the elementary school and the high school right there. We had to get on a bus and go down to Huntington, the first to get on the bus and the last to be picked up in the evening," Goines told me.

By 1939, the "colored" school attended by their parents had closed, so Barboursville's black youngsters attended Barnett Elementary and Douglass High School in Huntington. Until they graduated or moved away, Roy, Teddy, Gladys and seven or eight other African American students walked up Main Street to the steps in front of the junior high and boarded the same county school bus. They crossed over the Mud River bridge, through the underpass to Johnson's Hollow at "Wilson's Switch" to pick up other children, both black and white. Then it was through Altizer, over to the Colored Orphans' Home to pick up the residents there, and on to the fire station at Guyandotte to let off the white children and pick up more Barnett and Douglass students.

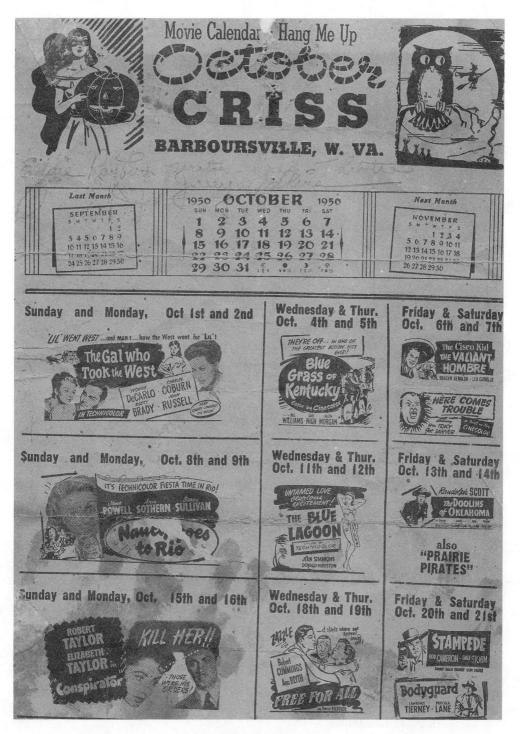

Criss Calendar
(Courtesy of Donna Brown)

Then, according to Carter, "It was down Fifth (Avenue) then, because it went both ways. They let the kids out at Barnett first in the mornings, and then took us. And in the evenings they picked up Douglas kids and Barnett last. And if there was any little kids in your family, you'd make sure they was on it."

In addition to school time with its long commute, neighborhood sports and other freewheeling boyhood amusements, Allen and Goines found jobs early in life.

"I've been selling something all my life," Allen said. "Yep, where there was a dollar to be made, I was trying to make it. When I was a kid, even before I was big enough to know anything, I was out selling Clover Leaf ointment on my bike up and down the street. The Burgesses were my biggest customers. I ordered it and I was supposed to have been 21 years old to order it. They sent it to me and I—at 11 years old, I went out on my bike and sold it.

"I also shined shoes at Clay's Barbershop. From the time I was 12 until I got out of high school, I'd go down there around eight o'clock on Saturdays and leave at about six. On a good Saturday, it would be about ten or eleven dollars. On an average Saturday, it was probably around five. Yeah, it was a little tiny place, had three chairs in the barber shop. Then in the back there was a shoe shine stand and a rest room, and that was where I had my business," Allen said.

Goines was equally enterprising from a young age:

As a kid I worked at the car wash, washing and drying the cars that came through…every time you turned around, I had a job. I kept busy. I worked at the George H. Wright clothing store, doing anything they would ask me to do. Anyway, let me tell you about it. I went down as a 13-year-old to get a part-time job. I put my age at 16, and told Mr. Wright that I wanted a job, and they asked if I had a Social Security card.

"Yeah, I have a Social Security card."

"How old are you?"

"Sixteen."

"You going to school?"

"Yes, I'm going to school."

They let me work!

They let me work, and I did such things as helping the decorator put the clothes in the window for display and fixing the signs showing this sells for such-and-such, and go down stairs and put those little plates in the machine that you could make those little signs off of, and I'd clean up the basement, sweep and make sure it stayed clean. I helped put cuffs on pants, you know making a cuff from the straight-leg pants. (Goines 2009)

By the time they were teenagers, the young men managed two worlds—Huntington life and Barboursville life—with relative ease. Reflecting back years later, both Allen and Goines generally found Barboursville of the 1940s and early 1950s a pleasant place to grow up. But there were some exceptions.

"Barboursville is a different kind of place," said Allen. "The people that lived there got along fine but (for) the outside people coming in, there was a difference…so no one really wanted to come to Barboursville to visit us."

Referring to his shine business at Clay's Barber Shop, he added, "I remember guys that would come into the barber shop when I was a kid used to make smart remarks and stuff. I remember that and I didn't like that, but there wasn't anything I could do about it."

Perhaps bolstered by the slightly older Allen and their sandlot friends, Goines's boyhood experiences were positive and nurturing, save for one memorable incident involving someone he referred to as "a very prejudiced" adult who pointedly told him he could not go into a public building in Barboursville to use the restroom.

Despite that one hurtful episode, Goines called his memories of Barboursville "very pleasant" and has returned many times to visit friends in the village. Allen agreed, saying Barboursville brings back some fine memories, and adding that many times he wished he could have afforded to buy his great-grandfather's home "and have it enshrined."

By the time the Barboursville Pirates made sports history in 1953, both young men had moved away. Allen graduated after playing football at Douglass, and joined his mother in Chicago. After a short stint in teacher's college, he joined the newly integrated Air Force and served peacetime duty in Germany for 18 months. Thanks to the favorable currency exchange rate in Germany, he said, "I enjoyed myself to pieces. I saw everything I could see." Allen returned to Illinois where he built a successful career in the insurance business and settled down with his gracious wife Mattie in the suburban community of Park Forest.

Goines became a Huntingtonian in 1952. As the younger African American families moved away from Barboursville, "there was nobody left but Mr. and Mrs. Washington, my grandmother and grandfather and Uncle Howard, and one of the descendents of Mr. Scott lived next door, Mr. Rotan," he said.

Goines brought his winning attitude to Douglass High School, and became a top student and star athlete. He would continue to spend time with his grandparents and uncle in Barboursville, and would from time to time spruce up the Smith family gravestones at Barboursville Cemetery (having been given a little money for the task by a teacher at Douglass who I believe was June Smith Thomas). He excelled at sports, playing football at Fairfield Stadium for the Douglass Wildcats against other black high schools. He was a teammate to future NBA player Hal Greer on the basketball and baseball teams, until Greer graduated in 1954.

Roy Goines
(Douglass High School yearbook photo courtesy of Huntington Public Library)

By the time he was a senior, Goines was student council president at Douglass. He took six "senior superlatives" in the 1955 *Blue and White* yearbook: friendliest, most likely to succeed, best looking, smartest, neatest and most studious. By the time Goines graduated from high school, preparation met opportunity—his door to the future was suddenly flung open, as his story continues.

Breaking the Color Barrier

Roy Goines, as an African-American youngster of the 1940s, was literally denied passage through the doors of the village grade school during a playground visit with friends, as he recalled in our interview. At the time, nobody apparently thought to question the clout of this unnamed white adult against a black child needing simply to use "the facilities." Trying to enroll such a student in Barboursville Elementary might have been even more unthinkable. Who in Barboursville knew that black families in other states were pressing at the time to change the status quo of racial division?

It was the Rev. Oliver Brown of Topeka, Kansas—he happened to be the first parent listed in the first of five combined lawsuits—whose name became associated with a landmark decision by the U.S. Supreme Court in 1954. After students and parents in Delaware, Kansas, South Carolina, Virginia and the District of Columbia unsuccessfully petitioned their school boards and district courts over inequitable conditions and forced segregation, the National Association for the Advancement of Colored People (NAACP) assisted in pushing appeals up the legal ladder.

As early as 1950, the "separate but equal" legal argument began to crumble under the evidence of deplorable conditions at many black schools across the country. It took nearly two years from the time 150 plaintiffs in five school desegregation cases were brought together before the U.S. Supreme Court as *Brown v. Board of Education*, for the Supreme Court to make its ruling. Under new Chief Justice Earl Warren, the court unanimously held that racial segregation of children in public schools violated the Equal Protection Clause of the Fourteenth Amendment. The decision was one of the most important of the twentieth century, and it galvanized America's civil rights movement.

Among Cabell County's public schools, effects of the Supreme Court decision were somewhat slow to materialize, and little attention was drawn to the issue by local news media. In August 1954, a delegation led by Mrs. Memphis Tennessee Garrison of Huntington approached the board with a petition asking them to act on the new decision. For the 1954-55 school year, the board decided that first and seventh grade black children could choose to attend the school in their district, and that black students in secondary grades who wished to take advantage of courses not offered in their school could be allowed to transfer to a "white" junior high or high school. By the time the 1956-57 school year commenced—following pressure from the Huntington NAACP Chapter, and a second Supreme Court ruling that desegregation proceed "with all deliberate speed"—the Cabell school board replaced its earlier policy with one of "complete but voluntary desegregation." Nevertheless, Douglass remained a school with entirely black enrollment until it was closed in 1961.

By that time, any potential debate about school integration in Barboursville became moot due to the outmigration of its younger black families. The 1960 and 1970 Census tables show black occupancy in town at an all-time low. Between 1960 and 1980, the Barboursville district's white residency hovered between 99.7 and 99.9 percent.

But for Roy Goines, *Brown v. Board of Education* was life-changing:

I was a junior in high school and then things opened up. And I had been wondering—I always had the desire and the motivation to go to college, so I was wondering as I was growing up where I was going to go. So I started corresponding when I was in 10th and 11th grade with schools such as Southern

Illinois and other smaller schools, where I could possibly have gotten a ticket and been able to attend.

And then, all of a sudden the Supreme Court decision came into play and I was able to go to Marshall. And things really happened in my favor. So I went over there, and never had a problem, never had a problem as I integrated in sports, athletics. But of course the year before, Hal Greer, who also went to Douglass with me and graduated the year before I did, (entered Marshall). Hal was a very good basketball player, as you may recall. They even named the street after him, Hal Greer Boulevard.

We didn't have any problems. Of course, I went to school and came home and didn't have any social life on campus. That wasn't a part of it, because there were only about a dozen blacks on the campus at that time in 1955, when I attended. There weren't many of us there, so there was no social life. We went to school, and we came on back home. But from playing football, I never had a problem there. (Goines 2009)

Goines, as an outstanding player and student athlete, was the only one of four black players from the 1955 JV squad to make varsity. On September 29, 1956, Roy Goines made history for Marshall University. In the season's first home game, Goines took the field at Fairfield Stadium as the first African American varsity football player to represent the Thundering Herd. Ironically, the Herd was playing against longtime rival Morris Harvey when Goines broke the football color barrier. One year later, when Jim Maddox of the 1953 BHS Pirates championship team transferred from Detroit to become MU's quarterback, the two boyhood buddies became college teammates.

Fifty years later, Goines, Maddox, head football coach Herb Royer and sports writer Ernie Salvatore were asked by a reporter how Marshall was able to integrate its football squad in such a racially-charged era without fanfare. They all gave essentially the same response: "It wasn't a big deal because we didn't make it a big deal."

Salvatore said the newspaper didn't play up the fact of black players being part of the Marshall program. Maddox emphasized that Coach Royer simply wanted the best football players he could find.

"Roy was such a good guy. Coach Royer was such a gentleman. The attitude was it didn't matter who you were, what mattered was what you could do to help the team. Roy, that guy could play!" Maddox said.

Goines cited several factors in his successful transition into Marshall. The fact that the Mid-American Conference consisted of other, previously-integrated, northern schools most likely prevented trouble on the field. Off the field, he credited a series of mentors, most notably his dean, Dr. J. Frank Bartlett, and Marshall's president Dr. Stewart H. Smith, for their early encouragement and friendship. In addition to Hal Greer, the future NBA Hall-of-Famer who had broken ground for black athletes the year before, Roy had the influence of his old Douglass coach Joseph Slash who received his Masters degree at Marshall long before *Brown v. Board of Education*. And there was his family, including his uncle Howard, a long-time maintenance worker at Marshall, who provided a comfort zone and a home base, as Roy played hard and studied hard.

Goines also credited his Barboursville upbringing: "I played sandlot, youth sports with the white kids in the neighborhood. When I got to Marshall, it was not strange to play with the whites I knew as kids, like Jim. It was not a strain to integrate."

From his beginnings at 905 Main Street, Roy Goines continued to break down barriers. He made the Dean's List and lettered in football for three seasons. He was second in command of the Marshall ROTC, also a first for African-Americans at Marshall. He changed his major from pre-med to accounting, and then became the first black student-athlete to graduate from Marshall in 1960.

Like his friend Ted Allen and many of Barboursville's "Champion Generation," Goines left West Virginia to pursue his potential. He served in the U.S. Army, and got his Master's degree at the University of Detroit. In 1967, Goines joined the Ford Motor Company as a human resource director at various plants and at the corporate headquarters. He retired from Ford in 1988 and embarked upon a second career teaching college students, most recently as a popular adjunct professor at the University of Laverne in San Dimas, California.

Vaya con Dios, My Pirates

Back in the village, most of Goines's boyhood playmates became the undefeated Barboursville Pirates of the early 'Fifties. These "brothers of the winning streak" took the 1952 Chemical Valley Championship, 1953 State Football title and 1954 State Runners-up. Most also excelled in basketball and track but still made time for Latin Club or Glee Club; several even had positions on All-State Choir.

The children of men who worked for the C&O, brickyard, nickel plant and American Car and Foundry, many followed opportunity beyond the borders of West Virginia. The village doctor's son Bill Curry (Class of '53 Pirate Co-Captain) married majorette Charlotte Browning, graduated from West Virginia University and became a pediatrician in Richmond, Virginia. Billy Foster settled in California, not too far from Goines. Teammates Lewis "Rhiney" Sang and Frank Wookey died young.

Jim Maddox's accolades at BHS rivaled Goines's popularity at Douglass. Voted the best-looking boy, best liked boy and best all-around athlete of the 1955 senior class, Maddox launched a successful career in sales and management after college and married Pam McCallister (Class of '54). Another big Pirate playmaker, Paul Hess ('55), married his classmate and Glee Club accompanist Carol Lantz and eventually became a bank president in Hinton, West Virginia. Ron Tickfer ('55) embarked upon a long career abroad with the U.S. Defense Department.

Decades later, the classes of '53, '54 and '55 celebrated numerous gatherings and kept up with each others' whereabouts and goings-on. "Our classmates, along with the Class of 1954, have a friendship that seems to go beyond that of other classes," the 50th Reunion Committee of the Class of '53 noted in its program book. Class leaders not only planned reunion weekends every five years, but also celebrated village history and led efforts to rebuild the WWII Honor Roll.

1954 BHS Majorettes (From Left to Right) Patty Mathews, Marlene McConkey,
Sheila Johnson, P. Ross, Sallie Taylor, Beryl Linthicum, Sandee Hatfield, Patsy Carson
and Nancy Newman, the BHS Majorette squad of 1954-1955
(1977 Treasure Chest Yearbook)

Post-war America was still a man's world to be sure, and Barboursville was no different. Considering that women of the era were typically objectified as beauty queens or leggy majorettes, the roles of the BHS female graduates were not quite as constrained as expected, judging by the classmates who submitted information to the reunion committees. Plenty of women proudly described themselves as homemakers, but there were also doctors, researchers and other women in professional roles.

Mostly though, Barboursville's "champion generation" joined their cohorts in contributing little bundles of joy to the "Baby Boom" generation. America saw a massive increase in births between 1946 and 1964, with United States births peaking in 1957. This social phenomenon reshaped the national landscape by spurring the growth of "suburban" housing developments across the country. Eastern Cabell County would lead West Virginia in the subdivision trend, with Barboursville schools reaping the consequences in rising enrollments.

America in 1955 was on the threshold of other cultural changes. The "champion generation" was the last to listen to what the adults were playing on the radio—Patty Page, Perry Como, Les Paul and Mary Ford, and big band sounds. My mom and her classmates might have learned some new dance moves to Bill Haley's "Rock Around the Clock," but the genre was basically considered a novelty until 1956, when Elvis suddenly conquered the radio charts.

Then there was television. In 1952, the village found itself within close range of one of the most powerful TV broadcast signals in the nation. At that time, the Federal Communications Commission ordered transmitter power boosts in 30 metropolitan areas, including the Huntington-Ashland area served by a lone station, WSAZ television. By 1955, there were three network affiliates in the Huntington-Charleston market, and 77 percent of American households owned a TV set. When the Class of '55 first entered high school, a family fortunate enough to buy a black-and-white TV set might line up rows of chairs in the living room for the neighbors to come and watch Texaco Star Theater or The Red Skelton Show. By the time they graduated, their generation's communal experience of watching the "picture show" at the Criss Theater had become passé, and the village movie house soon closed down.

By the end of the 1950s, most graduates of Barboursville's champion generation were in "the family way." Some (like my parents) found it necessary to relocate to out-of-state jobs so they could afford baby food and family cars. But many others stayed around, and the housing market grew up around them. With each new baby, the carefree high school days slipped further back into memory.

As they settled down on kid-filled streets in and around the village, their shifted values were reflected in another local phenomenon:

> Community growth and confidence in the future are evidenced in the church-building boom in the East Pea Ridge-Barboursville area. Church investment in real estate and building construction in that area for the period 1957-59—counting buildings completed, in progress, or to be begun in the immediate future—already has passed the quarter million mark, and is moving rapidly toward one half million dollars, a figure that would have seemed incredible to most persons familiar with the area ten years ago. (D. Miller 1958)

New brick churches that sprang up during the two-year construction boom of the late 1950s included Pea Ridge Baptist Church, Bates Memorial Presbyterian,

Lewis Memorial Baptist Church and the Church of Christ on Farmdale Road. Within village limits, Barboursville Baptist and Steele Memorial Methodist prepared larger new buildings for their congregations, First Methodist underwent improvements, and Kuhn Memorial Presbyterian constructed a new ranch-style minister's residence.

To Thee We Sing

In 1958, the student council decided Barboursville High School needed an Alma Mater. Several people submitted lyrics for consideration, including Mr. and Mrs. William Brownfield Sr., who suggested the old hymn tune "Finlandia." After a few alterations by BHS band director Joe Avis, the song of village graduation ceremonies and other formal functions was made official. It began, "To thee we sing, our gracious Alma Mater; Among the hills, our home so tranquil lies."

Barboursville High School
(Photo courtesy of Barbara Stephens Miller)

Barboursville High School continued to expand and modernize to accommodate young people from the village and its burgeoning outskirts. As the 1960s commenced, Barboursville schools filled up with young "Baby Boomers" raised on Sunday School, Scouting, Mootz's Sunbeam bread and Broughton's milk. More students fed in from Salt Rock, Beverly Hills and later Cox's Landing and Ona Junior High schools. From 1963 to 1971, the Pirates saw the additions of a wing of classrooms at the front of the main building; creation of a "girls' gym" from the old WPA bus garage; new band, music, wood shop and art facilities; a boy's athletic dressing room; and a large air-conditioned library. "Temporary" aluminum classrooms were built in back of the school in 1962, and these served BHS for 14 years.

In 1964, Norway's Torill Burge became the first foreign exchange student to attend BHS. The new, blue public library building was dedicated in 1967. National Merit recognition and other scholarships abounded.

In 1966, the Barboursville Boosters financed new bleachers at King Field, and volunteers provided construction free of charge. When Bob Estler converted his family's Orchard Hills farm into a 9-hole community golf course, villagers had the choice of playing there on the east side of town, the Knob Hill course (designed in 1950 by John "Patsy" Jefferson) west on Peyton Street, or at several other clubs within a ten-mile drive in the county. Barboursville's high school golf teams of the mid-'60s dominated state tournaments and shattered regional records. They included players Morgan Hargis, David Roach, Frank Sexton, Jack Sharp and, before he moved to Chapmanville, sophomore phenom Barney Thompson. Coach Harold McCarty was even able to put a girl's golf team together.

Joe Avis served as the state pageant director for Junior Miss and brought the glamour to Barboursville's auditorium in 1966, as America searched for the "ideal high school senior girl." At evening's end, the 1965 state winner Mary Hesson of Pea Ridge crowned Beverly Gwilliams of Lesage as West Virginia's representative to compete in the National Junior Miss Pageant. That same year, senior Barbara Owens headed to Columbus to represent West Virginia in the Miss USA-World Beauty Pageant.

Star Pirate athletes of previous generations became BHS coaches. For decades they helped mold the character of young Baby Boomers. These men also made sports headlines and became the public face of BHS, whether the season was glorious, miserable or middling.

James W. "Dink" Allen

Perhaps Barboursville's most prominent coach, James W. Allen became a local icon. He was known for a gruff, take-no-guff style that concealed what friends and family knew as the heart of a softie. The grandson of railroad-builder Captain Drury Allen, "Dink" was one of ten children of Edley H. Allen who owned the Wash-Rite Laundry on Depot Street. His mother Eula Thurmond Allen was widowed in 1941, while most of the children were young; relatives say the family lived through hard times after that. James nevertheless graduated from BHS in 1943, served in World War II on the USS Blue Ridge, played football under Cam Henderson at Marshall, and got a degree in 1950.

Allen served as head football coach at Barboursville High School from 1964 until 1985. He officially retired with more than 30 years as an educator and a coach in Mingo, Wayne and Cabell Counties. Post-retirement, he officiated at regional ball games and continued to substitute at Cabell Midland High School. There, he became a well-known presence to my sons and their classmates of the early 2000s.

My personal memories of Coach Allen involve hours behind the wheel of a driver's education vehicle in 1976. Two other student drivers and I nervously took turns practicing under his supervision. A typical class period might involve chauffeuring the coach to Burger Chef for coffee, the trophy shop on Ohio River Road, or the driveway of the Allen home where he would go in and feed his dogs. To us, he was indeed a man of few words. The classic 'Dink-ism' that springs to my mind is, "Put her in park and change drivers."

Dink's brother John Allen was also a coach in the county. He later became a school principal (which seemed to be a common Cabell County career path in the 1970s). "Big John" was principal of Ona Junior High School when I was a student there, and shared his brother's philosophy of gaining respect as a "wall of intimidation." Another old-school disciplinarian, John was outwardly grouchy but generally fair, with occasional flashes of dry humor.

In the mid-1960s, Dink was coaching the Pirates at the same time John was coach of the Huntington East Highlanders football team. It was inevitable that a "Battle of the Brothers" would pit the two giants of Allen Avenue against one another, generating a public volley of good-natured trash talk captured in the sports pages of the *Herald-Dispatch*:

Huntington East football coach John Allen is "out after" his brother Dink.

"He beat me last year and I've heard about it all year," John said Monday night. "I've been waiting a year to play him again and get revenge."

John's chance will come Friday night when his Highlanders will meet Dink's Barboursville Pirates at King Field in Barboursville.

Dink says he never mentions last year's 14-7 win over East to John, but he's worried about what will happen if the Highlanders should win Friday. "I'll never hear the last of it if he beats us," Dink said Monday night.

Both schools will take 2-0 records into the game, and both Allens have plenty of respect for the other's team.

"His backs are bigger than my tackles," John said. "They'll scare our little ole boys to death."

Dink, who has guided the Pirates to victories over Point Pleasant and Nitro, has a different idea who will be how scared.

"We know it's going to be our toughest game so far," Dink said. "They've got backs that can go all the way on one play."

…Dink isn't worried about getting the Bucs "up." "We're going to be ready," he said. If we can get these boys to play a ball game, I think we can win it."

And John, who has led the Highlanders to wins over Ceredo-Kenova and Milton, isn't as scared as he would like Dink to think. "I think we'll give a good account of ourselves," he said.

But John is cautious. He calls Barboursville "the biggest team, the roughest team, and the best team we've played so far,"

And he is taking no chances.

"I'm taking a deputy sheriff along to get us in and out of there as quickly as possible," he said. "The air's bad. Reminds me of a lot of bad memories."

John was kidding, but someone will have some bad memories after Friday night. (Schumacher 1966)

That someone turned out to be Dink; the Bucs lost that game 14-7 and John was "tickled to death" to even the score with his older brother. Nevertheless, the Pirates finished with a winning football season, and an even better basketball season.

Bill Dan Ray, who was the 1953 Pirates football co-captain with Bill Curry, became head basketball coach in 1963 and began producing a multi-year run of winning seasons. His 1975 squad, including the "tree-tall" trio of Steve Dillon, Ritchie Boyd and Mike Fortner, became the only Pirate basketball team to compete in a state tournament. Pandemonium broke out at the Charleston Civic Center when the team edged out St. Albans 58 to 57 for the West Virginia AAA Championship.

1975 West Virginia AAA Basketball Champions (front row from left) Will Bollman, Kenny
Bumgardner, John Pauley; (back row from left) Neal Johnson, Tim Urian, Bob McComas,
Mike Fortner, Steve Dillon, Ritchie Boyd, Chuck Derbyshire
(Courtesy of Barboursville Public Library)

In perhaps the most jubilant moment of a decade, fans take to the floor
of the Charleston Civic Center after Barboursville edges out St. Albans for the
1975 AAA State Championship.
(1977 Treasure Chest Yearbook)

Year in and year out, the Baby Boomers attended Barboursville High School, as did their children. Many students had the same teachers their parents did. Sports teams would rise and fall, and athletic programs would slowly expand to include girls. The Future Farmers and Future Homemakers faded as the district's rural acreage gave way to new housing and women's roles evolved. Across the street, Pirates Corner, the Rollyson's food truck and other nearby establishments served hot dogs, bags of chips, candy bars and soft drinks until new safety regulations kept all students strictly on-campus. Like any middle-American high school, Barboursville's student body always had its band kids, choir members, young artists, aspiring writers, jocks, cheerleaders, math nerds, and countless others just trying to find their place.

This would all change in 1994, when Barboursville and Milton high schools became the first in a series of dominos to fall as part of a county-wide school renewal process that continues in 2013 (most recently felling the former "Colored Orphans Home" on U.S. Route 60). The creation of Cabell Midland High School replaced the Pirates and Greyhounds with the scarlet and silver "Midland Knights," and was actually part of a second great wave of West Virginia school consolidation.

In the first wave, West Virginia's "county unit plan" of 1933 abolished hundreds of independent and magisterial school districts and created 55 county boards of education. This ultimately reduced the number of schools by more than half, to about 2,800 schools in 1959. Later, population losses and two legal decisions of the 1980s had a more dramatic impact, leaving fewer than 900 public schools in West Virginia by the end of the twentieth century. The Recht Decision, a 1982 judicial ruling, called for equity in school funding and equal instruction for all children in West Virginia. This led many counties to close smaller, more antiquated schools where it was harder to maintain standards. In 1989, Governor Gaston Caperton pushed for a School Building Authority to distribute state funds for counties to build and modernize schools. This was part of his administration's three-pronged approach, along with computer acquisition and teacher training, to boost West Virginia schools in the use of technology.

Once Barboursville High School was vacated, the Middle School moved into its place (as of 1989, the county no longer had junior high schools). In 2002, new construction again replaced the old, as the Village of Barboursville Elementary consolidated the primary grades of Barboursville and Pea Ridge Elementary schools. By 2010, the elementary school was the county's largest, holding more students than three of the county's five middle schools.

Each day of the 2012-2013 school year about 1,500 youngsters—over 700 children from pre-Kindergarten through fifth grade, and nearly 800 in sixth through eighth grade—would converge on two secure modern school buildings on Central

Avenue. The village's high school students would rise earlier in order to drive or catch a school bus to Ona.

In the time of Barboursville High School, four generations of adolescents passed through the high school's front doors on Central Avenue at the beginning of fall. Graduates of 68 senior classes of Barboursville High School paraded across the stage to receive their diplomas, after first rising to sing.

Alma Mater (Courtesy of Barbara Stephens Miller)

Our Special Correspondent Furnishes an Interesting Letter:
JULY 6, 1899— Jennie M—, a girl on Beech Fork, who has been pronounced
insane, imagines her head is made of glass, and constantly fears that some one
will break it.

CHAPTER 15

INSTITUTIONAL BARBOURSVILLE (1940s-2013)

The Other Side of the Coin

HERE'S a lingering question: why would a thinking person put a state mental institution on the same property as a junior high school?

When Morris Harvey College left Barboursville in 1935, the campus was split in two. The downhill buildings were converted for public school use. But up on "Fortification Hill" *aka* "Inspiration Ridge," the old dormitories sat vacant for seven years.

In 1942, West Virginia finally found a use for Rosa Harvey Hall and McDonald Hall. The state quickly filled a need and converted the space into the "Barboursville Unit of the Weston State Hospital." From that point until the mid-1970s, the village was book-ended by *two* state properties for the mentally ill. Just past the town's southern boundary, the Huntington State Hospital managed nearly 700 acres of farmland.

Local history has skimmed over Barboursville's role in caring for those at society's most pitiable rung. The most recent histories by Gunter and Hall each devoted half a sentence to the state hospital. Why bring it up, then? Why not just bask in the achievements of the Champion Generation and their relations—villagers who were healthy, well-educated and relatively fortunate? Why leave behind the celebrated soda fountain milkshakes to stare down the dreaded hospital rations?

"Holsteins and Bobby Soxers" – At the state hospital farm grounds just south of the high school, the 1954 BHS Speech Club enjoys a "senior day picnic" among the cows that supplied milk to the Huntington State Hospital. My late father, John W. "Jack" Rowsey, entertains his classmates by imitating a bullfighter.
(Photo Courtesy of Eugenia Damron)

Three reasons: First of all, there is just too much real estate to ignore here. In the mid-twentieth century, the state managed more local acreage for institutional purposes than was set aside in William Merritt's original town plan. Second, Barboursville's particular place in West Virginia's system of public institutions fits into a larger puzzle. It's a convoluted story, to be sure, but "Institutional Barboursville" can only be fully understood in relationship to Weston, Huntington and other connected centers of "involuntary commitment." Pulling back the curtain shows how far our society has come in dealing with marginalized individuals, but it also brings to light how far there is to go. And third, even though few have commemorated the hospital's 36-year existence, it slowly and subtly became part of the town's self-image.

Barboursville's neighbors on the hill were men and women whose lives were filled with unspeakable and unspoken tragedy, but Barboursville had something to offer them. The town was unique, and not just because "inmates" were in close proximity to school kids in the frenzy of adolescence. A glimpse of the Lost Village through the institutional prism reveals that Barboursville was, as ever, a distinctive and adaptable village.

"All Classes of Broken Humanity"

Before the hospitals evolved, early management of Cabell County's "unfortunates" was dictated by laws and traditions of Virginia.

Adults and children of the nineteenth century who were alone and helpless for various reasons—physical disabilities, alcoholism, abandonment or mental incapacity—were legally considered "paupers." Requiring paupers to live in tax-supported facilities called "poor houses" or "poor farms" was an idea imported from England. In the days of the early industrial revolution, it was commonly believed that rounding up and keeping people in this manner would not only be cost effective, but would somehow cure them of the bad habits and character defects assumed to be the cause of their poverty.

For nearly a century, county officials called Overseers of the Poor saw to the fate of these individuals. Elected officials of a district generally bound the paupers over to the person who offered the lowest bid. This meant the well-being of a pauper was almost entirely dependent on the kindness and fairness of the private bidder.

A commission named by the Cabell County court in 1853 was given the duty to procure at least 100 acres of land as a place to keep the poor. Richard McCallister of Tyler Creek in Salt Rock sold his farm to the county for this purpose when he moved away. Lambert described the property's location as "just beyond Enon church which stands on the divide between Tyler Creek and Trace Creek of Guyan" (very close to the present Lincoln County line). Existing accounts suggest the farm got off to a shaky first decade, punctuated by disputes among the overseers, bouts of mismanagement and an unsuccessful attempt by the county to sell the property. Many of the county's early paupers were lost to posterity; the locally-built caskets that held their remains were placed in unmarked graves on the farm.

It was a Barboursville man who ultimately stepped in, paid rent to the county and boarded the paupers. For an intermittent period before 1870, and during all the years between 1870 and 1929, a single family managed the Cabell County Poor Farm:

> Aaron Flood McKendree was born in Franklin County, Virginia, in 1805, and came to this section about 1835. He married Katherine Grubb, of German descent, and settled at Barboursville, where he formed a partnership with James H. Ferguson who afterwards became a well-known attorney, Judge Ferguson. Together they conducted a shoemaker shop. . . Mr. McKendree also worked in the old tannery with the late Mr. Leist or his predecessor.

> (Aaron's son) George William McKendree, the present owner of the place, was one of a large family. He married Mary C. Perry in 1885…During most of the long period of three quarters of a century, this devoted family has fathered and mothered the poor and unfortunate of this county. It has been a life of sacrifice such as is rarely equaled. (F. Lambert 1929)

According to county historian George Wallace, "this arrangement was continued through Mr. McKendree's lifetime and after his death his son, William McKendree, had the contract for keeping the Cabell County poor up to the year 1928. This arrangement could not of course have been a good one, but both of the McKendrees were good men and they faithfully performed their duties as is evidenced by the fact that they continued to have these contracts all of these years."

(Note: Lambert suggests a family connection between Aaron Flood McKendree and his son George William "Billy" McKendree of Salt Rock, and innkeeper Robert McKendree and *his* prominent son Major George W. McKendree of Barboursville. They were the only two McKendree households in the county in 1850, but the exact relationship is unconfirmed. Suffice it to say the two George W. McKendrees were different men, and were possibly cousins.)

The old McCallister farmhouse served as both the McKendree residence and the Poor Farm's "main house" until its closing, and was described by Lambert as "one of the most palatial of the old-fashioned country homes still in existence."

> Viewing the place from a little distance, one is impressed with its similarity to descriptions of the old Negro plantations. The master lived in the main house, while most of the inmates, or paupers lived in small outbuildings erected for the purpose. Nearby is the cemetery, in which the county lays its pauper dead….

No permanent record has ever been kept of the inmates, hence it would be difficult to tell who they were or whence they came. They represented all classes of broken humanity—human wreckage—many from good families. Even before the Civil war, Michael Loller, an old school teacher, was an inmate here. He remained till after the war and died here, and lies buried in an unmarked grave, in the pauper cemetery, near the house. In his better days, he was a very good carpenter. He worked for Dickie McCallister and helped to ceil and weatherboard the house, and joked that he was preparing a room for himself. This was before the poor farm was established. Little did he dream that his words would come true. He was crippled afterwards and compelled to walk on crutches. Like Ichabod Crane, his favorite drink was whiskey, and he kept account of his pints by cutting notches on a board which he kept in his room, at the house...

Several years after the war (about 1883) Dangerfield Bryant, another old school teacher, became an inmate. He came from North Carolina and was not only a school teacher but a teacher of singing and "instrumental" music. It was said that his fiddling was hard to beat. He was a cripple, smooth-shaven, low, heavy set, and weighed about 175 pounds. He was a good man and a perfect gentleman. He too lies in the cemetery there in a nameless grave. Many of the older people yet remember him as their teacher of years ago, for he taught in several of the country schools.

In contrast...Charley Jones was a large, powerful, high-tempered man who came some years ago from North Carolina, wandered around two or three years and settled on Madison Creek. He moved to Somerset, Kentucky, lost his second wife and returned to North Carolina, where he resided with a daughter. She clothed him well and treated him royally but he preferred the hills of West Virginia and came back. On one occasion, he had a fight with another man about his equal in strength. They pounded each other viciously for 15 or 20 minutes. Neither ever saw a well day afterwards. Charley came to the poor house, claimed his relatives abandoned him, lost his mind, and died there a few months ago. (F. Lambert 1929)

"Uncle Billy" McKendree
(Courtesy of Huntington Public Library)

By the twentieth century, the farm was known as the Cabell County Infirmary. Lambert visited the place shortly before its closing and interviewed 71-year-old caretaker George William McKendree. "Uncle Billy," as he was known, was described as a "typical Virginia gentleman of the olden days" who loved checkers, dominoes and baseball, and was known for his boundless hospitality. Over the years, the county paid him from $10 to $16 per month to board, clothe and house the county's paupers. The farm was self-sufficient though never profitable, and provided most of the food for McKendree's family and the residents. Many paupers were of "low mentality," but those "who had any feeling of self-respect whatever" ate with the family, and some had rooms in the main house. Many were able to do their own washing, ironing and cooking. Those who were able to help work on the farm were paid for their services. On Sundays, a "plantation atmosphere" prevailed, with visitors, ice cream, and even records on the Victrola in the main house.

Both adults and children lived at the poor farm, as recorded in seven point-in-time Census schedules. In 1860, the aforementioned Michael Loller, age 75, was the only pauper living in the household. From then, the headcount grew: There were four adults and one infant in 1870; 16 adults (one black) and 8 children in 1880; 15 adults and 15 children (one black) in 1900; 16 adults and 11 children in 1910; and 16 adults plus 20 children in 1920.

The youngest "inmates" ranged from 1-year-old babies to adolescents. Most, judging by their surnames, had been orphaned or separated from their parents.

In the year 1900, four of the children—17-year-old Margie, 5-year-old Stella, 4-year-old Willie and 1-year-old Mary—had no last names recorded, nor did a 38-year-old man listed only as "Mom's William." There were women and children with the same last names but all were simply recorded as "inmates" which suggests that being wards of the county negated any legal family relationship. There were only a small number of paupers identified with specific disabilities, yet most, even if they had no identified disability, were counted as illiterate.

In the 1920s, county welfare boards replaced overseers of the poor and the state began to play a greater role in indigent care, establishing agencies for the welfare of children and veterans. National programs such as the Salvation Army, as well as Social Security and other New Deal reforms, ultimately ended the practice of "putting away" individuals just because they were poor.

By 1927, there were two new places to send Cabell County's indigent citizens, both in Ona. County Court president T.H. Nash arranged purchase of the 156-acre Everett farm overlooking the present-day Cabell Midland High School campus. Once known as "Poore's Hill," the Cabell County Home was meant to house aged and infirm white people of Cabell County. In the 1930 Census, this included a few mothers and children as well. A few miles away, former coal magnate and Huntington hotel owner Fred C. Prichard opened "the Prichard School" for orphans in a stately stone mansion between Howell's Mill and Yates Crossing. When the Salt Rock "poor farm" closed in 1929, 31 remaining inmates were moved either to the old Everett farm, the Huntington City Mission, or an "unnamed county home" east of Huntington.

Before the departure of his paupers, McKendree shared his belief that poor families "should not be kept at a poor farm, but rather with private families, to spare the children the future disgrace."

Before their tearful departures, the last of the farm "inmates" were interviewed by Lambert who asked what they thought about Mr. McKendree.

> The writer went from cottage to cottage and one after another bore testimony to the same facts. Said one little old woman who had spent most of her life there, "Billy and his wife have been father and mother to me." Said another and another, "They have been father and mother to me." (F. Lambert 1929)

Labels and Life in the Shadows

The nineteenth-century system of poor houses and poor farms was unspecialized, in that it served as a catch-all for anybody who didn't "belong." The 1860 Census provided an unprecedented level of detail about adults who were unable to fit into productive society. Several residents of the County Poor Farm fit under one or more of the following classifications: "deaf and dumb," "blind," "insane," "idiotic," "pauper" or "convict." By 1880, the enumerator could use the additional descriptors of "maimed, crippled, bedridden, or otherwise disabled." By the twentieth century, these labels had been dropped from the Census schedule, although the term "feeble-minded" was written in for a handful of folks living at the county poor farm.

Medical science was barely contemplating disorders of the mind when a Boston school teacher named Dorothea Dix visited a city jail to teach a Sunday School class. There she found "insane" adults and even mentally disabled children tattered, hungry and chained up in filthy, freezing cells alongside hardened criminals. For 50 years, Dix visited those locked up in jails and prisons, and crusaded for states to build mental hospitals. "The Association of Medical Superintendents of American Institutions for the Insane," (forerunner of the American Psychiatric Association) was formed in 1844 in response to the efforts of Dix and other advocates.

With psychiatric science in its pre-infancy, citizens were not aware of what treatments might work or that people with serious mental illness could ever get better. History would reveal that many people suffering from mental illnesses could not only recover under the right conditions but could even achieve greatness. Abraham Lincoln and Charles Dickens both suffered from severe depression. Ludwig van Beethoven experienced what is now known as bipolar disorder, as did Isaac Newton and Winston Churchill. Charles Darwin is believed to have had obsessive-compulsive disorder; the list could go on. There was little such awareness at the time.

More typically—especially among families without education or means—a person who showed signs of emotional instability or intellectual incapacity would be treated with fear rather than compassion, shame instead of understanding. Family and neighbors might assume that the individual was weak, the "black sheep of the family," cursed, or possibly even possessed by demons. This stigma would lead to embarrassment and secrecy, which in turn often made the symptoms worse. Embarrassed or desperate family members might isolate, hide away or abandon their afflicted kin. The community might tolerate and feed a lone "village idiot" who roamed from place to place like a stray dog, but jail was always a possibility for those who could not be controlled. In 1880's Census, this included three "lunatics" housed at the county jail in Barboursville.

Strange behavior in the community was a cause for neighborly concern and sometimes made the newspapers. Between 1898 and 1900, the following local items appeared in *The Cabell Record*. Stigma being what it is even today, I have withheld last names:

DEMENTED MRS. ALLEN L— ADJUDGED TO BE INSANE AND SENT TO SPENCER—was brought to Milton and Drs. Love and Erwin and Squire Burke examined her and determined that she be sent to the asylum, leaving on the 6:30 p.m. train…was a lady highly respected by all who know her…is the mother of James L—, the story of whom Cabell people are all familiar with, which no doubt is the cause of Mrs. L—'s trouble.

WILD MAN IN THE WOODS—near Sanders mill on Fudge Creek, this county, there is said to be a wild man running at large. He has been seen by several persons and his screams at night are terrific.

Insanity developed in one of the inmates at the Home for the Incurables last Saturday, and the unfortunate will be sent to the Asylum for the Insane.

Miss Ada C—, a girl of this vicinity and an epileptic will be given a home at the institution for incurables near Huntington.

An unknown young woman, presumably insane, has been going up and down the C&O track for the past week. Mayor Ayers of Barboursville, was called to arrest her last Saturday. She had lain out in the rain all night and presented a pitiable sight. Before the officers could land her behind the bars she had skipped out. She should be taken care of. (The Cabell Record 1898-1900)

The Model Asylum

In 2008, when private owners bought the former Weston State Hospital in Lewis County and began fixing it up as a tourist attraction, there was plenty of controversy about the name they selected, the Trans-Allegheny Lunatic Asylum. This was the original name of the place, Virginia's third state mental institution. The new owners have stood their ground and attracted plenty of curiosity seekers and "ghost hunters" as a result.

As the institutional "mother ship" from which Barboursville State Hospital was created, the massive building in Lewis County was designed as a model "asylum" in the very best sense of that word. Dozens of state hospitals inspired by Dorothea Dix in the mid-1800s, including Weston, were the first attempt to provide "a pleasant and orderly place of refuge" for people with mental illness. The Gothic Revival building (still the nation's largest hand-cut sandstone structure) was designed inside and out to be place of calm, a serene retreat from the stressful world where patients could regain their "inner light." This seemingly "New Age" concept was advanced by one of the fathers of American psychiatry.

Thomas Story Kirkbride (1809-1883) was a physician and founder of the precursor to the American Psychiatric Association. Kirkbride was also a devout Quaker who advocated for a French philosophy known as "moral treatment" or "moral management," and put it into practice it at the Pennsylvania Hospital for the Insane from 1840 to 1880. Kirkbride maintained that those afflicted needed to be treated kindly and that harsh treatments only made patients worse.

In the retreat-like atmosphere of the hospital he supervised, restraints were avoided, self-control was encouraged, and patients were given comfortable living conditions, plenty of food, and kept occupied with tasks such as gardening, sewing and reading. As a doctor, he counseled his patients to take responsibility for their behavior, resist "mad thoughts," and help themselves become well. He also assured them that they were not doomed to be ill forever. As a lecturer, writer and consultant, he influenced a number of states to adopt his method, which became known as the "Kirkbride Plan."

This popular therapeutic philosophy of the day extended to every architectural and environmental detail of the new state asylums and hospitals, still known worldwide as "Kirkbride Buildings." Most were built between 1848 and 1890, and each followed the same basic floor plan and general arrangement of facilities. In addition to its placement on more than 100 acres of tillable land, orchards, woodlands, parks and walkways, the Weston asylum would feature the latest in ductwork to furnish centralized heating and cooling to the building. Eight wards were designed to house 30 people each with well-lighted, 9-by-12-foot bedrooms opening to a central hallway. Each ward had a parlor, dining room and bathroom. Kirkbride's plan restricted admissions to a maximum number of patients, recommended to be no more than 250 at Weston with one attendant on staff for every six patients.

Due to Civil War disruptions (including a raid on the partially-built hospital by General Jenkins in 1862) and the machinations of West Virginia statehood, construction was delayed. When West Virginia finally admitted 20 patients in 1864 (transferred from Staunton and Williamsburg because they were no longer Virginia's responsibility), the name changed to the West Virginia Hospital for the Insane. As construction continued in fits and starts, the number of admissions increased, as did the number of patients discharged from the hospital after treatment. By time of its formal opening in 1871, with a visit from the governor, a banquet and grand ball in the large ballroom in the central building, the hospital was considered one of the best buildings of its kind in the United States.

Weston's early "inmates" were well-attended-to:

> Some of the patients are suicidal and have to be carefully watched; others are homicidal and have to be restrained; but a large majority of them are peaceably disposed but are utterly incapable of taking care of themselves. Many of them, however, may work under direction of the attendants, and accordingly they are employed upon the farm and in many occupations about the house. The women do plain sewing and knitting; the men assist in the laundry, bakehouse, carpenter shop, quarry, etc. One of the patients, who was for a number

of years insane, and still has periods of occasional insanity, has made, with his own hands, nearly all of the finer furniture in the office and rooms of the Superintendent and other officers. The furniture is very beautiful in design and is very skillfully and substantially made. (The Asylum: Its Origins and Progress 1871)

Shortly after this grandest of openings, complaints came from around the state that too much money was being spent on the opulent building and splendid grounds of the Weston Hospital when what was needed were more beds. Within days, 86 new inmates came in, most of whom had languished in jails for years. After that, it seemed all roads led to the state hospital, carrying all ages and types of unfortunate West Virginians.

A 2008 graduate thesis by Kim Jacks at West Virginia University includes patient information from Weston Hospital's first 16 years of operation, when it was the sole destination for the "insane" of West Virginia. The "inmates" ranged from age 93 to 8 years—the mother of the eight-year-old said he had been insane since the age of three, then hurriedly handed the boy over at the Weston train station.

From 1864 to 1880, the most common disease attributed to Weston patients was chronic dementia, followed by acute mania, melancholia and chronic mania. Physicians—sometimes uneasily—assigned "supposed causes" for many of these maladies when they could, and Jacks ranked them by the most common. Heredity was at the top of the list (ascribed to 101 patients), followed by epilepsy (70 patients), and 40 to 50 patients each with "intemperance," "ill health," "menstrual," "traumatic injury," and "masturbation." Other cited reasons for admission were grief, "religious excitement," "mental perplexities," "the war," "hard study," "disappointed love," and "disappointment in business."

"As Full as Capacity Will Allow"

By the time of Dr. Kirkbride's death, his psychiatric ideal of a hospital with no more than 250 patients was forgotten as mental hospitals around the country admitted more and more patients. In 1880, Weston State Hospital was reported to be "as full as capacity will allow," with 491 patients. Through the next decade, as overcrowding became the norm, "cure" and discharge rates fell below Kirkbride-level expectations. Ironically, just as the public began to accept the idea of letting the state take care of those who they could no longer handle, standards of care deteriorated. Fewer employees cared for more and more patients. Custodial care became the norm. Information about treatments given to patients stopped appearing in reports to the state.

In the halls of government, the voices of psychiatric experts and social reformers were drowned out by "bean-counters" and back-scratching politicians. The West

Virginians who were "out of sight and out of mind" in Lewis County soon had counterparts at Spencer in Roane County (opened in 1893 to relieve overcrowding at Weston), and Huntington's "Home for Incurables," established in 1897 and renamed the West Virginia Asylum in 1901.

Rather than ushering in an enlightened age of mental health treatment, the new century only brought a compounding of problems at the state hospitals. State legislatures generally provided inadequate funding to maintain them despite the fact they were holding more and more patients. The superintendents not only had to make do with inadequate staff and materials, but complained that the quality of employees was declining because political parties were rewarding supporters with government jobs in the hospitals.

The West Virginia Board of Control was created by the legislature in 1909 to supervise the state's educational, charitable, correctional, and mental institutions. Until 1957, the Boards of Control consisted of gubernatorial appointees who filled the three seats for six-year terms. Few were ever physicians, and members typically had limited knowledge of medicine or disorders of the mind.

Conditions spiraled downward. Bereft of adequate resources, the hospitals were less and less likely to try and keep the patients busy. Classification of patients by illness broke down; sicker, more disruptive patients mingled with more peaceable ones. Entertainment, recreation and occupational therapies such as crafts and woodworking became more limited. Whereas in the early asylum days only physicians could order restraints, it became common ward-management practice to use straitjackets, cuffs, lock seats (to hold patients in a sitting position) and various other confining devices. In 1927, a hearing over the death of a restrained patient revealed that there were only three physicians for the 1,300 Weston inmates.

A new treatment for the mentally ill became widely used in state hospitals in the first half of the century. It was known as hydrotherapy, and tended to be used to induce fatigue in violent or agitated patients. There was the "continuous bath," which involved lowering a disruptive patient in a hammock suspended in a bathtub with only the head emerging above. Patients might remain in the tub for hours or even days, sometimes with bandages around their eyes and ears, sometimes with ice caps on their head. A "needle shower" involved pummeling the patient with cold pressurized water for a minute or two, purportedly to stimulate the heart and help the depressed patient. "Wet packs" were considered a beneficial treatment for "restlessness," and required swaddling patients in blankets or sheets that had been dipped in water, so only the head, fingers, and toes could move. A patient could be left in this condition for more than a day with the drying covers shrinking tight and hot around the body.

In 1940, electroshock therapy was introduced in American hospitals. This involved placing electrodes at the patient's temples and sending a jolt of electricity through the temporal lobes, resulting in convulsions. Patients subject to this treatment would seem to lose the cognitive processes and emotions that caused delusions and paranoia, but they also lost mental functioning and memory. The "curing" power of electroshock was only temporary and psychotic symptoms often returned, so many patients were treated repeatedly, even daily. Some eventually suffered serious, permanent brain damage. Even though the electroshock treatments were extremely painful; even though in their first years they caused 40 percent of patients to suffer broken bones from thrashing during the convulsions; and even though many patients would tremble, beg or make desperate attempts to escape when facing further treatments—the larger hospitals found it useful in quieting wards and sedating agitated patients. Physicians in state hospitals across the United States commonly administered the procedure for at least two decades.

Into these increasingly dreadful settings would come further advances in "treatment." West Virginia became the first state to carry out pre-frontal "ice pick" lobotomy surgeries on a large scale during the late 1940s and early 1950s. Always, more patients kept coming into the state hospitals, while the legislature kept cutting corners and denying additional staff and resources. In 1941, Huntington State Hospital, with a rated capacity of 600, held 953 children and adults. Weston had nearly 1,700.

Imagine spending monotonous years in a dank ward with 60 or 70 closely-confined neighbors whose dispositions might run the gamut from catatonic stupor to violent rage; how could one's "inner light" *not* be extinguished under the circumstances? It is clear that the Kirkbride theory of "moral treatment" had long been abandoned within the thick stone walls of Weston and its counterparts.

Handling the Overflow

As the state hospitals were forced to pack in more and more patients, the eyes of state government turned to vacant properties elsewhere in the state:

Five sanctuaries for the 1,936 tubercular patients and insane persons awaiting admittance to state hospitals were listed for a tour of inspection Saturday by a group of officials, including Governor Neely. Old Sweet Springs Hotel, Morris Harvey College buildings at Barboursville, old Pence Springs hotel, Alderson Collegiate Institute buildings at Alderson and the old Sheltering Arms hospital building at Hansford.

There are 230 bed available at Barboursville, near the Huntington state hospital.

The governor recently ordered the board of control to have all insane persons temporarily held in county jails pending admittance to state asylums in those institutions within 60 days. He suggested establishment of temporary receiving centers until the state's program of institutional expansion could catch up with the demand for facilities. (Associated Press 1941)

In 1941, the state purchased Rosa Harvey and McDonald Hall. "Weston State Hospital, Barboursville Unit" opened on January 20, 1942 to meet an urgent demand to house the "mentally defective" people being kept in county jails. Between 40 and 60 patients were moved that day from Weston, Huntington and Spencer state hospitals. By August, the hospital was practically filled to capacity, with a total of 270 patients. Later that year, additional bed space was provided through building renovations. A capacity of 315 was attained, and immediately filled through transfers from the other three hospitals.

Somewhere along the line, the status of Barboursville as a "temporary receiving center" for the state's "big three" hospitals changed, but not without a few howls of protest under the Capitol dome:

March 1943: Resolutions to annul the state's purchases of the Old Sweet Springs summer resort in Monroe county for a tuberculosis sanitarium and the old Morris Harvey college property at Barboursville for an insane asylum were introduced in the house of delegates yesterday by Majority Leader Harry L. Van Sickler (D-Greenbrier).

Contending the purchases were both illegal and unwise, the resolutions would direct the board of control to re-convey the properties to their former owners, and direct the attorney general to take any legal action necessary to recover "all moneys expended there for to the fullest extent that is lawful and practicable."

Both properties were purchased late in 1941, Old Sweet with $150,000 of an appropriation for a new wing at Hopemont sanitarium, and the Barboursville buildings with $125,000 of the money budgeted for capital improvements at Weston state hospital. Both places were designated as "units" of the institutions for which the money was originally appropriated. The resolutions, which require senate concurrence, will be up for action in the house today. They set forth that there is "no public need" for the continued use of the properties, contending there is "ample present capacity" at Pinecrest sanitarium for the tuberculars and at Weston for the insane. (Associated Press 1943)

October 1943: The state's purchase of the old Morris Harvey college property at Barboursville for an insane asylum was "just as illegal, unlawful and unconstitutional as the Old Sweet Springs deal," the house committee studying state spending declared today.

The committee, of which Delegate Rush D. Holt (D-Lewis) is chairman, declared there was no appropriation for Barboursville in 1941 and the money was taken from the funds of Weston Stale Hospital and used for a purpose foreign to the wording of the appropriations act. "It has been said," the group stated "that there was a grand jury investigation of these matters. A reading of the report of the jury would answer some of those who bring in this flimsy justification."

The 1943 legislature voted $214,000 for the operation of Barboursville in the current biennium, but in a rider to the budget act said that "in making this appropriation the legislature does not ratify the purchase of this institution." (Associated Press 1943)

The Sweet Springs tubercular facility was soon shut down as a result of the legislative maneuverings, but Barboursville somehow remained viable.

In July 1946, the Board of Control conferred with the heads of the five institutions and enacted a new policy to shift some of the state's patients around: all mental patients 16 years of age and under were to be transferred to the Huntington State and all "tubercular and criminally insane" inmates to Weston. It was also established that "the patients listed as feeble-minded will be segregated and sent to the "Barboursville Unit of the Huntington Hospital."

On January 8, 1949, a phalanx of members of the Grand Lodge of West Virginia, Ancient Free and Accepted Masons stood at attention for a ceremonial laying of the cornerstone for the Barboursville Unit's new administration building; the Masons placed a memorial box in the cornerstone. Within months, however, Barboursville State Hospital was fully established by legislative act as a separate state entity rather than a unit of Huntington State Hospital.

Through many of its years of operation, Barboursville's facility was a noted exception to the "general principal that each of the state hospitals will be asked to provide generalized psychiatric services to the region in which it is located." A certain kind of patient came to Barboursville, no matter if that person's family lived in Winfield, Welch or Wheeling. A report by the West Virginia Department of Mental Health in the 1960s summed up what was Barboursville's predominant niche from the outset: "Patients are admitted to this facility only after transfer from other institutions. The present population is composed largely of chronic regressed patients, many of whom have grown old in institutional settings, and includes a number of borderline or moderately retarded individuals. Patients are generally placid, docile and thoroughly adapted to institutional living."

Barboursville's establishment as a purely custodial facility, with no "treatment" and no psychiatrist on staff, set it apart. (A registered nurse served as de facto superintendent for at least four years.) As such, Barboursville became the first West

Virginia mental facility where a sort of truth in labeling prevailed: the state never even pretended to give its occupants a shot at rehabilitation. The state did pretend to justify Barboursville's lack of clinical personnel: "Psychiatric staff and other consultants can easily be shared when and where needed with Huntington State Hospital 12 miles away," wrote an official who must have been in denial about the ability of the staff and consultants at Norway Avenue to assist.

A *Herald-Advertiser* report written when Barboursville was still a unit of Huntington State Hospital cited severe overcrowding and under-staffing at Huntington: there was one psychiatrist per 150 patients, and a single trained nurse for all 1,150 patients. Huntington State Hospital attendants worked six 12-hour days per week and were paid half of what other hospitals offered for a regular 40-hour work week.

In 1949, a *Charleston Gazette* reporter named Charles Armentrout ran a three-week series of front-page exposés on West Virginia's state institutions for the mentally ill and mentally impaired:

> Scenes behind the facades of the sturdy-looking buildings wring the emotions dry. "Shocking" is an inadequate word to describe the conditions—or the nauseous smells—in every one of the hospitals.

> "They are crowded beyond the point of human decency," Joseph Z. Terrell, president of the state Board of Control, sadly acknowledged.

> Crammed into Weston State Hospital are 1,895 men and women, 590 more than capacity. At Spencer, 965 inmates are herded into space where only 540 were intended. The story is the same at Huntington State, the Barboursville unit and at Lakin State hospital for Negroes.

> Terrell and Board Members Dell White and L. Steel Trotter without hesitation gave their permission for a first-hand layman's inspection of all the hospitals.

> "You will find that West Virginia's mental hospitals are no worse, but certainly no better than the institutions of other states," Terrell said. "But go see for yourself and let the public know the facts." (Armentrout 1949)

What the reporters, along with several members of the Legislature who toured the facilities, discovered were "seas of beds, in many rooms so close together a hand can't be run between them." Men, women—even children, some of them nude—spending hours strapped onto chairs or beds for want of enough staff to attend to them. "The reek of odors of human filth" in some wards where a bucket placed on a rubber sheet in the middle of a room might serve as the toilet. At Huntington, 150 children considered "untrainables" were locked away on a bare third-floor ward with ragged garments and no toys save for a few crude mops they sometimes pushed back and forth for a semblance of activity. Segregated only by gender like the adults, children with volatile behavior disorders were grouped alongside children with physical birth defects or severe intellectual disabilities, as well as children with perfectly sound minds who were diagnosed with epilepsy. Many had not been outside in years. (Again, this was 1949.)

Whereas Armentrout's reports from Huntington, Lakin, Spencer and Weston were horrifying, Barboursville State Hospital came off as merely grim:

> The class of '30, Morris Harvey college, would never recognize the old alma mater that is now Barboursville State Mental hospital and from which the class of '49 will never graduate.

> There are 315 men and women cooped up in McDonald and Rosa Harvey Halls. They are the unsalvageable residue of Weston, Spencer and Huntington State Mental hospitals.

> They have been diagnosed and rediagnosed, given up as hopeless mental cases, then sent here. Now they are secluded in the former college dormitory halls.

> It looked like "visitors are coming day" on the second floor of McDonald Hall. The men—old and young—were in their places.

> Tiny rooms, perfect for two college chums, held four apiece, and every room was occupied.

> "There's nothing for them to do, but stay in their rooms or wander up and down the hall," said Charles E. Evans, Barboursville's efficient young financial secretary.

> They've jerked the doors off the closets in each of the rooms, leaving open alcoves with space for a chair.

> Silent, drawn old men peered out from the gloom of these spaces. There wasn't a sound from anyone except the voices and footsteps of the inspecting party.

> The second floor was reached unannounced, but here too there was nothing but men with deteriorated minds, rooms, beds and chairs.

In 1949, Charleston Gazette photographer Frank Wilkin took this photo of women in a remodeled third floor "cubicle" at Rosa Harvey Hall that served as their sleeping and living quarters. The newspaper retouched the photo to mask the patients' identities.
(Charleston Gazette Photo)

Tobacco, their only luxury, filled the jowls of many. Old, battered tin coffee cans served as spittoons.

About all the male patients at Barboursville have to do is sit and spit. (Armentrout, Forsaken and Forgotten: Hospital Has No Therapy But Plenty of Patients 1949)

The men did have an opportunity to get fresh air three times daily as they were marched up to Rosa Harvey's dining hall for meals, Armentrout noted in his single-day report on Barboursville. He pointed out that Barboursville, though legally designated as a unit of Huntington State, was "an altogether separately run and separately administered institution."

Mrs. Virginia Comstock, a registered nurse, is the superintendent, and a woman's intuitive desire for cleanliness is evident throughout the place.

There are no doctors on staff. When medication is needed, physicians from Barboursville are called upon to perform the service.

"Up until recently," said Evans, "we did not have any way to segregate the sick from the well. But I managed to haggle enough to set up isolation wards on each of the floors…" (Armentrout, Forsaken and Forgotten: Hospital Has No Therapy But Plenty of Patients 1949)

Despite the chronic and "hopeless" nature of the Barboursville patients—whether due to senile dementia, mental retardation, or perhaps having been hollowed out inside by the more radical "treatments" at the larger hospitals—nearly all the patients responded to the staff's efforts to modify behavior through a simple reward system:

"We have moving pictures for them about twice a week," Evans said. "They are shown in the dining room and it's quite an occasion. Only half of the patients can see the show at one time, so we have to run the film twice.

Tables must be pushed aside and chairs arranged so all can get a view. If a patient is "bad" during the days preceding the movies, then he doesn't get to go.

The threat of depriving them of this pitiful bit of recreation works wonders as a disciplinary measure, an attendant said.

"We have only one male patient in seclusion," he commented proudly, "and none, as you can see, is under restraint." (Armentrout, Forsaken and Forgotten: Hospital Has No Therapy But Plenty of Patients 1949)

Patients and Patience in the Village

Without diminishing the inherent tragedy of the place—old people who died "alone" in their crowded wards, far from loved ones; the 1950 overdose death of a distraught woman injected (in the absence of a supervising psychiatrist) with an undiluted sedative solution; people long abandoned by relatives whose pleading calls could be heard from the hilltop that they were ready to go home now—without diminishing all that, it should be recognized that the staff of Barboursville State Hospital took pains to reduce the crushing isolation of institutional life.

The village proved an accommodating host. As a result, Barboursville's "child-like" adult patients probably had more access to recreation and playtime than did the actual children warehoused at Huntington State Hospital. One villager recalled being at "the Criss" for movies on particularly noisy Saturday afternoons when the Barboursville patients would be seated on the front rows, some throwing their popcorn into the air. My sister was introduced one summer to the awkward attraction of hospital patients having their morning outing at the Barboursville swimming pool (while town kids gathered near the cemetery fence to gawk at their antics).

During the 1963 West Virginia Centennial, state hospital patients were included in a big way *(as described in the newspaper photo caption below)*.

FROM 1963: "The Junior Woman's Club of Barboursville will lend a helping hand when the Barboursville State Hospital Choir, consisting of 42 patients, presents 'Centennial Capers,' a variety show, Saturday. Planning the event are, from left, Henry King, music therapist; Dr. B.B. Gonzalez, clinic director; John Queen, business manager, and Mrs. Elsworth Smith of the Junior club, pianist."
(Courtesy of Barbara Stephens Miller)

Then there were the countless moments when the hospital patients and town residents, including junior high students, interacted in small ways. Church groups and others visited the hospital to provide worship services or entertainment for the patients. Students were sometimes given tours of the facility. On rare occasions, students would catch a glimpse across campus of an "inmate" trying to make an escape. Each witness no doubt came away from the encounter with a mix of emotions.

One memory came from a family friend who recounted a class tour of the hospital in the early 1950s, when a single hospital staffer acted as their tour guide.

"The people in the back of the group would get pretty nervous," she said. "I remember one patient put a death grip on my arm, demanding that I give her the white and red dotted swiss skirt I had on. Finally a worker came over and pried the woman's fingers away, explaining that I had to go back to school and couldn't take off the skirt, but maybe could send it later," she recalled.

I personally remember performing at the hospital around 1974 with the Ona Junior High choir; it was an uneasy but impactful experience. Today, we call them "teachable moments."

As was described by an area resident who visited once a month with her church,

"Now, as I look back on those days I find it so sad because some of the people there were far from insane. They were mentally retarded, developmentally delayed and perhaps abused (as) children."

Caregivers and Protectors

The unique relationship between the state hospital and the village extended to the town's healers and helpers. In the absence of a staff doctor, two particular men served as consulting physicians to Barboursville State Hospital. These were the same doctors who delivered the town's babies and attended the sick and dying from the 1930s through the 1960s. If someone in Barboursville broke a bone, ran a fever, got a smallpox shot, or needed any type of general medical care, odds are it was Dr. Curry or Dr. Bourne who took care of them.

Like village doctors of an earlier era—Benjamin L. Hume, S.E. McConkey, D.E. Musgrave and Walter Ross Spencer—Doctors Bourne and Curry each had medical practices in "downtown" Barboursville. As physicians and as neighbors, the two were unmatched by their predecessors in raising the quality of life in the village.

LEFT: Dr. W.D. Bourne with two other members of the Public Library Advisory Board
(courtesy of Barboursville Public Library)

RIGHT. Caption, Dr. Raymond Curry examines a young patient
(Treasure Chest 1977 Yearbook, Barboursville High School)

William D. Bourne (1898-1971) grew up in Braxton County, graduated from West Virginia University and got his medical degree at Emory University. He moved to Barboursville in 1935. In addition to his office and hospital practice, he served as a physician for the Barboursville State Hospital for a number of years. Dr. Bourne was active in fraternal organizations such as the Lions, Masons and Shriners, and belonged to the First Methodist Church of Barboursville. His proudest accomplishment, as evidenced by his obituary, was his leadership role in establishing the Barboursville branch of the public library.

Raymond H. Curry (1902-1976) was a Hamlin boy and descendent of "three pioneer Lincoln County families," who grew up to be one of the area's most esteemed physicians. After completing his medical training at Miami University in Ohio and West Virginia University, he started his practice in Barboursville as a young man in 1928. His early work included giving inoculations and examinations at the county's schools and serving as on-call doctor for both Morris Harvey College and the C&O Reclamation Plant. He spent many years serving as team physician for the Barboursville High School Pirates (of which his son Bill was a football co-captain during the championship years). Dr. Curry was an elder of Kuhn Memorial Presbyterian. He served as clinical consultant at the State Hospital from 1953 until his "official" retirement in 1974. In January of that year, "Dr. Curry Appreciation Week" was declared in the village; many in town turned out to honor him for his many achievements, including the decades of care and kindly concern he provided to "his children," as he called the nearly 5,000 local babies he delivered.

In 1956, another physician came to Barboursville as a young man. In March 1957, William S. Sadler (1930-1997) was appointed superintendent of the Barboursville State Hospital. At the time, the hospital was at its all-time peak of nearly 400 patients. About a year later, the new West Virginia Department of Mental Health (created to replace the Board of Control in managing the state mental hospitals) began "a general program of obtaining certified psychiatrists as heads of all state mental institutions," resulting in Dr. Sadler's replacement as superintendent. He returned to full-time family practice and, like his two predecessors, was rooted in the Barboursville community for many years.

Dr. Curry's Main Street neighbor—barber's son Max Clay—was another resident who took the well-being of the Barboursville community to heart. One fall evening in 1952, the 23-year-old BHS graduate joined a small group of men gathered at the town's city hall. They decided, Clay wrote, "that an organized volunteer fire department should be started and maintained for our growing community."

In 1953, the village passed an excess levy to buy a new pumper fire engine. The newly-organized crew of Barboursville volunteer firemen saw the need for additional equipment to make the truck complete, so they could finally replace the old Dodge hose truck that had served the village for 18 years. They solicited door-to-door, sold doughnuts at fairs and policed at football games until they met their goal, only to discover another glaring need:

When the new bright-red fire engine was delivered in September, 1953, the squatty city hall garage wasn't big enough to house it, so the fighting firemen began soliciting funds for a new firehouse.

"They'll never do it," some said. "It's illegal," said others. "A group of individuals can't own public property." But a way was found and the building was built. (Clay c. 1966)

By the time the present fire station was completed in 1954, Max Clay was chief of a volunteer core of firefighters that would grow to three dozen men by the mid-1960s. The department's response to fire calls in rural Cabell County necessitated more resources, larger equipment and expansion of its Central Avenue headquarters. According to longtime member Paul Hockenberry, over 300 have served Barboursville as volunteer firefighters, some of them second and even third-generation firefighters.

"The people of our community, rural area, City Council and the County Court have cooperated to the fullest in helping us. Without them and their aid the Barboursville Volunteer Fire Department wouldn't have been possible," wrote Clay.

Without Chief Clay and his fellow volunteers, the women's building at Barboursville State Hospital would have almost certainly been destroyed, ten years after a similar blaze at Huntington State Hospital ended in tragedy.

November 24, 1962

In the middle of the night on Thanksgiving weekend 1962, a patient in Ward B on the third floor of Rosa Harvey Hall notified nurse Ruth Thompson that the roof was on fire. At the same time, night watchman Ronald Adkins spotted flames leaping from the roof. "It looked as if they covered about 10 square feet. Then, the wind blew up, and they turned into a roaring furnace," he said.

Policeman Ott Reese also took notice and called the hospital's switchboard which also happened to be set up to answer night calls for the volunteer fire department. Reba Dailey, the night operator, pushed a button on her console that was linked directly to the department, immediately causing the signal at the top of the fire station to break the silence of the cold Saturday predawn. According to a neighbor's account, the siren (which to me has always sounded like the opening seconds of REO Speedwagon's "Ridin' the Storm Out") seemed to be stuck, blowing the same tone for about five minutes.

"Aerial Ladder Pours Water Onto Burning Roof"
(Huntington Advertiser Photo courtesy of Huntington Public Library)

By the time the "fire whistle" stopped, Max Clay and a number of fellow volunteers had already rushed to the scene. They immediately began to assist Nurse Thompson and the hospital staff in evacuating 187 female patients—30 of them bedridden—from the building. Drawing on muscle-memory honed through repeated hospital fire drills, the firemen and attendants moved instinctively and efficiently through the building to get the patients out. Within ten minutes, all the female patients were out of Rosa Harvey Hall without so much as a twisted ankle among them. (Some, through force of habit, at first tried to make their beds before leaving, said Dr. B.B. Gonzalez, acting hospital superintendent.) The Huntington Fire Department arrived to assist the village crew, which required more than two hours to put out the fire.

By morning's light, the third floor was gutted, the lower floors sustained water damage, and food supplies were lost. Damage was estimated at hundreds of thousands of dollars. After being initially gathered in to the men's ward and chapel areas, most of the displaced patients were temporarily accepted at Huntington, Lakin and Spencer while the hospital underwent repairs and improvements.

"Fire Chief Max Clay Describes Blaze, Business Manager John Queen Listens"
(Herald-Advertiser Photo courtesy of Huntington Public Library)

It was lost on nobody, including Chief Clay, that "it could have been a repetition of the 1952 fire at Huntington State Hospital." The Barboursville fire, which originated in a boiler room, occurred just two days before the tenth anniversary of the Huntington State Hospital fire, in which 17 women and girls perished.

"If it hadn't been for persistent fire drills, some people would have died," said Deputy State Fire Marshal C.A. Raper, of the rescue effort at Barboursville's overcrowded ward. Both Raper and Clay credited the hospital's longtime business manager, John Queen, for the hospital's state of preparedness. In its 1963 annual report, the West Virginia Department of Mental Health also recognized Queen's daughter Emily, "who proved herself a 14-year-old heroine" by assisting in the evacuation.

Less than 12 hours after the fire, the county mental health association and hospital volunteers, led by Mrs. Everett May, made a public appeal for donations to replace the clothing and "prized possessions" of the female patients. Explaining that nearly all the women kept dolls, the Cabell-Huntington Mental Health Association asked for small dolls to replace nearly 200 destroyed or damaged in the fire.

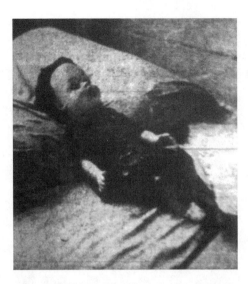

"This doll was the prize possession of one patient on the second floor
of the Barboursville State Hospital building damaged by fire.
The doll was left behind in the patient's flight to safety."
(Herald-Advertiser Photo courtesy of Huntington Public Library)

The "State Farm"

While people in Barboursville maintained some sense of connection with the hospital, another set of inmates toiled in obscurity a mile and a half away, in what must have seemed like the land that time forgot. Known by most townspeople only as the "state farm," the acreage just south of town was hidden away and inaccessible to the public. This mysterious parcel in West Virginia's institutional dominion served for more than three decades as a provider of food for Huntington State Hospital and other state facilities.

For about a century before that, the farm's hundreds of hilly acres served as a physical buffer between the southern edge of Barboursville and the northern side of the pastoral Martha community. Major George McKendree came into the possession of "Clover Valley Farm" in 1874 shortly after marrying Irene Octavia McComas. According to Frank Ball, the Major's farm "presented a fine, well kept appearance." It also served as a gateway from the village to the Martha Road farms where the Love, Moore, Rolf and Sanders families once kept "great flocks" of heavy-fleeced Southdown and Merino sheep on both sides of the county road. According to early landowner Charles Love, the area was graced by gigantic catfish swimming in the Guyandotte, "herds of fine Shorthorn cattle that grazed on the majestic hills and fertile valleys, smothering as it were in their fat. Also fine fat hogs that could scarcely walk."

After Major McKendree died in 1908, his 450-acre farm was purchased by road construction contractor C.O. Harrison. According to Frank Ball, Harrison was a first cousin twice removed from President William Henry Harrison. Contractor Harrison rented out the land until it was sold to the State of West Virginia in March 1935, to be used in connection with the Huntington State Hospital. A farm below it was also bought by the state, bringing the parcel to nearly 700 acres.

State Hospital Farm in 1942
(Courtesy of Barboursville Public Library)

The institutional pages of the annual West Virginia Legislature's *Blue Book* began providing fairly consistent descriptions of the farm beginning in 1942 *(when the above newspaper photograph was taken)*: "Thirty-two structures including residences, barracks for working patients, barns, storage houses, chicken houses, shops and many utility buildings have been provided on the farm." In 1952, the *Blue Book* stated that the "Huntington Hospital Farm is devoted to providing poultry, eggs, pork and milk for the patients at Huntington State Hospital. A registered herd of Holstein milk cows is maintained." In 1967, the farm continued to provide the hospital with pork and "an adequate supply of high-grade milk, processed in a pasteurizing plant fully approved by the State Board of Health." After 1967, no further mention was made in the publication about farm production for the Huntington State Hospital.

It would seem that the herd of Holsteins was the most enduring population on the farm, but what of these "working patients?" Who actually tended the cows, crops, pigs and chickens, besides young men of the 1935 "transient camp" who were hoping to get work with FDR's Civilian Conservation Corps? The 1940 Census shows two families living on the property, that of Huntington State Hospital Farm manager John Neel and gardener William A. Cook, as well as two men listed as hired hands. I have been told of other families who lived on the property to manage various farm operations in later decades.

What else can be known about the more transient human occupants? I might not have thought to ponder this but for the presence of an anachronistic two-story sandstone "guard shack" and observation deck at the community park. I still might have taken the *West Virginia Blue Book* at face value on the subject of the farm's "working patients," had it not been for two seemingly-random pieces of family information shared by my buddy Jill.

Jill grew up on Martha Road just a few hundred feet from the farm's southern boundary. She never knew much about what went on there. She did remember an uncle who worked there as a "warden" at the state farm. She also shared an early childhood memory from the early 1960s: "Prisoners escaped and came over the hill to our house on Martha Road. They hid across the street, then stole our car. I remember that it was the kind of car that could be started with a popsicle stick instead of a key. I was very young so my memory is vague. I do remember being sad that Mom couldn't take us swimming that day." Her older sister provided additional details, that the car was recovered after being found abandoned on a river bank with half a bottle of moonshine inside. After sharing this story with another local person who had farm family connections going back several decades, I heard of a similar incident involving high-jacking and hooch-making.

So what kind of inmates were we talking about here, patient inmates or prison inmates—jailbirds? How could people with severe mental illness pull off such a caper? Launched into detective mode by these revelations, I dug through statewide newspaper archives for clips of the Huntington State Hospital Farm at Barboursville, and was able to discover its origins:

March 9, 1943: With 6,000 acres of state-owned land available for cultivation this summer, the board of public works proposed to the legislature yesterday that it appropriate enough money to make state institutions self-supporting from a food standpoint. An item of $66,000 was included in a supplemental budget to buy fertilizer and equipment for the tilling of land during the war emergency...In cooperation with the federal government, the board proposed use of prison labor and any other available labor to grow as much food as possible in the coming season. (State Operated Gardens Proposed 1943)

I could not determine when state hospital labor gave way to correctional inmates at the Barboursville farm, or if patients ever actually handled the agricultural chores. The use of prisoners from the Huttonsville medium security prison near Elkins did take hold, though, and what began as a wartime austerity measure apparently became business-as-usual for West Virginia's institutional farms. Periodic state press reports of prisoner escapes and suspect behavior by government officials served as my trail of chronological breadcrumbs:

August 27, 1954: A man sentenced from 1 to 10 years by Kanawha County's Intermediate Court has escaped from a prison work farm near Barboursville, police reports showed yesterday. The convict was identified as Robert Paul Insford, 22, who was found guilty of breaking and entering. Prison authorities said the man's father lives at Hurricane and that an uncle lives in St. Albans. (Kanawha Man Escapes Barboursville Prison 1954)

September 1, 1954: Police are searching for Ezekial (Zeke) Myers, 22, of Charleston, who escaped yesterday from the Barboursville prison honor farm. Myers was acquitted on the latter charge after he was described as a "border-line mental case." ('Zeke' Myers Escapes From Prison Farm 1954)

July 1, 1958: William Racer, the captain of the guard which supervises Huttonsville Medium Security Prison trusties at the Huntington State Hospital farm, has been fired. Racer, a Boone County resident is being replaced by Dwight J .I. Orndoff of Arbovale. Racer's release was in connection with a new policy announced earlier by Institutions Commissioner Harold E. Neely. The policy is aimed at bringing supervisory personnel under control of the prison rather than the institution to which the trusties arc assigned on work details. The. policy was an outgrowth of an investigation by Neely into an alleged burglary ring that was being operated by five prison trusties from the Barboursville farm. (Associated Press 1958)

September 30, 1962: Two men who escaped from the Medium Security Prison's farm at Barboursville were lodged in the Kanawha County jail after being captured early Saturday by state police along U. S. 35 outside Charleston. . . Officers stopped a car being driven in a suspicious manner early today and arrested the men, who had fled Thursday night from the Barboursville institution. Both were serving one-to-10-year terms and had been assigned to duties at Barboursville State Hospital. (Two Escaped Inmates Held 1962)

April 25, 1967: BARBOURSVILLE, W.Va.—Police were still searching today for a 22-year-old Medium Security prisoner who escaped from a work detail at the Huntington State Hospital farm near here Monday. The escapee was Identified as Keith A. Bishop, serving a 1-10 year term from Kanawha County for breaking and entering. (Associated Press 1967)

As the 1960s progressed, overall stewardship of the old Clover Valley property became a matter of concern among at least one state government body:

October 28, 1965: State Agriculture Commissioner Gus Douglass has charged that the farms at some West Virginia mental institutions are being operated in a "haphazard" manner. The commissioner said Wednesday an investigation by his office, now being conducted, will continue at Weston and Barboursville State Hospitals, and agricultural operations at the state's correctional institutions will be reviewed in the near future. (United Press International 1965)

September 17, 1969: Gus R. Douglass, state commissioner of agriculture, is displeased with the method the Department of Mental Health used to dispose of a purebred dairy herd and blooded swine…"It almost amounts to a misappropriation of state funds," Douglass said…The 22 cattle at Barboursville State Hospital were sold on the livestock market at Point Pleasant April 6 for about $200 each. Their average value was placed at between $400 and $500, Douglass said and may have ranged up to $1,000 or more. The auctions and sales followed a recommendation by the governor's management task force that the Mental Health Department discontinued farming operations. (Associated Press 1969)

Eventually the land's function as a producer of food was found to be much less cost-effective than simply purchasing the food from outside vendors. In 1976, the Legislature transferred all West Virginia's institutional farms from the Commission of Public Institutions to the Department of Agriculture. By then, according to Frank Ball, the land lay "dormant and fallow."

I live on the avenue leading over to the State Farm. I saw a rustic gate swing across the entrance, a padlock put on it, and a lot of "No Trespassing" signs scattered about. Occasionally, I saw an ancient bus loaded with 25 or 30 people who likely hardly knew where they were going.. (F. Ball, Hospital Farm Move Sensible n.d.)

Even without the crops and livestock, the farm remained a "No Trespassing" zone. When the farm ceased operations, the buildings with all their furnishings were abandoned.

Advancements in Treating "The Other Ten Percent"

By the 1950s, some significant developments offered a ray of hope for Americans with mental illnesses. It would be too much to say the door immediately opened up for the patients to walk out and enjoy free lives in the community, but at least somebody was producing keys to the exit.

The first key was a national will to change the status quo after a million men had been rejected from service in World War II because of mental health problems. Forty percent of medical discharges from the armed forces had been for psychiatric disorders, the most common cause for rejection. After the war, half of disability pensions were for psychiatric problems. The number of mental patients had continued to rise with over 600,000 hospitalized for mental illness nation-wide. Investigators and reporters were publishing books and exposés about the poor conditions at state mental institutions across the country.

In 1946, President Truman signed the National Mental Health Act, creating the National Institute of Mental Health. Its mission was "to understand mind, brain, and behavior, and thereby reduce the burden of mental illness through research." With the Act's passage, the federal government began to issue grants to states for mental health services. This marked the first time that responsibility for treating and caring for individuals with mental health problems went beyond individual states and localities.

In 1954, another important key to freedom was introduced under the brand name Thorazine. The drug became one of the most widely used pharmaceuticals in mental institutions. Staff at Weston and other state psychiatric hospitals were shown films produced by the pharmaceutical manufacturers, as part of an educational effort to show the "miraculous" new treatments being offered. Antipsychotic medications began replacing the widespread use of shock treatments.

The effectiveness of Thorazine and other new drugs ended one of the darker periods in mental health history, "the lobotomy era." From 1948 to the mid-1950s, Dr. Walter J. Freeman made a number of visits to the state to operate and teach a ten-minute procedure he pioneered, the transorbital or "ice pick" lobotomy. Between the time Freeman introduced the prefrontal lobotomy and February 1967 (when his medical license was revoked), the zealous surgical pioneer traveled the nation in what he called his "lobotomobile" and performed more than 3,500 lobotomies (including one such procedure which left the sister of John F. Kennedy in a permanent infantile state). Freeman's life and work at state mental hospitals in West Virginia—where he performed about 150 lobotomies on patients at the isolated and under-resourced Lakin Hospital in Mason County—was featured in a documentary on PBS' nationally broadcast series, *The American Experience*.

Widespread use of the new psychoactive drugs made it possible not only to cease the practice of lobotomies and largely curtail electroshock therapy, but to increase discharges from state hospitals.

In 1955, Congress appropriated funds and passed the Mental Health Study Act of 1955. This second major federal initiative called for "an objective, thorough, nationwide analysis and reevaluation of the human and economic problems of mental health." The resulting Joint Commission on Mental Illness and Health issued a report which became the background for President John F. Kennedy's subsequent special message to Congress and the nation. JFK made the appeal "to arrive at a national program that would approach adequacy in meeting the individual needs of the mentally ill people of America."

The seeds planted by Congress in 1955 culminated in the Mental Retardation Facilities and Community Mental Health Centers Construction Act of 1963, beginning a new era in Federal support for mental health services. One Congressman said the community care plan would end "the warehousing of human beings" in vast and often overcrowded state mental institutions. In 1965, ten years after it authorized the mental health study, Congress provided appropriations for staffing the new community mental health centers.

One person is credited with doing more than any other individual in West Virginia to bring "full-time professional, non-political leadership" to the Department of Mental Health and open the doors to community mental health services in the state. Psychiatrist Mildred Mitchell-Bateman (1922-2012) came to West Virginia, worked for several years at Lakin Hospital, and became the first African-American woman to be named to a high-ranking office in West Virginia state government. In 1962, she became director of the Department of Mental Health and served in that capacity for 15 years. She is remembered as a trailblazer and an advocate for people with mental illness, and the Huntington State Hospital now bears her name.

Early on, Mitchell-Bateman advocated placing mentally ill patients at facilities nearest their homes and developing community mental health centers. Under her term as director, many state hospital patients were released. She is quoted as saying, "No one has a right to decide that patients aren't going to get any better." By the time she spearheaded a comprehensive mental health plan for the state, Mitchell-Bateman spoke out on the facts, chief among them that one in ten people has some form of mental or emotional illness and needs psychiatric treatment (a ratio that has remained constant through the years). In addition, she reported that about one-third of patients in the psychiatric hospitals were diagnosed as "mentally retarded."

Her department relied on regional planning meetings to address recommendations made by the first Governor's Conference of Mental Health in 1958, which had never been fully implemented due in part to West Virginia's economic woes at the time.

By1966, Mitchell-Bateman wrote, "Communities are moving rapidly toward organizing local services and about two-thirds of state's 55 counties are now providing some form of local mental health services." The comprehensive plan, as envisioned, would serve as a durable bridge between the state hospitals and community care. The goal was to supplement the state hospitals with a complex of local community and government services, both to "fight *against* mental illness" and "fight *for* mental health" with prevention, education and rehabilitation programs.

By this time, President Lyndon Johnson's "War on Poverty" legislation rivaled FDR's New Deal in the size and breadth of domestic federal aid. The enactment of Medicaid and Medicare was a major impetus in the movement toward "deinstitutionalization" of people with illnesses and disabilities; West Virginia realized $55 million in anti-poverty funding.

On the local front, the Cabell County Council for Retarded Children developed a four-county project on the former Lesage Tree Nursery, called the Green Acres Center for the Mentally Retarded. (For 28 years, Green Acres would serve my cousin Paula K. Brady who was born with Down Syndrome; I am certain the services she received there saved her from a "life sentence" in the state hospital and extended her lifespan far beyond mid-century expectations.)

By the end of 1960s, the flood of patients being admitted into the state hospitals finally receded. Though conditions were still overcrowded at Barboursville and the other facilities, things were improving:

> The growth of community health centers is another encouraging sign for reducing the number of patients in mental hospitals, Dr. Bateman said. She said the department now operates six full-time out-patient clinics and supervises 51 county programs. Dr. Bateman said the state's comprehensive mental health plan calls for the construction and staffing of 15 community mental health centers…one such at Elkins since 1966…another under construction near Huntington, will serve a three county area. (State Hospitals Treat More Despite 'Population' Decline 1969)

Under Mildred Mitchell-Bateman's watch, Barboursville State Hospital was poised for successful "de-hospitalization" of its most high-functioning patients.

Barboursville's Innovators

> "CAMP MAD ANTHONY WAYNE: It was a time of fun and games in the drab lives of 28 people who came here for a 10-day camping experience. They sang and danced and enjoyed the campfires. They did little chores, accepted new responsibilities. They ate heartily and slept well. No one got lost. No one got hurt. No one screamed in the middle of the night." (Morgan 1971)

Barboursville was the first hospital in West Virginia to try Sociotherapeutic Camping, an innovative "laboratory for change" patterned on programs in other states. Fifteen staff and five VISTA volunteers launched the camping program in 1967 with 32 Barboursville patients. Camps ranged from day trips to two-week programs. According to a summary in the *West Virginia Blue Book*, "The positive changes in patients were noticeable immediately. Patients who had not changed in years, began to respond. The therapeutic possibilities seemed unlimited."

In 1968, Governor Hulett Smith dedicated a new activities building at Barboursville State Hospital, and said that the state's mental hospitals "have been relieved of a tremendous burden. . . as a result of locally-provided services including counseling, diagnosis, treatment and rehabilitation." Barboursville was becoming a model for how to begin a sensible transition away from long-term institutional care.

In 1971, Charleston reporter John G. Morgan filed a two-part feature about the Sociotherapeutic Camping program. The campers from Barboursville State Hospital—during their stay at Camp Mad Anthony Wayne they were never called patients or "inmates"—aged from 34 to 64 years old. They were selected for their potential suitability for a new Patient Government Unit at the hospital. The 16 women and 12 men had been hospitalized for a decade or more, some for 30 years. The majority were diagnosed with mental illness, and the remainder with mental retardation.

The reporter accompanied state mental health director James McCullough in observing camp activities led by Mr. Paris Adkins, the hospital's recreation director. The staff included registered nurse Martha Waite, social worker William Dotson, and aides Don Mullins, Essie Chafin, Audrey Arthur and Clarice Dial. Morgan focused his story on eight specific campers, ranging from "a deeply depressed woman said to have lost six children" to "a smiling, slight, pale old fellow who used to teach music."

As the campers experienced life outside their crowded wards—they ate with knives and forks instead of using only spoons as in the hospital, sang around a campfire, danced and played games in the lodge, and selected their own group leaders—their staff counterparts supervised and observed, dispensed appropriate medications, and helped their "special people" break old behavior patterns. The overall purpose was to set up an atmosphere where independent thinking and decision-making would be encouraged in preparation for relocation to Barboursville's two-per-room "Self-Government Ward." Goals for the campers also included community involvement and ultimately supervised life outside the hospital.

Morgan followed up on the campers' progress at the end of the ten days.

The beautiful smile from the depressed woman was perhaps the most tangible evidence of the success of the camp. This bit of radiance was in sharp contrast to her sad face during the early part of the camping period. Paris Adkins, camp coordinator and recreation director here, said he felt that many of the patients had made noticeable improvements. Adkins said the patients had made an excellent adjustment in their new quarters. He said all quickly accepted their responsibility to keep their rooms clean and perform other tasks. "They take pride in their rooms," he said. "They have rearranged some of their furniture. Keeping the place clean is no problem." (Morgan 1971)

Based on the success of Barboursville's "laboratory for change," the state's six other mental institutions followed suit by 1974. That same year, the Department of Mental Health in its annual report recognized Barboursville's achievements, as well as its success in connecting patients with community mental health services:

> Barboursville State Hospital continues to serve a population of individuals whose condition is considered to be chronic and who have been transferred to this hospital from other state facilities. Despite the fact that this hospital serves essentially a hard-core chronic population, it has been been possible in the past three years to place 96 patients in extra-hospital settings. Several programs were initiated close to the end of the fiscal year...they include remotivation and re-socialization for patients, some adult basic education to improve their education level, and a number of group interaction programs designed to improve communication skills. (West Virginia Department of Mental Health 1973-74)

The downward trend in state hospitalizations continued, and the promise of a workable community mental health care system inched closer to reality in the late 1970s. Congress provided an added impetus with the passage of the Community Mental Health Center amendments of 1975. This was followed by an executive order by President Jimmy Carter to establish a commission to review the mental health needs of the Nation and then recommend how to best meet those needs.

In 1977, the Education for All Handicapped Children Act of 1975 was enacted. This federal law introduced the concepts of free appropriate public education, individualized education programs, least restrictive environment, and federal funding to provide for the education of children with disabilities. This law was perhaps the most significant development in bringing America's children with physical and mental disabilities out of the shadows, and keeping them from lives in institutions.

The policy of moving severely mentally ill people out of large state institutions and then closing part or all of those institutions became known as *deinstitutionalization*. This was based on the principle that mental illness should be treated in the least restrictive setting. The goal, the president said, was for individuals to "maintain the greatest degree of freedom, self-determination, autonomy, dignity, and integrity of body, mind, and spirit for the individual while he or she participates in treatment or receives services." Toward the end of Carter's four-year term, an unprecedented national field study gave an unprecedented picture America's mental and addictive disorders and service needs. In 1980, the Mental Health Systems Act—based on the report from the President's Commission on Mental Health—was passed by Congress.

By this time, however, the state decided Barboursville had served its 36-year purpose. In February 1978, new Governor Jay Rockefeller announced that the Barboursville State Hospital, called "the state's least efficient hospital" by the state department of health, would close its doors by the end of the year. Once a transition team determined how to relocate its 190 patients and 135 employees, the cluster of hilltop buildings stood empty once again.

"A Tradition of Financial Malnutrition"

In exploring Barboursville's role as a bit player in the state's institutional saga, one thing has become remarkably clear, and that is how decades of advocacy, scientific study and meticulous policy work on behalf of those with mental illness could be undone with the stroke of a pen.

As the state's pioneer mental health director, Dr. Mildred Mitchell-Bateman steered her vision of successful and supported deinstitutionalization through choppy and sometimes hostile bureaucratic waters. Federal government actions through the 1960s and 1970s provided a way to buoy up a mental health system that finally began to approach "adequacy." With the promise of an actual system of mental health prevention, intervention and treatment in American communities, hospitals like Barboursville did their part to speed up the de-institutionalization process, at least the half of the equation where people left the hospitals.

Then in 1981, with his presidential signature, Ronald Reagan essentially torpedoed the community "receiving" half of the de-institutionalization equation when he repealed the Mental Health Systems Act. Reagan's Omnibus Budget Reconciliation Act consolidated treatment and rehabilitation service programs into a single block grant that let each state administer its pot of funds however it saw fit. The federal role in services to the mentally ill was reduced to "technical assistance" for state and local providers of mental health services.

The 1981 budget act was just one more example of the same corner-cutting and short-changing that had been inflicted on Kirkbride's hospital plan a century earlier. Decade after decade, we have lived with the consequences of trying to do mental health care on the cheap. In 1953, Weston State Hospital ranked near the bottom nationally in almost every category measured to compare state mental institutions. Misappropriation and mismanagement of funds in many of the state institutions throughout the mid-century exacerbated problems, as did the fact that the hospitals served as a "dumping ground" for people without true mental illnesses. At one point, Dr. Mitchell-Bateman complained of food budgets that approached starvation levels.

In official reports preserved in the State Archives, her department attempted to maintain a hopeful tone, but amid the fiscal battles and the periodic eruptions of public outrage over hospital conditions, she told it like it was. She wrote in 1966 that "the daily maintenance expense per resident patient is little more than half the national average…the ratio of professional staff to patient is less than half the national average." Hitting the proverbial nail on the head, she added, "for the most part, the present situation can be traced to a tradition of financial malnutrition in these mental hospitals, resulting from lack of public concern and conviction that reasonable investments in services for the mentally ill can salvage a large portion of patients."

Barboursville State Hospital survived decades beyond its original intent as a "temporary receiving center" for Weston. Although its final years were marked by compassion for the people it served and innovations in care such as the therapeutic camping project, the facility also had its share of internal drama brought on by external forces.

Through years of substandard pay scales and chronic shortages of staff, the state improvised to get the work done. An additional set of administrative snags would spring from these "cost-saving measures." In 1966 for example, medium security prisoners were assigned to work at Barboursville Hospital. Their presence necessitated restrictions on outgoing mail, which somehow culminated in a series of letters from the state's Department of Public Institutions to journalist Bob Willis that were published in the *Raleigh Register*:

> Due to the obvious problem of censoring inmate mail, it is necessary to limit the amount of correspondence to and from the inmates. Inmates at Medium Security Prison assigned to State hospitals are permitted to write one free letter and two special letters a week to persons on their writing lists. We have attempted to relax the rule to provide for more exchange of correspondence between inmates and their families, but the relaxing of the rules resulted in an increased flow of mail between inmates and persons not on their writing lists.

> We have cases of inmates writing to the wives of other inmates in efforts to establish a relationship for the inmate who will soon be paroled. Other inmates write to girlfriends whose parents do not want the girls receiving such correspondence. Often, the content of the letter is highly objectionable. For example, correspondence relating to a planned escape cannot be allowed to go out of the institution. These are the reasons for the necessity of having a writing list for each inmate, and for limiting the amount of mail sent and received by the inmates. (Willis 1966)

Many of the physicians hired at bargain pay scales by West Virginia's state hospitals were graduates of foreign medical schools who had not passed qualifying exams to practice elsewhere in the United States. Subsequently there appeared flurries of news reports suggesting a veritable soap opera of cultural clashes, grievance procedures and reportedly petty behavior by the unlicensed physicians, including several husband-wife teams:

LAKIN. W.Va.—A physician at Lakin State Hospital who is being transferred to Barboursville State Hospital says he doesn't intend to go. Dr. Reynaldo Sotomayor claims he is being transferred because he filed a grievance against a superior at Lakin. James R. Clowser, Deputy director of administration for the state Department of Mental Health, said he understood that Sotomayor was being transferred because there was only one physician at the Barboursville institution. He said Dr. Sotomayor might be named acting clinical director at there. But Sotomayor described the transfer as "a slap in the face. I will starve before I will go to Barboursville," he said. Dr. Adoracion Sotomayor, his wife, was suspended without notice for a week in May because she allegedly called a superior a liar. (Associated Press 1974)

The last superintendent at Barboursville State Hospital, Dr. George Pozega, was embroiled in departmental controversy during his first years. As a result of low morale and high employee turnover, staff members organized a petition. (Among various complaints was that he tried to get rid of the "patients' mascot, a pet named Mama Cat," who lived on the grounds for many years.) Eventually, things settled down, Dr. Pozega stayed on, and the hospital stayed out of the headlines.

Then came Governor Rockefeller's February 1978 announcement that the state would save $600,000 by closing the hospital and putting the savings toward a new state veterans home. At the time, Barboursville was ruled out as a location for the veterans facility due to "the antiquated nature of the buildings," according to the governor's spokesperson.

Eight months later, Rockefeller would change his mind.

Balloons, Hospitals and Jails

According to Dr. E. Fuller Torrey, author of the 1997 book *Out of the Shadows: Confronting America's Mental Health Crisis,* "the magnitude of deinstitutionalization of the severely mentally ill qualifies it as one of the largest social experiments in American history." Thirty-five years after the closing of Barboursville State Hospital, the village is once again an institutional town, due in part to the haphazard nature of America's deinstitutionalization "experiment."

By 2003, America had experienced a 50-year decline in pubic psychiatric hospital beds, from 560,000 to 53,000. Cabell County did a laudable job opening its first community mental health and mental retardation programs so Barboursville's last patients to be transitioned had more options than most (and the county continues to have many dedicated professionals and human service agencies providing excellent services in the community). But for those diagnosed with severe mental illnesses and intellectual/developmental disabilities after deinstitutionalization went into effect, the number of long-term options are limited.

What's more, the community prevention and education programs envisioned in the National Mental Health Systems Act to reduce stigma and promote effective early treatment were eliminated before they ever had a chance to take root.

The state enthusiastically tackled the task of eliminating hospital beds, including all of Barboursville's. By 1997, West Virginia led the nation as one of eight states with "effective deinstitutionalization rates of over 95 percent," a number that adjusts for general population changes. With advances in psychopharmacology and behavioral treatment methods, this reversal in the use of "beds" as treatment should be considered a good thing, and it would be if funding of these less restrictive treatment options had been embraced with the same zeal by funders and policymakers.

On the contrary, research by Jacks showed that community mental health funding in the state suffered serious cutbacks. In the late 1990s, state agencies were accused of mismanagement of federal funds for community health care and told to repay ten million dollars. Medicaid, which was supposed to be used for "medical necessities" like doctor visits and prescription drugs, had been used for social programs such as running group homes where the mentally ill lived with supervision, and operating day treatment centers where clients learned life skills such as how to shop, cook, and make a budget. Rather than repay the federal debt and continue these promising approaches, the state agreed to drastically cut back on Medicaid funds used and turned the mental health payment system over to a managed care company, so the state lost about 40 percent of its funding.

With closed group homes and fewer caseworkers to assist clients, other systems filled the void. General hospitals increasingly began treating the mentally ill, some of whom would show up in emergency rooms several times a week. Increased homelessness and incarceration would also follow, as was predicted nearly 75 years ago by social scientists.

A 1939 study showed that European prison and psychiatric hospital populations were inversely correlated—as one rose, the other fell. This study gave rise to "the balloon theory." The premise (sometimes called "Whack-a-Mole," based on the fun arcade game) is simple: push in one part of a system and another part will bulge out. An extensive analysis of data on United States mental hospitals, jails and prisons for the years between 1904 and 1987 validated the balloon theory, according to Torrey. In 1995, he projected that at least ten percent of 483,717 inmates in jails and 1,104,074 inmates in state and federal prisons in the United States—approximately 160,000 people—were severely mentally ill.

Others have found that number to be too conservative. According to Jacks, more than a fourth of the prisoners in West Virginia's regional jails were treated for mental health problems in 2004, prompting one high-level corrections official to go on record saying, "De-institutionalization is a myth. We took them out of mental institutions, put them out on the street, and again and again, they've ended up in our jails."

In 1999, ground was broken for the latest institution to reshape Barboursville's physical and social landscape. Like the Barboursville Unit of Weston State Hospital, the Western Regional Jail filled up quickly. In 2004, West Virginia's psychiatric hospitals were once again full and the state had to spend $3.5 million dollars to have a thousand patients treated for mental problems at private facilities. So in a sad twist (fueled in part by rising drug crime), "Institutional Barboursville" is once again on the map, and in the newspapers, with daily reports of bookings at the regional jail.

Post-millennial Barboursville seems to have come full circle from its early years. Instead of poor farms and county lock-ups, however, twenty-first century West Virginia looks to its overcrowded jails and prisons, hospital emergency rooms and homeless shelters as the catch-all for its "classes of broken humanity."

What Might Have Been

Governor Rockefeller's announcement to close the Barboursville State Hospital left leaders once again to wring their hands, search their souls and explore other possibilities for the property.

Mayor Ted Kirk and county commissioner Bill Dunfee said they would like to see a "first class home for the elderly," to relieve the waiting list for senior high rises in Huntington. Somebody approached Marshall University about the property's use for School of Medicine, but M.U.'s spokesperson replied that they were "not interested at this point" and would "have to take a long, hard look at it." The State Department of Health said it was tentatively approached by some unnamed judges who suggested the grounds could be used as a home for delinquent youngsters.

Before any of these plans came to fruition, the Governor had a change of heart. After an October tour of the facility, Jay Rockefeller announced that the old state hospital "is an ideal site for the first veteran's home in West Virginia."

The *Herald-Dispatch* reported Jay's pronouncement after he strolled the grounds with hospital director George Pozega, veteran's group representatives and local dignitaries: "...the beautiful thing about Barboursville is that it won't cost that much money to turn this into an outstanding home," said Rockefeller. "A little paint and some minor repair work and this can be an excellent veteran's facility." Either it was one outstanding tour, or the governor's mind had been opened after his first few months in office. No other sites were thereafter considered for the home, which opened in Barboursville in 1981.

As for the neglected ground of the state hospital farm, it lay idle for more than a decade. Several officials had designs on the property, but opportunity would disappear as mysteriously as the auctioned dairy cows. The state's Comprehensive

Mental Health Plan of 1966 would have merged the Barboursville hospital and the farm:

> It is planned to convert this hospital into a residential facility for adult retarded, a change which can be accomplished with very little modification in the present program. A number of community family-type residences should be constructed on the farm near the hospital, each housing not more than ten patients, with facilities for approximately 130 in all. Patients selected will be those retarded who show potential for independent living...opportunity to live and learn in a family setting...(would include a) sheltered workshop facility, as well as vocational training and extra-hospital placements, and reduce service area from one which embraces the entire state to an eight-county region in the southwestern section. (West Virginia Department of Mental Health 1966)

Around the time of the hospital's closing, Frank Ball lamented the lack of action surrounding the state farm property, especially when there was such a shortage of parks and recreational facilities in the area. He reported about an inspired effort to transform the old farm for the greater public benefit :

> Several times since the State Hospital came into the ownership of the Barboursville State Hospital moves and suggestions have been made to turn it into something profitable, or at least, worthwhile. The greatest most forceful and most widespread effort was made in 1969 when men like Judge Ferguson of Wayne and Bill Dunfee of the Cabell County Commission along with others, held several assemblies in Barboursville and plans were made for a park that would have rivaled the 750-acre Oglebay Municipal Park at Wheeling.

> This move was backed by the local Lions Club, the Southwestern County Fair Association, the Saddle Club, several Huntington business firms, and it was rumored that the International Nickel Company was interested in putting money into it as a recreational place for their employees.

> Planned were a fairground, golfing course, skeet shooting, Olympic swimming pool, tennis courts, lakes and fishing, boating, hiking trails, bridle trails, horseshoe pitching, ball diamonds, gridirons, youth group meeting places: 4-H, FFA, FHA and others; garden clubs, forestry camp, exhibits of glass, antiques, etc.; a lodge, cabins, an assembly hall, industrial exhibits, Isaac Walton League meetings, fairground facilities; tours; farm exhibits – the list of proposed units was a long one.

> The director of Oglebay Park was called down to assess the physical probabilities. . .We had the rolling hills, the forested woodland, the bottom land, and overall, enough land.

Whereupon, four men: Dr. Wm. Sadler, George Cole (who trod the acres all as a boy when his father was overseer of the acreage for the state), Mayor Don Owens, and Phillip Vallandingham, went to Wheeling to look over Oglebay and get data as to its construction, cost and financing.

The men returned with a glowing report and set off for Charleston to see Governor Moore. He was sympathetic but felt that a long lease of the land from the state rather than outright purchase was the best course. They then returned to Barboursville to find that the hospital director had given notice that they had recreational plans of their own.

Thus did the long energetic planning for a park that would have rivaled Wheeling's come to naught.

Barboursville's plan were even greater than those that culminated in the creation of Oglebay Park. Among other extras was a footbridge across the Guyandotte that groups meeting at the 4-H Club grounds across the river could avail themselves of the privilege of the use of the park.

I am informed by one of the committee that there was set aside at that time $9,000,000…for parks and recreational facilities in West Virginia if used at once. It wasn't. So instead of a park known and used by people throughout the state and beyond, we have 679 acres of neglected land serving no purpose at all… With our hospital leaving us, the time to move toward putting something on the acreage left behind is now. (F. Ball, Hospital Farm Move Sensible n.d.)

The Barboursville Community Park, as a slightly less spectacular realization of earlier visions, would not be developed until after Ball's death.

In 1987, before transferring ownership of most of the old state farm to Barboursville, the Department of Agriculture reserved a patch of land on the property to accommodate the psychiatric residential treatment of adolescents. The Barboursville School, operating under the auspices of Joint-Commission-accredited River Park Hospital, is a reputable facility which fills a vital niche in West Virginia's service continuum for young people with the most serious mental health needs.

In 2013, the village of Barboursville embodies the opposite of "NIMBY-ism" or the "not in my back yard" mentality (to use an acronym from the 1980s that describes public opposition to undesired construction in a neighborhood). River Park Hospital's adolescent mental health facility sits peacefully in the field of vision of path walkers, fishing enthusiasts, little league families and pickup basketball players on the grounds of the community park. The West Virginia Veterans Home provides shelter on the hill for all manner of otherwise-homeless men after they have served our country. The regional jail, as well as the Robert L. Shell juvenile detention center, overlook Merritt's original grist mill site north of the Mud River. In a time when economic development is king, and in a place with a tradition of unquestioning service and patriotism, there is no record of villagers collectively kicking up a fuss over any of these state government assets.

As a relatively placid, docile and accepting twenty-first century community, Barboursville in 2013 remains an institutional mainstay for the region and the state.

There is a conclusion, if not an answer, to the question posed at the beginning of this unexpectedly long and sad chapter—why would a thinking person put a state mental hospital on the same property as a junior high school?

It turns out, I suppose, to be a trick question. Certainly, no single thinking person would have done so. Judging by the records that have been unearthed here, every official decision concerning the opening, operation and closing of the Barboursville State Hospital and the "state farm" seems to have been the result of political expediency and happenstance.

Nearly two centuries after the crusade of Dorothea Dix, true mental health care—the practice of helping every man, woman and child with mental, emotional and behavioral challenges to realize their full potential—is still an uncharted American frontier. Unfortunately, protection and care of the vulnerable will never be a profit-making concern.

As a lesser body in the constellation of "State Charitable and Corrective Institutions," the village served as the end of the line for a subgroup of West Virginia patients. Barboursville State Hospital had the task of caring for men and women who were considered too far gone for anything but institutional life.

What the hospital and surrounding community provided for 36 years was a spirit of compassionate independence in the face of meager resources and low expectations. The employees and volunteers of the Barboursville State Hospital—like their county "poor farm" predecessors and their overwhelmed contemporaries at Huntington, Lakin, Spencer and Weston—were good people who did the best they could with what little was provided.

Many were unsung heroes to those who depended on them.

Our Special Correspondent Furnishes an Interesting Letter (1898-1901):
FROM BLUE SULPHUR – A trio of our young people were buggy-riding
Sunday when in about two miles of home, the buggy broke down, and the result
was they had to walk home.

CHAPTER 16

TEENAGE WASTELAND (1960S-1970S)

Adolescence on the Outskirts

I N the 1970s, the crest of the wave of Baby Boomers entered the Clearasil Generation, and Barboursville High School landed on West Virginia's Top Ten in secondary school enrollment.

Five days a week during the school year, students outnumbered village residents. Buses carried about 2,700 children and teens from the unincorporated areas of Salt Rock, Guyan Estates, East and West Pea Ridge, Green Valley, Lesage and part of Ona. At the end of each school day and throughout the summer, most of those kids inhabited the rural routes and subdivisions, where life moved at a snail's pace.

Full disclosure: this is the point in the Lost Village timeline where local history merges with autobiography. Certainly, my take on the world a school bus ride away from Barboursville reflects my experience as a culture-shocked Indy-to-Ona transplant. Where posterity is concerned though, it doesn't matter whether it is my story or that of any young person with a view of life just outside Barboursville in the 1970s. Like Mildred McKendree Henderson's girlhood remembrances of the late nineteenth century, or Fred Lambert's early Turnpike vignettes, a coming-of-age portrait of eastern Cabell County life "Before The Mall" evokes quaint, bygone days.

I don't want the chapter title to leave the impression that Tri-State summers were a stone cold bummer. There were definite high points, and Baby Boomer kids had access to some pretty exciting attractions within five miles of the village.

There were triple features at the East drive-in movie theater (*Meatballs, Oddballs* and *Screwballs*, anyone?) and skating parties at Altizer's Whirling Wheels. Seasonal weekend favorites included miniature golf courses, some public swimming pools, early NASCAR venue International Raceway Park, and of course the "Tri-State's Favorite Playground" Camden Park, a nostalgic favorite.

For one brief shining moment we had "the Sears Slicky-Slide." Before the advent of water parks, this gigantic version of a children's playground slide provided burlap mats that riders held onto while swooping down their individual lanes, catching air as they bumped over a series of vertical drops. After a similar slide at Ohio's brand new Kings Island theme park was made famous in the opening montage of TV's *Banana Splits* show, similar slides were installed in locations across the United States. Huntington's version stood several stories high across the parking lot from Sears on 29th Street. It was to be short-lived; a critical mass of friction burns, bruised tailbones and other liabilities brought down these great American attractions.

When family vacation time was over, my contemporaries and I settled into Cabell County's version of the suburban summer routine—lounging on sculptured shag carpets glued to the TV, hanging on the end of a phone cord talking with friends, playing record albums on a big piece of furniture called the console stereo, washing the dishes before our moms got home from work, or spending drowsy visits watching *Concentration* or *The Lawrence Welk Show* with our grandparents. On balance, however, most of our waking hours outside of school involved searching for something to do within the confines of the subdivisions.

My corner of the outskirts was Indian Meadows, four miles east of the village along the banks of the Mud River. It is where I spent eight years of adolescence after my parents moved us back from Indianapolis. The little community was separated from U.S. Route 60 by a one-lane concrete tunnel under the C&O track, as well as a rusty and rackety steel bridge over the Mud River. The houses (roughly 200 of them in the original development) conformed to four different suburban floor models, including the ever-popular ranch and split-level, and sat close together on manageable lawns. The homes were in demand by parents who wanted their kids in the desirable Nichols-Ona-Barboursville school district.

A few miles west of the Ona Unincorporated sign, Indian Meadows was something of a demographic island. The development was populated with both returning West Virginians and non-native families, some with out-of-state or even foreign accents. As children of these "outsider" families, we were in our own world socially as well. Most of our classmates who got on the bus at Cyrus Creek and Blue Sulphur were different, more rural and from families who had occupied their respective hills and "hollers" for generations.

Indian Meadows Advertisement. The Setzer company advertised daily tours of model homes in eastern Cabell County's newest subdivision in July 1967.
(The Herald-Advertiser)

When our motley school-bus contingent made the transition from junior high to high school, we were thrown in as virtual strangers at BHS, after being pulled away from the majority of our Ona classmates who lived in the Milton High School district. Like our counterparts from Beverly Hills, Cox Landing and Salt Rock junior high schools, Indian Meadows students comprised a "third tier" of connectedness with our Barboursville peers. (Pea Ridge, Martha and Davis Creek kids would have been the "second tier" classmates, having attended junior high with the Barboursville Elementary students, who in turn had known each other since they had baby teeth. These anthropologic dynamics were never acknowledged, but in the flush of teenage insecurity they mattered.)

The Indian Meadows subdivision was created in the late 1960s by the same folks who divided the larger Thornburg farm into the 420 housing lots of Guyan Estates. The Guyan Estates land deed dictated that a neighborhood trustee be appointed by the bank board to see that streets were taken care of, and residents paid a small annual "street maintenance fee." The neighborhood boasted a swimming pool and an active community center. In a feature in the *Advertiser,* the community was described by its residents as close-knit.

Essentially, Indian Meadows was a smaller, newer, hillier version of Guyan Estates, but without trustees, a neighborhood association, ball fields, playgrounds or a swimming pool. It might have been a real estate developer's dream, but it wasn't a planned community in any real sense beyond home construction. Our amenities included a nondescript "community building," a neglected basketball court and not much else.

For adolescent children of two working parents—which itself was a new thing historically—dependable recreation options in the wasteland between Barboursville and Ona were few. The neighborhood didn't ever seem to have enough boys or girls in the same grade to sustain a scout troop. One enthusiastic adult tried to start a teen youth group at the community building in the early 1970s, but interest quickly faded after suspicions arose that he was running an Amway marketing scheme. One girl's dad organized a rural softball league, but it fizzled after one very short season.

The closest church was old Mud River Baptist, not exactly a hub for newcomers. Unlike Barboursville and Pea Ridge, Ona had no bus service so it was rare to take a trip all the way to Huntington outside of orthodontist appointments or special occasion shopping trips. Older youth with cars could get to either Snak Shak, Pizza Hut or Burger Chef to see and be seen. Otherwise, a young person could walk the big circle of the subdivision, up Cheyenne Trail and down Iroquois, or vice-versa. Like the unleashed neighborhood dogs, we roamed in small packs of two or three.

Weekends and summers on the outskirts left plenty of time for creative time-wasting. Then as now, when unsupervised young teens put their heads together, they sometimes followed their more adventurous impulses. There might be an attempted rowboat ride on the Mud River, or a climb up to the rock cliff that overlooked the community building and sewage works. With no barrier between us and the cliff's sheer 30-foot vertical drop, I found it remarkable that nobody had ever fallen or leapt to their doom on the hard ground below. Fortunately, Indian Meadows kids of the early Seventies were a fairly risk-averse lot. A few times we were able to put enough opposite-sex classmates together to throw an innocent but thrilling spin-the-bottle party in someone's garage or basement, but that was about as daring as things got in those days.

In nice weather, a half-day hike to the Ona countryside was an option (whether our parents knew it or not). Before the advent of joystick-guided travel through virtual mazes and lands, we laced up our Converse All-Stars or desert boots and improvised. The county's Boy Scouts might have had the impressive 32-mile Kanawha Trace hiking trail, but girls like me never knew anything about it. Pea Ridge boys and girls had their treks from Tallwood Acres to the "Dead Man's Desert," an expansive bulldozed and abandoned field that eventually was developed into Timberlake. My Barboursville cousins sought out "Jesse James's Cave." Surely the kids in Colonial Village and Williamsburg Colony had their own secret haunts. The exotic destinations for Indian Meadows kids followed the Mud River or the C&O.

My seventh-grade best friend Linda and I once packed some picnic snacks and made an exploratory journey to "Mohican Rock." To get there, one followed a weeded path which led under the I-64 bridge, then along the bank of the Mud River, over the slippery rocks in the shallows, to the present-day site of Blue Sulphur's Olde Farm Village. The rock formation discovered there was so named because it looked like a rugged Native American face in profile. The spot was probably a little more than a mile from our houses, but it might as well have been a world away. Once we arrived at our destination that afternoon, Linda and I found fresh evidence that it had been used as a place to drink alcohol, smoke cigarettes and who knows what else. Suddenly realizing we were two girls alone and out of earshot of civilization, we debated about what it all meant and concluded we were in the presence of an unseen sinister element. We scarfed down our provisions (probably Fluffer-Nutters and Fresca) then high-tailed it back along the river bank to our safe and familiar slab streets.

For those too young to drive, beautiful fall Saturdays inspired untold excursions on foot along the graveled C&O tracks from Blue Sulphur Gardens to Malcolm Springs, the other sizeable subdivision in our school district. This nifty shortcut to our friends' houses required a daring sprint across the Howell's Mill railroad trestle, a discovery that made it a one-time journey for my eighth-grade best friend "Donahue" and me. (Several months later, my blood ran cold after learning that a younger boy was killed during a similar hike when a fast-moving train struck him, flinging his body into the Mud River.)

By babysitting around the neighborhood, my friends, sisters and I were able to earn spending money. There were few places to spend it. The only consumer attraction within walking distance was the Blue Sulphur Market, which had a few groceries, some snacks and a Slush Puppy machine. For a few exciting junior high summers there was an ice cream truck that came around, operated by a really hunky driver-vendor whose recalled image brings to mind a young Billy Ray Cyrus. (I wonder how many other females planned their summer wardrobes around the popsicle man's route schedule like Donahue and I did.)

As we grew from junior high to high school students, my neighborhood companions and I continued to do countless other foolish things to relieve the tedium of life on the outskirts. Suffice it to say that nearly all of us survived and eventually matured.

The Roots of Suburban Sprawl

Indian Meadows kids comprised just a handful—less than one busload—of the "suburban" students who packed into Barboursville when school was in session. Our self-contained community was just one example of the area's market-based, developer-driven sprawl—instant rural settlements designed without consideration to the restless nature of young people who lived in them.

The epitome of this trend would be Pea Ridge. A densely-populated crazy quilt of small and large developments, the unincorporated neighborhood swallowed up most of the real estate around the old Kanawha Road "hog trail." The area began attracting "local people (who) thought they were moving to the boondocks" after World War II, according to C.D. Whitling, a man who built two small subdivisions there, Larchmont and Pembrooke. (True to the pattern, my dad's parents purchased a section of the old Wilson Dairy Farm on the main road and moved from Huntington's Highlawn Avenue in 1950.) By 1975, the unincorporated area had three times the population of Barboursville's—7,400 residents spread over 2.4 square miles. Pea Ridge was more populous than at least one West Virginia county.

Despite its relatively affluent homeowners, reputable grade school and progressive churches, Pea Ridge of the 1970s was beset by such rural inconveniences as spotty garbage service, inadequate sewage treatment and biting dogs. There weren't even any fire hydrants until a fund drive was conducted by the Women's Club to pay for them. In November 1975, the area was dubbed an "urban planner's 'I told you so' community" by *The Advertiser*, due to a number of ills that were the result of willy-nilly development without community planning or zoning laws.

As the building boom continued on the Ridge, land which might have been set aside for recreational use was gobbled up by development. The playground behind Pea Ridge Elementary was not of much community use since it required a hazardous walk along the narrow, blind curves of Mahood Drive. When the energy crisis hit, the president of the Women's Club said the neighborhood's parents were getting "tired of car-pooling it like crazy to the YMCA downtown." Huntington "Y" executives made noises about developing a small branch in the Pea Ridge-Barboursville area, but nothing came of it.

"Something for the Youth to Do"

Compared to the outskirts, Barboursville's recreational offerings were something to envy. The Criss Theater might have been long empty, but Barboursville had school athletic fields and tennis courts, a public library, a little league baseball field, and sidewalks.

Barboursville's elected officials continually raised the issue of providing "something for the youth to do." It was an ongoing campaign theme during the biannual village elections, but the lack of revenue required town leaders to be creative on a miniscule budget.

Considering that the polluted rivers no longer attracted swimmers, town leaders of the late 1950s and early 1960s saw the construction of a swimming pool as a "must," according to Frank Ball. After a Huntington architect set the price of construction at $64,000—a price beyond Barboursville's budget, even with help from the county commission—volunteers took on the job. By the summer of 1961, William Turman began having concrete poured for a 45-by-90-foot pool on the west side of the old cemetery. Materials and labor (including a railroad caboose for office and storage use) were either provided at cost or donated by men including Gus Stackpole, Jack Burton, William and Lester Roy. With support from other volunteers and two successive mayors, Jess Henderson and Emmett Mahaffey, the pool was completed at about two-thirds of the projected cost.

In addition to the seasonal attraction of a swimming pool, the nucleus of organized youth activity was Barboursville, as well as points south and west:

> We have the Boys' Club, the Boy Scouts, Girl Scouts, Brownie Scouts, Cub Scouts, four school 4-H Clubs and Rheta Keefer's Moonshiners 4-H Club; Pea Ridge is loaded with Scout troops meeting in the Pea Ridge United Methodist Church apparently. Barboursville and its area are organized to the hilt and seemingly have enough force to keep them all in motion.

> Little League baseball was set in motion in the spring of 1954...Since then other leagues have been formed, the Pee Wee League, the Babe Ruth League, the Minor Babe Ruth League, and the girls softball leagues, Major and Minor.

Young people whose parents did not shepherd them into 4-H, scouting and ball teams often went without such wholesome outlets. Tapping into this need, a newly-evangelistic branch of modern Christians sought to fill the recreational (and spiritual) void in the early 1970s. "Jesus rock" hit the scene, with long-haired bands occasionally touring churches and even local schools (I still have my autographed George King and the Fellowship *Shine* album from 1976).

When Fellowship Baptist church was newly established one mile east of Barboursville in June 1972, its outreach seemed geared to the youth of the subdivisions regardless of whether their parents were churchgoers. The new church had a bus to pick up kids from nearby neighborhoods, and advertised special incentives such as free Yo-Yo's. The large block building it occupied, however, had a secular past that could not quite be erased. For years it seemed, the bricked front and steeple could not mask the chapel's free-spirited heritage, bleeding through in huge capital letters that filled each of the ten cinderblock sections of the outside wall: H. U. L. L. A. B. A. L. O. O.

Digging (Up) the 'Sixties: From Street Dances to "Kaleidelic" Experiences

The years (and additional coats of paint) may have masked the sanctuary's past, but its origin as "TV's Hullabaloo Scene" dance club reveals that eastern Cabell County had a groovy streak. The village block parties and "street dances" of the late 1960s that preceded Oktoberfest/Fall Fest were a relatively inexpensive way to entertain the teenagers of the town and keep them out of trouble. They may have also inspired a local entrepreneur to cash in on the "youthquake."

My cousin Jeff remembers marveling at the first outdoor teen scene on the streets of Barboursville, where young folks thrashed about joyfully, doing the jerk and the pony to Martha Reeves and the Vandellas' "Dancing in the Street" and other hits of the day. Parents standing witnesss probably tapped their feet and smiled at the fact that their kids were having good clean fun and would sleep like babies that night. Somebody else took in what was going on in Barboursville and hundreds of other American towns, and saw dollar signs.

That someone was a New England businessman who purchased the rights to a name from NBC Television, shortly after its *Hullabaloo* show was cancelled in 1966. For those readers too young (or too square) to remember, *Hullabaloo* was one of two prime time "rock 'n' roll" shows to air in the mid-1960s (the other was ABC's *Shindig*) featuring popular recording artists who lip synced their current hits. Such iconic acts as the Supremes, Sonny and Cher and the Beatles appeared on the show. Performing behind each week's guest star was a troupe of ten frenetically-choreographed hipsters known as the Hullabaloo Dancers. One particular long-haired blonde danced in a cage each week as part of a segment called "Hullabaloo A-Go-Go."

When *Hullabaloo* was taken off its Monday 7:30 p.m. time slot (replaced in the fall of 1966 by a new youth-oriented comedy called *The Monkees*), Connecticut's John Angel saw an opportunity to strike Go-Go gold in the heartland, as reported in *Life* magazine:

The beauty of the idea is its simplicity: Take a big, empty barn, charge a dollar admission, self soft drinks in paper cups for a quarter, and have strict but minimal adult supervision. What happens is happy pandemonium: 800 kids, elbow to elbow, dancing themselves silly. (Youth/What They Need Is a Place To Go 1966)

Angel and a partner set up Teen Clubs International, Inc., and started advertising in business publications, offering franchise packages for $15,000 to $20,000 to entrepreneurs willing to open the teen clubs two nights a week. A 1967 full-page ad in *Billboard* magazine described what was provided in the franchise packet: signage, interior décor, a sound system, advertising, community relations and the all-important ingredient of musical talent:

THE HULLABALOO SCENE is not just a discotheque. Live talent will play the HULLABALOO circuit. Booking is done on a national basis. Big stars, too, will be making personal appearances from time to time at each Hullabaloo Scene. AND AT EVERY OPENING OF HULLABALOO— THE HULLABALOO DANCERS PLUS A MAJOR ROCK 'N ROLL STAR. (Teen Clubs International, Inc. 1968)

In 1967, there were about 250 Hullabaloo Scene clubs nationwide. In 1968, Barboursville got in on the action. The identity of the local licensee remains a Lost Village history mystery to this writer, but based on TCI's advertised standards, it was someone with "the highest degree of business ethics, flawless personal character references, and highest moral values."

In mid-May, *The Herald-Dispatch* carried the club's grand opening ad, complete with a photo of the *Hullabaloo* dancers and the following pronouncement:

Hey kids…from this day on there is a place for you…At HULLABALOO. It's a night club strictly for YADS that's really a groovy kind of fun. With your kind of music, your kind of entertainment, your kind of socializing…and your kind of people—YAD people. There are soft drinks, live music, records, special big name stars and plenty of fun for everyone.

*YAD means Young Adult—14 to 20. (Teen Clubs International, Inc. 1968)

If the Civil War re-enactors take a break from the Battle of Barboursville, or space is otherwise opened up on the village social calendar for another tribute to "way-back" times, I have a suggestion. By calling out for all the Ex-YADS who attended that Grand Opening, perhaps the glorious moments of May 17 and 18, 1968 could be re-created: Customers following the simple but strict Teen Club rules: "no liquor on your breath; wear what you like but don't be a slob; maintain your cool." Original TV *Hullabaloo* Dancers Peggy and Mickey showing off their moves to the excited clientele, followed by regional interpretations of "the frug," "the watusi" and "the swim" on full display. The event could be capped by the advertised "Kaleidelic Light Show," followed by a faithfully lip-synced tribute to the "Decca Recording Stars from New York"—Peppermint Rainbow—performing their new tracks.

Reminiscent of the harmonious soft rock of Spanky and Our Gang (the music group, not the 1930s movie urchins), Peppermint Rainbow is described by various rock historians as a "sunshine pop group from Baltimore that formed in 1967." The two-girl, three-guy ensemble cracked the Billboard Top 40 in 1969 with the title song from their only album, *Will You Be Staying After Sunday.* (A YouTube clip of their performance must be seen for the hair and matching costumes alone). The group may be most recognized for their Top 100 track "Don't Wake Me Up in the Morning, Michael." Unfortunately, details of the Peppermint Rainbow's West Virginia encounters and their weekend stay in Barboursville (whether at the Gateway Motel, Stone Lodge, or sleeping on a tour bus) never made the local newspapers, much less the pages of *Sixteen* or *Tiger Beat.*

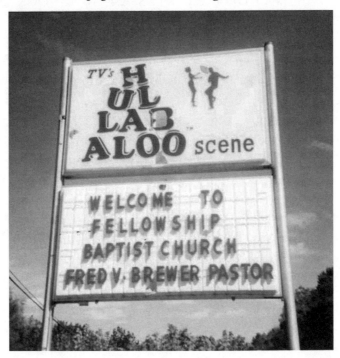

The first church sign at 3661 US Route 60 East in 1972
(Courtesy of Helen Alexander, Fellowship Baptist Church)

As a live music venue, Barboursville's Hullabaloo Scene entertained Tri-State youth for at least two years. In its first year, the club featured at least one other hit-making band, the Lemon Pipers of "Green Tambourine" fame. On most weekends, though, the club hosted regional bands that also made the rounds to places like Kenova's Dreamland Pool and Chesapeake's Riverside Club. The Hullabaloo also hosted private events such as the Milton High School Class of '69 after-prom.

A few of the area bands booked at Hullabaloo in its first heady year also recorded 45-RPM records that received airplay on WKEE Radio. Wearing matching ensembles that evolved from suits, to Nehru jackets and love beads, to star-and-stripes pullovers and fringed vests, the following groups offered up a buffet of Top 40 dance covers, original garage rock, James Brown-style soul and swirling keyboard jams: The Explosive Dynamiks, a racially-integrated rock and soul band from Huntington that released a hot track called "Whole Lotta Loving;" The Satisfied Minds, a Marshall University-based group that recorded "I Can't Take It;" The Outcasts from Ashland, Kentucky who got on the Billboard charts with "Loving You Sometimes;" King James and the Royal Jesters from Point Pleasant; and the Lovin' Kind from Ashland. (Happily, several of these bands' records have been uploaded to YouTube for your listening pleasure.)

As evidenced by a list of gig dates posted by "Battle of the Bands" winner Pegasus (on their tribute website *Pegasus Rocks)*, Cabell County's Hullabaloo club was open until at least April 18, 1970.

By the time my family moved back in the summer of 1971, the teen scene magic disappeared from "U.S. Route 60 near the Ona interchange." The Swingin' Sixties "discotheque" was by then as square as the word "square." "Disco," Go-Go's funky successor, wouldn't light up local dance floors until later in the decade. The hall went silent, and the outdoor sign became a target for roadside rock-throwing practice. In 1972, Rev. Fred V. Brewer's congregation moved in and gradually erased evidence of TV's Hullabaloo Scene.

As far as I can tell, the terms "YAD" and "Kaleidelic" never caught on. Kids born after 1956 could only drive past the barren stretch of Route 60 east of Barboursville, pass those tell-tale letters on cinderblock, and wonder what the Hullabaloo was about.

Unavoidable Psychology of the Times

It would be difficult to pinpoint how long it took for national fads, fashions and attitudes to seep into Cabell County of the 1960s and 1970s. As former city-dwellers, my sisters and I were awkwardly out of sync with our classmates (and local dress codes) when we arrived from Indiana. In the first weeks of school, I endured some minor harassment for a shorts ensemble I had on, and my sister was sent to the BHS office for a hem-to-knee skirt measurement.

Racial and ethnic diversity was not something to be seen in eastern Cabell County of the 1970s. All the students at Ona Junior High were white; I remember there being one black girl at BHS for no more than one school year.

Anyone with a television set or radio, however, would not have been able to escape the changes and turbulence that defined America of the 1960s and early 1970s. My West Virginia classmates were tuned in to the same TV networks and grew up listening to the same *Billboard Top 40* songs that I heard in Indiana— not just the upbeat British Invasion and "bubblegum" music, but protest songs and "black power" anthems. Ona Junior High social studies teacher John Paull Hogg was our resident renegade-hippy philosopher, assigning books by George Orwell and B.F. Skinner, and spinning folk-rock albums on his county-issue record player while we quietly and contentedly wore down our pencils on essay tests. At Barboursville High School, Linda Giles taught an excellent and enlightening Black Literature class.

Eventually, eastern Cabell County students got into the socially-conscious groove, at least superficially: by the time pictures were taken for the 1977 *Treasure Chest*, there may not have been any African American faces, but there were at least seven white kids (God bless them) sporting full-out, pick-worthy "Afro" hairdos.

On a deeper level, by the mid-1970s, the mood of the nation as a whole was at best subdued. People were worn down by high unemployment combined with economic inflation and gasoline shortages. And there was something else. To steal a phrase from dreamy 1970s troubadour Jackson Browne, the eyes of America's teenagers could not escape "the slow parade of fears" that came at us for more than a decade— starting with the assassination of John F. Kennedy and the escalation of military involvement in Southeast Asia.

West Virginians generally have weathered hardships with a sense of acceptance and even unflagging patriotism. As in other military conflicts, our state's citizens did more than their share in Vietnam, an "undeclared" war that lasted from the early 1960s to 1973. A total of 36,578 West Virginians served, with 1,182 killed. Forty-five soldiers from Cabell County died in Vietnam.

At least four of the names engraved on the West Virginia Veterans Memorial represent Barboursville men who gave their lives in Vietnam: Sergeant George "Butch" Eubanks attended Barboursville High School and was a member of the football and wrestling team. He became a dog handler in the war and was killed in action in Binh Dinh on his 21st birthday, Dec. 7, 1967. James Grayson Berry, son of James W. and Viola Osburne Berry, entered service in the U.S. Army a few months after graduating from Barboursville High School in 1963. He was killed in South Vietnam two years later, and is buried at White Chapel Memorial Gardens. Roger Dale Childers, son of Normal and Mildred Johnson Childers, was just 18 and in the U.S. Navy when he lost his life in Quang Ngai. He is buried at Ridgelawn Cemetery.

There were others. Arthur N. McMellon was a 33-year-old Sergeant in the U.S. Army who grew up in Lincoln County. He supplied Thanksgiving turkeys to feed 67 hungry youngsters near Ben Cat, and was killed by a grenade while riding in a jeep. McMellon is buried in Arlington National Cemetery. Rodney Kent Ranson was born on November 18, 1948, the son of Manford Kirby Ranson and Thelma Frances McCoy Ranson. He graduated from Barboursville High School in 1965 and attended Marshall University before entering the Army in February 1969. Ranson married Linda Sue Sexton in Kentucky the same month he entered service. He began his tour of duty on July 28, 1969, with the 7th Cavalry Regiment of the 1st Air Cavalry Division in Tay Ninh Province, Republic of Vietnam, near the Cambodian border. Private First Class Ranson was killed in action on November 20, 1969, in Tay Ninh Province, Republic of Vietnam, while on a mission with his platoon.

Upon returning home, the majority of servicemen who survived that long and unpopular war did not receive a public hero's welcome. In fact, eruptions of anti-war protest in American cities spilled over into hostility against the veterans themselves. With the exception of a few flare-ups on Marshall's campus during the heyday of American student unrest, Cabell County seemed to be unaffected by such gyrations. Barboursville families simply sent letters and care packages and, if they were lucky, welcomed home their young men.

Sadly—and shockingly—there was no local space left to etch these veterans' names for posterity. Barboursville's Veterans Memorial Roll of Honor on the corner of Main Street was vandalized in the early 1970s and subsequently removed. (The loving recreation of the wall on today's public square includes only the names of the original WWII veterans.) In recent years, however, new Barboursville bridges have been dedicated to the fallen Vietnam heroes, including Berry, Eubanks and Ranson, through acts of the West Virginia Legislature.

Even before Americans had a chance to absorb the full impact of the Vietnam War (United States military conscription, "the draft," ended in 1973), a new politically-charged term entered the national vocabulary: "Watergate." For more than two years, from the June 1972 arrest of "burglars" at the Democratic National Committee headquarters in Washington, D.C.'s Watergate Hotel, to the August 1974 resignation of President Nixon, the airwaves were dominated day and night by investigations, revelations and dramatic developments at the highest levels of government.

John Dean, one of the key players in the Nixon's cabinet during the aftermath of the Watergate break-in, recently described how attitudes changed after 1974. "Presidents before Watergate had been really…given a presumption of innocence. In the aftermath, they're almost presumed guilty." Dean may have been talking about the role of investigative journalism, but he also put his finger on a sense of skepticism that entered the national conscience and never really left.

In 1978, upon her retirement from a 31-year career as head librarian of the Barboursville Public Library, even the soft-spoken Sue Alexander reflected on changes she had observed. Over the years the resident of Union Avenue had used her vacation time to tour the world from Europe to the Orient. In an interview she said, "I wouldn't live anywhere else but this country, but I have seen many things I wish we would incorporate into America. Our tour guide in the Orient was so patriotic and so outspoken about it. I don't find such outspoken love of country here. We have gotten careless."

In the final year of President Jimmy Carter's administration, he was told by his pollster that the American people faced a "crisis of confidence" because of the assassinations of John F. Kennedy, Robert F. Kennedy and Martin Luther King Jr., as well as the Vietnam War and Watergate. Carter gave a nationally-televised address alluding to the national will and America's "longing for meaning." (This came to be labeled by opponents as his "malaise" speech, although Carter himself never actually used the word in his remarks.)

My generation may not have been aware of it, but the events of the years took a toll on our spirits. All the cataclysmic events could be viewed through different political or cultural prisms, but the cumulative effect cannot be denied. The assassinations of the 1960s, combined with the televised war, the mass protests, the chemically-enhanced "Woodstock generation," and the Watergate scandals left their psychological imprint.

So the Pirates of the mid-Seventies were not exactly our parents' "champion generation." Granted, Barboursville High School had unavoidably become a more impersonal place due to sheer numbers of students. For whatever reason, as far as the Class of '77 was concerned (at least as I experienced it), the AAA State Basketball Championship of 1975 and the jubilation surrounding it seemed like a momentary respite from the general cynicism that hung over Barboursville at the time.

CHAPTER 17

A SUDDEN REVERSAL OF FORTUNE (1970s-2013)

SOMETIMES the most trivial and random memories stick with us the most vividly. The year was probably 1972 or 1973. I remember getting a piece of "personalized" junk mail from the Fingerhut Company (my Columbia Record Club membership having landed me on a sucker list). I laughed out loud at the letter's claim that Fingerhut's luggage was superior to brands that could be found at the finest department stores in Ona, West Virginia. The very idea, that these advertising wizards thought there were department stores anywhere near Ona, was hilarious to me.

What a difference ten years would make.

Declining Economy and Diminishing Expectations

In 1975, Barboursville was dealing with typical small town issues. Being just ten miles from Huntington, the town considered itself "too close for a healthy local business community to flourish," according to a profile in *The Advertiser.* In general, the 2,340 residents were happy to live away from big city headaches, according to mayor Donald Owens. They were proud of their village, their schools and their Class AAA state basketball champions.

But aging sewer lines sometimes overflowed into the main streets. The town's two physicians, 73-year-old Dr. Curry and 44-year-old Dr. Sadler (working at the time for the new Marshall University Medical School), were no longer accepting new patients. The consolidated "Chessie System" was relying more on computerization and less on the workers in its Barboursville shops, so equipment was being moved out. There were not enough recreation facilities or activities in town.

Worse, the county's tax base was in a state of decline due to new property tax rules that withheld less from older homeowners. Industrial moves away from the village were also starting to hurt.

By the time Barboursville woke up to the impending loss of the state hospital in 1978, the town's economy had endured several swift kicks. "It's another thing gone," said the mayor in February 1978. "You get a community that loses things and they begin to feel like losers. The C&O had to leave the community. The Columbia Gas office left here. Over a period of years we see things drifting away from us."

One bright spot for manufacturing stood at the east end of Main Street. Cabell County native Leonard Sturm had grown his business, from a part-time operation out of a Depot Street garage in 1962, to what eventually became part of a global company, Sulzer Pumps. In 1977, the company expanded across Main Street into a large new facility on the former Moore-Brady farm property. (According to a spokesperson for the company, Mr. Sturm was a pioneer of the "hard coating method," and his Barboursville operation was at one time the leading such facility in the eastern half of the United States. Today the company serves the oil, gas, hydrocarbon, power generation and water industries.)

A development on the southwest side of town, however, would offset the employment gains realized through the Sturm expansion. More than 50 of the 60 workers of the Barboursville brickyard were suddenly laid off without explanation in the summer of 1979. Longtime workers interviewed by *The Cabell Record* were mystified. Production—with a capacity of about 70,000 bricks per day—had not slowed, and the owners had spent "tremendous amounts of money" modernizing the plant, according to the stunned employees. But they were not called back, and the owners began liquidating equipment from the 20-acre property.

The last red brick maker in West Virginia, the Peyton Street brickyard had not just been a source of industrial brick and union jobs. Barboursville red brick was elemental to village pride. It defined the look of Barboursville, from government buildings, businesses and churches to homes all over town, including the new homes on the heights of Brady Drive. Even the base of the "eternal flame" dedicated in 1970 was constructed of Barboursville brick. Frank Ball wrote of visiting his brother in the Washington, DC suburbs and scoffing at the brick homes in the neighborhood. "I told him that I didn't want to run the homes of his millionaire neighbors down but that we were filling mud holes in Barboursville with better brick than these."

It was later found that someone had embezzled a million dollars from the brick company, which led to its puzzling overnight demise. The abandoned ruin on the north side of Peyton Street sat vacant, teeming with industrial contaminants and legal landmines, for over a quarter of a century.

Barboursville needed a significant economic boost.

Opportunity Quietly Seized

Ted Kirk ran for mayor in Barboursville on the Republican ticket against incumbent mayor Boyd Hash in June 1977. The Huntington Alloys employee said he sought the office to address the lack of recreational facilities for the youth and the need for an upgraded sewer system in the village. After "walking all over town, knocking on every door and ringing every door bell," Kirk defeated Hash by a narrow 338 to 312 votes.

The Barboursville election did not make the front pages of Huntington's two newspapers. What *was* making front page news involved complaints and court actions by a group of downtown Huntington merchants who were trying to stop development of a large shopping mall targeted to open in 1979 just outside city limits, near the downtown exit of Interstate 64. Ultimately, the persistent opposition of the merchants caused the developers to lose interest in the site.

Back in quiet Barboursville, Kirk was sworn in alongside new recorder Sandra Walls, a Democrat, and three incumbent Democratic councilmen—49-year-old James P. "Paul" Dingess and 46-year-old Doliver T. McComas, both of whom worked for C&O; and 53-year-old Herman P. Grove who owned a religious bookstore. The two newcomers on the council were 50-year-old William E. Rucker, plant supervisor for the Allegheny Fire Equipment company, and the lone Republican, 35-year-old Glenn Holton. Holton was a BHS star athlete who had gone on to co-captain the WVU Mountaineers football team; in 1964 Holton was drafted into the National Football League by the Detroit Lions.

Kirk and the council were concerned with providing adequate police, garbage and sewer service on an annual revenue of $124,000. Expanding the geographic size of the village may not have been on top of their "to-do" list.

Councilman Doliver McComas later recalled, "We had very little to go on. We'd have to take money from the parking meters just to buy a case of oil for the garbage truck."

Then opportunity came knocking.

The Cafaro Company, a Youngstown, Ohio-based development firm specializing in shopping centers, purchased several large parcels of land about two miles east of the village. With plans abandoned for a shopping complex just outside of Huntington, Barboursville was approached at some point about the possibility of annexing what the Cafaros said would be the largest enclosed shopping mall in West Virginia. I have been told that contact was made with the village before Boyd Hash left office, and that he laid the groundwork for the sewage lagoon through the purchase of the old Brady family "low bottom" along the Mud River.

Under the agreement, Cafaro would pay for laying pipelines for a sewer system and upgrading the village's sewage treatment lagoon. In exchange, the Barboursville town council would provide sewer, water, garbage, fire and police service to the mall and to the thin strip of land connecting the two entities.

There were only a few signs of civilization on the two-mile stretch of U.S. Route 60 between the east end of Barboursville and Cyrus Creek Road. On the western end was the Colonial Village subdivision and White Chapel Memorial Gardens. On the eastern side stood an old stone diner beside Nichols School Road, some new construction by Rex Donahue (who in 1968 had begun purchasing land in that section), Holley's fishing lake, a Rich Oil station, Shirley Donahue's sewing shop, and the ever-popular "Our House Tavern," a beer and pool hall run by Frowde Carter and his brother J.D. The Snak Shak-turned-Country Squire restaurant graced the intersection of Route 60 and the Ona Interchange. The only building on the I-64 access road itself was Don Williams's full-service Exxon station. The horses on the rolling green land of "Melody T Farms" could be seen from the interstate.

Mayor Kirk appointed a task force, headed by Larry Perry, to study the idea of annexation. Assuming the proposed business and occupational taxes would be realized after the deal was made, the revenue potential for taking in this stretch of land was great. But so was the risk; considering that Barboursville still relied on a few men with push brooms to clean its streets, providing support for the huge construction project with no promise of revenue for several years was putting a lot on the line.

The council proceeded with due deliberation. The village Jaycees and the Junior Women's Club worked with Council to conduct a major outreach campaign to residents. A town hall meeting was scheduled at Barboursville High School's auditorium on October 2, 1978. About 120 people showed up to listen to village officials and the development company's vice-president, J.J. Cafaro, explain the project and answer their questions.

The next day the bipartisan Council met and voted unanimously to accept the annexation proposal. Applause exploded among a crowd of more than 80 persons while TV cameras rolled.

"I think this is wonderful—wonderful!" exclaimed Mayor Kirk, on the move that would start little Barboursville on its journey to an expected 590 percent increase on its annual budget.

Although the mayor and several of the council members served only a single two-year term (Glenn Holton's would be cut short by a tragic automobile accident that took his life less than two months later; the U.S. Route 60 bridge near Cyrus Creek is named in his memory), their decision on October 3, 1978 was the most significant event in twentieth century village history. Barboursville's "boom-and-bust" past, as well as the entire economic landscape of Cabell County, changed in that moment. Village citizens spoke through their elected representatives, and

Ted Kirk, James Paul Dingess, Herman Grove, Glenn Holton, Doliver McComas and William Rucker accomplished with the least amount of political drama what Huntington could not.

"The Mall Started It All"

Once the fateful vote was taken, other decisions still had to be made by council, with formal approval a month later by the Cabell County Commission. Given the resistance of downtown Huntington's merchants, and that city's fumbling of the development opportunity, the Cafaros' decision to name their new shopping complex "The Huntington Mall" had some local jaws flapping. Nevertheless, the county commission had no objections, considering the bigger picture.

"It would be asinine to be against something that's going to provide you with funding," said commission president Ted Johnson. "This is the future of Cabell County, things of this nature. West Virginia is losing population, but Cabell should gain."

By the end of 1978, county officials considered the mall agreement as part of a bright economic picture along with other new construction: a "Kmart mall" at the East Pea Ridge-U.S. 60 intersection, Sturm Machinery's expansion on east Main Street in Barboursville, and a new county airport in Ona. By the middle of 1979, an almost entirely new slate of Barboursville town officials was voted into office. Mayor Don Owens, recorder Betty Adkins and council members Becky Holton (widow of Glenn), Bill Plyburn, Mike Thompson, Roger Hesson and Tom Fife were tasked with the work of carrying out annexation on the village's tight budget.

County residents kept their eyes on the news to see what retail chains would sign on to occupy the million square feet of shopping space. The original plans called for five big "anchor" stores—Lazarus, Anderson Newcomb, Sears, J.C. Penney and the Diamond. Negotiations were complicated by the fact that three of the large retailers were firmly rooted in Huntington. Within months, the Diamond postponed then later cancelled its construction plan for the fifth large store at the back of the property. Huntington's Anderson Newcomb was purchased by the Wheeling-based Stone and Thomas department store chain, which announced it would continue to operate the downtown location in addition to a new Stone and Thomas at the mall.

In June 1979, the West Virginia Department of Highways announced it was working with the mall developers on a land acquisition and funding plan to redesign the Ona interchange—expanding, replacing and adding exit ramps and half-loops. The Cafaro construction had prompted the DOH to prevent potential traffic jams and hazards on the interstate. One of the new ramps would be designed specifically for easier access from the direction of Huntington, the spokesman said.

By the end of the summer of 1979, the Cafaro Company said 90 percent of its 120 smaller stores were signed.

The transition from small village to retail "boom town" brought growing pains and internal debate about Barboursville's identity. The formation of a Barboursville chapter of Rotary International in 1980, chartered with 28 service-minded business and professional members, was one sign of growing confidence. On the other hand, the city was still dealing with an antiquated sewer system , and struggled to increase its police force to deal with traffic, trespassing and theft around the mall construction site.

The annexation of the mall property divided Barboursville into two distinct main areas with two very different characters. By 1981, Barboursville was already being described as a "bi-polar" municipality. There was the old, tucked-away, pedestrian-friendly village as it always was, and two miles away a rising commercial section designed for ease of regional automobile flow and mass parking.

A succession of mayors and councils publicly pondered the annexation of additional areas, such as Guyan Estates and Pea Ridge, but encountered resistance from townspeople who liked their friendly little village just the way it was and opposed more wholesale change. Later annexation would take in additional miles of business property fronting Route 60 east and west of town, but on the question of taking the large residential areas into the fold, Barboursville essentially decided not to decide.

A glance through the Sunday pre-Christmas advertisements in the *Herald-Dispatch* from 1978 to 1983 tells the tale of Barboursville's rise and Huntington's demise as a retail center. In late 1978, as measured by column-inches, the big holiday players were: The Huntington Store, Anderson Newcomb, Mack and Dave's, Amsbary's, Nasser's, J.C. Penney, Delmar's, Corbin, Glenn's Sporting Goods, Star Furniture, Butler Furniture, Pied Piper, Wright's, The Smart Shop, Stationers, Frank's Shoes, Belle's, Super B and National Record Mart—all downtown—as well as Sears, Hatfield's & McCoy's, J.J.'s Factory Outlet (U.S. Rt. 60 across from the Gateway), the Chesapeake Kmart, and Hills "discount department store" on U.S. Rt. 60 between Huntington and Barboursville.

In 1979, Ethan Allen Carriage House and Kmart were new arrivals on Route 60 near Pea Ridge. Downtown, several stores including Lambros and Sons, Smart Shop and the Princess were promoting their locations on "Fashionable Fourth Avenue." By Christmas 1981, the first Mall holiday shopping season, the Princess Shop was having its "going out of business sale" and at least five downtown staples were co-located at mall: Stone and Thomas, Amsbary's, Wrights, J.C. Penney and Pied Piper. By1982, the Smart Shop had double-invested as well, with both downtown and mall stores.

The watershed year had to be 1983. A few of the downtown Huntington stores would hang on, but the writing was on the wall. People might be flocking to Huntington to capture the magic of "Huck's Herd" and Marshall basketball, but when "Black Friday" came they flocked in the other direction.

A mingling of two consumer trends that year seem to have firmly established Barboursville not just as the county's center of commerce, but as a regional attraction for America's new "conspicuous consumers." It turned out to be more than a phase; the 1980s heralded a seemingly-permanent change in the way people shop (and, some might say, the way we confuse "wants" with "needs"). Almost every new economic development in eastern Cabell County since that point has been merely quantitative—growth beyond expectation, and growth upon growth.

One of the first local clues to this phenomenon appeared in a small December 1983 advertisement by East End Cycle Sales: "Drawing for Cabbage Patch Doll." Nobody knew it yet, but this signaled the age of the "Must-Have" item.

NBC reporter Peter Hartlaub analyzed the creation of these homely surrogate children, and how they changed America:

> Up until this point, there had been fad toys, but people had mostly acted like members of a civilized society in their quest for them. That all ended in 1983, when Coleco's Cabbage Patch Kids became a huge media-fueled hit, causing a mad scramble for the few million of pudgy-cheeked dolls that were produced before Christmas. Demand from children who wanted to "adopt" a doll led to adult fistfights and price gouging, with some Cabbage Patch Kids selling on the black market for 10 times their retail price. The fad got even bigger the next year; 18 million Cabbage Patch Kids were sold in 1984. (Hartlaub 2010)

Other modern-age "Must-Have's" would follow: the Transformers (1984), Teddy Ruxpin (1985), Beanie Babies (1993), Mighty Morphin' Power Rangers (1994—a particularly insidious year for a mother of young boys), Tickle Me Elmo (1996), Furby (1998) and the Nintendo Wii (2006). Between the "instant collectible" hype and suspected supply manipulation by some of the companies, holiday shopping was elevated to a competitive sport.

While Coleco was adding fuel to an urgent sense of consumer demand, another corporation was lighting a fire on the supply end. One of the new "satellite businesses" built at the perimeter of the Huntington Mall parking lot, Children's Palace had distinctive battlements on the top like the Great Wall of China. When it opened in 1983—its warehouse-style merchandising of toys and baby items featured long aisles and "over-stock" storage that reached to the rafters—the store put department store "toy-lands" to shame. (The first time my husband and I walked into Children's Palace, he gazed in awe. After he was finally able to speak, he said, "If I had seen something like this when I was a kid, I would have passed out. My head would have exploded.")

The "Must-Have" product explosion of 1983 and the specialty warehouse shopping experience marked a national and local turning point. Barboursville was now a regional arena for the shopping gladiators. The eventual corporate demise of Children's Palace and other individual retailers did nothing to sap the strength of Barboursville's "eastern pole" as a powerful commercial magnet.

On the contrary, the footprint of Barboursville's regional shopping complex continued to expand over to Route 60 and beyond, drawing more customers and additional businesses. In 2003, Home Depot became an anchor of the Merritt Creek Farm center. Wal-Mart rose like a hilltop fortress at the old Melody T Farm in 2004. Outback Steakhouse and Cracker Barrel opened the way for other destinations along "Red Meat Row" including West Virginia's first Steak n Shake in 2007 and a new Fat Patty's (brainchild of BHS grad and burger-meister Clint Artrip) in 2010. In 2009, the popular highway pit stop Sheetz went in at the original Williams Exxon site, giving interstate travelers one more reason to get off at Exit 20 and spend some money.

In 2013, Barboursville continues to attract more restaurants, more hotels, more shopping complexes, professional buildings, condominiums, apartments and housing subdivisions. Its mall annexation has weathered the online shopping boom that brought down "brick and mortar" stores like my beloved Borders. It survived the Great Recession of 2008. In fact, the Cafaro Company did a $5 million remodel of the Huntington Mall in 2011 and in its 2013 brochure describes the Barboursville property as a "super-regional shopping center."

In a 2003 interview with the mall's general manager Joe Johnston, he explained that the Cafaro Company's original intent was to serve customers from a six-county metro area around Huntington, mainly from the west. Two decades in, a survey of zip codes from credit card transactions showed the mall regularly drew shoppers from 33 counties in a 75-mile radius. New shopping developments like Merritt Creek Farm and River Place were not seen by mall management as threats, but as giving "more reasons for people to come to Barboursville."

"The mall was the first proven entity in the county," Johnston said in 2003. "The mall started it all."

Fresh Air and Green Space: Barboursville's "Hidden" Jewel

While the mall was making headlines and bulking up Sunday newspapers with slick, colorful inserts, the village was quietly expanding into the wooded land on the south edge of town. Thanks to the business and occupation taxes rolling in from the retailers and a series of actions by village and state leaders, the old "Clover Valley" farm—off-limits and hidden from view for so many years—underwent a transformation that would make it one the largest municipal parks in the state.

In 1984, the state sold off a large share of "state farm" bottomland to the village (reserving a tract for use by the Barboursville School psychiatric residential facility for youth). During the administrations of mayors William Rucker, Don Owens and pharmacist William Plyburn, the land was re-contoured; all but one of the old state farm buildings disappeared.

The Barboursville Community Park made its first public splash with completion of a man-made lake. Lake William was dedicated in 1992 for three men who shared that first name—not the local nineteenth century greats Miller, Merritt and McComas, but late-twentieth-century movers and shakers Rucker, Plyburn and Turman.

William C. Turman (for whom the Route 60 bridge across the Guyandotte River was dedicated in 1995) was an engineer and business owner. His son, current mayor Paul Turman, referred to him as "the Cal Ripkin of bridge building." According to the West Virginia Division of Natural Resources, the 17-acre impoundment known as Lake William has a maximum depth of 10 feet and an average depth of 5 feet. The lake provides spring and winter fishing for stocked trout and a fishery for bluegill, channel catfish and largemouth bass.

A walking track around the lake, picnic shelters, basketball, volleyball, tennis courts and playgrounds were added during the 1990s. The Barboursville Little League and Barboursville Youth Football associations gained a well-appointed complex of sports fields.

In 2000, the village built an amphitheater in the park that could accommodate an outdoor audience of 4,000. Local artist Bill Dawson, a retiree from the U.S. Army Corps of Engineers, designed the $400,000 structure. (Incidentally, the same sloping area maintained for lawn chair seating at the amphitheatre provides access to the "legendary Jesse James Cave" rock formation).

In 2004, the council bid on a 99-year lease of 250 acres owned by the West Virginia Department of Agriculture, expanding park use for hiking, biking and geocaching. A firing range was added for local police to practice their skills, and soccer fields were laid out. In 2007, the first Civil War reenactment of the Battle of Barboursville set up camp at the park and became an annual happening.

Even so, it was not an easy destination to locate, especially for those who had never made the zig-and-zag through Barboursville's residential streets. In 2000, reporter and outdoor enthusiast Dave Lavender interviewed Tri-State area residents who were surprised to learn of the park's existence. Despite the fact that it was already larger than 16 state parks, forests and wildlife management areas in West Virginia, the Barboursville Community Park remained a "best-kept secret."

The awakening of eastern Cabell Countians to the great outdoors seems to have been part of a recent "fitness renaissance" that brought increasing numbers of parkgoers to Barboursville (which operates independently of the Greater Huntington Parks and Recreation District). Part of the trend might be attributable to an Emmy

Award-winning ABC network show taped in Cabell County in 2010 called *Jamie Oliver's Food Revolution.* The premise of the reality show was that Oliver, a feisty young British chef and health advocate, brought his crusade to Huntington because it was statistically marked as one of the unhealthiest cities in the country.

Another inspiration has been the memory of Paul Ambrose, a 1987 Barboursville High School graduate and class president whose stellar career as a physician and public health advocate was cut tragically short on September 11, 2001. At age 32, Dr. Ambrose was on a flight to Los Angeles to attend a national conference on youth obesity prevention when terrorists high-jacked and crashed the plane into the Pentagon. A few months later, Dr. Ambrose posthumously received the Surgeon General's Medal of Honor for his work on the *Surgeon General's Call to Action to Prevent and Decrease Overweight and Obesity.* That report initiated projects across the country to improve diet and increase exercise. (The Paul Ambrose Trail for Health (PATH), a growing urban bicycle and pedestrian trail system for the City of Huntington, is named after Dr. Ambrose.)

In 2010, the expanded Barboursville Park attracted the West Virginia 5-K Race Committee to schedule a number of events, and the local Lions Club added its own 5-K fundraiser.

Another team sport increased the useable space on the southern end of the 750-acre park. Through the dedication of soccer parents and other volunteers, Barboursville was awarded the U.S. Youth Soccer Region I Championship games. This provided impetus for Barboursville, state legislators and Governor Joe Manchin to foot the bill for a second sturdy "soccer bridge" to connect the original park space to 4-H Camp Road. In addition to use by the U.S. Youth Soccer and West Virginia Soccer associations, the new access point offers a complex of well-maintained grass fields, trails, restroom facilities and a paved roadway that attracts joggers, bike riders, dog walkers and model airplane flyers.

Things almost went a lot differently. A proposed development for the western end of the park rose and fell under two of the most "hands-on" mayors in Barboursville history.

Nancy and "Mayor T"

Barboursville's post-Mall growth spurt (one that continues into 2013), was aided and abetted by two powerful players in local affairs, mayors Nancy Cartmill and Paul Turman.

In 1993, Nancy Hunter Cartmill became the first woman to run for and to win the office of Barboursville mayor. As a former Barboursville elementary volunteer, state Parent Teacher Association president and educational lobbyist, "Nancy" had bipartisan appeal. A Republican in a village that voted about two-thirds Democratic, Cartmill held the position for eight consecutive years (four two-year terms), an unprecedented achievement. (Serving as village recorder for the duration of the Cartmill administration was Ann Stackpole Reed, the third-great granddaughter of William Clendenin Miller.)

Mayor Cartmill, a familiar fitness walker on the village sidewalks, made an impact early on. The downtown area got what many considered a much-needed "lady's touch" when floral hanging planters and new Christmas lights were purchased. Residents gained free garbage pickup service, and sidewalks and curbs were improved. In 1994, Cartmill applied for Barboursville to be designated as an official historic district. The village installed signs at all the village landmarks to coincide with veteran Robert Hall's historic tour book. Cartmill focused personal attention and city resources on the new Barboursville Senior Center (opened in 1999 on the old Merritt Homestead/Lions Club site), ruffling the feathers of some county agencies in the process. Throughout her tenure she also arranged for Barboursville school students to enjoy concerts, dances, musicals and other performances.

As B&O revenues grew and she continued to win re-election, Cartmill was not content for the village to rest on its laurels. At the same time downtown Barboursville was taking on a more attractive "Main Street USA" aesthetic, Cartmill took a bold stance toward development around the perimeter. She lauded the new Merritt's creek connector (briefly and erroneously identified as "Merrick Creek Road") and stressed to news media that the "key to attracting businesses is providing the infrastructure and economic development long before they commit to the area."

In 1997, under Cartmill's watch, the state Division of Highways cooperated with commercial developers to build a new bridge over the Guyandotte River, connecting Peyton Street to U.S. Route 60. With the land sitting empty, locals called it the "Bridge to Nowhere" until the Wyngate senior living and condominium complex and "Deer Creek's" luxury homes replaced the former Knob Hill golf course.

Two years later, Cartmill got behind a group of business leaders who had a vision for building a 92,000-square foot equestrian exposition center modeled after Lexington's Kentucky Horse Park. The desired location was on the land west of the Barboursville Park near Alternate Route 10. In preparation, a second new state bridge spanned the Guyandotte, leading to an empty field behind the 4-H Camp. The mayor joined a contingent led by businessman Ostie Mathisen, who presented a proposal to Governor Underwood. While the private commission sought funding, the council passed a budget to run utilities to the remote property. In the year 2000, as the Exposition Center seemed an inevitability, the outgoing mayor made her entrance in a stagecoach, wearing a white suit and "cowgirl hat" to welcome the Lone Star World Championship Rodeo to Barboursville Park.

Cartmill left office in 2001, after Barboursville voters refused to eliminate term limits. From that time on, the horse park proposal began to slowly lose momentum.

Paul Turman defeated Roger Hesson by just 87 votes in the 2001 mayoral primary, then went on to win the general election unopposed. The new mayor—president of the BHS senior class of 1959, All-Southern High School football scoring champ, MU gridiron stalwart, graduate of Greenbrier Military Academy, and a helicopter pilot cited twice for heroism in Vietnam—pledged to give his maximum effort to continue the economic success credited to Nancy Cartmill.

Turman, joined by a mostly-new village council, continued the utility work at the park that had been ordered under Cartmill's administration, but took a harder look at revenue projections that had been publicized for the exposition center. The new mayor refused to go into debt on the building projects, and members of the council began to peel away from full endorsement of the proposal. In 2002, the council voted to approve a $5 million grant application to the West Virginia Economic Development Grant Committee for the horse park project. When the grant was denied, the exposition center became a bridge too far, and the vision fizzled.

The Cabell County Planning Commission, the Huntington Area Development Council, and the editorial board of *The Herald-Dispatch* all saw the newly-accessible 40-acre parcel at the river bend as ripe for industrial or business development. Mayor Turman was convinced by then that the best use of the property was for recreation as part of the huge city park complex. "It is not a waste to keep it open space," said the former construction company president in 2003, a few months after he was elected to a second term. "My goal is to keep it an open area."

With friends in high places (his son was appointed deputy highway commissioner by Governor Joe Manchin), and continuing development that brought Barboursville's 2013-14 revenue to $5.3 million, "Mayor T" has scored on many fronts, both economic and political. In addition, Turman was able to accomplish what his predecessor could not—eliminating term limits in 2006 (upon a 336-to-297 decision by village voters). The mayor and council also put up successful ballot initiatives in 2007 and 2011 to do away with primary elections (citing an $8,000 cost savings to justify the move), and to extend the terms of elected service from two to four years.

Both Cartmill and Turman had their detractors, a few of them quite vocal. On the other hand, both mayors ran unopposed as incumbents in several of their primary and general races. (My dear mother, political one-timer Linda Brady, took it upon herself to run for mayor in 2011 to back up her stated conviction that "Barboursville's citizens are best served when offered a choice of candidates," and garnered several hundred votes.) Ultimately, the majority of active voters decided they were content to let "Nancy" and "Mayor T" hold the reins of municipal government as Barboursville crossed a sturdy bridge into the new millennium.

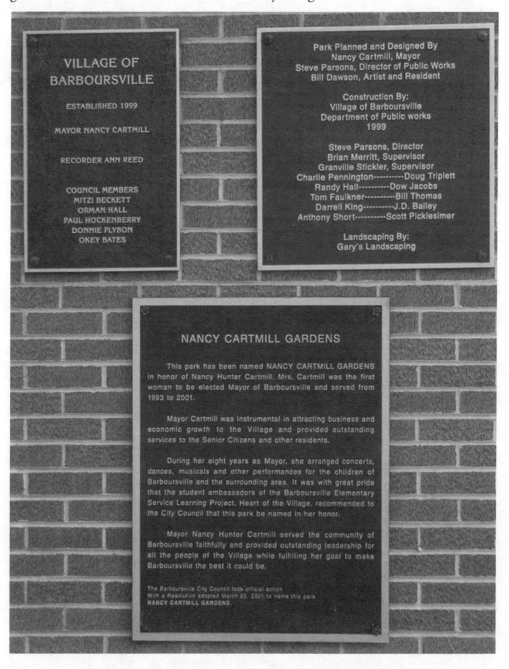

Wall and plaques erected at former courthouse square, 1999

At the Bicentennial Crossroads

Barboursville, West Virginia of 2013 still seems to be in a growth spurt. With the entire county redefining itself around Barboursville's strong commercial presence, the city seems to have had the "last laugh," after such a long rollercoaster ride of historic advances and declines.

Barboursville is no longer just a village, but a city— a Class 3 Municipality to be legally precise. Perhaps stubbornly, residents and leaders still prefer Barboursville to be known as "the best little village in the state." Those living in William Merritt's original settlement have been quoted again and again about being proud of their quiet streets, great neighbors and historic buildings. There seems to be a desire to take the wealth and conveniences that came from annexation, but not to be corrupted by them.

What will the future hold? Will all the desirable qualities that define "the best little village" exist 20, 50, or 200 years from now? Without a specific plan to identify and preserve the things people value most about Barboursville, one may as well dig through the old toy chest and consult a Magic 8-Ball: "Reply hazy, try again."

As measured by those who have abdicated their civic responsibility to vote in municipal elections, it is fair to say that Barboursville of the twenty-first century is not a politically active town. Allow the numbers to tell the story: West Virginia was ranked second to last in voter turnout for the 2012 General Election (voters measured against citizens eligible to vote), calculated at 45.1 percent. In the 2011 Barboursville municipal election, 618 people voted in the Turman-Brady race out of an eligible population of 3,297 adult residents, a measly turnout rate of 18.7 percent.

The villagers who have gotten involved show Barboursville to be a progressive little city with a "moral" streak. Even though many years have passed since Barboursville was a dry town, it has not been an "anything goes" town. People voiced their satisfaction when the village council voted to charge the two "strip clubs" off U.S Route 60 an extra $3,000 annual fee to maintain their city license, and in 2005 to strictly limit the number of video lottery machines in city limits. Since 1952, Barboursville's voters have consistently approved its municipal excess levies for sewer and street maintenance, even in recent years when Barboursville's budget showed funds carried over. In 2006, Barboursville precincts helped make the difference in passage of a county-wide school bond levy to fund new buildings. Barboursville's 2008 "drop-off" recycling initiative was an immediate success and set a standard that the county solid waste authority has emulated.

Barboursville's biggest boosters of the recent past, "the Champion Generation" have left their mark. As they age out of their once-active roles, however, the village-city is once again at a crossroad. Looking back at the 1950s and 1960s, it is hard to imagine (with the possible exception of the Volunteer Fire Department and youth sports associations) that same level of local volunteerism today—funding a public library, helping build the community swimming pool, moving and reconstructing the 1837 Toll House. Judging by the decline in local voter turnout, church attendance and participation in civic groups, perhaps it is just too difficult to draw attention to larger "quality of life" issues, when so many other things (and jobs to pay for those things) beckon every hour of every day.

Will future historians look back at Barboursville's children and grandchildren of "the Champion Generation" as people who neglected to get involved in village affairs because they were too busy being "marketed to?" Face it, being born in eastern Cabell County after 1980 means being able to take for granted that almost anything that *can* be purchased is right here handy. What does it mean to grow up so close to such a large consumer engine? On the one hand, what a great way to live! On the other hand, members of Barboursville's Millennial Generation are immersed in marketing messages, not only from their various electronic screens but also through their car windows.

Where does this leave preservation of local heritage? In the shadow of Barboursville's annexed lands—the Mall, the celebrated city park, the new housing communities, even the regional jail—it seems that the historic core of the community, the old "downtown," has been the easiest to pass by and ignore. Without the kind of organized promotion that places such as West Huntington's Old Central City have benefitted from, downtown Barboursville does not seem to have found a clear identity as a "destination."

Consider the "mom and pop" businesses along Main and Central. Since the year 2000, several antique stores, bakeries, cafés, farmers market vendors, specialty and consignment clothing stores have come and gone. The Great Recession, high property costs and a lack of steady foot traffic continue to take their toll. Village residents within walking distance can take advantage of the Dollar General Store, the post office, library, the barber and beauty shops, but they don't necessarily patronize the upscale Black Hawk Grill or other "boutique" businesses that dot Main and Central.

In the meantime, the small and sometimes struggling businesses that occupy the old buildings serve as the only stewards of these historic properties. Two present-day businesses—ZBA and WV Quilters—are examples of downtown landmarks that have been lovingly preserved and showcased. Others are occupied by people who know little about the origins of their workplaces.

What will be the fate of "historic Barboursville?" If the past practices of village leaders are any indication of what the future holds, take heed.

Our Special Correspondent Furnishes an Interesting Letter:
MARCH 9, 1899—Merrits Mill washed out by high water....
nearly the entire town turned out and watched the large structure float away.

CHAPTER 18

EPILOGUE: 'TWAS EVER THUS...

Barboursville High School (1929-2009)

The old Barboursville Middle School will start coming down during the next few weeks as Master Mechanical Insulation gets its heavy equipment ready for demolition. The old school will become a parking lot and bus loop for the new school, which opened in late-January behind the old facility. (Major demolition set to begin at old Barboursville school 2009)

Thomas Thornburg Home (1862-2009)

Michele and Eric Hankins clean their yard at 635 Water St. The Hankins' home is the No. 1 stop on the walking tour of historic houses sponsored by the city of Barboursville. (D. Peyton, Stroll Into History Offered 1994)

Thomas W. Thornburg's home was built in 1862 and was located at 635 Water St. This charming Victorian Queen Anne structure has been the home to the Peytons, Townsend and Hankins families and was recently demolished. (D. D. McMillian 2009)

Barboursville Clay Manufacturing Company (1904-2007)

Phase two of the old brickyard cleanup project in Barboursville is nearly complete after six kiln stacks were demolished Thursday afternoon. According to George Carico, coordinator of the Southern West Virginia Brownfields Assistance Center, a $200,000 grant from the U.S. Environmental Protection Agency Brownfields Program in 2006 has allowed the village to clean up the dilapidated Barboursville Clay/Brick Manufacturing Company...Carico said the debris from the demolition will be piled into an on-site landfill and covered with a soil cap. (Alexandersen, Old stacks come down at Barboursville brickyard 2007)

Old stacks come down at Barboursville brickyard.
(Photo courtesy of The Herald-Dispatch)

Cabell County Court House (1852-1996) and Methodist Episcopal Church South (1884-1996)

Memories flood back when Richard Spencer looks back at the old Barboursville Middle School.

A lifelong resident of Barboursville who can trace his family's roots there to the early 1800s, Spencer walked the school's narrow halls as a student.

His uncle fought the 1945 fire that destroyed the school's bell tower. His children all attended the school. His wife, Joyce, taught there. Yet, last Tuesday Spencer joined Barboursville City Council's unanimous decision to tear down Cabell County's oldest existing school building.

"It was tough," Spencer says. "We've talked about what we should do with that school ever since it closed two years ago. Ideas have been flying around town all that time. Now, it's come to this, sad to say."

Mayor Nancy Cartmill and other council members say refurbishing the school would cost much more than anyone is willing to pay.

"It was really difficult for me to vote for demolition," the mayor says. "I went to school in that building. So did nearly everyone on council.

"The problem is that no one has come up with a use for the school that would bring revenues back to the town. A lot of people want to use the building, but they want to use it for free."

Only two original walls of the old chapel remain intact. The inside, which served as a library, is more deteriorated than any other room.

"I would like to see the chapel preserved," City Councilman Paul Hockenberry said. "But, I don't think it would stand by itself if we tore down other parts of the school.

"Maybe we can build a replica of the old church once the buildings come down. It could be the start of a museum we need in town."

Bill Russell of Barboursville wanted the council to hear more discussion before they voted to tear down the historic building.

"With all the money in the village coffers, can't they spare a bit to save our village's history," Russell said. "I think out of a sense of fairness they ought to have a public hearing."

Spencer, however, says the council had two public hearings on the old school, one two years ago and another one before last week's meetings.

"No one had anything to say," he says. "I know we'll get some criticism, but I don't know how we could do anything else.

"I wanted to save that school myself. I just don't see how the city can afford to do that." (Massey 1996)

"Old Abraham" The Village Sycamore (circa 1820s-1995)

A poet's prose illuminated it, an unknown artist sketched it, presidents rode underneath its branches and Barboursville residents dozed in its shade.

Now, Old Abraham is gone.

On Friday, a tree company hired by the Village of Barboursville dismantled the 170-year-old sycamore at 813 Main Street known as Old Abraham.

All that was left Saturday was a 5-foot-wide rotted, hollow stump. Only the day before it stood at about 85 feet.

Although the tree grew into a historic landmark during the years, Sara Thomas is glad it's gone. For 21 years, it was nothing but a bellyache in her front yard.

"I'm one happy lady," said Thomas, 79. "I've spent almost 21 years raking leaves. I have raked leaves and picked up limbs; and it's ruined the roof." (Rake 1995)

Barboursville C&O Train Station (circa 1900-?)

The last Chessie System timetable to advertise stops at the Barboursville passenger station is dated April 29, 1956.

Today, ghosts of memories inhabit this skeleton of a building, sharing space with stored lighting fixtures, switching machines, wires and pipes. Time has blacked it, rotted away its ceiling and floorboards.

What once was a stately train station has lost its dignity. The wooden structure was converted to a storage area more than 20 years ago, said a 40-year employee of the Chessie System.

Once the king of the neighborhood, the Barboursville station now is a subject, serving only a minor purpose for the Chessie System reclamation plant that has sprung up around it.

Windows are broken and boarded. The paint is peeling from the sign proclaiming "Barboursville."
Train cars are stilled on the tracks around the station. Giant coils of cable are strewn around it and even the wild flowers grow tall in its shadow.

Several employees working at Chessie's Barboursville operation said they never even knew the history behind the rickety warehouse. (M. Bernstein 1985)

William McComas Home at "Mulberry Grove" (1837-1986)

As flames bellowed from the second floor of the old McComas-Sellers house on Knob Hill last night, a dusty oil painting of the pre-Civil War homestead rested against a faded green antique chair standing off by itself in the surrounding yard dimly lit by the blaze.

The house, nearly 150 years old, was fully engulfed in flames last night by the time firefighters from the Barboursville Volunteer Fire Department arrived, Chief Steve Parsons said.

Neighbors and residents who remember the old house as a landmark stood in its spacious front and adjacent yards watching the fire and talking about the times they had visited its last occupant—the late Winnie Sellards…

The McComas-Sellards homestead, apparently one of the first brick houses in Cabell County, was built no later than 1837, family members have said.

Mrs. Sellards had lived at the home until she died last December, Parsons said. (Rose, Old Cabell home destroyed by fire 1986)

Tivoli/CrissTheater (1926-1985)

Police cruisers blocked off Main Street just above the scene of what Steve Parsons, chief of the Barboursville Volunteer Fire Department, called the largest fire the town has seen in the last few years.

On a hillside across the street from 811 Main St., where an old brick building was engulfed by flames, local residents sat in rows as if watching a movie or outdoor concert. They gazed attentively as busy firefighters battled the blaze.

Standing among the crowd with his hands in his pants pockets was a man watching more than just an old building burning down. For Robert "Poky" Anderson, the burning building, built in the early 1920s as a movie house, was part of his family history.

"My dad, S.V. Anderson, built that building," said the 72-year-old Barboursville native. (Rose, Flames licking old Tivoli Theater spark memories of days gone by 1985)

John G. Miller and Holderby Store/Blume Hotel (1840s-1981)

During the last week in June, Barboursville's controversial "Old B Building" was razed and now is being carted away, brick by brick. For more than 140 years this sturdy building stood on a trail that served the public for nobody knows how long.

The building was the town's oldest structure and lovers of the nostalgic and the antique wanted it braced and kept for its historical interest. Others said that it was too old and frail for preservation. It had been condemned as unsafe by state fire and safety officials within recent years.

And now Old B Building is gone. But before its demise, it had served as a haberdashery, hotel, law offices, printing shop, classroom, adult learning center and, of course, music hall. For that it is best known to Morris Harvey alumni, who still remember the strains of violins and notes from pianos wafting out over the village green. (F. Ball, B Building. . . 140 years of Barboursville history razed 1981)

Barboursville Cemetery (1830s-Present)

It is believed to be 175 years old. It is the final resting place of many in this book. It sits less than two blocks from the village square, the current Nancy Cartmill Gardens. And it is sad in its decrepitude.

Melissa Reed in 1967 at the graves of Joseph
and Marie Gardner in the Barboursville Cemetery
(Photo by Frank Ball, Courtesy of Barboursville Public Library)

I have come to think of the Barboursville Cemetery as the Rodney Dangerfield of town graveyards. The village cemetery has gotten so little respect for so many years that a lot of it looks like the photos below (taken in 2009, before I got acquainted with so many of its occupants.) Regardless of whether the damage to the plot fences and monuments has been done by vandals, heavy equipment, soil erosion, the years, the weather or a combination of these elements, suffice it to say that care of these sites has not been perpetual.

Images of Barboursville Cemetery photographed in 2009.
(Photos by the author)

In the march of progress through time, other local cemeteries stand in contrast to Barboursville's. Old rival Guyandotte has it all over Barboursville in the way it honors its dead (its cemetery is currently maintained by the Huntington park board). The privately-maintained Thornburg family plot in Guyan Estates not only presents a stark contrast to the village burial ground, but demonstrates that it is possible to keep equally-ancient and weathered headstones upright and unbroken.

According to Barry Huffstutler who maintains the excellent local history website *Doors to the Past,* the Barboursville Cemetery was started around 1812 and most of the early graves were field stones. The first marker is said to belong to a Dusenbery. It is also said that when new graves were dug traces of old graves were found. Huffstutler's website relies on several sources and lists over 200 cemetery occupants, including several whose remains are believed to be in unmarked graves.

His lists do not include some of the African-Americans, including the original Washington and Hicks family settlers whose death certificates indicate they were indeed buried at Barboursville Cemetery. (Perhaps the disappearance of these twentieth century graves explains the vague nature of African American history in Barboursville.)

Ted Allen told me he remembered placing flowers on his great-grandparents' graves on Memorial Day, and that these and other black gravesites were located just behind the backyards of the Hicks-Washington-Scott families at the rear side of 901 and 905 Main Street.

"They tore all that down and made a housing area out of it. So I don't know what they did with the graves," Allen said.

The Barboursville Cemetery may not be host to paranormal research, but it is haunted in a sense—even cursed, dare I say—by bureaucratic neglect of years past. The history of the cemetery itself holds multi-generational conflict, outrage and ultimately resignation over exactly who was responsible for protecting it. Generations of legal minds have tried to sort out the ambiguous ownership of the cemetery, and I will not make the attempt.

I will, however, share a couple of interesting news clips. The first is a 1915 *Herald-Dispatch* report concerning the present-day Oaklawn Cemetery on East Pea Ridge:

BOARD OF TRADE PURCHASES NEW CEMETARY PLOT

- Barboursville Problem Has Been Solved by Recent Addition -
- Secure 20 Acres from Mounts Farm -
- Board of Trade Will Meet Tonight to Form Cemetery Association -

Barboursville will soon have a new cemetery if the board of trade, at the regular meeting tonight, ratifies the action of D. Blain Shaw, a representative, who has signed a deed for twenty acres of ground opposite Barboursville across the Guyan river on the paved road. The plot is a part of the Mounts farm, owned by Cecil Mounts. It was formerly the J.G. Miller estate.

The land was purchased for $200 an acre, it was stated, and the deed was signed yesterday. It is expected that the board of trade will take favorable action tonight and will in addition form a company to be incorporated later.

The new company will be known as the Barboursville Cemetery association and will be made up of members of the trade body. Barboursville was forced to secure a new cemetery plot. The present graveyard has been filled and it was impossible to secure a portion of the Kuhn estate, which adjoins it, without condemnation proceedings. It is said that in the will of Mrs. Kuhn the land was bequeathed to charitable institutions and would have made the condemnation a very hard matter.

Now that Barboursville has a new cemetery it is believed suggestions will lead to all of the bodies being exhumed and transferred to the new plot. However a mass meeting of the citizens of Barboursville will decide the matter. (Board of Trade Purchases New Cemetery Plot 1915)

The second clip, undated, was found in a scrapbook from the Stephens collection and is believed to have been published in the mid-1950s:

CENTURY-OLD BARBOURSVILLE CEMETERY TO BE RENOVATED
Barboursville's 118-year-old cemetery on the north side of Cemetery street, untended and neglected for many years, has been taken over by the Barboursville town council which will renovate it and give it perpetual care.

At a meeting of the town council last week, a resolution was adopted whereby the council accepted a deed to the cemetery known as the "Barboursville Old Cemetery," from trustees appointed by Judge John Hereford of Cabell County circuit court.

The cemetery consists of approximately 2.1 acres of land. Buried there are the forbears of some of Barboursville's leading contemporary citizens who have had twinges of conscience over the fact that weeds and undergrowth have run wild over the last resting places of grandfathers, great-grandfathers and great-great grandfathers.

Attorney Will H. Daniel, town counsel of Barboursville, who handled the legal details whereby the village took over the cemetery, said that the cemetery dates from October 25, 1835, when the first parcel of two comprising the burial ground was conveyed by trustees of the pre-war Methodist Episcopal Church to the church for use as a church and school.

Ultimately, the church and school were abandoned, disappeared and the land was used as a cemetery. The Civil War came on, the Methodist Episcopal Church became the Methodist Episcopal Church South and the Methodist Episcopal Church (North).

After the Civil War, the pre-war Methodist Episcopal Church became extinct in the vicinity of the Barboursville Old Cemetery, the original trustees died without conveying the land to any new organization and the cemetery fell into disuse. (H. Maxwell circa 1956)

To quote from a web-based community of preservationists: "Old cemeteries are markers of human history; of all the love, sweat, toil, tears, joys and triumphs of the past. They are links to family we never knew, they are sources of history and they tell us a great deal about ourselves culturally and socially."

Despite all the admirable qualities of its people, perhaps the greatest flaw in Barboursville's collective character is its carelessness with history. The village has allowed one after another of its treasures to be squandered, from the places described above to other lost landmarks such as "Colored Baptist Church" on Depot Street (now a fenced parking lot for city cars), and the round lighthouse that stood at the banks of the Guyan just south of U.S. Route 60.

It's an unfortunate trait, but one that's all-too-American. In the sadness of coming across decaying and disappearing historic properties, maybe the easiest thing is to feel helpless to do anything about it.

A Humble Proposition

Yet, there are things that can be done to restore Barboursville's rich heritage, and to regain a sense of the Lost Village's place in time.

Some recent projects represent a promising start. In 2007, Robert E. Frazier of Huntington painted a colorful mural along the interior wall of the overpass on Central Avenue, titled "Glimpse Into The Past." A few years later, the West Virginia Civil War Trails program placed an interpretive marker near the fountain at Nancy Cartmill Gardens to recognize the Battle of Barboursville.

By building on these two ideas, as well as protecting existing structures and providing some tender loving care to the cemetery, Barboursville could both commemorate its past and attract more historic tourism. Two relatively easy instal-lations would make a great difference, should village leaders be compelled to make the investment: a solid paneled gate at the front of the lot just east of the Toll House could both hide the big trucks that mar its appearance and serve as the "canvas" for another historic mural. With the addition of more interpretive markers around the fountain and along the walkways, the Cartmill Gardens could be transformed into a true Bicentennial Park. Interpretive signs could even be extended to the sidewalks of Barboursville to mark other historic sites, if someone wanted to get really serious about it.

All it would take to make a difference is a small group of passionate individuals and some dedicated volunteers. Taking inspiration from those buried in the sad old cemetery, Barboursville's future could hold another Marie Gardner, who made so many educational and cultural developments possible. Maybe someone will emulate town postmaster and empire-builder William Clendenin Miller, or the man who cleared the way for the Chesapeake and Ohio tracks, Irishman James S. Brady. Or the Reverend William Washington Scott, who built a school house for all the African American children of the town.

As I stated before, in terms of capitalizing on local history, many American towns have done much more with much less.

Hail to West Virginia's Best Village—Lost or Found

With or without a lasting physical legacy, let Barboursville be remembered for what it has always been, a town uniquely weathered and shaped by America's destiny and West Virginia's evolution. It is not the story of buildings, roads or bridges. It's the story of individuals and families who learned how to "go with the flow" and capitalize on the opportunities presented.

The first settlers were American Revolutionary veterans who arrived at Virginia's western border at the end of George Washington's presidency. The new village, officially founded during the height of America's second battle for independence, attracted educated young patriots who forged Cabell County's political and educational institutions and influenced an entire region.

From the beginning of westward expansion, the village stood smack dab at the national crossroads. Geographically seated at the junction of two rivers, a national turnpike, two railroads and the major highway systems of the twentieth century, Barboursville offered its residents an ever-changing glimpse of America on the move.

In the course of West Virginia's social and political birth pangs, including the sectional divisions of the Civil War, Barboursville's people stood at a junction as well, finding themselves divided for a short but painful time. Then, as America passed from the Agricultural to the Industrial era, the people of the village learned to pull together and let bygones be bygones.

First they welcomed the thunderous arrival of Collis P. Huntington's transcontinental railroad through the center of town, then suddenly found themselves in the shadow of his bustling namesake city, the city that took away Barboursville's identity as the county seat. Church and business leaders led the charge as Barboursville quickly and purposefully redefined itself.

The village operated simultaneously as a rough-and-ready gateway to the coal fields and a reverent college town. At the turn of the century, diverse new faces mingled with rural farm dwellers and more established founding families.

Just as Barboursville ushered in its own second century, the automobile changed everything. Main and Depot Streets receded alongside a faster thoroughfare. The Great Depression took its toll and a college was lost. The federal government provided a New Deal to America, and a needed boost in local construction and conservation work. Young men of the village answered the call to military service and returned as heroes of two "Great Wars." A contingent of bright young "Morris Harveyans" made Barboursville their permanent home and carried a proud educational tradition into its public schools.

Residents watched the town's fortunes shrink in the mid-twentieth century, but took pride in "B-ville" as a safe, nurturing bedroom community that was close to city jobs and conveniences. Villagers celebrated the achievements of the healthy, well-rounded youth who put Barboursville back on the map as the home of state champions; in turn, this high-spirited generation gave birth to the Baby Boomers. During these same decades, the village found itself host to state-run properties for West Virginia's marginalized people. From the town doctors to the volunteer firefighters, Barboursville's citizens did all that was in their power to provide safety, comfort and dignity to those at the forgotten fringes of society.

After one hundred years of being dwarfed by Huntington, what went around came around during America's late-century consumer boom. The shift of economic momentum from Barboursville to Huntington that began in the 1870s suddenly reversed itself after the people of the cash-strapped village pulled together to annex the Huntington Mall. As a result of the retail bonanza that followed, Barboursville not only weathered the economic storm brought about by two foreign wars, a stock market crash and a Great Recession, but has continued to grow and prosper.

Through all the years and changes, the gently rolling landscape combined with close access to a near-constant stream of travelers has surely molded the character of Barboursville's people. Villagers not only embody the quintessential Appalachian values—love of the home place, sense of humor, modesty—but most have seen enough of the world to recognize how precious these qualities are. Given the choice to move a few miles either way, out to the country or into the bigger city, residents of "old Barboursville" have not only chosen but cherished the spirit of small town life.

Through the ups and downs of two American centuries, the people who made this West Virginia village their home have been neighborly, tolerant, educated, enterprising and resilient individuals and families. They are the soul of the Lost Village. Let's hope that current and future generations will step up and celebrate, protect and preserve the memory of those "who made Barboursville Barboursville."

Thank you, reader, for joining me on this Barboursville odyssey. Thanks as well for enduring this writer's particular take on local history, as I did my best to carry the torch picked up from Lambert, Ball and others, and put it into context.

If this work inspires other grandkids and great-grandkids to ask more questions, solve more mysteries, or fill in missing details of the ongoing chronicle of "The Best Little Village in West Virginia," I will consider it a grand success.

A Timeline of Barboursville, County, State, National and World Events

Year	Barboursville	Cabell County	Virginia/ West Virginia	United States	World
1770-79	Land where Mud and Guyandotte Rivers meet, stands as wilderness and likely hunting ground for Shawnee, Mingo and Seneca tribes	1772:England's King George III grants land in this area to John Savage and other Colonial Solders for their service in French and Indian War in the 1750s	1771: Natural gas discovered in the Kanawha Valley 1774: Defeat of Chief Cornstalk at Point Pleasant signals end of Indian presence in western Va.	1773: Boston Tea Party protest against British Tax 1775: Revolutionary War begins 1776: U.S. Declaration of Independence signed	1771: Russia, under Empress Catherine the Great, conquers Crimea
1780-89			1780: Richmond becomes capital of Virginia 1787: James River and Kanawha Turnpike authorized	1783: George Washington leads U.S.to win war of Independence 1787-89: U.S. Constitution and Bill of Rights ratified	1789: French Revolution begins with storming of the Bastille
1790-99				1794-95: Battle of Fallen Timbers ends Northwest Indian War, leads to treaty ceding much of Ohio to U.S.	1796: Napoleon Bonaparte's campaign to conquer Europe 1791: Slaves in French Colony of Haiti rebel

1800-09	1802: William C. Merritt and Jeremiah Ward purchase land on both sides of the Guyandotte. Future site of Barboursville is called "Merritt's Mill."	1809: County created in honor of Gov. Wm. Cabell; area includes land from current Boone, Lincoln, Logan, Mingo, Putnam and Wayne counties.	1800: Martha Washington sets all her slaves free 1806: First salt well drilled in Great Kanawha Valley	1800: White House completed 1803-1806: Lewis and Clark Expedition sets out to explore west in search of route to Pacific Ocean	1804: Napoleon crowns himself Emperor of France
1810-19	1813: Town created by Act of Virginia Assembly 1813: Barboursville becomes county seat 1814: James River and Kanawha Turnpike extended to Barboursville	1810: Substitute County Census contains 487 households and 122 slaves	1810: Western Virginia protests unequal represen- tation in Virginia legislature.	1812-1814: U.S. at War with Britain; Washington, DC burned 1819: U.S. purchases Florida from Spain	1812: Bonaparte fights way to Moscow with 450,000 men – 440,000 die of cold and hunger
1820-29	1824: Va. General Assembly authorizes sale of lots in the public square 1824: Land deeded for construction of Methodist Church 1828: Town hosts Andrew Jackson who passes through during presidential campaign	1824: Part of county goes to forma- tion of Logan county	1829: Virginia counties west of the Allegheny Mountains protest constitu- tion that favors the slave-holding counties.	1823: With Monroe Doctrine U.S. asserts freedom from European Intervention	1821: Liberia founded for freed slaves 1829: First steam loco- motive built in England

1830-39	1830: Town has its own postmaster 1837: Land deeded by William C. Merritt's daughter to James River and Kanawha Turnpike for Toll House	1830: Additional land parceled to Logan county 1831: Daily stagecoaches and mail run between Richmond and the Ohio River on James River and Kanawha Turnpike 1837: Marshall Academy founded as "subscription school"	1830: Separation of western Virginia from eastern Virginia proposed by The Wheeling Gazette 1834: First commercial coal company in the Kanawha Valley	Advent of Electric telegraph and vulcanized rubber 1836: Texas wins independence from Mexico	Photography invented in France 1830: Charles X of France overthrown 1837: England's Queen Victoria begins her 63-year reign
1840-49	Barboursville becomes a regional center for manufacture of fans, furniture, wagons, buggies and harnesses; Timber becomes big business 1849: Large family of Sanders slaves manumitted and aided in resettlement to northern state.	1842: Wayne County created from Cabell 1847: Part of Boone County taken from Cabell 1848-50: Putnam county formed in part from Cabell parcels 1849: Guyandotte Navigation Company forms to build locks and dams on namesake river		1844: Methodist Church divides over issue of slavery 1845-49: Mass immigration of Irish escaping potato famine 1848: First women's rights convention in New York State 1848: California's gold rush opens up American west	1845-46: Failure of Ireland's potato crop kills more than a million people 1848: Last King of France abdicates 1848: Germans Marx and Engels publish Communist Manifesto
1850-59	1852: Two-story brick courthouse erected on public square -Locks and dams built from Barboursville to Branchland to aid in timber and product shipping downriver; -Steamboat era brings hotel trade to village	1854: First steamboat put into service on Guyandotte River 1857: Massachusetts abolitionist Eli Thayer speaks to county citizens; Richmond newspapers chide county; residents are divided over slavery	1853: State Board of Public Works plans C&O Railroad 1859: John Brown and followers attack the U.S. Federal Arsenal at Harpers Ferry in effort to incite a slave insurrection	1850: California becomes U.S. state 1853: Railroad completed from New York to Chicago	1853-54: Japan forced by U.S. to open its ports to Western trade

1861-63	1861: Battle of Barboursville at Fortification Hill results in several casualties 1862: Second skirmish at Barboursville leaves Union soldier dead near William C. Miller home	1860-61: Some South-leaning citizens form Border Rangers militia 1861: Cabell County votes to remain in Union 1861: Guyandotte torched by soldiers who destroy business section	1861: Richmond is made Capital of the Confederacy 1861-62: Wheeling Convention splits Virginia's counties over Ordinance of Secession	1860: Lincoln elected President 1861: Deep divisions between northern and southern states plunge country into open warfare	1861: Britain's Prince Albert, husband of Queen Victoria, dies at age 42
1863-69	1863: Barboursville becomes part of newly formed state 1863: Bitterness lingers between families of 27 Union volunteers and 67 Confederate volunteers from the village -Village's Methodist congregations split, Steele Mem. built for "northern" families 1869: Baptist and Episcopal churches allowed to have services in courthouse	1867: Cabell contributes land to formation of Lincoln County 1869: Collis P. Huntington begins two decades as president of Chesapeake and Ohio Railroad Co.	1863: West Virginia admitted to the Union as a key Civil War border state 1865: First free public school opens in Charleston 1865: Governor approves an act abolishing slavery and provides for emancipation of all slaves 1866: Hospital for the insane completed at Weston 1866: Voters ratify constitutional amendment denying citizenship to all who aided the Confederacy.	1865: Union wins Civil War after more than 600,000 die in fight 1865: President Abraham Lincoln is shot at Ford's Theatre and dies the next morning	

1870-79	C and O in Barboursville, major construction and freight activity on Depot Street 1876: Mob hangs Ed Williams from tree on courthouse lawn after Charles Meehling murder	1870: City of Huntington founded as western terminus of C&O Railway 1873: Completion of C&O Rail line from Richmond to Huntington	1871: Suffrage granted to all male citizens regardless of race; Citizenship restored to all persons stripped of voting privileges in '66 1875: State Capitol moved to Wheeling	1870: Georgia becomes the last of the Confederate states to reenter the Union. 1871: The Great Chicago Fire destroys much of that city 1876: Alexander Graham Bell makes the first successful telephone call	1870: The Franco-Prussian War begins, provoked by Prussian leader Otto von Bismarck, as part of his plan to unite Germany
1880-89	1887: County Seat moves from Barboursville 1888: Barboursville Seminary opens its doors; town's two saloons are closed	1884: Ohio River floods Huntington 1886: Huntington get electric streetlights 1887: Huntington becomes the new county seat 1889: Huntington Advertiser begins publication	1880: First major coal strike results in governor sending militia to Hawks Nest	1886: The Statue of Liberty is dedicated in New York Harbor	1881: Czar Nicholas II of Russia is assassinated 1887: Britain celebrates the 50th year of Queen Victoria's reign
1890-99	1890: Seminary reorganizes as Barboursville College	1893: Huntington Herald, later the Herald-Dispatch, begins publication	1897: Mary Harris "Mother" Jones sent into West Virginia to organize miners 1899: First state execution at Moundsville	1890: United Mine Workers of America formed	1898: Spanish American War begins

1900-09	1900: Guyan Valley Railway begins construction at Barboursville 1901: College renamed after major endowment from Raleigh Co. coal man Morris Harvey 1904: Barboursville Clay Manufacturing Company founded as major producer of bricks		1902: Mother Jones campaigns to unionize 7,000 miners in Kanawha Valley 1904: Guyan Valley Railway completed to Logan, opening up southern WV coal industry 1906: Over 600 miners killed in eight separate mine disasters across the state		
1910-19	1918: Presbyterian church forms	1913: Ohio River flood leaves thousands in Huntington homeless	1917: West Virginia Selective Service registrants number nearly 325,000	1912: Titanic sinks on its maiden voyage 1916: Amendment allowing suffrage for women rejected by voter 1917: US enters World War I	1914-18: World War I fought in Europe, killing more than 2 million

1920-29	Farmdale Fairgrounds host horse races C&O Reclamation Plant expands	1920: Canada-based International Nickel Co. builds facility by Guyandotte River 1924: Palatine Missionary Society opens St. Mary's Hospital 1926: Huntington first bridge across Ohio River opens at 6th Street 1928: Second largest theater in U.S., Keith-Albee, opens in Huntington	1920-21: Coal wars in an effort to unionize West Virginia coal miners 1925: Black leaders protest and prohibit showing of D. W. Griffith's Birth of a Nation at a Charleston theater.	1929: Market crash ushers in 12-year Great Depression in America	
1930-39	1935: Morris Harvey College abandons Barboursville and moves to Charleston	1937: County residents among more than 25,000 in region affected by record flooding; 6000 left homeless in Huntington	1933: Legislature abolishes magisterial and indepen-dent school districts, merging them into 55 county school boards	1933: President Franklin Roosevelt launches "New Deal" to get Americans back to work	1933: Adolph Hitler becomes chancellor of Germany 1938-39: Germany's invasions lead England and France to declare War
1940-49	1942: Barboursville Unit of Weston State Hospital opens on prop-erty formerly used by College. 1949: Legislative act establishes Barboursville State Hospital.	1943: Huntington floodwall project is completed 1949: WSAZ becomes state's first TV station	1946: Major chemical industries begin oper-ating in the Ohio River valley	1941: Japanese attack Americans at Pearl Harbor, leading to U.S. declaration of war 1945: FDR dies	1945: German and Japanese forces surrender, after World War II claims over 50 million lives 1945: Hitler commits suicide 1949: Mao Tse-tung proclaims new Communist Republic of China

1950-59	1953: Barboursville High School wins State High School Football championship	1952: Nearby Tri-State airport opening, bringing scheduled air service to area 1953: Ground broken for Cabell Huntington Hospital 1957: WV's interstate highway construction begins in Cabell County	1952: Construction begins on the West Virginia Turnpike 1954: Law allowing blacks to attend state colleges and universities enacted	1953: 1954: Landmark Supreme Court decision overturns public school segregation of black and white students	1950-53: Korean War between China-supported North and U.N.-supported South.
1960-69	1960: West Virginia's first large housing subdivision, Guyan Estates, built on Thornburg farmland near Davis Creek 1962: Fire damages Rosa Harvey Hall at Barboursville State Hospital	1961: Marshall College is designated a university	1965: Capital punishment abolished in West Virginia 1967: Silver Bridge at Point Pleasant collapses, killing 46	1963: JFK is assassinated 1964: Civil Rights Act outlaws racial discrimination 1968: Sen. Robert Kennedy and Rev. Martin Luther King are killed	1965: U.S. troops sent to South Vietnam to help fight Communist North.
1970-79	1975: BHS wins state AAA basketball championship 1978: Barboursville State Hospital is closed by the state 1978: Governor Jay Rockefeller announces plans to locate State Veterans Home at former hospital site 1978: Barboursville town council votes to annex property for planned shopping mall	1970: 75 people die in plane crash at Tri-State airport, including Marshall's football team members, coaches and fans. 1971: Amtrack passenger rail service begins 1976: Medical school established at Marshall University	1972: Logan County coal waste dam fails, killing 125 people and injuring thousands at Buffalo Creek 1974: Kanawha County school board removes controversial textbooks amid student protests	1973: U.S. suspends actions against North Vietnam. 1974: Watergate scandal results in President Nixon's resignation	1979: Iranian students take 52 U.S. diplomats hostage for 444 days

1980-89	1981: Huntington Mall opens in Barboursville 1981: West Virginia State Veterans Home dedicated	1983-89: MU Head Coach Rick Huckabay leads "Huck's Herd" to four Southern Conference titles, three NCAA Tournaments and an NIT berth 1985: East Huntington bridge opens	1984: Fairmont's Mary Lou Retton became the first woman to win a gold medal in gymnastics at the Los Angeles Olympics	1981: Personal Computers (PCs) introduced by IBM 1984: Vietnam War Memorial opened in Washington 1986: Space Shuttle challenger breaks apart after launch	1985: Mikhail Gorbachev calls for restructuring of Soviet Union 1989: Berlin Wall falls 1989: Student protesters killed in China's Tiananmen Square
1990-99	1992: Lake William dedicated in new Barboursville Community Park 1993: Village elects its first female mayor, Nancy Cartmill 1994: Barboursville and Milton High Schools are closed as Cabell Midland school opens in Ona 2001: Construction begins on Western Regional Jail	1992: Marshall University wins NCAA I-AA National Basketball Championship 1993: Production stops at Owens Illinois glass bottle factory 1999: Nearby Ashland Oil moves it corporate offices out of Ashland	1990: Former Governor Arch Moore pleads guilty to felony charges and serves three years in prison	1999:Two students go on a shooting spree at Columbine High School in Colorado, killing 13 people and then themselves. -	1990: U.S. launches Operation Desert Storm in response to Iraqi aggression against Kuwait 1990:South African anti-apartheid activist, Nelson Mandela is freed after spending 27 years as a political prisoner.

2000-09	Two new "Bridges to Nowhere" draw interest and development to west side of village near Alt. Rt. 10 2004: Council bid results in acquisition of former WV Dept. of Agriculture land , adding 250 acres to Community Park 2006: "Big Ben Bowen Highway" dedicated as connection between U.S. Route 60 and Rt. 2	2001: Cabell County native Dr. Paul Ambrose is killed in the September 11 crash at the Pentagon 2004: Opening of Pullman Square helps revitalize downtown Huntington 2007: Nine are killed in a fire at Huntington's Emmons Jr. Apartment building	2003: Private Jessica Lynch, a West Virginia native, is rescued from captivity in Iraq	2001: Al-Qaeda terrorists hijack four commercial airliners, crashing into New York City's two World Trade Center Towers, the Pentagon and rural Pennsylvania, killing 3,000 2008: Stocks nosedive as credit crisis throws nation into financial recession 2008: Barack Obama elected first African American U.S. president	2001: U.S. and British forces launch war in Afghanistan in response to Al-Qaida attacks 2003: Multi-national forces invade Iraq 2006: Saddam Hussein executed
2010-2013	2010: City Park expansion attracts WV 5-K Race Committee events, regional youth soccer, dirt biking and Relay for Life to Barboursville 2011: Longest-serving mayor Paul Turman wins sixth term	2010: Huntington and Cabell County schools spotlighted in Jamie Oliver's Food Revolution on ABC-TV. 2012: Rare "derecho" windstorm leaves 30,000 county homes and businesses without electricity during week-long heat wave.	2010: WV Senator Robert Byrd, longest serving Congress member in U.S. history, dies at age 92 2010: Explosion at Massey Energy Upper Big Branch mine leaves 29 dead	2010: U.S. continues to endure "Great Recession" with slow economic recovery and persistent high unemployment	2011: U.S. ends military involvement in Iraq 2011: Triple disaster in Japan after an earthquake generates a tsunami that sets off major damage to a nuclear power plant

BARBOURSVILLE MAYORS 1898-2013

1898	G.W. Ayers
1903-1904	Andrew Jackson Burns
1905	James Skinner
1906	S. E. Steele
1907-1908	D. O. Snyder
1909, 1913	James Brady
1910, 1926-1927	P. A. Vallandingham
1911	W. H. Stowasser
1911	W. S. King
1912	Jesse Green
1912	W.S. Hefner
1913	D. Blain Shaw
1914-1919	V. G. Shipe
1919-1920	C. R. Miller
1921, 1929-1930	H. S. King
1922-1923	T. W. Peyton
1924-1926	James Brady
1927-1928	John W. Jackson
1928-1929	E. L. McCue
1930-1931	C. T. Jimison
1931-1933	G. E. Welch
1933-1939, 1941-1943	C. C. Swann
1939-1941	R. W. Nelson
1943-1945, 1953-1955	G. P. Vallandingham
1945-1947	D. B. Nelson
1947-1949	C. T. Jimison
1949-1951	Harley Townsend
1951-1953	G. E. Welch
1955-1961	Jesse L. Henderson
1961-1969	Boyd Hash
1969-1971	Don Owens
1971-1973	Emmitt Mahafey
1973-1975	Don Owens
1975-1977	Boyd Hash
1977-1979	Ted Kirk
1979-1981	Don Owens
1981-1987	William Rucker
1987-1989	Don Owens
1989-1993	William Plyburn
1993-2001	Nancy Cartmill
2001-2013	Paul Turman *(elected term is through 2015)*

Source: Mayors' Wall, Nancy Cartmill Gardens, Barboursville, WV

SOURCE NOTES

Refer to the Bibliography for complete citations of the information sources used in this book. Sources are listed by chapter and noted at each subsection where they are cited.

Dedication
D. C. Miller 1976
Lowery 1984

CHAPTER 1—At 200 Years, Finding the Soul of the Lost Village
Frommer 1988

CHAPTER 2—"Our Special Correspondent Furnishes an Interesting Letter (1898-1901)
Cabell Record Newspaper 1898-1901

CHAPTER 3—Rivers, Trails and First Settlers (1700s to 1810)
Upriver and Up a Tree
WV Humanities Council 2006-2009
F. B. Lambert Collection n. d.
Land Grants and Treacherous Years
KYOWVA Genealogical and Historical Society, 2010
Dr. Robert Jay Dilger n. d.
George S. Wallace 1935
Captain Merritt and his Mill
Wallace 1935
Freeman n. d.
McEntee 2001
Blazing a Trail through a New Nation
F. B. Lambert Collection n. d.
Eldridge, Atlas of Appalachian Trails to the Ohio River 1998
Influence of Local Settlers
F. B. Lambert Collection n. d.
Simmons 2005
Wallace 1935
Eldridge, Cabell County's Empire for Freedom: The Manumission of Sampson Sanders' Slaves 1999
Roots Web 2000
Wallace 1935
Vogt 2011
J. Miller 1925

CHAPTER 4—A Frontier Town Takes Shape (1810-1820s)
Consider the word "frontier"
Chambers 2011
Maxwell 2009
Turman 2009
Meat—It's not just what's for dinner
Wikipedia
America's Original "Wild West"
Greater Kanawha Resource Conservation Development Council
Dunaway 1996
Pathway to the Mississippi
John E. Findling and Frank W. Thakeray 1997
Life around a Frontier Town
F. B. Lambert Collection n. d.
Mrs. Philip Richmond 1976

Wresting the County Seat from Guyandotte
Ball, History of Barboursville 1949
Gunter 1986
Mrs. Philip Richmond 1976
F. B. Lambert Collection n. d.
Wallace 1935
Matthews 1949-50
F. B. Lambert Collection n. d.
Mrs. Philip Richmond 1976
"The Sons of 1791"
Roots Web 2000
CrossSargent 2010
Mrs. Philip Richmond 1976
McMillian 2008
V. A. Lewis 1912
Kanawha Valley Star 1859
F. B. Lambert Collection n. d.
M. M. Johnson 1929
J. E. Smith 1996
Sellers 1991

CHAPTER 5—American Parade along Main Street (1820s to 1840s)
Completion of the Pike
F. B. Lambert Collection n. d.
Frank Ball, History of Barboursville, Wayne County News 7-7-1949
Meet the Travelers
F. B. Lambert Collection n. d.
Wallace 1935
Richard G. Stone 1978
Reniers 1941
Elliott and Nye 1852
Reniers 1941
An "Ordinary" Town
F. B. Lambert Collection n. d.
Calling the Tune
F. B. Lambert Collection n. d.
The Refining Influence of a French Noblewoman
D. J. Miller 1902
Gunter 1986
Roots Web 2000
Oberholtzer 1922
J. Miller 1925
D. J. Miller 1902
Matthews 1949-50
Religious Awakenings
Gunter 1986
Withers 2010
Connor n. d.
Steele 2010
Francis Asbury Society n. d.
Withers 2010
Wallace 1935
Otis K. Rice 1993
West Virginia Heritage Encyclopedia, Supplement Volume #6 1974
Cook, Monacans and Miners: Native American and Coal Mining Communities in Appalachia 2000
Barboursville on the Map
WVGenWeb n. d.
Thompson 1971
F. B. Lambert Collection n. d.

CHAPTER 6—Four Golden Years (1849-1852)

A Sleepy Stream Gets a Closer Look
Sedgwick 1976
J. Miller 1925
D. C. Miller, Herald Dispatch 1976
M. M. Johnson 1929
Greater Kanawha Resource Conservation Development Council 2011
A World in Flux
Wikipedia
The Guyandotte Navigation Company
Wallace 1935
Greater Kanawha Resource Conservation Development Council 2011
M. Beckett, Barboursville's Early History Recalled by Uncle Billy Miller 1933
Order for a New Courthouse
Wallace 1935
J. Miller 1925
A Splendid Home for a Growing Family
Roots Web 2000
Matthews 1949-50
Reasons-Pyles 2010
M. Beckett, Barboursville's Early History Recalled by Uncle Billy Miller 1933
Bozzelli 2009
Exodus on the River
F. B. Lambert Collection n. d.
Eldridge, Cabell County's Empire for Freedom: The Manumission of Sampson Sanders' Slaves 1999
Friedman 2011
Fain 2009
KYOWVA Genealogical and Historical Society 2011
Portrait of a western Virginia River Town at Mid-Century
F. B. Lambert Collection n. d.
KYOWVA Genealogical and Historical Society 2011
Valentine Leist, Pioneer Tanner, Taken by Death 1916
Wallace 1935
Elliott and Nye 1852

CHAPTER 7—Life on the Civil War Fault Line (1853-1861)
Moral Tensions over the South's "Peculiar Institution"
Schweiger 2000
F. B. Lambert Collection n. d.
Cabell County's Oldest Church Mud River Baptist 1967
Minutes Bloomingdale Salem Baptist church 1855-2005 - transcribed by T. Franklin May 2005
Shanks 1934
Spirit of Concession and Compromise
Manarin n. d.
P. Johnson 1997
Local Preoccupations
West Virginia Division of Culture and History 2011
Ball, History of Barboursville 1949
F. B. Lambert Collection n. d.
Greater Kanawha Resource Conservation Development Council 2011
M. M. Johnson 1929
Planitz 2010
Turner 1998
Wallace 1935
Ball, Steamboats on the Guyan 1966
Matthews 1949-50
Ball, Avenue of Antiquity Series 1973
Rising Passions and Deepening Divides
Wikipedia n. d.
P. Johnson 1997
Eldridge, Cabell County's Empire for Freedom: The Manumission of Sampson Sanders' Slaves 1999
Ceredo and Guyandotte

J. J. Geiger, Civil War in Cabell County, West Virginia 1861-1865 1991
Prochnow 2009
Marshall Turns to the Southern Methodists
F. B. Lambert Collection n. d
Matthews 1949-50
Roots Web 2000
Obituary of George Franklin Miller 1922
J. Benjamin 1953
V. A. Lewis, A History of Marshall Academy, Marshall College and Marshall College State Normal
    School 1912
The Noose Tightens
Wallace 1935
Shanks 1934
Gunter 1986
WV Division of Culture and History 2011
Dickinson 2011
Geiger, Civil War in Cabell County, West Virginia 1861-1865 1991
P. Johnson 1997
Barboursville in the 1860 Census
Heritage Quest Online 2011
Friedman 2011
Remember the *Fannie McBurnie* Chronology to Chaos
Geiger, Civil War in Cabell County, West Virginia 1861-1865 1991
V. Lewis 1906
P. Johnson 1997
An Ex Congressman Turned Highwayman 1861
Wallace 1935
Heritage Quest Online 2011
July 13, 1863
WV Division of Culture and History 2011
Wallace 1935
Heritage Quest Online 2011
Turner 1998
Geiger, Civil War in Cabell County, West Virginia 1861-1865 1991
M. M. Johnson 1929
Gunter 1986
J. Miller 1925
Ball, This Old House n. d.

CHAPTER 8—Barboursville's "Children of the Storm (1861-1869)
Raids, Ravages, Retaliation—and Four Yankee Teens
Geiger, Civil War in Cabell County, West Virginia 1861-1865 1991
Wikipedia n. d.
Heritage Quest Online 2011
Ball, The Everettes 1974
Gunter 1986
Ball, History of First United Methodist Church of Barboursville n. d.
KYOWVA Genealogical and Historical Society 2011
3-5-1975 Picture from the Past, Barboursville Bulletin
M. Beckett, Barboursville's Early History Recalled by Uncle Billy Miller 1933
F. B. Lambert Collection n. d.
Greater Kanawha Resource Conservation Development Council 2011
Baumgartner, The rides of Cabell County's 'Paul Revere' 1978
Dickinson 2011
 Baumgartner, First 'damnyankee gentleman' in Guyandotte n. d.
Joe Geiger n. d
West Virginia Division of Culture and History 2011
The Divergent Loyalties of the McComas Clan
P. Johnson 1997
Gunter 1986
Geiger, Civil War in Cabell County, West Virginia 1861-1865 1991

H. J. Baumgardner Obituary 1926
Simmons 2005
F. B. Lambert Collection n. d.
Wallace 1935
Mary Beth Pudup 1995
V. Lewis 1906
W. C. Smith 2011
Malin 1958
Kansas State Historical Society 1918
Heritage Quest Online 2011
Turner 1998
Baumgartner, Death in the Desert: The McComas Massacre of 1883 1977
Attack on the Miller Home
Reasons-Pyles 2010
Wallace 1935
J. Benjamin 1953
Geiger, Civil War in Cabell County, West Virginia 1861-1865 1991
Messy Affairs of County and State
Wallace 1935
Geiger, Civil War in Cabell County, West Virginia 1861-1865 1991
J. J. Geiger, Lecture 2011
Rice n. d.
WV Division of Culture and History 2011
War Grinds to a Bitter End
P. Johnson 1997
National Park Service 2011
Geiger, Civil War in Cabell County, West Virginia 1861-1865 1991
F. B. Lambert Collection n. d.
Matthews 1949-50
Dusenberry n. d.
Welsh 1995
Ball, Avenue of Antiquity Series 1973)
A Slow Return to Peacetime
H. R. Smith 1995
Wallace 1935
F. B. Lambert Collection n. d.
Gunter 1986
J. J. Geiger, Civil War in Cabell County, West Virginia 1861-1865 1991
WV Division of Culture and History 2011
M. M. Johnson 1929

CHAPTER 9—Village Booms and Busts (1870-1900)
Dawn of a New Age
The Library of Virginia
Wikipedia n. d.
P. Johnson 1997
Morison 1994
Barboursville's Shifting Labor Patterns
P. Johnson 1997
Heritage Quest Online 2011
Roots of A Striving New Generation
Roots Web 2000
F. B. Lambert Collection n. d.
F. Lambert 1929
Cabell County Courthouse n. d.
Wallace 1935
Engle 1993
Railroad Starts and Stops
D. C. Miller, Herald Dispatch 1976
P. Johnson

Morison 1994
D. C. Miller, "Huntington City Followed In Tracks of C&O Railway Growth": 1976
C. Fain 2012
Heritage Quest Online 2011
James I. Kuhn Obituary 1910
F. B. Lambert Collection n.d.
M. M. Johnson 1929
Ball, Avenue of Antiquity Series 1973
WVa-USA.com 2001
Yeatman 2008
Wallace 1935

A Man with a Printing Press
P. Johnson
Morison 1994
Heritage Quest Online 2011
Cabell County Press 1873

The New City of Huntington
City of Huntington 2011
Morison 1994
Wallen 1976
Bozzelli 2009

What About Jesse James?
Weaver 2008
Yeatman 2008
Great Bank robbery of 1875—Was It Jesse James? 1971

The George F. Miller Confusion
Ball, Old House Gets 'New Look' 1969
Roots Web 2000
Wallace 1935
WV State Historic Preservation Office 2008
Heritage Quest Online 2011
McMillian, Miller Homes an Early Piece of Area History 2008
Ball, Barboursville Bulletin 1966

Barboursville Babylon—The Meehling Affair
Heritage Quest Online 2011
Bloomingdale Salem Baptist Church Minutes 1855-2005 2005
Wallace 1935
Mrs. Philip Richmond 1976
WV Humanities Council 2006-2009
Cabell County's Greatest Tragedy and First Execution 1909
F. B. Lambert Collection n. d.
Gunter 1986

Colorful Life of the McKendree Twins
Heritage Quest Online 2011
Baumgartner, Mosaics from Barboursville's Past n. d.

The Rough and Rowdy "Guyan" Boatmen
Greater Kanawha Resource Conservation Development Council 2011
M. Beckett, The Guyandotte River n. d.
F. B. Lambert Collection n. d.
M. M. Johnson 1929
Baumgartner, Mosaics from Barboursville's Past n. d.

Among The President's Inner Circle
Rootsweb Family Histories n. d.
F. B. Lambert Collection n. d.
Roots Web 2000
United States Department of the Interior, National Park Service, National Register of Historic Places -
    Registration Form 748 Beech Street, Kenova 1989
West Virginia Legislature's Office of Reference and Information 2012
Morison 1994
P. Johnson 1997
Hensel 1892

Gunter 1986
Losing the Courthouse
M. E. Beckett 1935
Wallace 1935
D. C. Miller, Transportation Industry Carried Cabell Changes 1976
Baumgartner, Founding a College on a five dollar shoestring n. d.
Gunter 1986
W. Smith 1946
Old Water Mills Have Succumbed during Steady March of Progress 1939
Ball, History of Barboursville 1949
Barboursville Takes on a New Identity
Baumgartner, Founding a College on a five dollar shoestring n. d.
M. E. Beckett 1935
F. B. Lambert Collection n. d.
Day 1976
Mrs. Philip Richmond 1976
P. Johnson 1997
The Gilded Age Goes Out in a "Panic"
Morison 1994
White 1976
PBS 2000
Central Pacific Railroad Photographic History Museum 2012

CHAPTER 10— Here Lies Mary E. Brady
F. B. Lambert Collection n. d.
Out of the Frying Pan
Herald-Dispatch n. d.
Heritage Quest Online 2011
Roots Web 2000
F. B. Lambert Collection n. d.
Turner 1998
Brady 2012
One of a Million Irish Refugees
F. B. Lambert Collection n. d.
Anti-Irish Sentiment 2003
Historical Society of Pennsylvania n. d.
Laidley 1911
A Youth Tossed in Turmoil
F. B. Lambert Collection n. d.
Matthews 1949-50
World Health Organization 2012
National Center for Biotechnology Information, U.S. National Library of Medicine 2012
Wallace 1935
West Virginia Division of Culture and History 2011
Ball, Avenue of Antiquity Series 1973
Into the Fire—Savage Times for the Moore Men
Heritage Quest Online 2011
F. B. Lambert Collection n. d.
J. Geiger 2009
Wallace 1935
Childers 2008
Cabell County Courthouse n.d.
West Virginia Division of Culture and History 2011
Brady 2012
Land Deeds and Diapering Cloth
Cabell County Courthouse n. d.
F. B. Lambert Collection n. d.
West Virginia Division of Culture and History 2011
Town and Country Living
Ball, Avenue of Antiquity Series 1973
Laidley 1911

Heritage Quest Online 2011
F. B. Lambert Collection n. d.
"Hurled Into Eternity"
Herald-Dispatch 1912

CHAPTER 11—Beyond the Slave Kitchen – Barboursville's African American Family History
Debunking the Slave Kitchen
Heritage Quest Online 2011
Barboursville's "Free People of Color"
Olafson n. d.
Heinegg 2009
F. B. Lambert Collection n. d.
Dundas 1938
C. M. Fain 2009
Heritage Quest Online 2011
"A Society with Slaves" in Virginia's "Slave Society"
C. M. Fain 2009
Heritage Quest Online 2011
A State in Limbo
C. M. Fain 2009
West Virginia Sesquicentennial Commission 2013
Educational Broadcasting Corporation 2004
KYOWVA Genealogical and Historical Society 2010
Post-Bellum: Who Remained?
Ball, Old Morris Homestead Built 120 Years Ago 2011
Heritage Quest Online 2011
New Citizens Migrate to Cabell County
Engle 1993
C. M. Fain 2009
F. B. Lambert Collection n. d.
Educational Broadcasting Corporation 2004
Wikipedia n. d.
Heritage Quest Online 2011
The Arrival of Mrs. Mattie Fliggins
West Virginia Division of Culture and History 2011
Estler 1935
A. Turman 2010
West Virginia Division of Culture and History 2011
Heritage Quest Online 2011
"Moments in Early Negro Education"
Bickley 1979
Isaac Vinton Bryant - History of the American Negro: West Virginia Edition n. d
C. M. Fain 2009
Swann 2000
F. B. Lambert Collection n. d.
Woodson 1921
"A Wheelbarrow Full of Dimes"
Washington 1996
F. B. Lambert Collection n. d.
M. E. Johnson, Descendents of Billy Hicks 2010
Heritage Quest Online 2011
Veteran Barber of Barboursville Dies 1920
Cabell County Courthouse n. d.
Ball, Avenue of Antiquity XXV 1973
Deeds to "Higher Ground"
WV Division of Culture and History 2011
C. M. Fain 2009
Bickley 1979
Woodson 1921
Haught 1971
Racial Snippets from *The Cabell Record*

Cabell Record Newspaper 1898-1901
Barboursville Families: Hamler, Hill, Smith, Washington and Whirls
Cabell County Courthouse n. d.
West Virginia Division of Culture and History 2011
Heritage Quest Online 2011
Bryan 2003
W. Smith n. d.
F. B. Lambert Collection n. d
Ball, Unknown n. d
Goines 2009
Colored Students Engaged in Debate 1917
Jackson n. d
Sargent 2007
The Legacy of Reverend William Washington Scott
A. Caldwell 1923
A. B. Caldwell 1917
West Virginia Division of Culture and History 2011
M. E. Johnson, Descendents of Billy Hicks 2010
Mr. and Mrs. Ted Allen of Park Forest 2010
Cabell County Courthouse n. d.
Mrs. Philip Richmond 1976
Mixed Origins and Labels of Race
U.S. Census Bureau 2002
Washington 1996
Heritage Quest Online 2011
F. B. Lambert Collection n. d.
The Sorrells: Finding Refuge from "Jim Crow
.J D. Smith 2002
WV Division of Culture and History 2011
Konhaus 2007
Marshall University 2007
Good Neighbors
Washington 1996

CHAPTER 12—Turn-of-the-Century Bustle (1898-1920)
A Diverse Mix in the Village
Bozzelli 2009
Mrs. Philip Richmond 1976
Cabell Record 1899
Cabell Record 1898-1901
Morison 1994
Baumgartner, Mosaics from Barboursville's Past n. d.
F. B. Lambert Collection n. d.
Heritage Quest Online 2011
A Line to the Coalfields
F. B. Lambert Collection n. d.
Gunter 1986
Ball, Avenue of Antiquity Series 1973
West Virginia Division of Culture and History 2011
Coal Exhibit at Chief Logan State Park n. d.
Baisden 1976
Heritage Quest Online 2011
C. M. Fain 2009
Ball, Avenue of Antiquity Series 1973
Ball, History of Barboursville 1949
Bernstein 1985
Cabell County Courthouse n. d.
Chesapeake and Oho Historical Society 2012
M. Beckett, The Railroad n. d.
Tyler n. d.
"B" Stands For...

West Virginia Division of Culture and History 2011
Cabell Record 1898-1901
Bozzelli 2009
Gunter 1986
U.S. Department of Agriculture, Soil Conservation Services 1989
Barboursville Clay Manufacturing Company 2012
F. B. Lambert Collection n. d.
Heritage Quest Online 2011
West Virginia Division of Culture and History 2011
WV State Historic Preservation Office 2008
T. Sedgwick n. d.
Ball, Four Barboursville Businesses Stay in Same Families for 50 Years 1958
Vallandingham 2012
Ball, Avenue of Antiquity Series 1973
Dilley, The Vallandingham Family of Barboursville, West Virginia n. d.
Heritage Quest Online 2011
Mrs. Philip Richmond 1976
M. Beckett, The Barboursville Baptist Church n. d.
M. Beckett, Barboursville History 1996
UMC General Commission on Archives and History n. d.
M. Beckett, Morris Harvey College n. d
Midwest PHC 2004
Ball, Photographic Scrapbook n. d.
Cabell County Farm Women's Clubs 1961
Mrs. Philip Richmond 1976
Baumgartner, Whizzing around town at 8 miles per hour n. d.
Signs of the Times
P. Johnson 1997
Morison 1994
(Intense Excitement at Reno on Eve of Greatest Battle in History of Pugilism 1910
Nevada Historical Society 2010
Minnesota Public Radio 2012
Heritage Quest Online 2011
A Late Centennial Observance
Barboursville 100 Years Old 2013
Barboursville to be made terminal for G.V. Division 1913
Barboursville 1913
Barboursville to have Ice Plant 1913
Heritage Quest Online 2011
Mrs. Philip Richmond 1976
H. Maxwell 1899
Celebration over and Barboursville feels justly proud 1913
Entry into Europe's "Great War"
P. Johnson 1997
Morison 1994
W. Smith 1920
Holtby 2008
Morris Harvey to Have Good Outfit 1917
Midkiff 2012
Negroes Enlisting in the U.S. Army 1917
Nettie Woodyard of the Army Red Cross Nurse Corps
American Red Cross n. d.
W. Smith 1920
Heritage Quest Online 2011
West Virginia Division of Culture and History 2011
Swann Family Genealogy Notebook n. d.
The American Journal of Nursing, Vol. 18, No. 16 1918
Donahue 1985
W.W. Herrick 1918
Oscar T. Schultz 1918
U.S. Department of Health and Human Services n. d.

Casto 2009
M. Beckett, When We Were Sick 1996
Huffstutler 2007
From Tom's Creek to Belleau Wood—Barboursville's Gold Star Son
Heritage Quest Online 2011
Roots Web 2000
W. Smith 1920
Arnold-Friend 2010
16th Infantry Regiment 2005
The Great War Society 2000
Ferguson 1918
South Bank of Marne Cleared; Drive Goes On 1918
Duffy 2009
Farwell 1999
American Gold Star Mothers, Inc. n. d.
Potter 1999
American Battle Monuments Commission n. d.

CHAPTER 13—Tucked Away (1920s-1970s)
Motoring into the Modern Age
Morison 1994
Bozzelli 2009
F. B. Lambert Collection n.d.
F. Ball, The Country Squire 1973
Orders C.andO. to build a viaduct at Barboursville 1926
Barboursville Enjoys Period of Prosperity 1918
M. Beckett, Barboursville History 1996
W. Smith, Barboursville: Some Interesting Historic Facts About Former County Seat 1921
KYOWVA Genealogical and Historical Society 2011
Morison 1994
Fast Times at Farmdale Road
M. Beckett, Barboursville History 1996
Ball, Ye Olde Racetrack 1970
Gunter 1986
Mrs. Philip Richmond 1976
Herald-Advertiser 1971
Bozzelli 2009
Anderson n.d.
Memories and Mysteries—Keller Washington and His Notorious "In-Law"
Heritage Quest Online 2011
West Virginia Division of Culture and History 2011
Washington 1996
Greater Kanawha Resource Conservation Development Council 2011
WV Humanities Council 2006-2009
Lee 1969
United States Department of the Interior, National Park Service, National Register of Historic Places -
    Registration Form for Chafin House 1994
Blue Sulphur, Famous Old Resort, Will Open Doors 1923
Ball, Records Are Vague But Memories Warm As Old Blue Sulphur Hotel Wing Is Razed 1959
A. Caldwell 1923
Downriver Impact of the Coal Boom
Harmon 1927
Ball, There Was a Knock on the Door n. d.
WV Department of Environmental Protection 2004
White 1976
M. Beckett, The Guyandotte River n. d.
WV Humanities Council 2006-2009
DellaMea 2001-2012
M. Beckett, The Guyandotte River n. d
Heritage Quest Online 2011
The Crash

Morison 1994
M. Beckett, 850 Lee Street 1996
WV Humanities Council 2006-2009
R. L. Lewis 1998
West Virginia Archives and History 2012
Francis 1934
Morris Harvey Relocates to Charleston
M. Beckett, Morris Harvey College 1980
Yoak 1964
Ball, Morris Harvey College Reunion Has Versatile Turnout 1979
M. Beckett, Morris Harvey College n. d.
Barboursville's "Bread Basket"
M. Bernstein 1985
CSX Transportation n. d
Withers, Chessie holds open house 1981
Gunter 1986
Ball, C&O Reclamation Plant Fire Recalled 1979
A New Deal Legacy
Morison 1994
Pricketts Fort Memorial Foundation n. d.
Barry 2009
Town of Eleanor, W.Va. n. d.
WV Humanities Council 2006-2009
Associated Press 1935
National Archives 2012
Cabell County Farm Women 1963
Franklin D. Roosevelt American Heritage Center, Inc. 2007
Treasure Chest - Barboursville High School 50th Anniversary Yearbook 1977
U.S. Bureau of the Census n. d.
Morison 1994
Nation is Pulled into a Second World War
Morison 1994
Barbara Miller Collection n. d.
Extraordinary Service—the Daniel Family
Barboursville Future Farmers Contributing To War Effort n. d.
Barboursville Band to Get MWCA Award n. d.
West Virginia Division of Culture and History 2011
Heritage Quest Online 2012
Saxton 2000
Barboursville's World War II Honor Roll
Barboursville World War II Honor Roll n. d.
West Virginia Department of Archives and History 2012
Worldwide Struggle Forges the "Greatest Generation"
Morison 1994
Barboursville Tar Watched Japs Give Up In Tokyo Bay 1945
West Virginia Department of Archives and History 2012
West Virginia Division of Culture and History 2011
America's Big Mid-Century Rebound
P. Johnson 1997
Morison 1994
U.S. Census Bureau 2002
Treasure Chest Yearbook 1947
Hysell n. d.

CHAPTER 14—We've Got School Spirit
Barboursville's Champion Generation
Treasure Chest—Barboursville High School Yearbook 1955
Nineteenth Century Schooling
Powers c. 1958
F. B. Lambert 1910
F. B. Lambert Collection n. d.

Barboursville's "Common" and Private Schools
Powers c. 1958
New State, New Educational Foundations
F. B. Lambert 1910
D. C. Miller, Transportation Industry Carried Cabell Changes 1976
The "Alley School."
Miami University, Oxford, OH 2007
Solomon's Legacy
F. B. Lambert 1910
Conservation Loses Friend - Death of H.B. Thornburg 1966
West Virginia Division of Culture and History 2011
Claud H. Thornburg Obituary 2003
Cabell County Board of Education 1933-1990
Evolution of Village Schools
Torch - Barboursville High School Yearbook 1934
Treasure Chest - Barboursville High School 50th Anniversary Yearbook 1977
Torch - Barboursville High School Yearbook 1931
Scions from the Stock of Morris Harvey
 Brady 2012
V. Ball n. d.
Dorothy May Stackpole Obituary 1997
Gunter 1986
Alberta Cummings Obituary 2003
Faculty Meeting is 'Surprise' n. d.
Cabell County Death Registers 1988
Treasure Chest - Barboursville High School 50th Anniversary Yearbook 1977
Rites for Fannin at Barboursville Sunday 1968
John T. Fife Obituary 1971
Treasure Chest - Barboursville High School 50th Anniversary Yearbook 1977
Treasure Chest - Barboursville High School 50th Anniversary Yearbook 1977
Excellence In and Out of the Classroom
Garrett 2013
Cabell County Schools 1963
Segregated at School Time, Integrated at Play
Mr. and Mrs. Ted Allen of Park Forest 2010
Goines 2009
Carter 2010
Cabell County Board of Education 1933-1990
Yearbook Photo 1955
Woodrum 2006
Breaking the Color Barrier
National Park Service 2013
Crow 2011
U.S. Census Bureau 1900, 1910, 1920, 1930, 1940, 1950, 1960, 1970, 1980
Treasure Chest - Barboursville High School 50th Anniversary Yearbook 1977
Goines 2009
Vaya con Dios, My Pirates
Treasure Chest—Barboursville High School Yearbook 1955
Barboursville High School Reunion Committees n. d.
Baby Boom Generation n. d.
TV Coverage: RTMA Predicts Expansion 1952
Lefky 2007
D. Miller 1958
To Thee We Sing
Barboursville High School Reunion Committees n. d.
Treasure Chest - Barboursville High School 50th Anniversary Yearbook 1977
Pirateer 1967
Pirates Shatter Regional Records 1966
'Junior Miss' Pageant Near 1966
Barbara Owens Aiming for Beauty Title 1966
Pageant Day Proclaimed (Photo Caption) 1967

Wallace Funeral Home 2011
West Virginia Division of Culture and History 2011
A. Turman 2010
Schumacher 1966
Cade 1966
Treasure Chest 1975
WV Humanities Council 2006-2009
West Virginia Department of Education n. d.

CHAPTER 15— Institutional Main Street
The Other Side of the Coin
West Virginia Division of Culture and History 2013
"All Classes of Broken Humanity"
Crannell 2012
Wallace 1935
Cosco 1979
F. Lambert 1929
Heritage Quest Online 2012
Huffstutler 2007
Thomas n. d.
H. Beckett n. d.
Labels and Life in the Shadows
American Psychiatric Association 2003
National Alliance on Mental Illness 2013
Cabell Record 1898-1900
A Model Asylum
Jacks 2008
Associated Press 2012
McElroy 2013
The Asylum: Its Origins and Progress 1871
"As Full as Capacity Will Allow"
Jacks 2008
Handling the Overflow
Jacks 2008
Associated Press 1941
West Virginia Senate Multiple Years
Associated Press 1943
Charleston Gazette 1946
W.T. Chambers 1949
West Virginia Division of Culture and History 2013
West Virginia Department of Mental Health 1962-63)
Tour of Huntington State Hospital Shows Overcrowding, Utterly Inadequate Care 1949
Armentrout 1949
Armentrout, Forsaken and Forgotten: Hospital Has No Therapy But Plenty of Patients 1949
Patients and Patience in the Village
Associated Press 1950
Caption 1963
Caregivers and Protectors
West Virginia Senate Multiple Years
Gunter 1986
West Virginia Division of Culture and History 2011
William D. Bourne Obituary 1971
Raymond H. Curry Obituary 1976
S. Peyton 1974
Dr. William Samuel Sadler Obituary 1997
Barboursville State Hospital Gets New Chief 1958
Clay c. 1966
Redekopp 2003
November 24, 1962
West Virginia Department of Mental Health 1962-63
Alley 1962

Hospital Fire Here Recalled 1962
Patients' Prize Possessions Lost in Blaze 1962
Leonard 1962
The "State Farm"
F. Ball, Hospital Farm Move Sensible n. d.
Love 1925
Wallace 1935
West Virginia Senate Multiple Years
Heritage Quest Online 2012
State Operated Gardens Proposed 1943
Kanawha Man Escapes Barboursville Prison 1954
'Zeke' Myers Escapes From Prison Farm 1954
Associated Press 1958
Two Escaped Inmates Held 1962
Associated Press 1967
United Press International 1965
Associated Press 1969
West Virginia Legislature n. d.
Ball, Hospital Farm Move Sensible n. d.
Advancements in Treating "The Other Ten Percent"
Jacks 2008
Sargent 2007
Rogers 2011
American Psychiatric Association 2003
Mental Health Bill Passed By House; Compromise Due 1963
American Psychiatric Association 2003
West Virginia Archives and History 2013
West Virginia Department of Mental Health 1966
State Poverty Funds Near $55 Million 1967
Green Acres Project Director Hired 1967
E. Fuller Torrey 1997
State Hospitals Treat More Despite 'Population' Decline 1969
Barboursville's "De-Institutional" Innovators
Morgan 1971
Ramsey 1964
The News in Brief 1968
West Virginia Senate Multiple Years
"A Tradition of Financial Malnutrition"
West Virginia Department of Mental Health 1973-74
Jacks 2008
Associated Press 1976
West Virginia Department of Mental Health 1966
Willis 1966
Associated Press 1974
M. Smith 1975
American Psychiatric Association 2003
Balloons, Hospitals and Jails
E. Fuller Torrey 1997
National Institutes of Health 1999
WV Humanities Council 2006-2009
Jacks 2008
What Might Have Been
Berkeley, Barboursville Hospital: Buildings were deserted before but closing leaves sense of loss 1978
Seamonds 1978
West Virginia Department of Mental Health 1966
F. Ball, Hospital Farm Move Sensible n. d.
West Virginia Legislature 1921

CHAPTER 16—Teenage Wasteland (1960s-1970s)
Adolescence on the Outskirts
Heritage Quest Online 2012

Koenig 1975
The Roots of Suburban Sprawl
Chaff 1975
"Something for the Youth to Do"
Barboursville Voters To Decide Renewal Of Levy Tomorrow 1976
F. Ball, When a Town Wakes Up, Part IX n.d.
F. Ball, When A Town Wakes Up Part XIII c 1978
Digging (Up) the 'Sixties: From Street Dances to "Kaleidelic" Experiences
Hullabaloo Dancers 2012
Tim Brooks and Earle Marsh 1984
Youth/What They Need Is a Place To Go 1966
Teen Clubs International, Inc. 1968
L. Smith 2012
Wikipedia n.d
GarageHangover.com n.d.
Teen Clubs International, Inc. 1968-1969
Pegasus Rocks 2008
Unavoidable Psychology of the Times
Pinkston 2006
WV Humanities Council 2006-2009
West Virginia Department of Archives and History 2012
West Virginia Legislature 2012
Jeffrey 2013
Dean 2013
Berkeley, Librarian: Soft-spoken Sue Alexander retires after 31-year career 1978
Wikipedia n. d.

CHAPTER 17—A Sudden Reversal of Fortune (1970s-2010s)
Declining Economy and Diminishing Expectations
Goodman 1975
Berkeley, Barboursville Hospital: Buildings were deserted before but closing leaves sense of loss 1978
Leonard Sturm Obituary 2004
Sulzer Pumps (US) Inc 2013
F. Ball, When a Town Wakes Up, Part VII 1979
Wartman, Sale of land may hinge on cleanup 2007
Bonzo-Savage 1979
Opportunity Quietly Seized
Newcomer Victorious 1977
Barboursville, Milton Go To Polls Tuesday 1977
Morris 1977
Editorial - Huntington mall? 1978
Polk's City Directory 1977
West Virginia Legislature 2010
Chambers, Barboursville Embraces Growth 2001
Duane Rosenlieb, Mall Annexation Hearing Tonight In Barboursville 1978
Wartman, Mini golf, restaurant slated for Barboursville 2005
White, Few Voice Opposition to Mall's Annexation 1978
Houston 1978
Berkeley, 'Pleased' Mall developers react to vote 1978
"The Mall Started It All"
Ross 1978
Berkeley, Vote winners not surprised 1979
Moran 1979
New I-64 exit planned for Ona mall 1979
Dilley n.d
Duane Rosenlieb, Barboursville. . . a city in transition 1981
Hartlaub 2010
Wikipedia n.d.
Cafaro Company 2013
Wartman, Huntington Mall Retail drives growth in eastern Cabell County c 2003

Fresh Air and Green Space: Barboursville's "Hidden" Jewel
Chambers, Village closer to acquiring park site 2002
Bridge Dedicated 1995
West Virginia Division of Natural Resources 2003
Lavender, Herald-Dispatch 2000
Houvouras 2011
Paul Ambrose Trail for Health 2013
Nancy and "Mayor T"
D. Peyton, Stroll Into History Offered 1994
Chambers, Barboursville embraces growth 2001)
Council 2001
Chambers, Barboursville competing 2002
Wartman, Denied exposition center considered for other uses 2003
Withers, Council members, mayor get salary raises in Barboursville 2003
Henson, Cartmill comes to a crossroads 2000
At the Bicentennial Crossroads
Bipartisan Policy Center 2012
Barboursville, West Virginia Population: Census 2010 and 2000 Interactive Map, Demographics,
    Statistics, Quick Facts 2012
Lavender, Barboursville ups ante against strip clubs 2000
C. Johnson 2005
Alexandersen, Recycling initiative begins - Barboursville provides paper, plastic dropoff 2008
Rosenberger 2011
50-year-old Barboursville levy to stay in effect; mayor relieved at voter results 2011
Henson, Barboursville residents to vote on extended levy 2000

CHAPTER 18—'Twas Ever Thus...
Barboursville High School (1929- 2009)
Major demolition set to begin at old Barboursville school 2009
Thomas Thornburg Home (1862-2009)
D. Peyton, Stroll Into History Offered 1994
D. D. McMillian 2009
Barboursville Clay Manufacturing Company (1904- 2007)
Alexandersen, Old stacks come down at Barboursville brickyard 2007
Cabell County Court House (1852-1996) and Methodist Episcopal Church South (1884-1996)
Massey 1996
"Old Abraham" The Village Sycamore (circa 1820s-1995)
Rake 1995
Barboursville Cand O Train Station (circa 1900-?)
M. Bernstein 1985
William McComas Home at "Mulberry Grove" (1837-1986)
Rose, Old Cabell home destroyed by fire 1986
Tivoli/Criss Theater (1926-1985)
Rose, Flames licking old Tivoli Theater spark memories of days gone by 1985
Miller and Holderby Store/Blume Hotel (1840s-1981)
F. Ball, B Building. . . 140 years of Barboursville history razed 1981
Barboursville Cemetery (1830s-Present)
Huffstutler 2007
Mr. and Mrs. Ted Allen of Park Forest 2010
Board of Trade Purchases New Cemetery Plot 1915
H. Maxwell circa 1956
Sophie von Teschen et. al. 2013
A Humble Proposition
Sophie von Teschen et. al. 2013
Wolfe 2008
Hail to West Virginia's Best Village—Lost or Found

BIBLIOGRAPHY

"Anti-Irish Sentiment." Irish Emigration. 2003. http://www.rzuser.uni-heidelberg.de/~el6/presenta-tions/Irish_Americans_S2_WS2003/Anti_Irish_Sentiment.htm.

"Barboursville Band to Get MWCA Award." Cabell County news clippings - Barbara Miller Collection.

"Barboursville Clay Manufacturing Company." Abandoned. 2012. http://www.abandonedonline.net/industry/barboursville-brick/?nggpage=2.

"Barboursville Future Farmers Contributing To War Effort." Cabell County news clippings - Barbara Miller Collection.

"Barboursville Tar Watched Japs Give Up In Tokyo Bay," 1945. Cabell County news clippings - Barbara Miller Collection

"Bloomingdale Salem Baptist Church Minutes 1855-2005." Transcribed by T. Franklin May, September 2005.

"Cabell County's Oldest Church Mud River Baptist." April 5, 1967. *Barboursville Bulletin*.

"Faculty Meeting is 'Surprise'." Cabell County news clippings - Barbara Miller Collection

"Isaac Vinton Bryant - History of the American Negro: West Virginia Edition." http://www.wvculture.org/history/histamne/bryant.html.

"John T. Fife Obituary." 1971. Cabell County news clippings - Barbara Miller Collection

"Leonard Sturm Obituary." *Time for Memory*. 2004. http://www.timeformemory.com/fh_obitu-aryprint.cfm?obitid=23141.

"Minutes Bloomingdale Salem Baptist church 1855-2005 - transcribed by T. Franklin May." September 2005.

"Raymond H. Curry Obituary." 1976. Cabell County news clippings - Barbara Miller Collection

"Rites for Fannin at Barboursville Sunday." May 10, 1968. Cabell County news clippings - Barbara Miller Collection

"Swann Family Genealogy Notebook." Huntington, WV: KYOWVA Genealogical and Historical Society.

"Valentine Leist, Pioneer Tanner, Taken by Death." February 4, 1916. Cabell County news clippings - Barbara Miller Collection

"William D. Bourne Obituary." 1971. Cabell County news clippings - Barbara Miller Collection

16th Infantry Regiment. Historical Era: WWI. 2005. http://www.16thinfantry-regiment.org/History/HistoricalEras18611898/WW1/tabid/84/Default.aspx.

Alexandersen, Christian. "Old stacks come down at Barboursville brickyard." *Herald-Dispatch*, November 16, 2007.

Alexandersen, Christian. "Recycling initiative begins - Barboursville provides paper, plastic dropoff." *Herald-Dispatch*, June 9, 2008.

All the President's Men Revisited. Directed by Robert Redford, The Discovery Channel, 2013.

Allen, Mr. and Mrs. Ted, of Park Forest, IL, interview by Jeanette Rowsey. (May 2010).

Alley, Homer. "180 Patients Flee Blaze at Barboursville Hospital." *Huntington Advertiser*, November 24, 1962.

American Battle Monuments Commission. "Aisne-Marne American Cemetery and Memorial Booklet." American Battle Monuments Commission. http://www.abmc.gov/publications/CemeteryBooklets/Aisne-Marne_Booklet.pdf.

American Gold Star Mothers, Inc. History. http://www.goldstarmoms.com/WhoWeAre/History/History.htm (accessed 2012).

American Psychiatric Association. History. 2003. http://www.psychiatry.org/about-apa--psychiatry/more-about-apa/history-of-the-apa.

American Red Cross. World War I Accomplishments of the American Red Cross. http://www.redcross.org/museum/history/ww1a.asp (accessed 2012).

Anderson, Robert. Handwritten letter to Barboursville Public Library.

Armentrout, Charles R. "Forsaken and Forgotten: Hospital Has No Therapy But Plenty of Patients." *Charleston Gazette*, February 2, 1949.

Armentrout, Charles R. "The Price of Economy—Misery! Mental Patients Doomed to Lives of Neglect, Monotony, Indecency." *Charleston Gazette*, January 23, 1949.

Arnold-Friend, Louise. The U.S. Army's International Debut: Battle at the River Marne. July 16, 2010. http://www.army.mil/article/42423/The_U_S_Army_039_s_International_Debut_Battle_at_the_River_Marne/ (accessed 2012).

Associated Press. "Bateman To Get Accrediting Data." *Beckley Post-Herald*, January 23, 1976.

Associated Press. "Conditioning Center For CCC Candidates Goes Into Production." *Charleston Gazette*, August 7, 1935.

Associated Press. "Holt Says Purchase of M.H. Property Illegal." *Sunday Register*, Beckley, October 10, 1943.

Associated Press. "Jury Convicts Hospital Chief." *Charleston Gazette*, December 7, 1950.

Associated Press. "Lakin Doctor Won't Go To Barboursville." *Charleston Daily Mail*, June 28, 1974.

Associated Press. "Livestock Sales Displease Head of Agriculture." *Charleston Daily Mail*, September 17, 1969.

Associated Press. "Old Sweet Deal Annulment Sought ." *Charleston Gazette*, March 2, 1943.

Associated Press. "Patients Will Be Moved to Barboursville Today." *Charleston Gazette*, January 20, 1941.

Associated Press. "Police Searching For Escapee, 22." *Charleston Daily Mail*, April 25, 1967.

Associated Press. "State Hospital Guard Captain Loses His Job." *Charleston Daily Mail*, July 1, 1958.

Associated Press. "State Officials Seek Space For Insane and 'TB' Patients." *Charleston Daily Mail*, August 10, 1941.

Associated Press. "Transient Dies in Fall." *Bluefield Daily Telegraph*, June 11, 1935.

Associated Press. "West Virginia asylum owners welcome kindred spirits." *Wisconsin State Journal*, March` 3, 2012.

Baby Boom Generation. http://www.u-s-history.com/pages/h2061.html (accessed 2013).

Baisden, Harry L. "Impact of Coal Felt in Wallets, and Cemeteries." *Herald-Dispatch*, March 28, 1976.

Ball, Frank. "Avenue of Antiquity Series." *Barboursville Bulletin*, Various 1973.

Ball, Frank. "B Building...140 years of Barboursville history razed." *Herald-Dispatch*, June 1981.

Ball, Frank. "*Barboursville Bulletin*." To Be Razed For Library, December 14, 1966.

Ball, Frank. "C&O Reclamation Plant Fire Recalled." *Cabell Record*, January 24, 1979.

Ball, Frank. "Four Barboursville Businesses Stay in Same Families for 50 Years." *Herald-Advertiser*, August 3, 1958.

Ball, Frank. "History of Barboursville." *Wayne County News*, July 7, 1949.

Ball, Frank. "History of First United Methodist Church of Barboursville." *Cabell Record*.

Ball, Frank. "Hospital Farm Move Sensible." Undated news clips, Barboursville Public Library.

Ball, Frank. "Morris Harvey College Reunion Has Versatile Turnout." *Cabell Record*, 1979.

Ball, Frank. "Old House Gets 'New Look'." *Barboursville Bulletin*, December 10, 1969.

Ball, Frank. "Old Morris Homestead Built 120 Years Ago." KYOWVA Genealogical and Historical Society Newsletter, Spring 2011.

Ball, Frank. "Photographic Scrapbook." Barboursville Public Library

Ball, Frank. "Picture from the Past." *Barboursville Bulletin*, March 5, 1975.

Ball, Frank. "Records Are Vague But Memories Warm As Old Blue Sulphur Hotel Wing Is Razed." August 1959. Barboursville Public Library

Ball, Frank. "Steamboats on the Guyan." *Barboursville Bulletin*, December 14, 1966.

Ball, Frank. "The Country Squire." *Barboursville & East Huntington Bulletin*, November 28, 1973.

Ball, Frank. "The Everettes." *Barboursville & East Huntington Bulletin*, April 17, 1974.

Ball, Frank. "There Was a Knock on the Door." Undated news clips, Barboursville Public Library.

Ball, Frank. "This Old House." *Barboursville Bulletin*.

Ball, Frank. "Unknown." Undated news clips, Barboursville Public Library.

Ball, Frank. "When A Town Wakes Up Part XIII." *Cabell Record*, 1979

Ball, Frank. "When a Town Wakes Up, Part IX." *Cabell Record*, 1979

Ball, Frank. "When a Town Wakes Up, Part VII." *Cabell Record*, 1979.

Ball, Frank. "Ye Olde Racetrack." *Barboursville Bulletin*, August 26, 1970.

Ball, Vernon. "Barboursville Teacher to Retire After 35 Years." *Herald-Advertiser*.

Barbara Miller Collection, on loan to Jeanette Rowsey, 2012-2013.

Barboursville High School Reunion Committees. "Reunion Programs, Classes of 1951, 1953, 1954, 1955." Barboursville, WV.

Barboursville World War II Honor Roll at Nancy Cartmill Gardens, Barboursville, WV.

Barboursville, West Virginia Population: Census 2010 and 2000 Interactive Map, Demographics, Statistics, Quick Facts. 2012. http://censusviewer.com/city/WV/Barboursville.

Barry, Dan. "From New Deal to New Hard Times, Eleanor Endures." *New York Times*, December 24, 2009.

Baumgartner, Rick. "Death in the Desert: The McComas Massacre of 1883." *Herald-Advertiser*, 1977.

Baumgartner, Rick. "First 'damnyankee gentleman' in Guyandotte." *Huntington Advertiser*.

Baumgartner, Rick. "Founding a College on a five dollar shoestring." *Herald-Advertiser*.

Baumgartner, Rick. "Mosaics from Barboursville's Past." *Herald-Advertiser* .

Baumgartner, Rick. "The rides of Cabell County's 'Paul Revere'." *Herald-Advertiser*, June 15, 1978.

Baumgartner, Rick. "Whizzing around town at 8 miles per hour." *Herald-Advertiser*.

Beckett, Harry. "Sheaves of Loving Care: A History of the Prichard School." *Cabell County WV Doors to the Past.* http://www.rootsweb.ancestry.com/~wvcccfhr/history/prichard.htm (accessed 2013).

Beckett, Maurice E. "Village of Barboursville Resigned to Removal of Morris Harvey College." *Herald-Advertiser*, August 2, 1935.

Beckett, Maurice. "850 Lee Street." Barboursville, WV, 1996.

Beckett, Maurice. "Barboursville History." Barboursville, WV, 1996.

Beckett, Maurice. "Barboursville's Early History Recalled by Uncle Billy Miller." *Herald-Advertiser*, June 4, 1933.

Beckett, Maurice. "Morris Harvey College." Barboursville, WV, 1980.

Beckett, Maurice. "The Barboursville Baptist Church."

Beckett, Maurice. "The Guyandotte River."

Beckett, Maurice. "The Railroad." Barboursville, WV.

Beckett, Maurice. "When We Were Sick." 1996.

Beckley Post-Herald. "The News in Brief." May 6, 1968.

Benjamin, J.L. "Action at Barboursville Changed Civil War." *Huntington Herald-Advertiser*, December 20, 1953.

Berkeley, Sara. "Barboursville Hospital: Buildings were deserted before but closing leaves sense of loss." *Huntington Advertiser*, May 3, 1978.

Berkeley, Sara. "Librarian: Soft-spoken Sue Alexander retires after 31-year career." *Huntington Advertiser*, February 20, 1978.

Berkeley, Sara. "'Pleased' Mall developers react to vote." *Huntington Advertiser*, October 4, 1978.

Berkeley, Sara. "Vote winners not surprised." *Huntington Advertiser*, June 6, 1979.

Bernstein, Margarent. "Glory Days gone on Depot Street." *Herald-Dispatch*, July 7, 1985.

Bickley, Ancella R. *History of the West Virginia State Teacher's Association.* Washington, DC: National Education Association, 1979.

Bipartisan Policy Center. "2012 Election Turnout Dips Below 2008 and 2004 Levels..." *Bipartisan Policy Center.* November 8, 2012. http://bipartisanpolicy.org/news/press-releases/2012/11/2012-election-turnout-dips-below-2008-and-2004-levels-number-eligible-vo.

Bonzo-Savage, Elizabeth. "Brick Firm Layoffs, Future Go Unexplained." *Cabell Record*, 1979.

Bozzelli. *Cabell County Architectural Guide.* Huntington, WV: John D. Drinko Academy Marshall University, 2009.

Brady, Marjolee, interview by Jeanette Rowsey. (2012).

Broadcasting. "TV Coverage: RTMA Predicts Expansion." May 19, 1952: 78.

Bryan, Jami. "Fighting for Respect: African-American Soldiers in WWI." MilitaryHistoryOnline.com. 2003. http://www.militaryhistoryonline.com/wwi/articles/fightingforrespect.aspx (accessed April 29, 2012).

Cabell County Board of Education, School Board Minutes. Huntington, WV, 1933-1990.

Cabell County Courthouse. *Cabell County Deed Books.*

Cabell County Death Registers. Huntington, WV: Cabell County Courthouse, 1988.

Cabell County Farm Women. "1963 Historic and Scenic Tour 2." Barboursville, WV, 1963.

Cabell County Farm Women's Clubs. "Historic and Scenic Tour 1." Barboursville, WV, April 12, 1961.

Cabell County Schools. "Golden Horseshoe Winner." 1963.

*Cabell Record.*1898-1900.

*Cabell Record.*1898-1901.

Cabell Record. March 30, 1899.

Cade, Lowell. "John Allen 'Tickled," Even with McNeers Step Out of Bounds." *Herald-Advertiser*, September 17, 1966.

Cafaro Company. "Huntington Mall Brochure." Cafarocompany.com. 2013. http://www.cafarocompany.com/website/MallRealEstateBrochures/HTM%20REB.pdf.

Caldwell, A. B. *History of the American Negro and his institutions, Vol. I.* Atlanta, GA: A.B. Caldwell Publishing Company, 1917.

Caldwell, A.B. *History of the American Negro - West Virginia Edition, Vol. VII.* Atlanta, Georgia: A.B. Caldwell Publishing Company, 1923.

Caption, Photo. "The Junior Woman's Club of Barboursville will lend a helping hand..." 1963.

Carter, Gladys, interview by Jeanette Rowsey. (April 15, 2010).

Casto, James E. "Deadly 1918 Flu Hit Huntington Hard." *Herald-Dispatch*, May 1, 2009.

Central Pacific Railroad Photographic History Museum. "Maps Showing the Progressive Development of U.S. Railroads - 1830 to 1950 ." 2012. http://cprr.org/Museum/RR_Development.html#6.

Chaff, Lin. "Pea Ridge." *Huntington Advertiser*, November 24, 1975.

Chambers, Bryan. "Barboursville competing." *Herald-Dispatch*, July 3, 2002.

Chambers, Bryan. "Barboursville embraces growth." *Herald-Dispatch*, August 3, 2001.

Chambers, Bryan. "Barboursville Embraces Growth." *Herald-Dispatch*, August 3, 2001.

Chambers, Bryan. "Census: City, County Show Losses." *Herald-Dispatch*, March 23, 2011.

Chambers, Bryan. "Village closer to acquiring park site ." *Herald-Dispatch*, July 18, 2002.

Charleston Daily Mail . "Barboursville State Hospital Gets New Chief ." June 23, 1958.

Charleston Daily Mail. "Mental Health Bill Passed By House; Compromise Due ." September 11, 1963.

Charleston Gazette. "Kanawha Man Escapes Barboursville Prison." August 27, 1954.

Charleston Gazette. "State Hospitals Treat More Despite 'Population' Decline." August 7, 1969.

Charleston Gazette. "State Operated Gardens Proposed." March 9, 1943.

Charleston Gazette. "'Zeke' Myers Escapes From Prison Farm ." September 1, 1954.

Charleston Gazette. July 4, 1946.

Chesapeake and Oho Historical Society. C&O Structures. 2012. http://www.cohs.org/history/structures.shtml.

Childers, P.H. "Answers by P.H. Childers." *KYOWVA Genealogical and Historical Society Newsletter*, Fall 2008: 11.

City of Huntington. "Huntington is Born." Official Website of the City of Huntington. 2011. http://www.cityofhuntington.com/pages/history8.asp.

Clay, V. Max. "A Short History of "The Barboursville Volunteer Fire Dept."." c. 1966.

Coal Exhibit at Chief Logan State Park, 2010.

Connor, Rev. Dr. Mark.

Cook, Samuel R. *Monacans and Miners: Native American and Coal Mining Communities in Appalachia*. Lincoln, NE: University of Nebraska Press, 2000.

Cosco, Joe. "Cabell County Poor Farm, 1853 to 1929." *Goldenseal*, April-June 1979.

Council, Barboursville City. Resolution of March 20, 2001.

Crannell, Linda. Historical Overview of the American Poorhouse System . 2012. http://www.poorhousestory.com/history.htm.

CrossSargent, Martha. "PARoots.org." June 25, 2010.

Crow, Nathaniel. The Integration of Douglass High School, Cabell County, WV. *Academic*, Huntington, WV: The Carter Woodson Project, Marshall University Department of History, 2011.

CSX Transportation. Our Evolution and History. www.csx.com (accessed 2012).

Day, Jeff. "Barboursville college...once upon the Cabell village was home for Morris Harvey institution." *Herald-Advertiser*, June 28, 1976.

DellaMea, Chris. "Logan Field." Coalfields of the Appalachian Mountains. 2001-2012. www.coalcampusa.com.

Dickinson, Jack. "Lecture." Guyandotte Civil War Days. Huntington, WV, 2011.

Dilger, Dr. Robert Jay, Institute for Public Affairs and Professor, Department of Political Science, West Virginia University. Steve Kovalan, undergraduate history major, West Virginia University.

Dilley, Jack "The Vallandingham Family of Barboursville, West Virginia." Barboursville, WV.

Dilley, Jack. "Rotary Club of Barboursville, West Virginia U.S.A."

Dollarhide, William. *The Census Book: A Genealogists Guide to Federal Census Facts, Schedules and Indexes*. Heritage Quest, 1999.

Donahue, M. Patricia. *Nursing, The Finest Art*. Saint Louis: C. V. Mosby Company, 1985.

Douglass High School Yearbook. 1955.

Duane Rosenlieb, Jr. "Barboursville...a city in transition." *Herald-Dispatch*, March 8, 1981.

Duane Rosenlieb, Jr. "Mall Annexation Hearing Tonight In Barboursville." *Herald-Dispatch*, October 2, 1978.

Duffy, Michael. The Second Battle of the Marne, 1918. August 22, 2009. http://www.firstworldwar.com/battles/marne2.htm.

Dunaway, Wilma A. *The First American Frontier: Transition to Capitalism in Southern Appalachia, 1700-1860*. Chapel Hill, NC: University of North Carolina Press, 1996.

Dundas, Francis de Sales. *Hesselius Dundas*. Philadelphia: Historical Publication Society, 1938.

Dusenberry, William F. "William F. Dusenberry Diaries - Special Collections Department, Marshall University." Huntington, WV.

E. Fuller Torrey, M.D. *Out of the Shadows: Confronting America's Mental Illness Crisis*. New York: John Wiley & Sons, 1997.

Eldridge, Carrie. *Atlas of Appalachian Trails to the Ohio River*. Huntington, WV: CDN Printing, 1998.

Eldridge, Carrie. *Cabell County's Empire for Freedom: The Manumission of Sampson Sanders' Slaves*. Huntington, WV: Marshall University, 1999.

Elliott and Nye. *Virginia Directory and Business Register. Cabell County, 1852.*

Engle, Stephen D. "Mountaineer Reconstruction: Blacks in the Political Reconstruction of West Virginia." *The Journal of Negro History*, Vol. 78 Issue 3, 1993: 1.

Estler, William C. "Aunt Mattie Fliggins, at 95, remembers many incidents of slave days." *Herald-Advertiser*, April 21, 1935.

Fain, Cicero M. III. "Dissertation: Race, River & Railroad: Black Huntington, West Virginia, 1871-1929." Columbus, OH: The Ohio State University, 2009.

Fain, Cicero. "WV Genealogy Club Lecture: Into the Crucible." Charleston, WV, May 2012.

Farwell, Byron. *Over There: The United States in the Great War.* New York, NY: W.W. Norton & Co., 1999.

Ferguson, Fred S. "Guns of Allies Pound Hun Communications as Armies Sweep On." *Huntington Advertiser*, July 21, 1918.

Francis Asbury Society Website: www.francisasburysociety.com.

Francis, Henry W. ""Dear Mr. Hopkins"." New Deal Network. December 7, 1934. http://newdeal.feri.org/hopkins/hop04.htm (accessed 2012).

Franklin D. Roosevelt American Heritage Center, Inc. New Deal Resource. 2007. http://www.fdrheritage.org/links.htm.

Freeman, Candie. http://freepages.genealogy.rootsweb.ancestry.com/~cabell/fowsndx.html.

Friedman, S. Morgan. 2011. http://www.westegg.com/inflation/.

Frommer, Arthur. "Historic Preservation and Tourism." *Preservation Forum 2*, Fall 1988: 10.

GarageHangover.com.

Garrett, Shirley McMellon. "Email Correspondence." 2013.

Geiger, Joe Jr. "Lecture." Guyandotte Civil War Days. 2011.

Geiger, Joe Jr. "The Tragic Fate of Guyandotte." Guyandotte Civil War Days. 2009. http://www.guyandottecivilwardays.com/Tragic_Fate.htm.

Geiger, Joe Jr. *Civil War in Cabell County, West Virginia 1861-1865.* Charleston: Pictorial Histories Publishing Co., Inc., 1991.

Goines, Roy, interview by Jeanette Rowsey. Telephone Interview with Roy Goines of San Dimas, CA (November 5, 2009).

Goodman, Al. "The Village certainly has problems, but people like freedom." *Huntington Advertiser*, July 7, 1975.

Greater Kanawha Resource Conservation Development Council. 2011.

Gunter, Frances B. *Barboursville.* Barboursville, WV: Frances B. Gunter, 1986.

Hall, R.C. "History of George Wilson - 3 Part Series." *Ironton Tribune*, July & August 1938.

Harmon, Roy Lee. "Aged Historian Gets Letter From Former 'Village' Resident." December 11, 1927.

Hartlaub, Peter. "12 must-have toy hits from Christmases past." nbcnews.com. 2010. http://www.nbcnews.com/id/40059786/ns/business-retail/t/must-have-toy-hits-christmases-past/#.UaPiYZwlnbx.

Haught, James A. "Institute: It Springs From Epic Love Story." *West Virginia History* Vol. 32, No. 2, 1971: 101-107.

Heinegg, Paul. "Free African Americans of North Carolina, Virginia, and South Carolina, Foreword by Ira Berlin." Genealogical.com. 2009. http://www.freeafricanamericans.com/foreword.htm.

Hensel, William Uhler. *Life and Public Services of Grover Cleveland.* Edgewood Publishing Co. (Google eBook), 1892.

Henson, Jeff. " Cartmill comes to a crossroads ." *Herald-Dispatch*, February 25, 2000.

Henson, Jeff. "Barboursville residents to vote on extended levy ." *Herald-Dispatch*, February 3, 2000.

Herald-Advertiser. "Barbara Owens Aiming for Beauty Title." August 21, 1966.

Herald-Advertiser. "Conservation Loses Friend - Death of H.B. Thornburg." January 23, 1966.

Herald-Advertiser. "Great Bank robbery of 1875—Was It Jesse James?" July 11, 1971.

Herald-Advertiser. "'Junior Miss' Pageant Near." February 11, 1966.

Herald-Advertiser. "Old Water Mills Have Succumbed during Steady March of Progress." August 27, 1939: 1939.

Herald-Advertiser. "Pageant Day Proclaimed (Photo Caption)." January 1, 1967.

Herald-Advertiser. "Tour of Huntington State Hospital Shows Overcrowding, Utterly Inadequate Care." February 20, 1949.

Herald-Advertiser. July 11, 1971.

Herald-Dispatch Visitor's Guide - Golf. http://www.*Herald-Dispatch*.com/specialsections/visitorsguide/x337880985/Golf (accessed 2012).

Herald-Dispatch. "50-year-old Barboursville levy to stay in effect; mayor relieved at voter results ." February 9, 2011.

Herald-Dispatch. "Alberta Cummings Obituary." December 31, 2003.

Herald-Dispatch. "Barboursville Enjoys Period of Prosperity." December 6, 1918.
Herald-Dispatch. "Barboursville to be made terminal for G.V. Division." March 19, 1913: 10.
Herald-Dispatch. "Barboursville Voters To Decide Renewal Of Levy Tomorrow." March 8, 1976.
Herald-Dispatch. "Barboursville, Milton Go To Polls Tuesday." June 4, 1977.
Herald-Dispatch. "Board of Trade Purchases New Cemetery Plot." March 2, 1915.
Herald-Dispatch. "Bridge Dedicated." September 19, 1995.
Herald-Dispatch. "Celebration over and Barboursville feels justly proud." June 7, 1913.
Herald-Dispatch. "Claud H. Thornburg Obituary." June 2003.
Herald-Dispatch. "Dorothy May Stackpole Obituary." November 1997.
Herald-Dispatch. "Dr. William Samuel Sadler Obituary." 1997.
Herald-Dispatch. "Editorial - Huntington mall?" October 4, 1978.
Herald-Dispatch. "H.J. Baumgardner Obituary." June 17, 1926.
Herald-Dispatch. "Intense Excitement at Reno on Eve of Greatest Battle in History of Pugilism." July 3, 1910.
Herald-Dispatch. "James I. Kuhn Obituary." September 11, 1910.
Herald-Dispatch. "Major demolition set to begin at old Barboursville school ." March 25, 2009.
Herald-Dispatch. "Morris Harvey to Have Good Outfit." April 4, 1917.
Herald-Dispatch. "Newcomer Victorious." June 8, 1977.
Herald-Dispatch. "Obituary." June 17, 1926.
Herald-Dispatch. "Obituary." September 11, 1910.
Herald-Dispatch. "Orders C.&O. to build a viaduct at Barboursville." September 21, 1926.
Herald-Dispatch. "Pirates Shatter Regional Records." June 7, 1966.
Herald-Dispatch. "Say War Will Not Halt Huntington's Y.M.C.A. Campaign." April 6, 1917.
Herald-Dispatch. Huntington, West Virginia, April 2011.
Herald-Dispatch. May 11, 1912.
Heritage Quest Online. 2012. http://cabell.lib.wv.us/pages/resourc.htm.
Historical Society of Pennsylvania. "Exploring Diversity in Pennsylvania History ." www.hsp.org.
Holtby, David V. *World War I and the Federal Presence in New Mexico*. Albuquerque: University of New Mexico Center for Regional Studies, 2008.
Houston, Patrick. "Barboursville Approves Mall Annexation Plan." *Herald-Dispatch*, October 4, 1978.
Houvouras, Jack. "He Was Ours." *Huntington Quarterly* Issue 75, Autumn 2011.
Huffstutler, Barry. 2007. http://www.rootsweb.ancestry.com/~wvcccfhr/ (accessed 2011).
Hullabaloo Dancers. August 31, 2012. https://www.facebook.com/pages/Hullabaloo-Dancers.
Huntington Advertiser. "Colored Students Engaged in Debate." April 10, 1917.
Huntington Advertiser. "Green Acres Project Director Hired." June 7, 1967.
Huntington Advertiser. "Hospital Fire Here Recalled." November 24, 1962.
Huntington Advertiser. "Negroes Enlisting in the U.S. Army." April 13, 1917.
Huntington Advertiser. "New I-64 exit planned for Ona mall." June 1, 1979.
Huntington Advertiser. "Patients' Prize Possessions Lost in Blaze." November 24, 1962.
Huntington Advertiser. "South Bank of Marne Cleared; Drive Goes On." July 21, 1918.
Huntington Advertiser. "State Poverty Funds Near $55 Million." June 10, 1967.
Huntington Advertiser. "Veteran Barber of Barboursville Dies." February 4, 1920.
Huntington Daily Herald. "Thomas Thornburg Obituary." November 1, 1897.
Huntington Herald-Advertiser. "Aunt Patsy is Dead." March 29, 1899.
Huntington Herald-Dispatch. "Barboursville 100 Years Old." January 15, 2013.
Huntington Herald-Dispatch. "Barboursville to have Ice Plant." March 29, 1913.
Huntington Herald-Dispatch. "Barboursville." July 27, 1913.
Huntington Herald-Dispatch. "Cabell County's Greatest Tragedy and First Execution." February 14, 1909: 1.
Huntington Herald-Dispatch. "Obituary of George Franklin Miller." May 10, 1922.
Huntington Herald-Dispatch. "Obituary." May 10, 1922.
Hysell, Violet Bowen. "The Old Toll House, Main St., Barboursville, W.Va." Barboursville, WV: Daughters of the American Revolution, Barboursville Chapter.
Jacks, Kim. "Weston State Hospital." Master's Thesis, Morgantown, WV: West Virginia University Eberly College of Arts and Sciences, 2008.
Jackson, Vanessa. "Separate and Unequal: The Legacy of Racially Segregated Psychiatric Hospitals." Scirbd.Com. http://www.scribd.com/doc/27594207/Separate-and-Unequal-The-Legacy-of-Racially-Segregated-Psychiatric-Hospitals (accessed 2012).
Jeffrey, James K. Email Correspondence. Denver, CO, January 11, 2013.
John E. Findling & Frank W. Thakeray, editors. *Events That Changed America in the Nineteenth Century*. Westport, CT: Greenwood Press, 1997.

Johnson, Curtis. "Barboursville limits video lottery terminals ." *Herald-Dispatch*, May 18, 2005.

Johnson, Marvin E. "Descendents of Billy Hicks." East Orange, NJ: Descendents Tree, August 14, 2010.

Johnson, Mary McKendree. *Representative Men and Women of Cabell County, W.Va.* Parkersburg: Johnson, 1929.

Johnson, Paul. *A History of the American People.* New York, NY: HarperCollins, 1997.

*Kanawha Valley Star.*1859.

Kansas State Historical Society. *A Standard History of Kansas and Kansians.* Chicago: Lewis Publishing Company, 1918.

Koenig, John. "Guyan Estates." *Huntington Advertiser*, December 22, 1975.

Konhaus, Tim. ""I thought Things Would Be Different There": Lynching and the Black Community in Southern West Virginia, 1880-1933." *West Virginia History: A Journal of Regional Studies*, Vol. 1, Number 2, 2007: 25-43.

KYOWVA Genealogical and Historical Society. *200th Birthday of Cabell County: The Bicentennial 1809-2009.* Huntington: KYOWVA Genealogical and Historical Society, 2011.

Laidley, W.S. *History of Charleston and Kanawha County, West Virginia and Representative Citizens.* Chicago, IL: Richmond-Arnold Publishing Co., 1911.

Lambert, F.B. "Abandonment of Old 'Poor Farm' on Tyler's Creek Recalls Century and Half of Service Rendered by the McKendrees." *Herald-Advertiser*, April 14, 1929.

Lambert, Fred B. Collection. Huntington, WV: James E. Morrow Library, Marshall University - Special Collections.

Lambert, Fred B. *First Annual Catalog and Statistical Report of the Barboursville District Public Schools.* Barboursville, WV, 1910.

Lavender, Dave. "Barboursville ups ante against strip clubs ." *Herald-Dispatch*, June 7, 2000.

Lavender, Dave. "*Herald-Dispatch.*" Village park ready to blossom, May 25, 2000.

Lee, Howard B. *Bloodletting in Appalachia: The Story of West Virginia's Four Major Mine Wars and Other Thrilling Incidents of Its Coal Fields.* Parsons, WV: McClain Printing Company, 1969.

Lefky, Adam. Number of Televisions in the US. 2007. http://hypertextbook.com/facts/2007/TamaraTamazashvili.shtml.

Leonard, Dick. "Readiness Averts Major Fire Disaster." *Herald-Advertiser*, November 25, 1962.

Lewis, Ronald L. *Transforming the Appalachian Countryside: Railroads, Deforestation, and Social Change in West Virginia, 1880-1920.* Chapel Hill, NC: University of North Carolina Pres, 1998.

Lewis, Virgil A. "A History of Marshall Academy, Marshall College and Marshall College State Normal School." Manuscript, Charleston, West Virginia, 1912.

Lewis, Virgil. *Biennial report of the Department of Archives and History of the State of West Virginia.* Charleston, WV: WV Department of Archives and History, 1906.

Life. "Youth/What They Need Is a Place To Go." August 9, 1966.

Lion Television & Oregon Public Broadcasting. *History Detectives.* PBS, August 30, 2011.

Longbored Surfer. 2013. http://longboredsurfer.com/charts/.

Love, Charles. "History of Martha Community (Cabell County, West Virginia)." 1925.

Lowery, Charles D. *Dictionary of American Biography: James Barbour, a Jeffersonian Republican.* Alabama: University of Alabama Press, 1984.

Malin, James C. "Three Kansas Philosophers The Philosophy of Wesley McComas.*" Kansas Historical Quarterly*, 1958.

Manarin, Louis H. Constitution of 1851. http://www.wvhumanities.org/Statehood/reformconvention.htm (accessed 2011).

Marshall University. *General Undergraduate Catalog.* Huntington, WV, 2007.

Mary Beth Pudup, Dwight B. Billings and Altina L. Waller, editors. *Appalachia in the Making: The Mountain South in the Nineteenth Century.* Chapel Hill, NC: University of North Carolina Press, 1995.

Massey, Tim R. "Decision Came Hard." *Herald-Dispatch*, January 22, 1996.

Matthews, Madge Lester. "Ante-Bellum Barboursville." *West Virginia History Quarterly Magazine* Volume XI, 1949-50: 271.

Maxwell, Bob. "Voice of the People," *Herald-Dispatch*, 31 May, 2009.

Maxwell, H. *The History of Barbour County, West Virginia: From Its Earliest Exploration to the Present Time.* Morgantown, WV: Acme Publishing, 1899.

Maxwell, Hugh. "Century-Old Barboursville Cemetery To Be Renovated." circa 1956.

McElroy, Ethan. Kirkbride Buildings. 2013. http://www.kirkbridebuildings.com/.

McEntee, Sheila. "Excavating Clues to the Past." *Wonderful West Virginia Magazine*, March 2001.

McMillian, Don D. "Huntington sits on old Beuhring plantation." *Herald-Dispatch*, August 17, 2008.

McMillian, Don D. "Miller Homes an Early Piece of Area History." *Herald-Dispatch*, November 9, 2008.

McMillian, Don D. "Thornburg family active in Cabell County history." *Herald-Dispatch*, August 2, 2009.

Miami University, Oxford, OH. William Holmes McGuffey Museum . 2007. http://www.units. muohio.edu/mcguffeymuseum/index.html.

Midkiff, Ernest. "World War One." Cabell County Doors to the Past. 2012. http://www.rootsweb. ancestry.com/~wvccfhr/military/page2.htm.

Midwest PHC. History of the Pilgrim Holiness Church. 2004. http://www.midwestphc.org/History. html.

Miller, Doris C. ""Huntington City Followed In Tracks of C&O Railway Growth":." *Herald-Dispatch*, March 28, 1976.

Miller, Doris C. "Confidence Reflected in a Church Building Boom." *Herald-Advertiser*, August 24, 1958.

Miller, Doris C. "Transportation Industry Carried Cabell Changes." *Herald-Dispatch*, March 28, 1976.

Miller, Doris C. *The Herald Dispatch*, 1976.

Miller, Dr. Joseph Lyon. "The Millers and Their Kin." *West Virginia Historical Magazine Quarterly*, 1902.

Miller, J.W. "History of Barboursville Community." Barboursville, WV, 1925.

Minnesota Public Radio. "The Fertility Race." 2012. http://news.minnesota.publicradio.org/ features/199711/20_smiths_fertility/part1/f4.shtml.

Moran, Kevinne. "A-N details Ona mall plans." *Huntington Advertiser*, May 22, 1979.

Morgan, John G. "The Other One-Tenth: Camp Therapy 'Lifts' Patients." *Sunday Gazette-Mail*, January 17, 1971.

Morison, Samuel Eliot. *The Oxford History of the American People, Vol. Three: 1869 through the Death of John F. Kennedy*. New York, NY: Meridian Books, 1994.

Morris, Helen. "City, Merchants Argue Over Mall Contract." *Herald-Dispatch*, June 4, 1977.

National Alliance on Mental Illness. People With Mental Illness Enrich Our Lives. 2013. http://www. nami.org/Template.cfm?Section=Helpline1&template=/ContentManagement/ContentDisplay. cfm&ContentID=4858.

National Archives. Official 1940 Census Website. 2012. 1940census.archives.gov (accessed 2012).

National Center for Biotechnology Information, U.S. National Library of Medicine. 2012. http://www. ncbi.nlm.nih.gov/pubmedhealth/?term=rheumatic%20fever.

National Institutes of Health. "Important Events in NIMH History." NIH 1999 Almanac. September 1999. http://www.nih.gov/about/almanac/archive/1999/organization/nimh/history.html.

National Park Service. "Battle of Antietam." www.nps.gov. 2011. http://www.nps.gov/anti/historycul-ture/upload/Battle%20history.pdf.

National Park Service. Brown v. Board of Education National Historic Site. 2013. http://www.nps.gov/ brvb/historyculture/kansas.htm.

Nevada Historical Society. Johnson-Jeffries Fight: A Centennial Exhibit. July 2010. http://knowledge-center.unr.edu/digital_collections/exhibits/johnson_jeffries/aftermath.aspx.

New York Times. "An Ex Congressman Turned Highwayman." July 15, 1861.

Oberholtzer, Frances W. "Ball Invitations, Tinted with Yellow of Century's Time, Unearthed." *Sunday Advertiser*, February 19, 1922.

Olafson. "Cabell County Tax List, 1810 ." KYOWVA Genealogical & Historical Society. Huntington, WV.

Paul Ambrose Trail for Health. 2013. http://paulambrosetrail.org/.

Pegasus Rocks. Pegasus Rocks, Gigs. 2008. http://pegasusrocks.com/gigs.html.

Peyton, Dave. "'Mr. Barboursville High' John Fife Closes Long Career." *Herald-Advertiser*, June 4, 1967.

Peyton, Dave. "Stroll Into History Offered." *Herald-Dispatch*, September 10, 1994.

Peyton, Susan. "'Appreciation Week' Honors Dr. Curry, Barboursville's 'Semi-Retired' Physician." *Herald-Dispatch*, January 20, 1974.

Pinkston, Antwon. "Bridge named after Barboursville native." *Herald-Dispatch*, July 22, 2006.

Pirateer. Barboursville, WV: BHS, June 2, 1967.

Planitz, Nancy Warner. "Boggs-Bussey-Stewart Family History, vol. 3." http://www.planitz.org/. 2010. http://www.planitz.org/genealogy-records/boggs-family-and-bussy-family-and-stewart-family/ volume-3-of-3-family-groups-and-pedigree-charts/-boggs-bussy-stewart-family-history-vol-3-of-3. pdf (accessed September 2011).

Pocahontas Times. "Statue of Bishop Asbury Erected in Washington." April 30, 1925.

Polk's City Directory. Huntington, WV, 1977.

Potter, Constance. "World War I Gold Star Mothers Pilgrimages, Part I. " *National Archives Prologue Magazine*, Vol. 31, No. 2, Summer 1999.

Powers, Griffis & McConkey. "History of Barboursville Schools." Barboursville, West Virginia, c. 1958.

Pricketts Fort Memorial Foundation. "West Virginia New Deal." Prickettsfort.org. http://www.prick-ettsfort.org/wvnd.htm (accessed 2012).

Prochnow, Matt. "The Massacre and Burning of Guyandotte." Guyandotte Civil War Days. 2009. www.guyandottecivilwardays.com/Burning.htm.

Rake, Melissa. "Village leaves nothing of tree." *Herald-Dispatch*, August 20, 1995.

Ramsey, Glenn V. "Sociotherapeutic Camping for the Mentally Ill." *Oxford Journals: Social Work* Vol. 9, Issue 1, 1964: 45-53.

Reasons-Pyles, Katherine. "A Perfect Getaway. " *Huntington Quarterly*, Summer 2010.

Redekopp, Christina. "Barboursville VFD celebrates 50 years." *Herald-Dispatch*, June 22, 2003.

Reniers, Percevel. *The Springs of Virginia: Life, Love and Death at the Waters, 1775-1900* . Chapel Hill, NC: University of North Carolina Press, 1941.

Rice, Otis K. & Stephen W. Brown. *West Virginia: A History*. Lexington, KY: University Press of Kentucky, 1993.

Richard G. Stone, Jr. *The Brittle Sword: The Kentucky Militia, 1776-1912*. Lexington, KY: University Press of Kentucky, 1978.

Richmond, Mrs. Philip & Mrs. John (Ruth) Daulton. *A History of Barboursville, West Virginia*. Barboursville: GFWC Woman's Club of Barboursville, 1976.

Rogers, Kara. "Walter J. Freeman II and Lobotomy: Probing for Answers ." Encyclopaedia Britannica Blog. September 14, 2011. http://www.britannica.com/blogs/2011/09/walter-freeman-ii-lobotomy-probing-answers/.

Roots Web. Family Ties of Cabell County. 2000. http://freepages.genealogy.rootsweb.ancestry.com/~cabell/index.html (accessed 2011).

Rootsweb Family Histories. Family Ties of Cabell County. freepages.genealogy.rootsweb.ancestry.com/.../d146.html (accessed 2011).

Rose, Mara. "Flames licking old Tivoli Theater spark memories of days gone by." *Herald-Dispatch*, July 6, 1985.

Rose, Mara. "Old Cabell home destroyed by fire." *Herald-Dispatch*, May 14, 1986.

Rosenberger, Bill. " Recycling set to take first step in county ." *Herald-Dispatch*, April 13, 2011.

Ross, Jim. "OK Is Given To Annexation Of Mall Site." *Herald-Dispatch*, November 3, 1978.

Sargent, Beth. "Lakin Hospital." *Point Pleasant Register*, 2007.

Saxton, Michelle. "Barboursville family mourns loss of seven WWII brothers." *Herald-Dispatch*, May 28, 2000.

Schultz, Oscar T., M.D. "Two Cases of Human Anthrax at Camp Jackson." *The Journal of the American Medical Association*, 1918.

Schumacher, Bob. "John Allen "Out After" Dink." *Herald-Dispatch*, September 13, 1966.

Schweiger, Beth Barton. *The Gospel Working Up: Progress and the Pulpit in Nineteenth Century Virginia*. New York, NY: Oxford US, 2000.

Seamonds, Jack. "Barboursville Hospital 'Ideal' for Vets—Jay." *Herald-Dispatch*, October 18, 1978.

Sedgwick, Todd. "Only One: Success attributed to variety at W.Va.'s red brick factory." *Herald-Dispatch*.

Sedgwick, Todd. "Wanderlust of Economic Gain Lured Early Explorers Westward." *Herald-Dispatch*, March 28, 1976.

Sellers, Charles. *The Market Revolution: Jacksonian America, 1815-1846*. New York: Oxford University Press, 1991.

Shanks, Henry T. *The Secession Movement in Virginia, 1847-1861*. Richmond, VA: Garrett and Massie, 1934.

Simmons, Mark. *Massacre on the Lordsburg Road: A Tragedy of the Apache Wars*. 2005.

Slavery and the Making of America, Vol. 4: The Challenge of Freedom. Directed by PBS. Produced by Educational Broadcasting Corporation. 2004.

Smith, Harold R. "Falls of Guyandotte remember as a historic place." *Lincoln Journal/Weekly News Sentinel*, Oct. 25, 1995.

Smith, J. Douglas. *Managing White Supremacy: Race, Politics, and Citizenship in Jim Crow Virginia*. Chapel Hill, NC: University of North Carolina Press, 2002.

Smith, Jean Edward. *John Marshall: Definer of a Nation*. New York, NY: Henry Holt & Company, 1996.

Smith, Leanne. "Peek Through Time: Granny's A-Go-Go, Hullabaloo made the teen scene in 1960s Jackson." MLive—Jackson, MI News. August 9, 2012. http://www.mlive.com/news/jackson/index.ssf/2012/08/peek_through_time_grannys_a-go.html (accessed 2013).

Smith, Martha. "Superintendent on Probation; No Criticism Leveled By Hospital Employees." *Charleston Gazette*, January 4, 1975.

Smith, W.W. Honor Roll of Cabell County, W.Va. - *An Illustrated Biographical Record of Cabell County's Part in the World War 1914-1918*. Chicago, IL: Severinghaus Printing Company, 1920.

Smith, Wiatt. "Barboursville: Some Interesting Historic Facts About Former County Seat." *Herald-Dispatch*, March 13, 1921.

Smith, Wiatt. "Your Friends and Mine." *Herald-Dispatch*, March 28, 1946.

Smith, Wilma Cox, interview by Jeanette Rowsey. (September 22, 2011).

Sophie von Teschen et. al. WikiHow: How to Restore an Abandoned Cemetery. 2013. http://www.wikihow.com/Restore-an-Abandoned-Cemetery.

Steele, Aaron. March 30, 2010. www.genealogywise.com (accessed 2011).

Sulzer Pumps (US) Inc. "Sturm History." Brookshire, TX, June 3, 2013.

Sunday Advertiser. "Blue Sulphur, Famous Old Resort, Will Open Doors." July 8, 1923.

Sunday Gazette Mail. "Two Escaped Inmates Held." September 30, 1962.

Swann, George S. "A Brief History of the Ousley's Gap Community." Cabell County Doors to the Past. 2000. http://www.rootsweb.ancestry.com/~wvcccfhr/history/ousleysgap1.htm (accessed 2012).

Teen Clubs International, Inc "Advertisements, various." *Herald-Dispatch*, 1968-1969.

Teen Clubs International, Inc. "Advertisement." *Billboard*. March 18, 1968.

Teen Clubs International, Inc. "Advertisement." *Huntington Advertiser*, May 17, 1968.

The American Journal of Nursing, Vol. 18, No. 16.March 1918.

The Church of Jesus Christ of Latter-day Saints. *West Virginia County Death Records*. 2011. (accessed September 6, 2011).

The First Measured Century: A Look at American History by the Numbers. Directed by PBS. 2000.

The Great War Society. Doughboy Center: The Story of the American Expeditionary Forces. Second Battle of the Marne. 2000. http://www.worldwar1.com/dbc/2marne.htm.

Thomas, Jerry Bruce. "County Poor Farms." e-WV . http://www.wvencyclopedia.org/articles/1649 (accessed 2013).

Thompson, Margaret. "The People: Early Settlers to Imports." *Herald Advertiser*, July 11, 1971.

Tim Brooks & Earle Marsh. *The Complete Directory to Prime Time Network TV Shows, 1946-Present, Third Edition*. New York, NY: Ballantine Books, 1984.

Torch - Barboursville High School Yearbook. Barboursville, WV, 1934.

Torch - Barboursville High School Yearbook. Barboursville, WV, 1931.

Town of Eleanor, W.Va. Town of Eleanor, West Virginia. http://www.eleanorwv.com/history.html (accessed 2012).

Treasure Chest. Barboursville High School 50th Anniversary Yearbook, 1977.

Treasure Chest. Barboursville High School, 1947.

Treasure Chest. Barboursville High School, 1975.

Treasure Chest—Barboursville High School, 1955.

Turman, Ann, interview by Jeanette Rowsey. (April 15, 2010).

Turman, Paul. "Notes from Mayor "T"." *Village People* Issue 185, April 2009: 1.

Turner, Ronald Ray. "Cabell County WV 1850 Annotated Census." Manassas, VA, 1998.

Tyler. "Railroad Surveys: History and Curve Computations." Student, Big Rapids, Michigan: Ferris State University.

U.S. Bureau of the Census. "Historical Statistics of the United States of the United States, Colonia Times to 1957." U-S History. http://www.u-s-history.com/pages/h1528.html (accessed 2012).

U.S. Census Bureau. "Reports of the Population of the United States." Government, Washington DC, 1900, 1910, 1920, 1930, 1940, 1950, 1960, 1970, 1980.

U.S. Census Bureau. *Measuring America: The Decennial Censuses from 1790 to 2000*. Washington, DC: U.S. Department of Commerce, 2002.

U.S. Department of Agriculture, Soil Conservation Services. "Soil Survey of Cabell County, West Virginia." Government, 1989.

U.S. Department of Health and Human Services. The Great Pandemic: South Carolina. http://www.flu.gov/pandemic/history/1918/your_state/southeast/southcarolina/index.html (accessed 2012).

UMC General Commission on Archives & History. United Methodist Church Timeline. http://www.gcah.org/site/pp.aspx?c=ghKJI0PHIoE&b=3504153 (accessed 2012).

United Press International. "Agriculture Chief Blasts Farm Operation." *Morgantown Post*, October 28, 1965.

United States Department of the Interior, National Park Service, National Register of Historic Places - Registration Form 748 Beech Street, Kenova." 1989.

United States Department of the Interior, National Park Service, National Register of Historic Places - Registration Form for Chafin House." 1994.

Vallandingham, Samuel V. "Testimony Before Congress of the U.S., Subcommittee on Financial Institutions and Consumer Credit." Washington, DC, May 9, 2012.

Vogt, John. "Cabell County, Va. 1810 Substitute Census (Abstracts from the 1810 Personal Property Tax List." 2011.

von Teschen, Sophie et. al. WikiHow: How to Restore an Abandoned Cemetery. 2013. http://www.wikihow.com/Restore-an-Abandoned-Cemetery.

W.T. Chambers, Photographer. "Cornerstone Laid for Barboursville Hospital." *Herald-Advertiser*, January 9, 1949.

W.W. Herrick, M.D. "The Epidemic of Meningitis at Camp Jackson, Preliminary Report." *Journal of the American Medical Association*, 1918.

Wallace Funeral Home. "James. W. Allen 1924-2011." Time for Memory. August 2011. http://www.timeformemory.com/fh_obituary.cfm?obitid=35635&fhid=17.

Wallace, George Seldon. *Cabell County Annals and Families*. 1935.

Wallen, James A. "Riverboats Brought Commerce, Growth to Area." *Herald-Dispatch*, March 28, 1976.

Wartman, Scott ."Mini golf, restaurant slated for Barboursville." *Herald-Dispatch*, July 27, 2005.

Wartman, Scott. "Denied exposition center considered for other uses." *Herald-Dispatch*, October 8, 2003.

Wartman, Scott. "Huntington Mall Retail drives growth in eastern Cabell County." *Herald-Dispatch*, c 2003.

Wartman, Scott. "Sale of land may hinge on cleanup." *Herald-Dispatch*, February 13, 2007.

Washington, Harry B. "Roots of the Washington Family 1881-1996." Barboursville, WV: Personal manuscript given to Janet Altizer, April 1996.

Weaver, H. Dwight. *Missouri Caves in History and Legend*. Columbia, MO: University of Missouri Press, 2008.

Welsh, Jack D. *Medical Histories of Confederate Generals*. Kent, OH: Kent State University Press, 1995.

West Virginia Archives & History. "Federal Relief in West Virginia During the Great Depression: Journal of the House of Delegates 1933." West Virginia Division of Culture and History. 2012. http://www.wvculture.org/history/greatdepression/federalrelief03.html.

West Virginia Archives & History. http://www.wvculture.org/history/bateman.html.

West Virginia Archives and History. West Virginia Veterans Memorial Database. Charleston, 2012.

West Virginia Department of Education. West Virginia Report Cards . http://wvde.state.wv.us/data/report_cards/ (accessed 2013).

West Virginia Department of Environmental Protection. "An Ecological Assessment of the Lower Guyandotte River Watershed." May 2004. www.wvdep.org.

West Virginia Department of Mental Health. "Annual Report." Charleston, WV, 1973-74.

West Virginia Department of Mental Health. "Annual Report." Charleston, WV, 1969-70.

West Virginia Department of Mental Health. "Annual Report." Charleston, WV, 1962-63.

West Virginia Department of Mental Health. "Comprehensive Mental Health Plan for West Virginia." Charleston, WV, 1976.

West Virginia Department of Mental Health. "Comprehensive Mental Health Plan of West Virginia." Charleston, WV, 1966.

West Virginia Department of Mental Health. "Mental Health in West Virginia 1958-68." Charleston, WV, 1968.

West Virginia Department of Mental Health. "State Directory." Charleston, WV, 1968.

West Virginia Division of Culture & History. "The Civil War in West Virginia - 2011 Calendar." Charleston, WV: State of West Virginia, funded by U.S. National Park Service, 2011.

West Virginia Division of Culture & History. "WV Vital Research Records." www.wvculture.org. 2011. http://www.wvculture.org/vrr/.

West Virginia Division of Culture and History. "A Timeline of African-American History in West Virginia." West Virginia Archives and History. 2011. http://www.wvculture.org/history/timeline.html.

West Virginia Division of Culture and History. "West Virginia Counties." West Virginia Archives and History. 2011. http://www.wvculture.org/history/wvcounties.html.

West Virginia Division of Culture and History. West Virginia Highway Markers Database . Charleston, WV, 2013.

West Virginia Division of Natural Resources. Cabell County - Barboursville Lake. 2003. http://www.wvdnr.gov/fishing/public_access.asp?county=Cabell&type=Lakes&point=I4.

West Virginia Heritage Encyclopedia, Supplement Volume #6. Hardesty's - Jim Comstock, 1974.

West Virginia Humanities Council. *e-WV: The West Virginia Encyclopedia*. 2006-2009.

West Virginia Legislature. "House Concurrent Resolution 89." Charleston, WV, 2012.

West Virginia Legislature. "House Concurrent Resolution 72." 2010.

West Virginia Legislature. "West Virginia State Code." Charleston, WV.

West Virginia Legislature. *West Virginia Legislature Handbook, Manual and Official Register*. Charleston: State of West Virginia, 1921.

West Virginia Legislature's Office of Reference & Information. W.Va. Legislature's Kids' Page: Fun Facts About West Virginia. 2012. http://www.legis.state.wv.us/educational/Kids_Page/fun_facts. cfm.

West Virginia Senate. *West Virginia Blue Book*. Charleston, WV, Multiple Years.

West Virginia Sesquicentennial Commission. "A Sesquicentennial Moment March 22-28, 1863." *Herald-Dispatch*, March 22, 2013.

West Virginia State Historic Preservation Office. "Nomination of Barboursville Historic District." National Register of Historic Places Registration Application. Charleston, WV, 2008.

Weston Democrat. "The Asylum: Its Origins and Progress." November 13, 1871.

White, Rodney A. "Few Voice Opposition to Mall's Annexation." *Herald-Dispatch*, October 3, 1978.

White, Rodney A. "Huge Rafts of Timber Fueled River Sawmills." *Herald-Dispatch*, March 28, 1976.

Willis, Bob. "It Sometimes Takes a While." *Raleigh Register*, June 13, 1966.

Withers, Bob. "Chessie holds open house." *Herald-Dispatch*, August 21, 1981.

Withers, Bob. "Council members, mayor get salary raises in Barboursville." *Herald-Dispatch*, May 28, 2003.

Withers, Bob. "History of Methodism in Guyandotte." *Guyandotte1810-2010 Bicentennial Program Book*. Guyandotte & Carroll House Bicentennial Committee and Madie Carroll House Preservation Society, 2010.

Wolfe, Lori. "Gallery: Barboursville Mural." *Herald-Dispatch*.com. May 23, 2008. http://www.*Herald-Dispatch*.com/multimedia/x996201414.

Woodrum, Woody. "Roy Goines Broke MU Football Color Barrier." *Herd Insider Magazine*, September 28, 2006.

Woodson, Carter Godwin. *Early Negro Education In West Virginia*. The West Virginia Collegiate Institute, 1921.

World Health Organization. 2012. http://www.who.int/topics/en/): .

WVa-USA.com "The Building of the C&O Railway." WVa-USA.com. 1999-2001. http://www. wva-usa.com/history/mthope/cando.php.

WVGenWeb. www.wvgenweb.org (accessed 2011).

Yeatman, Ted. *Frank and Jesse James: The Story Behind the Legend*. Nashville, TN: Cumberland House Publishing, 2008.

Yoak, J.B.F. "Speech at Morris Harvey Alumni Banquet." 1964.

INDEX

About the Author

J EANETTE Rowsey is a writer and nationally-accredited strategic communications consultant from Huntington, West Virginia. She graduated from Marshall
University and has worked in public relations practice for over 30 years. She is also
a seventh-generation descendent of early Barboursville settlers.

The Lost Village of Barboursville is her first book.

Want additional copies of
The Lost Village of Barboursville?

Order direct online from: www.lostvillageofbarboursville.com
(Bulk and group discounts are available)

Mail correspondence and requests to:
JRC, P.O. Box 548, Barboursville, WV 25504

Email the author-publisher at:
lostvillageofbarboursville@gmail.com